48: *American Poets, 1880-1945,* Second Series, edited by Peter Quartermain (1986)

49: *American Literary Publishing Houses, 1638-1899,* 2 parts, edited by Peter Dzwonkoski (1986)

50: *Afro-American Writers Before the Harlem Renaissance,* edited by Trudier Harris (1986)

51: *Afro-American Writers from the Harlem Renaissance to 1940,* edited by Trudier Harris (1987)

52: *American Writers for Children Since 1960: Fiction,* edited by Glenn E. Estes (1986)

53: *Canadian Writers Since 1960,* First Series, edited by W. H. New (1986)

54: *American Poets, 1880-1945,* Third Series, 2 parts, edited by Peter Quartermain (1987)

55: *Victorian Prose Writers Before 1867,* edited by William B. Thesing (1987)

56: *German Fiction Writers, 1914-1945,* edited by James Hardin (1987)

57: *Victorian Prose Writers After 1867,* edited by William B. Thesing (1987)

58: *Jacobean and Caroline Dramatists,* edited by Fredson Bowers (1987)

59: *American Literary Critics and Scholars, 1800-1850,* edited by John W. Rathbun and Monica M. Grecu (1987)

60: *Canadian Writers Since 1960,* Second Series, edited by W. H. New (1987)

61: *American Writers for Children Since 1960: Poets, Illustrators, and Nonfiction Authors,* edited by Glenn E. Estes (1987)

62: *Elizabethan Dramatists,* edited by Fredson Bowers (1987)

63: *Modern American Critics, 1920-1955,* edited by Gregory S. Jay (1988)

64: *American Literary Critics and Scholars, 1850-1880,* edited by John W. Rathbun and Monica M. Grecu (1988)

65: *French Novelists, 1900-1930,* edited by Catharine Savage Brosman (1988)

66: *German Fiction Writers, 1885-1913,* 2 parts, edited by James Hardin (1988)

67: *Modern American Critics Since 1955,* edited by Gregory S. Jay (1988)

68: *Canadian Writers, 1920-1959,* First Series, edited by W. H. New (1988)

69: *Contemporary German Fiction Writers,* First Series, edited by Wolfgang D. Elfe and James Hardin (1988)

70: *British Mystery Writers, 1860-1919,* edited by Bernard Benstock and Thomas F. Staley (1988)

71: *American Literary Critics and Scholars, 1880-1900,* edited by John W. Rathbun and Monica M. Grecu (1988)

72: *French Novelists, 1930-1960,* edited by Catharine Savage Brosman (1988)

73: *American Magazine Journalists, 1741-1850,* edited by Sam G. Riley (1988)

74: *American Short-Story Writers Before 1880,* edited by Bobby Ellen Kimbel, with the assistance of William E. Grant (1988)

75: *Contemporary German Fiction Writers, Second Series,* edited by Wolfgang D. Elfe and James Hardin (1988)

76: *Afro-American Writers, 1940-1955,* edited by Trudier Harris (1988)

Documentary Series

1: *Sherwood Anderson, Willa Cather, John Dos Passos, Theodore Dreiser, F. Scott Fitzgerald, Ernest Hemingway, Sinclair Lewis,* edited by Margaret A. Van Antwerp (1982)

2: *James Gould Cozzens, James T. Farrell, William Faulkner, John O'Hara, John Steinbeck, Thomas Wolfe, Richard Wright,* edited by Margaret A. Van Antwerp (1982)

3: *Saul Bellow, Jack Kerouac, Norman Mailer, Vladimir Nabokov, John Updike, Kurt Vonnegut,* edited by Mary Bruccoli (1983)

4: *Tennessee Williams,* edited by Margaret A. Van Antwerp and Sally Johns (1984)

5: *American Transcendentalists,* edited by Joel Myerson (1988)

Yearbooks

1980, edited by Karen L. Rood, Jean W. Ross, and Richard Ziegfeld (1981)

1981, edited by Karen L. Rood, Jean W. Ross, and Richard Ziegfeld (1982)

1982, edited by Richard Ziegfeld; associate editors: Jean W. Ross and Lynne C. Zeigler (1983)

1983, edited by Mary Bruccoli and Jean W. Ross; associate editor: Richard Ziegfeld (1984)

1984, edited by Jean W. Ross (1985)

1985, edited by Jean W. Ross (1986)

1986, edited by J. M. Brook (1987)

1987, edited by J. M. Brook (1988)

Concise Series

The New Consciousness, 1941-1968 (1987)

Colonization to the American Renaissance, 1640-1865 (1988)

Realism, Naturalism, and Local Color, 1865-1917 (1988)

Dictionary of Literary Biography • Volume Seventy-six

Afro-American Writers, 1940-1955

Dictionary of Literary Biography • Volume Seventy-six

Afro-American Writers, 1940-1955

Edited by
Trudier Harris
University of North Carolina at Chapel Hill

Associate Editor
Thadious M. Davis
University of North Carolina at Chapel Hill

A Bruccoli Clark Layman Book
Gale Research Inc. • Book Tower • Detroit, Michigan 48226

Manufactured by Edwards Brothers, Inc.
Ann Arbor, Michigan
Printed in the United States of America

Library of Congress Cataloging-in-Publication Data

Afro-American writers, 1940-1955 / edited by Trudier Harris.
     p. cm.–(Dictionary of literary biography; v. 76)
"A Bruccoli Clark Layman book."
Includes index.
ISBN 0-8103-4554-4
    1. American literature–Afro-American authors–Bio-bibliography. 2. American literature–Afro-American authors–History and criticism. 3. American literature–20th century–Bio-bibliography. 4. American literature–20th century–History and criticism. 5. Afro-American authors–Biography–Dictionaries. 6. Authors, American–20th century–Biography–Dictionaries. I. Harris, Trudier.
PS153.N5A386 1988
810'.9'896073–dc19   88-21423
                         CIP

In Memory of
George E. Kent
(31 May 1920-2 September 1982)
and
Wallace Ray Peppers
(29 August 1948-22 May 1987)

Contents

Plan of the Series

. . . Almost the most prodigious asset of a country, and perhaps its most precious possession, is its native literary product—when that product is fine and noble and enduring.

Mark Twain*

The advisory board, the editors, and the publisher of the *Dictionary of Literary Biography* are joined in endorsing Mark Twain's declaration. The literature of a nation provides an inexhaustible resource of permanent worth. We intend to make literature and its creators better understood and more accessible to students and the reading public, while satisfying the standards of teachers and scholars.

To meet these requirements, *literary biography* has been construed in terms of the author's achievement. The most important thing about a writer is his writing. Accordingly, the entries in *DLB* are career biographies, tracing the development of the author's canon and the evolution of his reputation.

The purpose of *DLB* is not only to provide reliable information in a convenient format but also to place the figures in the larger perspective of literary history and to offer appraisals of their accomplishments by qualified scholars.

The publication plan for *DLB* resulted from two years of preparation. The project was proposed to Bruccoli Clark by Frederick G. Ruffner, president of the Gale Research Company, in November 1975. After specimen entries were prepared and typeset, an advisory board was formed to refine the entry format and develop the series rationale. In meetings held during 1976, the publisher, series editors, and advisory board approved the scheme for a comprehensive biographical dictionary of persons who contributed to North American literature. Editorial work on the first volume began in January 1977, and it was published in 1978. In order to make *DLB* more than a reference tool and to compile volumes that individually have claim to status as literary history, it was decided to organize volumes by topic, period, or genre. Each of these freestanding volumes provides a biographical-bibliographical guide and overview for a particular area of literature. We are convinced that this organization—as opposed to a single alphabet method—constitutes a valuable innovation in the presentation of reference material. The volume plan necessarily requires many decisions for the placement and treatment of authors who might properly be included in two or three volumes. In some instances a major figure will be included in separate volumes, but with different entries emphasizing the aspect of his career appropriate to each volume. Ernest Hemingway, for example, is represented in *American Writers in Paris, 1920-1939* by an entry focusing on his expatriate apprenticeship; he is also in *American Novelists, 1910-1945* with an entry surveying his entire career. Each volume includes a cumulative index of subject authors and articles. Comprehensive indexes to the entire series are planned.

With volume ten in 1982 it was decided to enlarge the scope of *DLB*. By the end of 1986 twenty-one volumes treating British literature had been published, and volumes for Commonwealth and Modern European literature were in progress. The series has been further augmented by the *DLB Yearbooks* (since 1981) which update published entries and add new entries to keep the *DLB* current with contemporary activity. There have also been *DLB Documentary Series* volumes which provide biographical and critical source materials for figures whose work is judged to have particular interest for students. One of these companion volumes is entirely devoted to Tennessee Williams.

We define literature as the *intellectual commerce of a nation:* not merely as belles lettres but as that ample and complex process by which ideas are generated, shaped, and transmitted. *DLB* entries are not limited to "creative writers" but extend to other figures who in their time and in their way influenced the mind of a people. Thus the series encompasses historians, journalists, publishers, and screenwriters. By this means readers of *DLB* may be aided to perceive litera-

*From an unpublished section of Mark Twain's autobiography, copyright © by the Mark Twain Company.

ture not as cult scripture in the keeping of intellectual high priests but firmly positioned at the center of a nation's life.

DLB includes the major writers appropriate to each volume and those standing in the ranks immediately behind them. Scholarly and critical counsel has been sought in deciding which minor figures to include and how full their entries should be. Wherever possible, useful references are made to figures who do not warrant separate entries.

Each *DLB* volume has a volume editor responsible for planning the volume, selecting the figures for inclusion, and assigning the entries. Volume editors are also responsible for preparing, where appropriate, appendices surveying the major periodicals and literary and intellectual movements for their volumes, as well as lists of further readings. Work on the series as a whole is coordinated at the Bruccoli Clark Layman editorial center in Columbia, South Carolina, where the editorial staff is responsible for accuracy of the published volumes.

One feature that distinguishes *DLB* is the illustration policy–its concern with the iconography of literature. Just as an author is influenced by his surroundings, so is the reader's understanding of the author enhanced by a knowledge of his environment. Therefore *DLB* volumes include not only drawings, paintings, and photographs of authors, often depicting them at various stages in their careers, but also illustrations of their families and places where they lived. Title pages are regularly reproduced in facsimile along with dust jackets for modern authors. The dust jackets are a special feature of *DLB* because they often document better than anything else the way in which an author's work was perceived in its own time. Specimens of the writers' manuscripts are included when feasible.

Samuel Johnson rightly decreed that "The chief glory of every people arises from its authors." The purpose of the *Dictionary of Literary Biography* is to compile literary history in the surest way available to us–by accurate and comprehensive treatment of the lives and work of those who contributed to it.

The *DLB* Advisory Board

Foreword

DLB 76: Afro-American Writers, 1940 to 1955 is the third in a series of three volumes covering the work of black American writers from the colonial period up to 1955. The first volume, *DLB 50*, covers Afro-American writers before the Harlem Renaissance; and the second volume, *DLB 51*, treats Afro-American writers from the Harlem Renaissance to 1940.

DLB 76 is the sixth and final volume in a series devoted exclusively to Afro-American writers. The earlier three volumes treat black American writers after 1955 and are divided as follows: *DLB 33: Afro-American Fiction Writers After 1955; DLB 38: Afro-American Writers After 1955: Dramatists and Prose Writers;* and *DLB 41: Afro-American Poets Since 1955.*

The current volume includes twenty-six authors and covers major and minor writers who first published significant works in the period between 1940, so marked because of Richard Wright's publication of *Native Son,* and 1955, which marks the beginning of the era of the civil rights movement. These writers form a bridge between the burst of creative energy in the 1920s and more widely based creative work of the 1960s.

With the waning of the Harlem Renaissance, due in part to the Depression and in part to the dissolution of the center of energy identified with young writers in Harlem, Afro-American literature experienced a brief hiatus in which fewer, but more lasting, new reputations were made and only a handful of the older writers remained in the limelight. While Langston Hughes continued to travel and read his work throughout the United States and other countries in the 1930s, the voices of Countee Cullen and Claude McKay were much quieter than they had been in the 1920s; indeed, criticism had already been leveled at Cullen that he was not living up to the expectations and quality shown in his early work. By 1946 both Cullen and McKay were dead. After the publication of *Moses, Man of the Mountain* in 1939, Zora Neale Hurston was not to publish another volume until 1948, and that novel, *Seraph on the Suwanee,* was not well received. The Harlem Renaissance had indeed given way to quieter times, especially in terms of the poets.

The folk poetry of Hughes and Sterling A. Brown gave way to the poets of academe, represented in the 1940s and 1950s by Gwendolyn Brooks, Robert Hayden, and Melvin B. Tolson. Brooks and Hayden remained within established poetic traditions instead of militantly severing ties with tradition while they earned their reputations. Tolson was consciously an iconoclast, deliberately outside of what he identified to be either black or white traditions, but clearly drawing upon them even as he made his claims. All college trained, indeed frequently college teachers themselves, these three poets brought an array of classical, mythical, literary, and historical allusions to their work. Their initial efforts convinced critics that black poets could indeed produce works comparable to those of significant poets such as T. S. Eliot and Wallace Stevens. Brooks's winning of the Pulitzer prize in 1950 for *Annie Allen* (1949) was a testament to that position. Laced with the texture of poetic tradition and the careful crafting that has become Brooks's trademark, the volume presents, in grand language, the heroic lives of black people living in poverty in Chicago and, by implication, other parts of the urban North to which they had fled in an effort to escape poverty and lack of opportunity in the South.

The historical poetry of Hayden, with its tightly woven lines and allusions, was a clear signal to his reading audience–as Tolson's was to his– that he was also an academic, a fact that could sometimes "produce poetry that has more intellectual brilliance than poetic content; philosophic profundity sometimes replaces passionate simplicity." That influence yielded, in "A Ballad of Remembrance," such lines as "Contrived ghosts rapped to metronome clack of lavalieres."

Tolson was so anxious to attack the status quo that he deliberately sought obscurity in classicism and foreign phrases, as well as in references to music, painting, and a body of other materials that formed his particular brand of eclecticism. In other moments, however, he could comment lucidly upon black history, producing in "Dark Symphony" such lines as "Black Crispus Attucks taught/Us how to die/Before white Patrick Henry's bugle breath/Uttered the vertical/Transmitting cry:/'Yea, give me liberty, or give me death'." Despite such instances of clarity, the majority of his poetry was clearly not poetry for the masses, as was the work, a short time later, of poets such as Nikki Giovanni, Etheridge Knight, and Don L. Lee (Haki R. Madhubuti), who arrived on the scene in the 1960s. With the waning of the political fervor of the 1960s, however, Hayden and Tolson, along with such poets as Michael Harper, have received more critical attention, as the recent round of scholarly books published about their works reveals. Novelist Margaret Walker, who was a Yale Younger Poet in the 1940s, is also receiving more attention for her verse.

The dramatists of the period 1940 to 1955 continued the trend that Hughes had started with *Mulatto* in the 1930s. It was not only a time to produce plays on Broadway, but a time for black actors and playwrights to form their own companies. One of these was the American Negro Theatre, founded in 1939, which would introduce performers such as Canada Lee, Alice Childress, Sidney Poitier, and others. The company's production of *Anna Lucasta* in 1944 was famous, and for many years thereafter the company brought to prominence many of the names that would be identified with black drama for the next couple of decades.

Playwrights such as Owen Dodson and Theodore Ward, like Hughes, were influenced by Afro-American history and culture in their depictions of the drama of black life. Ward's first two plays were produced by black companies formed during this period, *Big White Fog* (1938) by the Negro Playwrights Company (1940) and *Our Lan'* (1947) by the American Negro Theatre. In *Our Lan'*, his most ambitious play, Ward drew upon the specific situation of the blacks who had been abandoned on the sea islands by Southern slaveholders in the wake of the advance of Union troops; he depicts the efforts of those newly freed individuals to hold on to what became theirs by default rather than return the land they had cultivated for years to the persons who held titular claim to it. Dodson, in more general depictions of Afro-American history, portrayed the effects of race relations upon his characters, frequently with a poetic quality lining his prose. His *The Garden of Time* (1939) was also produced by the American Negro Theatre (1945).

The Committee for the Negro in the Arts, founded in 1947, and the Harlem Council on the Theatre, founded in 1950, were instrumental in getting a number of plays produced, including William Branch's *A Medal for Willie* (1951) and *In Splendid Error* (1954), and Alice Childress's *Just a Little Simple* (1950), *Florence* (1949), and *Gold Through the Trees* (1952). Generally, the climate was one in which black playwrights and authors were mutual advocates for black theater.

Louis S. Peterson would join Ward and Dodson in the early 1950s in picking up on themes centering upon history and race relations with *Take a Giant Step* (1953), a drama exploring the interactions of a black high school student in Connecticut with his fellow white students. Although race provides the subtle undertones to the drama, other themes are equally relevant; they include the problems attendant upon growing up, such as sexual awareness and alienation from parents. Peterson's play was rather palatable in comparison to the themes that would dominate black drama less than a decade later, but *Take a Giant Step* was in keeping with the integrationist climate of the 1950s.

The dominant voice in Afro-American fiction in the 1940s was Richard Wright. Having won the *Story* magazine contest for fiction in 1938 for "Fire and Cloud," which would be published in *Uncle Tom's Children* (1938), Wright lived up to his expected potential by publishing the controversial *Native Son* in 1940. The naturalistic bent of the novel shows the influence of Theodore Dreiser and others upon Wright, and its political focus shows the influence of much of the proletariat fiction of the 1930s, as well as Wright's involvement with the Communist party. The naturalistic vein in black fiction would culminate in 1946 with the publication of Ann Petry's *The Street*, a look at the effects of poverty and determinism upon the black female psyche in an urban environment.

Though Wright did not dramatize the migration of blacks from the South to the North, he did use that archetypal pattern to explain how Bigger Thomas's family arrived in the North. William Attaway would use the dream of a better life in the North in *Blood on the Forge* (1941) to show how his protagonists are lured into becoming strikebreakers in an urban industry. Chester Himes would also portray dreams gone sour in the midst of urban expectations in *If He Hollers Let Him Go* (1945), a novel about the war industry and racial discrimination in urban California.

Dorothy West, in *The Living Is Easy* (1948), would go to the East Coast–Boston, specifically–to show another kind of soured urban living, one created by the greedy personality of the major female character. The legacy of the fiction of this period, therefore, is more a study of dreams deferred than dreams realized; the characters are stifled by a variety of forces: the legal system, poverty, racism, and their own shortsightedness.

Other writers saw America as a place where dreams could never be fulfilled, and continued an exodus out of the country that some earlier writers, such as Claude McKay, had flirted with in the 1920s, and that James Baldwin had followed in the late 1940s. Wright, Himes, William Gardner Smith, and Frank Yerby became expatriates. Of these novelists, however, perhaps Yerby was the one who came closest to making the dream of American success come true, at least financially. With his costume novels and typically raceless plots, he found a formula for dictating success on his own terms, though some critics have judged him harshly for it.

Of the writers who remained in America, Ralph Ellison would dominate the scene in the 1950s. Ellison's *Invisible Man* (1952) and Baldwin's *Go Tell It on the Mountain* (1953) were comparable in presenting black lives rich with folk culture and history, and grounded in the oratory of the church. Less conspicuously problem novels than those of a few years before, these were frequently required reading. Indeed, in the mid 1960s, more than two hundred editors and critics revealed in a poll that they judged *Invisible Man* to be the best novel published in America during the preceding twenty years.

The fifteen years between 1940 and 1955, therefore, were ones in which many prominent black writers whose works are regularly taught and written about today came to the forefront of the American literary scene. In the essays in this volume, scholars and critics have tried to capture the nuances of the lives and the literature of that period.

–Trudier Harris

Acknowledgments

This book was produced by Bruccoli Clark Layman, Inc. Karen L. Rood is senior editor for the *Dictionary of Literary Biography* series. Charles Lee Egleston was the in-house editor.

Production coordinator is Kimberly Casey. Art supervisor is Cheryl Crombie. Copyediting supervisor is Joan M. Prince. Typesetting supervisor is Kathleen M. Flanagan. Laura Ingram and Michael D. Senecal are editorial associates. The production staff includes Rowena Betts, Charles D. Brower, Joseph Matthew Bruccoli, Patricia Coate, Mary Colborn, Holly Deal, Mary S. Dye, Sarah A. Estes, Cynthia Hallman, Judith K. Ingle, Maria Ling, Warren McInnis, Kathy S. Merlette, Sheri Neal, Joycelyn R. Smith, Virginia Smith, and Jack Turner. Jean W. Ross is permissions editor. Joseph Caldwell, photography editor, and Penney Haughton did photographic copy work for the volume.

The editors are grateful for the help of Karen L. Jefferson, curator, and Paul Coates of the Moorland-Spingarn Research Center; Edward D. Manney of the Vivian G. Harsh Research Collection of Afro-American History and Literature, the Chicago Public Library; Thomas Goldwasser of Serendipity Books, Berkeley, California; the reference staff at the Benjamin F. Payton Learning Resources Center of Benedict College, Columbia, South Carolina; and Craig Werner of the University of Wisconsin.

Walter W. Ross and Rhonda Marshall did the library research with the assistance of the reference staff at the Thomas Cooper Library of the University of South Carolina: Daniel Boice, Cathy Eckman, Gary Geer, Cathie Gottlieb, David L. Haggard, Jens Holley, Dennis Isbell, Jackie Kinder, Marcia Martin, Jean Rhyne, Beverly Steele, Ellen Tillett, Carol Tobin, and Virginia Weathers.

Dictionary of Literary Biography • Volume Seventy-six

Afro-American Writers, 1940-1955

Dictionary of Literary Biography

William Attaway

(19 November 1911-17 June 1986)

Samuel B. Garren
North Carolina Agricultural and Technical State University

BOOKS: *Let Me Breathe Thunder* (New York: Dou-
bleday, Doran, 1939; London: Hale, 1940);
Blood on the Forge, A Novel (Garden City, N.Y.: Dou-
bleday, Doran, 1941);
Calypso Song Book, edited by Lyle Kenyon Engel
(New York, Toronto & London: McGraw-
Hill, 1957);
Hear America Singing (New York: Lion Press,
1967).

PLAY PRODUCTION: *Carnival*, Urbana, University of Illinois, 1935.

PERIODICAL PUBLICATIONS: "Tale of the
Blackamoor," *Challenge*, 1 (June 1936): 3-4;
"Death of a Rag Doll," *Tiger's Eye*, 1 (October
1947): 86-89.

With the 1939 publication of his first novel,
Let Me Breathe Thunder, William Attaway was
hailed by Stanley Young in the *New York Times
Book Review* as a writer of great promise, "an authentic young artist not to be watched tomorrow
but now." His second novel, *Blood on the Forge*
(1941), not only confirmed his promise but has
been called by critic Robert A. Bone "by far the
most perceptive novel of the Great Migration,"
the period spanning the 1920s and 1930s, when
Afro-Americans in large numbers moved from
the agrarian South to the industrial North. The
notion, repeated in some later criticism, that
Attaway's novels were neglected by the critics is untrue. Upon publication both works were reviewed
in major critical journals, and both received high

*William Attaway (courtesy of the Schomburg Center for Re-
search in Black Culture, the New York Public Library, Astor,
Lenox and Tilden Foundations)*

praise. Indeed, the most striking feature of the
original reviews is the prediction of a great future for Attaway as a writer. Attaway wrote no
more novels, however, and for several decades
made his living by writing scripts for television,

radio, and film. He virtually was forgotten by reading audiences until the 1960s. During the resurgence of interest in Afro-American culture, Attaway was rediscovered as a novelist of power and penetration.

William Alexander Attaway was born in Greenville, Mississippi, on 19 November 1911, the son of William A. Attaway, a physician, and Florence Parry Attaway, a schoolteacher. Attaway's father was a formidable man. In 1909 he formed the first legal reserve insurance company for blacks, and in 1921 he was one of the principal founders of the National Negro Insurance Association. By that time, not wanting his children to grow up in the segregated South, he had moved the family to Chicago, thus participating in the migration northward which his son would chronicle in his second novel.

Attaway rebelled against his father's hard-earned success and his parents' encouragement to learn a profession. He attended a vocational rather than an academic high school, planning at that time to be an automotive mechanic, but eventually he gave in to family pressure. He had been introduced to the poetry of Langston Hughes by a high-school teacher and decided to become a writer. Bowing to his father's wishes, he entered the University of Illinois, but he did not remain there. After his father's death he dropped out of school to live as a vagabond for two years. His activities during this period reflect his continued rebellion against respectability. In his attempt to absorb a wide variety of experiences in preparation for a writing career, he worked as a seaman, salesman, and labor organizer. In November 1935, while Attaway was involved in the Federal Writers' Project guide to Illinois, he became friends with Richard Wright, who was also with the project. That same year his play, *Carnival*, was produced at the University of Illinois, where he had returned to his studies.

Attaway graduated with a B.A. degree in 1936. During this year he also published his first story, "Tale of the Blackamoor," in the June 1936 issue of *Challenge*. A lonely black boy waits upon a duchess in a great European court. The boy dances a minuet in secret with his mistress's Dresden china doll to escape his sense of being insignificant. Slight as the story is, it prefigures the author's refusal to treat black life in isolation from the relentless pressure on it of the dominating white culture.

After graduation Attaway moved to New York City, working at odd jobs while writing his first novel. For two years he even tried acting, helped by his sister Ruth, whose dramatic career had begun in 1936 with the role of Rheba in the original Broadway company of Moss Hart and George S. Kaufman's *You Can't Take It with You*. Attaway was acting with the traveling production of this play when he learned that his first novel had been accepted.

Let Me Breathe Thunder is the story of two white hoboes, Step and Ed, who are traveling by rail across the western United States at the end of the Depression. The story is narrated by Ed and focuses largely upon the contagious influence of Step upon a nine-year-old Mexican known as Hi Boy, whom they have picked up in New Mexico. The first part of the novel depicts the typical hard life of hoboes and the subtle changes in that life-style brought about by the boy's presence. Hi Boy, whose name derives from his habitual friendly greeting to all living things, is as "bright and joyful as the sunlight." His innocence and optimism contrast sharply with Step's bitter cynicism. The action in the novel revolves around the ways in which Hi Boy's goodness works to redeem the harshness of Step's life and character. The central tragedy is Hi Boy's "corruption" from contact with Step and his death before decisively altering the hobo's condition.

Setting plays a large part in this novel. The harsh world in which the hoboes live is depicted through several sharp scenes, including one in which the hoboes are shown to be sexually attracted to Hi Boy. Another scene involves a trip to see Mag, a black prostitute whom Step once saved from a mob. She now lives with her business manager, Cooper, her former pimp. Trying to prove his courage to Step during this visit, Hi Boy stabs himself in the hand. Although treated immediately, the wound never heals and later causes Hi Boy's death. The three leave for an Edenic ranch, the setting for the second part of the novel, but they carry with them the infection of Step's former life. The ranch belongs to a man named Sampson who has helped the hoboes out of trouble and offered them work. The situation at Sampson's ranch seems ideal: a beautiful rural setting, hard but satisfying work, ample food, and a kindly owner. Temptation exists, however, in the form of Anna, Sampson's teenage daughter. Despite Ed's warnings, Step takes advantage of the girl.

In stressing the novel's thematic parallels with the mythic Eden, Attaway betrays the overly insistent hand of a beginning writer. Events at the ranch occur against a repeated background of old and new apple orchards. Anna mentions that her father sees her as one of his apples, as yet unfallen. Ed hopes that she only wants to be kissed "in some garden," and he cautions that encouraging Step is comparable to stirring up a nest of rattlesnakes beneath the house. To clinch the parallel with Eden, after Anna and Step have become lovers, Ed searches the orchard for them, only to step on a "fallen apple."

Hi Boy's condition worsens. He cannot keep his wounded hand free from dirt, and with a gun given him by Mag the boy, who was originally identified with love for all creatures, turns to killing—rabbits, hawks, even a nest of rattlesnakes. He learns to lie, and Step uses him to hide his meetings with Anna. Finding Anna's attentions too demanding, Step frets to leave. In the boy's best interest he almost heroically agrees to leave him with Sampson, but events undo the fine intention. Out of compassion for the boy's sorrow at their departure, Sampson suggests that the men take the boy to town one last time. In a violent scene at Mag's, Anna is shot and Step and Ed flee by train, taking Hi Boy.

The unduly prolonged conclusion of the novel takes place on the train. The description of Hi Boy's dying is vivid but too drawn out. Despite Step's heroic attempts, when the train stops, the boy is dead. After placing the corpse on a train car bound for New Mexico, the two men, devastated and guilty, plan wearily to resume their traveling. At the end of the novel they stand defeated, all pretense of worth having crumbled.

Let Me Breathe Thunder was given full reviews in both the *New York Times Book Review* and the *New York Herald Tribune Books*. Both reviews judged the novel to be heavily influenced by the naturalism then popular, the *New York Times Book Review* finding these influences well handled. The *New York Herald Tribune Books* reviewer upbraided Attaway for weak imitation of the "hardboiled" school of writers, such as James M. Cain, Ernest Hemingway in his early stories, and John Steinbeck. Both critics noted similarities between Attaway's novel and Steinbeck's *Of Mice and Men* (1937)—as would later critics.

Ulysses Lee, writing in *Opportunity*, concentrated upon race in Attaway's novel. He regretted the publisher's note at the front of the book heralding it as "that rare thing, a novel by a Negro about whites." First, Lee points out, the novel needs no special claim, and, second, it is no

more about whites than blacks. Alone of the first reviewers, Lee noted the important presence of black characters throughout the novel. For him the two main characters might as well have been black because of their marginal existence in society and their deep yearning for stability. Lee's other comments shed light on some of the controversies concerning Afro-American writing in 1939. By making the main figures hoboes, Lee felt, Attaway wisely avoided the chief danger for a black writer: imagining characters—white or black—whose way of life is so remote from the author's that they become absurd. By drawing upon his own life as a vagabond, Attaway, according to Lee, had retained "artistic truth" in the novel. He felt that Attaway's black characters were his most effective, and he eagerly awaited a novel by him "primarily of Negro life."

Discussion of *Let Me Breathe Thunder* in the studies of Attaway's work in the late 1960s through the mid 1970s is usually brief. Critics like Addison Gayle, Jr., maintained that while Attaway gained immediacy through his use of a limited point of view, in doing so he sacrificed a greater range of characterization, style, and description. J. Saunders Redding and Hugh M. Gloster both applauded Attaway's use of white characters. Noel Schraufnagel and Edward Margolies both believed that Attaway sidestepped racial issues in the novel.

Attaway worked quickly on his second novel, *Blood on the Forge* (1941), substantially aided by a two-year grant from the Julius Rosenwald Fund for 1939 and 1940. The tragic plot centers on the Mosses, three black half brothers who move in 1919 from a poor farm in Kentucky to the steel mills of Pennsylvania. The transition is devastating for all three: Big Mat is killed; Chinatown is blinded; and Melody is demoralized.

Blood on the Forge is an ambitious novel in many ways. Two sharply contrasting settings—the rural South and the industrial North—are described with the thoroughness and authenticity of close personal observation. The book chronicles the impact of the Great Migration upon individual lives and depicts the struggle of workers in the major northern industries of the period. The cast is wide: white farmers and black sharecroppers in the South; immigrant workers of diverse ethnic and racial groups in the North; agents of the company owners; labor organizers; and the women whose lives in various degrees affect the men. The three Moss brothers differ widely in personality, as if Attaway sought to represent in one family the most common types of response among Afro-Americans to these historical events. For Ralph Ellison, Big Mat represents the religious, Melody represents the artistic, and Chinatown represents the pagan. Big Mat, the eldest brother and core of the family, in his strength, courage, and erupting anger toward whites, is comparable to Richard Wright's Bigger Thomas, in *Native Son* (1940), in terms of tragic stature.

Blood on the Forge is divided into five parts. Part 1, set in the hills of Kentucky, describes the plight of blacks trapped and victimized by a cruel, racist society. Big Mat sharecrops an exhausted piece of land for a cruel white farmer. He lives in a shack with his wife, Hattie, and his two half brothers, Melody and Chinatown. Melody, a sensitive and poetic dreamer, delights in playing the blues guitar. Chinatown, playful, happy, and idle, loves his one gold tooth above all else. Big Mat, tall, strong, and generally silent, longs to deliver God's word but feels cursed by an inability to preach and by Hattie's six miscarriages.

Big Mat's severe beating of a white overseer, who has insulted his dead mother, sets the stage for part 2. Just after the beating the men are recruited by a Jackleg, an agent for an Allegheny Valley steel mill intent on destroying the labor movement through the importation of cheap labor. Attaway describes a nightmarish ride north in a sealed train car. By evoking the horrors of the Middle Passage—the transportation of Africans to slavery in the New World—Attaway suggests that the brothers are exchanging one master for another.

The next part introduces the brothers to the life in the steel mills that will destroy them. They are shaken by the awesome machinery and the hostility of the white workers, whose jobs and hopes for a union are threatened by imported blacks. Big Mat quickly adapts, his strength and willingness to work winning a grudging respect among the whites. Chinatown and Melody give themselves over to dissipation in their rare times of leisure. Learning of Hattie's seventh miscarriage, Mat gives up his Bible, begins to drink, and begins living with Anna, a young prostitute from Mexico. She is determined to rise socially and chooses Big Mat because he is the strongest man she knows.

In the last two parts of the book the family is destroyed. Melody becomes hostile toward Big Mat, in part because he has abandoned Hattie, lost his desire to preach, and given himself up to his passions but mostly because he is jealous of Big Mat's relationship with Anna. One evening he goes to Anna to persuade her to leave Big Mat, but they end up having sexual intercourse. Calamities happen to each of the brothers which temporarily bring them together, but their unity does not last. Melody accidentally smashes his playing hand. Chinatown, serving as his replacement on the job, is permanently blinded by an explosion. Big Mat, realizing that Anna has cheated on him, is arrested for assaulting a man whom he wrongly suspects. The explosion fuels talk of strikes and unions, but the Moss brothers, their own judgment clouded, distance themselves. Indeed, Big Mat's belief that his life is better than it was in the South leads him to become a strikebreaker and, finally, a deputy. His newly found sense of power ends tragically, however. Learning that Anna has returned to prostitution, Big Mat beats her, then turns his fury on the strikers, finally killing one old worker. He is in turn beaten to death by a striker. His dying insight is that instead of having thrown off white dominance, he has become the overseer of the mill owners. Following Big Mat's death and the end of the strike, Melody and Chinatown leave for the slums of Pittsburgh to join other black "castoffs of the mill."

Most of the immediate and subsequent criticism found *Blood on the Forge* superior to *Let Me Breathe Thunder* in range of characters, control of events, and seriousness of theme. Ellison, the first of many critics to note Attaway's strategy of differentiating the three brothers, faulted the ending for being too pessimistic. Gayle questioned the credibility of Big Mat's insight, finding Attaway's failure to be the backing away from the true import of black violence: "Attaway does not have enough faith in his character to accept him as the black outsider become rebel." For Margolies, Attaway's emphasis on the destructive power of the "life-denying machine" questioned the credibility of his protagonists. Robert A. Bone praised the novel, noting that Attaway had included Zanski, a Ukrainian who represents a "superior adjustment to the new industrial environment" and who understands, as the brothers do not, that their lives can only gain value if they put down roots. In spite of the fact that almost all of the reviews immediately following publication of *Blood on the Forge* were strongly encouraging, the book sold poorly.

Perhaps because of the poor sales Attaway turned his main efforts at publication to more lucrative forms of writing. He wrote two books about music: *Calypso Song Book* (1957), a collection of songs, and *Hear America Singing* (1967), a history of popular music in America for young people. He also composed and arranged songs, including several for his friend Harry Belafonte, at whose home he married Frances Settele on 28 December 1962. Attaway and his wife had two children, a son and a daughter.

In addition to his musical publications, Attaway wrote scripts for radio, television, and motion pictures. He was involved with the civil rights movement and participated in the 1965 march for voting rights to Selma, Alabama. After working on the television script for a special on black humor entitled *One Hundred Years of Laughter* (1966), he went with his family to Barbados for what he thought would be a week's vacation. Instead, they lived there for eleven years, fulfilling a lifelong desire of his to live in a country with a black government, black law enforcement, and black professional people. In Barbados he continued to write, especially for television, but he also worked on American and foreign films. He was involved in the film version of Irving Wallace's best-selling novel *The Man* (1964), which deals with the first black man to become president of the United States. Early in 1968 the company owning the film rights to the novel hired Attaway to write the screenplay. Meeting Attaway at this time, Wallace found him to be "serious and intense" and an "excellent choice." Attaway subsequently wrote three drafts. Speaking of them in an interview, Wallace recalled that the film producers found them powerful "but too long and too rough." Wallace continued, "Rough they may have been, but he was damn good–he had passion. And because he was black, he understood those characters in the book." Largely because his drafts lacked enough polish, Attaway was dropped from the project, and Rod Serling wrote the final version.

The last years of Attaway's life were spent in California, initially in Berkeley and then in Los Angeles. In 1982 Greenville, Mississippi, honored him during an arts festival. While working on the script for *The Atlanta Child Murders* (1985) he had a heart attack from which he never fully re-covered. He died in Los Angeles on 17 June 1986.

References:

Robert A. Bone, *The Negro Novel in America*, revised edition (New Haven: Yale University Press, 1965), pp. 132-140;

Ralph Ellison, "Transition," *Negro Quarterly*, 1 (Spring 1942): 87-92;

Robert Felgar, "William Attaway's Unaccommodated Protagonists," *Studies in Black Literature*, 4 (Spring 1973): 1-3;

Addison Gayle, Jr., *The Way of the New World: The Black Novel in America* (New York: Anchor/Doubleday, 1975), pp. 192-201;

Hugh M. Gloster, *Negro Voices in American Fiction* (Chapel Hill: University of North Carolina Press, 1948), pp. 249-250;

Sam L. Grogg, Jr., Interview with Irving Wallace, in John Leverence, *Irving Wallace: A Writer's Profile* (Bowling Green, Ohio: Popular Press, 1974), pp. 184-256;

Carl M. Hughes, *The Negro Novelist* (New York: Citadel, 1953), pp. 79-82;

Ulysses Lee, "On the Road," review of *Let Me Breathe Thunder*, *Opportunity*, 17 (September 1939): 283-284;

Edward Margolies, Introduction to Attaway's *Blood on the Forge* (New York: Collier, 1970);

Margolies, *Native Sons: A Critical Study of Twentieth-Century Negro American Authors* (Philadelphia: Lippincott, 1968), pp. 52, 63-64;

J. Saunders Redding, "The Negro Writer and American Literature," in *Anger, and Beyond: The Negro Writer in the United States*, edited by Herbert Hill (New York: Harper & Row, 1966), pp. 1-19;

Noel Schraufnagel, *From Apology to Protest: The Black American Novel* (De Land, Fla.: Everett/Edwards, 1973), pp. 17, 52-53;

James O. Young, *Black Writers of the Thirties* (Baton Rouge: Louisiana State University Press, 1973), pp. 225-229.

Papers:
The University of California, Berkeley, contains six letters from Attaway. The Schomburg Center for Research in Black Culture, New York City, holds page proofs.

William Blackwell Branch

(11 September 1927-   )

Clara Robie Williams

PLAY PRODUCTIONS: *A Medal For Willie,* New York, Club Baron, 15 October 1951;
In Splendid Error, New York, Greenwich Mews Theatre, 26 October 1954;
Experiment in Black, New York, 1955;
Light in the Southern Sky, New York, Waldorf Astoria, 1958;
Fifty Steps Toward Freedom, New York, New York Coliseum, 14 July 1959;
The Man on Meeting Street, New York, Waldorf Astoria, 1960;
A Wreath for Udomo, adapted from Peter Abraham's novel, Cleveland, Ohio, Karamu Theatre, Spring 1960; London, Lyric Hammersmith Theatre, November 1961;
To Follow the Phoenix, Chicago, Civic Opera House, 1960;
Baccalaureate, Hamilton, Bermuda, City Hall Theatre, 1975.

MOTION PICTURES: *Decision in Hong Kong,* narration by Branch, Broadcast and Film Commission of the National Council of Churches, 1955;
Benefit Performance, story outline by Branch, Universal, 1969;
Together for Days, screenplay by Branch, Olas, 1971.

TELEVISION: *The Way,* ABC, 1955;
What Is Conscience?, CBS, 1955;
Let's Find Out, syndicated, 1956;
Light in the Southern Sky, NBC, 1958;
Legacy of a Prophet, Educational Broadcasting Corporation, 1959;
"The Explorer's Club," *The City,* Educational Broadcasting Corporation, 1963;
"Fair Game," *The City,* Educational Broadcasting Corporation, 1964;
"Gypsy in my Soul," *The City,* Educational Broadcasting Corporation, 1964;
Still a Brother: Inside the Negro Middle Class, National Educational Television, 1968;

William Blackwell Branch

The Case of the Non-Working Workers, NBC, 1972;
The 20 Billion Dollar Rip-Off, NBC, 1972;
No Room to Run, No Place to Hide, NBC, 1972;
Build, Baby Build, NBC, 1972;
The Black Church in New York, NBC, 1973;
Afro-American Perspectives, PBS, 1973-1974;
Black Perspectives on the News, PBS, 1978-1979;
"A Letter from Booker T.," *Ossie & Ruby,* PBS, 1987.

RADIO: *The Alma John Show,* syndicated, 1963-1965.

OTHER: "Marketing the Products of American Negro Writers," in *The American Negro Writer and His Roots,* edited by John A. Davis

(New York: American Society of African Culture, 1960), pp. 46-60;

Excerpt from *To Follow the Phoenix,* in *Black Scenes,* edited by Alice Childress (Garden City, N.Y.: Doubleday, 1971), pp. 57-66;

In Splendid Error, in *Black Theater: A Twentieth Century Collection of the Work of Its Best Playwrights,* edited by Lindsay Patterson (New York: Dodd, Mead, 1971), pp. 145-206;

A Medal for Willie, in *Black Drama Anthology,* edited by Woodie King, Jr., and Ron Milner (New York: Columbia University Press, 1972), pp. 439-473.

PERIODICAL PUBLICATIONS: "Changing Roles in a Changing Society," *Spelman Messenger,* 84 (November 1957): 12-22;

"The Yale-ABC Project: Three Views," by Branch, David Davidson, and Tim Kelly, *Television Quarterly,* 5 (Summer 1966): 9-24;

"The Need for True Involvement," *New York Times,* 14 July 1968, D: 17;

"The Challenge of the Black Writer," *Black Scholar,* 10 (July-August 1979): 9-11.

As a playwright, producer, director, and lecturer, William Branch is best noted for his moralistic stage productions that have won acclaim from audiences in the United States and parts of Europe, Africa, and the Far East. During the 1950s Branch was one of the leading black playwrights in America along with Alice Childress, Langston Hughes, Loften Mitchell, and Louis Peterson. Most of his work since that time has been in television and film.

William Blackwell Branch was born in New Haven, Connecticut, on 11 September 1927, the son of James Matthew Branch, an African Methodist Episcopal Zion minister, and Iola Douglas Branch. He attended high schools in Charlotte, North Carolina, and Washington, D. C., and enrolled at Northwestern University. While still a college freshman he joined the national cast (in Chicago) of Philip Yordan's Broadway success, *Anna Lucasta.* At Northwestern, from which he would graduate with a B.S. degree in speech in 1949, Branch enrolled in one semester of play writing. He later admitted that "far more helpful were extensive readings of plays and seeing plays on and off Broadway." From 1949 to 1950 he was a representative for *Ebony* magazine, and he served in the army from 1950 to 1953. In 1958, subsequent to his first two produced plays, Branch received an M.F.A. in play writing from

Columbia University. From 1965 to 1966 he was a Yale/American Broadcasting Company Fellow at the Yale University School of Drama.

As a playwright, Branch first became known for his handling of the theme of the black soldier in wartime. At twenty-four Branch wrote *A Medal for Willie,* his first play. It was produced by the Committee for the Negro in the Arts at Harlem's Club Baron on 15 October 1951.

A Medal for Willie is set at the memorial service in honor of a black soldier, Corporal Willie Jackson, who died a hero's death fighting for his country. The nation honors him with the public presentation of a medal to his mother. Willie's mother is upset about the attention her son is receiving after death; the community should have draped him and others with love and guidance while they were alive. She says bitterly, "Where was they when your father and me was strugglin' to feed him and put clothes on his back and bring him up decent? . . . An' where was they when he was walkin' the street lookin' for work?" Loften Mitchell articulates the major theme of Branch's play: "Should the Black soldier fight and die abroad or should he take up arms against the prejudiced southland?" For Donald T. Evans the central issue of the play is that "the oppressed cannot fight a battle for the oppressor and come out victorious." *A Medal for Willie* succinctly shows that the families, especially the black American women, who have lost their loved ones in war cannot be expected to hail their country or give total allegiance to it when racial oppression and suffering are ever prevalent. Black families deserve to have a better legacy than a mere medal in the name of democracy; they deserve democracy itself.

While stationed in Germany in 1952 and 1953, the twenty-six-year-old Branch completed "Frederick Douglass," later retitled *In Splendid Error.* Branch gathered the bulk of his material from Frederick Douglass's autobiography, *The Life and Times of Frederick Douglass* (1881), Shirley Graham's *There Was Once A Slave* (1947), and Leonard Ehrlich's *God's Angry Man* (1941). Branch says Douglass's autobiography furnished "the core of the story-line itself although . . . certain dramatic licenses were taken in order to more effectively dramatize what I consider to be the basic conflict: that of two ways of fighting for a cause."

The three-act *In Splendid Error* takes place in the parlor of Douglass's home in Rochester, New York, during the 1850s. It re-creates a discussion Douglass had with John Brown, the white abolitionist. Brown argues for guerrilla warfare so that the "plantation owners will have no choice but to consider a system more economically secure than slavery." Douglass agrees but later breaks with Brown over the tactic of attacking a federal arsenal at Harpers Ferry, West Virginia, which was not part of the original plan.

In Splendid Error opened to mixed reviews at the Greenwich Mews Theatre in New York on 26 October 1954; it had a four-month run. Lewis Funke, in the *New York Times*, found the scenes between Douglass and Brown "full of spirit and force." Henry Hewes in the *Saturday Review* called the play stimulating and said it was "a play to be revived by groups everywhere." Some critics felt the characters were less than lifelike, but others strongly disagreed. Branch openly stated that he intended to make a racial and political statement in the play:

> I saw in the Douglass-Brown story certain parallels . . . between the climate and events of the 1850's and those of the 1950's. Like Douglass, I found it hard to discard an ingrained belief that change could somehow take place without the necessity of outright overthrow of the government. . . . *In Splendid Error* eventually became more and more of a personal statement in contemporary terms as to the differing roles people could play in a revolutionary movement. I believed then, and believe now, that society needs both its id and its super-ego.

Branch's 1960 drama, *A Wreath for Udomo*, is a play about Udomo, an African leader. He moves from exile to become prime minister of his nation; and, at play's end–due to the difficult decisions he has had to make while governing–he is ritually murdered by his own people. The reviewer in the London *Times* said that after an expository scene in London, the play moved to Africa and "came alive," adding that the African scenes were beautifully done.

The poor market for black theater in the 1950s and early 1960s was an impetus for Branch to begin writing for radio, television, and motion pictures. As he said, white colleges were not "interested in plays with Negroes as leading characters . . . and by and large, Negro colleges

are so busy trying to keep up with the white ones, by doing the classics and Broadway hits, that they avoid Negroes also–except for the Broadway hit, *A Raisin in the Sun*." Community theaters had the same biases. During 1959 and 1960 Branch was awarded a Guggenheim Fellowship in creative dramatic writing; in those years he also directed the *Jackie Robinson Show* for NBC radio and from 1959 to 1961 wrote a syndicated "Jackie Robinson Column" for newspapers. One of his earliest television dramas, *Light in the Southern Sky* (1958), the story of Mary McLeod Bethune, won the Robert E. Sherwood TV Award and a citation from the National Council of Christians and Jews. His television documentary *Still a Brother: Inside the Negro Middle Class* (1968) was nominated for an Emmy Award and won a blue ribbon from the American Film Festival.

Branch has held visiting teaching positions at the University of Ghana, the University of Maryland, Smith College, North Carolina Central University, and Williams College and since 1985 has served as a professor of black theater and dramatic literature at Cornell University. He currently lives in New Rochelle, New York, where he is president of his own media development, production, and consulting firm.

References:
Doris E. Abramson, *Negro Playwrights in the American Theater, 1925-1959* (New York: Columbia University Press, 1969), pp. 171-188, 255-258;
Herbert Aptheker, *Toward Negro Freedom* (New York: New Century, 1956), pp. 68-72;
"Black Writers' Views on Literary Lions and Values," *Negro Digest*, 17 (January 1968): 30;
Donald T. Evans, "Bring It All Back Home," *Black World*, 20 (February 1971): 41-45;
Paul Harrison, *Drama of Nommo* (New York: Grove Press, 1972), p. xvii;
Loften Mitchell, "Three Writers and a Dream," *Crisis*, 72 (April 1965): 219-223;
Carleton W. and Barbara J. Molette, *Black Theatre: Premise and Presentation* (Bristol, Ind.: Wyndham Hall, 1986), pp. 122-123;
Mary Spradling, *In Black and White* (Detroit: Gale, 1980), p. 108.

Gwendolyn Brooks

(7 June 1917-)

George E. Kent
University of Chicago

See also the Brooks entry in *DLB 5: American Poets Since World War II.*

BOOKS: *A Street in Bronzeville* (New York & London: Harper, 1945);
Annie Allen (New York: Harper, 1949);
Maud Martha (New York: Harper, 1953);
Bronzeville Boys and Girls (New York: Harper, 1956);
The Bean Eaters (New York: Harper, 1960);
Selected Poems (New York: Harper & Row, 1963);
In the Mecca (New York: Harper & Row, 1968);
Riot (Detroit: Broadside Press, 1969);
Family Pictures (Detroit: Broadside Press, 1970);
Aloneness (Detroit: Broadside Press, 1971);
The World of Gwendolyn Brooks (New York: Harper & Row, 1971);
Report from Part One (Detroit: Broadside Press, 1972);
The Tiger Who Wore White Gloves: Or, What You Are You Are (Chicago: Third World Press, 1974);
Beckonings (Detroit: Broadside Press, 1975);
Primer for Blacks (Chicago: Black Position Press, 1980);
Young Poet's Primer (Chicago: Brooks Press, 1980);
Black Love (Chicago: Brooks Press, 1981);
to disembark (Chicago: Third World Press, 1981);
Mayor Harold Washington and Chicago, the I Will City (Chicago: Brooks Press, 1983);
Very Young Poets (Chicago: Brooks Press, 1983);
The Near-Johannesburg Boy, and Other Poems (Chicago: David, 1986).

OTHER: "The Life of Lincoln West," in *Soon, One Morning: New Writing by American Negroes*, edited by Herbert Hill (New York: Knopf, 1963), pp. 317-319;
A Broadside Treasury, edited by Brooks (Detroit: Broadside Press, 1971);
Jump Bad; A New Chicago Anthology, edited by Brooks (Detroit: Broadside Press, 1971);
A Capsule Course in Black Poetry Writing, edited by Brooks and others (Detroit: Broadside Press, 1975).

PERIODICAL PUBLICATIONS: "Poets Who Are Negroes," *Phylon*, 2 (December 1950): 312;
"Why Negro Women Leave Home," *Negro Digest*, 9 (March 1951): 26-28;
"How I Told My Child About Race," *Negro Digest*, 9 (June 1951): 29-31;
"They Call It Bronzeville," *Holiday* (October 1951): 60-67.

Gwendolyn Brooks holds a unique position in American letters. Not only has she combined a strong commitment to racial identity and equality with a mastery of poetic techniques, but she also has managed to bridge the gap between the academic poets of her generation in the 1940s and the young black militant writers of the 1960s. She generally is recognized as one of the most distinguished American poets of the twentieth century. For almost three decades now Brooks also has been a teacher, both in formal classroom situations and in more informal settings. As early as 1963 she was asked to conduct a poetry workshop at Columbia College in Chicago, and she would teach there intermittently until June of 1969. During this period she also taught at Elmhurst College in Elmhurst, Illinois, and at Northeastern Illinois State College. She was also Rennebohm Professor of English at the University of Wisconsin at Madison. Though she had resolved to quit teaching in 1969, she returned when she was invited to become Distinguished Professor of the Arts at the City College of New York. Although a "small indisposition" forced her to give up that position in 1971, she nonetheless has maintained a teaching relationship with many young poets, especially those in the state of Illinois, for whom she established the Illinois Poet Laureate Awards, grants of various amounts to encourage young talent.

Brooks was born in Topeka, Kansas, on 7 June 1917. Her mother, Keziah Corinne Wims, and her father, David Anderson Brooks, were descendants of blacks who had migrated to Kansas. David Brooks was the son of Lucas Brooks, a run-

Gwendolyn Brooks (UPI/Bettmann Newsphotos)

away slave who fought in the Civil War and settled in Oklahoma City. Lucas Brooks and his wife Elizabeth had twelve children; in spite of their own poverty they took in boarders and frequently fed others who came to their door hungry. David Brooks was the one family member who graduated from high school, delivering a speech and singing a song as part of the graduation ceremony. He then migrated to Nashville, Tennessee, where, with hopes of becoming a doctor, he attended Fisk University for a year. Back in Topeka in 1914, he met Keziah Corinne Wims, a schoolteacher; they were married after a two-year courtship and moved to Chicago. Keziah Brooks, however, decided that she wanted to have her first child at home in Kansas, so several weeks before the birth, she returned to Topeka, where Gwendolyn was born. Shortly thereafter, she rejoined David in Chicago. Sixteen months later, in 1918, Gwendolyn's brother Raymond was born.

Brooks's mother and father were contrasting and powerful influences in her life as she was growing up in Chicago. Keziah Brooks, who had taken courses to prepare for a career as a concert pianist, settled into being a nurturing wife and mother who was committed to duty and order. Be-

cause he could not afford tuition, David Brooks had turned from the expectation of becoming a doctor to being a janitor for the McKinley Music Company. He sang songs, told stories, and shared his meager fare with those less fortunate. His zest for life turned out to be a great influence upon Brooks, and he became the subject of several of her poems. At his death on 21 November 1959 she celebrated him in her poem "In Honor of David Anderson Brooks, My Father," in which she sought to express her sense of the essence of his life; the poem appeared in *The Bean Eaters* (1960). "A dryness is upon the house/My father loved and tended./Beyond his firm and sculptured door/his light and lease have ended." She concluded: "He who was Goodness, Gentleness/And Dignity is free/Translates to public Love/Old private charity."

The beginning of school for Brooks was the beginning of her awareness of racial and color issues that would be prominent in her poetry. Her six-year-old excitement dampened when she found that she was spurned by members of her own race because she lacked social or athletic abilities, a light skin, and good grade hair. The security she had developed at home, especially that sense of specialness she felt on her back porch contemplating her dream world, was shattered by intraracial prejudice. Problems tied to color created anxiety for her throughout most of her elementary and secondary school life, and the theme of intraracial and interracial prejudice frequently appears in her mature works.

Brooks found an alternative to peer rejection in her writing. From the age of seven she was supported in her vocation by her mother and father. Finding her daughter writing a page of rhymes, Keziah Brooks was astonished by their clarity and originality and said, "You are going to be a poet." Brooks recalled that she "believed every word she said and just kept on writing." Her early poems, especially those written between the time she was thirteen and the time she was sixteen, deal with a universe in which order and beauty largely prevail. She read avidly, and her early poetry is influenced by William Wordsworth, John Keats, William Cullen Bryant, Henry Wadsworth Longfellow, and many others. Brooks depicts herself as the girl of quiet games, of wild inner delight over the patterns of physical nature, and of occasional rebelliousness. She was also the prancing and dancing figure of her imagination. "Eventide," her first published poem, appeared in *American Childhood* magazine in 1930, when Brooks was thirteen. She began publishing poetry in the *Chicago Defender*'s weekly variety column, "Lights and Shadows," in 1934.

Brooks graduated from the integrated Englewood High School in 1934. By 1935 she was making considerable progress in mastering traditional poetic forms. She worked with different possibilities in syntax and frequently used startling beginnings, sharp comparisons and contrasts in her descriptions, analogy, and color symbolism. Occasionally, the imagery went beyond the atmospheric and the ornamental and became suggestive of mind-states. There were some hints of themes of racial pride in her work of this period, but she was concerned overwhelmingly with nature and love. Incorporating the influence of Sara Teasdale, she spoke with knowing composure of the vagaries of love: "Two years now, and going on three,/Sweet, you have been known to me./I remember every grave/Glance, or merry, that you gave/To me carelessly, and all/Your mild smiles. . . . " Like many adolescents, she was seething inwardly and making the most of imaginary pains.

In the 1930s and early 1940s Brooks progressed rapidly in mastering the techniques that would characterize her first volume of poetry.

Brooks at age nineteen (courtesy of the author)

She was encouraged by three teachers: Ethel Hurn responded to a book report on Paul Leicester Ford's historical novel, *Janice Meredith* (1899), by telling her that someday she might be a poet; her journalism teacher, Margaret Anderson, took time to talk with Brooks about her writing; and Horace Williston, who taught American poetry, admired her poems and her love for poetry, and generally inspired her. Brooks also corresponded with the Harlem Renaissance poet James Weldon Johnson, who complimented her talent and suggested that she read modern poetry. She read the works of T. S. Eliot, Ezra Pound, and E. E. Cummings. When Johnson came to Chicago for a lecture in 1933, Keziah Brooks took her daughter to hear and meet him.

Brooks was already familiar with some of the works of Countee Cullen and Langston Hughes through her reading of *Caroling Dusk: An Anthology of Verse by Negro Poets*, edited in 1927 by Cullen. She had heard Langston Hughes read when he came to Metropolitan Community Church, Brooks's home church. She shared some of her poems with him and was surprised when he read them in her presence and encouraged her to continue writing; Brooks was sixteen at the time. By the late 1930s she had a considerable body of poems as apprentice work, including seventy-five that had been published in the *Chicago Defender*.

Graduating from Wilson Junior College in 1936, Brooks worked briefly as a maid, an experience she found painful and inhumane, and one that would serve as the basis for future poems portraying women in domestic service. She also drew upon this experience for a chapter in her novel, *Maud Martha* (1953). She judged her next job to be worse than the domestic job; the Illinois Employment Service sent her to work as a secretary for a spiritual advisor, Dr. E. N. French, who operated in a huge slum structure known as the Mecca building and exploited the misery of the occupants and others by selling them "Holy thunderbolts, charms, dusts of different kinds, love potions, heaven knows what all." Trapped because she hated to go home a failure, Brooks said this job was "the most horrible four months of my existence." The misery obsessed and haunted her; though she periodically tried to incorporate the experience into fiction and poetry, she was unsuccessful in doing so until her seventh volume of poems, *In the Mecca*, was published in 1968.

In 1938 Brooks joined the NAACP Youth Council, which gave her associations for the first time with aspiring young people who accepted her and valued her talents. At one of the meetings that year she met Henry Lowington Blakely II, about whom she declared, "That is the man I am going to marry." They were married on 17 September 1939. On the one hand, the marriage provided early fulfillment and companionship. On the other, it took her from a spartan, but warm and secure, home affording human space and dignity and made her a participant in the stark realities of crowded living in one-room kitchenette apartments and in the meager employment afforded the black masses of Chicago. The experiences raised the artistic tension within her to a high point. Out of this experience would come the kitchenette poems, the varied portraits of ordinary struggling people, which in turn reflected the artist's growth in sensibility.

On 10 October 1940 Brooks's son, Henry Lowington Blakely III, was born, signaling what would become a productive and highly creative decade for the poet. In 1941 Inez Cunningham Stark, a rebel socialite from Chicago's Gold Coast and reader for *Poetry* magazine, offered a workshop at the South Side Community Art Center,

which she called "The Poetry Class." Brooks and her husband attended, as did other writers and poets, such as William Couch, Margaret Taylor Goss Burroughs, and Margaret Danner. Stark taught Brooks a good deal about the techniques of modern poetry; indeed, many of the poems in Brooks's first collection, *A Street in Bronzeville* (1945), were written while she was part of the workshop in 1941 and 1942. Stark was adamantly opposed to cliché and stressed that every word should work, even strain, and that language must be pushed to its furthest limit. As a result of incorporating Stark's advice Brooks won first prize in a workshop contest. She also won the 1944 Midwestern Writers Conference prize with the sonnet, "Gay Chaps at the Bar," and the 1945 prize from the same organization with "the progress," both of which would eventually appear in *A Street in Bronzeville*.

Initially, Brooks tried publishing her collection of poems through Emily Morison of Knopf; Morison advised Brooks to concentrate upon materials from her own background. Brooks consequently gathered nineteen poems about blacks, the subject in which Morison had found her most successful, and sent them to Harper. Harper editors, excited about the unsolicited poems that had arrived, showed them to Richard Wright, the novelist, who was one of their outstanding writers. Wright was impressed by the authenticity of the poems, but he suggested that the collection be expanded, particularly to include a long poem that would exhibit more of the personal feeling of the author. Brooks added several poems to the volume, including "The Sundays of Satin Legs Smith," the longest poem in the volume. *A Street in Bronzeville* was published on 15 August 1945.

The book was well received. Coming home from their weekly outing at the movies, on 26 August 1945, Brooks and her husband stood under the streetlights to read the review that appeared in the Sunday *Chicago Tribune*'s book review magazine. The reviewer, Paul Engle, himself a poet and teacher, essentially launched Brooks's reputation; it was Engle who had awarded her prizes at Northwestern University's Annual Writers' Conference and who had sent several of her poems to *Poetry* magazine. Other reviewers focused less on the racial themes in the collection and paid tribute to Brooks's artistry. Amos N. Wilder, writing in *Poetry* (December 1945), concluded that Brooks had revealed "a capacity to marry the special qualities of her racial tradition with the best attain-

Gwendolyn Brooks with her husband, Henry Lowington Blakely II, and their son, Henry Lowington Blakely III, in early 1945 (courtesy of the author)

ments of our contemporary poetic tradition." Starr Nelson, in the 19 January 1945 issue of the *Saturday Review*, felt that the book was both "a work of art and a poignant social document."

Brooks maintained that *A Street in Bronzeville* had "a rather folksy narrative nature, and I guess that is one way to get poetry in front of people; to tell stories. Everyone loves stories, and a surprising number of people can be trapped into a book of verse if there's a promise of a story. The legend on the cover of the book, 'Ballads and Blues . . .' promised excitement." The poetic stories were about the everyday lives of the black people who occupied a large section of Chicago that the *Chicago Defender* called "Bronzeville." The first poem in the collection, "the old-marrieds," is typical: "But in the crowding darkness not a word did they say/Though the pretty-coated birds had piped so lightly all the day." By emphasizing their silence and their inability to respond to events that would perhaps spark interest from "young-marrieds," Brooks suggests that the couple has not only grown beyond

loving, but almost beyond living. Familiarity with the routine of life and of their marriage has made them uninterested in responding to the natural sounds of the birds or to the humanity of the young lovers in the side streets (perhaps a suggestion of their own youth and falling in love); instead, they commune silently and are content with each other. This and other short poems in the volume leave the reader with some highly memorable details. Dark-skinned Mabbie of "the ballad of chocolate Mabbie" is jilted by Willie Boone for a light-skinned girl, and the poem ends: "It was Mabbie alone by the grammar school gates/Yet chocolate companions had she:/Mabbie on Mabbie with hush in the heart/Mabbie on Mabbie to be." Of the longer poems, "Queen of the Blues" and "Ballad of Pearl May Lee" remain close to ballad conventions for moving a story quickly but deliver their subtleties through ironic attitudes, striking diction, and modulations in the incremental repetition.

"Negro Hero" and "The Sundays of Satin Legs Smith" have a clear story movement, but they also exhibit the complexities of theme that are characteristic of Brooks's work. "Negro Hero" depicts a black war hero who must force democracy down the throats of his white fellow soldiers in order to risk his life for them: "I had to kick their law into their teeth in order to save them." His belief in democracy and his awareness that one must "deal devilishly" with drowning men urges him toward his goal in spite of "this possible horror: that they might prefer the/Preservation of their law in all its sick dignity and their knives/To the continuation of their creed/And their lives." "The Sundays of Satin Legs Smith" portrays a black man who turns life into battle and fights against the odds of having an interesting and fulfilling life in a ghetto. Through colorful clothes ("wonder-suits in yellow and in wine/Sarcastic green and zebra-striped cobalt"), a hip style ("Squires his lady . . ."), and sex ("His lady alters as to leg and eye/Thickness and height, such minor points as these/From Sunday to Sunday"), Satin Legs tries to control the environment that stands ever ready to defeat him. His sinking into the honey-imaged body of each new lady, however, suggests that he carries his trap within and can find no escape from it.

Brooks's world is thick with male and female heroes, unrecognized. Her premise is that life itself is good. Forced to live in a devitalizing space in which a dream is unable "to send up through onion fumes/Its white and violet, fight with fried potatoes/and yesterday's garbage ripening in the hall," the people of the "kitchenette building" nevertheless meet limited goals, such as paying the rent, "feeding a wife," "satisfying a man." Exploitation has not rendered them unaware of life's potential, though at present the most pleasurable triumph is a bath in lukewarm water in a bathroom shared by five apartments.

In "Gay Chaps at the Bar," the sonnet sequence on World War II in *A Street in Bronzeville*, Brooks uses Petrarchan and Shakespearean structures, but she loosens the forms sufficiently for them to accommodate the rhythms of speech ("I pull you down my foxhole. Do you mind?"). In the sequence war is the crucible through which innocence, love, and beauty must attempt to pass; there are triumphs, but there are also horrors. In "still do I keep my look, my identity . . . ," a dead body retains the form of the life it had. Soldiers triumph over racism in "the white troops had their orders but the Negroes looked like men" when they realize that no one will give "two figs" in the heat of battle or when it comes to the color of bodies in caskets.

Annie Allen (1949), her next book of poems, continued the movement of Brooks's poetry toward social issues. Before its publication Brooks was the recipient of several awards and prizes: the *Mademoiselle* Merit Award (naming her as one of the ten most outstanding women of the year) in 1945; Guggenheim fellowships in 1946 and 1947; a National Institute of the Arts and Letters Award in 1946; the American Academy of Arts and Letters award for creative writing in 1946; and *Poetry* magazine's Eunice Tietjens Memorial Prize in 1949 for several poems that would be published in *Annie Allen*. Brooks was enjoying her life as a mother, and she was pleased with her poetry, fiction, and the book reviews she began writing for Chicago newspapers in 1948, and later for *Negro Digest*, the *New York Times*, and the *New York Herald Tribune*. She tried to solve the problem of close and nomadic living in Chicago by purchasing a home in Kalamazoo, Michigan. She had to explain direct racial conflicts to her son when she walked with him east of Cottage Grove Avenue in Chicago, a territory in which blacks were not welcome; she captured this experience in a *Negro Digest* article entitled "How I Told My Child About Race." Most important for a full appreciation of *Annie Allen* is the fact that Brooks began to appreciate more the position of women in society, though her tensions tended to remain within the framework of the traditional woman.

Front cover for Brooks's 1969 volume of poetry (courtesy of the Afro-American Collection, Blockson Library, Temple University)

Her criticisms of the belittling effect of marriage on many women was articulated in a *Negro Digest* article, "Why Negro Women Leave Home."

Annie Allen is concerned with the maturation of a young black woman. In "Notes from the Childhood and the Girlhood" Annie grasps at life in typical childhood and youthful ways, as she undergoes a period of innocence. "Do not be afraid of no" portrays the young woman composing herself for more realistic encounters. Taking advantage of glimpses of Annie's personality given in the poems preceding it, "The Anniad," a mock-epic, takes her through the woman's epic cycle of romantic dreams, romantic love, marriage and children, and other confrontations that lead toward maturity. Annie is at once the would-be heroine of folk song and story and the black woman whose realistic situation negates such a possibility for heroic action. The imagery is thus a mixture of the romantic and the realistic.

> Think of ripe and romp-about
> All her harvest buttoned in,

All her ornaments untried;
Waiting for the paladin
Prosperous and ocean-eyed
Who shall rub her secrets out
And behold the hinted bride.

Yet Annie's "unembroidered brown" skin imprinted with "bastard roses" and her "black and boisterous hair" make it impossible for her to attain her original dream. "Appendix to the Anniad," a war interlude, and "The Womanhood" complete the cycle. Annie's triumph is not in terms of events but in the emergence of a thoughtful, humorous, and imaginative self.

Following the apparent simplicity of *A Street in Bronzeville*, *Annie Allen* startled its audience with its degree of difficulty and level of self-consciousness. Nonetheless, the stylistic developments and the sophisticated narrator are natural developments from Brooks's long apprenticeship and her first book. The imagery of *Annie Allen* is more symbolic and mythic. In "Beverly Hills, Chicago," a poem rendering the complex responses of a poor couple to the luxuries of the rich, fallen leaves become "The dry brown coughing beneath their feet," and refuse becomes "a neat brilliancy." The first sonnet in the sequence on "the children of the poor" speaks of people without children attaining "a mail of ice and insolence" and of those with children struggling "through a throttling dark," forced to make "a sugar of/The Malocclusions, the inconditions of love."

Despite reservations, *Annie Allen* was well received. The sonnets received high praises, with "The Anniad" being censured for difficulty, partly praised, or highly praised. In the 22 January 1950 *New York Times Book Review*, Phyllis McGinley found "The Anniad" outstanding and felt that when Brooks forgot "her social conscience and her Guggenheim scholarship" she created "unbearable excitement." Other reviewers mixed praise with complaints of obscurity and emerging propaganda. *Annie Allen* won the Pulitzer Prize in 1950, the first time that the award had been presented to a black honoree. Winning the prize certainly brought Brooks fame. She became established as a Chicago institution and as a poet of national reputation. She was interviewed constantly by the city's newspapers, called upon for public readings, appointed a judge in cultural affairs, enrolled in the Society of Midland Authors, and given various forms of civic recognition. The award did not, however, change Brooks's basic view of life, though it did perhaps encourage the preference for art over propaganda in her writing.

On 8 September 1951 Brooks's daughter Nora was born, a fact which brought happiness as well as the urgency of finding a new house. After selling her Kalamazoo house and borrowing five hundred dollars from her parents, Brooks and her husband moved into their own home in 1953; 7428 South Evans Avenue on Chicago's South Side has been Brooks's home ever since. In 1953 Brooks published *Maud Martha*, to date her only novel. Perhaps mirroring her own experiences as a young wife and mother, Brooks tells the story of a young woman emerging from romantic dreams to grasp realistically fulfillment as wife and mother. Maud Martha is a dark-skinned black woman who suffers prejudice because of her blackness. The novel is highly poetic and transcends naturalistic formulas.

Bronzeville Boys and Girls (1956) is a book of poetry for children in which poems with bouncing rhymes are intermixed with those of more subtle and varied sound patterns. The world Brooks creates is one in which childhood's disappointments are upstaged by the sheer drive for joy, beauty, companionship, freedom, love, and imaginative flights. For example, Otto hides from his father his disappointment in the meager Christmas presents he receives. John, desperately poor, lives "so lone and alone"; he is not to be bothered with questions about the beginning or ending or his hunger. Although the other girls at a party envy Mirthine, she turns out not to be prettier or different once she is no longer giggling or wearing her beads and bangles. Rudolph is tired of the city and wishes to escape into the country. Robert wonders about looking into the mirror and discovering a stranger—"A child you know and do not know." Lyle envies the "permanence," the rootedness, of a tree. And Luther and Breck transform the limitations of their city life by acting out the old knightly tales. Reviewers tended to emphasize the universality of the poems and to praise their rhythm and simplicity. Typical was the *New York Herald Tribune Book Review* which said: "Because Miss Brooks is a Negro poet, she has called these 'Bronzeville Boys and Girls,' but they are universal and will make friends anywhere, among grown-ups or among children from eight to ten."

Over the next few years Brooks worked on a novel she planned to call "The Life of Lincoln West." She reworked the same material as a story

Brooks and Nelson Algren

for the anthology *Soon, One Morning* (1963) and as a poem in *Family Pictures* (1970). Both published versions represent the first chapter of the unfinished novel and tell the story of a black-skinned child rejected by his family and the world at large. He comes to appreciate himself upon hearing that he is "the real thing," a label derisively contributed by a white man. Seven-year-old little Lincoln is being applauded for being the epitome of the stereotypical, unattractive "nigger," as the lines preceding the phrase "the real thing" suggest:

> THERE! That's the kind I've been wanting
> to show you! One of the best
> examples of the specie. Not like
> those diluted Negroes you see so much of on
> the streets these days, but the
> real thing.
>
> Black, ugly, and odd. You
> can see the savagery. The blunt
> blankness. That is the real
> thing.

The sad irony is that this is the *first* time that someone in Lincoln's life has "praised" him. With this incident Brooks shows the problems inherent in black people accepting standards of beauty imposed by those of another culture, for the results can be irrevocably damaging to the psyches of impressionable black children. Lincoln may be happy, but the base for his happiness is built upon layers and layers of racial intolerance.

Brooks began at this time to mine her experiences as secretary to Dr. E. N. French, who was eventually murdered. Images of toiling up the stairs in the Mecca building to deliver "Holy Thunderbolts" and Liquid Love charms to people whose lives were so often steeped in misery, frustration, and violence haunted Brooks. She tried unsuccessfully to build a novel around a girl named Giovanna, an ambitious person sharing the hardships of her family and questing for a high level of fulfillment. However, the naturalistic scenes tended to inject a grimness that lessened the work's suitability for the juvenile market for which Brooks intended it. By 1958, however, she was again attempting to create a novel regarding the Mecca experience. This time she used adults, but the melodramatic events made the story lose the quality to which she aspired. Not until the late 1960s would she be able to make out of the experience a work of art, but the struggle testified to the impact the experiences had made upon her confrontation with the rawness of life in Chicago.

In late 1958 Brooks was compiling a volume of poetry whose working title was "Bronzeville Men and Women." *The Bean Eaters* (1960), which was its final title, is pointedly articulate about Brooks's view of the complexities of the universe in which her people move and the ,variety of their responses; strength and self-reliance are keys to survival. "People," Brooks had written in 1958, "are stronger than they think. . . . They bring about events themselves. They can save themselves. They need not wail in the night or day, wanting and hunting some Love that will hold them like babies, and protect them from the stresses of nature, and from the strains imposed on themselves by themselves."

The book's title is meant to evoke association with Vincent van Gogh's *The Potato Eaters*. The title's direct source was Brooks's knowledge of a poor, elderly couple who "could make a pound of beans go further than a pound of potatoes." Brooks's father died in 1959 while she was writing *The Bean Eaters*. He had become a second father to her children. For Brooks he had always seemed the protector of the richer side of existence; now his very peaceful death made her feel that she would not again fear dying. She was overwhelmed by the simple finality of death having terminated communication with her father. Such feelings were behind her composition of "In Honor of David Anderson Brooks, My Father," in which she was determined to express what she felt was the essence of his living. It became the dedicatory poem in the new volume.

The book's opening poem, "The Explorer," presents the search for meaning to which so many of the personalities in *The Bean Eaters* respond. With diminishing hope for success the explorer hunts through the noise and confusions of people for "a still spot," "A satin peace," "a room of wily hush," and not for Eldorado. "So tipping down the scrambled halls he set/Vague hands on throbbing knobs. There were behind/Only spiraling, high human voices,/The scream of nervous affairs,/Wee griefs,/Grand griefs. And choices." In "My Little 'Bout-town Gal' " a man speaks resignedly of his wife's questings about town and the deficiencies that prevent his offering her a heart or humanity sufficient for her needs. The grand picture of heroes in a western movie reminds an urban male viewer of his own littleness and paralysis: "I am not like that. I pay rent, am addled/By illegible landlords, run, if robbers call." In appropriately jerky rhythms and monosyllables, "We Real Cool" presents youths' evasions of the usual challenges of life and says that their confusion and naiveté will lead to physical or spiritual destruction. "The Contemplation of Suicide: The Temptation of Timothy" and "Leftist Orator in Washington Park Pleasantly Punishes the Gropers" emphasize the triumph of life over death, with the speaker of the first poem clinging to life because something out of the daily round suggests vitality. In "The Bean Eaters" the poverty-stricken couple enjoys the memories they have accumulated. By engaging each other with an intensity that makes religion of their passion, the lovers of "A Lovely Love" triumph over their setting of tenement alleys and hallways.

The poems on interracial and intraracial conflict and prejudice in *The Bean Eaters* dramatize sharply the ways in which man compounds his problems. The white woman in the poem "A Bronzeville Mother Loiters in Mississippi. Meanwhile, a Mississippi Mother Burns Bacon" realizes that a meaningless, self-serving myth has confused her about the realities of her life and has convinced her brutal husband that he is a hero for killing a fourteen-year-old boy who allegedly whistled at a girl as she stood in the door of a country store. The poem was inspired by the Emmett Till murder case in 1955 which had a special impact upon Brooks because her son was a Chicagoan, too, and the same age as the murdered youth. Other poems satirize whites whose oppressive acts are a form of ill-based pride or ego-building. "The Chicago Defender Sends a Man to Little Rock" presents the idea that the real tragedy of the people in Little Rock, Arkansas, who abused black children attempting to integrate a school, is that they are like people everywhere. Intraracial conflict emerges in "Jessie Mitchell's Mother," in which the frustrated yellow-skinned mother attempts to see her own abused life as superior to that of her black-skinned but youthful daughter: ". . . her way will be black, and jerkier even than mine." She relishes in memories of "Her exquisite yellow youth."

The importance of *The Bean Eaters* derives from Brooks's continued mastery of poetic forms and her movement away from autobiographical tensions and toward social concerns. Although several reviewers were uneasy with the social poems in *The Bean Eaters*, most agreed with Harvey Curtis Webster who said that, of Brooks's first three books of poetry, her best social poems were in *The Bean Eaters*.

The 1960s brought changes in consciousness for Brooks. The catalyst was the racial strug-

Brooks and President Jerome Sachs at the Northeastern Illinois State College celebration of her appointment to the Illinois poet laureateship (photograph by Roy Lewis)

gle, which initially brought a new sense of the possible for blacks, then, as protests failed, revolt. In February 1962 Brooks protested New York radio station WNEW's refusal to allow Oscar Brown's musical setting of her poem "Of De Witt Williams on his way to Lincoln Cemetery" to be aired because it contained the word *black*. The station maintained that blacks would be offended, but Brooks could not believe that Negroes, who were gaining so much pride in the emergence of Africa, could resent a word Africans exulted in recognizing. She resented the implication that she would do anything against the progress paid for so dearly by blacks and whites, and she pointed out that she had long been part of the struggle: "For seventeen years. Without ever detouring from my Business—which is being a writer. Many of the banners so brightly (and originally, they think) waved by today's youngsters I waved twenty years ago, and published sixteen years ago."

Brooks's popularity and national visibility continued to increase in the 1960s, as did her contact with the young. In 1962 President John F. Kennedy invited her to read at a Library of Congress poetry festival. She met Robert Frost,

whose praise for her work was inspiring. She became a spiritual mother to countless young people; she also gave money for schools to award prizes in creative writing. In the fall of 1963 she began a sustained teaching period, initially with a poetry workshop at Chicago's Columbia College. During her teaching experiences she captivated young college students and inspired them to create their own poems, stories, and essays. She wrote a commemorative poem for Malcolm X that was included in *The World of Gwendolyn Brooks* (1971). Inspired by her contact with young readers, Brooks wrote new material for *Selected Poems* (1963). Among the new poems was "Riders to the Blood Red Wrath," which satisfied her desire to salute the Freedom Riders of 1961. Rigorously winnowed from earlier volumes, *Selected Poems* made possible judgment of Brooks's achievement to date. With very little dissent, critical response judged the volume the work of a major poet. The *New York Times* said that "Miss Brooks won a Pulitzer Prize in 1950 and deserved it." Robert D. Spector in the *Saturday Review* observed that "it is in her ability to feel and make others feel that she truly reveals the essential qualities of a poet." In *Poetry* magazine Bruce Cutler admired her wide-ranging technical resources, her ability "to exploit the spoken language and make it work for her," and her existence as "a whole person behind the poems"; he concluded that "she is one of the very best poets."

Brooks's work on *Selected Poems* had meant suspension of still another attempt to get her youthful experience of the old Mecca building into a work of art. In a 22 August 1962 letter to her Harper editor she spoke of having begun a projected two thousand-line poem: "I can't give up the thing; it has a grip on me." By late 1963 she had renewed her struggle with "In the Mecca," while continuing to write other poems, teach, and give readings at colleges and cultural affairs. What seems to have given her inspiration and additional content was the Second Fisk Writers Conference of April 1967 and her subsequent intense interactions with young black artists of Chicago. At the conference, which featured writers such as LeRoi Jones (Amiri Baraka), Margaret Danner, and John Oliver Killens, Brooks was aware of "a general energy, an electricity, in look, walk, speech, *gesture* of the young blackness I saw all around me." The conference owed much to the current conception of America as a broken community in which institutionalized racism worked toward the destruction of blacks, a view arising from the breakdown of the civil rights movement. Thus, the black power movement, which had absorbed the energy once given to the civil rights movement, began to merge with the arts to give blacks the strength and images of themselves necessary for survival. Questioned regarding this black aesthetic and cultural nationalism, Brooks responded: "Is that what you call it? You may use any label you wish. All I know is when people started talking about Blacks loving, respecting, and helping one another, that was enough for me." In this spirit she returned to Chicago and sponsored writing workshops for a street gang (The Blackstone Rangers) and such young writers as Don L. Lee (Haki R. Madhubuti), Walter Bradford, Carolyn Rodgers, Jewel Latimore (Johari Amini), and Sharon Scott, among others. In this "electric" atmosphere she completed the long poem "In the Mecca" and published it in a volume of the same title in 1968; she included with it a section entitled "After Mecca," which consisted of ten shorter poems that brought her feelings and encounters up to date.

Brooks spends little time evoking the Mecca, the half-a-block-long apartment building once located between Chicago's State and Dearborn streets, but focuses upon the people who live in this corrupting environment. What happens to Mrs. Sallie Smith, a domestic worker and sole supporter of her nine children, and how she responds provides the framework through which the poet portrays the struggles and the loneliness characteristic of those dwelling in the building. The disappearance of Pepita, her youngest child, leads Mrs. Sallie, her children, and the police on a search for her. Jamaican Edward, a tenant, has murdered the small girl and shoved her under his cot with the dust and roaches. During the extensive search for Pepita a representative group of the occupants display heroism, lostness, isolation, or inhumanity. Mrs. Sallie's power is suggested early: "She plans/to set severity apart,/to unclench the heavy folly of the fist./Infirm booms/and suns that have not spoken die behind this low-brown butterball." Some of her children resist the Mecca; the others succumb. Yvonne, the oldest, is a person of "bald innocence and gentle fright" and the "undaunted" who once "pushed her thumbs into the eyes of a thief." Briggs, though doomed to eventual resignation, resists gang life. Melodie Mary is only lightly moved by the troubles represented in headlines but deeply sympathizes with the nearby rats and roaches whose fate represents the threats terrorizing her own life: "Trapped in his privacy of pain/the worried rat expires,/and smashed in the grind of a rapid heel/last night's roaches lie."

Though several adult tenants are visionaries, their vision is no guarantee of escape. Alfred can articulate the ills of the Mecca and the world but remains trapped within his frustrations and reveries. Loam Norton connects the Mecca's troubles with universal evil. Amos and Way-Out Morgan envision bloody and healing revenge upon America. Most important, Don Lee has a grasp of the sweep of reality and envisions the construction of a new world; in him, black consciousness enters the poem.

Brooks adopts a range of language and postures in this poem. For example, she frequently directs sentiments toward her characters and sometimes approaches the aphoristic. For Briggs having to face gangs, she comments: "Please pity Briggs. But there is a central height in pity/past which man's hand and sympathy cannot go . . . / and is all self-employed,/concerned with Other,/not with Us." For the murderer Jamaican Edward, she says: "Hateful things sometimes befall the hateful/but the hateful are not rendered lova-

Brooks, circa 1970 (courtesy of Contemporary Forum)

ble thereby." From stately deliberative language, the poet ranges to that of unlettered speech. Her achievement in creating a highly flexible free verse is thus far beyond that appearing in *The Bean Eaters* and *Selected Poems*.

Except for "To a Winter Squirrel" the poems in the "After Mecca" section of *In the Mecca* are largely about the newer consciousness in the black community in the 1960s. Brooks's pictures include a boy breaking glass in protest of his condition; Medgar Evers, the civil rights leader assassinated in Mississippi; Malcolm X; the Blackstone Rangers and a Rangerette. Technically, "The Chicago Picasso" seems to introduce a foreign note, with its discussion of man and art, but its emphasis on the individual really undergirds the idea of community portrayed in "The Wall," a description of the large mural painted in 1967 by many black Chicago residents. Two sermons on the "warpland" (America) from this section represent the high point in the poet's struggle to move to the new center of the black struggle. The first urges blacks to build solid

bases for the unity and communion needed in the struggle and afterwards. The second urges blacks to bear up under the pains of the struggle and to "Live!/and have your blooming in the noise of the whirlwind."

To reviewers, *In the Mecca* was often a somewhat startling work, although most acknowledged that it was a powerful work. M. L. Rosenthal, writing in the *New York Times*, felt that the title poem was "overwrought with effects" and that the poet seemed to back away from her "overpowering subject." But he concluded that the poem "had the power of its materials and holds the imagination fixed on the horrid predicament of real Americans whose everyday world haunts the nation's conscience intolerably." William Stafford of *Poetry* magazine felt that Brooks achieved a "special kind of complexity" and that, although the poems were sometimes confusingly local in reference, "portions of the book come through strong." James N. Johnson in *Ramparts* magazine judged it Brooks's best work since *A Street in Bronzeville*.

The greatest influence on her life and writing since 1967 has been Brooks's commitment to black solidarity and redemption. On 8 January 1968 Gov. Otto Kerner appointed her poet laureate of Illinois. She has made the post into an instrument to encourage creativity among elementary and high-school youth by sponsoring writing contests and underwriting the cost of prizes. She has offered numerous scholarships, given young writers the leisure to write, financed trips for youth to visit Africa, and made her own journey to East Africa in 1971 and West Africa in 1974. She showed her commitment to the development of black publishing companies by having her work published by Broadside Press, founded in Detroit by black poet Dudley Randall, and Third World Press, headed in Chicago by black poet Haki R. Madhubuti. She has written nonfictional works on the art of writing poetry and edited several volumes displaying works by other black writers, particularly the young. Her commitment was recognized by black writers in a public tribute on 28 December 1969 at the Afro-Arts Theater, on Chicago's Southside. From this celebration came a book, *To Gwen With Love* (1971), comprised of testimonials by local black writers and those of note from all across the country.

In 1972 Brooks published her autobiography, *Report from Part One*, with prefaces by Don L. Lee and George E. Kent. Brooks provides information on her family history, her marriage and children, the influences in her life, and her teaching and publishing successes. She also chronicles her transformation from *Negro* to *black* poet, as well as her trip to Africa. She further includes excerpts from reviews she wrote in the 1960s, as well as three interviews conducted between 1967 and 1971. Written in her characteristic style of fragmented prose bordering upon poetry, Brooks nevertheless packs the impressionistic account with substantial details that illustrate her philosophy as a wife, mother, critic, and poet.

In the 1970s and 1980s Brooks produced a succession of slim volumes, many of them for children and many of them occasional pieces. *The Black Position,* a 1971 magazine, had four numbers. In *Aloneness* (1971) she makes a distinction between being alone and being lonely. The illustrations accompanying the sparse lines picture a boy about six years old, who initially asserts that "Once in a while alone is delicious. Almost like a red small apple that is cold. An apple that is small and sweet and round and cold and for just you," but who finally concludes that the aloneness with a loving mother is preferable to being alone.

Young Poet's Primer (1980) is a ten-page listing of thirty-three rules for young poets. Brooks draws upon her lecturing and teaching experiences to encourage creativity in the younger generation, including such advice as the fourth item: "Your poem does not need to tell your reader everything. A *little* mystery is fascinating. *Too much* is irritating." In *Mayor Harold Washington and Chicago, the* I Will *City* (1983), which comprises a small volume, Brooks writes in honor of her hometown two long poems in one volume and in celebration of the changing political times that enabled Harold Washington to be elected mayor.

Brooks also published a succession of small volumes of poetry: *Riot* (1969), *Family Pictures* (1970), *Aloneness* (1971), *Beckonings* (1975), and *Primer for Blacks* (1980); she made selections from the first three volumes for inclusion in *to disembark* (1981). The title "to disembark" had special significance for Brooks; she had first applied it to an unsuccessful attempt to write a verse biography of Phillis Wheatley, the eighteenth-century black poet. Brooks's choice of poems was designed to reflect some key struggles and experiences of Afro-Americans. From *Riot* she selected the title poem, which depicts white response to black anger. White John Cabot, symbolic of European culture, lapses into panic upon contemplat-

ing black rioting in his neighborhood. "The Third Sermon on the Warpland" treats the implications of Chicago street disturbances after the 1968 assassination of Martin Luther King, Jr.; the section ends with a portrait of love "alive in the ice and the fire." From *Family Pictures* Brooks chose "The Life of Lincoln West." Brooks selected, among others, "The Boy Died in My Alley," a startling and conscience-stirring piece that functions as a summons to the awareness that, in spite of ignoring a boy being shot to death, we are "each other's magnitude and bond." The *Beckonings* section concludes the volume with "Another Preachment to Blacks," a poem which asserts that the struggle for freedom is not a part-time occupation. Five previously unpublished poems are presented in *to disembark* under the heading, "To the Diaspora"; they focus on the struggles of spiritually endowed black women and black prisoners. "To the Diaspora" also includes a welcoming birth song in the African tradition. As D. H. Melhem points out in her studies of Brooks, the poet assumes the role of prophet in these later poems, pointing to the direction by which blacks can avoid disaster and achieve health.

Brooks also showed the teacher and prophet role in some of her nonfiction books from this period. In *A Capsule Course in Black Poetry Writing* (1975) she advised beginning poets: "Try telling the reader a little less. He'll, She'll love you more and will love your poem more, if you allow him to do a little digging. Not *too* much, but *some*." In 1975 Brooks defined poetry as "the very sifting of life . . . Think of life as a rough powder that you pour through a sieve. Well, the finest part of it that comes through will be the poetry. Poetry is a concentration; you can get the essence of a novel into a short poem."

In 1973 Brooks was appointed honorary consultant in American letters to the Library of Congress. The 1980s have continued to bring Brooks honors and awards. On 3 January 1980 she read her works at the White House with Robert Hayden, Stanley Kunitz, and eighteen other distinguished poets. She was appointed to the Presidential Commission on the National Agenda for the Eighties. On 24 November 1981 the Gwendolyn Brooks Junior High School in Harvey, Illinois, was dedicated. In 1983 she revisited England to judge the Sotheby's International Poetry Contest. She was made poetry consultant to the Library of Congress in 1985.

Brooks's ability to touch "the workaday vein of human sympathy" has sustained for her a wide popularity as a poet talking to people, instead of to a coterie. In readings across the country her ability to communicate with her audiences brings consistent standing ovations. Her books continue to reach a wide audience, and, among blacks, she has become an institution. Although critics and criticism may divide in opinions regarding periods or specific books that represent Brooks's greatest effectiveness, there is no doubt that she is recognized as one of the most distinguished poets of the twentieth century. Her increasing popularity is attested to by the appearance of her works in more and more mainstream American anthologies. Feminist readers find that her early treatment of themes such as abortion aligns her with issues important to them. Afro-American readers note her ability to change with the times without violating her fundamental philosophy, thereby making her works relevant to younger and younger audiences. Brooks is therefore a poet for many people and many generations; her stature will surely continue to grow.

Bibliographies:

Jon N. Loff, "Gwendolyn Brooks: A Bibliography," *College Language Association Journal*, 17 (September 1973): 21-32;

Heidi L. Mahoney, "Selected Checklist of Material by and about Gwendolyn Brooks," *Negro American Literature Forum*, 8 (Summer 1974): 210-211.

References:

Houston A. Baker, Jr., *Singers of Daybreak: Studies in Black American Literature* (Washington, D.C.: Howard University Press, 1974), pp. 43-51;

Keziah C. Brooks, *The Voice and Other Short Stories* (Detroit: Harlo, 1975);

Arthur P. Davis, "The Black and Tan Motif in the Poetry of Gwendolyn Brooks," *College Language Association Journal*, 6 (December 1962): 90-97;

Davis, "Gwendolyn Brooks: Poet of the Unheroic," *College Language Association Journal*, 7 (December 1963): 114-125;

William H. Hansell, "Gwendolyn Brooks's 'In the Mecca': A Rebirth into Blackness," *Negro American Literature Forum*, 8 (Summer 1974): 199-207;

Cleonora F. Hudson, "Racial Themes in the Poetry of Gwendolyn Brooks," *College Language Association Journal*, 17 (September 1973): 16-20;

Gloria T. Hull and Posey Gallagher, "An Interview With Gwendolyn Brooks," *College Language Association Journal*, 21 (September 1977): 19-40;

James N. Johnson, "Blacklisting Poets," *Ramparts* (14 December 1968): 48-54;

George E. Kent, "Aesthetic Values in the Poetry of Gwendolyn Brooks," in *Black American Literature and Humanism*, edited by R. Baxter Miller (Lexington: University of Kentucky Press, 1981), pp. 75-94;

Kent, *Blackness and the Adventure of Western Culture* (Chicago: Third World Press, 1972), pp. 104-138;

D. H. Melhem, *Gwendolyn Brooks: Poetry and the Heroic Voice* (Lexington: University of Kentucky Press, 1987);

Melhem, "Gwendolyn Brooks: the Heroic Voice of Prophecy," *Studies in Black Literature*, 8 (Spring 1977): 1-3;

R. Baxter Miller, "Define the Whirlwind: In the Mecca–Urban Setting, Shifting Narrator and Redemptive Vision," *Obsidian*, 4 (Spring 1978): 19-31;

Miller, " 'Does Man Love Art?': The Humanistic Aesthetic of Gwendolyn Brooks," in his *Black American Literature and Humanism* (Lexington: University of Kentucky Press, 1981), pp. 95-112;

Miller, *Langston Hughes and Gwendolyn Brooks: A Reference Guide* (Boston: G. K. Hall, 1978);

Maria K. Mootry and Gary Smith, eds., *A Life Distilled: Gwendolyn Brooks, Her Poetry and Fiction* (Urbana: University of Illinois Press, 1987);

Roy Newquist, *Conversations* (Chicago: Rand McNally, 1967);

Eugene B. Redmond, *Drumvoices: the Mission of Afro-American Poetry* (New York: Doubleday, 1976), pp. 270-284;

Harry B. Shaw, *Gwendolyn Brooks* (Boston: Twayne, 1980).

Papers:

Atlanta University, Atlanta, Georgia, holds papers and letters by Brooks. The State University of New York at Buffalo holds the typescript for *Annie Allen*.

Frank London Brown

(7 October 1927-12 March 1962)

Kathleen A. Hauke
University of Nairobi

BOOKS: *Trumbull Park, A Novel* (Chicago: Regnery, 1959);
Short Stories by Frank London Brown (N.p., 1965);
The Myth Maker (Chicago: Path Press, 1969).

OTHER: "Singing Dinah's Song," in *Soon One Morning: New Writing By American Negroes, 1940-1962*, edited by Herbert Hill (New York: Knopf, 1963), pp. 349-354.

PERIODICAL PUBLICATIONS:
FICTION
"Night March," *Chicago Review*, 11 (Spring 1957): 57-61;
"A Cry Unheard," *Chicago Review*, 13 (Autumn 1959): 118-120;
"In the Shadow of a Dying Soldier," *Southwest Review*, 14 (Autumn 1959): 292-306;
"A Matter of Time," *Negro Digest*, 11 (March 1962): 58-60;
"The Ancient Book," *Negro Digest*, 13 (March 1964): 53-61;
"McDougal," *Phoenix* (Fall 1969).
NONFICTION
"More Man Than Myth," *Down Beat*, 45 (30 October 1958): 13-16, 45-46;
"Mahalia the Great," *Ebony*, 14 (March 1960): 69-76;
"Chicago's Great Lady of Poetry," *Negro Digest*, 11 (December 1961): 53-57;
"An Unaccountable Happiness: For Kermit Eby," *New City Magazine* (1 April 1962): 14-15.

Frank London Brown, winner of a John Hay Whitney Award for creative writing, was a writer who showed the resilience, hidden resources, and beauty of black people rising from the despair of the Chicago streets. He flowered during the civil rights movement that culminated in the 1960s. In his novels, short stories, and journalistic essays Brown comes through as resolute in the midst of a hostile racial climate, with a special appreciation for women.

Frank London Brown, circa 1959 (photograph by Lacey C. Crawford)

The eldest of three children, Brown was born in Kansas City, Missouri, to Myra Myrtle and Frank London Brown, Sr. The family moved to Chicago when he was twelve. According to Sterling Stuckey, Brown, as a student at Colman Elementary School and DuSable High School, "battered his way into manhood" in "the bleak and deadly jungle of the South Side." His perspective was formed during the hours he spent in Morrie's Record Shop under the elevated tracks on Fifty-eighth Street, listening to such jazz and blues performers as Thelonious Monk, Joe Williams, and Muddy Waters.

After graduating from high school in January 1945, Brown went to Wilberforce University in Ohio for a few months. He joined the army in January 1946; during this time he sang baritone in a band. On 30 November 1947, at age twenty, he married his high-school sweetheart, Evelyn Marie Jones. The couple had three daughters, and a son who died shortly after birth. Brown attended Roosevelt University on the GI Bill while his wife worked. They lived in a trailer park. Evelyn Brown Colbert remembers that he "used to say, 'Let's *both* go to school.' He loved to read and learn and study. He was always in a hurry. He seemed aware that he didn't have enough time, so he never wasted it." Brown got his B.A. degree in 1951; then he spent 1953 and 1954 at the Kent College of Law.

Brown interspersed his studies with jobs as a machinist, a postal clerk, a loan interviewer, and a tavern owner. He read his short stories to jazz accompaniment at the Gate of Horn nightclub in Chicago from 1952 to 1953. He wrote record-cover liner notes, book reviews for the *Chicago Sun-Times* and the *Chicago Tribune,* and short stories for the *Chicago Defender,* before his involvement in the trade union movement. For a time he was program coordinator for the United Packinghouse Workers of America, AFL-CIO.

Brown's most significant publication was a 1958 interview with Thelonious Monk in *Down Beat* magazine. As his widow recalls, the writing of it "filled him with joy." He and Monk both "swung with the special beat of Chicago." Brown felt privileged when Monk invited him to read some of his short stories to the accompaniment of Monk's music at the Five Spot in New York City while Brown was in town for their interview.

Trumbull Park (1959), named for a Chicago housing development, is the novel which gained Brown entry into American letters. It is a fictionalized account of racial violence in the years 1954 to 1957, when the Browns were the tenth black family to take up residence in the development. The blacks in the book are harassed by anonymous, screaming, bomb-throwing whites, but they receive only callous police attention—clanging, smelly paddy wagons in which they are transported through the white mobs to and from bus stops, work, and the market. The police paddy wagons even carry the women to the hospital to bear their children.

Brown illuminates the psychology of a people besieged. He describes the whites as "drunk on something that only white folks could get a hold of . . . that made them hate all colored folks." Name-calling, bricks thrown through windows, and the fire-bombing of black homes which brought police cars and fire engines that "screeched around corners" while "sirens went and bells danged like everybody was having a hell of a good time" are constants in the book. The unrelenting racial tension encourages the physical and mental disintegration of some Trumbull Park inhabitants: "The boys on the street say of a man whom a woman has begun to rule, whose boss can and does cuss him eight hours a day, whose neighbors bump into him without saying 'I'm sorry,' whose children talk back to him, and whose dog won't come to him when he calls—the boys say that a guy like that has been denutted. Carl had been denutted." When the first family to integrate Trumbull Park, the Arthur Davises, has succumbed to despair and decided to move back to the ghetto, having "held the perimeter" until the other blacks came, Helen Martin, the wife of Buggy Martin, the protagonist, comments, "Those people died for us just as surely as they say Christ did."

The fecund woman as leader emerges as a secondary theme of *Trumbull Park.* As one of the male characters says, "They had put in 24 hours a day in good ol' T. P.—no husbands, no nothing—and had faced up to the mob AND the policemen, all day, every day. We had not given or taken what the women had." Sometimes the weight of everything white scares Buggy Martin, but Helen Martin provides a constructive attitude: "We got to take this foolishness of these white folks in stride. Live in spite of them." And when the small group of blacks at Trumbull Park frets at its own impotence, it is Helen who articulates the need for a more aggressive response: "We ought to start having a few meetings of our own—figure out something to do to *them.* No need to be always fighting *defense.*"

Published criticism of the work of Brown is based on *Trumbull Park.* The *New Yorker* found the novel "vigorous and exciting" because it paints a psychological picture of blacks in stress, and it shows how courage must confront the breakdown of self-respect, submission to the white man's hostile or patronizing image, and the guilt of forcing resolution on those who lack the strength. Novelist Alan Paton wrote in the *Chicago Sunday Tribune* that Brown causes an outsider to marvel at the inner resources of the American Negro, and that "hatred does not guide his pen." The *Christian Century* reviewer

Dust jacket for Frank London Brown's 1959 novel

thought that *Trumbull Park* improves the white reader's empathy for the black community and acquits passive resistance as an effective social force. The *New York Times* agreed that the real drama is not in what the white people try to do to their neighbors but in the self-restraining heroism of the blacks.

In November 1959 *Ebony* magazine listed Brown on its masthead as an associate editor. A note in the "Backstage" column of this issue describes Brown's first visit to *Ebony* fourteen years earlier: "One sunlit afternoon in the spring of 1944, a thin, intense and rather brash teen-ager walked into the office, identified himself as Frank London Brown and asked for a job as an editor. He had not yet finished high school, couldn't have been more than sixteen, had no experience, and wanted to be a writer." He turned down the offer of a position as delivery boy at that time.

Brown earned his master's degree at the Uni-

versity of Chicago in 1960; his novel *The Myth Maker* (1969), published posthumously to small sales and few reviews, had been his thesis. Its protagonist, Ernest Day, "never without a book in his hand," is a drug addict underneath the "el" who strangles an old black man for smiling at him. The largest portion of the book occurs after the murder. Day meditates on the meaning of life, on the randomness of crime, on life's contradictions—why some of us are black and given to suffer more, on whether or not there is a god or guide, and whether or not life has any order. He tries to figure out why he killed the benign stranger who had extended to him only the "random kindness" of a smile. "I like a country that makes me feel like I'm shit? . . . I hated being guilty for being a Negro. . . . Death is everywhere. It walks the streets and it looks for life just so it can eat it. . . . I thought these things when I strangled that man."

Because of its death-obsessed multiple personality, John U. Nef compares *The Myth Maker* to Dostoyevski's *Crime and Punishment* in a black American urban setting. Ernest Day's meditation illustrates the conflict between a person's rational self and his emotional sensitivity. Like Dostoyevski, Brown says that human behavior cannot be prescribed by rational calculation, that the emotional, irrational side of man's nature is far more powerful, but that each person has his own intrinsic value however sinful, useless, or obnoxious he may appear to be.

The other main character in *The Myth Maker* is Freda, a self-sufficient black woman. Freda gives Day responsive sexual love and the thing he wants most of all, "to hear someone call his name again–someone in the throes of love." Day becomes more human because of her. He begs Freda to remember him if something happens to him. In the book's ironic conclusion the police pound in the door during his orgasm with her.

The implied answer to the problem the novel sets is that despite disorder and evil, life is precious, "a thing warm and moving and striving with good feeling." The real landscape of *The Myth Maker* is the protagonist's mind rather than the gloom underneath the "el." Ernest Day earnestly struggles to make sense of and to use the day which God has allotted him. The book's title and conclusion suggest that to cope with the harsh, insane world, man must make myths.

The vignette was Brown's forte. Lynching, the loneliness of the unwed teenage mother, the danger of the South for blacks before the civil rights movement of the 1960s, the possibility of racial communion through jazz, and the prevalence of drugs on city streets are some of the themes of Brown's stories.

In "Night March" (1957) tension rises over an impending lynching. The conflict for the protagonist, Geeter, is whether to help save the lynching victim or to play the white man's game by knowing his place and withdrawing from the action, thereby saving himself. In choosing the latter course, he finds that by failing to give himself completely on his people's behalf, his suffering is unbearable. Through concise dialogue and description Brown imbues the reader with the sequence of feelings of emotion going through Geeter.

"A Cry Unheard" (1959) is a story treating intraracial and intrafamily failures in love. A proud, unmarried, bespectacled child-mother kills herself and her beloved baby. She does not seek help from her parents or her brother (the unnamed narrator) because they disapprove of her pregnancy and she vows to make it on her own. She has written to her brother, so he knows of her anguish and of her sacrifices for her baby. He expresses his feelings of guilt following her death. The irony, Brown implies, is that despair can engulf despite the inherent love of the family.

Brown's long, first-person story, "In the Shadow of a Dying Soldier" (1959), may be autobiographical. It concerns a black journalist who is asked to go into the South to cover the trial (1955) of Emmett Till's murderer. The journalist reluctantly accepts the assignment and feels terror merely from being in the South. The atmosphere weighs threateningly. When the reporter is threatened for telling the truth, the black woman who owns his hotel manages to protect him until he can reach the airport and the safety of flight to Chicago and home. The story is reminiscent of Ted Poston's "My Most Humiliating Jim Crow Experience," which also reports a southern trial. Brown effectively conveys the emotions that go through a person experiencing what later generations know only as historical fact.

The powerful "McDougal" (1969), written in hip idiom, depicts a jam session in which black musicians recognize that their white trumpet player, who is married to a black woman and lives on "the stroll," has "told the truth" in music. He "knows the happenings . . . I mean about where we get it. You dig? . . . the man's been burnt."

"A Matter of Time" (1962) evokes the sensation of a person with a terminal disease who realizes that the beauty of his world and loved ones will vanish for him soon, and the lovely scenes he views of children laughing and playing must go on without him.

Brown wrote encomiums to two fellow artists in "Mahalia the Great" (1960) and "Chicago's Great Lady of Poetry" (1961). He saw his own attitude toward life in Mahalia Jackson's absence of cynicism and in her humility: "Mahalia Jackson is the symbol of . . . the shifting spirit that is causing nations to change, and dark people to aim higher than the pot of beans and a soft bed." In his essay on Gwendolyn Brooks, Brown is awed by her sensitivity, toughness, and innovation. Brown so adulates his fellow black artists that his language borders on hyperbole.

Brown was a candidate for a Ph.D. and a fellow of the Committee on Social Thought at the University of Chicago under John U. Nef. He was also director of the university's Union Research Center, when, during the summer of 1961 at age thirty-three, he discovered he had leukemia. While his energy lasted, he pushed himself. For example, he participated in a wade-in at Chicago's Rainbow Beach on Lake Michigan. He died at the University of Illinois Educational Research Hospital on 12 March 1962.

Brown's posthumously published essay, "An Unaccountable Happiness," expresses his particular voice. It describes his family's journey from Missouri to Chicago, where they had been led to believe they would find such things as "a park . . . which we needed no permission to traverse." The family found such parks, but also, "We had an equal opportunity to stagger and fall beneath the knives of the men in the tight cars and the women in fast dresses. Indeed, if we chose (and sometimes we 'chose' while kicking and crying all the way down) we could even become men in tight cars and women in fast dresses." He concluded that "the fault is believing that the world can be park all the way through. That there can be a cushion deep enough to soften the hurt that collision between chimes and reality does engender." Brown's widow believes that Brown "saw and felt and lived the essential sadness of the world."

Gwendolyn Brooks has written a poetic memoir of him:

Petitions denied,
We let our spirited and our venturesome go—
Our liberator and our insevere

Armed arbiter, our scrupulous pioneer—
Out from the lushness of his legacy.

References:
"Backstage," *Ebony*, 14 (March 1959): 20;
Ulli Beier, "The Whole Truth," *Black Orpheus* (1964): 71-73;
Gwendolyn Brooks, "Of Frank London Brown: A Tenant of the World," *Negro Digest*, 18 (September 1962): 44;
Les Brownley, "Frank London Brown: Courageous Author," *Sepia*, 8 (June 1960): 26-30;
"The Departed," *Negro Digest*, 18 (September 1962): 50;
Robert E. Fleming, "Overshadowed by Richard Wright: Three Black Chicago Novelists," *Negro American Literature Forum*, 7 (Fall 1973): 75;
Alphonso Pinkney, *Black Americans* (New York: Prentice-Hall, 1969), p. 150;
J. Serebnick, "New Creative Writers," *Library Journal*, 84 (1 February 1959): 507;
Sterling Stuckey, "Frank London Brown," in *Black Voices*, edited by Abraham Chapman (New York: New American Library, 1968), pp. 669-676;
Dempsey J. Travis, *An Autobiography of Black Chicago* (Chicago: Urban Research Institute, 1981).

Papers:
There are two letters from Brown to Willard Motley in a collection of Motley's papers at the University of Wisconsin. Some of Brown's letters and manuscripts are located in the Vivian G. Harsh Collection of Afro-American Literature, Woodson Regional Library, Chicago. The rest are privately held.

Owen Dodson

(28 November 1914-21 June 1983)

James V. Hatch
City College of New York

BOOKS: *Powerful Long Ladder* (New York: Farrar, Straus, 1946);

Boy at the Window (New York: Farrar, Straus & Young, 1951); republished as *When Trees Were Green* (New York: Popular Library, 1967);

The Confession Stone (Ontario, Canada: Leeds Music, 1968); revised and enlarged as *The Confession Stone: Song Cycles* (London: Breman, 1970);

Come Home Early, Child (New York: Popular Library, 1977);

The Harlem Book of the Dead, by Dodson, James Van Der Zee, and Camille Billops (New York: Morgan & Morgan, 1978).

PLAY PRODUCTIONS: *Divine Comedy*, New Haven, Yale University Theatre, 16 February 1938;

The Garden of Time, New Haven, Yale University Theatre, 17 May 1939; revised for the American Negro Theatre, New York, Library Theatre, 7 March 1945;

New World A-Coming, New York, Madison Square Garden, 26 June 1944;

Bayou Legend, Washington, D.C., Howard University Theatre, 5 April 1948;

Till Victory Is Won, Washington, D.C., Kennedy Center Opera House, 4 March 1974.

RADIO: *Dorie Miller*, CBS, 7 December 1944.

OTHER: *Epithalamion for Evelyn Boldes Young and Joseph Henry Jenkins* (Boston: Hale, Cushman & Flint, 1942);

Bayou Legend, in *Black Drama in America: An Anthology*, edited by Darwin T. Turner (Greenwich, Conn.: Fawcett, 1971), pp. 205-295;

Divine Comedy, in *Black Theatre, USA*, edited by James V. Hatch and Ted Shine (New York: Free Press, 1974), pp. 322-349:

The Shining Town, in *Roots of Black Drama*, edited by Leo Hamalian and Hatch (Detroit:

Owen Dodson (photograph by Kurt Ammann)

Wayne State University Press, forthcoming 1989).

PERIODICAL PUBLICATIONS:

POETRY

"Someday We're Gonna Tear Them Pillars Down," *Harlem Quarterly*, 1 (Summer 1942): 161-166;

"Black Mother Praying in the Summer of 1943," *Common Ground*, 4 (Winter 1944): 79-82;

"Jonathan's Song," *New Currents*, 2 (August 1944): 12;

"Martha Graham," *Theatre Arts*, 28 (September 1944): 534;

"Pearl Primus," *Theatre Arts*, 28 (December 1944): 713.

DRAMA

The Ballad of Dorie Miller, *Theatre Arts*, 27 (July 1943): 436;

Dodson at the 19-24 October 1952 Festival of Negro Poets in Jackson, Mississippi. Standing at rear (left to right): Arna Bontemps, Melvin B. Tolson, Jacob Reddix, Dodson, and Robert Hayden. Seated: Sterling Brown, Zora Neale Hurston, Margaret Walker, and Langston Hughes (by permission of the Tolson family).

Everybody Join Hands, Theatre Arts, 27 (September 1943): 555-565;

The Third Fourth of July, by Dodson and Countee Cullen, *Theatre Arts,* 30 (August 1946): 488-493;

Freedom, the Banner, Callaloo #21, 7 (Spring-Summer 1984): 57-71.

FICTION

"The Summer Fire," *Paris Review,* 12 (1956): 62-78;

NONFICTION

"Color USA," *Twice a Year,* no. 14-15 (Fall 1946-Winter 1947): 354-364;

"College Troopers Abroad," *Negro Digest,* 8 (April 1950): 47-49;

"Playwrights in Dark Glasses," *Negro Digest,* 17 (April 1968): 31-36;

"Who Has Seen the Wind?," *Black American Literature Forum,* 11 (Fall 1977): 108-116; 13 (Spring 1979): 20-23; 14 (Summer 1980): 54-59.

By the time of Owen Dodson's death in 1983 he had published three volumes of poetry; his fiction and drama had been anthologized in over sixty texts and translated into Japanese, Italian, German, Czech, and Dutch. He was twice invited to read his poems at the Library of Congress; Richard Eberhart introduced Dodson at the 1968 Dartmouth College Black Arts Festi-

val as "the best Negro poet in the United States." The next year *Time* magazine wrote that Dodson's poetry "stands peer to Frost, Carl Sandburg and other white American poets."

In 1956 George Plimpton awarded Dodson's short story "The Summer Fire" second prize in a contest sponsored by the *Paris Review* and subsequently included it in *Best Short Stories from the Paris Review* (1959). Twenty-seven of his plays and operas have been produced—*Till Victory is Won* (March 1974) at the Kennedy Center. President Lyndon Johnson invited Dodson to the White House. He was a recipient of Guggenheim, Rosenwald, and Rockefeller fellowships and two honorary doctorates; his friends included W. H. Auden, Countee Cullen, Langston Hughes, and Richard Wright, all of whom influenced his writing. Insisting that art and literature are essential for the survival of human beings, he influenced two generations of theater students at Howard University, and his poetry is evidence of his ability to adapt literary tradition to express his own vision of life.

Owen Vincent Dodson was born in Brooklyn, New York, on 28 November 1914 to Nathaniel Barnett Dodson, a free-lance writer for black newspapers, and Sarah Elizabeth Goode Dodson, a volunteer church and community social worker. He was the ninth child in his family. His father, director of the National Negro Press Association, introduced his son to Booker T. Washington, W. E. B. Du Bois, and James Weldon Johnson. Every Sunday the Dodson family attended the Concord Baptist Church, where the elder Dodson was Sunday school superintendent and where the young Owen Dodson sang traditional black church music. Dodson's discovery of poetry began under the tutelage of poet Elias Lieberman, principal of Thomas Jefferson High School, where Dodson won medals for declamation of verse. The idea that poetry was meant to be read aloud never left him.

Awarded a scholarship, he enrolled at Bates College in Lewiston, Maine, where his classmates included John Ciardi and Edmund Muskie. In a freshman English class taught by Robert Berkelman, Dodson had the temerity to suggest that he could write a sonnet as good as any by John Keats. Berkelman responded to this impertinence by assigning him the task of writing one sonnet a week until his graduation with a B.A. in 1936. By the time of his commencement Dodson had published his verse in the *New York Herald Tribune*, *Opportunity*, and *Phylon*.

After graduation Dodson entered the Yale Drama School on a fellowship. His play *Divine Comedy*, produced there in 1938, portrays the folly of giving one's wealth and devotion to self-styled prophets who, like Father Divine, claim to be God. This play received the Maxwell Anderson Award for verse drama. Dodson's second production at Yale, *The Garden of Time* (May 1939), retells the classical Medea story in terms of American racism. The play opens in Greece and seems to be a retelling of the story of Jason and Medea. However, by act 3 the characters and their conflict transmogrify to postbellum South Carolina, where a black Medea and a white Jason fulfill their tragic destiny. In both *The Garden of Time* and *Divine Comedy* can be found features that were to remain benchmarks for his later work. His writing remained basically oral and poetic in style. His sense of delight in human foibles and his belief of the saving power of love are darkened by a melancholy approaching fatalism: "Why we sailed and how we prosper/will be sung and lived again/all the lands repeat themselves/shore for shore and men for men."

By the time Dodson received his M.F.A. from Yale in 1939, he had made several lifelong friends, including cartoonist Ollie Harrington, Auden, and Anne Cooke, who asked Dodson to join her in teaching speech and drama at Spelman College in Atlanta, where he went in

Dodson, circa 1933 (courtesy of the Schomburg Center for Research in Black Culture, the New York Public Library, Astor, Lenox and Tilden Foundations)

1938. He remained until 1941, when he accepted a position with the communications department at Hampton Institute in Virginia, where he taught only briefly before enlisting in the United States Navy in November 1942.

Assigned to the racially segregated Great Lakes Naval Training Station, Dodson met others who were important in his life: Chicago artist Charles Sebree, actor Frank Silvera, Edwin Embree, head of the Rosenwald Foundation, and Peggy and Leonard Reiser, to whom he would dedicate his first novel. Shortly after Dodson's enlistment, his commander, Daniel Armstrong, appointed him to write and produce a series of naval-history plays "to raise the morale of the Negro seaman." Dodson set about staging eight short pageants on Sundays. *Theatre Arts*, the most prestigious theater monthly in America at the time, published two: *The Ballad of Dorie Miller* (July 1943), a verse chorale portraying the heroism of the black seaman who shot down several Japanese planes during the attack on Pearl Har-

Sadie Brown and Gordon Heath in Dodson's 4 August 1944 production at Howard University of Eugene O'Neill's Mourning Becomes Electra *(courtesy of the Hatch-Billops Collection, New York)*

bor; and *Everybody Join Hands* (September 1943), which praises the struggles of China's people against their Japanese oppressors.

A major race riot exploded in Detroit in 1943; angry and hurt by American racism, Dodson composed "Black Mother Praying in the Summer of 1943," a poem that was to become his most popular. In it a black mother implores God to end racial discrimination against black servicemen. The opening lines mold contemporary objects into incongruous, disturbing spiritual metaphors, a technique that was to become characteristic of Dodson's style: "My great God, You been a tenderness to me/through the thick and through the thin/you been a pilla to my soul/ . . . a elevator to my spirit."

Following Dodson's medical discharge from the service because of asthma, Embree arranged for the Rosenwald Foundation to award Dodson a fellowship. In 1944 Dodson wrote and directed *New World A-Coming*, a Negro-history pageant designed to demonstrate the black-American contribution to the war effort. The pageant, presented at Madison Square Garden in New York City to an estimated twenty-five thousand people, succeeded so impressively that Dodson was appointed executive secretary of the newly created Committee for Mass Education in Race Relations

at the American Film Center. The committee of film producers and writers, which included Langston Hughes, Richard Wright, and Arna Bontemps, was charged with encouraging the production of films that would present America's ethnic minorities in nonstereotypical roles.

In August 1946 Dodson saw the publication of his first collection of poetry, *Powerful Long Ladder*, which established his reputation as a poet. The book is divided into five sections; its theme is expressed in its epigraph: "It takes a powerful long ladder to climb to the sky/and catch the bird of freedom for the dark." The last poem in the book, "Open Letter," concludes with a plea for racial harmony: "Brothers let us enter that portal for good/when peace surrounds us like a credible universe/bury that agony, bury this hate, take our black hands in yours." M. L. Rosenthal, reviewing the volume for the *New York Herald Tribune Weekly Book Review* (16 March 1947), praised "its vividness, its solid strength in picturing pain and disgust without losing the joy of life which marks the best artist. . . . " Several poems in the volume have become well known; and it contains one of Dodson's most memorable lines: "Sorrow is the only faithful one."

In 1947, feeling that its influence on the Hollywood establishment had been negligible,

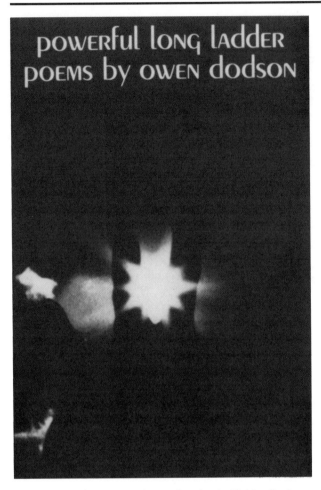

Dust jacket for a later edition of Dodson's 1946 collection of poetry

Dodson resigned his position with the Committee for Mass Education in Race Relations and, at the invitation of Anne Cooke, moved to Washington, D.C., to join Howard University's newly established drama department. He remained there for the next twenty-three years, directing, producing, and teaching students such as Earle Hyman, Hilda Simms, Gordon Heath, James Baldwin, Roxie Roker, Marilyn Berry, Shauneille Perry, Zaida Coles, Graham Brown, Alfredina and Bill Brown, Debbie Allen, Ted Shine, Vantile Whitfield, Richard Wesley, LeRoi Jones (Amiri Baraka), Robert Hooks, Glenda Dickerson, Clayton Corbin, and Clinton Turner Davis.

Dodson's first Howard University success came with the 1948 production of his *Bayou Legend*, a dramatic-verse adaptation of Henrik Ibsen's *Peer Gynt* (1867) set in a Louisiana bayou. In September 1949 he, Cooke, and James Butcher led the Howard Players on a tour of Norway, Denmark, Sweden, and Germany. Their performances of Ibsen's *The Wild Duck* (1884) and

DuBose Heyward's *Mamba's Daughters* (1929) were praised in the European press. A report in *Berlingske Tidende*, a Copenhagen daily, was typical: "The ability of the Howard Players to express the play . . . fascinated the audience. There was hearty applause and many curtain calls." The three-month tour concluded with Drew Pearson presenting the American Public Relations International Award to the troupe. The Howard Players were the first American college-theater group to tour Europe, and their success influenced the United States Congress to establish a nationally funded cultural exchange program.

In February 1951 *Boy at the Window*, Dodson's first and best novel, was published. The review in the *Washington Star* was headed "A Sensitive Writer Gives New Color to an Old Theme," while the headline in the *Washington Post* read "Eloquent Writing: Child's Eye View of the Adult World." The semi-autobiographical novel concerns the growth to puberty of a sensitive nine-year-old boy named Coin Foreman, "a copper penny," growing up in the 1920s in a working-class neighborhood of Brooklyn, where West Indians, Jews, Italians, and blacks have vital and integrated lives. The central event in the novel is Coin's response to the death of his beloved mother, which he feels his conversion to the Baptist church should have prevented. Her death leaves his spirit forever scarred. The prose, rich in image and metaphor, captures the intimate thoughts and voice of a maturing child.

In 1952 Dodson received a Guggenheim Fellowship to write a sequel to *Boy at the Window* which he called *Come Home Early, Child*; he spent his fellowship year in Ischia, Italy, living and writing in the villa of W. H. Auden. In this second novel, which did not find a publisher until 1977, Coin Foreman leaves home, joins the navy, has a love affair in Italy, and returns to Brooklyn to discover his estrangement from the past. His passage into manhood is described in a rich poetic language; the second of its two sections is surrealistic.

At Howard University Dodson directed several premiere productions, including James Baldwin's *Amen Corner*, produced at Howard in 1953. He also insisted that his students perform the classics; he directed three productions of *Hamlet* during his career. In 1974 the Kennedy Center Opera House in Washington, D.C., presented Dodson's opera, *Till Victory Is Won*, written with composer Mark Fax to celebrate Howard University's centennial, and *Owen's Song*—se-

REMEMBERING OWEN DODSON

Cover for a 1984 tribute to Dodson

lections from his poetry and excerpts from *Bayou Legend* arranged by Glenda Dickerson and Mike Malone.

It was not until some years after his retirement, when he moved to New York City, that Dodson was able to return to poetry. He considered *The Confession Stone: Song Cycles* (1970) to be his masterpiece. Spoken by the Holy Family, this series of monologues concerning the life of Jesus is often performed at Easter services and has developed a devoted following. The simple language suggests the common humanity of the Holy Family. For example, sending the boy Jesus on a household errand, Mary tells him, "Jesus, don't stop to play with Judas and his friends along the way." For *The Harlem Book of the Dead* (1978), visual artist Camille Billops contracted with the Harlem photographer James Van Der Zee for a series of his funeral photographs, and Dodson agreed to write poems as captions to the photos. The result, with its excellent poem "Allegory of Seafaring Black Mothers," displays Dodson's talent for combining ideas with startling images: "How many mothers with their grit/with their bony and long dreams/have dared to splash with us out to sea?" Dodson's final collection of

poems, "Life on the Streets," has never been published; in May of 1982, however, the New York Public Theatre staged a reading of the poems, with performances by Gloria Foster and Roscoe Lee Brown.

For all his achievements Dodson's poetry and plays have been accorded little critical attention. (An authorized biography is now in process.) He was too young to be part of the Harlem Renaissance and too traditional in perspective to be one of the angry, militant, black writers of the 1960s. Because he wrote drama, fiction, and poetry, his achievement has been difficult to categorize.

Dodson's reputation may also have suffered from his divided energies. Students and former students demanded much of his time. In his last years he became the dean of black theater, in demand as a speaker at fund-raisers and artistic occasions. He directed plays at the Harlem School of the Arts and served as board member for the Frank Silvera Writers' Workshop and for the Hatch-Billops Collection. He traveled, gave readings, and lectured widely despite crippling arthritis requiring him to use canes, a walker, or a wheelchair. Sometimes he would say, "Child, I'm a mess." Much of Dodson's best poetry was written in his final years, when he saw beyond the particular present into the malaise of all human activities. He never stopped working; until he had a heart attack in 1983, he was writing chapters for a new novel and telephoning his friends to read new poems to them.

Dodson did not write Negro folk literature like Paul Laurence Dunbar, or Negro protest literature like Langston Hughes or Richard Wright; nor was he erudite in the style of Robert Hayden or Melvin Tolson. Inconsistent in style and subject, Dodson's stories, plays, and poems range from racial protest to art for art's sake, and from social to personal, from secular to religious. Like Countee Cullen before him, Dodson mastered the English sonnet, but he did more: he welded the astonishing images of the black vernacular and gospel rhythms to European forms. His poetry should be read aloud to catch these nuances. As Karl Shapiro has written, "Dodson represents a new stage in the development of Negro letters. Politically and racially he seems more advanced in his approach to his material than his predecessors. When formal, his poetic language is not merely proper and dignified, but original in the sense that matters, that is as a fusion of his total ex-

Dodson near the end of his life (photograph by Mary Ellen Andrews)

perience as a man with his talent as a maker of poems."

Interviews:

John O'Brien, "Owen Dodson," in *Interviews with Black Writers*, edited, with an introduction, by O'Brien (New York: Liveright, 1973), pp. 54-61;

Curt Davis, "The Human Poetry of Owen Dodson," *Encore: American & Worldwide News*, 6 (4 April 1977): 32-35;

James V. Hatch, "Remembering Owen Dodson," in *Artist and Influence 1985*, edited by Leo Hamalian and Judith Wilson, no. 3 (New York: Hatch-Billops Collection, 1985), pp. 61-106.

Bibliographies:

James V. Hatch and OMANii Abdullah, *Black Playwrights, 1823-1977: An Annotated Bibliography of Plays* (New York & London: Bowker, 1977), pp. 66-70;

Hatch, Douglas A. M. Ward, and Joe Weixlmann, "The Rungs of a Powerful Long Ladder: An Owen Dodson Bibliography," *Black American Literature Forum*, 14 (Summer 1980): 60-68.

Biographies:

Bernard L. Peterson, Jr., "The Legendary Owen Dodson," *Crisis*, 86 (November 1979): 373-378;

Sallee W. Hardy, ed., *Remembering Owen Dodson* (New York: Hatch-Billops Collection, 1984);

James V. Hatch, "Owen Dodson: Excerpts from a Biography in Progress," *Massachusetts Review*, 28, no. 4 (Winter 1987): 627-641.

References:

Robert A. Bone, *The Negro Novel in America*, revised edition (New Haven & London: Yale University Press, 1965), pp. 185-187;

Noel Schraufnagel, *From Apology to Protest: The Black American Novel* (De Land, Fla.: Everett-Edwards, 1973), pp. 76-77.

Papers:

Most of Dodson's papers are at the Moorland-Spingarn Research Center, Howard University; in the Countee Cullen-Harold Jackman Collection, Atlanta University; in the James Weldon Johnson Collection, Yale University; and in the Hatch-Billops Collection, New York City.

Ralph Ellison

(1 March 1914-)

Leonard J. Deutsch
Marshall University

See also the Ellison entry in *DLB 2: American Novelists Since World War II*.

BOOKS: *Invisible Man* (New York: Random House, 1952; London: Gollancz, 1953); republished with an introduction by Ellison (New York: Random House, 1982);
Shadow and Act (New York: Random House, 1964; London: Secker & Warburg, 1967);
Going to the Territory (New York: Random House, 1986).

OTHER: "Afternoon," in *American Writing*, edited by Hans Otto Storm and others (Prairie City, Ill. & Rochester, N.Y.: J. A. Decker, 1940), pp. 28-37;
"Flying Home," in *Cross Section*, edited by Edwin Seaver (New York: L. B. Fischer, 1944), pp. 469-485;
"Did You Ever Dream Lucky?," in *New World Writing*, no. 5 (New York: New American Library, 1954), pp. 134-145;
"A Coupla Scalped Indians," in *New World Writing*, no. 9 (New York: New American Library, 1956), pp. 225-236;
"Society, Morality and the Novel," in *The Living Novel*, edited by Granville Hicks (New York: Macmillan, 1957), pp. 58-91;
"Out of the Hospital and Under the Bar," in *Soon, One Morning*, edited by Herbert Hill (New York: Knopf, 1963), pp. 242-290.

PERIODICAL PUBLICATIONS: "Slick Gonna Learn," *Direction*, 2 (September 1939): 10-11, 14, 16;
"The Birthmark," *New Masses*, 36 (2 July 1940): 16-17;
"Mister Toussan," *New Masses*, 41 (4 November 1941), 19-20;
"That I Had the Wings," *Common Ground*, 3 (Summer 1943): 30-37;
"In a Strange Country," *Tomorrow*, 3 (July 1944): 41-44;

"King of the Bingo Game," *Tomorrow*, 4 (November 1944): 29-33;
"February," *Saturday Review*, 1 (January 1955): 25;
"And Hickman Arrives," *Noble Savage*, 1 (Spring 1960): 5-49;
"The Roof, the Steeple and the People," *Quarterly Review of Literature*, 10, no. 3 (1960): 115-128;
"It Always Breaks Out," *Partisan Review*, 30 (Spring 1963): 13-28;
"Juneteenth," *Quarterly Review of Literature*, 13, nos. 3-4 (1965): 262-276;
"Tell It Like It Is, 'Baby,' " *Nation*, 201 (20 September 1965): 129-136;
"Night-Talk," *Quarterly Review of Literature*, 16, nos. 3-4 (1969): 317-329;
"A Song of Innocence–Excerpt from Novel in Progress," *Iowa Review*, 1 (Spring 1970): 30-40;
"Cadillac Flambé," *American Review*, 16 (February 1973): 249-269;
"Backwacking: A Plea to the Senator," *Massachusetts Review*, 18 (Autumn 1977): 411-416.

Centuries hence, when the important Afro-American writers of our day are studied, perhaps Ralph Ellison–novelist, short-story writer, and essayist–will be considered the most indispensable. Already, a great many critics think that his *Invisible Man* (1952) is one of the most significant American novels of the twentieth century.

Ralph Waldo Ellison was born in Oklahoma City, Oklahoma, on 1 March 1914 to Lewis Ellison and Ida Millsap Ellison. Lewis Ellison, a native of Abbeville, South Carolina, had traveled to Cuba, the Philippines, and China as an enlisted soldier. Returning to Abbeville, he and a partner operated an ice-cream parlor until he moved to Chattanooga, Tennessee, where he found employment with a construction firm. When Lewis and Ida Ellison moved to Oklahoma a few years after statehood was attained, Lewis put his skills to work in helping to build some of the first steel-and-

Ralph Ellison in 1939 (photograph by Richard Wright, courtesy of Ralph Ellison)

concrete structures in Oklahoma City. After serving as a construction foreman, he ventured out on his own, starting a small ice and coal business.

Ida Millsap, originally from White Oak, Georgia, met and married Lewis Ellison in Abbeville. A political activist, Ida Ellison–or "Brownie," as she was commonly called–canvased Negro voters for Eugene Debs's Socialist party during the gubernatorial campaign of 1914, the same year her son Ralph was born. During the 1930s she went to jail for violating zoning ordinances.

When Ralph was three and his only surviving sibling, Herbert, was four months old, Lewis Ellison died as the result of an accident. Their resourceful mother worked as a domestic in white homes and served as an apartment-house custodian. She brought home magazines and books for the boys to read and was able to supply her sons with chemical and electrical sets, a phonograph and records, a rolltop desk and chair, and a toy typewriter. In terms of material needs and spiritual heritage, Ralph Ellison never considered himself deprived.

Even the policies of Oklahoma's white supremacist governor, "Alfalfa Bill" Murray, did not prevent Ellison from having white friends or doing what he wanted to do. While still a boy, he and a few friends resolved to become Renaissance men. They would, they decided, conquer all realms of knowledge that interested them and become well-rounded individuals. "My friends and I," he said, "were exploring an idea of human versatility and possibility which went against the barbs or over the palings of almost every fence which those who controlled social and political power had erected to restrict our roles in the life of the country." Ellison simply refused to be restricted to prescribed roles or limited by Jim Crow regulations. When he did not have some books or sheet music under his arms, he was building crystal radio sets or expanding his horizons in other ways.

There is a tension in Ellison's work between the concept of geography as fate and the concept of human volition as destiny. Ellison has observed, "It is not geography alone that determines the quality of life and culture. These depend upon the courage and personal culture of the individuals who make their homes in any given locality." One's geography presents as givens certain raw materials which individuals accept passively or dynamically transform by an assertion of their human will. Within his community certain individuals served as positive models for Ellison because, even as they were being conditioned by their environment, they knew how to take what they needed from the life around them and leave their own imprint upon it.

Among those who inspired the young Ellison–besides his determined mother–were the men who frequented the local drugstore and barbershop, swapping tales and believing in "the spirit of the law, if not in its application." There were also the jazz musicians who "stumbled upon the freedom lying within the restrictions of their musical tradition." Later in his career Ellison would write essays about some of these jazzmen, including blues singer Jimmy Rushing, who at one time worked for Lewis Ellison as an ice carrier, and guitarist Charlie Christian, who was a classmate of Ellison's younger brother Herbert in elementary school.

One of the anecdotes from Ellison's early life concerns his name. His father—perhaps "aware of the suggestive power of names and the magic involved in naming"—decided to call his son Ralph Waldo in honor of Ralph Waldo Emerson, the great American philosopher-poet. Such a meaningful name caused endless embarrassment for him when adults would "invariably repeat my first two names and then to my great annoyance, they'd add 'Emerson.' " As it happened, a little boy by the name of Emerson did live next door. When the adults were told this, they only laughed louder. " 'Oh no,' they'd say, 'you're Ralph Waldo Emerson,' while I had fantasies of blue murder." In school he disguised his middle name by using an innocuous W, and he avoided Emerson's works "like the plague." Only later did he come to terms with his name and with the moral obligations that Emerson assigned to American writers.

Even if he vowed to avoid Emerson, Ellison was an avid reader in his youth. He was also an ardent musician. The trumpet was his forte, although he was able to play several brass instruments and the soprano saxophone as well. His school featured band, orchestra, a brass quartet, glee club, chorus, and European folk dancing, but Ellison chose to learn more about music by taking private lessons from Ludwig Hebestreit, conductor of the Oklahoma City Orchestra. Ellison paid for these lessons by mowing Hebestreit's lawn. To help out at home he sold newspapers, operated an elevator, worked as a soda jerk, and took other odd jobs.

Ellison left Oklahoma in 1933, at the age of nineteen, under honorable but financially strained circumstances: he had been awarded a scholarship by the state of Oklahoma, "supposedly on merit," he reports, "but the scholarship program itself was a device through which the state hoped to circumvent applications by Negro students for enrollment in the state universities of Oklahoma." Ellison chose to attend Tuskegee Institute in Macon County, Alabama, but he did not have enough money to travel in style so, like many others during the Great Depression, he

hopped a freight train. While he was hoboing, two white railroad detectives carrying .45 revolvers forced him off the train in Decatur, Alabama, the town where the Scottsboro Boys were being tried at that time for crimes allegedly committed while hoboing. Ellison recalls: "I had no idea of what the detectives intended to do with me, but given the atmosphere of the town I feared that it would be most unpleasant and brutal." He never found out what they had in mind, however, because when some of his traveling companions began running for their lives, so did he.

Tuskegee, founded by Booker T. Washington in 1881 as a technical institute, had evolved into a liberal arts college under presidents Robert M. Moton and Frederick Douglass Patterson. Here Ellison, majoring in music and music theory, expected to become a professional musician. While studying under the composer William L. Dawson he aspired to write a symphony by the time he was twenty-six equal to anything Richard Wagner had written by that age. He continued to explore other interests as well, including starring in the school play as a sophomore and reading widely. In 1935 he read T. S. Eliot's *The Waste Land* (1922), a poem which impressed him with its jazzlike rhythms and its "hidden sense of organization." With his discovery of Eliot came Ellison's realization that the humor, energy, and creativity of black Americans, so well seen in their music, churches, and daily life, had been largely ignored in poetry and fiction.

Unlike the protagonist of his novel, *Invisible Man*, Ellison was not expelled from Tuskegee; experiencing some financial difficulties at the end of his junior year, he went to New York in the summer of 1936 to earn money, fully expecting to return for his senior year, although he never did. Arriving in New York with only seventy-five dollars, he stayed at the Harlem YMCA, where he got a job behind the food counter. On his second day in New York he happened to meet Alain Locke, whom Ellison had heard speak at Tuskegee. Accompanying Locke was Langston Hughes, who subsequently would go to Harlem's Apollo Theater with Ellison on numerous occasions. At this meeting Hughes asked Ellison if he would deliver two books to a friend, André Malraux's *Man's Fate* and *Days of Wrath* (both translated, 1936), indicating that he could read them first if he wanted to. As Ellison's essays demonstrate, he not only read *Man's Fate*, but it had a profound impact upon him.

Ellison, Archibald MacLeish, Frederick Lewis Allen, and Bernard DeVoto at the National Book Awards presentation, 27 January 1953 (AP/Wide World Photos)

Initially, Ellison expected a career in music or sculpture. A Tuskegee teacher gave him a letter of introduction to Harlem sculptor Augusta Savage, but when she could not accept any new students, Ellison studied under Richmond Barthé for about a year. To support himself during the late-Depression years he free-lanced as a photographer, worked as a file clerk-receptionist for a psychiatrist, and later built and sold hi-fi systems. When he was out of work, he slept in the park below City College. His job in the psychiatrist's office inspired him to reread Freud on dream symbolism, providing knowledge he was to put to use in his fiction. The challenge to attempt fiction was issued by Richard Wright, whom Ellison had met through their mutual friend, Hughes. Ellison began his literary career by writing a review of Waters E. Turpin's *These Low Grounds* (1937) for the autumn 1937 issue of *New Challenge*, edited by Wright. Ellison contributed a short story, "Heine's Bull," to the winter issue, but the magazine folded and the story never got beyond the galleys. In February of 1937 Ellison at-

tended his mother's funeral in Dayton, Ohio, where she had moved from Oklahoma City in 1935. She died of tuberculosis of the hip which had been misdiagnosed by an incompetent doctor as arthritis. Ellison and his brother Herbert were so short of money that they slept in an automobile by night and hunted quail by day, selling some of their catch to General Motors executives and eating the rest to stay alive.

Ellison joined the Federal Writers' Project in 1938 and received $103.50 per month. With Sterling A. Brown serving as editor of Negro affairs, the project offered Ellison a number of assignments which required research and writing. While working with the Living Lore Unit–"a group consisting of twenty-seven writers who were to document New York's Urban and industrial folklore"–Ellison collected many tales, including the story of Sweet-the-Monkey, who could make himself invisible and perform all sorts of devilish acts. Besides acquiring information that would later serve as source material, Ellison was developing a greater appreciation for the function of folklore. As Robert G. O'Meally puts it, in Ellison's fiction "lore is more than local color; it is ritualistic and reflective of a whole lifestyle."

As Ellison moved toward a literary career by submitting reviews and essays for publication, he was surrounded by friends and acquaintances who shared his left-leaning political point of view; however, unlike some of them, he never joined the Communist party, and he always insisted that art should never be subverted by the dictates of partisan politics. Even in his earliest critical commentaries he expected the artist to exemplify a dauntless integrity and independence and to master the techniques of his or her craft. To acquire such a background for himself, he systematically scrutinized the prefaces of Henry James and Joseph Conrad, studied William Faulkner, James Joyce, Ernest Hemingway, Mark Twain, and Fyodor Dostoyevski, and held long conversations with Richard Wright.

His first two published short stories are clearly apprentice pieces. "Slick Gonna Learn," which appeared in the September 1939 issue of *Direction,* is an excerpt from a novel Ellison conceived but never wrote. "The Birthmark" appeared in *New Masses* on 2 July 1940. Both stories protest police brutality in a rather direct manner. His next three stories, however, are built on dialogues between two young boys, Buster and Riley, and deal with the aspirations of those whose spirits remain irrepressible despite a repressive environment. In "Afternoon" (*American Writing,* 1940), "Mister Toussan" (*New Masses,* 4 November 1941), and "That I Had the Wings" (*Common Ground,* Summer 1943) Buster and Riley seek and find positive role models within their own folklore and ethnic history.

After serving as managing editor of the *Negro Quarterly* in 1942 under editor Angelo Herndon, Ellison returned to story writing and produced his two most famous, successful, and widely anthologized stories before *Invisible Man:* "Flying Home" (*Cross Section,* 1944) and "King of the Bingo Game" (*Tomorrow,* November 1944). The protagonist of "Flying Home," an aviator named Todd, learns to gain strength from his folk roots when he reconciles himself to Jefferson, the humanistic old black peasant who befriends him in his hour of need. "King of the Bingo Game" seems a rehearsal for *Invisible Man* in that it features a nameless character who, despite the absurdity of his situation, tries desperately to manipulate his fate and forge his own

identity. In this story Ellison relies heavily on symbols and surrealistic techniques.

In 1944 Ellison met Fanny McConnell in New York City. Born in Louisville, Kentucky, and raised in Pueblo, Colorado, and Chicago, McConnell had served as secretary to James Weldon Johnson when she attended Fisk University in Nashville, Tennessee, and graduated from the University of Iowa, where she studied drama and speech. They married in 1946. It was Ellison's second marriage. Details of his first marriage are unavailable.

During World War II Ellison produced one patriotic story, "In a Strange Country" (*Tomorrow,* July 1944), and served as a cook in the merchant marine. When he returned to the United States in 1945 exhausted from his Atlantic voyages, he accepted an invitation to recuperate on a farm in Waitsfield, Vermont, where the idea for *Invisible Man* began to germinate in his mind. About the same time that he was reading Fitz Roy Raglan's *The Hero* (1936) and "speculating on the nature of Negro leadership in the United States," he reveals, "I wrote the first paragraph of *Invisible Man.*" With the assistance of a 1945 Rosenwald grant, he continued working on the book until its publication in 1952, although chapter 1 (England's *Horizon,* October 1947, and America's *'48*) and the prologue (*Partisan Review,* January-February 1952) appeared in earlier installments. An abortive short novel about World War II–to which he had devoted a year–was jettisoned during this period.

Invisible Man begins with the prologue, the penultimate stage in the unnamed main character's development. He has been on the run; now he is in his underground hole. Faced with his enforced hibernation, his impulses at first are vindictive: he siphons electricity from the Monopolated Light & Power Company, and he ascends to ground level where he engages in an act of personal terrorism. Repelled by his own violent behavior, he returns to this warm underground shelter, gets high, and listens to jazz records such as Louis Armstrong's "What Did I Do to Be So Black and Blue?" As he begins a mental descent through layers of consciousness, he encounters images from his racial past: a sermon on the "Blackness of Blackness" and a dialogue between a slave woman and her mulatto children; into his dream state also comes a character named Ras the Destroyer, from whom he had fled until he plunged into his dark sanctuary. Returning to waking consciousness, the invisible man believes that

Ellison as a witness at a Senate subcommittee hearing on the problems of big cities, 30 August 1966 (AP/Wide World Photos)

the music he has been listening to demands action, and "I believe in nothing if not in action."

Before he can act in a meaningful way, however, the invisible man must confront and come to terms with his identity and his life. The best way to order the chaos of his experience, he reasons, is to tell the tale of how he got into the hole in the first place. His narrative then proceeds on two levels: on the first level, episodes from his life are reconstructed so readers can share them as the naive boy experienced them; simultaneously, on the second level, the voice of the older, wiser, and judgmental narrator is heard as he interjects his satirical asides. This dual perspective, in part, accounts for the novel's complexity.

Another source of the novel's complexity is its symbolism. Ellison has remarked that during the years he wrote *Invisible Man* "the symbols and their connections were known to me. I began . . . with a chart of the three-part division. It was a conceptual frame with most of the ideas and some incidents indicated." The symbolic patterns are so dense and the symbols are so ubiquitous that literary scholars continue to produce myriad explications of the work.

Some of the primary symbols in the novel are introduced in the first chapter, the battle royal scene, which R. W. B. Lewis labels "a 'representative anecdote,' that is, an episode in which the entire novel is implicit." The battle royal consists of a group of blindfolded black youths fighting before a crowd of rich white men who pay the combatants by throwing what appear to be gold coins, but are in fact only brass slugs, on an electrified rug that shocks the youths when they touch it. The battle is itself an initiation ritual which symbolizes many aspects of race relations in a socially segregated society, including white sadism and the hostile black reaction that is channeled into intraracial violence. The young protagonist allows himself to be blindfolded, symbolic of his moral myopia (blindness becomes a major motif of the novel), for he naively expects the rich white men in the smoker to give him something of great value for his efforts. What they *do* give him as a reward for his accommodationist speech that follows the battle is a briefcase. Emblematic of his middle-class aspirations, this briefcase will eventually contain a number of symbolic documents–such as his high school diploma, his scholarship to a state college for Negroes, letters of reference, and a sambo doll–some of which the narrator will later burn in a symbolic gesture of repudiation. That night in a dream about his grandfather he sees a circus (symbolic of absurd reality), clowns (symbolic of the role assigned to blacks as entertainers), and a series of envelopes that represent years in the invisible man's life; the last envelope contains a prophetic and symbolic message: "To Whom It May Concern, Keep This Nigger-Boy Running."

The next series of events occurs at a black college campus clearly modeled on Tuskegee Institute. The college is a symbolic wasteland, although the naive youth prefers to see it as an Edenic paradise. The whitewashed buildings represent the socialization process which has been designed to whitewash the minds of the college's students. Down the road is the black powerhouse, "with its engines droning earth-shaking rhythms in the dark, its windows red from the glow of the furnace." Like most of the other images employed in the novel, the powerhouse functions as a symbol–here representing, among other things, the demonic, machinelike college president, Dr. Bledsoe (whose name suggests the deracinated quality of his racial allegiance). The main character inadvertently crosses Dr. Bledsoe by allowing the white philanthropist, Mr. Norton (whose face, "pink like St. Nicholas'," ironically hints of Santa Claus, another mythical gift giver), to meet black sharecropper Jim Trueblood (whose name suggests his function as symbolic foil to blood-drained Bledsoe). When Trueblood relates a dream that accompanied his commission of incest with his daughter, Freudian symbols– doors, hills, rooms, and grandfather clocks– present themselves in an unrestrained tumult. Norton is unsettled by the revelation he experiences after listening to his black counterpart's story, and while he collapses, some children, appropriately enough because both Norton and then later the invisible man come "falling down," sing "London Bridge Is Falling Down"–a tune which also suggests the dissolution of the invisible man's Edenic world.

Like the first two chapters, the other twenty-three chapters are awash with symbols and symbolic dates, scenes, episodes, and characters. There are, in fact, very few, if any, passages devoid of symbolic overtones. One of the novel's most overtly symbolic encounters occurs in chapter 11 when the invisible man undergoes a lobotomylike operation in the hospital of the paint factory where he has gone to work. The contraption he is strapped into–more sophisticated than the electrified rug in chapter 1 but similar in its emasculating function–is designed to neutralize the hero, transform him into an "amiable fellow." The shock therapy does not work as the white "doctors" intend it to, however, because in peeling away surface veneers of superficial experience the invisible man returns to a more basic identity. The device in which he is entombed turns out to be an ironic womb: "A huge iridescent bubble seemed to enfold me.... I was laved with warm liquids.... The sterile and weightless texture of a sheet enfolded me. I felt myself bounce, sail off like a ball thrown over the roof into the mist, striking a hidden wall beyond a pile of broken machinery and sailing back." When he emerges from this amniotic sac, his umbilical cord is severed–"I felt a tug at my belly and looked down to see one of the physicians pull the cord which was attached to the stomach node, jerking me forward"–and he is reborn. Lest the reader overlook the symbolism of this incident, Ellison has his protagonist focusing "upon the teetering scene with wild, infant's eyes" at the beginning of the next chapter.

The rest of the hero's adventures–with Tod Clifton, Rinehart (whose name comes from a song by Jimmy Rushing), Brother Jack, Sybil, and numerous others–culminate in a surrealistically rendered race riot. In the last chapter the invisible man takes refuge in the dark hole. The narrator's tale is now told except for the epilogue. In this final section of the novel the protagonist meditates upon the meaning of his experience. He has, in terms Ellison borrows from Kenneth Burke, moved from purpose to passion (or conflict) to perception. The hero's perception, or insightful self-understanding, is symbolized by the 1,369 light bulbs that illuminate his underground home. Devoid of any illusions, he still has much to affirm because, as shaping artist of his tale, he sees more clearly the relationship between personal responsibility and individual identity. A new sense of self emerges from this assessment. Having transformed himself from ranter to writer, the invisible man is prepared to engage with American society on a new footing. In the epilogue the novel's fictional narrator seems finally to comprehend that the U.S. Constitution, embodying "sacred" democratic principles, is a

Ellison presenting the William Dean Howells Medal to John Cheever, 1965 (UPI/Bettmann Newsphotos)

"vital covenant" offering unlimited possibilities for "individual self-realization."

Although Ellison's art transcends any simplistic cultural pigeonholes, one may discern the way the author draws upon a variety of literary traditions, including over a century of Afro-American lore and literature. The reader unacquainted with Frederick Douglass, Booker T. Washington, W. E. B. Du Bois, James Weldon Johnson, Alain Locke, Marcus Garvey, Richard Wright, and black folklore may miss a dimension of the novel's art, for all contribute to the meaning of the invisible man's quest and all enrich the rhetorical texture of the work.

The protagonist's youthful desire to become another Booker T. Washington testifies to his misguided ambitions early in the novel. Indeed, the speech he delivers after the battle royal–his valedictorian speech–is lifted *verbatim* from Washington's 1895 Atlanta Exposition address, an address Du Bois contemptuously dubbed "the At-

lanta Compromise." "Cast down your bucket where you are," Washington had frequently advised; later in the novel two characters literally cast down their kerosene-filled buckets during a race riot and set ablaze some buildings. During the college campus chapters, the novel takes satirical swipes at the Founder (based on Washington) and his disciple, Dr. Bledsoe, whom the students surreptitiously call "Old Bucket-head." The bronze statue of the "cold father symbol" puzzles the narrator, who cannot decide whether the founder is lifting the veil of ignorance from the kneeling slave or lowering it more firmly in place. Such a statue of Booker T. Washington still stands on the grounds of Tuskegee University.

Standing in stark opposition to a deceptive, opportunistic, kowtowing Booker T. Washington figure is the image of Frederick Douglass, a heroic paragon whose spirit hovers in the background throughout the novel. The radical organization, the Brotherhood, welcomes the protagonist as the new Booker T. Washington, but it would not be likely to tolerate a Frederick Douglass in its midst. Douglass was committed to the Constitution and never lost faith in the promise of American democracy; he personifies manly assertiveness and unobtrusive self-esteem. The narrator's grandfather and Douglass are linked together as crafty, dignified, rebellious, and fiercely independent men. Near the end of chapter 17 when Brother Tarp, who is also associated with these figures, gives the invisible man a portrait of Douglass, the hero contemplates the life of the man he would choose, at that point in his career, to emulate:

> Sometimes I sat watching the watery play of light upon Douglass' portrait, thinking how magical it was that he talked his way from slavery to a government ministry, and so swiftly. Perhaps, I thought, something of the kind is happening to me. Douglass came north to escape and find work in the shipyards; a big fellow in a sailor's suit who, like me, had taken another name. What had his true name been? [Frederick Bailey.] Whatever it was, it was as *Douglass* that he became himself, defined himself.

There are numerous ironies here, not the least of which is that it took a long time for Douglass to be appointed to a government ministry–he was over fifty years old at the time; that the invisible man triumphs as an introspective author quietly meditating upon the meaning of his experiences rather than as a crowd-rousing orator; and that Douglass chose his own name while the invisible man's "identity" is conferred on him by the Brotherhood. Perhaps the crowning irony is that the invisible man has much farther to go before he approaches Douglass's standards of forthright independence, for the fugitive slave refused to accept a subordinate position in anyone else's organization–he was always his own man.

W. E. B. Du Bois is never explicitly mentioned in *Invisible Man* but his presence, nevertheless, makes itself felt. Both Du Bois and Ellison's narrator are troubled by a sense of double consciousness. The invisible man becomes aware that "there were two of me: the old self that . . . dreamed sometimes of my grandfather and Bledsoe and Brockway and Mary, the self that flew without wings and plunged from great heights; and the new public self that spoke for the Brotherhood . . . I seemed to run a foot race against myself." Similarly, in *The Souls of Black*

Folk (1903) Du Bois experiences a "peculiar sensation": "one ever feels his twoness–an American, a Negro; two souls, two thoughts, two unreconciled strivings; two warring ideals in one dark body, whose dogged strength alone keeps it from being torn asunder." Despite this sense of dichotomy, however, both Du Bois and the invisible man ultimately achieve a unified vision, one strong enough to merge the dual selves. In discussing the Negro's relationship to America, the invisible man at one point reflects, "we . . . [are] snarled inextricably within its veins and sinews"; at another point he says, "America is woven of many strands." Both metaphorical expressions recall Du Bois's assertion: "we have woven ourselves with the very warp and woof of the nation," in the "Of the Sorrow Songs" section of *The Souls of Black Folk*. "I am," Ellison once said, "a man who shares a dual culture." Du Bois asks the rhetorical question that haunts much of Ellison's writing: "Would America have been America without her Negro people?" Ellison's reply, like Du Bois's, is that such a premise is inconceivable: there simply wouldn't *be* a recognizable America or an American culture under such circumstances.

Houston A. Baker, Jr., who has studied the relationship between James Weldon Johnson's *The Autobiography of an Ex-Colored Man* (1912) and *Invisible Man*, calls the former a prototype of the latter. His governing thesis is that "the cultural situation that produced *The Autobiography of an Ex-Colored Man*, the manner in which the story is set forth, and the antecedent works that influenced its author lead one easily to the informing sensibility and significant patterns of action in *Invisible Man*." The anonymous narrators of both novels offer retrospective accounts of their lives "from a position of impunity." Other parallels abound. Both novels recapitulate the various stages of Afro-American history from slave days, to Reconstruction, to the migration north, to, finally, the disillusioning experiences in an urban milieu. In both works the narrators are caught in patterns of circular movement: they are haunted by a sense of déjà vu because they keep running into the same demeaning situations–no matter how different the surface circumstances of those situations may seem. Finally, both works are predicated upon a shared perception: that the "achievements of the folk cannot be minimized" in reaching the goal of freedom.

Ellison first read Alain Locke's *The New Negro* (1925) while he was still in high school. At

Ellison and Clifford Geertz on 13 June 1974, when they were both awarded honorary degrees at Harvard
(UPI/Bettmann Newsphotos)

Tuskegee he met Locke and then, on his second day in Harlem, renewed his acquaintance. Although Ellison eventually became critical of the New Negro movement, parts of *Invisible Man* seem a gloss upon Locke's famous essay. Locke believed that in the process of being transplanted from the South to the North, the Negro was becoming transformed, that is, psychologically liberated from the strictures of the past. Locke expected many advantageous developments to follow from the improved condition of the Negro. However premature his prognosis, Locke's views still have many points of correspondence with *Invisible Man*. Both works praise the initiative of the common folk, acting as individuals or en masse, while sneering at the feeble efforts of the putative leaders. Both works portray blacks as reluctant rebels. Locke says, "the Negro is radical on race matters, conservative on others, in other words, a 'forced radical,' a social protestant rather than a genuine radical." The invisible man admits to a similar disposition when he yearns for "peace and quiet, tranquillity, but was too much aboil inside." He, too, is not a rebel by nature. Most important of all, Locke believed the Negro should develop a more positive self-

Dictionary of Literary Biography

concept which would permit him to take full responsibility for his actions and his mental life: "he must know himself and be known for precisely what he is. . . . we rejoice and pray to be delivered both from self-pity and condescension." This is precisely the conclusion Ellison's narrator comes to when he assumes responsibility for what has happened to him, and he says, "my problem was that I always tried to go in everyone's way but my own." The political solution for both the New Negro and the invisible man is to exploit what Locke calls the "new democracy in American culture," for "the Negro mind reaches out as yet to nothing but American wants, American ideas." The same glorification of cultural pluralism and political liberalism is found in the work of both authors.

Locke had little patience with "quixotic radicalisms," and so he denounced Garveyism–the militant politics and the separatist philosophy of Marcus Garvey. Although Garvey was the original spearhead of the New Negro movement, when he was sent to jail for alleged mail fraud in 1925 (the same year Locke's essay appeared), he and his radical approach to racial problems were discredited. Garvey was a flamboyant figure who wore colorful military regalia–braids, plumes, and all–when he appeared in public. Among the three most prominent ideas he espoused were that black is beautiful, that black people in America should return to Mother Africa, and that they should be willing to die for their beliefs. The character Ras the Destroyer in *Invisible Man* (whose name pointedly resembles "race") is clearly based upon Garvey. Ellison draws upon the diction and cadences of Garvey's speech when he has Ras address Tod Clifton with: "You *my* brother, mahn. Brothers are the same color; how the hell you call these white men *brother?* . . . Brothers the same color. We sons of Mama Africa, you done forgot? You black, BLACK! . . . You African, AFRICAN!" Both in image and substance Ras the black nationalist is a latter-day Garvey.

Ellison at one time was a close friend of Richard Wright's, and, arguably, *Invisible Man* incorporates more biographical incidents from Wright's life than from Ellison's own. Like the invisible man, Wright was from the South and lived for a while with his Uncle Clark in Greenwood, Mississippi; at the smoker the invisible man is introduced as "the smartest boy we've got out there in Greenwood." Wright once worked at an optical factory; the invisible man helps to make Optic White when he works at the Liberty Paints factory. While Ellison was never involved in a battle royal, in *Black Boy* (1945) Wright recounts his fight with a black acquaintance, Harrison, for five dollars (the same sum awarded the invisible man after his bout with Tatlock):

> The white men were smoking and yelling obscenities at us. . . . The fight was on, was on against our will. I felt trapped and ashamed. . . . We fought . . . slugging, grunting, spitting, cursing, crying, bleeding. The shame and anger we felt for having allowed ourselves to be duped crept into our blows and blood ran into our eyes, half blinding us. The hate we felt for the [white audience] went into the blows we threw at each other.

Wright's description is strongly echoed in the battle royal scene of *Invisible Man*. Despairing of justice in the South, Wright pinned his hopes on going north where he joined the Communist party. In *American Hunger* (1977), the second part of his autobiography, Wright reports that he was told in an interview with a comrade in the late 1930s: "Look, we want to make you a mass leader," to which Wright replied: "But suppose I'm not that kind of material?" He realized that the comrade had not seriously considered anything he had said: "Our talk was a game; he was trying to outwit me. The feelings of others meant nothing to him." The Brotherhood's desire to mold the invisible man into a new Booker T. Washington prompts him to ask, "What was I, a man or a natural resource?" Wright came to distrust the authoritarian operations of the party. He especially objected to their efforts at mind control: "I had fled men who did not like the color of my skin, and now I was among men who did not like the tone of my thoughts." His run-ins with his comrades frequently sound like the invisible man's skirmishes with Brother Jack and Brother Wrestrum. Eventually Wright felt betrayed by the party; in return he denounced it. The invisible man in time comes to a similar conclusion about the Brotherhood.

Both Wright and Ellison dealt with the concept of invisibility. "The White South said that it knew 'niggers,' and I was what the White South called a 'nigger,' " Wright relates in *Black Boy*. "Well, the White South had never known *me*– never known what *I* thought, what *I* felt." Bigger Thomas, in *Native Son* (1940), complains that he, too, feels "naked, transparent." An added ironic dimension to the narrator's invisibility in *Invisible Man* is that for a long time he had been blind to

Lane Kirkland, Ellison, and Senator Walter Mondale at a political dinner in New York City (AP/Wide World Photos)

his own true nature—he had been invisible to himself. A novella by Wright, "The Man Who Lived Underground," which appeared in part in 1944, one year before Ellison began writing his novel, provides numerous similarities to *Invisible Man.* Both main characters choose to be underground men, and they live surrealistic lives in symbol-laden surroundings.

While all of these literary sources play an important role, no Afro-American source is so pervasively infused into *Invisible Man* as black music, folklore, and folk culture. These folk elements affect the very structure and texture of Ellison's book. As Ellison has observed, "Great literature is erected upon [a] humble base of folk forms." He had already used folkloric and mythic materials in his early stories such as "Mister Toussan" (with its references to black history) and "Flying Home" (with its title from a Lionel Hampton composition and its manipulation of Jim Crow imagery), but *Invisible Man* is a veritable compendium of folktales, folk songs, spirituals, bebop, jive (and other elements of jazz), sermons, jokes, boasts, riddles, street rap, conundrums, aph-

orisms, eulogies, political oratory, and the dozens. From the beginning of the novel, when, in the prologue, the invisible man listens to Armstrong's "What Did I Do to Be So Black and Blue?" and in a hallucinatory state imagines a slave woman's tale about miscegenation, until the end of the novel, when, in the epilogue, the narrator ponders whether to "Open the window and let the foul air out" or say "It was good green corn before the harvest," black music, and especially the blues, continually informs and confirms the novel's meaning. ("Open the window and let the foul air out" comes from "Buddy Bolden's Blues," which was frequently performed by Armstrong, who was nicknamed "Bad Air"; "It was good green corn before the harvest" derives from a Leadbelly song.) Elsewhere in the narrative Mary Rambo sings Bessie Smith's "Back Water Blues"; the mourners sing "There's Many a Thousand Gone" at Clifton's funeral; "Who Killed Cock Robin" becomes a mock dirge in the narrator's mind; and Peter Wheatstraw sings "She's got Feet like a Monkey/Legs like a Frog - Lawd, Lawd!" from "The Boogie Woogie Blues"

by Count Basie and Jimmy Rushing. Albert Murray claims, "It was as if Ellison had taken an everyday twelve bar blues tune (by a man from down South sitting in a manhole up North singing and signifying how he got there) and scored it for full orchestra." O'Meally sees the invisible man as having achieved the perspective of a blues singer who "recounts his story with style, irony, and a sense of absurdity" as he views "his trials and glories in terms of adventure and romance." The tensions that are captured in the novel may be compared to the "antagonistic cooperation" which Ellison says characterizes the way jazz musicians combine individual and communal impulses.

Among the greatest legacies of the folk culture are the folktales, many of which originated in the slave era. Often these tales take the form of animal fables that pit Brer Rabbit against Brer Bear. To complicate matters, Ellison seems to assign his hero the role of Brer Rabbit at certain times while assigning him the role of Brer Bear at others. The invisible man, for example, is identified with Brer Bear when he hibernates in his underground home ("Bear with me," he puns) and when he runs afoul of the Brer Rabbit characters—Bledsoe, Brother (i.e., Brer) Jack, Brockway (also referred to as Tar Baby)—who constantly try to trick and trap him. Concomitantly, he becomes identified with Brer Rabbit when he scampers from misadventure to misadventure but manages to make the world his briar patch all the same. He does this, for example, in the hospital scene when he realizes that "somehow I was Buckeye the Rabbit." He is the trickster figure who, at the very moment the "doctors" think they have neutralized him, wins a significant moral victory over them; he has regressed to an old folk-based identity which liberates him from his fear of all slave drivers and oppressive father figures: "Knowing now that there was nothing which I could expect from them, there was no reason to be afraid." The outcome proves to be ironic because the hero is not the mindless automaton they intended him to be but a stronger and far more dangerous individual than they realize. Beethoven's Fifth Symphony (used as the Victory-Day theme during World War II), which has been playing in the background during this ordeal, provides an appropriate accompaniment to the hero's victory. By the end of his tale, the narrator becomes both Brer Rabbit in his warren (who cunningly enjoys his private joke by stealing electricity from the power company) and Brer Bear in his den (hiber-

nating before his inevitable reemergence in the spring)—signifying his ability, finally, to manipulate roles rather than be manipulated by them.

Ellison has expertly grafted the vernacular style—utilizing all the energy, insight, and poetry of an oral folk tradition—onto the body and into the substance of his work. *Invisible Man* continues the Afro-American literary tradition by selecting from it, synthesizing the enduring aspects of it, and expanding it to new parameters. In devising a new epic form supple enough to contain a remarkably diverse set of materials, Ellison has made unprecedented use of black culture as a literary source.

At the same time, Ellison insists that as an American writer he works out of a tradition too complex to restrict itself solely to Afro-American sources. In fact, it is not even possible to isolate an Afro-American tradition that exists independently of the other traditions which help shape the American character. He continues to use the word *Negro* and insists that Negroes are not an African people, but Americans of eclectic cultural traditions and mixed bloodlines whose history and destiny are indigenous. Talking about a distinct "white culture" and "black culture" is glib, he argues, "because the truth of the matter is that between the two racial groups there has always been a constant exchange of cultural, of stylistic elements. Whether in the arts, in education, in athletics, or in certain conceptions and misconceptions of democratic justice, interchange, appropriation, and integration—not segregation—have been the constants of our developing nation." The "concord of sensibilities"—cultivated in churches, in sports stadiums, on radio stations, on dance floors, and in the very home itself—is too intricately knotted for it ever to be disentangled.

The reviews of *Invisible Man* were overwhelmingly laudatory—the book was commonly hailed as a masterpiece—but there were voices of dissent. Communists, naturally, were incensed by Ellison's *reactionary* portrait of the Brotherhood; school boards banned the book for being too candid in its depiction of sexual and racial reality; and black nationalists attacked Ellison for being too obsessed with the writer's craft and too devoid of revolutionary fervor. Descriptive terms—such as "existential," "transcends race," "complex," "ambiguous," and "universal"—used by certain critics to praise the novel were inverted by detractors to condemn it. To the degree that *Invisible Man* could be read as the picaresque odys-

sey of Everyman, these detractors charged, Ellison was abandoning the protest tradition and shirking his proper racial commitments as a writer. Such critics were not impressed when Ellison was favorably compared to Saul Bellow and J. D. Salinger, writers who also emphasized the primacy of personal integrity in an existentially absurd universe.

Ellison fed the polemical fires by fighting back. He rejected Wright's naturalism, he said, because naturalism deals with "everything except the nature of man." He argued that naturalism "conditions the reader to accept the less worthy values of society, and it serves to justify and absolve our sins of social irresponsibility." Those who want to write sociology, he admonished, should not write novels. His affinity for the great nineteenth-century American authors like Emerson, Herman Melville, and Nathaniel Hawthorne is based upon what Ellison perceives to be their willingness to confront significant moral issues, including the issue of black humanity, without sacrificing style or compromising craft. For these reasons he considered Richard Wright a "relative" rather than a literary "ancestor," explaining: "while one can do nothing about choosing one's relatives, one can, as artist, choose one's 'ancestors.'" Authors he consciously sought out and chose to learn from did not include naturalists or propagandists.

After *Invisible Man*, two more pieces showcasing the character Mary Rambo appeared: "Did You Ever Dream Lucky?" (*New World Writing*, 1954) and "Out of the Hospital and Under the Bar" (*Soon, One Morning*, 1963), the second of which had originally been intended to be part of *Invisible Man*. In 1956 Ellison published one of his best stories, "A Coupla Scalped Indians" (*New World Writing*), which, in the vein of the earlier Buster and Riley stories, centers on two boys, one of whom is explicitly referred to as Buster. Determined to become Indian Scouts (not mere Cub Scouts), they work on their tests (in swimming, endurance running, cooking) independent of any troop–despite the fact that they bear the additional burden of having recently been "scalped," that is, circumcised. The familiar Ellisonian theme, initiation into manhood, plays itself out against an encounter with the sphinxlike Aunt Mackie, portrayed alternately as appealing and repugnant, young and old, angel and devil, seductress and seduced–in short, a symbol of human experience. The story achieves a perfect and self-contained expression of its theme.

Shadow and Act (1964) collects essays and interviews written over a twenty-two-year period. Taking his title from lines in T. S. Eliot's 1925 poem "The Hollow Men," Ellison sets out to probe the meaning of experience, to understand what lies below the surface of the act. He arranges his materials according to three general themes: the first third of the book investigates literature and folklore; the second third deals with Negro music and the blues and jazz artists who have created it; and the last third offers a cultural and political examination of the relationship of the Negro subculture to the rest of the nation. *Shadow and Act* is essential reading for anyone who wishes to plumb the depths of the author and his work, for it is filled with precisely argued statements concerning Ellison's own literary theories and practice and with his evaluation of other writers. In the course of the book Ellison deflates the definitions and assessments of American life which he considers inadequate; he also engages in public debate with Irving Howe (over the nature of the black experience in America), with his friend Stanley Edgar Hyman (about the nature of Negro folklore), and with LeRoi Jones (whom he castigates for misreading the nature of the blues). In addition to presenting his reformulation of what the novel is and what it should attempt to do, and offering a celebrated definition of the blues, Ellison argues for the interrelatedness of all experience and proclaims that, at least on the level of the imagination, integration has been achieved in the United States.

Many accolades and honors followed in the wake of *Invisible Man* and *Shadow and Act*. Ellison received the National Book Award, the Russwurm Award, and a Certificate of Award from the *Chicago Defender*, all in 1953; the American Academy of Arts and Letters Fellowship to Rome for 1955-1957; the Medal of Freedom in 1969; and the Chevalier de l'Ordre des Artes et Lettres from André Malraux, French minister of cultural affairs, in 1970. He lent prestige to many academic institutions by accepting posts at Bard (where he taught Russian literature and American literature, 1958-1961), Rutgers (where he taught creative writing and comparative literature, 1962-1969), the University of Chicago (where he was Alexander White Visiting Professor, winter of 1961), and New York University (where he served as Albert Schweitzer Professor in the Humanities, 1970-1979, and is now professor emeritus). He

Ellison, circa 1985 (courtesy of Leon Russell)

has also lectured at Columbia University, at Yale (where he is an honorary fellow), at the Salzburg Seminar in Austria (where he spoke on American literature and Negro folklore in 1954), and at dozens of schools, including Amherst, Antioch, Carnegie Mellon, Fisk, and Princeton. Honorary doctorates came at a rapid and regular pace to the college dropout: from Tuskegee (1963), Rutgers (1966), University of Michigan (1967), Grinnell (1967), Williams College (1970), Adelphi (1971), Long Island University (1971), College of William and Mary (1972), Wake Forest (1974), University of Maryland (1974), Harvard (1974), Bard College (1978), Wesleyan University (1980), and Brown (1980).

In addition to being a world-renowned writer—*Invisible Man* has been translated into fourteen languages and his first two books have remained in print continuously since publication—and a respected presence in American intellectual circles, Ellison is a gourmet cook, a photographer, a musician, an art collector, a builder of hi-fi sets, and a designer of his own furniture. It would seem that with all these accomplish-

ments Ralph Ellison has achieved his childhood ambition of becoming a Renaissance man.

Off and on since 1955 Ellison has been working on a second novel. Sections have appeared as "And Hickman Arrives" (1960), "The Roof, the Steeple and the People" (1960), "It Always Breaks Out" (1963), "Juneteenth" (1965), "Tell It Like It Is, 'Baby'" (1965), "Night-Talk" (1969), "A Song of Innocence" (1970), "Cadillac Flambé" (1973), and "Backwacking: A Plea to the Senator" (1977). By 1966 Ellison reportedly had written over one thousand pages of the new novel, enough to fill four bound volumes of typescript. Then, in 1967, a fire struck the Ellisons' recently acquired summer home in Plainfield, Massachusetts, destroying about 350 pages, which contained almost a year's worth of revisions. The political assassinations of 1968 may further have dampened the comic spirit that imbued the new work. Still, restoration of the text had progressed to such an extent by 1970 that Ellison was pondering how best to handle his gigantic manuscript and was considering whether to publish it as a trilogy.

The excerpts indicate that the novel will involve Rev. Alonzo Zuber Hickman; Bliss, his adopted son, who renounces Hickman and becomes a Negro-baiting senator known by his alias, Sunraider; Severen, the black assassin who shoots Sunraider; Cliofus, friend of Severen and an aspiring writer; Minifees, a black musician who burns his white Cadillac on Sunraider's lawn; and McIntyre, a white reporter. In a headnote to one of the excerpts—the one in which Hickman is at Sunraider's bedside following the assassination attempt on the senator's life—Ellison describes the scene as "an anguished attempt to arrive at the true shape and substance of a sundered past and its meaning." One is tempted to speculate that this may be one of the major themes of the entire novel-in-progress.

In addition to his ongoing efforts to finish this work of fiction, Ellison completed *Going to the Territory* (1986), a collection of sixteen speeches, reviews, and essays written since 1957, all except two of them previously published in newspapers and magazines. Most of these pieces were written during the 1960s; only one, an essay commemorating Erskine Caldwell on his eightieth birthday, was written as late as 1983. The subjects range from literature to sociology, from the responsibilities of the artist to homages to Duke Ellington, Richard Wright, and Romare Bearden. Ellison continues to explore "Americanness" and to analyze America's uniquely pluralistic culture. In "The Little Man at Chehaw Station" he observes, "we are, by definition and by the processes of democratic cultural integration, the inheritors, creators, and creations of a culture of cultures." To illustrate his ideas, he provides autobiographical vignettes. The reader will not quickly forget Ellison's hilarious recollection of the disputatious opera critics he stumbled upon in the basement of a Harlem tenement; besides serving as furnace stokers in the bowels of a slum building, they did double duty as extras at the Metropolitan Opera House. This anecdotal narrative, in revealing how these "four huge black men" acquired an expert knowledge of opera, demonstrates for Ellison that the American writer should never sell his audience short.

The acquisition of style occurs on all social levels, according to Ellison: "the word play of Negro kids in the South would make the experimental poets, the modern poets, green with envy" ("What These Children Are Like"), because "within the bounds of their rich oral culture, they possess a great virtuosity with the music, the poetry, of words." As enamored as he is of the classical Western literary tradition, he nonetheless celebrates this facility with the vernacular.

Elsewhere in the volume Ellison defines the artist as "a lightning rod attracting unexpected insights and a warning against stale preconceptions." For those critics who scorn him as too disengaged and effetely belletristic an artist, he offers a disarming characterization of himself "as a novelist interested in that area of the national life where political power is institutionalized and translated into democratic ritual and national style" ("The Myth of the Flawed White Southerner").

Going to the Territory is elegantly written. Often aphoristic ("What one reads becomes part of what one sees and feels"; "most American whites are culturally part Negro American without even realizing it"; "in this country it is always wise to expect the unexpected"), Ellison unremittingly and sometimes brilliantly explores "the mystery which haunts American experience, and that is the mystery of how we are many and yet one." In their review of this volume, *American Visions: The Magazine of Afro-American Culture* refers to Ellison as "the dean of black American writers." The collection reaffirms Ellison's stature as a social and literary critic.

Ellison's reputation has undergone a remarkable metamorphosis over the years. His liberalism was considered out of step with the times by the New Left and Third World spokespersons of the late 1960s and early 1970s. He incurred their displeasure in 1965 when he participated in President Johnson's White House Art Festival—a function which Robert Lowell conspicuously boycotted. The selection of *Invisible Man* that same year as the single most distinguished work published since World War II in a Book Week poll of two hundred (predominantly white) authors, critics, and editors was taken as further evidence that Ellison was "on the wrong side." By contrast, a *Negro Digest* poll in 1968 of black writers indicated that Richard Wright was *their* number one choice; Ellison and James Baldwin tied for third place behind second-place Langston Hughes. As black militancy grew in the 1960s, LeRoi Jones assailed Ellison in "Philistinism and the Negro Writer" for silently "fidgeting away in some college" while the ghettoes burned. The editors of *The Militant Black Writer* (1969) pointed out that "black self-consciousness has traveled [since the publication of *Invisible Man*] from self-knowledge to self-determination." Perhaps the most virulent

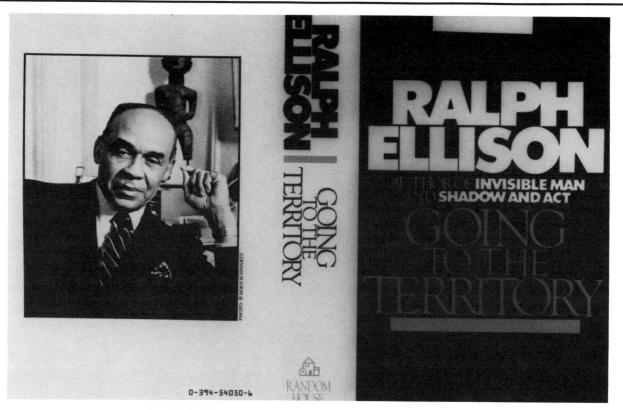

Dust jacket for Ellison's 1986 book of speeches, reviews, and essays

diatribe was launched by Ernest Kaiser, who charged: "Ellison has become an Establishment writer, an Uncle Tom, an attacker of the sociological formulations of the civil rights movement, a defender of the criminal Vietnam War of extermination against Asian (and American Negro) people, a denigrator of the great tradition of Negro protest writing and, worst of all for himself as a creative artist, a writer of weak and ineffectual fiction and essays mostly about himself and how he became an artist." Even though Langston Hughes, James Baldwin, and James Farmer (of CORE) continued to speak well of his work, Ellison was often the scapegoat of the black militant's rage.

As times change, so do attitudes. A number of young black writers who had distanced themselves from Ellison earlier have come full circle. Larry Neal, for example, who with LeRoi Jones edited *Black Fire*, a 1968 anthology of Afro-American writing (from which they excluded Ellison), subsequently admitted to "wincing" when he reread his comments about Ellison in the afterword to *Black Fire*. Refusing to be coopted by white critics who analyzed *Invisible Man* in formalistic terms, black critics increasingly marvel at Ellison's treatment of Afro-American life;

they find his monumental novel a profound examination of the richness and beauty and heroism of the black experience. According to John Wright, by the late 1970s, in reaction to the black arts movement, Ellison had become "reluctant father figure to the new generation of black writers." The 1980 *Carleton Miscellany* entitled "A Ralph Ellison Festival" contains only glowing tributes from fellow black writers and critics.

Very few literary events have aroused greater anticipation than the long-awaited appearance of Ellison's second novel. But even if Ellison never publishes another word, his *Invisible Man* is secure as a classic of literature, for it not only evinces an extraordinary command of language but it also contains both literal and symbolic truths about black people in particular and human beings in general.

References:

Michael Allen, "Some Examples of Faulknerian Rhetoric in Ellison's *Invisible Man*," in *The Black American Writer*, edited by C. W. E. Bigsby (De Land, Fla.: Everett-Edwards, 1969), I: 143-151;

Houston A. Baker, Jr., "A Forgotten Prototype: *The Autobiography of an Ex-Colored Man* and *In-*

visible Man," *Virginia Quarterly Review*, 49 (Summer 1973): 433-449;

John Z. Bennett, "The Race and the Runner: Ellison's *Invisible Man*," *Xavier University Studies*, 5 (March 1966): 12-26;

William Bennett, "Black and Blue: Negro Celine," *American Mercury*, 74 (June 1952): 100-104;

Bernard Benoit and Michel Fabre, "A Bibliography of Ralph Ellison's Published Writings," *Studies in Black Literature* (Autumn 1971);

Harold Bloom, ed., *Modern Critical Views: Ralph Ellison* (New York: Chelsea House, 1986);

Martin Bucco, "Ellison's Invisible West," *Western American Literature*, 10 (November 1975): 237-238;

David L. Carson, "Ralph Ellison: Twenty Years After," *Studies in American Fiction*, 1 (Spring 1973): 1-23;

Earl A. Cash, "The Narrators in *Invisible Man* and *Notes from Underground*: Brothers in Spirit," *CLA Journal*, 16 (June 1973): 505-507;

Barbara Christian, "Ralph Ellison: A Critical Study," in *Black Expression*, edited by Addison Gayle, Jr. (New York: Weybright & Talley, 1969), pp. 353-365;

Jacqueline Covo, *The Blinking Eye: Ralph Waldo Ellison and His American, French, German and Italian Critics, 1952-1971: Bibliographic Essays and a Checklist* (Metuchen, N.J.: Scarecrow, 1974);

Leonard J. Deutsch, "Ellison's Early Fiction," *Negro American Literature Forum*, 7 (Summer 1973): 53-59;

Deutsch, "Ralph Waldo Ellison and Ralph Waldo Emerson: A Shared Moral Vision," *CLA Journal*, 16 (December 1972): 159-178;

Deutsch, "*The Waste Land* in Ellison's *Invisible Man*," *Notes on Contemporary Literature*, 7 (September 1977): 5-6;

Leigh A. Ehlers, " 'Give Me the Ocular Proof': *Othello* and Ralph Ellison's *Invisible Man*," *Notes on Contemporary Literature*, 6 (November 1976): 10-11;

Barbara Fass, "Rejection of Paternalism: Hawthorne's 'My Kinsman Major Molineux' and Ellison's 'Invisible Man,' " *CLA Journal*, 15 (December 1971): 171-196;

Russell G. Fischer, "*Invisible Man* as History," *CLA Journal*, 17 (March 1974): 338-367;

Leon Forrest, "Racial History as a Clue to the Action in *Invisible Man*," *Muhammad Speaks*, 12 (15 September 1972): 28-30;

Frances S. Foster, "The Black and White Masks of Franz Fanon and Ralph Ellison," *Black Academy Review: Quarterly of the Black World*, 1 (Winter 1970): 46-58;

Donald B. Gibson, "Ralph Ellison and James Baldwin," in *The Politics of Twentieth-Century Novelists*, edited by George A. Panichas (New York: Hawthorne, 1971), pp. 307-320;

Ronald Gottesman, ed., *Studies in Invisible Man* (Columbus, Ohio: Merrill, 1971);

Maxine Greene, "Against Invisibility," *College English*, 30 (March 1969): 430-436;

Edward M. Griffin, "Notes from a Clean, Well-Lighted Place: Ralph Ellison's *Invisible Man*," *Twentieth Century Literature*, 15 (October 1969): 129-144;

Allen Guttman, "Focus on Ralph Ellison's *Invisible Man*: American Nightmare," in *American Dreams, American Nightmares*, edited by David Madden (Carbondale: Southern Illinois University Press, 1970), pp. 188-196;

Trudier Harris, "Ellison's 'Peter Wheatstraw': His Basis in Black Folk Tradition," *Mississippi Folklore Register*, 9 (1975): 117-126;

Gary Haupt, "The Tragi-Comedy of the Unreal in Ralph Ellison's *Invisible Man* and Mark Twain's *Adventures of Huckleberry Finn*," *Interpretations*, 4 (1972): 1-12;

Peter L. Hays, "The Incest Theme in *Invisible Man*," *Western Humanities Review*, 23 (Autumn 1969): 335-339;

John Hersey, ed., *Ralph Ellison: A Collection of Critical Essays* (Englewood Cliffs, N.J.: Prentice-Hall, 1974);

Floyd Ross Horowitz, "The Enigma of Ralph Ellison's *Invisible Man*," *CLA Journal*, 7 (December 1963): 126-132;

David C. Howard, "Points in Defense of Ellison's *Invisible Man*," *Notes on Contemporary Literature*, 1 (January 1971): 13-14;

Abby Arthur Johnson, "Birds of Passage: Flight Imagery in *Invisible Man*," *Studies in the Twentieth Century*, 14 (Fall 1974): 91-104;

John H. Johnson, ed., "Ralph Ellison: His Literary Works and Status," special issue, *Black World*, 20 (December 1970);

E. M. Kist, "A Langian Analysis of Blackness in Ralph Ellison's *Invisible Man*," *Studies in Black Literature*, 7 (1976): 19-23;

George Knox, "The Totentanz in Ellison's *Invisible Man*," *Fabula*, 12, nos. 2-3 (1971): 168-178;

Richard Kostelanetz, "Ralph Ellison: Novelist as Brown-Skinned Aristocrat," in his *Master-*

minds (New York: Macmillan, 1969), pp. 36-59;

James B. Lane, "Underground to Manhood: Ralph Ellison's *Invisible Man*," *Negro American Literature Forum*, 7 (Summer 1973): 64-72;

F. H. Langman, "Reconsidering *Invisible Man*," *Critical Review*, 18 (1976): 114-127;

L. L. Lee, "The Proper Self: Ralph Ellison's *Invisible Man*," *Descant*, 10 (Spring 1966): 38-48;

Howard Levant, "Aspiraling We Should Go," *Mid-Continent American Studies Journal*, 4 (Fall 1963): 3-20;

Todd M. Lieber, "Ralph Ellison and the Metaphor of Invisibility in Black Literary Tradition," *American Quarterly*, 24 (March 1972): 86-100;

Marcia R. Lieberman, "Moral Innocents: Ellison's 'Invisible Man' and 'Candide,'" *CLA Journal*, 15 (September 1971): 64-79;

Stewart Lillard, "Ellison's Ambitious Scope in *Invisible Man*," *English Journal*, 58 (September 1969): 833-839;

Charles T. Ludington, Jr., "Protest and Anti-Protest: Ralph Ellison," *Southern Humanities Review*, 4 (Winter 1970): 31-40;

Barbara S. McDaniel, "John Steinbeck: Ralph Ellison's Invisible Source," *Pacific Coast Philology*, 8 (1973): 28-33;

Kerry McSweeney, *Invisible Man: Race and Identity* (Boston: G. K. Hall, 1988);

Louis D. Mitchell, "Invisibility: Permanent or Resurrective," *CLA Journal*, 17 (March 1974): 379-386;

Mitchell and Henry J. Stauffenberg, "Ellison's B. P. Rinehart: 'Spiritual Technologist,'" *Negro American Literature Forum*, 9 (1975): 51-52;

Alan Nadel, *Invisible Criticism: Ralph Ellison and The American Canon* (Iowa City: University of Iowa Press, 1988);

R. W. Nash, "Stereotypes and Social Types in Ellison's *Invisible Man*," *Sociological Quarterly*, 6 (Autumn 1965): 349-360;

C. W. Nettlebeck, "From Inside Destitution: Celine's Bardamer and Ellison's Invisible Man," *Southern Review* (Australia), 7 (November 1974): 246-253;

William W. Nichols, "Ralph Ellison's Black American Scholar," *Phylon*, 21 (Spring 1970): 70-76;

Therman B. O'Daniel, ed., "Special Ralph Ellison Number," *CLA Journal*, 13 (March 1970);

Raymond M. Olderman, "Ralph Ellison's Blues and *Invisible Man*," *Wisconsin Studies in Literature*, 7 (Summer 1966): 149-159;

Stuart E. Omans, "The Variations on a Masked Leader: A Study on the Literary Relationship of Ralph Ellison and Herman Melville," *South Atlantic Bulletin*, 40 (May 1975): 15-23;

Robert G. O'Meally, *The Craft of Ralph Ellison* (Cambridge, Mass.: Harvard University Press, 1980);

Janet Overmyer, "The Invisible Man and White Women," *Notes on Contemporary Literature*, 6 (May 1976): 13-15;

Paul A. Parrish, "Writing as Celebration: The Epilogue of *Invisible Man*," *Renascence*, 26 (Spring 1974): 152-157;

Marjorie Pryse, "Ralph Ellison's Heroic Fugitive," *American Literature*, 46 (March 1974): 1-15;

Frederick L. Radford, "The Journey Towards Castration: Interracial Sexual Stereotypes in Ellison's *Invisible Man*," *Journal of American Studies*, 4 (February 1971): 227-231;

"A Ralph Ellison Festival," special issue, *Carleton Miscellany*, 18 (Winter 1980);

John M. Reilly, ed., *Twentieth Century Interpretations of Invisible Man* (Englewood Cliffs, N.J.: Prentice-Hall, 1970);

Stewart Rodnon, "*The Adventures of Huckleberry Finn* and *Invisible Man:* Thematic and Structural Comparisons," *Negro American Literature Forum*, 4 (July 1970): 45-51;

Rodnon, "Henry Adams and Ralph Ellison: Transcending Tragedy," *Studies in the Humanities*, 3, no. 2 (1973): 1-7;

Richard Ross, "*Invisible Man* as Symbolic History," *Chicago Review*, 14 (November 1967): 24-26;

Roger Sale, "The Career of Ralph Ellison," *Hudson Review*, 18 (Spring 1965): 124-128;

Jerold J. Savory, "Descent and Baptism in *Native Son*, *Invisible Man*, and *Dutchman*," *Christian Scholar's Review*, 3 (1973): 33-37;

Hartmut K. Selke, "An Allusion to Sartre's *The Flies* in Ralph Ellison's *Invisible Man*," *Notes on Contemporary Literature*, 4 (May 1974): 3-4;

Isaac Sequeira, "The Uncompleted Initiation of the Invisible Man," *Studies in Black Literature*, 6 (Spring 1975): 9-13;

V. D. Singh, "*Invisible Man:* The Rhetoric of Colour, Chaos, and Blindness," *Rutgers University Studies in English*, 8 (1975): 54-61;

Raney Stanford, "The Return of the Trickster: When a Not-Hero Is a Hero," *Journal of Popular Culture*, 1 (Winter 1967): 228-242;

John Stark, "*Invisible Man:* Ellison's Black *Odyssey*," *Negro American Literature Forum*, 7 (Summer 1973): 60-63;

Shelby Steele, "Ralph Ellison's Blues," *Journal of Black Studies*, 7 (1976): 151-168;

Jeffrey Steinbrink, "Toward a Vision of Infinite Possibility: A Reading of *Invisible Man*," *Studies in Black Literature*, 7 (1976): 1-5;

Carolyn W. Sylvander, "Ralph Ellison's *Invisible Man* and Female Stereotypes," *Negro American Literature Forum*, 9 (1975): 77-79;

Joseph A. Trimmer, ed., *A Casebook on Ralph Ellison's Invisible Man* (New York: Crowell, 1972);

J. M. Waghmare, "Invisibility and the American Negro: Ralph Ellison's *Invisible Man*," *Quest*, 59 (1968): 23-30;

James Walker, "What Do You Say Now, Ralph Ellison," *Black Creation*, 1 (Summer 1970): 16-18 ff.;

William Walling, " 'Art' and 'Protest': Ralph Ellison's *Invisible Man* Twenty Years After," *Phylon*, 34 (June 1973): 120-134;

Walling, "Ralph Ellison's *Invisible Man:* 'It Goes a Long Way Back, Some Twenty Years,' " *Phylon*, 34 (March 1973): 4-16;

Sharon R. Weinstein, "Comedy and the Absurd in Ralph Ellison's *Invisible Man*," *Studies in Black Literature*, 3 (Autumn 1972): 12-16;

Joe Weixlmann and John O'Banion, "A Checklist of Ellison Criticism, 1972-1978," *Black American Literature Forum*, 12 (Summer 1978): 51-55.

Papers:

Some of Ellison's papers are held in the archives of the Julius Rosenwald Fund, Fisk University, Nashville, Tennessee.

Lorenz Graham
(27 January 1902-   )

Ora Williams
California State University, Long Beach

BOOKS: *How God Fix Jonah* (New York: Reynal & Hitchcock, 1946);
Tales of Momolu (New York: Reynal & Hitchcock, 1946);
South Town (Chicago: Follett, 1958);
North Town (New York: Crowell, 1965);
I, Momolu (New York: Crowell, 1966);
Whose Town? (New York: Crowell, 1969);
A Road Down in the Sea (New York: Crowell, 1970);
David He No Fear (New York: Crowell, 1971);
God Wash the World and Start Again (New York: Crowell, 1971);
Carolina Cracker (Boston: Houghton Mifflin, 1972);
Detention Center (Boston: Houghton Mifflin, 1972);
John Brown's Raid: A Picture History of the Attack on Harpers Ferry, Virginia (New York: Scholastic Book Services, 1972);
Runaway (Boston: Houghton Mifflin, 1972);
Stolen Car (Boston: Houghton Mifflin, 1972);
Song of the Boat (New York: Crowell, 1975);
Return to South Town (New York: Crowell, 1976);
John Brown: A Cry for Freedom (New York: Crowell, 1980).

OTHER: Walter van Tilburg Clark, *The Ox-Bow Incident*, adapted by Graham for Classics Illustrated comics, 125 (New York: Gilberton, 1955);
William Shakespeare, *Macbeth*, adapted by Graham for Classics Illustrated comics, 128 (New York: Gilberton, 1955);
The Story of Jesus, adapted by Graham for Classics Illustrated comics, special edition, 129A (New York: Gilberton, 1955);
H. G. Wells, *The Time Machine*, adapted by Graham for Classics Illustrated comics, 133 (New York: Gilberton, 1955);
The Ten Commandments, adapted by Graham for Classics Illustrated comics, special edition, 135A (New York: Gilberton, 1956);

Lorenz Graham (courtesy of the author)

"Flies," "Girlfriend," and "No Hop," in *Happenings* (Los Angeles Public Schools, 1965);
"Rainy Night," in *Voices of Youth* (Los Angeles: Los Angeles Public Schools, 1965);
"Dropout," "Home Run," "It Takes Some Brass," "Only Forty-Nine Ninety Five," and "Telephone Girl," in *Directions 1*, compiled by Graham, John Durham, and Elsa Graser (Boston: Houghton Mifflin, 1972);
"African Storyteller: A Liberian Tale," "County Fair," "No Damn Lie," "Rock Bottom," and "You Figure How the Parts Go," in *Direc-*

tions 2, compiled by Graham, Durham, and Graser (Boston: Houghton Mifflin, 1972);
"Alfonso," "Hitchhiker," "Money," "Showdown," and "Superstar," in *Directions 3,* compiled by Graham, Durham, and Graser (Boston: Houghton Mifflin, 1972);
"Accent," "Brothers," and "Twins," in *Directions 4,* compiled by Graham, Durham, and Graser (Boston: Houghton Mifflin, 1972).

Lorenz Graham, folklorist, lecturer, novelist, short-story writer, former social worker, and educator, has written four novels, four novelettes, and more than twenty-eight short stories, largely for an adolescent audience. He has also written Classics Illustrated comic-book adaptations of *Macbeth, The Ox-Bow Incident, The Story of Jesus, The Time Machine,* and *The Ten Commandments.*

A contemporary of Richard Wright, Zora Neale Hurston, Ralph Ellison, W. E. B. Du Bois (the second husband of his sister, author Shirley Graham), Virginia Hamilton, Margaret Walker, and Alice Walker, Graham was encouraged to become a writer after complaining to his sister that black writers only presented distorted images of black people. Agreeing with him, she insisted that artists must be allowed artistic freedom and that he should write the positive works he longed to see in print. For more than fifty years he has been presenting positive images of black people and of their experiences. In well-structured works he writes purposefully and sensitively about blacks he has known in the United States and in Africa, about racial problems in our country, about difficulties in growing up in America and in Africa, about relations between parents and children, and about adolescents and society.

Graham has won the Charles W. Follet Award and the Child Study Association Award, both for *South Town* (1958). He won the Book World First Place Award for *Whose Town?* (1969). His reputation as an author of fine books for children brought him an invitation to speak in South Africa at a 1987 symposium on children's literature.

Lorenz Bell Graham was born in New Orleans, Louisiana, on 27 January 1902 to Etta Bell Graham and David Andrew Graham. Because Graham's father was an African Methodist Episcopal minister whose assignments took the family to various parts of the country, he attended public schools in Illinois, Tennessee, Colorado, and the state of Washington. While in Tennessee, Gra-

Graham and his wife, Ruth Morris Graham, on their wedding day, 20 August 1929 (courtesy of the author)

ham was brutally beaten by a group of white boys as he returned home from school. When his father protested to the police about the incident, the police responded with racial epithets. When he matured, Graham came to understand that such hatred as he had experienced at the hands of the boys and the police destroys the hater: "people are people, whether black, white. . . . there are fast learners and slow learners, cruel people and kind, strong and weak."

Graham pursued undergraduate study at the University of California, Los Angeles, at the City College of New York, and at Virginia Union University, Richmond, Virginia, where he received his B.A. degree. He did graduate work in sociology at Columbia University between 1952 and 1955 and at New York University between 1956 and 1957. His social work studies and his subsequent jobs as a social worker became important subjects in his fiction for adolescents.

One of the first interruptions in Graham's education came when he went to Liberia, West Af-

rica, from 1924 to 1928, as a missionary-teacher at Monrovia College. There he met Ruth Morris, another missionary-teacher. On 20 August 1929 they married. Five children were born to this marriage: Lorenz, Jr.; Charles M.; twins, Jean and Joyce; and Ruth.

Before going to Africa, where his father went in 1926 to become president of Monrovia College, Graham held the traditional stereotypes of Africans. He admits he went "believing that I would be able to help the poor benighted Africans, that I could bring light to that dark land." He soon realized that what he had read about Africans being depraved, lazy, vicious, and stupid was identical to commonly written descriptions of American Negroes. When he failed to enlist his friends in efforts to rewrite the African story, he decided he would write honest stories about the Africans he knew.

How God Fix Jonah (1946), which retells the biblical story of Jonah in West African idiom, is Graham's first major work. It depicts Africans as the thinking people he knew. Graham suggests that the story be read aloud and that the reader picture "an African lad who has heard the stories of gods and devils, stories of loud-spoken kings and fearless slaves." In his foreword W. E. B. Du Bois writes that Graham's portrayals give "insight into the workings of the minds of men." Du Bois continues, "This is the stuff of which literature is made; and in the lore of the world, the literature of Africa has its place although it is often forgotten." The reviewer for *Commonweal* found parts of *How God Fix Jonah* had "amazing new vitality, emotion, and meaning in their dramatic, rhythmical renditions between God and his people," and recommended it for adults and children.

Graham's second African book was *Tales of Momolu* (1946), whose protagonist, Momolu, is featured in two other works. Momolu's name comes from an ironic incident in Graham's life. In Africa Graham spoke to a group of Liberian students, urging them to become doctors and nurses. After his talk his superiors cautioned him against overstimulating the children. Twenty years later, when Graham had to be treated for malaria in Norfolk, Virginia, his doctor was one of the students he had addressed, a Dr. Momolu Tugbah.

The Momolu stories are set in Africa, the place of man's beginnings, and one major theme in the works is Momolu's initiation into manhood or to various levels of maturity. Momolu is trained for manhood by listening to what his fa-

ther says and by observing the older men. From them he learns that strength, courage, and cooperation are some of the qualities men possess. "The Return of Flumbo," which introduces Momolu and his family, provides vignettes of family unity, love, concern, loyalty, and respect. Episodes highlighting these themes foreshadow events in subsequent tales and works, such as *I, Momolu* (1966). One example of such foreshadowing is that of Flumbo, Momolu's father, being attacked by an alligator. Flumbo's leg never really heals, a fact that receives much attention in subsequent stories. "Momolu Faces Danger," "Momolu Helps Make a Canoe," "The Alligator Fight," and "Momolu Helps on the Farm" all record Momolu's quest for manhood or knowledge. Each tale contains one or two experiences that contribute to Momolu's growth; and each story shows how his African family, tribal customs, and relationships help shape him.

I, Momolu, the second in the Momolu series, is about a Liberian boy who is initiated into manhood through a series of incidents that culminate in his exposure to the Western civilization encroaching upon Liberia. Flumbo helps Momolu learn about worlds outside their native village as the two travel together to the government seat. When they return to their native village, Momolu helps his father accept the civilization that must come to their village. As Momolu makes his odyssey into modern Liberia, the reader is exposed to African folklore, historical events, and the dilemmas people experience when confronted with change.

Graham's first big success in writing came with the acceptance by the Follett Publishing Company of *South Town*, a novel for adolescents, which for twelve years made the rounds of publishers, who, although they liked the work, felt this novel did not conform to their notions of how black characters should be depicted. One editor disliked the fact that the black family in *South Town* took baths in a tin tub on Saturday night, the kind of thing that a rural white family would do. This editor felt that Graham should find some way to distinguish a southern black family from a southern white one. Graham refused. *South Town* has met with considerable success. It has been republished by two companies and translated into German. All editions have sold well.

In *South Town* the Williams family, a hardworking, closely knit family that wishes to fulfill the American Dream, has its goals thwarted and life disrupted by a series of critical racial inci-

Advertisement for three of Graham's books. Every Man Heart Lay Down *(1970) is an excerpt from* How God Fix Jonah, *his 1946 collection of Bible stories written in West African Pidgin English.*

dents which force the family to go north. The Boyds, a white family, are the antagonists who represent the oppressive South. Harold Boyd's attempt to run over David and David's sister foreshadows some of the ordeals the Williamses are to experience. Mrs. Williams and Mrs. Boyd have a serious argument which eventually causes Mr. Williams to lose his job with the city and which prevents him from getting other jobs. After the Williams family is harassed by night riders, a white friend and supporter is killed, and their home is firebombed, the family leaves for the North, where life will have to be better.

South Town is the first in a quartet of novels unified by a number of constants. David Williams and his family are the protagonists in the four works. From *South Town* to the last work in the se-

ries, *Return to South Town* (1976), David and his family seek a normal life. In each work prejudice is a major force which at times becomes life threatening to the Williamses and their friends. And, in each of the novels, the home, church, school, and work are settings. David, the major protagonist in these works, is introduced in *South Town* at sixteen. He announces his goal of becoming a doctor and of returning to practice in South Town. The novels follow David's quest most particularly.

The second novel in the series, *North Town* (1965), examines the adjustment David, still sixteen years old, has to make in a northern industrial town. In this new setting David, from the rural South, must adjust to apartment living, to a high school that is predominately white, and to

Covers for three of Graham's comic-book adaptations for Classics Illustrated

subtle and overt forms of prejudice and discrimination. The old and new challenges require him to make some important decisions. When he makes the wrong choices, as he does on several occasions, he and his family suffer. They all accept these challenges and work together to resolve their problems.

The friends David acquires are also important in this work and in subsequent works. The Crutchfields help the Williamses through various crises. The Lenoirs have a daughter whom David dates. Alonzo Wells is a pessimistic black lad who befriends David. Buck Taylor is a young black who dislikes blacks less fortunate than himself. Then, there is Mike Connor, a young white friend who helps David become a star football player.

North Town has many important themes: the adjustments a black adolescent male and his family must make to a northern industrial town, the importance of a strong, supportive family to growing black teenagers, and problem solving in the single-parent home. The work explores the seemingly omnipresent confrontation between young black males and the police and stresses the need to examine all sides of crucial issues.

In *Whose Town?* protagonist David Williams is still an innocent, although he has learned much from his experiences in the South and in the North. Now eighteen and almost a man, David has to be initiated further into the ways of the world. Fighting, losing, winning, and resolving racial conflicts do not mean the end of racism, Graham seems to say; overcoming racism is a continuous battle. Eventually David is caught up in a series of racial problems. A typically vulnerable black American youth, he is attacked by a white youth, falsely accused, and arrested. In a related incident he witnesses the murder of his friend Alonzo Wells. David almost fails to complete high school because of his encounter with the police. David's personal encounters with racism are forces which help to mold him. He witnesses racial tensions in his town which escalate into a full-blown riot as whites and blacks fight for power. David observes and participates in events. This exposure enables him to see options for his behavior and the value of weighing decisions. His awareness of racism is peaked at black-nationalist meetings when he hears militant statements about race relations.

Whose Town? has numerous themes such as how to deal with prejudice and the hopes black parents have for their children, the threat and impact of joblessness, and assaults on family unity. After Mr. Williams loses his job, he begins staying away from home, stops going to church, and seems indifferent to what is happening in the home. He complains that he is not doing a man's part—"not working, depending on unemployment money, same as relief. . . ."

In *South Town* the David Williams family journeys to North Town in search of a better life which would enable David to become a doctor. In *Return to South Town* David has finished medical school and returns to South Town to fulfill the dream of practicing medicine in his former home. He is pleased to see such obvious changes as school integration and mixed social affairs. He soon discovers, however, that the same Harold Boyd who, years before, had deliberately tried to run over David and his sister, is now a major obstacle to David's establishing a medical practice. Although Boyd, also a medical doctor, realizes integration is the law of the land, he resists and circumvents the new law, typifying the manner in which integration edicts were ignored, especially in the early 1970s.

Just as integration in South Town is obvious to David, so also are changing attitudes. A waitress is polite to him and addresses him as "Sir." A student at the community college would like for David to meet his sociology teacher, who is black. Nurse Manning, white, cries because of the insults Boyd directs to David. The white nurse Pegram joins "in the angry protest" when she learns that David has been arrested. Red Boyd, whom David saved from drowning during their childhood, is instrumental in negotiating for the property David buys. The supportive Dr. Tennant informs David that his license has been granted.

In *Return to South Town* the number of blacks who exhibit great confidence in themselves and are willing to venture is much larger than in *South Town*. Israel Crawford knows his veterans' rights, and this knowledge enables him to hold on to his family property and to pay off the mortgage. He also buys land that the younger generation of blacks does not want. His neighbors provide David with room, board, and transportation. They discuss his plans with him, make helpful suggestions, and offer to lend him money or to borrow some for him. Junior, Israel Crawford's son, has such pride in David's accomplishments that he takes his friends to David's office and provides whatever help David needs. David becomes Junior's role model.

Covers for two Classics Illustrated special issues. These issues are significant because Graham is credited with the adaptations.

Perhaps the change of attitude is greatest in David, who has gained confidence in himself:

Velvet, you know I used to be afraid of what white folks could do, but if I've learned anything, I've learned that even the meanest of them, the most rebbish, are people too. They aren't giants and they aren't great brains. Most of them are small and weak. I know I've got what it takes to deal with them. They can't hurt me.

David rejects Harold Boyd's offer to see patients in a segregated wing of the Boyd Memorial Hospital. When his application for his medical license is delayed, he has too much pride to ask the Boyds to intervene on his behalf: "I am my father's son and I am not about to beg Harold Boyd . . . or any other white man for anything."

The David Williams series may be seen as a fictional account of the black struggle for civil and human rights. They represent Graham's response to the fact that, while stories had been written about heroic and degenerate Negroes and while much had been written about the "awful and heartrending subnormal conditions under which many Negroes suffer," he did not find much written about the kind of people he "most often saw."

Critics have responded favorably to the individual volumes, but the Williams series has been little looked at as a whole. Robert Small hailed *South Town* as an "especially good example of a book for junior literature. . . , a junior novel with a serious and very current literary theme and genuine literary excellence." The reviewer in the children's issue of *Book World* found *Whose Town?* an enlightening book and hoped that "parents, teachers, librarians [would] take note of it." This reviewer also applauded Graham's use of suspense and his style.

In the mid 1950s Graham did five adaptations for Classics Illustrated. Dan Malan, a Classics Illustrated historian, says that the average adapter spent ten months on a project to insure ac-

curacy of costumes and settings. Graham's *The Story of Jesus* (1955) was the first Classics Illustrated special edition. His *The Ten Commandments* (1956) was promoted along with the movie of the same name starring Charlton Heston, but it differs from the movie in closely following the biblical narrative.

Carolina Cracker, Detention Center, Runaway, and *Stolen Car,* four novelettes for and about juveniles, were published separately in 1972. Like so many of Graham's works, they grew out of his experiences with, and deep concerns for, youth. As an employee of the New York Welfare Department and as a probation officer in Los Angeles, he searched for ways to reach those prone to delinquency. He saw literacy as a major step toward making any meaningful change in the lives of these young people. As a consequence, he wrote these books for them.

The four novelettes are to be used in conjunction with the four *Direction* textbooks which Graham helped compile. The target readers are seventh and eighth graders, especially those students who are in the largest American minority groups–blacks, Hispanics, orientals, and American Indians. The compilers state that "under the surface lies similarity; everyone's membership in the human family."

In *Carolina Cracker* Bill Martin, a poor, white sixteen-year-old, has been providing for himself since he ran away when he was thirteen. Sensitive about being called a poor white, Bill is determined to become somebody, but he must get a job first. He selects the restaurant at which he wishes to work, goes to the black chef, asks for a meal, and then starts working. Major themes in this work are the plight of the poor white, his high visibility, the similarity of his condition to that of racial minorities, and the empathy that blacks have for poor whites.

Detention Center, although depicting some facets of existence in a detention center, is mostly about a romance between two juveniles detained at the center. The two fall in love at first sight and manage to communicate through forbidden notes. Juanita, the heroine, experiences a crisis when Valentino, her newfound love, is released from the center before she is. A counselor helps Juanita through this difficult period and provides Juanita with insights that help her make a reasonable adjustment to the outside world. Although Juanita and Valentine are reunited after her release, Graham suggests that their future to-

gether depends on the behavior and the choices each makes.

Runaway is a moving story about a sixteen-year-old girl whose home life becomes so unbearable that she runs away. The protagonist, Marybell, is introduced to the reader through Ted Robinson, a classmate, whose mother is a friend of Marybell's mother. Marybell has an English teacher, Mr. Locker, who insists "anybody can write" and inspires his students, including Marybell, to do so. She writes beautiful and deeply moving poetry in which she alludes to her dilemmas. Her poetry provides an outlet, while Ted's family offers Marybell hope by taking her in. Graham had difficulty with his publisher who did not feel Marybell, a black girl from the ghetto, should write "so poetically." Again, Graham refused to make the recommended changes.

Ted Robinson's family is also important in *Stolen Car.* The Robinsons experience a crisis when Leola Robinson's car disappears from her night job at the telephone company. The problem escalates when Leola thinks her unemployed brother has been involved in the alleged car theft. The tensions are relieved, and the anguished family reconciled, when they learn that the car was taken by mistake and the accused brother finds a job.

John Brown: A Cry for Freedom (1980) is a historical biography. In his introduction to this well-documented work Graham makes several very important statements that speak to the stature and commitment of John Brown, that indicate the significance of this work at this time in history, and that touch on some of Graham's previous themes. Graham writes, "The story of John Brown and his cry for freedom are now given again because his life did indeed help to make his country what it is today, and his beliefs, his words, and his prophecies apply to present conditions." Graham's John Brown is no fanatic, but a man who fought slavery because he thought its free labor would keep Americans from finding work and because he was convinced that the keeping of slaves was a sin.

The relevance of Graham's works is to be found in the various awards and citations he has won, including the Thomas Alva Edison Foundation Citation in 1956 for his adaption of *The Ten Commandments.* He has also been recognized by the Association for the Study of Negro History and by the California Council on Literature and Young People. In 1968 the latter organization presented him with its annual award for his contribu-

Graham and his wife (courtesy of the author)

Graham, circa 1975 (photograph by Warren Williams)

tions to children's literature. In 1977 the city of Anchorage, Alaska, showed its appreciation for Graham's works by presenting him with a citation.

Lorenz Bell Graham continues to write for young people with the purpose that motivated his earlier works: to present people so that they can be understood by others. The sincerity, commitment, and inspiration in his works make them attractive to more and more teachers of adolescent literature. Although he writes primarily for the young, as did his sister Shirley Graham, his reviewers often insist that his suspenseful, realistic

books are also appropriate for adults. Graham's fiction provides guidelines so that youth, in particular, black males, can avoid the pitfalls into which too many black males traditionally fall–a series of arrests and serious legal problems. An inspirational, didactic writer, Graham has created an enduring legacy with his work.

Papers:

Most of Graham's manuscripts are at the University of Minnesota, Minneapolis; other manuscripts are in the North Carolina Central University Library in Durham.

Shirley Graham

(11 November 1896-27 March 1977)

Kathy A. Perkins
University of California, Los Angeles

BOOKS: *Tom-Tom* (Cleveland, 1932);
Dr. George Washington Carver, Scientist, by Graham and George D. Lipscomb (New York: Messner, 1944);
Paul Robeson, Citizen of the World (New York: Messner, 1946);
There Once Was A Slave: The Heroic Story of Frederick Douglass (New York: Messner, 1947);
The Story of Phillis Wheatley (New York: Messner, 1949);
Your Most Humble Servant (New York: Messner, 1949);
Jean Baptiste Pointe de Sable, Founder of Chicago (New York: Messner, 1953);
The Story of Pocahontas (New York: Grosset & Dunlap, 1953; London: Sampson Low, 1960);
Booker T. Washington, Educator of Hand, Head and Heart (New York: Messner, 1955);
His Day Is Marching On: A Memoir of W. E. B. Du Bois (Philadelphia: Lippincott, 1971);
Gamal Abdel Nasser, Son of the Nile (New York: Third Press, 1972);
Zulu Heart: A Novel (New York: Third Press, 1974);
Julius K. Nyerere: Teacher of Africa (New York: Messner, 1975);

Du Bois: Pictorial Biography (Chicago: Johnson, 1978).

PLAY PRODUCTIONS: *Tom-Tom,* Baltimore, Morgan College, circa 1929-1931; revised as *Tom-Tom: An Epic of Music and the Negro,* Cleveland, Cleveland Stadium, 30 June 1932;
Coal Dust, Baltimore, Morgan College, 1930; revised as *Dust to Earth,* New Haven, Yale University, January 1941;
Elijah's Ravens, Cleveland, Gilpin Players, circa 1930;
Little Black Sambo, by Graham and Charlotte Chorpenning, Chicago, Federal Theatre Project, 1938;
I Gotta Home, Cleveland, Karamu Theatre, November 1939;
It's Morning, New Haven, Yale University, 1940.

RADIO PRODUCTIONS: *Tom-Tom* [excerpts], New York, Station WJZ, 26 June 1932;
Track Thirteen, New Haven, Conn., Station WICC, Mutual Radio Network, 1940.

OTHER: *Track Thirteen,* in *Yale Radio Plays: The Listener's Theatre,* edited by Constance Welch

Shirley Graham (courtesy of the Schomburg Center for Research in Black Culture, the New York Public Library, Astor, Lenox and Tilden Foundations)

and Walter Prichard Eaton (Boston: Expression, 1940), pp. 131-163;

W. E. B. Du Bois, *In Battle for Peace*, comment by Graham (New York: Masses & Mainstream, 1952).

PERIODICAL PUBLICATIONS: "Black Man's Music," *Crisis*, 40 (August 1933): 178-179;

"Oberlin and the Negro," *Crisis*, 42 (April 1935): 118, 124;

"Spirituals to Symphonies," *Etude*, 54 (November 1936): 691-692;

"Towards An American Theatre," *Arts Quarterly* (October-December 1937): 18-20.

Shirley Graham's role as the wife of W. E. B. Du Bois, whom she married on 14 February 1951, has overshadowed her significant contributions to the arts. Throughout the 1930s and early 1940s, a period when music and theater provided little opportunity for black women, Graham achieved distinction as a biographer, playwright, musician, composer, stage director,

and educator. She first received national recognition in 1932 when she became the first black composer in the United States to have an opera, *Tom-Tom*, professionally staged. Graham was also one of few black women to have had all of her plays performed, although they were never published. During this same period she lectured widely on the influence of African music in western culture and the role of blacks in American theater. During the mid 1940s and the 1950s Graham wrote children's books which focused on famous blacks.

Lola Bell Graham was born 11 November 1896 in Indianapolis, Indiana, to Rev. David A. and Etta Bell Graham. Her father, an African Methodist Episcopal (A.M.E.) minister, and mother raised their daughter and four sons in parsonages throughout the country. Graham's father, who would read aloud stories relating to the lives of famous blacks such as Frederick Douglass, Jean Baptiste Pointe de Sable, and Phillis Wheatley, was a major influence in her life. When she was young, her father also instilled in her an appreciation for the people and cultures of Africa. Graham learned how to play the piano and pipe organ, sing spirituals, and conduct a choir in her father's churches. Graham's only comedy and one of her first plays, *Elijah's Ravens* (circa 1930), is a three-act play that takes place in the home of an A.M.E. minister and his large family. The household consists of the parents, four enterprising boys, and a precocious young girl; the play is undoubtedly based on her father's family. She revived it in 1941 in Cleveland, Ohio.

Graham entered business school after graduating from Lewis and Clark High School on the eve of World War I in Spokane, Washington, where she was class poet and the first-prize winner in an essay contest on Booker T. Washington. Until her 1921 marriage to Shadrach T. McCanns, Graham secured a variety of government jobs in Spokane and Seattle. During her marriage to McCanns, Graham taught private music lessons and played the pipe organ for white movie houses, where she was hidden backstage. The couple divorced in the mid 1920s. The marriage produced two sons, Robert and David, whom Graham raised with the assistance of close relatives.

When her father was appointed president of Monrovia College in Monrovia, Liberia, in 1926, Graham accompanied the family as far as Paris, where she remained to study music at the

Scene from the 1940 Yale University production of Graham's play It's Morning *(courtesy of Yale School of Drama, Yale University)*

Sorbonne. Graham was fascinated with the traditional rhythms and music she learned from Africans living in France; and African music was important throughout her career in the arts. Returning to the United States in the late 1920s, Graham furthered her musical studies at Howard University's music department. As a nonmatriculating student Graham studied privately under Prof. Roy W. Tibbs and served as music librarian. Tibbs encouraged her to continue her musical training and recommended her for a teaching position at Morgan College (later Morgan State University) in Baltimore, Maryland, where she headed the music department from 1929 to 1931. Recognizing that a degree would increase her opportunities in academia and enable her to better support her sons, Graham entered Oberlin College during the fall of 1931 to work on her A.B. in music. Oberlin accepted her as a sophomore because of her many years of private music training, along with teaching experience at Morgan.

At Morgan, Graham wrote and produced her first one-act play, *Tom-Tom*, which she sent to the famed Karamu Theatre in Cleveland, for production consideration. At the time she submitted the script, the season had been filled. However, in the spring of 1932, white producer Laurence Higgins came to Cleveland to prepare for a huge

summer season at the Cleveland Stadium called "Theatre of Nations," which was to include operas of various cultures. He solicited the help of Russell and Rowena Jelliffe, directors of Karamu, in seeking an opera composed by a black, only to find that the Jelliffes were not aware of any such works. Rowena Jelliffe suggested that Graham's one-act play, *Tom-Tom*, be reviewed for conversion into an opera. Taking a leave of absence from Oberlin, Graham transformed her one-act into a sixteen-scene, three-act opera, writing a solid and imaginative libretto and music, despite the tightness of her deadline.

Tom-Tom: An Epic of Music and the Negro premiered 30 June 1932, before a crowd of ten thousand; and on 9 July it played before an audience of over fifteen thousand, including the governor and other dignitaries. The opera traces African music from its origins through its twentieth-century manifestations in the United States, arguing that despite slavery and their many decades out of Africa, black Americans retain strong remnants of African culture and traditions. The production consisted of a cast of close to five hundred people, with elaborate staging, authentic African costumes, and musical instruments, in addition to live elephants. Act 1 takes place in the jungle prior to the beginning of the slave trade in 1619. Act 2 is set in North America dur-

ing slavery; and Act 3 occurs in Harlem. The chant of the old-style Negro preacher is used in place of the traditional opera recitative, and tom-toms are featured prominently. The major characters include a witch doctor in the first act who becomes the plantation voodoo man in Act 2; in the final act this character emerges in Harlem as a Marcus Garvey-type leader of the Back-to-Africa Movement.

Tom-Tom received mixed reviews. The notion of a black opera drew attention from the national press. Black newspapers took great pride in informing readers that Shirley Graham was a "race girl" or "one of our own." The *Cleveland Plain Dealer* (the leading white paper) announced in its 26 June advertisement: "Though it is second in the series of four operas to be presented– 'Tom-Tom' stands first in interest and importance, because nothing quite like it has ever been attempted. There have been plenty of all-Negro plays in recent years. But who ever heard of an all-Negro opera?" Herbert Ewell, reviewing the opera in the *Cleveland Plain Dealer* (10 July 1932), praised the music but criticized the production as weak in places.

Tom-Tom established Graham as an authority on Afro-American culture. During her remaining years at Oberlin she lectured widely at colleges and wrote articles regarding the impact of African culture in the United States. She also presented small scenes from *Tom-Tom* at various institutions.

Graham completed her Oberlin A.B. in 1934. She forwarded Du Bois a copy of her master's thesis on survivals of Africanisms in modern music, knowing that if it met with his approval, it would easily be accepted by her graduate committee. It was, and she completed her M.A. in 1935. As a young girl Graham had met Du Bois when he was a guest in her parents' Colorado home. From the time she left Oberlin until their 1951 marriage, she was to seek him out constantly for advice, approval, and employment referrals.

After graduation from Oberlin Graham accepted the position as head of the fine arts department at Tennessee Agricultural & Industrial State College in Nashville. For the fall of 1936 she was invited to teach at Talladega College in Alabama. She was considering accepting this position when she changed her plans. Under the administration of Franklin D. Roosevelt, Congress had created the Works Progress Administration in 1935, out of which was born the Federal Theatre Project. The project was a godsend for

Cover for the 1932 printing of Graham's opera Tom-Tom

the numerous out-of-work black artists and craftspeople because it provided them an opportunity to learn various aspects of theater production, play writing, and administration from professionals. Through the project several Negro units were set up around the country. While visiting relatives that summer in Chicago, Graham spoke with the regional director to inquire about work possibilities. To her surprise, she was offered the directorship of the foundering Chicago Negro Unit. Her first few months there were highly frustrating, primarily because she was viewed by key members of the unit as an outsider as well as a person difficult to please. In a 27 November 1937 letter to friend Harriet Gibbs Marshall of the Washington Conservatory of Music, Graham notes: "The city as a whole is utterly devoid of cultural interests. Standards are set by Joe Louis and Al Capone."

Graham was often perceived by her peers throughout most of her life as antisocial, aggressive, and curt. Those well acquainted with her knew she was obsessed with achieving monumental goals such as presenting *Tom-Tom* and her plays on Broadway, in addition to becoming the leading expert on Afro-American music. As she emphasized in a letter to Du Bois on 25 April 1940: "Some one of us must be in a position of au-

thority. Until that happens we get no plays produced and most of our acting is turned into a burlesque. . . . Eventually, I know I'll arrive if I keep plugging." Graham was constantly at race with time because of her age. She was thirty-five years old when she entered Oberlin in 1931, although she always documented her age as being ten to eleven years younger. Concerned with the welfare of her two sons, Graham secured minor jobs after work, in addition to devoting what free time she had to writing plays and articles. It is therefore understandable that the Chicago unit viewed Graham in the manner in which they did.

In spite of the problems she encountered with the Chicago unit, Graham elevated the nearly defunct group to a level of national recognition and importance. Between 1936 and 1938 she directed, adapted plays into musicals, conducted, and designed and organized classes. It was while director of the unit that her talents as a writer were recognized, for in 1938 she was awarded a Rosenwald Fellowship in creative writing, which she used at Yale University.

At Yale from 1938 to 1940 Graham wrote four plays: *Dust to Earth, I Gotta Home, It's Morning,* and a radio play, *Track Thirteen,* while taking courses and working after school concurrently. She told Du Bois, in a letter of 30 December 1939, that she was under great stress at Yale: "Never have I been under such a severe strain of work, but that is my own fault. It isn't that I am exceptionally dumb–the Ph.D. work alone here would not stump me. But, against advice, I have insisted on doing a great deal of playwrighting also. And not a bit of credit is accorded toward my degree for that."

Graham's first full-length play, *Coal Dust,* had been produced in 1930 at Morgan College. It was revived at the Karamu Theatre in 1938. Revised and retitled *Dust to Earth* by Graham, it was produced at Yale in January 1941. *Dust to Earth,* a three-act tragedy set in a West Virginia mining town, deals with love and racial tension. Writing in dialect, Graham attempts to capture the true language of the blacks and whites of a rural mining community. Typical of all of Graham's plays, the script required a large cast and elaborate staging–in this case, a coal-mine opening with a working elevator.

One of Graham's most interesting and better-written plays, *It's Morning,* was produced at Yale in 1940. The quality of this play benefited from extensive revisions required by a Yale University production. *It's Morning,* according to Graham in an unpublished 1975 interview with James V. Hatch, "juxtaposes the personal anguish of a mother's decision as to whether she should kill her daughter who has just been sold into slavery against the Emancipation Proclamation, which comes a few minutes too late."

It's Morning commands special attention because Graham displays her experience as a composer and designer, in addition to illustrating her pride in her African heritage, as her "Note on the Play" in the script indicates:

> The dialect in *It's Morning* is not uniform. It is not intended to be. Many African languages express different meanings by changes in pitch and volume. The most primitive of American Negroes indicate slight changes in meanings by changing vowel sounds. Also, the old type of Negro preacher used a biblical mode of expression which cannot be expressed in dialect. The song used in Scene II, "Ah want Jesus to walk wid me," is one of the oldest of the Spirituals. As are most of these older songs, it is in the minor mode.

Graham's designing ability is evident in her application of light, shadow, and color. Through these media she creates strong visual images, as exhibited in the opening of the first scene of *It's Morning*:

> Bright morning sunshine streams through the open door and frameless window in the back of a rather large, sparsely furnished room. The walls are crudely plastered with old newspapers, but through the knotholes and cracks come bits of light, pointing up the strings of bright red peppers hanging near the fire and reflecting in the piece of broken mirror above the hearth. The left wall is almost taken up by the wide, open fireplace which burns heaps of pine cones.

Properly staged, *It's Morning* is a highly emotional drama, reminiscent of a Greek tragedy. The slave women function like a Greek chorus, setting the scene and informing the audience of what has occurred. The slaves also provide the audience with information about Cissie, the mother who must decide whether or not to murder her child. As with all Greek tragedies, the murder takes place offstage. *It's Morning* was a very personal work for Graham, as noted in part to Du Bois in her letter of 30 December 1939: "They are doing a one-act play of mine here at Yale in February. Honestly, I wish they wouldn't. It was written for a Negro cast. It is highly emotional

Scene from the 1941 Yale University production of Graham's play Dust to Earth *(courtesy of Yale School of Drama, Yale University)*

and has an impressive dignity which I do not believe these young students can achieve. I think the same play will be done at Fisk this winter. Although, I know Yale's production will have all the advantages of superior staging I [*sic*] haven't the slightest doubt which will actually be the better performance."

Graham's radio play, *Track Thirteen,* aired over New Haven's station WICC in 1940. This fast-paced comedy takes place aboard "Train 27," out of Chicago, that accidentally leaves on track thirteen. A highly superstitious black porter, referred to only as Porter, is petrified that a disaster will occur before the train reaches its destination. Ironically, thirteen proves to be Porter's lucky number. He receives a five-thousand-dollar reward when he captures a disguised, wanted bank robber on board.

While at Yale, Graham made vain attempts to have her plays and *Tom-Tom* produced on Broadway. She was perhaps a little naive in thinking that her years at Yale, work with the Federal Theatre, and success with *Tom-Tom* would warrant her acceptance on Broadway.

Graham did not complete her Ph.D. at Yale; from 1940 to 1941 she directed a YWCA theater group in Indianapolis. Her next appointment was as director of a YWCA-USO group at Fort Huachuca in Arizona where she directed productions and started a camp magazine. During this period her interest in the arts gave way to her commitment as a civil rights activist. At Fort Huachuca Graham witnessed blatant discrimination

against the black soldiers, some of whom were court-martialed for minor offenses and given long jail sentences. She was also outraged by the spectacle of young black college graduates being supervised by whites with only high school diplomas. She began writing to Washington, speaking out against these injustices and having cases reopened. After being cited as un-American, a "trouble maker," a "rabble rouser," and accused of using her position with the YWCA-USO as an excuse to stay at the fort and agitate, Graham was dismissed from her job in 1942. In a 9 November 1942 letter to Du Bois she comments:

> I did not leave Fort Huachuca of my own free will. I was literally torn away. . . . They ordered me to come to New York for a conference. When I got there they coolly informed me that the USO was not interested in some of my activities which were outside the recreational program of USO. They could not consider race problems, etc. etc. . . . No, I didn't want to leave Fort Huachuca. I knew I was getting worthwhile things done out there.

Back in New York she became a field secretary for the NAACP from 1942 to 1944. With the untimely death, while he was in uniform, of her elder son, Robert, she became more outspoken in the civil rights field. It was also during this period that Graham began writing books on black heroes for young people. She was becoming increasingly aware of the ignorance of black his-

tory among young adults and sought to aid in rectifying the problem with her biographies.

In 1944 Graham collaborated with George D. Lipscomb to produce *Dr. George Washington Carver, Scientist,* the first of several biographies she would publish about famous black Americans. Graham succeeds in capturing Carver's mission and sense of commitment as well as his eccentricities. The book is generally an appreciative celebration of a man of humble beginnings who made a significant contribution to humanity. It is informative and absorbing, and it succeeds in carrying out its goal of being inspirational to young people.

Paul Robeson, Citizen of the World (1946) is the first singly authored and the second of Graham's biographies of famous Afro-Americans. It set a pattern that Graham would follow through several more volumes, depicting famous lives to serve as role models for adolescent black Americans. Written with this intended audience in mind, the volumes stress the high points and the successes in the subjects' lives, rather than the disappointments and tragedies. In the Robeson volume, for example, Graham traces his many triumphs in overcoming racial discrimination in schools, public facilities, on the stage, and in films (his size and dazzling smile win as many battles as his great baritone voice). The treatment ends on a peak in 1944, when more than eight thousand people in New York join in giving Robeson a fabulous forty-sixth birthday party replete with a cake so large that it had to be carried by two men. When Graham wrote a foreword to the fourth printing of the volume, in 1971, there was no hint of the many troubles that beset Robeson after that great celebration at Madison Square Garden.

Graham begins her account of Robeson's life when he is twelve, shortly after his nomadic preacher father settles in Somerville, New Jersey, after having dragged his small son practically all over the state; the elder Robeson had used the travel to overcome his despondency following his wife's death. The volume marks various peaks in Robeson's life, including his anticipation of his eighth-grade graduation speech, his summer jobs, meeting his future wife, his first attempts to sing and perform on stage, his acceptance in Europe, his trip to Africa, and his much-hailed return to America. Graham casts Robeson in the tradition of the gifted black individual who carries the burden of his race upon his shoulders; his individual triumphs become triumphs for

black people, and his failures, though some of them must have been excruciating, diminish in comparison. The roles and skills Robeson perfected–football and baseball player, track star, singer, stage and film star, lawyer, linguist, historian–made him a Renaissance man in his day and a legend to black people then and now.

Viewed from its perspective of providing a model for young black Americans, there is little that is problematic about the volume. As biography, however, there is the critical problem of the author adoring her subject so much that she is almost blinded by his legendary status. In fact Graham is herself an actor in the biography. During a trip to Paris she heard that Robeson was performing in *Othello* in London; she flew there, presented herself at rehearsal, was invited and warmly received into the Robeson home, and provided with tickets for the show. Years later, when she expressed her desire to write a biography of Robeson, he was apparently flattered but did not participate in the gathering of information for the book. Though Graham emphasizes that she talked with hundreds of people who knew him (some of whose voices interrupt the flow of the narrative) and gathered information from a variety of other sources, there is still a noticeable gap in the absence of the contributing voice of the subject. Graham is never fully able to nail down the human being behind the legend, which is perhaps an acceptable idea for role-modeling, but a problematic one for readers interested in getting substantive information through a biography that was written during Robeson's lifetime.

In his review of *Paul Robeson* (*Crisis*, February 1947), Arthur Spingarn echoed Graham's intent when he said, "Miss Graham has done many things and all of them with distinction, but it is as a biographer that she is at her best. She has written in a kind of *musical* form a warm, *dramatic*, and affectionate life, with the quality of fictional suspense."

The Story of Phillis Wheatley (1949) is more adulatory than *Paul Robeson*. Gathering information about this Boston slave poet has been difficult for all of her biographers; Graham, therefore, had to rely as much upon imagination and conjecture as fact in trying to present Wheatley's life to her audience. She begins with the young Wheatley being sold at auction in Boston just as John and Susanna Wheatley are out for a morning of shopping. Mrs. Wheatley buys the frightened young girl, and her son and daughter consent to teach her English, manners, and more

Shirley Graham and W. E. B. Du Bois at their public marriage ceremony, seven days after their secret wedding on 14 February 1951 (courtesy of Archives, University Library, University of Massachusetts, Amherst)

formal book learning. From the young girl who hid in the rose bushes and hugged the earth in the Wheatley yard because they reminded her of home after months on a slave ship, Phillis grows to read the Bible and Latin and to produce poems for almost every mournful occasion in the city of Boston.

As a result of writing a poem upon the death of Rev. George Whitefield, Phillis is invited to London by the Countess of Huntingdon, and she is given the opportunity to accompany Mr. Whitefield's widow and the young Mr. Wheatley there. Celebrated widely, she returns to Boston to her secure place in the Wheatley household, only to have that disrupted by war and by the deaths of various members of the Wheatley fam-

ily. Shortly before the last of the family dies, she finally marries a freed black man who is financially unable to take care of her and, in later years, their two children. She dies in 1784 while her husband is in debtors' prison.

To offset the tragedy of Phillis's life Graham emphasizes how much the Wheatleys loved and cared for her. She also makes Phillis's relationship with her husband John Peters, whom many have presented as a rogue of a man, the epitome of a romance destroyed only by indigence. Rather than end the volume with Wheatley's death, Graham includes a lengthy poem that the poet wrote, which concludes on this upbeat note:

To every realm shall peace her charms display,
And heavenly freedom spread her golden ray.

So ended, the book suggests that Wheatley's triumphs in publishing her volumes of poems while yet a slave, her celebration by George Washington and others, and her general acceptance into the Boston community should overshadow the more tragic details. In 1950 Graham's biography on Benjamin Banneker, *Your Most Humble Servant* (1949), won the Anisfield-Wolf Award, and the same year Graham was presented the Academy of Arts and Letters Award for contribution to American literature.

Graham's first and only novel, *Zulu Heart,* was published in 1974 under the name Du Bois. Set in South Africa, it tells the story of Kirkcudbright Johannes Vermeer, a rich Afrikaaner who, at thirty-six, seems to have a bright future as a newly wed surgeon. Stricken suddenly with a massive heart attack, the young Vermeer faces death unless he agrees to accept the heart of a black miner. Choosing life over caste–but keeping the transplant a secret from his nationalistic family, especially his stern father–Kirk begins to experience some unusual things. Initially, he has disturbing dreams about African villages and playful encounters with young black boys. Then, in an evening out on the town, he discovers rhythms in his blood and in his dancing feet that he did not have prior to the operation. He is distraught and wonders if he is possessed or insane until it becomes clear that the owner of the heart was the son of a Zulu chief and that the heart has a destiny that Kirk must now carry out.

To the consternation of those who know him, Kirk becomes sympathetic to the black miners, makes pilgrimages to the Bantustans to discover more about their lives, and eventually finds the village to which the donor of the heart had belonged. He discovers that he can speak Zulu and understand an elder in the village who unlocks his destiny. He defies all odds about the longevity of those with transplanted hearts, and, with money, time, and commitment, he becomes one of the leaders of black African resistance. Doc Zulu, as he is affectionately called by the blacks who recognize his mission, raids Robben Island, the country's notorious prison, and frees many of leaders of the resistance, including the young man who has been selected chief of Doc Zulu's village. Although Kirk is killed in the raid, his mission is accomplished, and, through the son whom he has fathered by a native woman, his spirit will continue to live.

Zulu Heart has enough of the plausible to be thoroughly engaging and just enough of the fan-tastic to maintain suspense. Though shifts in point of view sometimes interrupt the flow, Graham is nonetheless able to sustain an interesting and timely story. She is knowledgeable about African landscape and politics, and she draws her characters with admirable detail. With brief scenes all over Europe and in New York, the story unfolds with the richness of a drama and indeed would seem to be perfect for adaptation to film. Although the central issues focus upon black lives and culture, *Zulu Heart* is one of the few novels in which an Afro-American author makes non-black characters her primary focus.

Other than *Zulu Heart,* whatever remaining aspirations Graham may have had in the music, theater, and literary world were halted in 1951 when her husband, Du Bois, was indicted for his activism in the movement for world peace. In *The Autobiography of W. E. B. Du Bois* (1968) he discusses the negative impact that Graham's marriage to him had on her career after the indictment: "My wife's work and income were seriously curtailed by her complete immersion in this case." Graham assisted Du Bois in his writings, attended rallies and meetings, and supported him in every way. She essentially spent the rest of her life vindicating his name. Graham became the founding editor of *Freedomways* magazine, a quarterly review of the freedom movement, from 1960 to 1963. In 1961 the Du Bois were invited to live in Ghana to begin work on an "Encyclopedia Africana." After the death of W. E. B. Du Bois in 1963 Graham continued to assist with the research on this encyclopedia. From 1964 to 1966 she was organizing director of Ghana Television. Shirley Graham died on 27 March 1977 in Beijing, China, at the age of eighty.

The many accomplishments of Shirley Graham in the areas of music, theater, and literature have been overlooked or forgotten, but Graham deserves great praise as a pioneer and role model. Few blacks have succeeded simultaneously as a writer, composer, director, playwright, and conductor. To achieve success in just one of these areas would have been noteworthy for a black woman during her lifetime.

Interview:
"Conversation: Ida Lewis & Shirley Graham DuBois [*sic*]," *Essence,* 1 (January 1971): 21-27.

References:
W. E. B. Du Bois, *The Autobiography of W. E. B.*

Du Bois, edited by Herbert Aptheker (New York: International, 1968);

Kathy A. Perkins, "The Unknown Career of Shirley Graham," *Freedomways,* 25, no. 1 (First Quarter 1985): 6-17.

Papers:

Shirley Graham's papers can be found in the W.

E. B. Du Bois Manuscript Collection, University of Massachusetts, Amherst, Massachusetts; the Federal Theatre Project Collection, George Mason University, Fairfax, Virginia; and the Washington Conservatory of Music Collection in the Moorland-Spingarn Research Library, Howard University, Washington, D.C.

Robert Hayden

(4 August 1913-25 February 1980)

Norma R. Jones
Alcorn State University

See also the Hayden entry in *DLB 5: American Poets Since World War II.*

BOOKS: *Heart-Shape in the Dust* (Detroit: Falcon Press, 1940);

The Lion and the Archer, by Hayden and Myron O'Higgins (Nashville: Hemphill Press, 1948);

Figure of Time: Poems (Nashville: Hemphill Press, 1955);

A Ballad of Remembrance (London: Breman, 1962); revised as *Selected Poems* (New York: October House, 1966);

Words in the Mourning Time (New York: October House, 1970);

The Night-Blooming Cereus (London: Breman, 1972);

Angle of Ascent: New and Selected Poems (New York: Liveright, 1975);

American Journal (Taunton, Mass.: Effendi Press, 1978; revised and enlarged edition, New York: Liveright, 1982);

Collected Prose: Robert Hayden, edited by Frederick Glaysher (Ann Arbor: University of Michigan Press, 1984);

Robert Hayden: Collected Poems, edited by Glaysher (New York: Liveright, 1985).

OTHER: Introduction to *Counterpoise Series* (Nashville: Hemphill, 1948);

Robert Hayden

Kaleidoscope: Poems by American Negro Poets, edited, with an introduction, by Hayden (New York: Harcourt Brace Jovanovich, 1967);

Preface to Alain Locke's *The New Negro* (New York: Atheneum, 1968);

Afro-American Literature: An Introduction, edited by Hayden, David J. Burrows, and Frederick Lapides (New York: Harcourt Brace Jovanovich, 1971);

American Models: A Collection of Modern Stories, edited by Hayden, James E. Miller, Jr., and Robert O'Neal (Glenview, Ill.: Scott, Foresman, 1973);

The United States in Literature, edited by Hayden, Miller, and O'Neal (Glenview, Ill.: Scott, Foresman, 1973; revised, 1979);

Person, Place, and Point of View: Factual Prose for Interpretation and Extension, edited by Hayden, Miller, and O'Neal (Glenview, Ill.: Scott, Foresman, 1974);

The Lyric Potential, edited by Hayden, Miller, and O'Neal (Glenview, Ill.: Scott, Foresman, 1974);

The Human Condition: Literature Written in the English Language, edited by Hayden, Miller, and O'Neal (Glenview, Ill.: Scott, Foresman, 1974).

PERIODICAL PUBLICATIONS: "A Portfolio of Recent American Poems," *World Order,* 5 (Spring 1971): 33;

"Recent American Poetry–Portfolio II," *World Order,* 9 (Summer 1975): 44-45.

Robert Hayden faced in the mid twentieth century the dilemma that Countee Cullen, one of his literary mentors, had faced during the Harlem Renaissance. Hayden and Cullen were both black, both poets, both very much desirous of being known by their professional appellation rather than their racial one. While Cullen eventually escaped–or at least transcended–the dilemma by writing children's books, Hayden attacked head-on those who attacked him and refused to subordinate art to race even during the turbulent 1960s, when many younger black writers considered him superfluous. Like Gwendolyn Brooks, Hayden became a poet of academe by mastering traditional poetic forms; he could write sonnets and heroic couplets as easily as free verse, and he could invoke literary allusions from ancient Grecian, European, and American literary history. Consistently refusing to believe that there had to be a separate language or some special approach from which to depict the experiences of Afro-Americans, Hayden wrote about them in poems as complex and complicated as those in which he treated other subjects. Contrary to how those mired in trends have judged

him, there is no doubt that Hayden was sympathetic to black experiences, whether they involved the middle passage, slavery, discrimination, heroism, literary personalities, the blues, poverty, or political injustice. While Hayden may have been made uncomfortable by some of the critical judgments leveled against his works during his lifetime, his desire to follow his muse has ultimately worked in his favor; there are several new critical studies treating his work and a new generation of critics who are reevaluating, in more constructively sympathetic terms, his place in the American literary canon.

As a black American who avidly pursued models judged to be some of the best in writing poetry, such as modernists Ezra Pound, William Carlos Williams, and Wallace Stevens, Hayden was in a unique position to comment on American life. He had the dual vision of the dreamer as well as those who lived within the dream; his own knowledge of Afro-American life and culture, combined with forms taken from outside that culture, enabled him to create strikingly memorable poems. He appreciated the metaphysics of Elinor Wylie, and he drew upon the works of several other poets to create what he refers to as his "baroque" poetry, an eclectic blending of influences upon him. Clearly, Hayden was among the most technically sophisticated American poets who began their careers during or immediately following World War II. As receptivity to black poets increased, and as the civil rights movement ushered in a new awareness of black artists, Hayden's works were widely anthologized, making him readily accessible to a large reading audience.

Robert Hayden's early life conforms to the stereotype of growing up in the ghetto. He was born in Detroit, Michigan, 4 August 1913 to Asa and Ruth Sheffey. They named him Asa Bundy Sheffey. When the Sheffeys separated during his infancy, he became the foster son of Sue Ellen Westerfield Hayden and William Hayden, sharing their home in the St. Antoine slum of Detroit, ironically nicknamed Paradise Valley. Robert Hayden was their only child. As a teenager he became acquainted with his natural mother who moved in next door, and the resulting emotional tug-of-war for his affections between Sheffey and the Haydens tortured the young boy. Moreover, the Hayden marriage was unhappy, chiefly because Mrs. Hayden was still in love with her deceased first husband. She had had three children by him, including the alco-

Robert Hayden, age eight

holic Roxie, who also lived with the Haydens. Most of the time, all the women (even Ruth Sheffey, who moved in with the Haydens for a while) and Robert were allied against William Hayden. On other occasions, it was the Haydens and Robert allied against Ruth Sheffey, whose promiscuity the Haydens despised. Robert Hayden loved her anyway, just as he loved Mrs. Hayden, who took out her frustrations by whipping him and condemning his ingratitude. Only as an adult would Hayden begin to sympathize with his sometimes violent, often inarticulate foster father, William Hayden.

Robert Hayden was severely myopic as a child, and this prevented his participation in normal children's games. In spite of having to hold books six inches away from his face, he became an avid reader. The Haydens were uneducated, but Ruth Sheffey sent him books from Buffalo, New York, where she moved during his childhood. The Haydens' poverty and strife-ridden marriage did not prevent their giving Hayden whatever advantages they could. He was active in

the Baptist church, and William Hayden encouraged him to attend school in summer whenever possible. Hayden played the violin in the Sunday school orchestra until his vision problem forced him to stop. He graduated from Detroit Northern High School in 1932 and entered Detroit City College (now Wayne State University) on a scholarship arranged by the family's caseworker. He majored in Spanish and minored in English, hoping to become a teacher. While acting in a play by Langston Hughes, he showed Hughes some of his poetry, only to be told that his work was derivative. In a 1977 interview he agreed with Hughes, but at the time, he said, he was crestfallen.

Hayden worked with the Federal Writers' Project in Detroit from 1936 to 1938, researching local black folklore and history. Afterward, he compiled information on the Underground Railroad in Michigan while working part-time as a theater, movie, and music critic for the *Michigan Chronicle,* a black weekly. The paper's editor, Louie Martin, later founded Falcon Press to publish Hayden's first book of poems, *Heart-Shape in the Dust* (1940). Hayden's engagement to Erma Morris, a promising concert pianist who had ambitions to become a composer, was disapproved of by her parents, middle-class Episcopalians, because of Hayden's impoverished working-class Baptist background, but the couple married anyway on 15 June 1940. He pursued his historical research in the summer of 1941, which he and his wife spent in New York City while Erma Hayden studied at Juilliard. Erma Hayden taught in the Detroit public school system when the couple returned to Michigan from New York, but Robert Hayden was jobless because the Work Projects Administration, which funded the Federal Writers' Project, was being dismantled.

In 1941, determined to get his master's degree, Hayden began attending the University of Michigan. He officially became a graduate student in 1942, the year the Haydens' only child, Maia, was born. At Michigan he was able to continue a longtime interest in acting and play writing. But even more important to him was his opportunity to study poetry with W. H. Auden, who was then a visiting professor. Auden gave him personal advice as well as valuable criticism of his poems, which Hayden credited with helping him to develop his own individual style: "He stimulated us to learn more about poetry and even to search ourselves. He made us aware of other literatures, and he made us aware of poet-

ry in a way that we never would have been had it not been for him," Hayden wrote. Hayden was two times winner of the university's Hopwood Award for poetry by a student, which carried with it a financial prize. After completing his master's degree in 1944 Hayden remained at Michigan for two years as a teaching fellow, the first black member of the English Department's teaching staff. An administrator warned him that he would have to leave should his appointment cause "any difficulty of a racial nature." When a position as assistant professor of English opened at Nashville's black Fisk University, Hayden and his family moved to the segregated South in 1946.

The mature Hayden regarded the poems of *Heart-Shape in the Dust* and the unpublished collection, "The Black Spear," which had won his second Hopwood Award, as apprentice efforts. Many of the poems in the 1940 volume are clearly derivative of the poets of the Harlem Renaissance. Thus, Hayden's "The Negro to America" ("Till that eagled-winged/Day be come/When liberty/Also means me,/You are not free. . .") recalls Langston Hughes's "I, Too, Sing America" and "Let America be America Again" in its assertion that until democracy applies to the least of Americans, no American can truly claim to be free; until blacks have been fully incorporated into the "dining room" of plenty of American society, then whites must also "eat in the kitchen." "Poem for a Negro Dancer" is indebted to Countee Cullen's "Heritage" and Claude McKay's "Harlem Dancer" in that Hayden joins Cullen in advocating the value of a heritage that should not be corrupted by contact with the West, and he joins McKay in emphasizing that, like the dancer who performs for the lurid eyes of customers in a Harlem cabaret, black people must hold some part of themselves free from the degrading implications that compensation for their art can sometimes bring; art from the souls of black people cannot be bought and sold.

Hayden's lifelong concern with social protest and his pride in his Afro-American heritage are evident in *Heart-Shape in the Dust,* but his handling of these themes shows little of his eventual mastery. "These Are My People" is strongly influenced by his interest in leftist ideology, which he held in common with many black intellectuals of the 1930s and early 1940s: "It's spring, spring, spring/down in the slums,/and the rats gnaw at the houses/and disease crawls into the beds." Eighteen of the forty-seven poems in the volume

deal with specifically black subject matter, and the best of these embody the blues tradition, as in "Shine, Mister?": "Standing on the corner/Tryin to make a dime–/Lawd, a po workin man/Has a helluva time."

"The Black Spear" collection (1942) originated out of Hayden's interest in black history, particularly the era of slavery and the Civil War, which he had researched for the Federal Writers' Project. The style of the poems in "The Black Spear" is influenced by Stephen Vincent Benét; indeed, the title was conceived in response to a passage in Benét's Civil War epic *John Brown's Body* (1928) where the narrator calls for a black poet who will sing the "blackskinned epic, epic with the black spear." Hayden reworked the poems in this collection for several years, improving his technique, but he never found a publisher. Eventually, some, but not all, were published in the final section of *Selected Poems* (1966) along with "Middle Passage," which had not been completed in time to be included in "The Black Spear" collection. ("Middle Passage" first appeared in almost its present form in a 1945 issue of *Phylon.*) The multiple personae of some of the history poems reflect Benét, as does the counterpointing of narrative and lyric; but the wealth of accurate historic fact (the product of long hours in the Schomberg Center in New York City) and the heaped up dramatic ironies are Hayden's alone.

The history of Hayden's researching, writing, and revising of "Middle Passage" tells much about how he worked. He was never satisfied that the final polish had been given. In fact, in a 1971 interview, Hayden noted that he was still not satisfied with the ending of "Middle Passage": "I would like to change it somewhat, make it stronger. I have the feeling now there's something more I should say in order to round the poem off." He also recalled that there had been about fifteen different drafts of "A Ballad of Remembrance." In addition to a perfectionist temperament, which slowed output, Hayden's writing was also hampered by his job's demands. At Fisk University, where he was on the English faculty for twenty-three years (1946-1969), he taught a full class schedule (at the time, five courses per semester). In addition to all the normal academic busywork, he also served as adviser to the student literary publication, the *Herald,* whose staff included a number of students who would have significant literary careers of their own (such as William Demby, Lonne Elder, and Julius Lester).

The cast of a play Hayden directed for the Alpha Kappa Alpha sorority in Detroit, circa 1939. Hayden is in the middle of the back row (photograph by Langford P. James).

In addition to the teaching load and life in a Jim Crow society, Hayden was further burdened by the straitlaced, southern black middle-class environment of Fisk, which did not quite know what to make of an avant-garde Negro intellectual from the North. A major point of friction with the college administration was the subject matter of some material published in the *Herald* with Hayden's permission. In the 1940s four-letter words and sexual frankness were enough to put Hayden's job in jeopardy.

There were compensations for Hayden in Nashville, in particular, a satisfying friendship with fellow writer Arna Bontemps, the librarian of Fisk, who helped Hayden receive a Julius Rosenwald Fellowship for Creative Writing in 1947. Another Fisk associate was art curator Myron O'Higgins, with whom Hayden privately published a small poetry collection in pamphlet form, *The Lion and the Archer* (1948).

Although the Hayden contribution to *The Lion and the Archer* totals only six poems, it represents a vast alteration in his technique from *Heart-Shape in the Dust*. In the years since his first contact with Auden, Hayden studied the work of

Gerard Manley Hopkins, Stephen Spender, C. Day Lewis, and Rainer Maria Rilke. The six poems are from what Hayden called the work of his "baroque" period. They are not a montage of styles; rather, they reflect the liberating influence of his awareness of new technical possibilities. The effect of these poems can be as startling as those of the late-Renaissance metaphysical poets to whom the term *baroque* is usually applied. "A Ballad of Remembrance," for example, exhibits the dramatic characteristic of the baroque whereby "a tentative attitude is expressed and then, through interaction of the several dramatis personae, it is gradually modified until in the end a new attitude is achieved." The poet uses a New Orleans Mardi Gras dance-parade to present the general state of insanity in the world: "Tight streets unfolding to the eye/like fans of corrosion and elegiac lace/crackled with their singing"; "masked Negroes wearing chameleon/satins gaudy now as a fortuneteller's/dream of disaster." Instead of closing the poem in the same vein, however, Hayden turns to its real intent: a tribute to Mark Van Doren for his voice of sanity in the crazy world in which Hayden lives. Van

Robert Hayden at Fisk University, circa 1958

Doren, "richly human," has enabled Hayden to release himself "from the hoodoo of that dance" and to speak "with my true voice again."

The poems in *The Lion and the Archer* exhibit a much more sophisticated use of language than *Heart-Shape in the Dust.* Some critics have called the language of "A Ballad of Remembrance" and similar poems perfervid and overblown, as in "the sallow vendeuse/of prepared tarnishes and jokes of nacre and ormolu"; but this language serves the purpose of showing the fancy facade behind which lurks the dehumanizing reality of discrimination. The language of the six poems is much more condensed than Hayden's earlier work. Thus, in "Homage to the Empress of the Blues," a lyric about Bessie Smith, there are "dollfaced heaven" (pictures torn out of magazines or church papers to cover the holes in plaster walls of poor people's homes) or "alaruming fists of snow" (real snow, but also a metaphor for the white policeman), and "the riot squad of statistics" (official violence, often the statistical tools of the social work establishment). It is condensation

rather than the baroque elements which becomes more typical of Hayden in his prime. The collection received a favorable mention in the *New York Times Book Review,* where the poems were praised for "experimental vigor" and for eschewing both the old protest tradition as well as a "limited minstrel quaintness" which the reviewer thought characterized too many black poems. Yet, while none of the poems are protest poems in the traditional sense, two out of the six deal with effects of white racism on a sensitive spirit (other subjects are Bessie Smith and the role of the poet in war).

The 1940s saw the appearance of most of Hayden's black history poems in various periodicals and in an important Langston Hughes and Arna Bontemps anthology, *The Poetry of the Negro* (1949). Although all of the history poems relate to "The Black Spear," only one is from that collection, "O Daedalus, Fly Away Home," based on a Sea Island folk legend of flying Africans, which held that some slaves had the power to fly back to the homeland.

Hayden's best-known black history poem is the fairly long (177 lines in the final version) "Middle Passage," which blends lyric, dramatic, and narrative techniques. It is composed of three sections which offer different slants on the slave trade: (1) the sometimes uneasy, sometimes complacent thoughts of slave ship officers, ending with the horrible story of a fire aboard ship; (2) the recollections about Africa of a retired slave trader; and (3) the story of the slave rebellion aboard the Cuban vessel *Amistad* and the blacks' eventual return to Africa, thanks to United States justice. Particularly striking is the poem's use of many forms of discourse: lists (of ships' names), diaries, prayers, ship's logs, hymns, legal depositions, oldster's yarns, parodies, and orations. All these are joined together by lyric commentary which tries to come to terms with this "voyage through death/to life upon these shores." Another notable aspect of the poem is the objective presentation of white personae, for in this drama of the slave trade, not one of the speakers is black. The poem is laden with irony, which, in part, depends upon the ships' names (*Jesus, Esperanza, Mercy*), a sailor's hymn ("Jesus, Savior, Pilot Me"), and a parody of a song from Shakespeare's *The Tempest* (circa 1611):

Deep in the festering hold thy father lies,
of his bones New England pews are made,
those are altar lights that were his eyes.

Possibly even more dramatic than "Middle Passage" is "Runagate Runagate" (the word *runagate* is a corruption of *renegade*), which first appeared in the Hughes-Bontemps anthology. Using collage, it evokes the Underground Railroad and Harriet Tubman. A sense of urgent flight predominates. Most of the lines are unhampered by punctuation, and there is a run-on effect reinforced by a series of "ands";

Runs falls rises stumbles on from darkness into
    darkness
and the darkness thicketed with shapes of terror
and the hunters pursuing and the hounds pursuing
and the night cold and. . . .

Indeed, the movement slows only in the passage devoted to a reward notice for fugitive slaves.

The experimental sonnet, "Frederick Douglass," has fourteen lines but does not rhyme. Its irregular rhythm shows Hopkins's influence. The basic pattern is a five-stress line; and through the use of periodic sentences, parallelism, and repetition, Hayden manages to produce the tight, wound-up effect of a conventional sonnet. His cadences reverberate with an oratory like Douglass's:

When it is finally ours, this freedom, this liberty,
    this beautiful
and terrible thing, needful to man as air,
usable as earth; when it belongs at last to all, . . .

The three major history poems of the 1940s mark Hayden's maturity as an artist. The burden of teaching duties and his personal troubles—to the end of his life his sleep was interrupted by nightmares replaying the events of his conflict-ridden childhood home—kept his poetic output small. But what he did produce was the painstaking work of the conscious artist.

His artistic development continued through the 1960s, as seen in the little pamphlet *Figure of Time* (1955), the only collection of poems Hayden published in that decade. Like *The Lion and the Archer*, it was privately printed and received little critical attention. *Figure of Time* contains eleven new poems and reprints three published previously; the subject of most of them is suffering humanity: victims of war and racial oppression, the ghetto poor, loveless families, and those who face final defeat at the hands of time. One new emphasis is an expression of Hayden's religious belief. In 1943 the poet had become a Bahá'í, a follower of the Persian prophet Bahá'u'lláh (1817-1892)

whose central teachings are the unity of all religions and the brotherhood of mankind. Hayden found the Bahá'í emphasis on social ethics, practical uplift, and world peace ideal for twentieth-century man. The Bahá'í outlook is shown in "In Light half nightmare, half vision," where human suffering in Germany, South Africa, Korea, and America are related to the suffering of Bahá'u'lláh.

Figure of Time has poems about Hayden's childhood. He said he finally had achieved the necessary "psychic distance and craftsmanship" to deal appropriately with this subject. The most noteworthy of these poems is "Summertime and the living . . ." with its sunflower images representing the only kind of beauty tough enough to survive in a slum. The narrator longs for roses, but these "only sorrow could afford" (for funerals). The daily struggle left his elders "shouting-angry" each evening. But there were compensations: the vitality of street life, and the hope of glory embodied in black boxer Jack Johnson.

Eleven new poems which the poet deemed worth publishing do not seem much to show for all of the 1950s. Hayden said that much of his time at Fisk was spent in self-imposed isolation so that he could devote himself as completely as possible to his art. Students and colleagues from these years who did not know him well recall him somewhat with awe, as one set apart from the campus community.

The 1960s began the most significant phase of Hayden's literary career, combining to bring the middle-aged poet both unanticipated recognition and rejection. In addition to growing recognition and publication opportunities (particularly in anthologies) the temper of the times seemed to give the poet fresh creative drive, even as their violence tortured his spirit. A catalyst in the growing interest in Hayden's work was the enthusiastic appreciation of Dutch scholar and popularizer of Afro-American literature, Rosey E. Poole. A Baháí and survivor of the Nazi occupation of Holland, through witnessing the extermination of the Jews she had become sensitive to the oppression suffered by American blacks. Poole, in turn, introduced Hayden's work to another Dutch Bahá'í, the publisher Paul Breman, who had immigrated to England. Breman published *A Ballad of Remembrance* in 1962; it brought Hayden international recognition when it won the Grand Prize for Poetry at the First World Festival of Negro Arts at Dakar, Senegal,

Hayden reading at the Library of Congress, circa 1971

in 1966. An American version of *A Ballad of Remembrance* was published as *Selected Poems* in 1966. It contains a total of forty-one poems, the majority from *A Ballad of Remembrance*, and several poems revised by Hayden for it. Thirteen poems were new. The volume represents the finished artist, a view which Hayden himself shared.

Selected Poems is arranged thematically. The themes are black history, the quest for the meaning of human existence, Mexico, racism, and autobiographical poems. The best known of the quest poems is "The Diver," in which a scuba dive into a submerged wreck and nitrogen narcosis become metaphors for despair and a death wish. The lines of the poem are a series of sentence fragments, the verbs of which are sometimes just participles:

> Swiftly descended
> into canyons of cold
> nightgreen emptiness.
> Freefalling, weightless
> as in dreams of
> wingless flight,
> plunged through infra-
> space and came to
> the dead ship, . . .

Ongoing critical debate surrounds this poem, some interpretations seeing it only in psychoanalytic terms, others seeing it as only a Negro's reaction to racism. Asked about the poem, Hayden remained noncommittal. "Electrical Storm" relates a specific experience, a brush with death in the form of a fallen power line. Here superstitious folk religion expresses the human predicament:

> They hunched up, contracting in corners
> away from windows and the dog;
> huddled under Jehovah's oldtime wrath,
> trusting, afraid.

Over against human fear are held the musings of the erudite professor: "Who knows if it was heavenly design/or chance . . . ?" "Dawnbreaker" argues for spiritual certainty. The subject is the Báb, a martyred Bahá'í prophet whose redemptive sufferings

> Fed the
> fires that consume
> us now, the fire that
> will save.

Hayden, 1967

Another group of the *Selected Poems* reveals Hayden's response to the period spent in Mexico (1954-1955) under a grant from the Ford Foundation. Since his days as a college Spanish major he had been interested in Latin American culture and spoke the language fluently. Yet the Mexican sojourn appears not to have been altogether happy, partly due to his being the intended victim of a confidence scheme and partly due to some unspecified inner turmoil. (In this latter connection it may be significant that about this time, when Hayden applied for a visa, he first discovered he had never been legally adopted by the Haydens, as they had always led him to believe.) The exotic always appealed to Hayden, so there was much in the Mexican scene to incite his imagination: semipagan religious processions ("Day of the Dead"), the pageant of a marketplace, bullfights ("La Corrida"), alien art forms, and the people themselves, such as the pathetic beggar of "Market" and an appealing street urchin in "Kid." Yet, while the Mexican poems exhibit tech-

nical competence and evocative imagery, critics seldom list them among Hayden's best.

The other two sections of *Selected Poems* deal with recollections of the past, both of the Negro, and of the man Robert Hayden. "Tour 5" describes a motor trip and potentially lethal encounter with a white man in preintegration Mississippi. Whites have supplanted the Choctaws and Chickasaws, who have left only their names behind; now black tourists ask directions of a white man "whose eyes revile us" while "shrill gorgon silence breathes behind/his taut civility." Another set of memories is in "Witch Doctor," a portrait of religious cult leader Prophet Jones. More personal is "Those Winter Sundays," a description of the atmosphere in Hayden's boyhood home. Understatement heightens the touching tribute to Hayden's foster father, who was unable to express love directly because of "the chronic angers of that house." The son is indifferent

> to him
> who had driven out the cold
> and polished my good shoes as well.

Hayden once confided that he never read this poem publicly without fearing he might break down.

The civil rights era brought Hayden both overdue praise and unexpected enmity. Hayden took advantage of a critical climate more willing to judge minority writing on merit rather than ethnicity. However, even as the white literary establishment began to lose its racism, a new racial emphasis dominated the critical judgment of some blacks, particularly the young. This artistic nationalism rejected the idea that the black writer should speak for or to anyone other than those of his own race (and perhaps other oppressed peoples). It focused on the search for a *black aesthetic,* a notion with political overtones, based on the conviction that the sensibilities of blacks and whites are fundamentally different. Such a philosophy was anathema to Hayden, both as Bahá'í and artist, and he had made his opposition clear as early as 1948 in a little manifesto written for an introductory leaflet to the *Counterpoise Series,* of which *The Lion and the Archer* was the first booklet:

> as writers who belong to a so-called
> minority we are violently opposed
> to having our work viewed, as the
> custom is, entirely in the light of
> sociology and politics
> . . .

Hayden receiving an honorary degree at Brown University, 1976

we believe in the oneness of
mankind and the importance of the
arts in the struggle for peace
and unity

Ironically, the first Black Writers' Conference held at Fisk in the spring of 1966 turned into a virulent attack upon Hayden from which he did not soon recover. The militant black nationalists at the conference, followers of Ron Karenga's philosophy that "black literature should be didactic and propagandistic for the purpose of indoctrinating the masses in their revolutionary cause," considered Hayden's well-crafted works and his refusal to be categorized as a "black poet" antirevolutionary at best and dangerously close to being antiblack at worst. It would be four years later, in *Words in the Mourning Time* (1970), before Hayden could deal artistically with those attacks. Hayden never deviated from his 1948 stance, even when many writers of his age group hedged on the issue of a black aesthetic or even followed the lead of young militant propounders of such fatuous statements as: "the only audience which will listen to anything that takes *guts* to be said is a black audience." In a 1973 interview Hayden lamented the confusion between poetry and politics and reaffirmed his identity as artist:

> There's a tendency today–more than a tendency, it's almost a conspiracy–to delimit poets, to restrict them to the political. . . . I can't imagine any poet worth his salt today not being aware of social evils. . . . But I feel I have the right to deal with these matters in my own way. . . . I know who I am, and pretty much what I want to say.

As the 1960s drew to a close, many predominantly white universities began actively recruiting black students and faculty, and in 1969 Hayden returned to his alma mater, the University of Michigan, as professor of English. The return to Michigan did not mean a retreat from conflict. For Hayden, this was "the mourning time" which Bahá'u'lláh had prophesied, an "age of blindness" when the evils of war and racism would wreak havoc on all mankind. After passing through disasters, man would be purified so that a new order of peace and justice could prevail. But, for Hayden, suffering was more real than the hoped-for redemption, thus the agonized tone of his *Words in the Mourning Time*.

Words in the Mourning Time does not represent any change in poetic technique from *Selected Poems;* in tone, it is something of a step backward. The poems chosen for reprint are not Hayden's best. The title poem is typical; while hardly strident, it lacks Hayden's customary detachment. "Words in the Mourning Time" is a long and angry poem about the assassinations of Martin Luther King and Robert Kennedy and about the Vietnam War. Hayden later expressed doubts as to its enduring worth and excised seven of its ten sections when "Words in the Mourning Time" was revised for *Angle of Ascent: New and Selected Poems* (1975).

Hayden's best poems in *Words in the Mourning Time* deal with man's quest for liberation. "Soledad" is about a young drug addict whom the Haydens tried to help, but failed: "Naked, he lies in the blinded room/chainsmoking, cradled by drugs, by jazz/as never by any lover's cradling flesh." In "The Dream," Sinda, an old slave woman, waits to be freed according to her private dream of "great big soldiers marching out of gunburst." She expects their faces to be those of Cal and Joe, fellow slaves who have long since been sold away. Between the sections describing Sinda are prose passages, letters written home by black Union soldiers. Ironically, Sinda expires before she meets her liberators. A further irony is that the letters show the black troops to be ordinary young men, not the glorious figments of Sinda's dream. Two other poems, "Zeus over Redeye" and "Unidentified Flying Object," deal with the horrifying effects of space-age technology on humanity, a theme that took on greater importance in Hayden's later work.

The best poem in *Words in the Mourning Time* is "El-Hajj Malik El-Shabazz," a summation of the life of Malcolm X (the title is the name Malcolm X took after his pilgrimage to Mecca). One of its most associative lines is the epigraph "O masks and metamorphoses of Ahab, Native Son," because it recalls *Moby-Dick* and Richard Wright. Yoking Malcolm X with Wright's Bigger Thomas and Herman Melville's Captain Ahab, Hayden asserts that the Black Muslim who became the quintessential embodiment of black rage is also quintessentially American. The poem follows the outline of Malcolm X's life given in Alex Haley's *The Autobiography of Malcolm X* (1964): the murder of his Garveyite father and subsequent dissolution of the family, Malcolm's drift into crime, followed by imprisonment, where he achieves a "false dawn of vision" by becoming a Muslim and

a hater of whites–"Rejecting Ahab, he was of Ahab's tribe." Finally, breaking with the Black Muslims, he goes to the holy city of Mecca, "hejira to/his final metamorphosis" where

> He fell upon his face before
> Allah the raceless in whose blazing Oneness all
> were one. He rose renewed renamed, became
> much more than there was time for him to be.

For Hayden, Malcolm X achieved a vision of brotherhood much like his own.

Hayden's *The Night-Blooming Cereus* (1972) signals the preoccupation with metaphysical issues which increasingly marked his artistic maturity. The focus in the volume is on metamorphosis. Hayden begins with the myth of girl-become-spider captured in the work of a black sculptor (Richard Hunt's "Arachne"). The horror of "Arachne" is contrasted with unfolding-to-fulfillment in the title poem, "The Night-Blooming Cereus," about the spectacular blooming of a cactus. Hayden seems to suggest that the answer to metaphysical questions is that the questions themselves are wrong; reality does not correspond to rational categories. All is Yeatsean flux, mutability, oneness, known only through the imagination. "The Peacock Room," visited by Hayden in the Smithsonian, is a timeless art object, transcending the brutal realities of "Hiroshima Watts My Lai" and also the "Med School/cadaver," which is all that remains in time of Hayden's beloved friend, artist Betsy Graves Reyneau (whose twelfth birthday party had been held in the Peacock Room). In art, all disparate realities are joined; time and eternity are one. Knowing this secret of ultimate unity is the reason for "a bronze Bodhisattva's ancient smile." (In Buddhism, a Bodhisattva is one who has achieved spiritual enlightenment.) Thus, the answer to the questions posed in the final stanza, "What is art?/ What is life?," is metamorphosis; they cannot be separated.

Several critics have concluded that *The Night-Blooming Cereus* represents Hayden's final departure from black history and retreat into private symbol. This estimate is forcefully countered by Wilburn Williams in one of the most illuminating pieces of Hayden criticism published to date. Agreeing with those who view the later Hayden as primarily a symbolist, Williams argues, however, that a symbolist is what he always had been. There is no conflict between the symbolist Hayden and the author of the history poems,

Hayden at Your Heritage House in Detroit, 1979 (photograph by Hugh Grannum)

where black history itself becomes metaphor of the struggles and suffering of all humanity. In the later poems, Hayden gave up panorama in favor of personalized, but still symbolic, portraits.

The eight poems in *Angle of Ascent: New and Selected Poems* contain two of Hayden's best symbolic portraits. A brief moment in past history, or a relatively obscure life, now is seen to have the same symbolic import as some vast movement. In "Free Fantasia: Tiger Flowers," the black boxer who became middleweight champion in 1926, only to die shortly thereafter following eye surgery, reminds humanity of the inevitably losing fight with time. Flowers, called the "Georgia Deacon" because of his Bible reading and clean living, made an indelible impression upon teenage Robert Hayden. When Flowers died

> Hardshell believers
> amen'd the wreck
> as God A'mighty's
> will. I'd thought
> such gaiety could not
> die. Nor could our
> elegant avenger.

As with Betsy Reyneau of the Peacock Room, so with the artist of the ring; transient life is transmuted into lasting art, of which the emblem is an exotic landscape by Rousseau:

> *The Virgin Forest*
> by Rousseau—
> its psychedelic flowers
> towering, its deathless
> dark dream figure
> death the leopard
> claws—I choose it
> now as elegy
> for Tiger Flowers.

The imaginative connection, the changing of the temporal into the eternal, is the narrator's contribution.

"For a Young Artist" describes the situation when the world rejects the artist's gift which has united the eternal with the physical world of time, an undoubtedly autobiographical reference. Using the frame of a short story by Gabriel García Márquez, the poem describes the plight of an elderly angel who, due to a mid-flight accident, has crashed on earth, where humans put him in a chicken house and charge admission to

see the "freak." The angel's efforts to take off again are ludicrous:

> He leaps, board wings clumsily flapping, big sex flopping, falls.

But somehow (the poem does not say how) there is the liberating metamorphosis from "awk-/ward patsy" to master of the art of flight:

> silken rustling in the air,
> the angle of ascent
> achieved.

Ironic humor and criticism of the American penchants for materialism and violence prevail in the last collection of new poems, mostly symbolic portraits, published before Hayden's death, *American Journal* (1978). "A Letter from Phillis Wheatley" humorously recounts England's reception of America's first black published poet when she visited there in 1773. The theme of the poem is that for survival, a poet must learn to accept a segregation that is only more evident when the poet is black: "At supper–I dined apart/ like captive Royalty–."

The mellow tone of "Phillis Wheatley" probably reflects some of the happy experiences which came Hayden's way in the 1970s: he won the Russell Loines Award in 1970, and he was elected to the American Academy of Poets in 1975. In 1976 he was the first black appointed Consultant in Poetry to the Library of Congress (the American equivalent to England's poet laureate). The appointment was renewed for the following year. In the 1970s three scholars made his work the subject of doctoral dissertations, an experience gratifying to Hayden. In addition to writing and teaching, Hayden in his last years managed to devote time to readings, lecturing, being interviewed, and advising younger poets. Many of his students at Michigan were Hopwood Award winners.

Two of the more somber poems in the 1978 *American Journal* are the symbolic portraits "Astronauts" and "American Journal." A reliance on technology dehumanizes the astronauts. They become "Armored in oxygen/faceless in visors"; they are those "to whom only/their machines are friendly." Cast in the form of a report by a space alien, "American Journal" is saved from preachiness by the naive reporter's objective style:

> item their vaunted
> liberty no body pushes me around i have heard
> them say land of the free they sing what do
> they fear mistrust betray more than the freedom
> they boast of in their ignorant pride have seen

> the squalid ghettoes in their violent cities
> paradox on paradox how have the americans
> managed to survive

Hayden's final years were troubled by failing health. As he grew older, his sight continued to worsen. The many demands on his time and energy often left him physically and emotionally drained. He was at work on a collection of new and selected poems which was published as a revised version of *American Journal* in 1982 when he was hospitalized in Ann Arbor, Michigan, with a heart ailment. He died on 25 February 1980.

Published criticism of Hayden's work is meager, most articles being mere explications of one or two poems. When comprehensive criticism of him is published it may well agree with his description of himself as "a romantic who has been forced to be realistic." Hayden's work deals with the awful realities of American history; yet, because he sees the future of the nation as a passage from death to life, he is more a poet of hope than of despair. His chosen role as an American poet, yet aware of the injustices perpetuated against his race, gives him a unique perspective in American letters.

Robert Hayden was among the first black poets to master the techniques of modernist verse. He was, as poet Michael Harper says, "a symbolist poet struggling with the facts of history." Although the demands of his teaching and his endless revising combined to limit the number of Hayden's poems, his influence seems likely to outweigh output. He has demonstrated that in one man the black poet and the American poet can be the same.

Interviews:

"Black Writers' Views on Literary Lions and Values," *Negro Digest*, 17 (January 1968): 33, 84-85;

"The Poet and His Art: A Conversation," in *How I Write*, volume 1 (New York: Harcourt Brace Jovanovich, 1972);

John O'Brien, *Interviews with Black Writers* (New York: Liveright, 1973), pp. 109-123;

"Conversations with Americans," *World Order*, 10 (Winter 1975-1976): 46-53;

Richard Layman, "Robert Hayden," in *Conversations with Writers*, 1 (Detroit: Bruccoli Clark/ Gale Research, 1977), pp. 156-179.

Bibliography:

Xavier Nicholas, "Robert Hayden," *Bulletin of Bibli-*

ography, 42 (September 1985): 140-153.

Biographies:

Robert M. Greenberg, "Robert Hayden 1913-1980," in *American Writers: A Collection of Literary Biographies,* edited by Walton Litz (New York: Scribners, 1981);

Pontheolla T. Williams, "Robert Hayden: A Life Upon These Shores," *World Order,* 16 (Fall 1981): 11-34.

References:

Arthur P. Davis, "Robert Hayden," in *From the Dark Tower: Afro-American Writers 1900-1960* (Washington, D.C.: Howard University Press, 1974), pp. 174-180;

Charles T. Davis, "Robert Hayden's Use of History," in *Modern Black Poets,* edited by Donald B. Gibson (Englewood Cliffs, N.J.: Prentice-Hall, 1973), pp. 96-111;

Howard Faulkner, " 'Transformed by Steeps of Flight': The Poetry of Robert Hayden," *CLA Journal,* 21 (June 1978): 282-291;

Fred M. Fetrow, " 'Middle Passage': Robert Hayden's Anti-Epic," *CLA Journal,* 22 (June 1979): 304-318;

Fetrow, "Portraits and Personae: Characterization in the Poetry of Robert Hayden," in *Black American Poets Between Worlds, 1940-1960,* edited by R. Baxter Miller (Knoxville: University of Tennessee Press, 1986), pp. 43-76;

Fetrow, *Robert Hayden* (Boston: Twayne, 1984);

Fetrow, "Robert Hayden's 'Frederick Douglass': Form and Meaning in a Modern Sonnet," *CLA Journal,* 17 (September 1973): 79-84;

Fetrow, "Robert Hayden's 'The Rag Man' and the Metaphysics of the Mundane," *Research Studies,* 47 (September 1979): 188-190;

Dennis Joseph Gendron, "Robert Hayden: A View of His Life and Development as a Poet," Ph.D. dissertation, University of North Carolina at Chapel Hill, 1975;

Michael S. Harper, "Remembering Robert Hayden," *Michigan Quarterly Review,* 21 (Winter 1982): 182-186;

John Hatcher, *From the Auroral Darkness: The Life and Poetry of Robert Hayden* (Oxford: George Ronald, 1984);

Julius Lester, "In Memorium: In Gratitude for Robert Hayden," *World Order,* 16 (Fall 1981): 50-55;

Charles Henry Lynch, "Robert Hayden and

Gwendolyn Brooks: A Critical Study," Ph.D. dissertation, New York University, 1977;

Michael P. Novak, "Meditative, Ironic, Richly Human: The Poetry of Robert Hayden," *Midwest Quarterly,* 15 (Spring 1974): 276-285;

Obsidian, special issue on Hayden, 7 (Spring 1981);

Fritz Oehlschlaeger, "Robert Hayden's Meditation on Art: The Final Sequence of *Words in the Mourning Time,*" *Black American Literature Forum,* 19 (Fall 1985): 115-119;

Maurice J. O'Sullivan, Jr., "The Mask of Allusion in Robert Hayden's 'The Diver,' " *CLA Journal,* 17 (September 1973): 85-92;

Gerald Parks, "The Baha'i Muse: Religion in Robert Hayden's Poetry," *World Order,* 16 (Fall 1981): 37-48;

Rosey E. Pool, "Robert Hayden: Poet Laureate (An Assessment)," *Negro Digest,* 15 (June 1966): 164-175;

Constance J. Post, "Image and Idea in the Poetry of Robert Hayden," *CLA Journal,* 20 (December 1976): 164-175;

Vilma R. Potter, "A Remembrance for Robert Hayden, 1913-1980," *MELUS,* 8 (Spring 1980): 51-55;

Lewis Turco, "*Angle of Ascent:* The Poetry of Robert Hayden," *Michigan Quarterly Review,* 16 (Spring 1977): 199-219;

Pontheolla Taylor Williams, "A Critical Analysis of the Poetry of Robert Hayden through His Middle Years," Ph.D. dissertation, Columbia University, 1978;

Williams, *Robert Hayden: A Critical Analysis of His Poetry* (Champaign: University of Illinois Press, 1987);

Wilburn Williams, Jr., "Covenant of Timelessness and Time: Symbolism & History in Robert Hayden's *Angle of Ascent,*" *Massachusetts Review,* 18 (Winter 1977): 731-749;

World Order, special issue on Hayden, 16 (Fall 1981).

Papers:

The manuscript of Hayden's play "Go Down Moses" is at the University of Michigan. Other materials are held at Fisk University, Nashville, Tennessee; Howard University, Washington, D.C.; the Library of Congress; and Xavier University of Louisiana, New Orleans, Louisiana.

Chester Himes

(29 July 1909-12 November 1984)

Ralph Reckley
Morgan State University

BOOKS: *If He Hollers Let Him Go* (Garden City, N. Y.: Doubleday, Doran, 1945; London: Falcon Press, 1947);

Lonely Crusade (New York: Knopf, 1947; London: Falcon Press, 1950);

Cast the First Stone (New York: Coward-McCann, 1952);

The Third Generation (Cleveland: World, 1954);

The Primitive (New York: New American Library, 1955);

For Love of Imabelle (Greenwich, Conn.: Fawcett, 1957); expanded as *La Reine des pommes*, translated by Minnie Danzas (Paris: Gallimard, 1958); revised as *A Rage in Harlem* (New York: Avon, 1965; London: Panther, 1969);

Il pleut des coups durs, translated by C. Wourgaft (Paris: Gallimard, 1958); republished as *The Real Cool Killers* (New York: Avon, 1959; London: Panther, 1969);

Couché dans le pain, translated by J. Hérisson and H. Robillot (Paris: Gallimard, 1959); republished as *The Crazy Kill* (New York: Avon, 1959; London: Panther, 1968);

Dare-dare, translated by Pierre Verrier (Paris: Gallimard, 1959); republished as *Run Man, Run* (New York: Putnam's, 1966; London: Muller, 1967);

Tout pour plaire, translated by Yves Malartic (Paris: Gallimard, 1959); republished as *The Big Gold Dream* (New York: Avon, 1960; London: Panther, 1968);

Imbroglio negro, translated by J. Fillion (Paris: Gallimard, 1960); republished as *All Shot Up* (New York: Avon, 1960; London: Panther, 1969);

Ne nous énervons pas!, translated by J. Fillion (Paris: Gallimard, 1961); republished as *The Heat's On* (New York: Putnam's, 1966; London: Muller, 1966); republished as *Come Back Charleston Blue* (Harmondsworth, England: Penguin, 1974);

Pinktoes (Paris: Olympia Press, 1961; expurgated

Chester Himes, circa 1969 (photograph by J. Mud)

edition, New York: Putnam's/Stein & Day, 1965; London: Barker, 1965);

Une affaire de viol, translated by André Mathieu (Paris: Editions Les Yeux Ouverts, 1963); republished as *A Case of Rape* (Washington, D.C.: Howard University Press, 1984);

Retour en Afrique, translated by Pierre Sergent (Paris: Plon, 1964); republished as *Cotton Comes to Harlem* (New York: Putnam's, 1965; London: Muller, 1966);

Blind Man with a Pistol (New York: Morrow, 1969; London: Hodder & Stoughton, 1969); republished as *Hot Day, Hot Night* (New York: Dell, 1970);

The Quality of Hurt: The Autobiography of Chester Himes (Garden City, N.Y.: Doubleday, 1972; London: Joseph, 1973);

Black on Black: Baby Sister and Selected Writings (Garden City, N.Y.: Doubleday, 1973; London: Joseph, 1975);

My Life of Absurdity: The Autobiography of Chester Himes (Garden City, N.Y.: Doubleday, 1976);

Plan B, translated by Hélène Devaux-Minie (Paris: Lieu Commun, 1983).

OTHER: "The Dilemma of the Negro Novelist in the United States," in *Beyond the Angry Black,* edited by John A. Williams (New York: Cooper Square, 1966), pp. 52-58.

PERIODICAL PUBLICATION: "A Letter of Protest to His Publishers from Chester Himes in Spain," *Negro Digest,* 18 (May 1969): 98.

Novelist, essayist, short-story writer, and journalist, Chester Himes made his mark as a satirist and as a writer of detective novels. In 1970 John A. Williams maintained that "Himes is perhaps the single greatest naturalistic writer living today." Himes does not moralize. He simply places his characters in an environment and records their actions and reactions. His first five novels were largely autobiographical protest novels. From 1957 to the end of his career he wrote detective novels, set in Harlem and *Pinktoes* (1961), a ribald satire on black-white relations.

Born 29 July 1909, in Jefferson City, Missouri, the third son of Estelle Bomar Himes and Joseph Sandy Himes, Chester Bomar Himes maintained that nothing was permanent in his life but change. His two older brothers were named Edward and Joseph. The first four years of his life were spent in Jefferson City. During the next nine years, however, he lived in Cleveland, Ohio; Alcorn, Mississippi; Augusta, Georgia; and Pine Bluff, Arkansas. When Chester Himes was thirteen the Himes family moved to St. Louis, Missouri, where they bought a house and remained for two years; they then moved to Cleveland, where Himes grew into adulthood.

Himes maintained that he was the product of two opposing traditions: the body-servant tradition and the field-hand tradition. His mother was almost white; her progenitors were related to a slave owner and became house servants. His father was a very dark man whose ancestors worked in the fields. What resulted was an intraracial family feud that disrupted Himes's early life. His mother felt that her white heritage made her superior to her husband whom she dominated and humiliated. Himes respected his father, but he maintained "my father was born and raised in the tradition of the southern Uncle Tom; that tradition derived from an inherited slave mentality which accepts the premise that white people know best, that blacks should accept what whites offer and be thankful." Himes resented his father's lack of courage and acquiescence to whites and to his wife. There is constant friction between a white female (or near-white female) and a black male in four of his first five novels, and this theme is undoubtedly autobiographical.

While the Himes family was living in Pine Bluff an accident occurred that changed their lifestyle. Mrs. Himes had no faith in the southern public school system; therefore, she educated Joseph and Chester herself. At Branch Normal College, where their father taught blacksmithing, the boys decided to give a demonstration in the use of explosives. Chester had misbehaved, and, as a result, his mother forbade him to participate. Performing the experiment alone, Joseph made a mistake and was blinded. Unable to get help from local physicians, the family moved to St. Louis in an attempt to get the proper medical attention. After the family was in Missouri for two years, the doctors informed the parents that there was very little hope for Joseph's ever recovering his sight. Mrs. Himes, who had always blamed herself for the accident, moved the family to Cleveland, where she had learned further medical help might be available.

The concern for Joseph undermined the family structure. Joseph Himes, the elder, who had been a teacher in the South, was forced to take a job as a handyman and later as a janitor in order to keep the family together, but these jobs undermined his confidence in himself. Joseph eventually was sent to a school for the blind (he later went to college and earned a doctoral degree in sociology despite the fact that he never fully regained his sight). The constant moves were detrimental to Chester, who had always been a shy, withdrawn person.

Himes graduated from Cleveland's Glenville High School in January 1926 before he was seventeen. He planned to enter Ohio State University in the fall to study medicine. In the meantime, his father got him a job as a busboy in the Wade Park Hotel so that he could defray some of his

Joseph and Estelle Bomar Himes with their three children (left to right) Joseph, Edward, and Chester

school expenses. After being on the job for two days, Himes fell down an elevator shaft and suffered a back injury that plagued him the rest of his life. By September 1926, with the aid of a back brace, Himes enrolled in the university.

Himes did not do well in his studies, he wrote in his 1972 autobiography, *The Quality of Hurt*, because he was oppressed by the white environment: "I was tired of Ohio State University and its policy of discrimination and segregation, fed up with the condescension, which I could never bear, and disgusted with myself for my whoremongering and my inability to play games. . . . It was much later in life that I came to understand I simply hadn't accepted my status as a 'nigger.'" Ohio State was on the quarter system. Himes completed his first quarter in December 1926 and returned for the second, but by that time he had acquired such a reputation for his carousing that the dean let him withdraw, as he says, "for reasons of ill health and failing grades."

On returning to Cleveland Himes continued the dissolute life-style he had begun in Columbus. He associated with members of the underworld, he gambled, and, though he never really became a pimp, he associated with pimps and learned "something of the hustling world." Little Katzi, as Himes was affectionately called by his friends, was arrested for burglary and forgery; he took drugs and became known for his vio-

lence: "I discovered that I had become very violent. I saw a glimmer of fear and caution in the eyes of most people I encountered. Squares, hustlers, gamblers, pimps, even whores. I had heard that people were saying 'Little Katzi will kill you.' I can't say what I might have done." His parents were divorced, and Himes lived with his father in Cleveland, paroled into his custody on the forgery conviction. Himes met Jean Johnson, who became his common-law wife. After again serving time, for burglary, Himes married her on 13 August 1937. The couple lived together until 1951.

In November 1928 Himes broke into the home of Samuel Miller in the suburbs of Cleveland and, at gunpoint, robbed cash and jewelry. He fled to Chicago, but he was arrested there and returned to Ohio. In December 1928 he was tried, found guilty, and sentenced to serve twenty years at hard labor: "I grew to manhood in the Ohio State Penitentiary. I was nineteen years when I went in and twenty-six years old when I came out. . . . I learned all of the behavior patterns necessary for survival, or I wouldn't have survived, although at the time I did not know I was learning them. On occasion, it must have seemed to others that I was bent on self-destruction." Himes began his writing career in prison. Most of his works at the time were short stories, some of which dealt with prison life. They were first published in black weekly newspapers such as the *Atlanta World*, the *Pittsburgh Cou-*

Himes, age seventeen

rier, and the *Baltimore Afro-American*. In 1934 the short stories "Crazy in the Stir" and "To What Red Hell" appeared in *Esquire*. His third novel, *Cast the First Stone* (1952), deals with prison life and discusses those behavior patterns which Himes found necessary for survival in prison. The novel, comprised mainly of white characters, was written after he left the penitentiary.

"To What Red Hell" is a fictional account of a 1930 fire that ravaged Ohio State Penitentiary. In the Easter Monday fire more than three hundred convicts were burned to death in their cells. Himes explains that he was almost a casualty of that fire. The story is narrated by Blackie, an inmate. The state of mind that overwhelms Blackie and reverberates throughout the story is confusion. The smoke, the fire, the screams, and the undirected activity create a sense of unreality. The

scene becomes "a dung hill of confusion." Or, again: "confusion was a tangible thing about him. He could feel it pressing in on his clothes." Through all of the chaos, however, Blackie becomes a careful observer of human nature, even of his own actions. For example, he knows that his cell mates are dying of asphyxiation, and inwardly he applauds the brave convicts who defy death to save their comrades, but he admits that "he really wanted to go up in that inferno where heroes were being made and angels were being born, but he couldn't, just couldn't, that's all."

In "The Night's for Cryin" (*Esquire*, 1937) Himes puts so much distance between himself and his characters that the reader almost comes to the conclusion that he hated his own creations. The main character, Black Boy, has the viciousness of a cold-blooded killer. There are no redeeming qualities in him. Even his loneliness and his nightly crying on death row do not help the reader to empathize with him. And while his victim, Marie, is not quite as detestable as Black Boy, she is a liar and a cheat and a cheap street woman who lives only for the thrill of the moment.

In May 1936, after serving just over seven years, Himes was paroled. Although he thought of himself as a writer, he could not make a living with his pen. He supported himself and his wife by working as a part-time waiter and as a bellhop. But even his part-time work was not enough. Himes said, "I did not want Jean to work and mostly we went hungry." He eventually was employed by the Works Progress Administration. First he worked as a laborer. Then he graduated to working as a research assistant in the Cleveland Public Library. Finally, Himes was employed as a writer on the Ohio Writers' Project. It was while he was on the project that he wrote unsigned editorial page fillers for the *Cleveland Daily News*.

From the early 1940s to the early 1950s Himes's increasing success as a writer was interspersed with manual labor. In 1942 he and Jean moved to California. He worked at more than twenty jobs in the next three years, mostly in the shipyards of Los Angeles and San Francisco. He received a fellowship from the Julius Rosenwald Fund and moved to New York City in 1944. The next year his first novel, *If He Hollers Let Him Go* (1945), was published by Doubleday, Doran; and he began work on *Lonely Crusade* (1947) at a ranch near Susanville, California, owned by Jean Himes's brother. In residence at Yaddo, the art-

Sterling A. Brown, Bucklin Moon, Himes, Owen Dodson, and John Bright, circa 1955

ists' colony in New York State, during part of 1948, Himes delivered a lecture at the University of Chicago that year titled "The Dilemma of the Negro Writer." He worked as a caretaker, porter, janitor, and bellhop from 1949 to 1951, the year he and Jean separated.

Himes's first novel, the partly autobiographical *If He Hollers Let Him Go*, is a hard, brutal story told in the language of black folk. The style, clear-cut and vigorous, employs shocking, sometimes explosive language which is characteristic of the psychological and emotional state of the protagonist, Bob Jones. The novel's setting is wartime Los Angeles, and the narrative covers a period of several days in his life. Jones has left Cleveland in the fall of 1941 and has come to California because at home he was being refused work while white men "in line behind him" were being hired. But California, in this respect, is no better.

In spite of the discrimination, after some time in California, Jones gets a job at Atlas Shipbuilders Corporation and works diligently until he becomes a "leaderman," or a supervisor for a group of black mechanics. One day he asks Madge Perkins, a white southerner who has teased him sexually, for help with a job. She becomes indignant and shouts, "I ain't going to work for no nigger." Jones rejoins, "Screw you, then, you cracker bitch." Madge reports the incident to the department superintendent who immediately demotes Jones to a regular mechanic. He

is told that if he apologizes to Madge and if he behaves himself, he will eventually be reinstated. Jones feels humiliated by what she has done and to avenge himself decides to demean her through rape. Jones goes to Madge's apartment and forces his way in—at least he thinks he is forcing his way in—but when he finds that Madge literally wants him to attack her sexually, he becomes deathly afraid and flees. Madge, who has to stop and put some clothes on, pursues him down the stairs and attempts to lure him back into her room to start all over again, but Jones feels that his manhood had been challenged and that he had failed, so he leaves.

Alice Harrison, Jones's black social-worker fiancée, tells him that his attitude toward whites is all wrong and persuades him to apologize to Madge, despite the fact that Madge first insulted him. Bob agrees, but he never gets the opportunity to apologize, for shortly after promising Alice that he would, he accidentally runs across Madge asleep in an isolated cabin generally used for assignations. Again she tries to seduce him, and again he declines. Before he can escape an inspector finds the door locked from the inside and demands that it be opened. Madge, realizing she is in an embarrassing situation, cries, "Help! Help! My God, help me! Some white man, help me! I'm being raped." Several men are called to break open the door. Jones tries to escape, but one of them strikes him with a ball-peen hammer. Eventually the charges are dropped; Jones

Himes (photograph by Carl Van Vechten, by permission of Joseph Solomon, the Estate of Carl Van Vechten)

is lectured on his lasciviousness, and he is forced to join the United States Army.

Bob Jones is tormented by fears which come as a result of racism. Awake or asleep, he is plagued with the hazard of being a Negro. He is fully aware that he is not a part of society, and he cannot accept this fact. He knows that he is circumscribed in his actions, that his life is determined by others, and that he is not free to be a man in the American sense of that term. "Sometimes," he says, "I get the feeling that I don't have anything at all to say about what's happening to me. I'm just like some sort of machine being run by white people pushing buttons." One of the major points made in *If He Hollers Let Him Go* is that the roles of the black male under racism and the white female (in their relationship with each other) have been so fixed by society that no matter how much a couple is attracted to one another, the social taboos prevent any kind

of positive relationship, a theme that is repeated in much of Himes's fiction.

Lonely Crusade, Himes's second novel, is like *If He Hollers Let Him Go* in setting, tone, and characterization. The novel is also set in Los Angeles, during World War II. The novel covers a period of fifty days in the life of Lee Gordon, who has been jobless for a long time. Lee finally is employed by a union because it needs someone to sell it to the black workers who, for the most part, distrust unionism.

Because of Lee Gordon's position, others try to use him, and his life becomes very complicated. Lewis Foster, vice-president of production of Comstock Aircraft, offers him a job in the personnel department at a salary of five thousand dollars a year, an incredible offer for a black man during the 1940s. Lee refuses to accept the obvious bribe to sell out the union, but his refusal infuriates his wife, Ruth, who sees no reason for Lee's rejecting the position. They quarrel, and Lee leaves the house. While working with Luther McGregor, another black man, Lee is waylaid by several of Foster's henchmen and again offered a bribe to sell out the union. Luther accepts, after being forced to admit that he has done so before. Lee refuses and, as a result, is severely beaten by the puzzled goons who cannot conceive of a black "boy's having such a thing as integrity."

The Communists, for whom Luther McGregor is supposedly a spy, agree that someone must be sacrificed to satisfy the workers, and Jackie Falks, a white woman, is chosen over McGregor because his symbolic value is important to the party; this further complicates Lee Gordon's life. Falks, a union member, an employee in the office of Foster, and a Communist spy who is strategically placed to report to the party on both the union and the management, is expelled from the party. Lee Gordon makes an unsuccessful attempt to defend her before the union members, who also oust her. When Lee Gordon persists in defending Jackie passionately, even to his wife, Ruth inquires why he is "so upset over what happens to a white tramp when the same things happen to Negro women every day." Gordon cannot explain his emotional state, and Ruth understands that he has "gone to bed with this woman." She becomes infuriated and refuses to sleep with him. Lee, guilty and swollen with indignation that his wife should suspect him, storms out of the house.

Lee Gordon loses control of his life, although, at the book's conclusion, he makes a

Himes in France, 1963

hero's gesture by marching to his death. Afraid of Ruth Gordon, Jackie Falks ejects him, and he moves onto skid row. McGregor recruits him to disrupt the union, and during negotiations, Paul Dixon, Foster's agent, is murdered by McGregor. When McGregor is killed while fleeing the police, Lee Gordon is betrayed by Falks and charged with the crime. At novel's end, wanted by the police who have orders to shoot him on sight, Lee Gordon heroically leads the union parade as a standard-bearer.

In *Lonely Crusade*, as in *If He Hollers Let Him Go*, the major characters do not control their own destinies. Himes argues that the black male who does not subjugate his will to the mainstream cannot survive in America. Each of his characters, in his own way, tries to survive in America with his manhood intact. Each fails and each is destroyed.

Critical reaction to *Lonely Crusade* was, for the most part, negative. Himes himself gave the best examples of the novel's reception:

Everyone hated the book. The communist review *The New Masses* hit the stands with a vitriolic three-page attack.... The *Daily Worker* and the *People's Voice* launched attacks, *Ebony* magazine ran an editorial ... in which it said: "The character Lee Gordon is psychotic, as is the author, Chester

Himes." The *Atlantic Monthly* said: "Hate runs through this book like a streak of yellow bile." *Commentary*, a Jewish journal, ran a long diatribe ... in which my book was compared to the "graffito on the walls of public toilets." James Baldwin wrote a review [for] ... the *New Leader*, headlined: "History as a Nightmare."

Himes further stated that Willard Motley "wrote a vicious personal attack charging me personally with statements taken from ... my characters." Writer and critic Carl Van Vechten, a personal friend, was one of the few who thought the novel was great.

Lonely Crusade has not fared much better since its first reviews. James Lindquist maintains that it leaves the reader with "an impression of power" but says that the novel is poorly structured. Stephen F. Milliken says that "it is, of all of Himes's books, the one that comes closest to failure due to the sheer abundance of things packed into it." For Carl Milton Hughes, both *If He Hollers Let Him Go* and *Lonely Crusade* are derivative of Richard Wright's *Native Son* (1940).

Himes's third published novel, *Cast the First Stone* (1952), was actually the first to be written. When World War II started, Himes could not find suitable employment in the war industry in

Cleveland, and novelist Lewis Bromfield asked him to work on his Malabar Farm. Bromfield, who became interested in the manuscript of the novel that Himes had written about prison, was going to Hollywood to write a screen adaptation of Ernest Hemingway's *For Whom the Bell Tolls* (1940). Bromfield took the manuscript with him and gave it to some producers. Himes followed him, trying to get work. Himes had no success with "Black Sheep," as the novel was called in manuscript in Hollywood, and he went to work in the shipyards. When *Lonely Crusade* received negative reviews, Himes reworked the novel, cutting it to half its original size.

In *Cast the First Stone* Himes suggests that only if the reader himself is without blame can he pass judgment on the protagonist, Jim Monroe. Set in an unnamed state prison during the 1940s and early 1950s, the plot of *Cast the First Stone* covers a period of five years in the life of Monroe, who is serving a twenty-to-twenty-five-year sentence for armed robbery. The novel begins with Monroe's entrance into prison and ends when he is transferred from the cell blocks to the prison farm.

During the novel Monroe is involved in a prison riot, a fire in which many prisoners die, gambling, numerous intrigues, and a significant love affair with another prisoner. He is the victim of senseless and calculated brutality, and he sees other prisoners and guards brutalized. He is punished several times for infractions of the rules. His most serious punishment is for his refusal to break off an affair with Dido, a prisoner whom Monroe finds irresistible. Since open homosexuality is a serious offense, Monroe and Dido are placed in solitary confinement. When they refuse to end their relationship, they are placed in a boy-girl company, a section of the prison especially reserved for known sexual perverts. However, Monroe affirms that the affair is innocent, and he is vindicated. He eventually is transferred from the cell blocks to the prison farm, the first step in his release from prison. Dido, however, takes his own life.

Milliken points out that in making Jim Monroe, the protagonist of *Cast the First Stone*, white, Himes "eliminated the entire subject of racism, the central theme of his first two novels." While it is true that the novel only deals with prison life, Himes makes it quite clear in *The Quality of Hurt* that racism did not affect him until he was out of prison; "under the mental corrosion of race prejudice in Los Angeles, I had become bit-

ter and saturated with hate." It was as a reaction to racism that he wrote *If He Hollers Let Him Go*. Perhaps it is more accurate to say he had not truly experienced racism when he wrote *Cast the First Stone* and, therefore, did not write about it, than to say that he eliminated the subject by creating a white protagonist.

There are many similarities between Jim Monroe and Himes. Jim Monroe suffers a broken back, as Himes did. He draws worker's compensation, and he enrolls at the state university. Jim's parents are divorced, and, following their separation, Jim lives a "wild and reckless year" hanging around a "gambling joint, going to bed with prostitutes, drinking whiskey and gambling." Like Himes, Monroe is convicted of forgery and is given a five-year bench parole. He later goes to prison for armed robbery. Milliken writes that Jim Monroe might be a " 'Mississippi white boy' but in every other respect he is Chester Himes."

Himes's next two novels, *The Third Generation* (1954) and *The Primitive* (1955), are also autobiographical in nature. In an interview with John A. Williams, Himes said that his mother had written an autobiographical novel, tracing her white lineage up to the Civil War and the Emancipation Proclamation. Himes felt that the information should have been included in his novel, *The Third Generation*, but he said he needed to get his novel published, and he feared that the story of a slave family "that had been interbred into a Southern white family would be offensive to the publishers and would make it difficult for publication at that time." Fearing censure, Himes ignored materials that could have made his novel a more honest portrayal of a family's history.

The Third Generation delineates the detrimental effects of racial dissension on the third son of a third generation black family, the Taylors. The father, William Taylor (generally referred to as Professor Taylor) is a black man whose ancestors come from the field-hand tradition. He marries partly white Lillian Manning, who is descended from the body-servant tradition. The couple has three sons: Thomas, the oldest, who goes away to school and never returns; William, the second, who is accidentally blinded and, as a result, is placed in a special educational institution; and Charles, the youngest, on whom the brunt of the parental feuds falls.

Professor Taylor marries Lillian Manning by default. He goes to court her younger sister but is drawn to Lillian because of her aloofness. Lillian, on the other hand, is drawn to Professor

Himes and James Baldwin, circa 1972

Taylor because of his condescending ways. She has reached a stage in which she believes that she can only give herself to a man she considers her inferior, for she could only give of herself "in the manner of bestowing grace." When their children are born, Mrs. Taylor inculcates them with the notion that they should cling to their white heritage and that they should deny their blackness. Her conjugal relationship with Professor Taylor ceases after the birth of Charles Taylor, and all of her affections are transposed to him. She pampers him, and through him she hopes to perpetuate her white ancestry. She massages his scalp and brushes his hair continually so that it will become straight. Once, when Charles gets paint in his hair, and his father has to shave off all of it, Mrs. Taylor becomes extremely agitated, for she "firmly believed that it had been the shaving of his skull that had changed its texture. It hurt her deeply to know that he would not have straight hair. She felt that he had been deprived of his birthright. Until her death she counted it as one of the tragedies of his life."

Lillian Taylor not only pampers and grooms Charles, but she encourages him to groom her. She allows him to brush her "long silky hair," to

"file her nails," and even to tenderly massage her feet. Moreover, she gives him a lock of her hair. Charles never forgets these experiences. As a young man he reminisces over "the tenderness of doing her nails, the soft delight of feeling her hair, the passion of her whippings." Eventually, Charles becomes so attracted to his mother that, when his parents fight, Charles physically attacks his father in order to protect her. In essence, Lillian Taylor, in her attempt to preserve her white heritage, destroys herself, her husband, and her favorite son, Charles.

The reception of *The Third Generation* was generally positive. John Brooks, reviewing the novel in the *New York Times* (10 January 1954), wrote that Himes kept "the reader in despair" but showed "how increasingly firm a position he deserves among American novelists." Milliken called it Himes's least contrived work.

The plot of *The Primitive*, Himes's fifth and final protest novel, is simple. It covers a period of seven days. Jesse Robinson, a none-too-successful black writer, wants to celebrate because he has just received an advance on his new book. As a result, he leaves his job as a porter in an upstate resort and comes to New York City, where

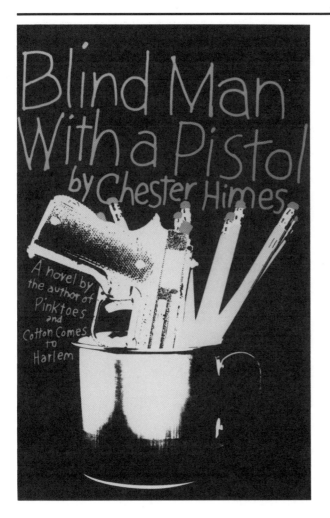

*Front cover for Himes's 1969 detective novel featuring
Coffin Ed Johnson and Grave Digger Jones*

he has been keeping a room in a slum boarding-house. After receiving his money and visiting movie houses, he calls Kristina (Kriss) Cummings, a white friend who is just getting over a love affair. She refuses to let him visit her immediately, telling him she has engagements for the next two days. Jesse stays with Kriss on Friday and returns to her apartment Saturday, where, with several acquaintances who move in and out of the apartment, they have a drunken orgy. In one of his drunken periods Sunday night, Jesse kills Kriss, but he does not realize she is dead until Monday.

Jesse Robinson and Kriss Cummings are symbols of the destructive force of prejudice and racism. Kriss sees in Jesse an exotic savage who is always capable of satisfying her physical appetites. Once when Jesse, the primitive, cannot meet Kriss's sexual needs, she threatens to put him out: "If you don't make good tonight . . .

you're fired." Jesse, on the other hand, sees in Kriss the ideal of feminine beauty and, like Faust, will sell his soul to make love to her. Both Jesse and Kriss have accepted the stereotypical myths society has taught them about white women and black men, and both are destroyed by those myths.

Throughout the novel Jesse continually reminds his friends that he has made a "separate peace." In other words, he has given up fighting for and writing about those things that he feels deeply about. To make such a peace is, of course, to admit defeat. And Jesse Robinson, like his brothers Bob Jones, Lee Gordon, Luther McGregor, and Professor Taylor, characters in Himes's other protest novels, is truly defeated.

The Primitive unravels the seamy side of an interracial love affair. At bottom, though, the work is not a study in the depravity of two lost souls. Rather, it is an oblique indictment against a society which has turned two intelligent, honest, and productive human beings into two misfits. As in his other novels, Himes focuses on environmental forces. But he does not throw his characters into direct contact with these forces as he does in his earlier novels. Instead, he uses flashbacks to make the reader aware of the characters' past experiences which have turned them into misfits. Like Himes's other novels, *The Primitive* describes the pernicious effects racism has on an individual and how it destroys meaningful relationships. Himes argued, "The final answer of any black to a white woman with whom he lives in a white society is violence."

Edward Margolies maintains that *The Primitive* "is Himes's most pessimistic work. He has lost faith in the human capacity to reason its way out of its dilemmas." Henry F. Wilson dismisses the novel as trash; he writes, "Set in New York City, it comes off as a sordid and unwholesome performance which never gets off its knees or out of the bathroom atmosphere which clings to it like the odor of squashed skunk."

During the 1950s Himes became an expatriate and began a new career as a writer of detective novels. His agent, Margot Johnson, sold *Cast the First Stone* to Coward-McCann publishers for twelve hundred dollars. With his wife gone and his parents both dead and encouraged by the favorable reception of *If He Hollers Let Him Go* and *Lonely Crusade* in French translation (and with the example of his friend Richard Wright to guide him), Himes decided to take his chances in France. He moved around in Europe, settling on

the island of Majorca, Spain, in 1954. After a short stay there he briefly returned to the United States with the manuscript of *The Primitive.*

In Europe Himes perhaps felt that he could say things as an expatriate that he could not say at home. He was known in European literary circles. His books were translated into French; editions had been printed in England, and as such, Himes was broadening his publishing affiliations; he no longer relied solely on American publishers.

Himes's first year in Europe was spent with Alva Trent, whom he called "a little crazy." Alva, who was married to Jan Van Olden Barneveldt of Holland, had suffered several nervous breakdowns while living with her husband. Living with her created problems for Himes. With other nationalities Himes and Alva suffered no humiliation, but the Americans and the British could not ignore the presence of an interracial couple in their midst.

In 1957, four years after Chester Himes first left the United States, he found it somewhat difficult to meet his expenses in Europe because his earlier publications were producing very few, if any, residuals. He had written a novel (later to be published as *Pinktoes*), and while looking for a publisher, he met Marcel Duhamel, who was then the director of Gallimard's detective story series, La Série Noire, the only one then successful in France. Duhamel convinced Himes that he should write detective stories. Himes, who had always considered himself a serious writer, eventually acquiesced. In his interview with John A. Williams, Himes admitted that he started writing a detective novel because he "was very broke and desperate for some money." In truth Himes was in such financial straits that he could not afford to purchase the necessary materials for writing.

He also gave up his serious writing because living in Europe, away from racism, had given him time to think and to build a new and different philosophical construct of America's racial problems. His Harlem detective novels, published between 1957 and 1969, include the following: *For Love of Imabelle* (1957), *The Real Cool Killers* (1959), *The Crazy Kill* (1959), *The Big Gold Dream* (1960), *All Shot Up* (1960), *Cotton Comes to Harlem* (1965), *The Heat's On* (1966), and *Blind Man with a Pistol* (1969). In novellas, Himes's Harlem detective novels (with the exception of *Run Man, Run*, which was published in 1966) feature the same two black police detectives, Grave Digger Jones and Coffin Ed Johnson, and, as Milliken notes,

they have formulaic plots. In each book everyone involved is searching for a mysterious object. Because there is a crime or they otherwise need one of the searchers, Jones and Johnson became involved. Invariably Jones and Johnson kill some of the searchers, solve the mystery, and return home to their families. The first Harlem detective novel, *For Love of Imabelle,* published in France as *La Reine des pommes,* with jacket blurbs by Jean Cocteau, Jean Giono, and Jean Cau, received the Grand Prix du Roman Policier in 1957. Two of the detective novels were made into films, *The Heat's On* (retitled *Come Back Charleston Blue*) in 1974 and *Cotton Comes to Harlem* in 1978.

Himes's detective novels are extremely violent. Raymond Nelson insists that the violence of these novels is organic: "What we have, then, is a literature of violence, growing naturally out of a particular place and time, and formed, not by self-conscious artistry but by a more organic aesthetic that permits the laws of a specific way of life to find their own expression." For Himes violence in New York City is a way of life. Black people have come to expect it even from law enforcement officers who have sworn to protect them. Therefore, for an artist to create a setting like New York, and not have violence in it, is to create a world without verisimilitude. Himes insisted that "American violence is public life; it's a public way of life, it became a form, a detective story form." Himes's use of violence in these novels goes much deeper than the fact that violence in America is pervasive. Himes came to realize that although violence was practiced by the mainstream, blacks were afraid to become violent, especially if that violence was directed at whites. Himes said, "That's one of the reasons I began writing the detective stories. I wanted to introduce the idea of violence. After all, America lives by violence, and violence achieves . . . its own ends." Believing that the mainstream understands and respects violence, in 1970 Himes said, "It is just an absolute fact that if the blacks in America were to mount a revolution in force with organized violence to the saturation point, that the entire black problem would be solved. But that is the only way the black man can solve it." In Himes's protest novels the protagonists are always planning retaliatory violence (on whites who had insulted and/or humiliated them), but they rarely dare to put these plans into action. In his Harlem detective novels Himes legitimizes black violence.

Lesley Packard, who became Himes's wife in the mid 1960s

Run Man, Run, unlike Himes's other detective novels, does not feature Coffin Ed Johnson and Grave Digger Jones. Rather, the novel is a study in terror. Himes had always been skeptical of the workings of justice in America, particularly at the street level where black men are at the mercy of white policemen. In *Run Man, Run* Himes takes a defenseless black law-school student and leaves him at the mercy of a drunken, emotionally unstable vice squad detective whose sole intent is to kill the student in order to cover up an earlier irresponsible murder.

Jimmy Johnson, in order to pay for his schooling, works as a night porter at Schmidt and Schindler Luncheonette, in downtown New York City. Detective Matt Walker, in one of his drunken stupors, is unable to locate his car, for he has forgotten where he has parked it. He terrorizes two of the night porters, Luke and Fat Sam, because he believes that they have stolen his

vehicle. In threatening Fat Sam, Walker's gun goes off accidentally and fatally wounds him. Luke, the second porter, discovers Sam's body, so Walker kills him, too. Johnson, the third porter, witnesses the second shooting but manages to escape the scene. Walker pursues Jimmy Johnson and wounds him. Jimmy escapes to an adjoining building, but when the proprietor of that building calls for a police officer, Walker doubles back and attempts to kill Jimmy before Jimmy can identify him as the killer. Walker is unable to implement his plans because Jimmy identifies him as the killer. Unfortunately, no one believes Jimmy. Rather, he is committed to Bellevue Hospital for psychiatric observation while the police department investigates the murders.

Walker has killed the two porters with an unidentifiable pistol from the "homicide museum." When he says, therefore, that he has not fired his official pistol, his superiors cannot prove him wrong. Walker is suspended because of Jimmy Johnson's accusations, but Walker's superiors can find no motive for his killing the porters; further, they respect Walker and think of him as the ideal officer because of his background. He has served in the army and is educated; therefore, even while under suspension he is allowed to pursue Jimmy, under the disguise of searching for the killer. Walker's brother-in-law, Sergeant Brock (who knows Walker is the killer), is in charge of the investigation, and to protect the family, he protects Walker.

The major thrust of *Run Man, Run* is to demonstrate the defenselessness of blacks against a system of justice that is sworn to protect blacks. Himes also demonstrates the indifference and the callousness of the judicial system at the street level where it affects the day-to-day living conditions of the poor. Walker, for example, can stalk Jimmy on crowded streets or in tenement houses, and no one interferes with his murderous plans. Jimmy lives in constant fear of the moment when Walker will catch him alone and kill him. The victim is forever looking over his shoulders, peering at faces in the crowd, worrying about a maniacal killer who relentlessly pursues him. Johnson fears being shot in a deserted alley, but Walker shoots him on a crowded street, with people all around, and still walks away undetected. The senseless killing of the two black porters, the merciless tracking of Jimmy, and the shooting incident support Himes's point that violence in New York City is a way of life for blacks. Since blacks are forced to live in a world of perpetual vio-

lence, Himes suggests through Jimmy's action (Jimmy Johnson acquires a gun with the intention of killing Walker before Walker kills him) that blacks must become violent if they are to survive in America. Johnson is different from Himes's protest novel protagonists in that he is willing, when everything else fails, to retaliate against his oppressor.

Himes's indictment of an indifferent, unfeeling law-enforcing agent (and hence a law-enforcing agency) is typified in Sergeant Brock. Brock knows that Walker has committed the murders, for shortly after the fatal shootings Brock finds the prostitute with whom Walker has spent most of the evening, but he does not reveal this information to anyone. Brock sits in on Walker's interrogation session and knows that Walker is lying, but Brock does not reveal the truth. While Walker was stalking Jimmy, Brock swears that he was at the precinct. Brock goes into the ghetto to talk to the spouses of the murdered men and observes the poverty and the filth in which the dead men's families live, and he must realize that with the men no longer there, the life-styles of these families must deteriorate; yet, he refuses to turn his brother-in-law in for the murder of these two men. In the obligatory scene between Brock and Walker, Brock admits that he knows Walker is the killer, and Walker inquires: "Why didn't you stop me before now?" Brock responds: "I thought you'd know I wanted you to get rid of the gun; I thought you'd have sense enough to see that." Brock further admits that he is not on Walker's side, but that he does not want his wife and children to suffer the consequences of knowing that they have "a murderer for a brother and an uncle."

In the late 1950s and early 1960s Himes's long relationship in Europe with a German woman, Marlene Behrens, ended with her mental breakdown and commitment. Shortly afterward he married an Englishwoman, Lesley Packard, who was with him until he died. Information on Himes's personal life and his friendship with Richard Wright is available from his two autobiographies, *The Quality of Hurt* and *My Life of Absurdity* (1976).

Pinktoes (1961) is Himes's most daring literary effort. A satirical novel originally published by Olympia Press, it is centered on the activities of Mamie Mayson, "the hostess with the mostest," who is determined to solve the "Negro Problem" single-handedly by serving Negroes up to white folk and being "loved by white people for this ser-

Front cover for Himes's 1973 collection of short fiction (courtesy of the Afro-American Collection, Blockson Library, Temple University)

vice." Mamie, who is preoccupied with sex and food, is famous for her interracial parties where more sex than food is served to her ravenous guests. All of the important people in New York who are interested in solving the race problem, black and white, come to Mamie's parties. But the guests come not to solve the race problem but to enjoy interracial sex.

The one person Mamie Mayson cannot lure to her socials is Juanita Wright. The "droopy-drawed" Juanita "had vowed never to set foot in" Mamie's house; therefore, Juanita's husband, Wallace Wright, "a small blond man with a small blond mustache who looks so much like a white man that his white friends found it extremely difficult . . . to remember he was colored," attends Mamie's parties alone. In order to get even with Juanita for slighting her, Mamie spreads gossip to the effect that Wallace has left his black wife to marry his white paramour, Peggy. Then Mamie works out an elaborate scheme for Juanita to catch Wallace and Peggy together. Juanita catches her husband and his lover in an embarrassing position. Humiliated, Juanita asks Art Wills, a white man-about-town who is in pub-

lishing, to take her home and "ease" her tension. The end result of Mamie's scheme is the polarization of blacks and whites.

Mamie is about to sponsor her masked ball, Harlem's integrated social event of the year, and not to have some white folk present would destroy the sense of racial solidarity. In order to prevent this catastrophe from occurring, Mamie presses into service the Reverend Mike Riddick, a rather burly, black preacher whose duty it is to wrestle the devil out of Peggy "so that she would give Wallace Wright back to his lawful colored wife." Riddick, who is an expert at this type of wrestling, jousts Peggy's devil for three days, an ordeal that leaves him quite weak; however, the reverend is so pleased with Peggy's overall performance that he decides to marry her, clearing the way for Juanita and Wallace to be reunited. This problem solved, Mamie reigns as queen of the masked ball; all of the important white folk attend the affair, and everyone is happy.

Pinktoes uses sex as a vehicle for satire. Through the antics of his characters, the novelist exposes the foibles of an outwardly respectable group of people who have deluded themselves into believing that they are improving black-white race relationships when, in reality, all they are doing is bed-hopping.

"Baby Sister," a scenario published with a collection of Himes's short stories in *Black on Black* (1973), was another literary experiment by Himes. It unravels the incestuous affair of a brother and sister. Baby Sister, seventeen, lives with her mother and three brothers: Susie who is twenty-one, Buddy who is twenty, and Pigmeat who is fourteen. The action begins with the burial of the father who has died trying to protect Baby Sister's virtue. Susie has to leave the funeral to protect Pigmeat who has insulted Slick, the pimp who is set on making Baby Sister a prostitute. Susie defends his brother, then he attacks Baby Sister for instigating the problem. As a result of the attack on her, Baby Sister, who is pregnant by her lover, police lieutenant Timme Fischer (although no one in her family knows of the pregnancy or the lover), leaves with Timme under the guise of finding evidence in the slaying of her father. Later that night Susie attempts to rape Baby Sister when she returns home. The family suspects Susie in the attempted rape so Lil, the oldest sibling, a singer who lives on her own, attempts to extricate Baby Sister through a career on the stage. In a contest she wins a one-

week singing engagement at Birdland. Meanwhile, Pigmeat, who also lusts after Baby Sister, attacks Timme who kills him. Susie also attacks Timme, and he is also killed.

The screenplay outlines all of the sexual ghetto-specific traits that are stereotypical of the black experience: the voluptuous, not-too-moral seventeen-year-old whose walking undulations disturb the entire male population of her neighborhood; the ever present pimp who is always looking for the innocent young girl to "turn her out"; the lecherous minister who is more zealous in the bedroom than he is in the pulpit; the common hustler who is always on "the make"; and even the protective brother who succumbs to seducing his sister. All of these ghetto-specific traits are evidenced in an extremely violent environment. Such fare could tickle the fancy of those who do not want to look at the problems of blacks seriously. Milliken maintains that if the script were "filmed in a determinedly 'realistic' style, *Baby Sister* would emerge as little more than a sordid and brutal chronicle of the seamier side of slum life."

Chester Himes died of Parkinson's disease in Spain on 12 November 1984. His last novel, the unfinished *Plan B* (1983), has been published only in France. Himes always believed that mainstream America did not take the black literary artist seriously. White Americans, he maintained, only wanted to be entertained by the black experience. He treated that experience seriously, refusing to compromise his belief that black survival in white America is an awful experience. Ralph Ellison, in *Shadow and Act* (1964), insists that the most insidious form of racism is that of the written word. Ellison believes that the literature of modern America tends to imprison blacks. "Thus it is unfortunate for the Negro," writes Ellison, "that the most powerful formulations of modern American fictional words have been so slanted against him that when he approaches for a glimpse of himself he discovers an image drained of humanity." All of his life Chester Himes fought against images that would give a distorted view of American blacks. At times he might have been repetitive in context; he might have presented readers with a painful truth that they were not quite ready to accept, but he always presented his reading public with words and images that objectified the black experience in America as he saw it.

References:

Robert A. Bone, *The Negro Novel in America*, revised edition (New Haven: Yale University Press, 1965), pp. 157-159, 173-176;

R. Chelminski, "Hard-Bitten Old Pro," *Life* (28 August 1970): 60-61;

Michel Fabre, "A Case of Rape," *Black World*, 21 (March 1972): 39-48;

Fabre, "Ecrire, une tentative pour révéler l'absurdité de la vie," and "Un redoutable argot," *Le Monde des livres* (13 November 1970), pp. 20-21;

Fabre, "A Tentative Check List, A Selected Bibliography of Chester Himes," *Black World*, 21 (March 1972): 76-78;

Hoyt W. Fuller, "Traveler on the Long, Rough, Lonely Old Road: An Interview with Chester Himes," *Black World*, 21 (March 1972): 4-22, 87-98;

Carl Milton Hughes, *The Negro Novelist* (New York: Citadel Press, 1953);

James Lundquist, *Chester Himes* (New York: Ungar, 1976);

Edward Margolies, "America's Dark Pessimism, *Blind Man with a Pistol* by Chester Himes," *Saturday Review* (22 March 1969): 59ff.;

Margolies, *Native Sons: A Critical Study of Twentieth-Century Negro American Authors* (New York: Lippincott, 1968), pp. 87-101;

Margolies, "The Thrillers of Chester Himes," *Studies in Black Literature* (June 1970): 1-11;

Margolies, *Which Way Did He Go? The Private Eye in Dashiell Hammett, Raymond Chandler, Chester Himes and Ross Macdonald* (New York & London: Holmes & Meier, 1982);

René Micha, "Les Paroissiens de Chester Himes," *Temps Modernes*, 20 (February 1965): 1507-1523;

Stephen F. Milliken, *Chester Himes: A Critical Appraisal* (Columbia: University of Missouri Press, 1976);

Raymond Nelson, "Domestic Harlem: The Detective Fiction of Chester Himes," *Virginia Quarterly Review* (Spring 1972): 260-276;

Ralph Reckley, Sr., "The Castration of the Black Male: A Character Analysis of Chester Himes' Protest Novels," Ph.D. Dissertation, Rutgers University, 1975;

Reckley, "The Oedipal Complex and Intraracial Conflict in Chester Himes' *The Third Generation*," *CLA Journal*, 21 (December 1977): 275-281;

Reckley, "The Use of the Doppelganger or Double in Chester Himes' *Lonely Crusade*," *CLA Journal*, 20 (June 1977): 448-458;

Ishmael Reed, "The Author and his Works, Chester Himes: Writer," *Black World*, 21 (March 1972): 24-38;

John A. Williams, "My Man Himes: An Interview with Chester Himes," in *Armistad 1*, edited by Williams and Charles F. Harris (New York: Random House, 1970), pp. 25-94;

Henry F. Winslow, "Review of *The Primitive*," *Crisis*, 60 (1956): 572.

Papers:
Many of Himes's papers are held at the Beinecke Rare Book and Manuscript Library, Yale University. Some materials are held in the archives of the Julius Rosenwald Fund, Fisk University, Nashville, Tennessee.

Naomi Long Madgett

(5 July 1923-   )

Robert P. Sedlack
DePauw University

BOOKS: *Songs to a Phantom Nightingale*, as Naomi
Cornelia Long (New York: Fortuny's, 1941);
One and the Many (New York: Exposition Press,
1956);
Star by Star (Detroit: Harlo, 1965; revised edition,
Detroit: Evenill, 1970);
Pink Ladies in the Afternoon: New Poems, 1965-1971
(Detroit: Lotus Press, 1972);
Exits and Entrances: New Poems (Detroit: Lotus
Press, 1978);
A Student's Guide to Creative Writing (Detroit:
Penway Books, 1980);
Phantom Nightingale: Juvenilia (Detroit: Lotus
Press, 1981);
Octavia and Other Poems (Chicago: Third World
Press, 1988).

In the foreword to *Phantom Nightingale: Juvenilia* (1981) poet, teacher, and publisher Naomi
Long Madgett notes: "I do not recall any time in
my life when I was not involved with poetry."
Since 1941 Madgett has published seven volumes
of poetry; she has taught in the public schools of
Detroit and at Eastern Michigan University; and
she has served as publisher and editor of Lotus
Press, also in Detroit, since 1974.

Born in Norfolk, Virginia, on 5 July 1923,
Naomi Cornelia Long spent her childhood in
East Orange, New Jersey, where her father, Clarence Marcellus Long, served as a Baptist minister. As a child, she often sat on the floor of his
study reading Aesop's fables or Robert T.
Kerlin's anthology *Negro Poets and Their Poems*
(1923). She also studied an elocution book that
her mother, Maude Hilton Long, had used as a
student at Virginia State College, memorizing
some of its poems for the impromptu recitations
that she, as a minister's daughter, was often
called to make.

At an early age, Madgett began to record
her experiences and express her feelings in
verse. In the first section of *Phantom Nightingale: Juvenilia*, which contains poems written between
1934 and 1943, she expresses the loneliness a
child feels without a playmate, a forced optimism

Naomi Long Madgett (courtesy of the author)

during the Depression, and the restive questioning of a child reared in an intensely religious
home. Many of her earliest works are nature
poems in which she either describes natural phe-
nomena directly, as in "Dusk," or uses nature to reveal emotion, as in "No Stars Tonight." Others,
such as "Escape #1" and "To My Lost Love," are
sentimental love poems. The primary influence
upon the poet at this stage in her life was the English romantic tradition, either directly from
John Keats and William Wordsworth or indirectly
through Paul Laurence Dunbar and Countee Cullen.

Shortly after Christmas 1937 Clarence Long moved his family from East Orange to St. Louis, Missouri, and Naomi, a high-school freshman, transferred from an integrated but racist school in East Orange to the all-black Sumner High School. In a 1982 interview she credits this transfer as "the turning point in my life . . . for the better," because for the first time she found that the achievements of Afro-Americans were respected and honored publicly. At her new school she was strongly encouraged to continue writing.

In the second section of *Phantom Nightingale: Juvenilia*, "The St. Louis Years, 1938-1941," Madgett includes poems that reflect both her formal, classroom education and her informal education. Titles like "Threnody," "Sonnet," and "Pianissimo," the use of Latin phrases, and mythological and classical allusions reflect her education. Poems about contemporary life include "On Democracy," an antilynching poem; "Market Street," which celebrates the vitality of black life in St. Louis; and "Refugee," one of her earliest uses of colloquial diction and rhythms, inspired by a street-corner conversation between two bums.

When selecting the twenty-two poems for her first volume, *Songs to a Phantom Nightingale*, published in June 1941 a few days after her graduation from Sumner, Madgett did not include any of her contemporary or colloquial poems. "To Autumn" and the mythological "Styx Before Crossing" are literary imitations. The love poems "Misconception" and "No Stars Tonight" may have been based on experience, but they are emotionally unconvincing. But if this collection is marred by the typical weaknesses of youthful imitation of romantic poetry, it also shows some promising experiments with language and technique.

During World War II Madgett attended Virginia State College, earning a B.A. in 1945. She then began graduate study at New York University, but she withdrew after one semester to marry Julian F. Witherspoon and moved with him to Detroit in 1946. In Detroit Madgett worked as a reporter and copyreader for the *Michigan Chronicle*, an Afro-American weekly, until the birth of her only child, Jill, in 1947. The following year she began work as a service representative with Michigan Bell Telephone Company, a position she held until 1954. She divorced Witherspoon in 1949. On 29 July 1954 she married William H. Madgett, and, though this marriage also

ended in divorce in 1960, she continues to use the name Madgett. She began teaching in the Detroit public high schools in 1955, completing study for an M.Ed. at Wayne State University in 1956.

The collection *One and the Many* (1956) is a record of Madgett's life to the mid 1950s and reveals her determination to pursue a career as a poet. One of the earliest poems, "Sarah Street (St. Louis)," recalls the exhilaration she felt as a teenager, leaving East Orange where she'd been "caged/And enraged/In my small New Jersey town" for "the gay/Honky-tonk and tin-horn rattle/Of the bars and dance halls" of St. Louis. "A Negro in New York" presents the deepened appreciation for southern black life by a speaker returning to the North, surely a result of the poet's years at Virginia State College. In "To Jill" Madgett expresses her feelings of a deep contentment with motherhood which enable her to understand the creativity of God. "Do Not Pass Me By" and "The Lost" reveal a fear that life is getting away, leaving her unfulfilled. "The Rut," with its tautness, sharp staccato rhythms, and childlike rhymes, expresses the quiet desperation of a trapped homemaker. "The Divorcee" is a poem that records the heartbreak and loneliness of failed love. In "The Ivory Tower" Madgett wonders whether to shift her focus from the romantic feelings of her lyric poetry, which she refers to now as "pretty, useless things," to social concerns for "the hungry, beaten throng,/The hopeless, the defeated ones." She resolves the problem by deciding to focus on her personal development, to "go my destined way,/Singing the stars and heralding the dawn."

The selection and ordering of poems in *One and the Many* suggest that Madgett was concerned, like Countee Cullen before her, with gaining recognition as a poet only, not being typed as a *Negro poet*. The nine poems in the collection with Afro-American themes, including the important "Refugee," written about 1941 and selected by Langston Hughes and Arna Bontemps for their important anthology, *The Poetry of the Negro: 1746-1949* (1949), appear at the very end of the book, as if added to fill it out. "Her Story" is the grim, despairing monologue of a "big and black and burly" waitress misnamed Grace who aspires to become an actress but is driven toward suicide by the cruel gibes of patrons; "Monkey Man" castigates black men who waste their lives and destroy their families by drinking and carousing; and "New Calvary" (an earlier poem revised for this

Madgett, circa 1928 (courtesy of the author)

Madgett at the time of her first book, 1941 (courtesy of the author)

volume) excoriates the brutality of whites during the first days of the civil rights movement. Perhaps the key to Madgett's attitude toward her heritage during the early 1950s can be found in the poem "Not I Alone," where she states: "not riots nor revolutions can do so much/In bitter years of bloodshed and hatred/As I can do in a brief moment of being myself–/Being my best self by which I would be characterized."

In 1959 Madgett wrote perhaps her best-known poem, "Midway." In it the black speaker represents all Afro-Americans: "I've prayed and slaved and waited and I've sung my song./You've bled me and you've starved me but I've still grown strong./You've lashed me and you've treed me/And you've everything but freed me/But in time you'll know you need me and it won't be long." Because of its relevance, this poem was widely quoted and misquoted, inaccurately attributed, published anonymously, and even reproduced without permission by one historian of the civil rights movement in the South.

Besides intensifying her own interest in contemporary events, another obvious effect of the civil rights movement for Madgett was a recognition that few black children had ever heard of Cullen or Langston Hughes. As a result, she offered the first course in Afro-American literature in the Detroit public schools during the summer of 1965. After spending 1965-1966 at Oakland University as a Mott Fellow, she returned to the classroom and began teaching the course as a regular part of the curriculum. Her energy and creativity were acknowledged in 1967 when she was honored by the Metropolitan Detroit English Club as the Distinguished English Teacher of the Year.

Star by Star (1965), Madgett's third collection, takes its title from her favorite poem, "Quest," previously published in *One and the Many*. The book begins with a series of lyrics, including a sequence of nineteen short love poems, and concludes with eight specifically Afro-American poems, most notably "Midway." Although a handful of these poems had appeared in her previous books, most of them are recent, and they show a marked improvement in technique, with stronger images, tighter phrasing, and didacticism without sentimentality. "Beginning and End," for example, opens with images reminiscent of Thoreau's remarkable obstetrical description of spring in *Walden* (1854) and a metaphysical linking of life and death symbolized by worms: "Spring's earliest suggestion was/A curling, stretching rope of slime/Regurgitated by a

morning-sick earth./And I wonder if all birth begins/With the throwing up of worms." In "Mortality" Madgett uses the short, clipped lines, the rhyme, and even the imagery of Emily Dickinson to present a typically Dickinsonian theme: "This is the surest death/Of all the deaths I know./The one that halts the breath,/The one that falls with snow/Are nothing but a peace/Before the second zone." In "Woman with Flower" Madgett takes a simple, household setting characteristic of Dickinson and combines it with her own penchant for natural images to convey a clearly didactic but unsentimental theme: "I wouldn't coax the plant if I were you./Such watchful nurturing may do it harm. / . . . /Give it a chance to seek the sunlight for itself./Much growth is stunted by too careful prodding,/Too eager tenderness./The things we love we have to learn to leave alone."

Star by Star contains the first long sequential group of poems published by Madgett. "Trinity: A Dream Sequence" is a coherent series of nineteen short poems, spoken by a woman and presenting the intense longing, secrecy, apparent consummation, adoration, guilt, and conclusion of an illicit romance. The paradoxical but effective use of religious imagery to describe her reaction and her lover, and the litanylike final poem distinguish "Trinity" from Madgett's simple, more straightforward early love poems.

The Afro-American poems in *Star by Star* continue to explore the black experience. From the perspective of a black mother, "For a Child" describes the poignant moment, depicted again and again by Afro-American writers, when a child suddenly realizes that he or she is different. "Violet" is a "proud black princess" who is psychologically crippled by white standards of beauty. "Nocturne" echoes both Hughes's "The Negro Speaks of Rivers" and Cullen's "Heritage" to emphasize the beauty of the black race. Recognizing the importance of the civil rights events in Montgomery, Birmingham, and Selma, Alabama, Madgett's narrator assumes the collective voice of the protesters in "Alabama Centennial." The cool, contained threat of younger black writers of the 1960s is anticipated in "Pavlov": "Is it this that makes you stand/A distance off/Afraid,/Because you find me dangerously/Independently/Passive?"

Madgett's fourth volume of poetry, *Pink Ladies in the Afternoon* (1972), reflects her life during the period of the late 1960s and early 1970s: her commitment to her dual career in the midst of civil disorder and the Vietnam War, her approach-

Madgett as a freshman at Virginia State College, 1943 (courtesy of the author)

ing middle age, and her ever deepening awareness of her heritage and identity. "Dedication" talks about the difficulties of pursuing poetry at this time. Nostalgia is evident in poems like "Last Look" and "Sunny," where she examines her relation to her mother and to her father. "Late," which begins, "I sip Pink Ladies in the afternoon,/ Peruse old yearbooks, wonder where/My old companions/ . . . /Went"; "Offspring" and "The Mother" explore the feelings of a parent whose children are grown.

The love poems in *Pink Ladies in the Afternoon* are quiet expressions of resignation. Typical is "Never Without Remembrance," which ends,

"Let it be sufficient that our hands' caress/Stirs embers still/When all our dreams are ashes."

Current events and a trip to Africa with Operation Crossroads Africa encouraged Madgett to continue using Afro-American themes in fourteen of the fifty-four poems in the collection. "Newblack" is a tough-minded rejection of the attacks by black militants on distinguished Afro-Americans from Booker T. Washington to Martin Luther King. Mimicking the style characteristic of the angriest black writers of the period, the poet argues that these attacks are divisive and destructive, ("whitey's last triumphal laugh/at Blackboy"). Given the atmosphere of the time, the

Madgett in 1954

publication of this poem was courageous. In "Eliza" her imagination seizes upon that character from Harriet Beecher Stowe's *Uncle Tom's Cabin* (1852) to stress her determination to escape the pursuing dogs and slave catchers; in "Simple" she describes Langston Hughes's famous character as he laments his problems with an angry landlady, lack of money, and an impatient girlfriend. "Culturally Deprived" is a dialogue between a young girl and her mother that reveals both the mother's material poverty and her emotional wealth, while "Black Woman" is the monologue of a sensuous woman, supremely confident of her own beauty, awaiting the arrival of her "beautiful/Black men." Three short lyrics entitled "Glimpses of Africa" are based upon Madgett's journey to her ancestral homeland. She recounts the hungry longing for her roots, the shock of being identified as a stranger, and her attempt to reconcile expectation and reality.

Dudley Randall, himself a poet and publisher, reviewed *Pink Ladies in the Afternoon* in the September 1974 issue of *Black World*. He credited Madgett's ability to write "good free verse" to her mastery of traditional verse, citing that quality as one of the "pleasures" of the volume. He also found Madgett's ability to evoke things in the reader's imagination another source of pleasure; the loneliness described in "Simple," for example, is successful because Madgett is able to strike chords in any reader who has experienced the death of a friend.

In 1968 Madgett resigned from the Detroit public schools to accept a position as an associate professor in the English department of Eastern Michigan University. After *Pink Ladies* appeared in 1972, she and her third husband, Leonard P. Andrews, whom she married that year, took over the newly founded Lotus Press. Although many of the earliest publications were run off on a duplicator, by 1978 all of the publications were typeset. Lotus Press has published over sixty-five titles, including the work of writers Randall, Gayl Jones, Ray Fleming, and Paulette White.

Exits and Entrances (1978), physically the most attractive of Madgett's six volumes, has three distinct sections, though they are not labeled as such: the first continues and enlarges the autobiography of *Pink Ladies*; the second reemphasizes the poet's interest in Afro-American themes; the third contains her most recent lyrics. "Family Portrait" is a sweet, anxious dialogue between a young girl and her mother looking at a photograph of her older brothers and mother taken before she was born. "Album: Photo 2," "Saturday Night at the Parsonage," "Deacon Morgan," and "Mufflejaw, I Remember You" recall Madgett's posing for a picture with her brothers, the ritualistic preparations for Sunday in her father's home, a crippled deacon faithful to and beloved of God, and a favorite cat that elicits an elegy to childhood. "Kin" and "Fantasia" are dedicated to Madgett's daughter; the former uses natural imagery–"Leaves of one vine entwine us utterly"–to emphasize the closeness of mother and daughter, while the latter, one of the longest poems in the collection, is a thumbnail biography of a girl who moves from a rich, imagined life as an Indian maiden, Princess of Siam, Rose of Spanish Harlem, and the lover of Black Orpheus to a rich, realized life as an Afro-American woman and mother.

In the final poems of the first section of *Exits and Entrances*, Madgett acknowledges the pastness of the past while savoring its memories. "The Silver Cord" recognizes the need "to tie the knot" of the severed umbilical cord "and let it fall away." "Fifth Street Exit, Richmond" returns to the Virginia city where Madgett spent many happy summers. It recalls the details of those summers while recognizing that time and a new freeway have changed things forever.

Lulled by the reminiscent warmth of the poems in the first part of *Exits and Entrances*, the reader may be surprised by the sudden plunge into the tensions, threatening violence, and contro-

Madgett at a benefit reading in Detroit, 1980 (courtesy of the author)

versy in the middle third of the collection. In "Catastrophe" and "City Nights" the narrators are temporarily secure on the front porch, yet fearful of the "weak light of a distant madness" that stalks the city streets. Madgett, like her Detroit contemporary, Joyce Carol Oates, captures the surrealistic nightmares of urban dwellers. "Phillis" recounts the life of Phillis Wheatley, who was seized from Africa, endured the brutality of the middle passage, and survived to "sing/A dual song" of Christian humility and African pride. Drawing upon the more recent past, Madgett pays indirect tribute to predecessors like Hughes, in the blues technique of "Monday Morning Blues," and direct tribute to Rosey Pool, the Dutch scholar who promoted Afro-American literature before it was fashionable to do so. In another poem, "In Search of Aunt Jemima (Alias Big Mama)," she associates herself with Don L. Lee (Haki R. Madhubuti), whose earlier "Big Momma" praises the strength and stability of the black mother; here, however, Madgett suggests that the public face of Big Mama, the Aunt Jemima face, was the mask she wore for whites, to conceal an ominous power.

Unlike Madhubuti and other militants who reject some, or much, of their past and change their names to symbolize their rejection, Madgett takes pride in her father's and his father's accomplishments and name. In "Nomen" she declares, "I will keep the name my father gave me/being neither anonymous nor poor/and having no need to let myself be robbed/a second time." And she excuses the ignorance of her younger contemporaries in "The Old Women" when she says, "They are young/and have not learned/the many faces of endurance, the furtive/triumphs earned through suffering." In the title poem of *Exits and Entrances* she emphasizes a central theme of the work, the successful quest for identity: "Through random doors we have come/home to our kingdom . . . / . . . armed with the invincible sword and shield/of our own names and faces."

The final third of *Exits and Entrances* consists of lyric poems: a brief tribute to Duke Ellington; a religious poem based upon dreamvisions of Christ's birth and life; several nature poems that elicit human responses; five poems about either writing or poetry; and a series of love poems.

Exits and Entrances was reviewed in the March-April 1980 issue of the *Black Scholar*. Although Melba Boyd spent more time talking about Madgett's life, travels, publishing endeavors, and the physical design of the volume than the poems themselves, she nonetheless praised the

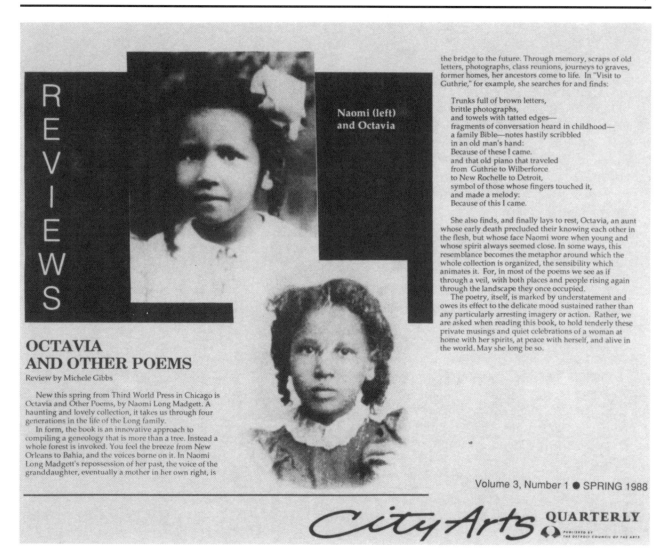

the bridge to the future. Through memory, scraps of old letters, photographs, class reunions, journeys to graves, former homes, her ancestors come to life. In "Visit to Guthrie," for example, she searches for and finds:

Trunks full of brown letters,
brittle photographs,
and towels with tatted edges—
fragments of conversation heard in childhood—
a family Bible—notes hastily scribbled
in an old man's hand:
Because of these I came.
and that old piano that traveled
from Guthrie to Wilberforce
to New Rochelle to Detroit,
symbol of those whose fingers touched it,
and made a melody:
Because of this I came.

She also finds, and finally lays to rest, Octavia, an aunt whose early death precluded their knowing each other in the flesh, but whose face Naomi wore when young and whose spirit always seemed close. In some ways, this resemblance becomes the metaphor around which the whole collection is organized, the sensibility which animates it. For, in most of the poems we see as if through a veil, with both places and people rising again through the landscape they once occupied.

The poetry, itself, is marked by understatement and owes its effect to the delicate mood sustained rather than any particularly arresting imagery or action. Rather, we are asked when reading this book, to hold tenderly these private musings and quiet celebrations of a woman at home with her spirits, at peace with herself, and alive in the world. May she long be so.

Naomi (left) and Octavia

OCTAVIA AND OTHER POEMS
Review by Michele Gibbs

New this spring from Third World Press in Chicago is Octavia and Other Poems, by Naomi Long Madgett. A haunting and lovely collection, it takes us through four generations in the life of the Long family.

In form, the book is an innovative approach to compiling a geneology that is more than a tree. Instead a whole forest is invoked. You feel the breeze from New Orleans to Bahia, and the voices borne on it. In Naomi Long Madgett's repossession of her past, the voice of the granddaughter, eventually a mother in her own right, is

Volume 3, Number 1 ● SPRING 1988

City Arts QUARTERLY

Advertisement for Madgett's 1988 volume of poetry

conciseness of the metaphors and Madgett's "gentle and distinguished . . . creative genius."

In reviewing *Exits and Entrances* for the Summer 1980 issue of *Black American Literature Forum*, Ray Fleming concluded that there were "some fine individual poems in the collection, poems with a wholeness of vision that uncovers the humor and complexity in human relationships. The best of Madgett's lyrics resonate with the vibrant, warm humanity of the poet and invite us, with an almost philosophic calm, to look honestly into ourselves." While he found much to praise about the volume, Fleming also noted some things that were "troubling," including "a disconcerting vagueness about many of these poems that makes it difficult, if not impossible, to locate with precision the dominant idea or emotion that motivates them." He cited "Mufflejaw" and "Fanta-

sia" as two of the problem poems but found "Reluctant Spring," "Kin," and "The Survivors," "in which the measured language and tone produce a beautiful haunting quality," to be some of the worthwhile pieces in the volume.

After the publication of *Exits and Entrances* Madgett continued her active career as a woman of letters. She participated in the Creative-Writers in the Schools program in Michigan and gave readings at universities across the country. In 1984 she retired from formal teaching at Eastern Michigan University and was accorded the title of professor emeritus. She has been honored by the Detroit City Council, the Michigan State Legislature, the Black Caucus of the National Council of Teachers of English, the Stylus Society of Howard University, Your Heritage House with the Robert Hayden Runagate Award, and Wayne

111

State University with an Arts Achievement Award. In late 1986 she received a Creative Artist Award from the Michigan Council for the Arts to underwrite her seventh book of poetry.

Octavia and Other Poems (1988), published by the Third World Press in Chicago, is a handsome collection divided into three sections: a sequence of thirty-three poems that explore Madgett's family history; a series of other recent poems; and an appendix of pictures, biographies, and a family tree that provides a context for the poems about her family. Although the poems in the second section reveal a variety of experiences, the emphasis in *Octavia* is upon Madgett's imaginative exploration of the quietly heroic struggles of her grandparents, uncle, aunts, and father during the first two decades of this century. The central figure of this family history, however, is Octavia Cornelia Long, an aunt who died of tuberculosis at the age of thirty-four, three years before Madgett was born. Identifying closely with her because of their physical resemblance and a shared middle name, she poignantly re-creates the life of this restless, defiant, and beautiful young woman. By re-creating her life, the poet also achieves a mystical union with her that frees Octavia's spirit from the grave and resolves the poet's own ambivalent feelings toward this long-dead woman.

During the past forty-seven years Naomi Long Madgett has published hundreds of poems in dozens of newspapers, magazines, and journals. The poems have been collected in seven volumes, reprinted in more than seventy anthologies, and translated into half-a-dozen languages. Yet, her work has never been the subject of an extended scholarly study. The reason for the neglect is not, however, difficult to fathom. Over the years Madgett has emphasized her lyric poetry at a time when such poetry, regrettably, has been regarded lightly. At the same time though much of the favorable attention she has received has come from Afro-American critics, journals, and organizations, she has tended to downplay her Afro-American verse. This was particularly true in *One and the Many, Star by Star,* and *Pink Ladies in the Afternoon,* where her Afro-American poems were placed at the ends of the volumes. But in *Exits and Entrances* and, most effectively, in *Octavia* she has emphasized her Afro-American heritage. With this emphasis, her poetry should receive the wider recognition it deserves, because by mining her own past she presents it as symbolic, in the broadest and best sense, of the past of her people.

Reference:

Eugene B. Redmond, *Drumvoices: The Mission of Afro-American Poetry* (Garden City, N.Y.: Anchor Press, Doubleday, 1976).

Papers:

Madgett's papers are housed in the Special Collections Library at Fisk University, Nashville, Tennessee.

Willard Motley

(14 July 1909-4 March 1965)

Robert E. Fleming
University of New Mexico

BOOKS: *Knock on Any Door* (New York & London: Appleton-Century, 1947; London: Collins, 1948);
We Fished All Night (New York: Appleton-Century-Crofts, 1951);
Let No Man Write My Epitaph (New York: Random House, 1958; London: Longmans, 1959);
Let Noon Be Fair (New York: Putnam's, 1966; London: Longmans, 1966);
The Diaries of Willard Motley, edited by Jerome Klinkowitz (Ames: Iowa State University Press, 1979).

OTHER: "The Almost White Boy," in *Soon, One Morning: New Writing by American Negroes*, edited by Herbert Hill (New York: Knopf, 1963), pp. 389-402.

Although his own origins were middle-class, Willard Motley became a naturalistic novelist who specialized in depicting the lives and concerns of proletarian America. In four massive documentary novels Motley explored problems as diverse as the American penal system, corruption in politics, narcotics addiction, and the American exploitation of Mexico. By the time he began his career in the 1940s, naturalism, with its emphasis on the methodical accretion of factual detail and a deterministic philosophy, was out of fashion. Nevertheless, Motley became famous on the strength of his first naturalistic novel, *Knock on Any Door* (1947), in which he traces the downfall of an Italian-American altar boy who is led by circumstances to become a murderer. Because he dealt with a variety of ethnic groups in addition to blacks, Motley is frequently grouped with other members of what Robert A. Bone has called the "raceless novel" movement of the late 1940s, but in many ways Motley's work is more comparable to the fiction of Frank Norris, Theodore Dreiser, and James T. Farrell.

Willard Francis Motley was born on 14 July 1909 in Chicago, Illinois, where he grew up in an ethnically mixed neighborhood on the South

Willard Motley, circa 1945 (courtesy of the Afro-American Collection, Blockson Library, Temple University)

Side. Because his father, Archibald Motley, Sr., was a Pullman porter who worked on a Chicago-to-New-York run, his mother, Mary, was the chief influence on him during his formative years. An older brother, Archibald John Motley, Jr., was already in the process of establishing a name for himself as a painter. The Motleys were the only black family in their immediate neighborhood, and although Willard was aware of racism during his childhood, he later recalled that he had seldom been the target of discrimination. On the contrary, during the 1919 Chicago race riots, the Roman Catholic Motleys were defended by their white neighbors. At Englewood High School Mot-

ley was active in extracurricular activities, from football, where he was called "The Little Iron Man," to the school newspaper. Although the Depression made it impossible for him to attend college, Motley wanted to go so badly that he attempted to win an athletic scholarship from the University of Wisconsin.

Motley had planned to be a writer from the time he was quite young. When he was thirteen, he submitted a short story to the *Chicago Defender*, which published it in three installments during September and October of 1922. By December of that year Motley, using the pseudonym Bud Billiken, had taken over a weekly children's column, which appeared in the *Chicago Defender* from 9 December 1922 through 5 July 1924. While most of his contributions were entertainment for children, such as stories and birthday greetings, occasional notes of racial pride and an awareness of human suffering suggest a growing social consciousness.

Thus, by the time of his high school graduation in 1929, Motley was firmly committed to a career as an author. However, his success as a juvenile writer had not sufficiently prepared him for writing for a more mature audience. The romantic and formulaic short stories he contributed to popular magazines met only with rejection. In an attempt to gain experiences on which to base his fiction, Motley left his parents' home behind, first in order to travel–once to the East Coast by bicycle and twice to the far West in an old car–and then to move out permanently, to a rat-infested slum apartment near Chicago's Maxwell Street market.

Motley's travels provided material for several publications, including articles on such adventures as climbing Oregon's Mount Hood and hiking over Catalina Island, spending a month in a Wyoming jail for stealing gasoline, and eating in a mission soup kitchen in Denver when he ran out of money. An article (*Commonweal*, 10 March 1939) that criticized the practices of mission soup kitchens is significant because Motley's interest in social issues, particularly the plight of the poor, gives his observations effective focus. However, his two most important works of this period, poised midway between fiction and nonfiction, arose out of his meeting a Mexican-American boy named Joe, who had been imprisoned in a Denver reformatory for stealing a bicycle. Published in two issues of the *Ohio Motorist*, "The Boy" (August 1938) and "The Boy Grows Up" (May 1939) contain the germ of Motley's major

work of fiction, *Knock on Any Door*, for Nick Romano, the protagonist, is modeled primarily on Joe.

Back in Chicago, Motley began to visit Hull House, the famous settlement house established by Jane Addams in 1889. There he helped to found a small literary journal, *Hull-House Magazine*, to which he contributed some of his experimental efforts at fiction dealing with society's lower classes. In these sketches Motley not only exercised powers of observation and description that would figure so significantly in his later career as a naturalist, but he developed what was to become one of his major themes, the presence of good even among members of the lowest strata of society: the prostitutes, tramps, and petty criminals of a slum neighborhood.

Undoubtedly the most fully developed short story that Motley wrote during this period was "The Almost White Boy," in which he dealt with an aspect of the racial situation in America. Although Motley was unable to find a publisher for the story in 1940, it was finally printed in *Soon, One Morning: New Writing by American Negroes* (1963). The story concerns Jim Warner, the product of a mixed marriage, who finds himself ostracized by both races. Jim courts a white girl named Cora, and the couple unsuccessfully attempts to bridge the racial gap; neither family approves of the match. Finally Cora makes it clear that Jim can have her sexually, but that she will not marry him. When Jim refuses her, Cora calls him a "nigger," and Jim is left alone, repeating the hollow motto he has learned from his father–"people are just people." This was to be Motley's only extensive treatment of racial relations until he wrote *Let No Man Write My Epitaph* (1958) in the 1950s.

During the years from 1939 to 1942 Motley benefited greatly from his friendship with those who shared his literary interests. At Hull House he met Alexander Saxton, also on his way to becoming a proletarian novelist, and William P. Schenk, who founded *Hull-House Magazine* along with Motley and Saxton. Both men were better educated than Motley and introduced him to books ranging from the classics of the nineteenth century to the works of such moderns as John Dos Passos, John Steinbeck, and Ernest Hemingway. Motley also became acquainted with Jack Conroy, already well established as a proletarian novelist and left-wing editor, when he submitted one of his stories to Conroy's periodical the *Anvil*. Motley's informal literary and social education was

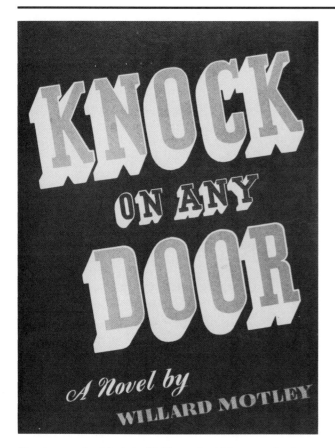

Front cover for Motley's 1947 novel which traces the downfall of an Italian-American altar boy (courtesy of the Afro-American Collection, Blockson Library, Temple University)

As sources for his main character, Nick Romano, Motley used three young criminals with whom he had come in contact. The first of these was Joe, the young Mexican-American prisoner Motley had met in Denver in 1937. By the time of Motley's second visit in 1938, Joe's character was already changing, and he was serving a second term. During this visit Motley toured the facility and made notes to supplement his subjective responses from the first meeting with Joe. Besides taking a literary interest in the boy and his family, Motley took a personal interest as well, arranging for Joe to stay with him in Chicago and finding him a job. However, his efforts were too late: Joe had already established a pattern of committing minor crimes. A second prototype for Nick was a young Polish Chicagoan named Mike. Motley worked at reforming Mike only to have Mike steal his camera and typewriter. Nevertheless, Motley remained sympathetic and grieved for Mike when he went to prison for a lengthy term. Finally, Motley found a story in the Chicago newspapers while he was actually writing his novel. During the fall of 1941 Bernard "Knifey" Sawicki went on trial for the murder of four people, including a Chicago police officer. Motley not only attended the trial but met with Morton Anderson, the public defender assigned to Sawicki, and eventually used parts of Anderson's closing argument in *Knock on Any Door*.

From 1940 to 1943 Motley, a conscientious objector, labored over his first novel, doing research to ensure its factual accuracy. He made visits to the St. Charles, Illinois, School for Boys to augment his knowledge of juvenile reformatories and interviewed the warden of the Cook County Jail to learn how executions were carried out. As part of his Writers' Project duties, Motley visited Little Sicily, Chicago's Italian district, taking pictures and notes, making friends, and learning Italian customs to use as background. In spite of the effort Motley put into the novel, however, it was not to see print for nearly four years. Rejected by two publishers and completely revised twice, the book finally came out in 1947.

Knock on Any Door is an interesting mixture of sociology and art. To support his social theory, Motley created an idyllic boyhood for Nick Romano. When Nick's father had owned a prosperous business in Denver, Colorado, Nick was a model of good behavior. After the family loses its money during the Depression, a move to a poor section of Denver puts Nick into an unfavorable environment, where he begins to learn antiso-

rounded out when, in 1940, he was accepted by the Work Projects Administration Writers' Project. Authors Richard Wright, Margaret Walker, Frank Yerby, Nelson Algren, and Arna Bontemps and sociologists Horace R. Cayton and St. Clair Drake were among the stimulating people who congregated at the Writers' Project offices. In 1940 Motley was still determined to be a writer, but he had gained a more realistic idea of what a writer's work entailed and had developed his own skills accordingly.

By the beginning of 1941 Motley had published only a dozen articles and stories, most of them in obscure magazines, but he had begun work on a novel. From the time of its conception *Knock on Any Door* was intended to illustrate the inadequacy of the penal system in dealing with young offenders and to advance the theory that boys guilty only of minor offenses were exposed in reform schools and prisons to sadistic officials and more experienced juvenile delinquents who together molded the relatively innocent youths into hardened criminals.

cial behavior. When Nick is sent to reform school he is brutalized by the jailers and the more experienced inmates. Nick is shaped by his experiences and by later contact with youthful gangs in Chicago. In and out of reformatories and jails from the time he is fourteen, Nick is finally executed at the age of twenty-one for the murder of a policeman named Riley.

A good deal of sociology informs *Knock on Any Door* and establishes the novel as part of the naturalistic tradition. Motley, himself a member of a minority group, shows the difficulties encountered by first-generation immigrants as Nick's father fruitlessly looks for work while his mother tries to uphold old-world standards within the family. Both church and school are depicted as harsh, authoritarian institutions. The tough urban environments of Denver and skid-row Chicago present microcosms in which the survivors are street-wise and aggressive, while their victims are the sort who work hard and turn the other cheek. The prison scenes, solidly grounded in research, interviews, and observation, are equally accurate.

Like Theodore Dreiser, Motley brought more to his writing than just research and sociological theory. Because the novel, like many of Dreiser's, was based on real people whom the author had known and liked, Nick Romano is much more than the subject of a case study. As Motley's diaries reveal, he was emotionally involved with his characters; after writing the scene of Nick's execution, he cried as if a real-life tragedy had taken place. Part of the author's identification with his characters is transferred to the reader through Motley's narrative technique of moving into the mind of a character, conveying scenes as they appear to that character rather than to the omniscient narrator who presents most of the story. Like Farrell, Motley frequently shifts into the idiom of the character involved in the action he is narrating to counteract the naturalist's tendency toward scientific reporting.

Despite minor themes and sympathetically created characters, *Knock on Any Door* is primarily a thesis novel whose main purpose is to expose and criticize society's method of dealing with crime. The police, epitomized by the murdered officer, Riley, are often corrupt and brutal. They are willing to employ unconstitutional means, such as torture, to extort confessions from the accused, and if the guilty person cannot be found, they have no scruples about improving conviction records by seizing any plausible candidate and building a case against him. Policemen like Riley are often sadists as well: Riley openly boasts about the number of people he has killed and notches his gun belt each time he adds a victim.

The court is similarly unfair to the accused. Motley depicts the prosecuting attorney as a vengeful man, intent on demanding an eye for an eye. The judge seems biased, allowing the prosecutor to present evidence such as Riley's bloodstained clothes to sway the emotions of the jury. Adverse pretrial publicity is allowed, and in spite of himself, Nick adopts the persona the newspapers have created: Pretty Boy Romano, handsome and tough, who goes to the electric chair with a contemptuous swagger. Members of the jury are presented as uninterested rather than vindictive. They finally agree on a guilty verdict only so they can return to their own homes and concerns.

But the prison system is Motley's chief target. As the gym director at the Denver reform school cynically remarks, his institution will reform nobody. The administration teaches brutality by example. Escape attempts are punished by public whippings which merely reinforce the defiance of the inmates. Some punishments actually result in death. School officials ignore the way bigger and stronger boys run dormitories according to their own rules so that younger boys are forced to pay bribes for protection, are homosexually assaulted, and are routinely beaten. Any boy who is to survive must learn to do what Nick does—become so dangerous to the other inmates that he will be left alone. Once a boy has been conditioned by the reform school, Motley suggests, he will never again fit into civilized society. Regardless of whether one can accept all of the author's environmentalist theories, Motley must be credited with being one of the earliest, and most effective, critics of the modern penal system.

Both the popular and the critical success of *Knock on Any Door* were phenomenal. Within three weeks of its 1947 publication the novel had sold 47,000 copies, and in the first two years, sales rose to 350,000 copies. *Look* magazine ran an extensive picture story made up of excerpts from the novel and photographs, set up by Motley, of actual residents of his adopted skid-row neighborhood. In 1949 Columbia Pictures released a motion picture version starring Humphrey Bogart.

Reviews in the *New York Times*, *Saturday Review*, *Atlantic Monthly*, and *Harper's* saw in Motley

Jack Conroy, Nelson Algren, Emmett Dedmon, and Motley, circa 1948 (courtesy of Jack Conroy)

a major new naturalist and compared his first novel favorably with Richard Wright's *Native Son* (1940). Black critics of the day were impressed by Motley's handling of white characters and hailed his "raceless" novel as a significant breakthrough. The book continued to enjoy critical esteem into the 1950s: Walter Rideout listed it as one of the ten major radical novels of its decade (*The Radical Novel in the United States*, 1956), and Blanche Gelfant and Alson Smith treated it as one of the landmarks of the naturalistic urban novel (*The American City Novel*, 1954; *Chicago's Left Bank*, 1953).

Later criticism has not been so kind to Motley. Robert A. Bone suggested that Motley had merely imitated Wright's *Native Son*. Bone also considered it a mark of weakness that Motley chose not to treat black life in the novel. It is a fact that Motley concealed his own race by refusing to be billed as a *Negro author* or to allow his picture to appear on the jacket of *Knock on Any Door*; however, once the merits of the novel had established it on the best-seller lists, Motley was quite willing to reveal his race. Throughout his life Motley contended that "people are just people," that the problems of any group are the problems of mankind, and that no author should be limited to the role of spokesman for a single ethnic or racial group.

When he sent the manuscript of *Knock on Any Door* to a publisher in 1943, Motley sought a subject for his next novel. The topic which sug-

gested itself immediately was World War II. As early as 1941 Motley noticed that war fever was causing Americans at home to become filled with hatred. He envisioned a pair of novels that would show first the advent of the war and then its aftermath through the lives of five Chicagoans. Conferences with his publishers resulted in several changes, and ultimately the two projected books were collapsed into *We Fished All Night* (1951).

We Fished All Night loosely combines the stories of three men in an attempt to convey the social, political, and cultural milieu of the characters. Don Lockwood, a Polish American who has changed his name from Chet Kosinski in order to sound more American, had been active in amateur theater before the war. After losing a leg in the North African campaign, he drifts until he accidentally becomes involved in Chicago politics. Lockwood's glibness and image as a wounded veteran help him to a position of power in the Chicago political machine, but by the end of the novel he has begun to realize the hollowness of his apparent success. Aaron Levin had been an aspiring poet before the war. He suffers a mental breakdown and deserts under fire in Europe, returning to Chicago to seek a faith to live by. When Judaism, Catholicism, and communism all fail him, Levin retreats into his own mind; under the delusion that he is a great writer, he wanders the city, writing fragments of "poems" on scraps of paper that he soon loses.

Jim Norris was a labor organizer before the war. He conducts himself bravely in the European theater of battle, but he suffers psychological damage, manifested after the war when he begins to molest young girls. He dies in an ironically conceived battle between the union (in which he no longer believes) and the police (who are attempting to uphold "the American Way of Life").

The loose structure of *We Fished All Night* allowed Motley the freedom to explore a more varied cross section of American life than he had in his first novel. Although the adverse effect of the war was his primary theme, he also treated politics, labor unions, the plight of ethnic and racial minorities, and the role of the writer in twentieth-century America. He stresses a sociological view of the world in his first novel, but he employs a psychological approach to character in *We Fished All Night*.

The Chicago political scene is mercilessly laid bare through Don Lockwood's story. The machine operates on money supplied by bribes and kickbacks from contributors who range from cheating contractors to real underworld figures. Votes are bought, and ballots marked in favor of opposing politicians are burned. Police guarding the polls spy on voters. Since money is the life blood of politics, especially crooked politics, the machine favors wealthy contributors in spite of its rhetoric about helping the masses. The susceptibility of politicians to bribes unites the political theme of the novel with the theme involving organized labor. Emerson Bradley, owner of the Haines Corporation, is able to use city police to break strikes against his company because he is a major contributor to the machine's campaigns.

Motley also attacks the melting-pot concept of America. First-generation immigrants such as Don Lockwood's Polish grandfather never feel at home in their adopted land; the second and third generations hurry to shed signs of their ethnic origins. Anti-Semitism still thrives even as Hitler is being condemned for his attacks on the Jews. Finally, Motley touches upon a subject that he avoided in *Knock on Any Door*—racism directed against black people. Racism was intended to be an even more important theme, but Dave Wilson, the autobiographical character who would have carried that section of the novel, was deemphasized during the rewriting of the book; nevertheless, racial prejudice is recognized as one of the ways in which American reality falls short of its promise.

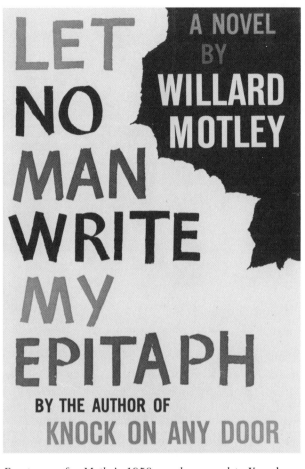

Front cover for Motley's 1958 novel, a sequel to Knock on Any Door *(courtesy of the Afro-American Collection, Blockson Library, Temple University)*

In spite of its greater complexity, or perhaps even because of it, *We Fished All Night* is not as successful a novel as *Knock on Any Door*. As reviewers were quick to point out, Motley had spread himself too thin in attempting a broadly panoramic novel and had failed to create characters that would come alive as Nick does in his first book. Furthermore, he had taken up too many themes and thus had done justice to none. The effects of the war on returning soldiers and the conflict between capital and labor are both oversimplified, partly because Motley did not know this material as well as he had known that of *Knock on Any Door*.

Soon after the completion of *We Fished All Night* Motley took a trip to Mexico; having visited various parts of the country, he bought a house near Mexico City in 1952, where he was to live for the rest of his life. He never married but adopted a Mexican boy, Sergio Lopez.

Let No Man Write My Epitaph, in part a sequel to *Knock on Any Door*, concerns two branches

of the Romano family, following the later lives of Nick Romano, Jr., an illegitimate son born after the execution of the protagonist of *Knock on Any Door,* and Louie Romano, Nick's baby brother in the first novel. Motley's purposes in returning to the material were to show the positive side of the lower-class Chicago neighborhoods, whose dark side he had plumbed in the earlier book, and to investigate the extensive effects of yet another corrupting influence—narcotic addiction. In one of the subplots Motley also deals more openly with interracial problems than in his previous books.

Nick Romano, Jr., born to Nellie Watkins, a waitress who had testified in Nick's defense in *Knock on Any Door,* is the major protagonist. Nellie carefully shelters Nick from the adverse influences of their tough neighborhood, but the strain of supporting Nick by a series of low-paid jobs and her tragic memories of the boy's father drive Nellie to alcoholism and later to heroin addiction. She becomes sexually captivated by Frankie Ramponi, the pusher who supplies her with drugs. As Nick matures, he learns more and more about his mother's life and eventually becomes an addict himself. Rather than end the novel tragically, however, Motley saves both Nick and Nellie by the intervention of a set of colorful skid-row characters, a sentimental narcotics detective and writer Grant Holloway, who is a friend of Nick Romano, Sr., in the first novel.

In the subplot of *Let No Man Write My Epitaph* young Louie Romano, who has been kept ignorant of his brother's execution, looks and acts much like his older brother. Louie is involved in gang warfare and the fringes of the underworld, but two things save him: his Aunt Rosa finally breaks the family's long silence and tells him about his brother, and Louie falls in love with Judy, a beautiful black woman. Louie reforms, and, although the love story is not resolved in the book, Motley's notes indicate that he planned a third Romano novel in which Louie and Judy would face the problems of an interracial marriage.

As in his first two books, Motley emphasizes the corrupting influence of the city, symbolized as a powerful jungle cat stalking its victims. Even though Nick Romano, Jr., has been raised properly, he eventually has to be tested by the evil that permeates the city. Similarly, though every effort has been made to protect Louie from the taint of the family tragedy, he too becomes infected by the crime and brutality of the city. This corruption theme correlates well with Motley's

new material on the narcotics problem, for the growing power of a narcotic over its user parallels the growing influence of a brutal environment over its inhabitants.

The novel's naturalistic depiction of the dehumanizing influences of both the corrupt city and narcotics is necessarily gloomy, but *Let No Man Write My Epitaph* is no unrelieved tragedy. The novel's cast includes such Dickensian characters as Judge Sullivan, an alcoholic who has abandoned his former way of life but whose eloquent grammatical English and perfect manners provide a model for Nick. The judge and other surrogate uncles befriend Nellie and help to bring up her fatherless boy in scenes that range in tone from comic to sentimental. These attempts to lighten the tone of the work often seem contrived, awkward, or unbelievable, and they detract from the unity of the novel.

Motley uses to much better effect another set of subordinate figures, the black characters who represent the spectrum of the race in a large city. Motley contrasts the antipathy between the black and the white middle classes, as exemplified by Judy and the Romano family, with the fellowship in the tenderloin district of Chicago, where black and white narcotic addicts share living accommodations and needles as they fight the same enemies: poverty, the police, and the narcotics pushers who bleed and cheat them.

Although *Let No Man Write My Epitaph* was something of a commercial success—Columbia Pictures used a simplified version of the story for a 1960 film starring James Darren, Shelley Winters, Ricardo Montalban, Ella Fitzgerald, and Burl Ives—it failed to impress the reviewers. Several noted rightly that the O. Henry characterizations of Nick's "uncles" seemed out of place in such a novel. Most critics saw the documentary portions of the novel as undigested facts, too similar to the sociological case study, and suggested that the novel's failure demonstrated how dated naturalism had become. However, Granville Hicks, reviewing the novel for *Saturday Review,* felt that *Let No Man Write My Epitaph* was a mixture of strengths and weaknesses and proved that naturalism could still be a vital movement in American fiction.

Let No Man Write My Epitaph is more clearly focused than *We Fished All Night,* and the major characters are more fully conceived. It is even more carefully written than the much revised *Knock on Any Door,* for Motley consciously supported his story with symbolic patterns and crea-

tively used popular songs to provide a meaningful counterpoint to events or emotions. However, it lacks its burning intensity and the personal commitment that resulted from Motley's friendship with the prototypes of Nick Romano.

During the last years of his life, Motley turned from Chicago to Mexico for his subject matter. Favorably impressed by his adopted country, he planned a good-natured, humorous novel set in Mexico. As he worked on the novel, his original conception changed so that he ultimately wrote two books about Mexico: an unpublished nonfiction book, "My House Is Your House," and a novel which he called "Tourist Town," published after his death as *Let Noon Be Fair* (1966).

"My House Is Your House" is many things—a travel book, an informal analysis of Mexican customs and society, an indictment of American manners abroad, and a confession of Motley's innermost thoughts about racism and prejudice. The five-hundred-page manuscript ranges from simple descriptions of Mexican food and drink—what the natives ate rather than what was produced for the tourists—to insightful views of Mexican racial attitudes. Regarding the latter, Motley noted that while he was never discriminated against as a black man, full-blooded Indians did suffer from discrimination. He observed with disapproval the domination of Mexican culture by the Catholic church, in which he himself had been raised, and considered the church another exploiter of the people. But most of all, he emphasized the adverse effects Americans had on Mexico, from the disrespectful tourists to the money-hungry developers and corporations. Motley was unable to find a publisher for "My House Is Your House" except for four chapters that appeared in *Rogue*, a men's magazine (August, October, and December 1964 and August 1965). Since Motley's death one further chapter has been published under the title "The Willard Motley Nobody Knows" in the scholarly journal *Minority Voices* (Spring 1978).

Let Noon Be Fair is similar in intent, if not in style, to Motley's earlier thesis novels. Motley marshals numerous facts to support his opinion that the United States is exploiting Mexico both economically and culturally. Motley also contends that, apart from the United States, Mexico's worst enemies are the Catholic church, the corrupt bureaucracy, and the Mexican upper class. *Let Noon Be Fair* is a panoramic novel that focuses on an entire town. Based on Puerto Vallarta, one of Motley's favorite towns, Las Casas is a quiet fishing village that has few accommodations for tourists at the beginning of the novel, but which has been virtually ruined by commercial development by the time of the last chapter, approximately twenty years later. Motley traces the changes that take place in the town and the effects of those changes on an enormous group of characters, who represent the entire social and economic scale of the town; they range from three wealthy families to Father Juan Campos and his mistress Maria Camacho, who becomes madam of a whorehouse catering to tourists, and finally down to the poorest peons of the village. In addition, Motley creates a cast of American residents who serve as witnesses to the changes the town undergoes.

Motley's attack on North American exploitation of the village catalogs not only major economic changes but also gradual moral and cultural changes. The Mexican government attempts to limit foreign involvement in the economy of Mexico by prohibiting foreign ownership of beach property, but the *norteamericanos* simply circumvent the law by taking Mexican dummy partners; eventually most commercial enterprises of Las Casas, from the major hotels to the brothels, are owned by Americans. The infusion of American money causes prices to rise, so that the original residents of the village are trapped by inflation. Since Americans demand the same foods and standard of living they enjoy at home, the native way of life is Americanized. Because tourists speak no Spanish, shopkeepers and hotel managers must learn English, and soon Spanish is regarded as an inferior language. The moral effects of the American presence are nearly all negative, for bored wealthy Americans seek sexual pleasures in a setting where they can remain anonymous. Throughout the village, except for a few stubborn reactionaries who cling to their old values, the people are motivated solely by materialism.

Motley completed the manuscript of *Let Noon Be Fair* just two weeks before his death, so he had no opportunity to improve the novel in the course of the final editing process, but it is doubtful whether he could have eliminated the flaws that critics found in the published work. For example, several reviewers objected to the novel's episodic nature and to the large number of characters and suggested that Motley had created only a series of superficial vignettes. Motley had already recognized the apparent lack of unity and attempted to correct the problem by designing

framing passages to go at the beginning and end of the novel; however, after his death his publisher wisely omitted these awkward and implausible sections. Less justifiable is the criticism by Charles Poore of the *New York Times,* who implied that Motley was guilty of sensationalism in his catalog of sexual misconduct. As a naturalistic writer, Motley would undoubtedly have defended his frank presentation of sexual exploitation, as he had always defended his use of explicit language and street slang, on the grounds that such material was essential to an honest depiction of real life. But the most undeserved criticism accused Motley of simply attempting to produce another best-seller. Motley was always sensitive to social justice, and *Let Noon Be Fair* was a sincere effort to save a way of life in the same way that *Knock on Any Door* was an effort to save a class of boys.

Motley died 4 March 1965 in a Mexico City hospital after a brief illness. His son, who was married and living in Merida, Yucatan, at the time, reported to the *New York Times* that because he had always been proud of his health and hated to consult a doctor, Motley delayed seeking the medical attention that might have saved his life; he died from intestinal gangrene. At the time of his final illness Motley was leading a hand-to-mouth existence, living from one meager royalty check to the next. His literary reputation, which had been so high in the 1940s after the publication of *Knock on Any Door,* dropped during the 1960s as critics placed more emphasis on black authors who addressed black life more directly than Motley had. However, since the 1970s interest in Motley has been on the rise, as evidenced not only by the growing number of secondary materials on Motley and his works, but also by the publication of new primary materials. An abridgment of the elaborate diaries Motley kept from 1926 until shortly before the publication of *Knock on Any Door* was published in 1979. The diaries offer a unique view of a naturalistic writer's creative processes and the genesis of his career.

Willard Motley deserves the attention he has lately received because his work is so representative of the "raceless novel" trend in Afro-American fiction, a movement that also involved authors such as Wright, Zora Neale Hurston, Chester Himes, Ann Petry, and James Baldwin. In the wider field of general American fiction, *Knock on Any Door* merits consideration as one of the last great naturalistic novels.

References:

Robert A. Bone, *The Negro Novel in America,* revised edition (New Haven: Yale University Press, 1965), pp. 178-180;

Robert E. Fleming, "The First Nick Romano: The Origins of *Knock on Any Door,*" *Mid America II* (East Lansing, Mich.: Midwestern Press, 1975), pp. 80-87;

Fleming, *Willard Motley* (Boston: Twayne, 1978);

Fleming, "The Willard Motley Nobody Knows: Reflections of Racism in 'My House Is Your House,'" *Minority Voices,* 2 (Spring 1978): 1-10;

James R. Giles and N. Jill Weyant, "The Short Fiction of Willard Motley," *Negro American Literature Forum,* 9 (Spring 1975): 3-10;

Thomas D. Jarrett, "Sociology and Imagery in a Great American Novel," *English Journal,* 38 (November 1949): 518-520;

Jerome Klinkowitz, Giles, and John T. O'Brien, "The Willard Motley Papers at the University of Wisconsin," *Resources for American Literary Study,* 2 (Autumn 1972): 218-273;

Klinkowitz and Karen Wood, "The Making and Unmaking of *Knock on Any Door,*" *Proof,* 3 (1973): 121-137;

Alfred Weissgarber, "Willard Motley and the Sociological Novel," *Studi Americani,* 7 (1961): 299-309;

N. Jill Weyant, "Lyrical Experimentation in Willard Motley's Mexican Novel: *Let Noon Be Fair,*" *Negro American Literature Forum,* 10 (Spring 1976): 95-99;

Weyant, "Willard Motley's Pivotal Novel: *Let No Man Write My Epitaph,*" *Black American Literature Forum,* 11 (Summer 1977): 56-61.

Papers:
The largest holding of Motley's papers is the Motley Collection, Swen Franklin Parson Library, Northern Illinois University, DeKalb, Illinois. Loaned by Motley's estate, this large collection includes letters, notes, clippings, journals, early manuscripts of *Knock on Any Door, We Fished All Night,* and *Let Noon Be Fair,* as well as a number of unpublished manuscripts such as "My House Is Your House." The Motley Collection, Memorial Library, University of Wisconsin, Madison, Wisconsin, contains letters, notes, clippings, and some manuscripts donated by Motley.

Beatrice M. Murphy

(25 June 1908-   )

Katherine H. Adams
Loyola University in New Orleans

BOOKS: *Love Is a Terrible Thing: Poems* (New York: Hobson Book Press, 1945);
The Rocks Cry Out, by Murphy and Nancy L. Arnez (Detroit: Broadside Press, 1969);
Get With It, Lord (Washington, D.C., 1977).

OTHER: *Negro Voices: An Anthology of Contemporary Verse,* edited by Murphy (New York: Harrison, 1938);
Catching the Editor's Eye (1947);
Ebony Rhythm: An Anthology of Contemporary Negro Verse, edited by Murphy (New York: Exposition Press, 1948);
Today's Negro Voices: An Anthology by Young Negro Poets, edited by Murphy (New York: Messner, 1970).

Beatrice Murphy has devoted her life to service to blacks, young people, the elderly, and those who are handicapped. Legally blind since the late 1960s, she has worked, and continues to work, as an editor, reviewer, poet, bibliographer, and speaker to further the needs and goals of minorities. Called a "genuine heroine" by the *Catholic Standard* in 1981, she certainly merits such a plaudit, if only for her role as a popularizer of black literature.

Beatrice M. Murphy was born in Monessen, Pennsylvania, on 25 June 1908, but she was brought up in Washington, D.C., and educated in the public schools there, graduating from Dunbar High School in 1928. While still a student she began publishing poems in *Prism,* the *Harp,* and *Crisis* magazines. Her poem "You, Too" won a second-prize award from *Embryo* in 1930; her editorial "I Don't Go to Church" was the prize letter of *Debate* magazine in 1934.

In 1933 she began writing the column "Think it Over" for the *Washington Tribune* in which she advocated realism for black youths. She stressed their need to experience life unprotected, to ignore criticism, and to pursue ambitious schemes ("Are you making a thing of beauty of the material given you?". . . for you, of

Beatrice M. Murphy (photograph by Scurlock)

all the world, can call your soul your own."). Here she pledged to follow the goals she set for others. A Roman Catholic since 1938, she often cited Christ's example of conviction and strength and criticized establishment churches that alienated their young members. Her commitment to young blacks also led her to form a young people's political study club so that they could become politically aware.

In the late 1930s Murphy began three new jobs. From 1935 to 1937 she served as feature and children's editor for the *Washington Tribune* with Nayden Taylor, responsible for two pages of features weekly. Until 1941 she was employed as secretary to Dr. Paul H. Furfey, head of the Department of Sociology at Catholic University, where she was the first black employed above a blue-collar level. Along with Naydon Taylor, she also conducted her own public stenography service and circulating library.

Murphy edited her first book in 1938, *Negro Voices: An Anthology of Contemporary Verse.* As in the *Washington Tribune* column her main intention

was to aid struggling unknown young black poets. Besides "new poems by old favorites" such as Langston Hughes, she collected short biographies and two or three poems from over eighty relatively unknown authors. In her preface she said, "It has been the editor's contention for a number of years that within the Negro race is a great deal of undiscovered talent, and that it was the duty of any member of our race in a position to do so, to help bring this talent to life," thus to offer "irrefutable evidence that the Negro is still singing, even more lustily than before, and that his song is a beautiful sound to hear."

Starting in 1938 Murphy wrote a book review column, "The Bookworm," carried in the *Afro-American, San Antonio Register, Richmond Planet,* and other newspapers. She reviewed mystery stories, children's stories, studies of black history, and anything that came across her desk. Reviewing Benjamin Brawley's history *Negro Builders and Heroes* (1937), she urged blacks to appreciate their past and give encouragement to living heroes.

In 1941 doctors diagnosed Murphy as having an inoperable spinal curvature which was becoming arthritic. She was given three months to live if she insisted on going back to work to support herself and her eleven-year-old son. Against medical advice she went back to her many jobs wearing a body cast, from under her arms to her hips, and using braces. In 1981 she recalled this decision: "One can and must carry on and do the best that he can; not give up because the doctors have made their pronouncements of doom. Think of what I would have missed: 40 full years of living!"

In 1942 she began work as a secretary, correspondence reviewer, and editorial clerk for the federal government. From 1943 to 1954 she also served as book review editor for *Pulse* magazine, and from 1947 to 1948 she reviewed books on black history for the *New York Times.*

While working as a reviewer and secretary Murphy continued to write poetry for *Interracial Review,* the *Christian Herald, Tan Confessions,* and other journals. Her first book of original verse, *Love Is a Terrible Thing,* appeared in 1945. Her poems cover the various stages of love from its glorious inception to the final disillusionment. In "The Letter," for example, the narrator begs the departed lover for the return of "something very precious": You see, it is my heart."

In 1948 Murphy edited a second poetry anthology, *Ebony Rhythm,* again publishing poetry of relatively unknown authors, including Melvin Tolson. In the preface she stressed the common experience of all poets ("Negro poets write, as poets have since they first began, about love, nature, and everyday events in the world they live in–which is an American, not a Negro, world") and described a new pitfall for young black poets then gaining critical attention: "Editors would do the young Negro writer a greater service by demanding of him what they would demand of any other writer, rather than being swayed, by sentimental considerations of race, to 'encourage' what sometimes turns out to be mediocrity rather than genius." Frequent requests from writers for advice also led her to publish *Catching the Editor's Eye* (1947), a pamphlet explaining the procedure for submitting poems to an anthology or journal.

In 1954 Murphy was suspended from government employment as a security risk, a move designed to punish her for her activism. She returned to her job in 1955 with the blessings of the Congress.

Because of declining health, Murphy retired from the federal government on disability in 1959, but her commitment to service continued undaunted. In 1965, working out of her home with limited funds, she and two friends, Myrtle Henry and Jesse Roy, established the non-profit Negro Bibliographic and Research Center, renamed the Minority Research Center in 1971, and continued it until 1977. She was managing editor of its *Bibliographic Survey: The Negro in Print,* published until 1972. This survey contained reviews of American and foreign publications–"adult and juvenile, fiction and nonfiction, bound and unbound"–with the aim of furthering "the knowledge of the history, aims, and problems of the race." Its subscribers included public school, college, and federal libraries throughout the United States and in some foreign countries. The center also provided information on publications concerning other minorities as well as research services. In 1968 the center gave three thousand books to the Martin Luther King Library in Washington, D.C.

In 1969, with Howard University's Nancy L. Arnez, Murphy published a second book of original poetry, *The Rocks Cry Out.* During this violent time for black Americans she stressed the necessity for nonviolent action and black unity: "I will bare my body to the bullwhip/And accept whatever fate/Awaits the black man in his fight/For equality and freedom./I will do anything in the world/You ask of me–but one:/I WILL NOT

Beatrice M. Murphy (Beatrice Murphy Campbell) has devoted two-thirds of her life to the promotion of literature by and about Blacks. She has been book critic for Pulse Magazine, The New York Times, The Washington Tribune, The Afro-American, and other Negro newspapers all over the United States. Writer and poet, she has conducted special feature columns, children's page, book review columns, poetry columns for various Negro syndicates. She is the author of three books of poetry: "Love Is A Terrible Thing," "Get With It, Lord," and, with Dr. Nancy Arnez, "The Rocks Cry Out;" the editor of three anthologies of poetry by known and unknown Black writers: "Negro Voices," "Ebony Rhythm," and "Today's Negro Voices."

She initiated and served as Managing Editor-Director of The Negro Bibliographic and Research Center, Inc. (later known as Minority Research Center, Inc.) and editor of its publication "Bibliographic Survey: The Negro in Print," a bi-monthly annotated bibliography of books by and about Negroes, which has been used by public school, college, and Federal libraries all over the U.S. and in many foreign countries. She is listed in "Who's Who Among Black Americans," The Literary Market Place," "Directory of British and American Authors," "Afro-American Encyclopedia," "Living Black American Authors," "Contemporary Authors," "Black American Writers, Past and Present"; "Selected Black American Authors," and many others.

In 1967, she began losing her sight, and is now legally blind.

Introducing THE BEATRICE M. MURPHY FOUNDATION

PURPOSE

1. The name of the corporation is:
   THE BEATRICE M. MURPHY FOUNDATION
2. The purpose or purposes for which the Corporation is organized will be:
   (a) To encourage the reading among the public of literature authored by Blacks through a wide use of public library facilities, and to foster an appreciation of such literature, both for pleasure and information.
   (b) To disseminate all types of information concerning literature authored by Blacks, by means of descriptive indexes, annotated bibliographies, and by other appropriate methods for the use of institutions and the public generally.
   (c) To promote and encourage the study of literature authored by Blacks by scholarships, contests, presentations, displays, and providing assistance in publishing writings thereon.
   (d) To encourage further works of literature by Black Authors; but the corporation shall not engage in the publishing of such works for profit.

BOARD OF DIRECTORS

Mrs. Janice Frey   Dr. Edward C. Mazique
Dr. Jerome N. Goldman   Rev. Lola Singletary
Mrs. Shirley Henderson

Mrs. Beatrice M. Murphy
Executive Director

The Beatrice M. Murphy Foundation is a non-profit, tax-exempt corporation established in 1977 to collect, distribute, and preserve literature by and about Blacks and to encourage the continued production of Black literature.

On December 14, 1977, the Board of Library Trustees of the District of Columbia was presented with the charter of the Beatrice M. Murphy Foundation together with a gift of 1700 books. These books were added to a collection previously donated from Mrs. Murphy's personal library and The Negro Bibliographic and Research Center, Inc.

At the present time the Martin Luther King Library, Washington, D.C., is the principal recipient of the Foundation's contribution of books. Other libraries are also in need of books. Library budgets are extremely limited and insufficient to meet adequate personnel levels or to purchase materials in keeping with the demand for them.

The persons most affected by these curtailments often have been the least assertive — the very poor, the young, the senior people, and the library users who have physical limitations. In response to their deprivation, the Beatrice M. Murphy Foundation has begun to augment the libraries' holdings.

The Beatrice M. Murphy Foundation is collecting funds for the purchase of appropriate new and used books, and, in addition, is endeavoring to acquire, by donation, new, used, and even rare books to augment existing circulating and reference collections.

WE SOLICIT YOUR CONTRIBUTIONS OF BOTH MONEY AND BOOKS
Send your contribution to:
The Beatrice M. Murphy Foundation
2737 Devonshire Place, N. W., #222
Washington, D. C.   20008.

All contributions are tax-exempt.   (202) 387-6053

Brochure for the Beatrice M. Murphy Foundation

FILL MY LIFE WITH HATE." Nikki Giovanni, in a review in *Negro Digest*, said *The Rocks Cry Out* misrepresents black youths as separate and violent and thus "seem[s] to just miss the whole point of being Black in the beginning of Blackness."

In 1970 Murphy edited a third poetry collection, *Today's Negro Voices: An Anthology by Young Negro Poets*, again encouraging unknown authors. In the preface she discussed the changed voice of the young and the new division in the black community and noted that poets had become "race saturated." She said she heard "a poignant cry for somebody to help" behind the militant rhetoric and lamented the failure of her generation to pass on its hope and courage to endure.

While working with these projects Murphy was stricken with diabetes and phlebitis, and she began losing her sight in 1967. After several unsuccessful operations in 1969 and 1970, she became legally blind. Since then she has given much of her time to volunteering, working as a counselor to others threatened with blindness and as a consultant to the government of the District of Columbia. In 1976 she served as a delegate to the White House Conference on Handicapped Individuals. Such extensive activities, as well as aid to the blind and elderly within her neighborhood, led to her selection as the District of Columbia's Handicapped Person of the Year in 1981, the International Year of the Disabled. At that ceremony she declared to a reporter: "As long as you can wiggle one little finger you're not handicapped."

In 1977 she published a collection of her inspirational poetry, *Get With It, Lord,* detailing "the struggles–the fighting, yearning, resisting, submitting, and fierce loving–of one soul in its relationship with God" to help others suffering from ill health and despair. A representative poem is "Simon The Cyrene":

> Perhaps it was a sign
> that he
> who bore your cross
> up the slopes of calvary
> was black–
> even as I–
> who bear another cross
> along life's rugged way
> upon my back!

Also in 1977 her friends incorporated the Beatrice M. Murphy Foundation to encourage the reading and study of black literature. The foundation contributes books to public libraries, sponsors scholarships and contests, and provides assistance to black authors. That year she gave seventeen hundred books to the Martin Luther King Library in Washington, D.C.. She is the foundation's executive director and is still collecting and contributing books to the library. Since 1977 much of her writing has been in the form of speeches before national and District of Columbia committees, community groups, and on radio and television advocating the rights of the elderly, the blind, and the handicapped.

References:

"Meet Beatrice Campbell, a Genuine Heroine," *Catholic Standard* (12 November 1981): 2;
"If You Can Wiggle a Finger . . . ," *Perspective on Aging,* 11 (January-February 1982): 8-9.

Effie Lee Newsome
(19 January 1885-12 May 1979)

Mary B. Zeigler
Kennesaw College

BOOK: *Gladiola Garden: Poems of Outdoors and Indoors for Second Grade Readers* (Washington, D.C.: Associated, 1940).

PERIODICAL PUBLICATIONS:
POETRY
"O Sea, That Knowest Thy Strength," *Crisis*, 13 (March 1917): 219;

"O Autumn, Autumn!," *Crisis*, 16 (October 1918): 269;

"Morning Light: The Dew-drier," *Crisis*, 17 (November 1918): 17;

"Bronze Legacy: To a Brown Boy," *Crisis*, 24 (October 1922): 265;

"Magnificat," *Crisis*, 25 (December 1922): 57;

"Sun Disk," *Crisis*, 26 (June 1923): 68;

"Exodus," *Crisis*, 29 (January 1925): 113;

"Cantibile," *Crisis*, 31 (December 1925): 65;

"Christmas Tree Land," *Opportunity*, 3 (December 1925): 373;

"Night of Great Holiness," *Opportunity*, 3 (December 1925): 373;

"Commodore Bonbon," *Opportunity*, 3 (December 1925): 373;

"Punchinello on the Tree," *Opportunity*, 3 (December 1925): 373;

"Chocolate Rabbits," *Opportunity*, 4 (April 1926): 127;

"Negro Street Serenade," *Crisis*, 32 (July 1926): 136;

"Capriccio," *Crisis*, 32 (September 1926): 247;

"The Bird in the Cage," *Crisis*, 33 (February 1927): 190;

"Spring Rain," *Crisis*, 40 (May 1933): 110;

"Ecce Ancilla Domini: An Old Colored Woman Goes to Prayer," *Crisis*, 41 (June 1934): 180;

"Wings Away," *Phylon*, 1 (1940): 336;

"In Winter," *Phylon*, 2 (1941): 75;

"Father and Son," *Crisis*, 48 (September 1941): 295;

"Arctic Tern in a Museum," *Phylon*, 3 (1942): 45.

FICTION
"The Wind's Christmas Story," *Opportunity*, 3 (December 1925): 372;

Effie Lee Newsome

"He Will Come Back at Easter," *Opportunity*, 4 (April 1926): 126-127.

NONFICTION
"The Loss of Ashlee Cottage," *Crisis*, 24 (June 1922): 28-85;

"Charcoal, Leddy, Charcoal: An Idyl of the South," *Crisis*, 24 (August 1922): 158-160;

"A Great Prelate: Bishop Lee at Home," *Crisis*, 32 (June 1926): 69-71;

"Early Figures in Haitian Methodism," *Phylon*, 5 (1944): 51-61.

Effie Lee Newsome's poetry appears beside that of Langston Hughes, Frank Horne, and Countee Cullen in *Crisis* and *Phylon*, journals edited by W. E. B. Du Bois. Anthologized by Hughes, Cullen, Arna Bontemps, and Arnold Adoff, Effie Lee Newsome is virtually unknown today. During the 1940s, after the publication of *Gladiola Garden* (1940), Newsome became known as a nature poet for children, and her reputation, or lack of it, generally rests on that label.

Mary Effie Lee was born 19 January 1885 in Philadelphia, Pennsylvania, to Mary Elizabeth Ashe Lee and Benjamin Franklin Lee. A clergyman, Benjamin Lee was chief editor of the *Christian Recorder*, the official publication of the African Methodist Episcopal (A.M.E.) church. She lived the first seven years of her life in Philadelphia, not many miles from the Gouldtown, New Jersey, settlement that her father's free-black ancestors had founded in the eighteenth century and where her father was reared and received his early lessons in literature from his mother, Sarah Gould Lee. Benjamin Lee loved literature and the other fine arts and encouraged his daughter's efforts toward literary and artistic expression. Mrs. Lee read stories to her children about nature and taught them to draw pictures of birds, flowers, and insects. Newsome enjoyed these subjects more than any other.

In 1892, when her father was elected twentieth bishop of the A.M.E. church, Mary Effie Lee moved to Waco, Texas, with her family. During her four years there she continued to read about and explore the plant and animal life of the region, trying her hand at poems and sketches that were sent away to magazines or newspapers. In 1896 the family moved to Xenia, Ohio, where Newsome's father established their permanent home in a rural area and where she received most of her adult education. From 1901 to 1904 she attended Wilberforce University, the African Methodist Episcopal institution that had given her parents their start. Her parents had graduated from the university, her mother in 1873 and her father in 1872. Bishop Lee had also taught there for three years, 1873 to 1876, and had served as its president from 1876 to 1884. His daughter's explorations kept her busy filling notebooks with sketches, descriptions, and poems about the birds, insects, and other woodland activity. She was encouraged to continue her projects and became active in the church and community life, helping children "appreciate nature and God's creatures." Newsome had professional train-

Newsome's father, Benjamin Lee, during his presidency of Ohio's Wilberforce University, 1876-1884

ing as an artist. She also studied at Oberlin College and at the University of Pennsylvania, where, she said, her work was "well-rated."

In 1915 Newsome's nonfiction, poems, and short stories began appearing in the *Crisis*. Her works can be found in *Crisis* and in other major publications such as *Opportunity* from 1925 to 1927 and *Phylon* from 1940 until 1944. In 1918, at the close of World War I and the opening of the Harlem Renaissance, "Morning Light: The Dew-drier," her most anthologized poem, appeared in the November issue of *Crisis*. In later years it was included in Countee Cullen's *Caroling Dusk* (1927), Hughes and Bontemps's *Poetry of the Negro: 1746-1970* (1970), Adoff's *Poetry of Black America* (1973), and Bontemps's *American Negro Poetry* (1963). "Morning Light" reflects Newsome's early interest in Africa and her African-American heritage. From her study of African lore she learned about young boys who were used by explorers and hunters on safari to clear paths through the tall African grasses. Some-

times, in the half-light of dawn, the young defense-less pathfinders, called "dew-driers," encount-ered unexpected dangers. This poem celebrates the dew-drier and foretells a role for those of African ancestry as guides toward peace and human understanding, important international goals in the years following World War I.

In the first stanza of the poem Newsome paints an exotic picture of the native boy–"brother to the firefly"–bravely leading the way through the "heavy menace" of the thicket:

> Brother to the firefly–
> For as the firefly lights the night,
> So lights he the morning–
> Bathed in the dank dews as he goes forth
> Through heavy menace and mystery
> Of half-waking tropic dawn,

With a comparison of the native boy to a firefly Newsome anticipates an analogy between the boy and the Negro race.

> May not his race, even as the dew-boy leads,
> Light onward men's minds toward a time
> When tolerance, forbearance
> ....
> Shall shape the earth for that fresh dawning
> After the dews of blood?

In "Morning Light" Newsome voices the prevailing mood of the times, that of the Harlem Renaissance.

During the 1920s Effie Lee Newsome focused her attention on children's poetry. On 4 August 1920, she married Henry Nesby Newsome, an A.M.E. minister teaching at Wilberforce University. Shortly thereafter they moved to Birmingham, Alabama, when he was assigned a church there. Newsome began to write verses for children, wrote and edited the children's poems and sketches in "The Little Page" of the *Crisis* magazine from 1925 to 1927, organized the Boys of Birmingham Club, and became an elementary school teacher and children's librarian.

The poems in her 1940 volume, *Gladiola Garden*, describe flora and fauna and connect their existence to the lives of humankind. The narrator is cast as an innocent child who is involved in the process of discovery. The poems are typically four to six lines long and frequently depend on meter and rhyme for balance and emphasis, as well as for appeal to young readers.

Newsome uses two techniques for organizing and developing her poems. In poems with

one or two short stanzas, the stanza opens with a vivid picture filled with details of color, shape, and proximity, illustrated particularly well in "White Clover":

> In their rounded snow-white caps,
> Scented pleasantly,
> Little clover ladies meet
> In a sewing bee.

Then, into that picture of the natural flora or fauna, the poet mixes comparatively human characteristics, either implied or explicit in metaphor or simile.

> In their rounded snow-white caps
> And their great green bows,
> Clover ladies meet and meet
> Till the summer goes.

With longer poems Newsome begins in a similar manner, but she ends with a stronger anthropomorphic image. "My Lady Cardinal Steals Blue Grapes!" illustrates this point. At first the bird acts as birds of her kind should: "I saw her sorrel self this day/Flit to the vines and peck at grapes. /I watched her when she went away." Then the bird begins to be relational. "I'd caught her silver, softer chirp/Answering her lord bird's deep-toned 'Chuck.'" Finally, the poem unfolds into an image that not only links natural instinct to intelligence but also unites it with human motive. Recognizing the female cardinal's partiality to the male cardinal, the speaker observes, "I'd heard his rich song at the dawn./Blue grapes were small pay for such luck!"

Newsome's best expression of her views of the world's contradictions as well as its wondrous glories appears in "At the Pool." The creek's pool is a microcosm of the larger world, the world outside of the garden. It contains the humming life of insects and the plants that depend on it for nourishment and, in exchange, "keep the pool life stirred." The pool beckons the innocent child to step into it:

> Beside some forest pool.
> The reeds around it smell so fresh,
> The waters look so cool.
> I just hop in and wade,
> And have a lot of fun
> Playing . . . in the sun.

But once in the creek, the child sees at close view the true character of nature. The calmness

changes to intense activity; the "bugs and things" dart, scamper, swim, and hop about on the water top and the shady banks. Finally, death makes its appearance:

> Then all at once kingfisher comes,
> That fearless, royal bird!
> ....
>
> He swoops and swallows what he will,
> A stone-fly or a frog.
> Winged things rush, frightened, through the air,
> Others to hole and log.

Flowers, birds, and insects figure prominently in *Gladiola Garden*. Newsome describes almost thirty different flowers and uses their names in the titles of twenty-one poems. Some of these names would be rather difficult to pronounce for the second-grade reader for whom the poems are intended. The childlike persona of the poem "Names" recognizes the difficulty:

> I wish the flowers' names were plain
> And easy, just like Jean and Jane,
> Or like flower names of pink and rose,
> The kind that everybody knows.

There are more than sixteen different kinds of birds in the *Gladiola Garden* poems. Newsome usually describes the colors of their feathers, their place in nature, and their humanlike activities, making the birds seem friendly and familiar. A typical poem, "Scarlet Trimming," pictures woodpeckers as little people playing dress-up:

> The woodpecker folk are quite fond of bright red—
> Poinsettia scarlet for neck or for head.
> And whether the costume is brown, black or gray,
> They count on red hats or red scarfs to make gay.
> The dignified *flicker*, with linings of gold,
> The black and gray *downy* that weathers the cold,
> The jaunty old *red-head* in jockey outfit—
> All choose blurs of scarlet to cheer up a bit.

Many of the insects—including spiders, beetles, hawkmoths, and mud-dauber wasps—have human or fairy qualities. The monarch butterfly lives "in royal halls" while the bagworm lives in its "log cabin" ("Home"). In "Two Firefly Songs" a firefly "at dull blue dusk/. . . flashes [its] silver green"; later it becomes "a lemon-golden spark,/a dancing rhinestone in the sky,/a jewel in the dark." While bees "buzz on like small brown cars" ("Bees"), little spiders "dress in black velvet blouses" ("Spider Dress"). The nature trail through the grass ends when the ants in "long strings . . . return from their marketing" ("In the Grass"), and "Johnny Greenjacket" the grasshopper invites the ducks and is eaten for dinner.

Newsome's poetry lacks scope and experimentation that would give it variety. In few instances, as in "Morning Light" (1918) and "Father and Son" (1941), does she dare to express directly her opinion of the cruelties of life. She chose to accept and be known by the role of quiet, nurturing mother gardener. While she does not ignore nature's ugly side, she prefers, instead, to help children experience the beauty of nature and poetry. The editors of the *Negro History Bulletin* (February 1947) were accurate when they said that Newsome's "aim is not only to help children to appreciate the good and the beautiful but to express themselves accordingly."

References:
"The Lees from Gouldtown," *Negro History Bulletin* (February 1947): 99-100, 108;
Charlemae Rollins, *Famous American Negro Poets* (New York: Mead & Company, 1965), p. 57;
Horace Talbert, *The Sons of Allen* (Xenia, Ohio: Aldine Press, 1906), pp. 180-181.

Papers:
Most of Newsome's papers were lost in a 1974 tornado which destroyed her home in Xenia, Ohio. A biographical sketch that she wrote for Arna Bontemps is in the Harold Jackman Collection, Atlanta University Center Library, Atlanta, Georgia.

Carl Ruthven Offord
(10 April 1910-)

Thelma Barnaby Thompson
University of the District of Columbia

BOOKS: *The White Face* (New York: McBride, 1943);
The Naked Fear (New York: Ace Books, 1954).

OTHER: "Low Sky," in *Cross Section: A Collection of New American Writing*, edited by Edwin Seaver (New York: Fischer, 1944), pp. 304-313;
"So Peaceful in the Country," in *Black Hands on a White Face*, edited by Whit Burnett (New York: Dodd, Mead, 1971).

PERIODICAL PUBLICATIONS: "So Peaceful in the Country," *Story*, 25 (May-June 1945): 81-86;
"Gentle Native," *Masses and Mainstream*, 1 (September 1948): 8-16;
"The Green, Green Grass and a Gun," *Masses and Mainstream*, 2 (February 1949): 39-43.

Carl Ruthven Offord, novelist, short-story writer, and newspaper editor and publisher, is best known in the literary world for his existential treatment of the problems southern blacks faced when they migrated north and for his fictional treatment of Fascist activities in Harlem during World War II.

Born in Trinidad, West Indies, on 10 April 1910 to upper middle-class parents, Offord was one of five children. His father, George Offord, a machinist, was from a family of talented engineers. His socialite mother, Ottie Simmonds Offord, died while her children were still young. The family was separated, and Carl lived with his paternal grandmother, while George Offord migrated to the United States.

Without either parent's direct supervision Offord was at the mercy of a grandmother who made her disapproval of his late mother apparent. Her attitude did not encourage him to stay in school, and he left at age eleven. Even then, he was sure that he wanted to be a writer. Unconsciously, he prepared himself for that demanding role by reading everything that was available, which was mainly emotional, romantic novels, while he worked at odd jobs.

Offord's family tradition dictated that he become an engineer. With support from his uncle Archie, his mother's brother, who also was a master machinist, Offord left Trinidad in 1929 at the age of nineteen and did not return. In New York City he registered as an apprentice machinist with a company that paid him nothing for the initial three months of training. He would, however, receive three cents per hour for the first year, and, after this, his wages would be increased incrementally by three cents per hour for each successive year until he achieved certification as a capable machinist. Offord did not continue this training.

Offord wanted to be a writer. He studied for the New York Regents examination so he could earn a high school diploma, and while holding a variety of jobs, he joined a mobile theater. He was convinced that learning to act and learning about the theater would give him the necessary knowledge to write plays. He was disappointed with the theater, for black roles were imposed on him; and some of those roles required him to be deferential.

In the late 1930s Offord studied at the New School for Social Research in New York, where he concentrated on painting, drama, and writing; and he started to write for the *Crusader News*, a paper that presented a weekly digest of news pertinent to black people. At that time he began to write fiction. In 1943 his first novel, *The White Face*, was published by McBride.

The White Face portrays the dilemma of Chris and Nella Woods, who escape from Georgia after Chris, in a fit of anger, strikes Mr. Harris, his inhumane, white employer. The Woods are convinced that New York will be better. Nella says: "We going to leave all this mess, . . . we going where we could live like we ought to live. We going where we could work when we want to, and get paid for the sweat we put out. We going where we going to be free for once. . . . We going

Carl Ruthven Offord

where we could live. Know what that mean?. . . .
We going North."

Unfortunately, the Woods find New York
no better. Leaving their two older children in
Georgia, the Woods take only their sick child,
Baby Love, to New York. They travel in a stolen
car, driven by a cousin Tommy. They arrive in
Harlem safely but to a cold and hostile welcome.
Unable to stay with their relatives, they wander
from one dingy tenement to another, trying to
conceal the death and illegal burial of their child
on an open dump lot and to evade Fascist agents
who seek to subjugate and blackmail them. Nella
finds domestic day work through a casual labor
pick-up point, a "slave-market" in the Bronx.
Chris stays undercover during daylight and listens at nights to Reeves, a Fascist soapbox
speaker, who is supported by blacks and whites.
Blinded by hate, Chris eventually is won over to
fascism by Manny, a corrupt and powerful black
Fascist.

Nella works for Jews, the Wallmans, and confides her fears about the Fascists to her employer. She too becomes an enemy in Chris
Woods's distorted perception. Instigated by
Manny to kill Nella, Chris follows her to the
Bronx, beats the lawyer son of the Wallmans,
and is thrown into prison. While he is in prison,
the state of Georgia issues a warrant for his arrest for murder when Mr. Harris dies. Chris
breaks under the pressure: "his hate piled up
into a crunching volcano." Although the Fascists

use Chris's imprisonment as a rallying point, and
Nella, with the help of some liberal whites, is
able to save him through the legal system, it is
too late. Chris, maddened by hate and oppression, grabs an officer's gun in an attempt to kill
his wife and is in turn shot dead by the police.

In part, because it dealt with the subject of
subversion in the midst of World War II, *The
White Face* was widely reviewed. Most critics considered the work important in providing insights
into the political workings of Harlem. Diana Trilling, writing in the *Nation* (June 1943), termed
the book a "sociological report on one of the less
well-known aspects of the Negro problem–the activities of Fascist agents in Harlem." Trilling
noted that "Fascist agitators" were "finding Harlem fertile territory for their anti-Semitic propaganda" and called the book "a chilling account of
something that is much more than a footnote to
the problems confronted on the home front."
J. W. Holmes, writing for *Opportunity* (Winter
1944), said that, given the harsh realities of New
York, perhaps "the black peasant would be better
off if he had stayed where he was." In the *Library
Journal* (1 May 1943) Ernestine Rose called *The
White Face* a "powerful story" and added,
"Though bitterly realistic, the inherent propaganda is incidental to narrative which is solidly
constructed, convincingly motivated, and moves
swiftly and with mounting emotional impact to
tragic crisis. In less skillful hands, this would
have been just another raw and crude recital of

Front page of an issue of Offord's newspaper, the Black American

lower class negro life. It is amazingly not so. Sincerity and idealism shine through its somber pages." Henry Lee Moon credited Offord with producing something new by attempting to depict Harlem as "an American community differing from other American communities chiefly because of the restricted opportunities afforded its people for economic security, social welfare and cultural advancement" and for showing "the warping influence of these limitations." Writing in the *New Republic* (21 May 1943), Moon recognized the complexity inherent in depicting Harlem, but he did not believe that Offord had achieved a book of enduring quality. Lisle Bell (*Weekly Book Review*, 16 May 1943) found *The White Face* a convincing novel; he concluded that Offord's "bitterness" had led to "touches of exaggeration" but that the novel was "close enough to the grim truth to leave one depressed and shaken."

Despite stereotyping and episodic development *The White Face* succeeds in portraying the destruction of trusting relationships that racism causes. For example, Cousin May, experienced in the ways of New York, instructs the newcomer Nella Woods, "You got to hand them a line all the time. That's New York. Don't do no good to let them know your business." And again, when Nella seeks domestic work, she is told, "Don't give them your right address no time. Anytime sump'n's stolen you apt to have the cops right on your neck. That's the way it is." Offord's implication seems to be that racism perverts all human relationships, personal and political, across racial lines as well as within races; until it is eradicated, no one is exempt from its destructive influence. *The White Face* was reprinted in 1975. Labeled then as protest writing, it brought his fiction to the attention of a wide audience.

In the fall of 1943 Offord entered the United States Army. Assigned to the Negro Port Company, he gained new experiences, some of which were later used in his stories. He was discharged on 19 December 1945, having achieved the rank of first sergeant. After the war Offord started several businesses–such as the House of Offord and Imperial Coffee–dealing in spices and other exotic foods, but these did not last. Throughout this period of time he devoted his efforts to writing for newspapers and to writing short stories. "Low Sky," about life in Harlem,

was included in Edwin Seaver's anthology, *Cross Section* (1944). In 1948 and again in 1949 *Masses and Mainstream* published two of his short stories set in the Caribbean.

Offord's novel, *The Naked Fear,* was published in paperback in 1954 by Ace. This work is not of the same caliber as *The White Face.* The major characters are a white couple, George and Amy Sutton, both neurotics who thrive on each other's weaknesses. George comes home one day with an infant girl, whom he says he has found by the wayside. Amy does not believe him. She despises the child because it robs her of some of George's attention. When she learns, however, that the district attorney's baby is missing and that there is a handsome reward, she immediately thinks of how she can benefit. Although their infant is not the district attorney's child, to quell suspicion the couple moves into a dilapidated black tenement house. Amy tries to kill the baby. With new knowledge of blacks gained from his dealings with Ben, a respectable janitor, George recovers from a phobia of blacks that had been caused by a brutal wartime experience. He gains enough courage to hold a job and enough strength to take the child and leave Amy. *The Naked Fear* did not receive any critical attention.

After the publication of *The Naked Fear* Offord turned his major attention to newspaper work. He founded the weekly *Black American* in New York City in 1961. He organized and directed the first Black American Film Festival in 1977. His newspaper is a major sponsor of the United Black Appeal, a fund to provide food, clothing, and medical supplies to African countries affected by famine or political upheaval. Working in cooperation with twelve other U.S. voluntary agencies, the United Black Appeal has brought relief to thousands. Offord is writing his autobiography.

References:

Robert Bone, *The Negro Novel in America,* revised edition (New Haven: Yale University Press, 1965), p. 159;

John M. Hughes, *The Negro Novelist* (New York: Citadel Press, 1953), pp. 84-87, 212-215;

Noel Schraufnagel, *From Apology to Protest* (De Land, Fla.: Everett-Edwards, 1973), pp. 33-37.

Louis Peterson
(17 June 1922-)

Steven R. Carter
University of Puerto Rico

BOOK: *Take a Giant Step* (New York: French, 1954).

PLAY PRODUCTIONS: *Take a Giant Step*, New York, Lyceum Theatre, 24 September 1953;
Entertain a Ghost, New York, Actor's Playhouse, 9 April 1962;
Crazy Horse, New York, New Federal Theatre, 8 November 1979;
Another Show, Stony Brook, N.Y., State University of New York at Stony Brook, 1983.

MOTION PICTURES: *The Tempest*, screenplay by Peterson and Alberto Lattuada, Cinecitta, 1957;
Take a Giant Step, screenplay by Peterson and Julius Epstein, United Artists, 1958.

TELEVISION: "Padlocks," *Danger*, CBS, November 1954;
"Class of '58," *Goodyear Theatre*, NBC, December 1954;
"Joey," *Goodyear Theatre*, NBC, March 1956;
"Emily Rossiter Story," *Wagon Train*, NBC, September 1957;
"Hit and Run," *Dr. Kildare*, NBC, December 1961.

Louis Peterson (courtesy of the Schomburg Center for Research in Black Culture, the New York Public Library, Astor, Lenox and Tilden Foundations)

Louis Peterson remains best known for his only published play, *Take a Giant Step* (1954), a partly autobiographical portrayal of a middle-class black youth's painful, yet often comic, passage to manhood. Though frequently acclaimed as a universal depiction of adolescence, *Take a Giant Step* emphasizes the special stresses on a black growing up in a predominantly white neighborhood. One of less than a dozen plays by blacks to be produced on Broadway prior to Lorraine Hansberry's *A Raisin in the Sun* (1959), it has made an important contribution to the development of black drama. In his introduction to *A Black Quartet* (1970), Clayton Riley, a critic strongly supportive of black revolutionary theater, pointed out that "we need not agree with what . . . such playwrights as Loften Mitchell, Louis Peterson and Lorraine Hansberry have had to say in order to recognize the rigors of those battles they fought so that we who follow them might mount other campaigns . . . with different weapons."

Louis Stamford Peterson, Jr., was born in Hartford, Connecticut, and grew up in the predominantly white south end of the city. Like the parents of the black youth in *Take a Giant Step*, Peterson's father and mother both worked in a bank. Louis Peterson, Sr., according to his son in a *New York Times* interview with Seymour Peck, "took care of the coins" that came "in packages" and served as a guard. Later, in 1931 or 1932, Ruth Conover Peterson, to help send Louis and his brother through college, began to run the

club room for the bank employees. Both of the elder Petersons insisted on the importance of a college education, apparently considering it crucial for even the small amount of advancement that American society permitted to blacks. They also made their sons take piano lessons, probably as an aid to developing middle-class refinement.

Peterson's neighborhood contained mainly immigrant families, and his early friends included Swedish, Scottish, Italian, and Irish boys. In his 1953 interview with Peck, he remembered it as "a very pleasant place to grow up in," though "there were frictions. . . . You'd be walking along the street together [with your friends] and someone might yell something at you, or 'dirty wop' at your friend. Your friends defended you and you defended them, you were a gang linked against that sort of thing. But there were never any awful, destructive incidents as today when Negroes move into white neighborhoods in some places."

In 1940, after graduating from Bulkeley High School in Hartford, Peterson followed the wishes of his parents and attended college. At Morehouse College in Atlanta, Georgia, he was initially interested in music, and he had become so accomplished at the piano that he soon gave a recital. However, he eventually majored in English, receiving the Benjamin Brawley Award for Excellence in English in 1944, the year he graduated from Morehouse with a B.A. He also participated in the theater, acting in T. S. Eliot's *Murder in the Cathedral* and other productions, and liked this so much that he went on to study stage technique at the Yale University's school of drama from 1944 to 1945. Although he was unable to study play writing during that year, he did try to write a play on his own time.

Leaving Yale, Peterson studied drama at New York University and began to work as an actor in and around New York. His first leading role was that of a talented young black musician in the 1946 Blackfriars premiere of Edwin Bronner's *A Young American*. Of this production, Loften Mitchell wrote in *Black Drama* (1967), "Beyond establishing a measure of sincerity and musical ability, neither Mr. Peterson nor the rest of the cast helped the play, and the play certainly did not help them." In 1947 Peterson received his M.A. from New York University and appeared on Broadway in the very minor role of Emanuel Price in the important black drama *Our Lan'* (1947) by Theodore Ward.

Louis Peterson (photograph by Carl Van Vechten, by permission of Joseph Solomon, the Estate of Carl Van Vechten)

Although he continued his professional studies as an actor from 1948 to 1949 with Stanford Meisner at the Neighborhood Playhouse School of the Theatre in New York, Peterson was already having doubts about making acting his career. As he told Peck, "I had always been encouraged to write by teachers but other things–music, acting–occupied me and the impulse to write was forgotten. But after school I felt I was going to have to make a living and acting was a nebulous thing at best. I decided that if I could write, I should, and for the theatre." His first two completed plays dissatisfied him, but in 1950 he managed to get accepted into a play writing class taught by Clifford Odets at the Actors Studio, where he was also taking lessons in acting from Lee Strasberg. Odets, a well-known realistic playwright, gave Peterson much personal attention, sometimes working with him outside the

classroom until six in the morning. When Peterson went on the national tour of the dramatization of Carson McCullers's *The Member of the Wedding* as Honey Camden Brown in September of 1951, he was stimulated by what he had learned from Odets to begin writing *Take a Giant Step*, which he completed in 1952. On 21 July 1952 Peterson married Margaret Mary Feury.

Peterson was able to interest a group of young producers in optioning his play for Broadway. After a successful tryout in Philadelphia, *Take a Giant Step* moved to the Lyceum Theatre in New York, where it opened on 24 September 1953. Louis Gossett, Jr., then a high school senior and basketball player, was chosen from 445 applicants to play the lead. Other members of the cast included Estelle Hemsley as the grandmother, Frederick O'Neal and Estelle Evans as the parents, Dorothy Carter as Christine, Pauline Myers as Violet, and black playwright Frank Wilson as a bartender. Louis Kronenberger selected *Take a Giant Step* as one of the best plays of the 1953-1954 season for the *Burns Mantle Yearbook*, *The Best Plays of 1953-1954*, and it has been anthologized several times. Darwin T. Turner, in the introduction to his anthology *Black Drama in America* (1971), rightly claimed that "any representative history of Afro-American authorship in the professional theater must include Louis Peterson's *Take a Giant Step*." Although all the New York critics reviewed it favorably, except for the *Daily News* critic who found it overly long, the play ran for only seventy-six performances, closing on 28 November 1953.

In his interview with Peck, Peterson stated that he felt "almost defensive" because his play was not about "the real Negro problem, such as might exist in the South today." However, he believed it essential "to show hope for the Negro in terms of what you know." Inexperienced in the more overt and violent forms of racial oppression, he knew much about the quieter, subtler forms. In *Take a Giant Step*, he treated the wounds inflicted by the racist version of Afro-American history taught in the 1950s, the overwhelming isolation of blacks living away from other blacks, and the fear that made many black parents seek to hobble proud, gifted children lest their strength provoke white fury.

At the beginning of the play, Peterson's seventeen-year-old protagonist, Spencer "Spence" Scott, is smarting from his history teacher's assertion that the slaves had to be freed by white Northerners because they were too stupid to do anything for themselves. Incensed by the pointing fingers and jeers of his white classmates, he had responded by implying that either she or the college she attended was ignorant since she had not learned "about the *up*rising of the slaves during the Civil War–or Frederick Douglass" and by walking out of the classroom. Suspended from school for two weeks and ordered to apologize when he returns, Spence runs away from home, and when he comes back he finds that his parents, Lem and May Scott, are as unsympathetic as he had feared. Lem Scott, thinking only of the damage done to his son's chances for college, even sneers at Spence for being a "genius" who "knows more than his teacher." Even though Spence's understanding of history and reality sustains him, and his father eventually supports him, the original attitudes of his teacher, classmates, and parents exact a hefty spiritual and emotional toll.

Another matter distressing Spence is that he has had only whites for friends throughout his childhood, and they are now deserting him because their girlfriends' parents do not want any black near their daughters. The sole exception is a shy Jewish boy named Iggie who has shared his enthusiasm for collecting stamps. One friend is not enough to ease his appalling loneliness, however, and he feels very bitter about his abandonment. When a former friend named Tony is sent by the others to borrow Spence's baseball equipment, he gives all of it to them, sarcastically informing Tony that he is doing this because of the great friendship they have all demonstrated. Sarcasm failing, he adds a few insults, but afterwards he regrets that he exposed so much of what he felt. He resolves this conflict by bidding Tony and the others a more diplomatic farewell at a party that his mother has arranged, announcing that he must now concentrate exclusively on his studies to prepare himself for college. He is telling them the truth about his goals, but he also feels that he is only saying goodbye to them before they would inevitably say it to him. He retains only the friendship of Iggie, who is equally an outcast and who has never let him down. But his loneliness and pain have only been accepted, not banished; the cost of his upbringing among whites is clear.

Although his parents have instilled in Spence Scott a sense of his own worth, they afford little help to him in his time of crisis. Both of them work so hard at the bank that they have failed to observe his increasing isolation and have

contributed to it by giving him little companionship especially after his elder brother Mack has left for college. Of course, they have taken these jobs to get Spence and Mack out of the neighborhood and provide them with college educations, but these material benefits have had to be paid for with dignity as well as sweat. Lem Scott can scoff at his son for refusing to tolerate racial insults at school because he swallows such insults daily at the bank to keep his job. Moreover, Lem and May Scott know that if Spence had sassed a white woman in the South as he did his history teacher, he would have been lynched, and they could not have prevented this. They place security above pride and are terrified of behavior that they consider dangerous and irresponsible. However, when Spence's grandmother, who has been his closest companion and ally, points out that he was only doing "the things that [they] made it possible for him to do," Lem embarrassedly acknowledges that his son's actions were justified, though he would still like Spence to apologize for practical reasons. May Scott remains unconvinced that he acted correctly, and later, in the strongest speech in the play, she tells Spence that he will have to do worse things than he realizes: "You'll laugh at [whites] when you could put knives right into their backs without giving it a second thought–and you'll never do what you've done and let them know they've hurt you. . . . You think it's easy for me to tell my son to crawl when I know he can walk and walk well? I'm sorry I ever had children." This speech prompts Spence to apologize for doing things that worry her, and his subsequent tactfulness in dismissing his white friends thus becomes a compromise between her advice and his refusal to humble himself before whites. The play ends with May Scott's expression of her love for her son, suggesting the crucial importance of the bond between black parents and children to their mutual survival and strength.

The play also shows Spence facing the loss of his deeply beloved grandmother, having a humorously timid and unsuccessful encounter with a prostitute named Violet, and finally receiving his sexual initiation from a teasing, caring, and lonely widow named Christine, who nurses him after his grandmother's death. Because many white critics identified with Spence's sexual experiences and labeled the play *universal*, some blacks later denounced it as the work of a "hankyhead." Countering this attack, Donald T. Evans, in an article titled "Bring It All Back Home" in

Black World, contended that for all his universality Peterson "begins with Black particulars. *Take a Giant Step* graphically demonstrates the difficulties of growing-up Black in a white world. The added responsibilities and the need to know exactly who you are and where you have to go are brilliantly handled." Though the play contains too much chitchat and simpleminded schoolboy humor that fails to advance characterization or action, it is a moving, honest, well-constructed, often genuinely comic work that has much still to say to contemporary audiences.

After *Take a Giant Step* finished its run, Peterson completed a play based on a summer job he had had on a farm in Connecticut's tobacco valley. As he told Peck, the theme of this play was "the fear the people of the farm have for their security and the way this fear makes them behave." However, he was unable to get this play produced, and he began to write for television. His first script, "Padlocks," was for the CBS series *Danger* and was produced in 1954 with James Dean in the lead. His second script, "Class of '58," was also produced in 1954 for the *Goodyear Theatre* on NBC. According to Mitchell this show "utilized a white cast, although it was obviously a sequel to the *Take a Giant Step* boy who had college difficulties." These difficulties involved getting dropped from school because of his expression of anger at the world and himself. Peterson's third television show, "Joey," appeared on the *Goodyear Theatre* in 1956 and earned him a nomination for an Emmy Award. In spite of Peterson's success, Mitchell felt that such projects diminished his "creative forces," and he argued that "Mr. Peterson symbolizes what has happened to the Negro writer in the legitimate theatre. Fame is offered to him. He is *the* Negro dramatist–whether he wants to be or not. He can appear publicly to great acclaim, but a real appreciation of his work, of its intent, and rewards for it are not often forthcoming. And so the writer wanders off to television, radio, the movies or essay writing where the rewards are greater than those offered by the theatre."

On 25 September 1956 *Take a Giant Step* began its off-Broadway revival at the Jan Hus Auditorium with black playwright Bill Gunn in the lead and Beah Richards, Godfrey Cambridge, Rosetta LeNoire, and Raymond St. Jacques in the cast. This revival, which ran for 264 performances, was seen by actor Burt Lancaster and his associates Harold Hecht and James Hill, who liked it enough to purchase the movie rights.

Gordon Draft, Peterson, and Jeff Hayden, circa 1955 (courtesy of the Schomburg Center for Research in Black Culture, the New York Public Library, Astor, Lenox and Tilden Foundations)

Peterson and Alberto Lattuada cowrote *The Tempest* (1957), a film version of Aleksandr Pushkin's *The Captain's Daughter* (1836) and Peterson coauthored the film script of *Take a Giant Step* with Julius Epstein. The film was released in 1958 with ballad singer Johnny Nash as Spence, several members of the original Broadway cast, and Ruby Dee as Christine. Two years later, Peterson wrote an episode titled "Hit and Run" for the highly popular television series, *Dr. Kildare*. Amid this success, however, his marriage was dissolved in 1961.

On 9 April 1962 Peterson's second produced play, *Entertain a Ghost*, opened off-Broadway at the Actor's Playhouse to generally unfavorable reviews, forcing it to close after eight performances. Its plot centers around an actress rehearsing a play written by her husband about their life together. This play reveals his awareness that she is intent on sacrificing him and everyone else to further her career. The husband's play contains a subplot involving a romance between a swanky white girl and a black man. Peterson himself called *Entertain a Ghost* "a complete and utter failure" in a letter to Doris Abramson dated 16 February 1966, which she excerpted in her study *Negro Playwrights in the American Theatre, 1925-1959* (1969). In that letter he discussed the heart attack he suffered in June 1963, which forced him to rest for six months, and his dissatisfaction with the television writing he had felt compelled to do "to support a rather large apartment." Moving to a smaller apartment, he had taken a job preparing magnetic tapes and operating an electronic computer for an insurance company so that he would have more time free to write for the theater. Convinced now that he was "a theater writer," he felt

that "one of the things I loathed most in the period when I was writing successfully were the times spent away from the original sources of your productivity, namely everyday, honest people."

In 1978 *Take a Giant Step* was one of five steps selected for a retrospective series of the best black plays of the 1940s and 1950s at the New Federal Theatre. On 8 November 1979, Peterson's play, *Crazy Horse*, began a limited twelve-performance run at the New Federal Theatre, the Henry Street Settlement's training and showcase unit for black and Puerto Rican playwrights. According to the 12 November 1979 *New York Times* review by Mel Gussow, "the core of the work is an interracial marriage in the 50's between a black journalist and a white woman, a relationship that is based on the author's life." Spanning many years, the play depicts the disapproval of both sets of parents to the marriage; the highly emotional conflicts between the journalist, David, and his white wife, Kate; and the gradually developing insanity of David and Kate's young daughter. The cast included Joe Morton as David, Susan Warrick as Kate, black playwright Charles Gordone as David's uncle, Bob, and Minnie Gentry as David's grandmother. Gussow found "a dated, stilted quality" about the romance between David and Kate, regarding the subplots as "more intriguing," particularly the treatment of "black home life in Connecticut" and the "theatrical minor characters" of David's "flamboyant, alcoholic" uncle and his "randy, comic matriarch" of a grandmother.

In 1972 Peterson was hired by the Department of Theatre Arts at the State University of New York at Stony Brook. A *New York Times* interview (20 February 1983) spoke of a new production, a play called *Another Show*. *Another Show*, renamed *The Totaling of Zero*, deals with a college student who commits suicide and the effect of his death upon the people who are closest to him. They feel guilty because all of them think they are responsible in one way or another for the student's demise. Peterson calls the play a comedy. *Crazy Horse* and *Another Show* indicate that Peterson still considers himself primarily a playwright and will probably continue to create realistic plays mixing humor and drama. For the public and the critics, his most significant work is indisputably his stirring, insightful, and sensitive portrayal of a black adolescent modeled on himself in *Take a Giant Step*. However, he may yet dig deeply enough into his adult experiences and insights to produce a drama that rivals or excels it.

References:

Doris E. Abramson, *Negro Playwrights in the American Theatre, 1925-1959* (New York: Columbia University Press, 1969), pp. 221-238;

Barbara Delatiner, "Playwright Eyes a New Giant Step," *New York Times*, 20 February 1983, XXI, p. 19;

Donald T. Evans, "Bring It All Back Home: Playwrights of the Fifties," *Black World*, 20 (February 1971): 41-45;

Mel Gussow, "Stage: 'Crazy Horse,' Drama by Louis Peterson, at New Federal," *New York Times*, 12 November 1979, III, p. 13;

Loften Mitchell, *Black Drama: The Story of the American Negro in the Theatre* (New York: Hawthorn Books, 1967), pp. 163-166;

Seymour Peck, "The Man Who Took a Giant Step," *New York Times*, 20 September 1953, II, p. 1;

Clayton Riley, ed., *A Black Quartet* (New York: New American Library, 1970), p. ix;

Howard Taubman, "Theatre: Peterson's Work," *New York Times*, 10 April 1962, I: 48;

Darwin T. Turner, ed., *Black Drama in America: An Anthology* (New York: Fawcett, 1971), pp. 12-13, 22.

Ann Petry

(12 October 1908-   )

Sandra Carlton Alexander
North Carolina Agricultural and Technical State University

BOOKS: *The Street* (Boston: Houghton Mifflin, 1946; London: Joseph, 1947);

Country Place (Boston: Houghton Mifflin, 1947; London: Joseph, 1948);

The Drugstore Cat (New York: Crowell, 1949);

The Narrows (Boston: Houghton Mifflin, 1953; London: Gollancz, 1954);

Harriet Tubman, Conductor on the Underground Railroad (New York: Crowell, 1955); republished as *The Girl Called Moses* (London: Methuen, 1960);

The Common Ground (New York: Crowell, 1964);

Tituba of Salem Village (New York: Crowell, 1964);

Legends of the Saints (New York: Crowell, 1970);

Miss Muriel and Other Stories (Boston: Houghton Mifflin, 1971).

OTHER: "The Novel as Social Criticism," in *The Writer's Book*, edited by Helen Hull (New York: Harper, 1950), pp. 32-39;

"A Purely Black Stone" and "A Real Boss Black Cat," in *A View from the Top of the Mountain: Poems after Sixty*, edited by Tom Koontz and Thom Tammaro (Daleville, Ind.: Barnwood Press, 1981), pp. 75-76;

"Ann Petry on Langston Hughes' 'Sweet Flypaper of Life,'" in *Rediscoveries II*, edited by David Madden and Peggy Bach (New York: Carroll & Graf, 1988), pp. 203-207.

PERIODICAL PUBLICATIONS: "Harlem," *Holiday*, 5 (April 1949): 110-116, 163-166, 168;

"The Common Ground," *Horn Book*, 41 (April 1965): 147-151.

In many respects Ann Petry is a study in contrast. She came from a tiny town in New England to Harlem in 1938. She spent some years in Harlem learning of its people and transmitting their yearnings, feelings, and fears to the printed page. Her experiences in the inner city educated her to the economic hardships of the poor, deepened her sensitivity to the plight of millions of less fortunate black Americans, and made her

Ann Petry (photograph by Carl Van Vechten)

painfully aware of the degree to which bigotry can erode the personal lives of its victims. Petry is a product of New England, steeped in its values of hard work, independence, and fair play. Her dual personal history has given her an unusual literary vantage point from which she has been able to isolate and dramatize essential aspects of the human condition that transcend geographical and racial boundaries. While changing directions in literary taste in later decades have undercut the popular acclaim that she enjoyed in

140

the 1940s and 1950s, her works retain vitality for discriminating readers.

Ann Lane was born in Old Saybrook, Connecticut, to Peter C. Lane and Bertha James Lane on 12 October 1908. She was the youngest of three children, the oldest child having died at age two. The Lanes lived a rather comfortable and stable life. The family, early on, had established a tradition in the sciences, with specific concentration in chemistry, that was to extend for three generations. Her father, a native of New Germantown, New Jersey, was a pharmacist who had been apprenticed to a druggist and licensed in 1890. He owned a drugstore in Old Saybrook. Her aunt and uncle were also druggists, owning a drugstore in the neighboring town of Old Lyme, Connecticut. Equally accomplished in her own right, her mother, a native of Hartford, Connecticut, graduated from the New York School of Chiropody and was licensed to practice her profession in 1915. The Lanes were one of two black families in the small New England town, a fact which helped to shape Ann's perspective and provided her with raw materials for later stories and novels.

In 1925 Ann Lane, the only person of Afro-American descent in her class, graduated from Old Saybrook High School. She found that her classes at the Connecticut College of Pharmacy (now the University of Connecticut School of Pharmacy) had a similar racial composition. She graduated from this institution with a Ph.G. degree in 1931. For the next seven years Ann worked as a pharmacist in the family-owned drugstore.

In 1938 Ann Lane made some crucial decisions. On 22 February 1938 she married George D. Petry in Old Saybrook, and jointly they decided to sever ties with her native town. She resolved to go to New York, learn to write, and become good at it. In New York the need to earn money and an inclination toward writing led her to newspaper work. A job as a newspaper reporter for the *People's Voice*, a Harlem weekly, plunged her into the streets of Harlem. James W. Ivy of *Crisis* magazine wrote that in her years as a journalist Ann Petry "acquired an intimate and disturbing knowledge of Harlem, and its ancient evil, housing; its tragic, broken families; its high death rate." Marjorie Greene of *Opportunity* magazine wrote of those years that "she covered everything from teas to fires, with births, deaths, big shots, and picket lines interspersed. She wrote straight news stories, the more expansive dra-

matic feature; she edited and did rewrites and even ventured into the advertising end."

Not content with the writing experience provided by her stint with the *People's Voice*, Petry enrolled in creative writing courses at Columbia University in the evenings to learn about fictional technique, effective dialogue, and dramatic structure. A tireless, disciplined, and single-minded worker, Petry spent hours polishing her craft, writing and rewriting her stories. She deliberately set out to understand the anxieties and frustrations that stimulated abnormal behavior in the human species, reading voraciously in the fields of psychology and psychiatry. She taught in a Harlem experimental school, which gave her an opportunity to observe firsthand the degree to which ghetto existence affected the lives of black children. In those years Petry taught salesmanship, became a member of what is now the American Negro Theater, and became affiliated with Negro Women Incorporated, a political group, eventually becoming its executive secretary.

In the midst of a career and an active civic life, Petry was not prepared for the editorial rejections that came her way. In response she made up her mind to focus exclusively on her writing. "I decided," she said, "that I would work for nobody, and at nothing else–that I would spend every single minute of my day just writing. It wasn't an easy decision exactly. It meant that I had to live on my husband's allotment check–the only income I had."

In 1943 *Crisis* published her short story "On Saturday the Siren Sounds at Noon," which is set in the middle of New York's Harlem. Told in flashbacks through the consciousness of a nameless black father whose memory is triggered by the weekly Saturday noon air raid siren, the story depicts his returning home one day to find that a tragic fire has claimed the lives of all his children. He blames their deaths on the willful neglect of his good-time wife, Lilly Belle, whom he learns had left the youngsters alone to be with her boyfriend, and murders her. He throws himself into the path of an oncoming train.

The story is representative of Petry's early work in that it is based in part on true incidents. When asked by a *Crisis* writer how she came to write the story, Petry replied, "One Saturday I was standing on the 125th Street platform of the IRT subway when a siren suddenly went off. The screaming blast seemed to vibrate inside people. For the siren seemed to be just above the station. I immediately noticed the reactions of the people

on the platform. They were interesting, especially the frantic knitting of a woman seated on a nearby bench. . . . I began wondering how this unearthly howl would affect a criminal, a man hunted by the police. That was the first incident. The second was a tragedy I covered for my paper. There was a fire in Harlem in which two children had been burnt to death. Their parents were at work and the children were alone. I imagined their reactions when they returned home that night. I knew also that many Harlem parents, like Lilly Belle in the story, often left their children home alone while at work. Imaginatively combined the two incidents gave me my story."

When juxtaposed with "On Saturday the Siren Sounds at Noon," Petry's story "Doby's Gone" (*Phylon*, 1944) establishes the contrast between the metropolis and the small town that is a major theme in her writing. Set in small towns in upstate New York and Connecticut, "Doby's Gone" is based on the author's own experiences of growing up black in a predominantly white New England community. The central character, a young black girl named Sue Johnson, invents an imaginary friend and playmate, Doby, to fill her lonely hours and to compensate for her lack of companionship. The story centers around Sue's experiences on her first day of school and focuses on the ostracism she suffers because of her color. Being called a "nigger girl" spurs her to fight back, and for the first time, Doby disappears. Following the fight Sue is befriended by Daisy Bell, a white girl who had previously shunned her. Sue Johnson's initiation into adulthood is confirmed by her understated summary of that day's turbulent events: "Mama, Doby's gone." In renouncing the childhood fears that gave rise to Doby and by confronting racial bigotry head-on, she reaches maturity.

In 1945 Petry produced one of her best-known short stories for *Crisis* magazine, "Like a Winding Sheet." Set in Harlem, it chronicles a day in the life of Johnson, a black factory worker. At the beginning of the story she describes Johnson, who is lying in bed entwined in a sheet, as a "huckleberry" wrapped in a winding sheet (a white garment traditionally used as a burial garment). Petry's imaginatively introduces and foreshadow's the problem of black and white conflict and creates an air of foreboding that pervades the story. Throughout Johnson's difficult day he endures racial slurs and discrimination from white women, both on the job and off. Being denied a cup of coffee in a local restaurant cuts John-

son as deeply as his female boss's pejorative epithet, "niggers." It is more tragic than surprising, then, that Johnson, having been characterized as a man of integrity who "could never hit a woman," returns home at the end of a frustrating day to batter and destroy the one person he loves most, his wife, Mae. Petry's suggestion is that even the strongest crumble under the corrosive effects of racial oppression.

"Like a Winding Sheet" drew Petry national acclaim, winning her a place in Martha Foley's *Best American Stories of 1946*. Its publication kindled the interest of major book publishers. Within months after it appeared she had written the first five chapters and a synopsis of her first novel, *The Street* (1946), which had won a Houghton Mifflin Literary Fellowship Award of twenty-four hundred dollars in 1945.

After ten months of writing in near seclusion, Petry's first novel appeared in January of 1946. *The Street* tells the story of Lutie Johnson, an intelligent, industrious, and attractive young black woman who struggles to survive and maintain her dignity in a brutal environment. The action moves the main character from Long Island to Connecticut, via flashback, and then to Harlem in search of a better way of life for her and her son. The ambitious Lutie hires herself out through the mail as a maid to the wealthy Chandlers of Connecticut, leaving her son in Long Island in the care of her husband, Jim.

Lutie Johnson's unhappy experiences in the Chandler household mark the beginning of her increasing disillusionment with the American dream and foreshadow the violence and brutality that will obstruct her progress as she pursues it. Mr. Chandler drinks incessantly, and Mrs. Chandler is involved in an adulterous affair with a family friend. Complications increase when Mrs. Chandler's aristocratic friends hint that the pretty Lutie may make sexual advances to Mr. Chandler, though Lutie is repulsed by the idea.

Lutie's deteriorating relationship with her own husband adds further complication. Returning to Long Island at her father's urging, she is shocked to discover that Jim has brought another woman into her home and is supporting her on the money that Lutie has earned. Severing ties with both her husband and her employers, Lutie moves to Harlem. This background sets the stage for the narrative and explains the main character's presence on the ghetto street at the beginning of chapter 1.

Lutie's experiences in the inner city provoke emotions within her that range from humiliation and degradation to fright and terror. Her attempts to secure honest labor, whether through taking night classes to qualify for civil service employment or practicing to become a nightclub singer, all come to naught. Her attractive physical features are a liability in Harlem, where violence and sex prove easy partners. Rejecting on principle a neighbor's proposal to help her earn her living through prostitution, Lutie finds herself in danger from Jones, the building superintendent. A sexual degenerate who pursues Lutie with unbridled passion, he becomes madly enraged by her continued rejection and works to destroy her son, Bub, by introducing him to a life of crime. Lutie likewise counters the advances of Junto, a powerful white Harlem businessman, and is forced to kill his flunky, Boots Smith, to ward off a brutal sexual assault. At the conclusion of the story Petry indicates that Bub will probably be sent to reform school, and Lutie, on a train for Chicago, rationalizes abandoning her son and expresses a vague hope of salvaging the pieces of her life.

From the outset Petry's presentation in the novel is metaphorical. The story begins in the midst of a violent windstorm that alternately sucks, blows, stifles, blinds, and brutalizes Lutie as she makes her way through the filthy, paper-strewn street. The windblown street suggests the uncertainty that characterizes life in the urban inner city. Ultimately, it comes to symbolize the destructive, deterministic societal forces against which heroic figures like Lutie battle in vain for a dignified existence. Recalling Theodore Dreiser's *An American Tragedy* (1925), the novel ends in a condemnation of Lutie Johnson's environment: "The street will get them sooner or later, for it sucked the humanity out of people, slowly, inevitably."

When *The Street* first appeared, it won generally favorable reactions and drew commendable reviews. Writing in *Phylon* (March-June 1947), Alain Locke deemed it "the artistic success of the year. . . ." Alfred Butterfield, *New York Times Book Review* critic, noted that the novel was "a work of close documentation and intimate perception." Praising Petry for her artistry, he wrote, "It deals with its Negro characters without condescension, without special pleading, without distortion of any kind. . . . " Arna Bontemps, writing in the *New York Herald Tribune Weekly Book Review*, praised Petry for her "unblushing" realism and

noted that it was "part of her achievement, however, that the carnal life of the slums never seems to be hauled in for its own sake."

The general consensus seemed to be that *The Street* was, in the words of Henry Tracy (*Common Ground*, Summer 1946), "an outstanding novel from any angle." Even those who had begun to sour on social criticism acknowledged that Petry had breathed new life into the naturalistic novel. Noting the absence of sociological and political propaganda, and commending Petry for control and restraint, David Dempsey of the *Antioch Review* (September 1946) wrote: "Petry underscores her meaning with action rather than editorials and avoids the sentimentalization of character which one finds in such a 'protest' writer as Steinbeck."

Petry's early work is strongly naturalistic. Its focus is on racism as an environmental force adversely affecting human lives so that its victims can neither understand nor control the devastating effects upon them and those they love. Like Dreiser, Jack London, Stephen Crane, and Frank Norris, she trained in journalism, and characteristic of her work from this period is a detailed documentary style. Her short stories and *The Street* parallel the work during the 1940s of Richard Wright, Chester Himes, William Attaway, and Willard Motley, Afro-American naturalists.

Petry's second novel, *Country Place* (1947), derives much of its surface uniqueness from the fact that it is essentially raceless. The major characters are white, and many of the minor ones are of varying nationalities and ethnic origins. At its narrative core *Country Place* tells the story of two sets of characters in the quiet country town of Lennox, Connecticut. The narrative begins with Doc, the druggist, through whose eyes the action of the story is filtered; he introduces the town and its inhabitants. The center of dramatic interest is Johnnie Roane, a World War II veteran, who returns to his hometown to be reunited with his beautiful wife, Glory. Johnnie's anticipated reunion with his wife is spoiled at the outset, however, by the gossip and sordid suggestions of Weasel, the town cab driver, a Dickensian character who knows all the secrets of the townspeople and delights in promulgating personal scandal. At first Johnnie dismisses Weasel's implication that Glory has become sexually involved with Ed Barrell, even though she is noticeably cold and unresponsive to him upon his return. Mrs. Gramby, the town's pillar of aristocratic respectability, is the focus of a second set of characters. Mearns,

Petry autographing copies of her 1947 novel (courtesy of the Schomburg Center for Research in Black Culture, the New York Public Library, Astor, Lenox and Tilden Foundations)

her weak, indecisive son, lacks both motivation and direction. Lillian, his cheap, vulgar wife, is preoccupied with staving off approaching middle age and with the acquisition of wealth.

The tension of the story builds when Weasel arranges to drive Johnnie's mother and Mrs. Gramby past a rendezvous point where Glory and Ed are discovered making love. Further propelling the action, Weasel informs Johnnie that Glory and Ed have plans to meet at Ed's cabin in the woods. Stalking the lovers in a violent storm, Johnnie arrives at the cabin to find Glory nearly nude. Following a fight and an argument in which Glory reveals her true antipathy for her husband, Johnnie leaves for New York.

In the meantime the separate plot lines begin to entwine. Weasel discovers a letter in Ed's wallet that suggests his involvement with Lillian; he presents it to Mrs. Gramby and she promptly revises her will. Lillian, in desperation, makes a

thwarted attempt on Mrs. Gramby's life. While posting her will at the local courthouse, Mrs. Gramby, accompanied by Ed Barrell, makes a misstep, and both plunge down the steps to their deaths. When the will is read, Lillian finds that she has been disinherited, and Mearns gains the strength of character to dissolve the marriage. The story ends on a note of despair, with most of the major characters either dead or spiritually lifeless. Only Johnnie Roane, who has severed ties with the dead past and gone to New York to pursue a career in art, has managed to transform his loss into a source of hope for a better tomorrow.

Country Place is a story of the inevitability of change and of the tragic disillusionment that those who refuse to adjust to it must suffer. The novel has many distinctive features, notable among which are the technical devices the author uses to heighten the human drama: the point of

view that shifts and rotates among the major characters adds immediacy to the story, enabling the reader to see the town in its totality. Petry shows great skill in the selection of the two narrators. Doc, the stationary philosopher-narrator, like the leader in a Greek chorus, records and reflects on the action of the story, while Weasel, the roving gossip, not only spreads the news but becomes a catalytic agent, introducing complication and moving the story forward. Yet, the author's greatest technical feat may well be her presentation of the steadily intensifying rainstorm that parallels in exact proportions the human drama as it unfolds and heightens to a shattering climax at Ed Barrell's cabin hideaway.

Country Place, a selection of the British Book Club, enjoyed a warm reception from reviewers. *Herald Tribune Book Review* critic Rose Feld wrote (5 October 1947): "There is much that is exceedingly good in Petry's book, the feel of the small town, the integrity of the dialogue, the portrayal of Johnnie, of Glory, of Mrs. Gramby." *Atlantic Monthly* reviewer John Caswell Smith, Jr. (November 1947) saw a definite growth in the author. "Ann Petry's writing in the second novel," he stated, "shows much of the improvement one was led to anticipate on reading her first. . . . *Country Place* is a good story, worthy of the telling." Offering a less positive response to the novel, Bradford Smith of the *Saturday Review of Literature* (18 October 1947) saw its design as "a rather too skillful contriving," possessing the "quality of artificiality."

Respect for Petry's achievement in *Country Place* has increased rather than diminished. In 1953 Carl Milton Hughes described it as "a performance that exhibits a high level of competence in fictional writing" and called the work Petry's "assertion of freedom as a creative artist." Eleven years after the publication of the novel, Robert Bone termed *Country Place* a "distinguished achievement" and rated it one of the eight "major" and "superior" novels ever written by a black American.

Country Place was followed by a series of separately published stories. Two of the stronger stories, "The Necessary Knocking at the Door" ('47, 1947) and "The Bones of Louella Brown" (*Opportunity*, 1947), though radically different in tone, illustrate Petry's technical proficiency at its best. The first is the story of Ann Knight, a product of the urban-black middle class, who meets blatant racism head-on at a church conference in the form of Mrs. Gib Taylor, a conservative Missis-

sippi aristocrat steeped in the plantation tradition. Mrs. Taylor refuses to sit beside Ann in the conference dining hall, declaring that she had "never eaten with a nigger." Paralyzed by the fear of further degradation, Ann is unable to bring herself to help Mrs. Taylor, who becomes increasingly ill during the night in the room next to her own. The story ends with the maid's ironic statement: "If anybody'd known about her havin' a heart attack, they could a saved her." "The Bones of Louella Brown" is a rare display of Petry wit and humor. A satire of New England snobbery and intolerance, the story chronicles the zany attempts of two undertakers, Peabody and Wiffle, to distinguish between the remains of the Countess Elizabeth Bedford from those of Louella Brown, the Bedford family laundress.

One of Petry's favorite stories is "In Darkness and Confusion," a novella based on the Harlem riots of August 1943. "In Darkness and Confusion" is similar to "Like a Winding Sheet" in its structural outline. The story deals with an affectionate couple, William Jones and his wife, Pink, and the frustrations they feel after losing two children–a son to the bullet of a southern military policeman and a stepdaughter to the shallow glamour of the ghetto subculture. Their pent-up emotions erupt in the chaos of a violent street riot.

Petry returned to Old Saybrook in 1948. In 1949 for *Holiday* magazine she produced a long nostalgic essay entitled "Harlem," which reviewed in pictorial and historical form the world's most famous black community. That was followed by publication of her first children's book, *The Drugstore Cat* (1949). A delightful story for youngsters six to ten years of age, this piece marks the author's first departure from adult writing. Set in an environment Petry knew well, it focuses on Buzzie, the country cat who comes to live with the town druggist and emerges as a hero when he saves the store from robbers. *The Drugstore Cat* is alive with sound and visual imagery.

Another product of this reflective period was Petry's 1950 critical essay, "The Novel as Social Criticism," an eloquent defense of the problem or thesis novel, which she learned was regarded as "a special and quite deplorable creation of American writers of the twentieth century" long after having published *The Street*, her own novel of social criticism. In her essay Petry eschews the idea that art ought to exist for its own sake and asserts that most of the world's greatest novelists, from Charles Dickens to Leo Tolstoy to

William Faulkner, have written social criticism, for each suggests "how society affected the lives of his characters." Petry demonstrates some critical depth when she acknowledges that the problem novel is likely to have its shortcomings in the hands of a novice; for example, an evil society can be made to assume the "burden of responsibility" for actions ordinarily assigned to individual characters. Ending on a very personal note about her own formal preparation for the writing profession, Petry appears to have written the essay to soothe wounds of the past rather than with an eye toward the future.

In 1953 Petry's *The Narrows* was published. It is set in the black section of a small Connecticut community. The plot centers around black Link Williams and his relationship with Camilo Treadway, daughter of the town's most revered white family and heiress to an industrial fortune. The reader is told through endless flashbacks that young Link has been reared variously by the upright Miss Abbie Crunch, her entrepreneur friend F. K. Jackson, and Bill Hod, a local pub owner of the archetypal trickster variety who has sordid underworld connections. Link's innate intelligence apparently accounts for the academic success he enjoys as a star athlete and Phi Beta Kappa graduate of Dartmouth, but it is his weak, indecisive character, perhaps attributable to his unstable upbringing, that draws him back to Monmouth, Connecticut, where he takes a job tending bar for Hod. Shortly after his return he falls hopelessly in love with Camilo and only later discovers her real marital status and identity. At the close of the novel Link suffers for his indiscretions when he is killed by Camilo's husband and the family matriarch. There is much to be admired in *The Narrows*, especially its characterization and stylistic experimentation. Petry creates a number of minor characters, such as Weak Knees, Cat Jimmy, and Bug Eyes, that are uniquely memorable.

Generally unhappy with the lack of black nonfiction for juveniles, Petry wrote *Harriet Tubman, Conductor on the Underground Railroad* (1955). Dedicated to Petry's only child, Elisabeth Ann, *Harriet Tubman* is a moving and sensitive portrayal of the famous former slave and abolitionist who was personally responsible for delivering over three hundred slaves out of bondage in Dorchester County, Maryland. Petry's characterization of Tubman is made real by her sympathetic presentation of the fears and internal struggles that the underground railroad conduc-

tor must have suffered in her precarious, self-imposed occupation. The book has a wealth of historic detail, and its informational value is increased by the clever manner with which Petry juxtaposes Tubman's private history with the public history of the nation during the years before the Civil War.

Petry's last two children's books were *Tituba of Salem Village* (1964) and *Legends of the Saints* (1970). *Tituba of Salem Village* tells the story of a female slave from Barbados who finds herself branded a witch and caught up in the hysteria of the Salem witch trials of the late 1600s. Made vulnerable by her color, her servile condition, and her innocence, Tituba is accused and attacked by those with far less intelligence, perception, and talent. The book moves readers with poignancy and irony to the shocking disbelief with which Americans have had to view that tragic chapter in the nation's history. *Legends of the Saints*, illustrated by Ann Rockwell, presents in simple language the miraculous lives of ten holy people of varying nationalities and time periods.

Petry has produced some excellent short stories since 1953. "Has Anybody Seen Miss Dora Dean," published by *New Yorker* magazine in 1958, is a refreshing blend of humor, folklore, and suspense. Told in flashback, it depicts the unexpected suicide of Forbes, a gentlemen's butler, and the transforming effect of his death on his frivolous and flirtatious wife, Sarah. One thinly disguised autobiographical story, "The New Mirror," which appeared in the *New Yorker* in 1965, and another, "Miss Muriel," the lengthy piece that became the title story of *Miss Muriel and Other Stories* (1971), show evidence of a new thematic thrust. "The New Mirror" tells the story of a black family in an all-white town and their attempts to maintain privacy in an environment where color keeps them constantly on display. "Miss Muriel," told from the perspective of a young black girl, is a romantic story with racial overtones. It depicts the pursuit of an attractive aunt by two lovers of different ethnic origins. Both stories make a powerful comment about the barriers that prevent meaningful human relationships in modern society.

Perhaps the finest story to make its first appearance in *Miss Muriel and Other Stories* is "The Witness." Conceived in the symbolic tradition of fellow New England writers Nathaniel Hawthorne and Herman Melville, it tells the haunting story of a high-school teacher's discovery of the terrifying evil that lies within the human breast.

There can be little doubt that Ann Petry's fiction will continue to secure her a position as one of the most distinguished Afro-American writers of the twentieth century. Her greatest technical achievements lie in her power of characterization and her control of narrative flow and detail, whether depicting the plight of the tenement dweller or exposing the narrowness of the New England sensibility. Geography, however, remains the single determining factor in her career.

References:

George R. Adams, "Riot as Ritual: Ann Petry's 'In Darkness and Confusion,'" *Negro American Literature Forum*, 6 (Summer 1972): 54-57, 60;

Robert Bone, *The Negro Novel in America*, revised edition (New Haven: Yale University Press, 1965), pp. 157, 180-185;

Marjorie Greene, "Ann Petry Planned to Write," *Opportunity*, 24 (April-June 1946): 78-79;

Carl Milton Hughes, *The Negro Novelist 1940-1950* (New York: Citadel Press, 1953), pp. 160-163;

James W. Ivy, "Ann Petry Talks About First Novel," *Crisis*, 53 (January 1946): 48-49;

David Littlejohn, *Black on White* (New York: Grossman, 1966), pp. 154-156;

Clara O. Jackson, *Twentieth Century Children's Writers* (New York: St. Martin's, 1978), pp. 993-994;

Joyce Ann Joyce, "Ann Petry," *Nethula*, 2 (1982);

Margaret B. McDowell, "The Narrows, A Fuller View of Ann Petry," *Black American Literature Forum*, 14 (Winter 1980): 135-141;

John O'Brien, *Interviews with Black Writers* (New York: Liveright, 1973), pp. 153-163;

Sybil Weir, "The Narrows, a Black New England Novel," *Studies in American Fiction*, 15 (Spring 1987): 81-93.

Papers:

The largest collection of Petry's papers is at the Mugar Memorial Library at Boston University in Boston, Massachusetts.

J. Saunders Redding

(13 October 1906-2 March 1988)

Thelma Barnaby Thompson
University of the District of Columbia

See also the Redding entry in *DLB 63: Modern American Critics, 1920-1955.*

BOOKS: *To Make a Poet Black* (Chapel Hill: University of North Carolina Press, 1939);

No Day of Triumph (New York & London: Harper, 1942);

Stranger and Alone: A Novel (New York: Harcourt, Brace, 1950);

They Came in Chains: Americans From Africa (Philadelphia: Lippincott, 1950; revised, 1973);

On Being Negro in America (Indianapolis: Bobbs-Merrill, 1951);

An American in India: A Personal Report on the Indian Dilemma and the Nature of Her Conflicts (Indianapolis: Bobbs-Merrill, 1954);

The Lonesome Road: The Story of the Negro's Part in America (New York: Doubleday, 1958);

The Negro (Washington, D.C.: Potomac Books, 1967).

OTHER: *Reading for Writing,* edited by Redding and Ivan E. Taylor (New York: Ronald Press, 1952);

"The Negro Writer and His Relationship to His Roots," in *The American Negro Writer and His Roots* (New York: American Society of African Culture, 1960), pp. 1-8;

"The Alien Land of Richard Wright," in *Soon, One Morning: New Writing by American Negroes 1940-1962,* edited by Herbert Hill (New York: Knopf, 1963), pp. 48-59;

"The Negro Writer and American Literature," by Redding, and "Reflections on Richard Wright: A Symposium on an Exiled Native Son," by Redding, Herbert Hill, Horace Cayton, and Arna Bontemps, in *Anger, and Beyond: The Negro Writer in the United States,* edited by Hill (New York: Harper & Row, 1966), pp. 1-19, 196-212;

"Ends and Means in the Struggle for Equality," in *Prejudice U.S.A.,* edited by Charles Y. Glock and Ellen Siegelman (New York: Praeger, 1969), pp. 3-16;

J. Saunders Redding (courtesy of the Schomburg Center for Research in Black Culture, the New York Public Library, Astor, Lenox and Tilden Foundations)

" 'The Souls of Black Folk': Du Bois' masterpiece lives on," in *Black Titan: W. E. B. Du Bois, An Anthology by the Editors of Freedomways,* edited by John Henrik Clarke, Esther Jackson, Ernest Kaiser, and J. H. O'Dell (Boston: Beacon Press, 1970), pp. 47-51;

Cavalcade: Negro American Writing from 1760 to the Present, edited by Redding and Arthur P. Davis (Boston: Houghton Mifflin, 1971);

Langston Hughes, *Good Morning Revolution,* edited by Faith Berry, foreword by Redding (New York: Hill, 1973);

Dust jacket for Redding's 1954 account of his journey to India

"Portrait Against Background," in *A Singer In the Dawn: Reinterpretations of Paul Laurence Dunbar*, edited by Jay Martin (New York: Dodd, Mead, 1975), pp. 39-44.

PERIODICAL PUBLICATIONS: "Playing the Numbers," *North American Review*, 238 (December 1934): 533-542;

"A Negro Looks at This War," *American Mercury*, 55 (November 1942): 585-592;

"A Negro Speaks for His People," *Atlantic Monthly*, 171 (March 1943): 58-63;

"The Black Man's Burden," *Antioch Review*, 3 (December 1943): 587-595;

" 'Here's a New Thing Altogether,' " *Survey Graphic*, 33 (August 1944): 358-359, 366-367;

"The Negro Author: His Publisher, His Public, and His Purse," *Publishers' Weekly*, 147 (24 March 1945): 1284-1288;

"Portrait: W. E. Burghardt Du Bois," *American Scholar*, 18 (January 1949): 93-96;

"American Negro Literature," *American Scholar*, 18 (April 1949): 137-148;

"The Negro Writer-Shadow and Substance," *Phylon*, 11 (Fourth Quarter 1950): 371-373;

"Report from India," *American Scholar*, 22 (Autumn 1953): 441-449;

"No Envy, No Handicap," *Saturday Review*, 37 (13 February 1954): 23, 40;

"Up from Reconstruction," *Nation*, 179 (4 September 1954): 196-197;

"Tonight for Freedom," *American Heritage*, 9 (June 1958): 52-55, 90;

"Contradiction de la litterature negro-americaine," *Presence Africaine*, nos. 27-28 (August-November 1959): 11-15;

"Negro Writing in America," *New Leader*, 43 (16 May 1960): 8-10;

"In the Vanguard of Civil Rights," *Saturday Review*, 44 (12 August 1961): 34;

"J. S. Redding Talks About African Literature," *AMSAC Newsletter*, 5 (September 1962): 1, 4-6;

"Home to Africa," *American Scholar*, 32 (Spring 1963): 183-191;

"Sound of Their Masters' Voices," *Saturday Review*, 46 (29 June 1963): 26;

"Modern African Literature," *CLA Journal*, 7 (March 1964): 191-201;

"Man Against Myth and Malice," *Saturday Review*, 47 (9 May 1964): 48-49;

"The Problems of the Negro Writer," *Massachusetts Review*, 6 (Autumn-Winter 1964-1965): 57-70;

"The Task of the Negro Writer As Artist: A Symposium," *Negro Digest*, 14 (April 1965): 66, 74;

"Since Richard Wright," *African Forum*, 1 (Spring 1966): 21-31;

"A Survey: Black Writers' Views on Literary Lions and Values," *Negro Digest*, 17 (January 1968): 12;

"Equality and Excellence: The Eternal Dilemma," *William and Mary Review*, 6 (Spring 1968): 5-11;

"Literature and the Negro," *Contemporary Literature*, 9 (Winter 1968): 130-135;

"The Black Youth Movement," *American Scholar*, 38 (Autumn 1969): 584-587;

"The Negro Writer: The Road Where," *Boston University Journal*, 17 (Winter 1969): 6-10;

"The Black Revolution in American Studies," *American Studies*, 9 (Autumn 1970): 3-9.

As Richard Wright implies in his introduction to J. Saunders Redding's *No Day of Triumph* (1942), it is clear that his middle-class background, instead of isolating him from other blacks, provided Redding with a valuable perspective to understand, observe, chronicle, investigate, and criticize the workings of American society and, primarily, the place of the Negro in America. Redding, a prolific writer with a long and fruitful career, defies identification with any particular period; he lived through the Depression, the Harlem Renaissance, the black revolution of the 1960s and 1970s, and two world wars. He wrote boldly and objectively about the difficult and controversial issues of race relations and racial problems at a time when it was unpopular to do so. A scholar, teacher, novelist, historian, and critic, Redding achieved credibility by never

attempting to be a spokesman for his race. Yet, by speaking honestly for himself he won that place.

Born in Wilmington, Delaware, on 13 October 1906 to Lewis Alfred and Mary Ann Holmes Redding, Jay Saunders Redding was the third of seven children, two of whom died in infancy. His parents, both graduates of Howard University, provided for their children a comfortable home. Both his grandmothers were influential to him. His paternal grandmother bore permanent physical and psychological scars from slavery. Severe and uncommunicative because of her experiences, she related tales of personal suffering and cruelty to her grandchildren to inspire strength. His maternal grandmother, Holmes-Conway, a mulatto, born and reared free and sheltered from hardships, was excessively religious and also excessively conscious of her light skin.

Though a graduate of Howard University, Redding's father earned only twenty-five dollars a month as a schoolteacher in rural Maryland. During the summer he waited tables at the United States Hotel in Boston. He moved to Wilmington, Delaware, in 1898. In Wilmington he was president of the local branch of the NAACP and a Sunday school superintendent, posts he held for many years. Redding remembers that his father, who worked for the postal service, "was driven by more than the necessity to provide a living for his family."

Redding graduated from high school in 1923, entering Lincoln University in Pennsylvania with no career goal in mind. At Lincoln Redding secured a key to the library, where he spent much of his free time reading the novels of the English Victorians, the increasingly popular American realists, and Negro sociohistorical studies. After one year at Lincoln he transferred to Brown University, where his brother, Louis, had graduated the year before.

Redding was intellectually challenged at Brown, where he wrote for the campus magazine. When he graduated in 1928 he was appointed to teach at Morehouse College in Atlanta, where, in 1929, he was married to Esther Elizabeth James. Three years later he was fired because, as he said in *No Day of Triumph*, he was looked upon by the faculty as a "pariah who would destroy their societal bond, their asylum." Redding returned to Brown University for graduate study, receiving an M.A. in 1932. In 1933 he studied at Columbia as a graduate fellow and went on to fill a substitute lectureship in Louis-

ville, Kentucky, at Louisville Municipal College in 1934. Shortly thereafter in 1935 his first son, Conway Holmes Redding, was born. In 1936 he accepted the chairmanship of the English Department at Southern University in Baton Rouge, Louisiana. It was at Southern that he began to write his first book, *To Make a Poet Black* (1939).

To Make a Poet Black is one of the earliest critical works on Afro-American literature. The historical period covered is from colonial times through the early 1930s. In his preface Redding says that "literary expression for the Negro has not been and is not wholly an art" because this literature has been written for a purpose or out of necessity. For him most Negro writers lose critical distance in their desire to adjust to American life and write for blacks as well as whites.

In "The Forerunners," the first chapter of *To Make a Poet Black,* Redding addresses the work of Jupiter Hammon, Phillis Wheatley, and George Moses Horton. Like the other chapters this one opens with an overview of historical developments and examines the effects of these developments on black life and thought. For Redding, Hammon was not a good poet. His "life was motivated by the compulsion of obedience to his earthly and his heavenly master." Wheatley, a much better poet, is faulted for lacking "enthusiasm" and for failing to protest slavery. Redding considered Horton to be a very good poet who, at least, protested his own enslavement.

The second chapter, "Let Freedom Ring," looks at writers of the mid nineteenth century. Though poet Frances Ellen Watkins Harper was "a trailblazer, hacking, however ineffectually, at the dense forest of propaganda," most writers of the time "often sacrificed beauty of thought and of truth–the specific goals of art–to the exigencies of their particular purposes." In spite of their failures of art, Redding credits writers such as Charles Redmond, Frederick Douglass, James Madison Bell, and William Wells Brown with creating "in the Negro a core of racial pride without which no great endeavor is possible."

"Adjustment," the third chapter, considers writers from the turn of the century such as James E. Campbell, Paul Laurence Dunbar, Charles W. Chesnutt, W. E. B. Du Bois, Fenton Johnson, and William Stanley Brathwaite. The major focus in this chapter is on Dunbar, of whom Redding says, "No Negro of finer artistic spirit has been born in America." Chesnutt's *Conjure Woman* (1899) "proved that the Negro could be made the subject of serious esthetic treatment

without the interference of propaganda." The early Du Bois is credited with announcing in a clear and lucid style that blacks could be "a potential force in the organization of society," although in his later work he became "an avowed propagandist."

Redding finds much to condemn, but finally, much to praise in his analysis of the Harlem Renaissance, "Emergence of the New Negro." He is bothered by the exclusive attention to urban life and a focus on escapism or futility to the exclusion of art. The writings of Jessie Redmon Fauset and Countee Cullen are criticized as detached from reality, and even Langston Hughes's experiments with blues and shout are expressions of feeling rather than of thought. Claude McKay is praised for works such as "If We Must Die" and "To the White Fiends," but in general he is faulted, along with Eric Walrond, Wallace Thurman, and Walter White, for a "delineation of the defeatist attitude." Only five writers are hailed in *To Make a Poet Black:* Jean Toomer, author of *Cane* (1923); George Schuyler, author of *Black No More* (1931); Rudolph Fisher, author of *The Walls of Jericho* (1928); Sterling Brown; and Zora Neale Hurston.

Completed at Elizabeth City State Teacher's College, North Carolina, where Redding taught from 1938 to 1943, *To Make a Poet Black* was well received. E. V. Stonequist said it had a "high degree of sympathetic understanding combined with intellectual honesty and fairness in criticism." It was regarded by Theophilus Lewis as a "landmark of Negro literature" and by Alain Locke as having a "formula suitable mostly for the interpretation of the transitional generation."

After the publication of his first book, Redding received a Rockefeller Foundation fellowship in 1939. He was charged to travel through the South, "to look for people, for things, for something." No better eyes could have been chosen, for Redding could see even the minute details, and better yet, he could make others see them, too. In the partly autobiographical *No Day of Triumph* he records his feelings as he accepted the challenge:

> My mind was uneasy, bedeviled by vague doubts. It seemed to me that I was looking for stability in a world that had been slowly disintegrating for a dozen years, and now, half of it at war, was breaking up very fast. No one seemed to know the values that would be preserved or even worth preserving. The depression seemed a final paralysis before the death of a way of life that

Dust jacket for Redding's book-length essay, which examines the psychology of the Negro

men had thought enduring.... Perhaps, I thought, what you will find ... will not be valid for the world that comes after.

Redding structures *No Day of Triumph* in four stages, each named after a Negro spiritual. Part 1, "Troubled in Mind," recapitulates Redding's early years, his ancestry, and the values instilled in him as a young man. These values were processed in his own mind and filtered through the philosophies of both his grandmothers. His paternal grandmother, who had been deformed by her slavemaster, Caleb Wrightson, is quoted as telling God in prayer, "You ain't been here in my lifetime. You ain't been here in be't a thousan' years.... We had slav'ry sense you been here." His maternal grandmother prayed to God as the "Holy Father, chastiser of sin and evil, great maker of all things pure and good." As Redding set out on his journey, he fortified himself with a synthesis of both these beliefs and had pledged himself to objectivity tinged with compassion.

Parts 2 and 3, "Don't Be Weary, Traveler" and "Poor Way Farin' Stranger," report on the conditions of individuals as well as of black families, a format simultaneously like a travelogue, a picaresque novel, a history, and sociological research. Some of the persons that Redding meets—a doctor, a lawyer, a Negro college president—are representative; other characters are unique.

Redding traveled through North Carolina, Virginia, Tennessee, Mississippi, Arkansas, and Kentucky, where he examined the lives and fortunes of contemporary blacks, recording their dilemmas and their dreams. The hardships of segregation are presented through the voices of the people who suffer because of it. For instance, the unemployed day-laborer Leon declares, "The white folks has got us beat, man." Mike, the Communist labor organizer, moans, "I'd like to be a good American without being either middle class or Negro. You can't be good at all three." In Mississippi one black official revealed to Redding that

217,000 black children of primary age were not in school while 105,000 of high school age suffered the same fate. Black schools were open between three and seven months per year, and of the approximately seven thousand black trustees of schools, six thousand could not read or write their names. Redding found indifference, indulgence, and selfishness among most black professionals. The black doctor to whom he talked, for instance, looked out for himself: "He was the richest Negro in town, and the best educated. But it was because of this that he found himself being dragged into considerations of group problems for which he felt no real responsibility but which he nevertheless enjoyed for the sense of a new kind of power that it gave him. He admitted that he felt none of the spiritual qualities of leadership, no real concern, no honest humility."

"There is a Balm," the last section of *No Day of Triumph,* is hopeful. Phondus Midgett, the largest landowner in Mississippi, contradicts the stereotype of the successful southern black. He is not the mulatto son of a white father. He does not cater to whites and is not improvident. The students at Alcorn College have impeccable manners. They have a progressive leadership that teaches them to face life with "courteous courage and bulldog teeth sheathed in rubber discretion."

No Day of Triumph was a great success, receiving reviews of up to twelve hundred words in length. Critics viewed the work from several aspects. While most praised it for accuracy, eloquence, sanity, compassion, and honesty, some saw it as a statement of the evils of democracy. Typical was Malcolm Cowley, who said of the work's portrayal of the evils of racism, "It is a picture that ought to frighten us, for all Mr. Redding's unexcited style." In 1944 Redding received the Mayflower Cup Award given annually to the resident of North Carolina who writes the best book. He was the first black writer to be thus honored. He had not entered his book in the competition and was not aware that it was being considered along with twenty-eight others. With *No Day of Triumph* he established himself as an American writer and attracted the attention of several groups, most notably the Communists, who tried to recruit him, promising to make his works best-sellers.

Redding joined the faculty at Hampton Institute as professor of English and creative writing in 1943. By 1944 he received a Guggenheim Fellowship, and the *Amsterdam News* cited him for distinction. The New York Public Library also honored Redding for outstanding contributions to interracial understanding in 1945 and 1946. Redding kept pace as a book reviewer, a teacher, and a writer. He also continued his role as father; his second son, Lewis Alfred II, was born in 1945. In 1949 the National Urban League cited him for outstanding achievement. It was at this time, also, that Brown University, Redding's alma mater, invited him to be a visiting professor of English. Redding was the first black person to hold a full professorship in this institution.

Redding's *Stranger and Alone: A Novel* (1950) springs as much from his imagination as it does from his experience teaching at black colleges. The plot deals with a mulatto, Shelton Howden, who betrays his black friends. Howden, the insecure son of a white father and a black mother, feels inferior because of his ignorance of his background; he sets out to prove himself superior to other blacks. Void of common sense, gratitude, and compassion, Howden never grows in the humane or social graces. Though educated in both black and white colleges, Howden evades their civilizing influences by remaining a loner, jealous of the ease and pleasures of other students. When he joins Arcadia College, he meets an older and more ruthless version of himself, the mulatto president, Wimbush, who acts as Howden's mentor and instructs him, "People like us aren't answerable to the race of men. If we were, then there would be no balance to things. . . . People like us are the equilibrators. . . . It's not our fault that its unequal. We didn't set it up and we can't turn times back to year one. It's only common sense to accept the world as we find it." Thus, when Wimbush, with the help of his satanic daughter, Gerry, contaminates Howden's mind totally, so that when Howden marries for convenience and divulges to white Judge Reed the secret plan of the black group, his betrayal of his friends is no surprise.

In general *Stranger and Alone* was favorably reviewed. Negative criticism was limited mainly to the structure of the work and the lack of development in Howden's character. Ralph Ellison, reviewing the work for the *New York Times* (19 February 1950), wrote, "He has done a vastly important job of reporting the little known role of those Negro 'leaders' who by collaborating with the despoilers of the South do insidious damage to us all." Paul Pickrel, writing for the *Yale Review,* found the work uneven in quality but agreed with Ellison, because *Stranger and Alone* showed the "critically weak points in those very in-

Dust jacket for Redding's popular history of the Negro in America

stitutions which most of us look to as the solution–
in part, at least–of the problem of the Negro."

Redding's history of black Americans, *They
Came in Chains: Americans from Africa*, was originally published in 1950 as one of the Peoples of
America series. A revised edition was published
in 1973. He begins by stating the philosophy of
men who instituted and accepted slavery as a
means of achieving economic prosperity and
shows that blacks as well as whites raised opposition to it. Blacks were never content with their
lot, and the myth of the happy Negro was born
of the imagination of whites. Scrupulously honest, Redding points out that during slavery cruelty to blacks sometimes resulted in cruelty in
return. He pays special attention to the abolitionists and to blacks, such as David Walker and
Harriet Tubman, who contributed to the liberation of their people.

They Came in Chains had a mixed critical reception. Because the book lacked footnotes,
Redding was accused of making "errors in detail"
and of using "exaggerations." In general, however, he was commended. Youra Qualls in the
Christian Science Monitor (18 September 1950) said
he had made "a scholarly achievement of distinction and importance." Anne Whitmore of the *Li-*

brary Journal (1 June 1950) found that the work
was "adequately detailed . . . and written with restraint and authority" and recommended it. L. P.
Stavisky, writing for the *Survey* (November 1950),
was effusive in his praise: "In a fluid and imaginative style the author has given us a vivid commentary of the story of the Negro people in
America."

The theme of Redding's fifth book, *On
Being Negro in America* (1951), is that the American Negro is burdened and preoccupied with the
problems brought on by his color, and this burden and preoccupation sap creative energy and
create a "second ego." Echoing Du Bois's idea of
"double consciousness," Redding asserted that
blacks felt they must always think of themselves
in terms of color and not as men or women, thus
upsetting their psychological equilibrium. In support of his theme that this preoccupation needs
to be discarded Redding discusses integration,
the ignorance of each race about the other that results in harmful myths, and the unnecessary complications that racism brings to the lives of
children. He surveys the social and political gains
that blacks have made through the efforts of the
National Association for the Advancement of Colored People (NAACP), the Congress of Racial

Equality (CORE), the Student Non-Violent Coordinating Committee (SNCC), Dr. Martin Luther King, and others, and he laments that race problems are incurable in human terms. Education and law have failed, but Christianity offers hope if man would emphasize his relationship to man. Redding had set out to purge himself of the race problem, to write it out of his mind, but concludes: "Now that I come to the end of this essay, I realize that I have not done for myself all that I had hoped to do. I am not purged: I am not cured of my sickness. Perhaps it is not the sort that can be cured by individual home remedies."

Like all of Redding's works, this book was widely reviewed. One of the most insightful reviews appeared in the *Nation* (17 November 1951). There Rayford W. Logan classified the work as autopsychoanalysis and considered it "one of the most effective statements . . . of the constant conflict experienced by the Negro between his reactions as a normal human being and those which life in America requires of him." Logan goes on to say that the book "requires serious consideration for it is the mature, restrained, eloquent denunciation of an evil by a sensitive man of good will. . . . Redding's disturbing book has vital meaning not only for America in 1951 but for the world, and will have, I fear, for many years to come."

In 1952 Redding edited with Ivan E. Taylor of Howard University a book of readings called *Reading for Writing*. In that same year he was asked by the U.S. Department of State to be an emissary to India. *An American in India*, published in 1954, was the result of his trip. Redding was greeted with personal warmth and overwhelming hospitality in India. He learned as much as he taught. For three months he traveled through the country. He spoke at "dozens of university centers and villages." Thrown with the intellectuals, Redding discovered that the American image in India was one of imperialism and that even some of the benevolent American foundations were thought of as mere tools for achieving the end of imperialism. "Anglo-American Democracy is slow," they said. The Indians believed generally that they could be politically eclectic. They could take the best from communism, socialism, and democracy and develop a political system for themselves. Redding found what seemed to be a "hard, solid core of communism" among professors, writers, journalists, politicians, and students.

The book exposes a dichotomy in the Indian attitude. Individual Americans, the Indians thought, were generous and acceptable, but America as a country was base and lacking cultural achievement. As Redding states, "America, in short did not equal the sum of her parts. Evils mentioned in abstract terms had a greater validity than good that could be seen in concrete results." On several occasions Redding describes frustration in his attempts to correct the erroneous views that some Indians held about America and the American Negro.

Extensively reviewed and warmly received, *An American in India* probably accomplished, unconsciously, what Redding had often hoped for, the opportunity for a black writer to speak as an American, unencumbered by race. Although Redding acknowledged that his "Negroness" probably allowed him intimacy in certain Indian quarters and although the irony of a black man speaking on and for America did not escape some Indians, he was, for the first time in a book, able to subdue his preoccupation with the condition of the Negro in America and to practice his art as a writer.

Lewis Gannet, reviewing the work in the *New York Herald Tribune Book Review*, wrote: "Mr. Redding is never dogmatic, . . . He tells us of his own problems and unanswered questions. His book is lively, colorful, consistently thought provoking, bewilderingly honest. I know no other book dealing with India which remotely resembles it." Journalist Edgar Snow, writing in the *Nation* (30 October 1954), agreed.

Shortly after the publication of *An American in India* Redding was invited to join the editorial board of the *American Scholar*. He remained on the board for eight years, continuing his research, his teaching, and his writing. *The Lonesome Road: The Story of the Negro's Part in America* (1958) examines the military contribution of blacks in American wars and studies the life and times of Daniel Payne, Frederick Douglass, Sojourner Truth, Isaiah Montgomery, Daniel Hale Williams, Booker T. Washington, W. E. B. Du Bois, Robert S. Abbott, Marcus Garvey, A. Philip Randolph, Paul Robeson, Joe Louis, and Thurgood Marshall, blacks who have made a significant contribution to American history. The book captures a sense of the struggle in which the Negro leader has engaged, often with his own people.

Of eleven reviews of *Lonesome Road* published between March and June 1958 only one was unfavorable. Paula Snelling, writing in the *New Republic* (23 June 1958), criticized Redding

Dust jacket for Redding's 1958 history of Negro leaders

for not attending more fully to the role of the black church and for omitting those blacks who "kept their home base in the South and sought ways of communicating with white Southerners without relinquishing personal dignity or the aspirations of their race."

Typical of the favorable reviews were M. S. Byam's comments on the work (*Library Journal*, 1 March 1958): "This is no mere angry or shrieking picture of the poor Negro's plight but rather a documentation of his complete belongingness to America historically and culturally. It stands by itself since facts are used here to let the story tell itself."

In 1959 Redding was again offered a Guggenheim Fellowship. He continued his lecture tours, his teaching, and his book reviewing for *Afro* magazine. One of the highlights of his academic life that year was his participation in the First Conference of Negro Writers, when he spoke on "The American Negro Writer and His Roots."

In 1962 Redding made a six-month lecture tour at the universities of five West African countries. His lectures were the first in a series of a cultural exchange program sponsored by the Society of African Culture, of which Redding was a member of the executive council; his task was to lecture on American life and the status of American blacks. He interpreted for readers of *Afro* magazine his impressions of the new African nations, considering political policies and principles, social and religious habits, and discussing misconceptions such as Africa as the "Dark Continent." Shortly after his return from Africa, he was awarded a doctorate of literature from Brown University in 1963.

Redding was a fellow in the humanities at Duke University in 1964, the year he was awarded an honorary doctorate of humane let-

ters by Hobart College (Redding held six such degrees). He returned to Hampton Institute in 1965 but became director of the division of research and publications at the National Endowment as for the Humanities in 1966. In a *Washington Post* article (14 August 1968) Redding described his role at the National Endowment as seeking "involvement in the humanistic aspects of problems plaguing America, Europe, Asia and Africa . . . the search for freedom, dignity, equality and power." He was able to stimulate interest in research dealing with the black man in America and Africa and to introduce researchers to available materials in this field.

Meanwhile, *The Negro* (1967), Redding's eighth book, was written as one of the U.S.A. Survey Series, intended to present Americans with a clear interpretation of their own country and its traditions as well as to provide foreign readers with informative, realistic appraisals of contemporary life in the United States. Covering much the same ground as *They Came in Chains* and *On Being Negro in America*, this work presents an overview of the Negro's life in America. In line with the book's purpose one critic found this work suitable only as an introduction to anyone "wholly uninformed about the Negro in the United States." Redding, conscious of the purposes and the limited scope of the book, included suggestions for further reading.

In 1968 Redding accepted a professorship in history and American literature at George Washington University while remaining as a special consultant to the National Endowment for the Humanities. One of his aims at the university was to "wrap into the factual substance of American life, materials and ideas about the Afro-American, the Black American." Still in demand for interviews and speaking engagements, he worked with Arthur P. Davis at Howard University to compile an anthology of Negro American writing from 1760 to 1970; it was eventually published in 1971 as *Cavalcade*. In 1970 he accepted the Ernest I. White Professorship of American Studies and Humane Letters at Cornell University. In 1986 the university established a program of fellowships for minority students in his honor. Every year, this endowment provides up to ten stu-

dents with full tuition and a stipend of ten thousand dollars.

In 1969 Redding reminded America of the cost of ignoring part of its history and in the 1970s helped young people who suffered because of this memory loss. Speaking of Black Power and Black Studies programs, he said, "A part of the past is being repeated in the present. The popular interest in Black people . . . developed out of a real crisis of ignorance that this time did not have to be. For there were all those philosophical analyses and scholarly works of 30 and 40 years ago that, had they got the attention they should have, would have served as sufficient forewarning of the present 'Black Revolution.'" With psychologist Kenneth B. Clark, Robert C. Weaver, Federal Judge William Hastie, and historian John Franklin, Redding during the 1970s was a member of the Haverford Group, which met informally to find ways of helping young people avoid racial isolation.

Redding stands out as an American writer of distinction who dared repeatedly to show America her less democratic side. He labored unflinchingly for over four decades to clarify the experience of black people in America. In his varied attempts to tell the truth of this experience Redding offended some of his fellow blacks by attacking accepted value systems within Negro society. He spoke out on the color barriers within his race, the intellectual softness in some black colleges, and the lack of concern of the educated for the uneducated and questioned the value of Black Studies Programs and the concept of a Black Aesthetic. His works will remain germane in any study of the Negro in America.

References:

Arthur P. Davis, *From the Dark Tower: Afro-American Writers, 1900-1960* (Washington, D.C.: Howard University Press, 1974);

Jean Wagner, *Black Poets of the United States: From Paul Laurence Dunbar to Langston Hughes*, translated by Kenneth Douglas (Urbana: University of Illinois Press, 1973).

Papers:

Redding's papers are held at Brown University.

William Gardner Smith

(6 February 1927-5 November 1974)

Jacquelyn Jackson
Middle Tennessee State University

BOOKS: *Last of the Conquerors* (New York: Farrar, Straus, 1948; London: Gollancz, 1949);
Anger at Innocence (New York: Farrar, Straus, 1950; London: Gollancz, 1951);
South Street (New York: Farrar, Straus and Young, 1954);
The Stone Face (New York: Farrar, Straus, 1963);
Return to Black America (Englewood Cliffs, N. J.: Prentice-Hall, 1970).

PERIODICAL PUBLICATION: "The Negro Writer: Pitfalls and Compensations," *Phylon*, 11 (Fourth Quarter 1950): 297-303.

In spite of a lack of contemporary critical recognition for his work, journalist, novelist, and editor William Gardner Smith is linked to the black social protest novel tradition of the 1940s and the 1950s, which includes writers such as Richard Wright, Chester Himes, Willard Motley, and Ann Petry. Addison Gayle credits Smith with turning away from "much of the deterministic thought of his predecessors." His protagonists are fully sympathetic, and his third book, *South Street* (1954), is one of the first black militant protest novels.

Smith was born in Philadelphia, Pennsylvania, on 6 February 1927 to Edith Smith. In 1934 his mother married Douglass Stanley Earle, and this marriage produced three children—two daughters, Phyllis and Sydney, and a son, Douglass. Smith, the eldest, delighted in the care of his half sisters and brother, although he disliked his stepfather.

As a child living in the South Philadelphia ghetto during the 1940s, a recurring setting in his novels, Smith gained an acute sense of the pain of being black in America. He was, nevertheless, able to transcend the violence, racial abuse, and corruption that threatened him by focusing on part-time work and his studies. He was an excellent student throughout his elementary and junior high school years. An avid reader and an extremely talented storyteller, he had read all of Ernest Hemingway and much of Somerset

William Gardner Smith (photograph by Erich Hartmann, courtesy of the Schomburg Center for Research in Black Culture, the New York Public Library, Astor, Lenox and Tilden Foundations)

Maugham by the age of eleven. To supplement the family income, at age nine he worked in a grocery store; and at age thirteen he worked at a photography studio.

As a student at Benjamin Franklin High School Smith continued to excel in his studies. He was also active in school activities as captain of the fencing team; photographer; cheerleader; editor of the school paper the *Junto*, and of the yearbook the *Almanac*; and judge of the student court. Gerald Hamm, a white English instructor, encouraged Smith to become a writer. In Smith's senior year school principal Charles A. Williams helped him secure a part-time position with the *Pittsburgh Courier*. Smith graduated with honors

from high school in January 1944 at the age of sixteen, the second highest student in his class.

After graduation Smith began working full time as a reporter for the *Pittsburgh Courier*, where he was teamed with city editor John A. Saunders, but his journalism career was interrupted. On 8 January 1946 he was drafted into the army. After basic training he was sent to Europe where he was assigned as a clerk-typist in occupied Berlin.

On the return trip from Europe eight months later Smith began writing his first novel, *Last of the Conquerors* (1948), and completed it while attending Temple University as a full-time student. Inspired by Smith's experiences abroad, *Last of the Conquerors* is a story of race relations between black and white American troops in occupied Germany shortly after World War II. The protagonist Hayes Dawkins is a sensitive, intelligent, young black soldier who works as a clerk-typist in Berlin. At first Dawkins and other American soldiers are skeptical of the Germans; but after working with them they realize that the German people are simply human beings. The black troops find acceptance and soon discover a sense of freedom that cannot be found in America. They date white women, go to the opera and to clubs, and fall in love. Free from oppression, the black soldiers discover that life among the German people is preferable to life in America.

The theme of racism in the novel is brought sharply into focus through the love story of Dawkins and Ilse Mueller, his German girlfriend. When the black troops are transferred from the command of Captain Doyle in Berlin to the command of Captain Polke in Widsdorf, they find themselves in "Nigger Hell." Under the leadership of Captain Polke, a prejudiced southern commander, and his right-hand man first sergeant Brink, described as an Uncle Tom, the black troops are relegated to second class status. The army becomes a microcosm of American life. Polke is brutal in his discipline of the black troops, who are restricted from socializing with German women. Many of the soldiers are unjustly court-martialed, and half of the black troops are dishonorably discharged and sent back to the states on trumped-up charges. Ilse Mueller follows Dawkins from Berlin to Widsdorf, and the knowledge of his affair precipitates Polke's wrath against him. Ilse is imprisoned by the military police. The knowledge that they are to be sent back to America dishonorably forces the black troops to make very difficult decisions. One

soldier commits suicide with his lover. A second soldier flees to the Russian border. A third soldier goes berserk and deserts the army. Hayes Dawkins returns to America, abandoning Ilse to avoid court-martial proceedings.

Last of the Conquerors received an extensive, but primarily descriptive, review in the 28 August 1948 issue of the *Saturday Review of Literature*. Harrison Smith recognized the controversial quality of the book and felt it was "guaranteed to shock any reader who is at all apprehensive of the results of our continued discrimination against Negro citizens on ourselves and on public opinion throughout the world." He noted Smith's newspaper experience as being primarily responsible for his "reporting" style and, treating the book more as historical document than fiction, questioned whether the German women really welcomed black soldiers to the extent that Smith maintained, suggesting that perhaps they were just out to procure food and other "urgent necessities" for their families no matter the donors. The reviewer for the 17 August 1948 issue of the *Chicago Sun Times* judged the profanity in the novel to be excessive but recognized that it might be necessary in accompanying a novel with a "bitter message."

After the publication of *Last of the Conquerors* Smith briefly continued his studies at Temple University. The novel had attracted two New York theatrical producers who bought the stage rights, although a stage version of the novel was never produced. In 1949 he married his high school sweetheart Mary Sewell and began to write full time. From fall 1949 to mid 1950 he worked on and completed *Anger at Innocence* (1950).

In *Anger at Innocence* Smith abandons racial themes to focus on the problem of good and evil. Set in South Philadelphia, the novel centers around Ted Hall, a shy, frustrated, forty-year-old white man who falls in love with Rodina Beleza, a sensual young pickpocket. Hall has had little success in life, never having achieved anything that he wanted. His marriage is a failure, and his attempts as a writer are futile. Rodina's background is equally insecure and dismal. Living in the slums of Philadelphia, she is a defeated, neurotic young woman who seeks release through crime. Because she is stifled by the drudgery of taking care of her invalid mother, who constantly reminds her of her criminal nature and strongly condemns her, Rodina feels compelled to do evil things.

Leaving a diner one night in the rain, Ted is accosted by Rodina, who attempts to pick his pocket. He seizes her and, before releasing her, makes her promise that she will not pick pockets again. Ted and Rodina continue to see each other. After he meets Rodina's mother, Ted leaves his wife, Sylvia, and moves into Rodina's apartment building. They secretly begin living together platonically. He attempts to reform Rodina while torn by his guilt for leaving his wife. The novel becomes a kind of tragic duel between Ted Hall, who is predominantly good, and Rodina, who is predominantly evil. Rodina wants to be good; and for a while she tries to find a job, gives up her life of crime, and silently endures her mother's condemnation. But she is surrounded by undesirable people who have a tremendous influence on her. Hucks, a frustrated truck driver and her former lover, attempts to gain her back at any cost. He learns she has picked another pocket, and she agrees to submit to his advances in order to silence him. Juarez, a gossiping, sinister man with ungratified sexual designs on Rodina, tries to manipulate her into returning to crime. Rodina's mother continues to implant in her a sense of worthlessness.

Ted cannot reform Rodina, who begins to corrupt him. He loses his job, and his lack of money and mounting distrust slowly strain the relationship. Even after Ted finds another job, he continues to feel guilty about deserting his wife, and he corresponds with Sylvia much to Rodina's dismay. Later, Rodina falls in love with Ted. Sensing that she cannot be good and fearful that Ted will leave her, she attempts, with Juarez's guidance, to make Ted evil. First, she lies to him about her mother needing a sizable amount of money for an operation and volunteers to return to picking pockets for the money. Instead he steals two cameras from his job so she can sell them; his guilt, however, forces him to resign. She demands that Ted shoot Hucks. Added complications—the death of her mother, Sylvia's letter-writing campaign designed to increase Ted's guilt, and Juarez's gossip—increase the tensions between Ted and Rodina, who are now sleeping together. Her fears mount; he refuses to relinquish completely his decency even though he learns about her betrayals and lies. Sensing that he is leaving her to return to his wife, Rodina retaliates by killing both Ted and herself.

Anger at Innocence is artistically weak. Although the characterizations of Ted Hall and Rodina Beleza are clearly drawn, improbabilities seriously mar the work. Smith is, however, convincing in his depiction of the stranglehold of the environment, the sinister characters, and the economic deprivation that eventually keep Rodina away from a normal life.

Alain Locke, in his mid-century review of black American literature for a 1951 issue of *Phylon*, considered *Anger at Innocence* to be a "severe disappointment" because it was "largely journeyman reporting, with all the faults of melodrama, superficial stock characterization, banality and cliché situation." He blamed Smith for not bringing to fruition the tragic potential of the situations he created; instead, the writing was "psychologically naive and sociologically superficial," and the drama "unrolled" "in tabloid newspaper fashion, with little to commend it to serious readers anxious to explore the Negro 'lower depths' to which the author invites them." Carl Milton Hughes commented in *The Negro Novelist* in 1953 that the novel exhibited "competent writing," but that Smith operated from the "false premise" of assuming that good and bad were absolutes in human beings. Smith thereby weakened his story "with improbabilities" and made his novel "only partially successful."

During a month's stay at Yaddo, New York, the artist's colony, in June 1951 Smith examined his life in Philadelphia, particularly his troubled relationship with Mary, and they decided to go to France. Smith and his wife intended to stay in Europe possibly a year. Once there he found a way of life that stood in sharp contrast to the routine of American life. Although his major reason for leaving America was to attempt to save his marriage by starting anew, the need for personal freedom became a dominant one: "I am absolutely unhappy paying a mortgage, paying an insurance policy, buying furniture. . . . I cannot stand the confinement and the safety. . . . I can't stand to be settled for life. I want to move. I want to live, to discover something new. . . . " For Smith, Paris was a search for liberation.

Financial difficulties in Europe strained Smith's marriage. Although he had written an article for the *Pittsburgh Courier* and was working on his third novel, he did not have steady employment. Less than three months after their arrival Mary left Paris and moved to England in hopes of finding employment. Their marriage slowly collapsed; and after failing to find employment in England, Mary was forced to return to Philadelphia. Smith informed his family of their separation and pending divorce. Although he was fre-

quently without money and had no job possibilities, Smith found in Europe a tremendous sense of personal freedom and credibility as a writer. He met Richard Wright, James Baldwin, Ollie Harrington, Chester Himes, Art Simmons, and other black Americans, and these associations gave him intellectual sustenance and an active social life. He managed to keep writing by sending articles to *Ebony* and *Jet* magazines. His third novel was completed in 1954.

Planned as part 1 of an uncompleted trilogy, *South Street* is one of the first black militant protest novels. Unlike his first two novels, in which both protagonists are powerless in their efforts to overcome oppression, this novel ends optimistically with the protagonist choosing to resume active involvement in organized battle against white oppression.

South Street deals primarily with the three Bowers brothers in South Philadelphia. Claude, the eldest, a noted writer and civil rights activist, has just returned from Africa. He is weary of the struggle and seeks a rest. Michael, an intensely militant young man, has a passionate hatred for whites and is disenchanted with his passive brothers, particularly Claude, who is his idol and is now inactive. Philip, the youngest, is a sensitive, insecure intellectual who despises violence and shuns involvement. All three brothers are bound by the memory of their father who was lynched by a white mob. Each wears a carnation in his lapel as a reminder of his murder.

The major focus of the novel is on the relationship of the Bowers brothers as each struggles to define his life. Claude is tired of fighting and wants to live simply as a writer and enjoy life. He meets and marries Kristin, a young, white violinist. The marriage suffers from isolation and the pressures of ghetto life. In desperation he and Kristin prepare to flee to Canada where they hope to live without racial prejudice. Michael, who repudiates Claude because of his interracial marriage, organizes the Action Society to combat the violence and abuse committed against blacks in the city. He plans several unorganized retaliatory attacks that quickly get out of control and cause his followers to lose confidence in his leadership. Knowing that Claude has leadership abilities, Michael attempts without success to persuade him to return to active participation. Philip struggles to gain respect from both Claude and Michael by joining the Action Society. Caught between his love for them and his need to define his life without violence, Philip finally withdraws

into his own private world.

Philip's death, the pivotal point of the plot, brings the two remaining brothers together. He is killed by an angry white youth who has been beaten earlier by blacks in one of Michael's unorganized retaliatory attacks. Philip's murder causes Claude to rethink his position; he discovers that his place is on South Street with Michael. Claude leaves Kristin to resume leadership in the fight against oppression.

Smith integrates and maintains several plot lines expertly throughout *South Street*. He skillfully depicts the social and political lives of the characters. Henry F. Winslow, who reviewed it for the February 1955 issue of *Crisis*, called the novel "a fictional sight-seeing tour to the Negro sector of present-day Philadelphia." He considered the novel to be less effective than *Last of the Conquerors*, primarily because the "choice of a wide variety of characters . . . is made at the sacrifice of depth in any one." Nonetheless, he did applaud Smith for capturing the "sights and sounds" of Philadelphia. Doris Dungill Holmes, writing in *Phylon*, was somewhat more sympathetic to the novel. She applauded when characters transcended stereotypes to become individuals, and she generally praised the language and plot. While she recognized that the novel lacked the "surface centrality" that many readers may have preferred, she nonetheless found it "stimulating" and its treatment "impressive."

With the publication of *South Street* life for Smith improved. He became news editor of English language services for Agence France-Presse in 1954. One of the reasons for taking the job was that he had moved artistically to an impasse: "I had come to a dead end. I felt I couldn't go down the old road any longer. I mean the road of protest." In between the publication of *South Street* and securing a job, Smith had started a new novel, but it was rejected by his publisher. His work at the press agency gave him a much-needed respite.

By 1957 Smith's divorce from Mary Sewell became final. In 1959 he once more resumed his novel, completing a manuscript, "Pink Ballets," that was accepted by an American publisher and then a French publisher but was never published. In 1961 he married Solange Royez.

The Stone Face (1963) is Smith's last published work of fiction. It is the story of Simeon Brown, an American black, who has struggled with unrelenting racial prejudice and violence in America. As a young man he was accosted by a

William Gardner Smith (photograph copyright © Photo Pix, Paris)

group of white boys, severely beaten, and left blind in one eye. Brown is an amateur painter who has created a portrait, "the stone face," the unhuman face of racism. The novel's setting is in Paris where Brown has come to find freedom from oppression.

In Paris Brown soon finds friends and joins other American and African expatriates. Life there is relatively calm and peaceful for him. He meets Maria, a Polish lady, who suffers from fear of blindness. They fall in love and find that they both are fleeing from similar backgrounds: Brown from the emasculation and brutality of white America and Maria from the horrors of the concentration camps. Her ambition is to become an actress, visit Hollywood, and become wealthy. Simeon has no such ambitions; he simply wants to find freedom.

Simeon Brown's life is a continuous round of cafe society, parties, and enjoyment until he discovers the Algerian War. Most of his fellow black expatriates are content with life, but Brown sees the unjust treatment of the Algerian people by the French and the Algerian fight for liberation as parallel to the oppression of blacks in America. This discovery is crucial, for he now under-

stands that the sense of isolation he felt in America is shared by all oppressed peoples. Brown's frustrations and Maria's blossoming career, after a successful eye operation, lead him to examine his role as an expatriate. More important, the incidents taking place in conjunction with the integration of schools in Little Rock, Arkansas, heighten his frustrations. When Maria's career escalates and Brown finds himself involved repeatedly in conflict with Parisian police, he knows that he must return to America: "I can't sit by, comfortable, while others take the hard blows."

Reviews of *The Stone Face* were mixed. Jean Carey Bond, writing for *Freedomways*, considered the book "not a very good novel." She found the action "crudely contrived" with only "fleeting moments of technical originality." Nick Aaron Ford, writing for *Phylon* in 1964, asserted that the novel established Smith "as a serious contender for a place in the first rank of contemporary writers." He ultimately judged it to be "the best (not the most sensational) novel by a Negro writer since Ellison's *Invisible Man*." Joseph Friedman, the reviewer for the 17 November 1963 issue of the *New York Times Book Review*, shared some of Ford's feelings by asserting that the book was a

"solid achievement" and that Smith should be counted "among the most worthy young writers, Negro or white."

In 1964 Smith left France to take the position of assistant editor in chief of Ghana Television in Accra, working with Shirley Graham Du Bois. He was excited about his new responsibilities. Soon after his arrival he was promoted to director of the institute of journalism, and he and his wife had a son. In 1966 the government of Ghana was overthrown by military coup, and Smith was ordered to leave.

Smith returned to Paris and to his job with Agence France-Presse. He wrote an outline about his experiences in Ghana but could not interest a publisher in it. In 1967 he received an assignment to return to America and cover the race riots. For the first time in sixteen years Smith returned to his home. He spent the first few days visiting his family and seeing his relatives and friends. After approximately four weeks of investigating the conditions in Cleveland, New York, Detroit, Brooklyn, Chicago, Washington, D. C., San Francisco, Los Angeles, and Philadelphia, he returned to Paris.

Smith's report on the riots in America gave him immediate exposure; he was in demand on the lecture circuit, on radio and television programs, and at public meetings and conferences. The death of Dr. Martin Luther King, Jr., caused him to shelve the projected book on his African experiences and concentrate on his American experiences. He divorced his second wife, Solange, and in 1970 married Ira Reuben, a native of Ranchi, India.

Return to Black America (1970), Smith's fifth published book, examines the Black Power movement in the United States, its leaders, those who oppose it, and the effects of the movement on blacks and whites. It also examines "black America and the world," focusing on the time Gen.

Charles de Gaulle intervened to allow Stokely Carmichael to enter France. In the closing section Smith presents his solution for black unrest. Peace will come "only by a radical transformation of the surrounding white society itself." He predicts that America is in for "a long, hot decade or two."

A daughter was born to Ira Reuben and Smith in 1971, and in November of that year he returned to America for a brief time. On 30 October 1973, complaining of chest pains, he flew to Algiers for a complete medical examination by his friend, Dr. Jacques Tomasini. He remained there for about two weeks and was told that he had cancer. Smith underwent two operations, one in December 1973 and the other in November 1974. The last operation revealed that he was terminally ill. On 5 November 1974 William Gardner Smith died in Thiais, France.

References:

Robert A. Bone, *The Negro Novel in America*, revised edition (New Haven: Yale University Press, 1965), pp. 167, 176-178;

Jerry H. Bryant, "Individuality and Fraternity: The Novels of William Gardner Smith," *Studies in Black Literature*, 3 (Summer 1972): 1-8;

Addison Gayle, Jr., *The Way of The New World: The Black Novel in America* (Garden City, N. Y.: Anchor Press, Doubleday, 1975), pp. 239-247;

Leroy Hodges, *Portrait of An Expatriate—William Gardner Smith* (Westport, Conn.: Greenwood Press, 1985);

Stanley Schatt, "You Must Go Home Again: Today's Afro-American Expatriate Writers," *Negro American Literature Forum*, 7 (Fall 1973): 80-82;

Noel Schraufnagel, *From Apology to Protest: The Black American Novel* (De Land, Fla.: Everett-Edwards, 1973) pp. 47ff.

Melvin B. Tolson

(6 February 1898-29 August 1966)

Robert M. Farnsworth
University of Missouri at Kansas City

See also the Tolson entry in *DLB 48: American Poets, 1880-1945.*

BOOKS: *Rendezvous with America* (New York: Dodd, Mead, 1944);

Libretto for the Republic of Liberia (New York: Twayne, 1953; London: Collier-Macmillan, 1970);

Harlem Gallery: Book I, The Curator (New York: Twayne, 1965; London: Collier-Macmillan, 1969);

A Gallery of Harlem Portraits, edited by Robert M. Farnsworth (Columbia & London: University of Missouri Press, 1979);

Caviar and Cabbage: Selected Columns by Melvin B. Tolson from the Washington Tribune, 1937-1944, edited by Farnsworth (Columbia & London: University of Missouri Press, 1982).

PLAY PRODUCTION: *A Fire in the Flint,* based upon Walter White's novel, Oklahoma City, Okla., 28 June 1952.

OTHER: "Abraham Lincoln of Rock Spring Farm," in *Soon One Morning: New Writing by American Negroes, 1940-1962,* edited by Herbert Hill (New York: Knopf, 1963), pp. 572-577.

PERIODICAL PUBLICATION: "Richard Wright: *Native Son,*" *Modern Quarterly,* 11 (Winter 1939): 19-24.

With the publication of *Libretto for the Republic of Liberia* (1953) Melvin B. Tolson claimed a major role for Afro-American poets in the modernist literary revolution forged principally by such poets as Hart Crane, T. S. Eliot, Ezra Pound, William Carlos Williams, and Wallace Stevens. *Libretto for the Republic of Liberia* marked a dramatic change in poetic technique from Tolson's previous poetry, although in retrospect one can see many premonitory signals of this

Melvin B. Tolson, circa 1945 (courtesy of the Tolson family)

change. In mid career Tolson assumed the modernist revolution in literature was irreversible. For him the New Criticism, which sees a text as a "verbal icon," was an acknowledgment of a prior and more fundamental literary revolution. Thus, Tolson became an enthusiastic spokesman for accepting modernist literary tenets, although he was careful and definite about retaining a marked distinction between his own social and political views and the conservative views of many of the leading spokesmen of the New Criticism. He sometimes pictured himself in the forefront of a phalanx of black writers winning a share of a future international audience for the recognition of Afro-American culture. Allen Tate's enthu-

164

siastic praise for *Libretto* and later Karl Shapiro's even more unstinting praise for *Harlem Gallery: Book I, The Curator* (1965) brought Tolson substantial professional recognition, but his own enthusiasm for the modernist tenets of the New Critics was never shared by the younger generation of black writers.

The controversy emanating from Tolson's allegiance to modernism has severely restricted the number of scholars willing to assume the challenge of critically reading his demanding late works. It also has unfortunately caused Tolson's earlier achievements to be neglected. However, the last few years have shown promise that a new generation of scholars is willing to consider Tolson's work more objectively.

Melvin Beaunorus Tolson was born 6 February 1898, in Moberly, Missouri, to the Reverend Alonzo Tolson and Lera Hurt Tolson. Alonzo Tolson was a Methodist Episcopal minister, and it was common then for ministers of that denomination to be reassigned to churches within a fairly large district every few years. Thus Tolson grew up in the small towns of northern Missouri and central Iowa and at the age of fourteen published his first poem, on the sinking of the *Titanic*, in a local newspaper in Oskaloosa, Iowa. In 1916 the family moved to the Kansas City area for what was to become a more or less permanent residence. Tolson finished high school in Kansas City, Missouri, and wrote both stories and poems published in his high school yearbooks. In 1918 he began college at Fisk University but transferred a year later to Lincoln University in Pennsylvania, entering as a freshman. In his sophomore year at Lincoln, at a fraternity dance in Philadelphia, he met Ruth Southall from Charlottesville, Virginia. Following a courtship of several months, they were married 29 January 1922. A year and a half later Tolson graduated with a B.A. degree just about the time they had their first child, Melvin B. Tolson, Jr.

In 1924 Tolson was hired as an instructor of English and speech at Wiley College in Marshall, Texas. Because of his success as a speaker and debater at Lincoln, he was quickly invited to organize and coach a debate team at Wiley. In the years to come Tolson's Wiley Forensic Society became a legend. In approximately fifteen years Tolson's debate team lost only once, and that defeat was attributed to a biased jury. His teams early cracked the color line and defeated teams from such prestigious schools as the University of Southern California, the University of Kansas,

and even Oxford University, England. Tolson himself was in great demand as a speaker throughout his life.

Meanwhile, three more children, Arthur Lincoln, Wiley Wilson, and Ruth Marie, were all born by the end of 1928. He completed a novel, "Beyond the Zaretto," in these years, but the manuscript has been lost. In 1926 Tolson published a story in the Wiley College *Wild Cat*, "The Tragedy of the Yarr Karr," a fantasy adventure of a Greenwich Village bohemian in "pursuit of the red grape of existence," who moves through exotic adventures in Russia and North Africa only to choose at the end to become a mission worker in the slums of an eastern city. The combination of exotic fantasy and the raceless character of the story suggest that Tolson's imagination was not yet predisposed to literary realism or to expressing his racial feelings in literary form.

Tolson himself was later to point to the academic year 1931-1932 as pivotal in his development as a poet. He moved his wife and children to his parents' home in Kansas City and, with the aid of a fellowship, took leave from his faculty post at Wiley to live in Harlem and to enroll in an M.A. program in comparative literature at Columbia University. He wrote a thesis on the writers of the Harlem Renaissance and critically examined their writing and how collectively they formed a cultural movement. He became personally acquainted with many of the writers. By the end of his stay, at the age of thirty-three, he began writing *A Gallery of Harlem Portraits* (1979), his first book of poems.

Borrowing the suggestion from Edgar Lee Masters that a community could be represented through dramatic portraits of its citizens, Tolson attempted to create an epic picture of Harlem. Alain Locke in his *The New Negro* (1925) had emphasized the cultural and racial diversity of Harlem and had celebrated the sense of community which he found emerging from such diversity. For him Harlem was prophetic of a great cultural future for the Negro race, and Tolson responded in kind in his *A Gallery of Harlem Portraits*. Following the lead of Langston Hughes, whom he called "the most glamorous figure in Negro literature," Tolson incorporates blues lyrics liberally throughout his book. While the cast of characters is from all classes and a great variety of racial hues, there is an insistent proletarian identification. The racial oneness which the people of Harlem are in the process of realizing–amidst much

Tolson in 1918 (courtesy of the Tolson family)

The Tolson family in 1930: (front) Arthur, Wiley Wilson, and Melvin, Jr.; (back) Ruth Marie, Ruth, and Tolson (photograph by Horace Mann Bond, courtesy of the Tolson family)

Tolson and his wife in Marshall, Texas, 1946 (courtesy of the Tolson family)

conflict–is only a prelude to a oneness of under-dogs everywhere:

> Then a kike said: *Workers of the world, unite!*
> And a dago said: *Let us live!*
> And a cracker said: *Ours for us!*
> And a nigger said: *Walk together, children!*
> WE ARE THE UNDERDOGS ON A HOT TRAIL!

In the 1930s poems from the book were published in *Arts Quarterly, Modern Monthly,* and *Modern Quarterly.* V. F. Calverton, the editor of *Modern Monthly* and of the Modern Library *Anthology of American Negro Literature* (1929), became a staunch friend and supporter of Tolson. He introduced him to important editors and in his column "The Cultural Barometer" in *Current History* (February 1938) described him as "a bright, vivid writer who attains his best effects by understatement rather than overstatement, and who catches in a line or a stanza what most of his contemporaries have failed to capture in pages and volumes."

Throughout his life Tolson loved an argument, and he seldom backed off from controversy. Early in 1933 when Langston Hughes's poem "Good-Bye Christ" created a public furor,

Tolson defended his religious and social views in a piece published in two parts in the *Pittsburgh Courier* (26 January and 2 February). In September 1937 he also published a caustic article, "Wanted: A New Negro Leadership," in the *Oracle.* That article, plus his growing reputation as a speaker, an extraordinarily successful debate coach, and a beginning-to-be published poet, probably led to his invitation to write a weekly column, "Caviar and Cabbage," in the *Washington Tribune.* Selections from the column were published in 1982. For most of seven years he wrote freely and challengingly on a miscellany of topics. Tolson himself best describes the persistent voice of these columns:

> I am an optimist. I believe a better world is coming by and by. I believe that human nature can be converted, changed, reconditioned, I do not believe man is born to be selfish, poverty-stricken, ignorant, unthinking.
>
> There are critics who say that I hit with the kick of a Missouri Mule. If I fail to do this, it aint no fault of mine. I don't hold malice. I don't hate persons.

I hate ideas and customs that keep people from happiness.

In 1939 Tolson's "Dark Symphony" won first place in the national poetry contest sponsored by the American Negro Exposition in Chicago. *Atlantic Monthly* published the poem in 1941. Mary Lou Chamberlain, then an editor on the *Atlantic Monthly* staff, was so impressed with his work that when she later moved to Dodd, Mead, she invited Tolson to submit a collection of his poems for book publication. *Rendezvous with America* was published during World War II in 1944 and quickly went to three editions.

Thematically, *Rendezvous with America* argues for the inevitability of the people's triumph through class struggle; the meek—the proletariat—shall inherit the earth. But Tolson characteristically added a countervailing dose of Missouri skepticism, "but only if they work and fight for it." He saw hope in the breakdown of racial barriers and in the class unity emerging from the hardships of the Depression. The greed of the capitalists would lead to their own destruction. World War II amplified this same lesson to the international scene. The European civilizations had made a mockery of the very civilization they pretended to represent. Those peoples and nations abused and exploited by colonialism and racism would emerge as leaders after the war.

Tolson arranged his poems into eight sections to shape his message to the nation and the world at war. The long opening poem, "Rendezvous with America," reminds the reader of the strength America draws from being a nation of peoples from widely different national, social, and racial experiences. "Woodcuts for Americana" praises America for its strengths and condemns it for its inequities. "Dark Symphony," which celebrates specifically the historic contribution of black Americans and their struggle to gain recognition for their achievements, ends with a proud and defiant prediction of black accomplishment and cultural realization. "A Song for Myself," which includes the poem by the same title, argues that art gives the artist the strength to survive. The "Sonnets," with their emphasis on a poetic form as a principle of organization, suggest that the health of a society depends on the personal integrity of its members plus the group realization of a democratic ethos. "Of Men and Cities" views world history as a drama of human aspiration and failure. "The Idols of the Tribe" focuses on the corruption of man's

dreams by his prejudices and his creation and worship of false gods. "Tapestries of Time" threads a sturdy faith in human progress through the wreckage of man's history, particularly through the chaos and destruction of World War II.

The reviews of *Rendezvous* were many and generous in their praise. Representative was Arthur E. Burke in *Crisis* who measured Tolson against the major black poets of the time and marked out his particular contribution:

> Melvin Tolson's *Rendezvous with America* . . . carries one back to Cullen's *Color* and Hughes' *Fine Clothes to the Jew.* No Negro poet save Sterling Brown, in his *Southern Road,* has published in volume so much that is remarkable for its freshness, its poetic imagination, and above all, its reflection of American life as it affects Negroes. The reader will not find here the same sort of color consciousness found in Cullen, the same rawness of life in Hughes, or the same satirical humor in Brown. All these elements are here but in a mood peculiar to Tolson. Tolson exhibits a vigorous Americanism, a fine catholicity, a generous humanity seldom met with.

In 1947 Tolson left Wiley College to join Langston University in Oklahoma. That year he was named poet laureate of Liberia by Pres. William S. V. Tubman and commissioned to write a poem for Liberia's centennial in 1956. The *Libretto for the Republic of Liberia,* with an effusive introduction by Allen Tate, expands the themes of *Rendezvous with America.* Liberia is invoked as "the quicksilver sparrow that slips The Eagle's claw!" Liberia is an effort by Americans, white and black, to establish a new nation on what is perhaps the most ancient site of human habitation in the world. Liberia, as its name implies, is a part of an emerging universal brotherhood of freedom that makes a mockery of the divisive idols of the tribe of race, caste, and class.

Tolson eschews any suggestion that the founding of Liberia is akin to European colonialism. Instead, he recounts the heroic efforts of Elijah Johnson and Jehudi Ashmun to establish a new nation. As Tolson tries to draw the line that evidences the evolutionary force of democratic freedom at work in history, he links these events to Liberia's role in World War II as a base for American bombers in Africa. Tolson argues strongly that World War II must mark the end of colonialism if there is to be world peace.

On 19 October 1940, in "Caviar and Cabbage," Tolson described the Ferris wheel theory

Tolson and Egbert McLeod, president of Wiley College, circa 1950 (courtesy of the Schomburg Center for Research in Black Culture, the New York Public Library, Astor, Lenox and Tilden Foundations)

Tolson and Robert Frost (courtesy of the Tolson family)

of history; a nation which becomes stronger than another becomes deluded with a sense of superiority that leads inevitably to its own defeat. He suggested it should be replaced with a merry-go-round theory of history based on economic and racial brotherhood. "On the merry-go-round all seats are on the same level. Nobody goes up; therefore, nobody has to come down. That is democracy as I see it." The themes are repeated in the *Libretto for the Republic of Liberia*:

> The ferris wheel
> of race, of caste, of class
> dumped and alped cadavers till the ground
> fogged the Pleiades with Gila rot. . . . .

In contrast, the new day dawning is a triumph of the world's previously despised, the *vile canaille*, the *Gorii*, the *Bastard-rasse*, the *uomo-qualyque*, the *hoi-barbaroi*, the *vsechelovek*, the *descamisados*, and the *hoi polloi*. All of these "Unparadised nobodies with maps of Nowhere/ride the merry-go-round!" Tolson is well aware of the challenge man's history poses to any optimistic belief in the emergence of utopian order. In *Libretto for the Republic of Liberia* he cites instance after instance of man's barbarism and self-destructiveness, his worship, wittingly or unwittingly, of the false idols of the tribe of race, caste, and class, all of which are in turn the product of the competition for economic power or the lust of money.

> below the triumvirate flag & tongue & mammon
>   while *blut und boden* play the anthem *iron masters*
>   *gold*
>   ruble shilling franc yen lira baht and dime
>   brass-knuckled (*la légalité nous tue*)
>   wage armageddon on the temple of *dieu et*
>   *l'état.*

Tolson closes his poem with a surreal tour, by auto (the Futurafrique), by train (the United Nations Limited), and by plane (*Le Premier des Noirs*), which leads its passengers to the Parliament of African Peoples, where the "Iscariot cuckolded four freedoms" are given new life, and the axiom *unto each according as any one has need* is brought out of storage and made ready for use. The economic and cultural dominance of Europe ultimately gives way to a liberated and fruitfully peaceful universal order of mankind. Man's imagination is freed from the self-inhibiting restrictions with which generations of history have shackled it:

> The Parliament of African Peoples signets forever
> the recessional of Europe and
> trumpets the abolition of itself
> and no nation uses *Felis leo* or
> *Aquila heliaca* as the emblem of
> *blunt und boden* . . . and the
> deserts that gave up the ghost
> to green pastures chant in the
> ears and teeth of the Dog in
> the Rosh Hashana of the Afric
> calends: "*Honi soit qui maly*
> *pense!*"

The 1950s were a time of increasing success for Tolson. In 1951 his poem "E. & O. E." won *Poetry* magazine's Bess Hokin Prize. The next year he was elected mayor of Langston, one of several historic all-black communities in Oklahoma. He was reelected three times, and his family had difficulty persuading him not to run for a fifth term. Tolson wrote and directed a dramatic version of Walter S. White's *Fire in the Flint* (1924), which was performed at the national convention of the NAACP in Oklahoma City on 28 June 1952. In 1954 Tolson was admitted to the Liberian Knighthood of the Order of the Star of Africa. A short time later Pres. William S. V. Tubman of Liberia made a ceremonial visit to Langston. Tolson was appointed permanent fellow in poetry and drama at Bread Loaf in 1954 and there began a friendship with Robert Frost. In 1956 Tolson was an honored guest at the ceremonies inaugurating Tubman for another term as president of Liberia. On his return trip from Liberia he stopped in Paris, where Melvin Tolson, Jr., was studying at the Sorbonne, and spent an afternoon sharing experiences with Richard Wright.

Planned as a five-book epic poem which would tell the history of black America, *Harlem Gallery: Book I, The Curator* is Tolson's last major work. The present, the chronological end of the story, was to be represented in the first book. Harlem was to be its setting. Instead of representing a diverse citizenry of Harlem as poetic portraits hanging in a fictional gallery as in *A Gallery of Harlem Portraits*, Tolson assumed a literal art gallery functioning within the Harlem community. The Curator of the gallery provides the central point of view.

The Curator's friends, three major characters who are all practicing artists, dramatically amplify the reader's view of the black artist's dilemma and achievement. John Laugart's painting *Black Bourgeoisie* is in keeping with Tolson's view that the artist, the true ape of God, must

Tolson in 1965 (courtesy of the Tolson family)

Dr. Nkomo carry on a running debate on the relation of the artist to his milieu. It is through this debate and its extension in the lives of the artists, Laugart, Starks, and Heights, that Tolson attempts to picture the achievements and dilemmas of contemporary black American culture.

It is a world marked by thwarted ambition and absurd conflict, as the inevitable collapse of the idols of the tribe brings confusion and chaos in its wake, and it is a world of hope, where the new order is prefigured. The Curator opens the poem by observing that "The Harlem Gallery, an Afric pepper bird,/awakes me at a people's dusk of dawn." The echo of W. E. B. Du Bois's *Dusk of Dawn: An Essay Toward an Autobiography of a Race Concept* (1940) is meant to remind the reader of Du Bois's prophecy that the twentieth century is the century of the color line. At the close of *Harlem Gallery* the Curator indicates the future by the contrasting nature of the flowers of the black and white communities. Symbols of life grow in the ghetto, but symbols of death "blow in the white metropolis."

> In the black ghetto
> white heather
> and the white almond grow,
> but the hyacinth
> and the asphodel blow
> in the white metropolis!

As Tolson told Jack Bickham (*Oklahoma's Orbit*, 29 August 1965): "I say that the flowers representing decay and death are found in the white metropolis, but the flowers of hope grow in the black belt. I speak here of the masses of poor people. They are on the move. Most American writers are cynical. But even in the violence of Richard Wright there is something that lifts you. There is no despair." The Curator, too, does not despair at the cruel dilemmas that the black American artist faces:

> I hazard—yet,
> this allegro of the Harlem Gallery
> is not a chippy fire,
> for here, in focus, are paintings that chronicle
> a people's New World odyssey,
> from chattel to Esquire!

Karl Shapiro's introduction to *Harlem Gallery* appeared as a prepublication review in the *New York Herald Tribune* on 10 January 1965. He gave high praise to the book: "A great poet has been living in our midst for decades and is al-

cleanse this world with his searing portrayal of the enervating prejudices of the idols of the tribe. The Curator sees himself and Laugart as "the Castor and Pollux of St. Elmo's fire,/on Harlem's Coalsack Way." Mister Starks—*Mister* is his given name—is a former jazz pianist and now conductor of the Harlem Symphony Orchestra and composer of "Black Orchid Suite," dedicated to his wife, whose infidelity causes him to choose suicide. Starks is a poet, and his "Harlem Vignettes," reminiscent of Tolson's *A Gallery of Harlem Portraits*, gives penetrating insight into the other characters of *Harlem Gallery*. Hideho Heights, the bold and popular "Redskin beatnik bard of Lenox Avenue," also has a hidden self, which the Curator discovers when he comes across the manuscript of Hideho's "E. & O. E.," a private poem in the modern vein, a dramatically ironic reference to Tolson's own poem.

The Curator is both professionally and personally interested in the lives and achievements of these artists. He shares his views and concerns with Dr. Obi Nkomo, an alter ego whose challenging observations Tolson sometimes gives more authority than the Curator's. Nkomo is a native African, educated in the West and at sophisticated ease in Harlem, although still retaining an authentic African perspective. The Curator and

most totally unknown, even by the literati, even by poets." Shapiro has reiterated his praise for Tolson as "one of the great architects of modern poetry" on many subsequent occasions, but only one book-length analysis of the poem has been done.

Tolson achieved much recognition in 1965. His alma mater, Lincoln University, granted him an honorary doctorate. He was elected to the *New York Herald Tribune* book review board. He gave a reading at the Library of Congress under the auspices of the Gertrude Clark Whittall Poetry and Literature Fund. The District of Columbia gave him a citation and award for cultural achievement in the fine arts. And upon his retirement from Langston University he became the first appointee to the Avalon Chair in Humanities at Tuskegee Institute for the academic year 1965-1966. However, all this gratifying public recognition came against a backdrop of ominous concern for his physical health. In 1964 Tolson had two separate operations for abdominal cancer. His recovery at times appeared almost miracu-lously complete as he thrived on the public attention that now seemed lavish compared to that of previous years. In 1966 he won the National Institute and American Academy of Arts and Letters Award in Literature which carried with it a grant of twenty-five hundred dollars. He entered St. Paul's Hospital in Dallas, Texas, in June 1966 for the first of three more operations over the next three months which were a vain effort to save his life. He died 29 August 1966.

References:

Robert M. Farnsworth, *Melvin B. Tolson, 1898-1966: Plain Talk and Poetic Prophecy* (Columbia: University of Missouri Press, 1984);

Joy Flasch, *Melvin B. Tolson* (New York: Twayne, 1972);

Mariann Russell, *Melvin B. Tolson's Harlem Gallery* (Columbia: University of Missouri Press, 1980).

Papers:

The principal collection of Tolson's papers is in the manuscript division at the Library of Congress.

Margaret Walker

(7 July 1915-   )

Joyce Pettis
North Carolina State University

BOOKS: *For My People* (New Haven: Yale University Press, 1942);
Jubilee (Boston: Houghton Mifflin, 1966; London: Hodder & Stoughton, 1967);
Prophets for a New Day (Detroit: Broadside Press, 1970);
How I Wrote Jubilee (Chicago: Third World Press, 1972);
October Journey (Detroit: Broadside Press, 1973);
A Poetic Equation: Conversations Between Nikki Giovanni and Margaret Walker, by Walker and Nikki Giovanni (Washington, D.C.: Howard University Press, 1974);
For Farish Street Green (Jackson, Miss., 1986);
This Is My Century: New and Collected Poems (Athens: University of Georgia Press, 1988).

OTHER: "New Poets," in *Black Expression,* edited by Addison Gayle, Jr. (New York: Weybright & Talley, 1969), pp. 89-100;
"Willing to Pay the Price," in *Many Shades of Black,* edited by Stanton L. Wormley and Louis H. Fenderson (New York: Morrow, 1969), pp. 117-130;
"Richard Wright," in *Richard Wright: Impressions and Perspectives,* edited by David Ray and Robert M. Farnsworth (Ann Arbor, Mich.: University of Michigan Press, 1973), pp. 47-67;
"On Being Female, Black, and Free," in *The Writer on Her Work,* edited by Janet Sternburg (New York: Norton, 1980), pp. 95-106.

PERIODICAL PUBLICATIONS: "The Humanistic Tradition of Afro-American Literature," *American Libraries,* 1 (October 1970): 849-854;
"Some Aspects of the Black Aesthetic," *Freedomways,* 16 (Winter 1976): 95-102.

Margaret Walker, poet, novelist, teacher, and essayist, published poetry in the 1930s in the prestigious magazine *Poetry, Opportunity,* and in *Crisis.* Having published her first volume of poems in 1942, her second one in 1970, and a prize-

Margaret Walker, 1942 (courtesy of the Schomburg Center for Research in Black Culture, the New York Public Library, Astor, Lenox and Tilden Foundations)

winning novel in 1966–and having continued writing into the 1980s–her career spans five decades. Throughout this time, the themes, images, and subjects of her work have remained consistently pertinent to a changing society. Her work is suffused by a complete historical perspective and humanism.

Much of Walker's responsiveness to the black experience, communicated through the realism of her work, can be attributed to her growing up in a southern home environment which emphasized the rich heritage of black culture. Margaret Abigail Walker was born 7 July 1915 in

Birmingham, Alabama, to the Reverend Sigismund C. Walker and Marion Dozier Walker. The family moved to New Orleans when Walker was a young child. A Methodist minister who had been born near Buff Bay, Jamaica, Walker's father was a scholar who bequeathed to his daughter his love of literature–the classics, the Bible, Benedict de Spinoza, Arthur Schopenhauer, the English classics, and poetry. Similarly, Walker's musician mother played ragtime and read poetry to her, choosing among such varied authors and works as Paul Laurence Dunbar, John Greenleaf Whittier's "Snowbound," the Bible, and Shakespeare. At age eleven Walker began reading the poetry of Langston Hughes and Countee Cullen. Elvira Ware Dozier, her maternal grandmother, who lived with her family, told Walker stories, including the story of her own mother, a former slave in Georgia. Before she finished college, at Northwestern University in Evanston, Illinois, in the early 1930s, Walker had heard James Weldon Johnson read from *God's Trombones* (1927), listened to Marian Anderson and Roland Hayes sing in New Orleans, and, in 1932, heard Hughes read his poetry in a lecture recital at New Orleans University, where her parents then taught. She met Hughes in 1932, and he encouraged her to continue writing poetry. Her first poem was published in *Crisis* in 1934.

As a senior at Northwestern in 1934 Walker began a fruitful association with the Works Progress Administration. She lived on Chicago's North Side and worked as a volunteer on the WPA recreation project. The project directors assigned her to associate with so-called delinquent girls, mainly shoplifters and prostitutes, in order to determine if Walker's different background and training might have a positive influence on them. She became so fascinated by an Italian-Black neighborhood that she eventually chose it as the setting and title for an unpublished novel that she began writing, "Goose Island." On Friday, 13 March 1936, Walker received notice to report to the WPA Writer's Project in Chicago as a full-time employee. Classified as a junior writer–her salary was eighty-five dollars a month–her work assignment was the Illinois Guide Book. Other writers on the project were Nelson Algren, Jacob Scher, James Phelan, Sam Ross, Katherine Dunham, Willard Motley, Frank Yerby, Fenton Johnson, and Richard Wright. In 1937 the WPA office allowed her to come into the downtown quarters only twice weekly so that she might remain at home working on her novel.

Perhaps her most rewarding interaction with a writer at the project was Walker's friendship with Wright, a liaison that, while it lasted, proved practical and beneficial to both fledgling writers. Before she joined the project, Walker had met Wright in Chicago in February 1936, when he had presided at the writer's section of the first National Negro Congress. Walker had attended solely to meet Hughes again, to show him the poetry she had written since their first meeting four years earlier. Hughes refused to take her only copy of the poems, but he introduced her to Wright and insisted that he include Walker if a writer's group organized. Wright then introduced her to Arna Bontemps and Sterling A. Brown, also writers with the WPA.

Her introduction to Wright was the beginning of a three-year association and friendship which Walker remembers as a "rare and once-in-a-lifetime association . . . rather uncommon in its completely literary nature." During those years both Walker and Wright worked diligently to publish for the first time in national books and magazines. Walker's poems "For My People" (1937), "We Have Been Believers" (1938), and "The Struggle Staggers Us" (1939) were published in *Poetry*. She and Wright collaborated on the structure of her poetry, particularly the free verse pieces, deciding on a long line or strophic form, punctuated by a short line. They revised Walker's "People of Unrest," collaborated on revisions of Wright's "Almos a Man" and *Lawd Today* (1963), and discussed Negro dialect, folk materials, spirituals, and work songs. Wright supported Walker's decision to delay writing the Civil War story that eventually came forth as *Jubilee* (1966) and suggested books that she might read to further her political education, such as John Reed's *Ten Days that Shook the World* (1919).

Although Wright left Chicago for New York on 28 May 1937, neither his friendship with Walker nor their literary interdependence ended immediately. Walker provided him, in fact, with important help on *Native Son* (1940), mailing him (as he requested) newspaper clippings about Robert Nixon, a young black man accused of rape in Chicago, and assisting Wright in locating a vacant lot to use as the Dalton house address when Wright returned to Chicago briefly the next year. Furthermore, Walker was instrumental in acquiring for him a copy of the brief of Nixon's case from attorney Ulysses S. Keyes, the first black lawyer hired for the case. (He was later replaced by an NAACP attorney.) Together, Wright and

Cover for Walker's 1970 volume of poetry (courtesy of the Afro-American Collection, Blockson Library, Temple University)

Walker visited Cook County jail, where Nixon was incarcerated, and the library, where on her library card they checked out a book on Clarence Darrow and two books on the Loeb-Leopold case, from which, in part, Wright modeled Bigger's defense when he completed his novel in the Spring of 1939.

"Goose Island" was also completed in 1939, but it was never published. Walker readily admitted that it was inexpertly done because she had not at that time mastered the techniques of fiction. Moreover, she felt that her novel was doomed after she discovered in 1938 the similarities of plot between her novel and *Native Son*. Doubleday rejected the novel, telling Walker that its tone resembled a social worker writing condescendingly about poor people.

In June 1939 Walker saw Wright for the last time in New York, where she went to attend the League of American Writers convention. For Walker the friendship with Wright ended abruptly and painfully when Wright believed gossip that he thought Walker had spread and demanded that she not see him further. As late as 1973, in an essay titled "Richard Wright," Walker said the "memory of that trip [was] still too painful to discuss." Wright's biographers also minimally discuss the end of the friendship. In *A Poetic Equation* (1974) Walker says, "Some mutual 'friends' told him some kind of lie. They said that I had said something. I don't know what they told him, but he became inarticulate with rage." In his *Richard Wright* (1980) Addison Gayle, Jr., reports that Wright accused Walker of betraying him, refused to identify the informers, and ordered her to leave the city. Wright also refused to help her with "Goose Island" as he had promised, saying, "I'm not interested in your

novel anymore . . . the relationship is over." Michel Fabre, in *The Unfinished Quest of Richard Wright* (1973), stops short of saying that unfulfilled romantic expectations contributed to the split, although Walker has always maintained that the friendship was "completely literary [in] nature." Fabre says that "in her frankness, she apparently committed indiscretions which almost lost Wright some of his friends in Chicago. . . . She would certainly not have suffered such shock and disappointment if Wright had admitted to her sooner that he was in love with and on the point of marrying someone else." Although Wright wrote Walker later, for her the friendship was over, and she never communicated with him again.

The termination of the friendship with Wright was only one of several endings awaiting Walker in 1939. That year Congress passed a law that WPA employees had to leave if they had been employed as long as eighteen months. Although she could have resumed employment after an interim period, Walker decided to enroll in graduate school for an M.A. in English. She reasoned that with an advanced degree she could teach in college and continue to write. As a result of some assignments with the WPA, she knew she was unsuited for newspaper work or for survival as a free-lance writer.

Walker left Chicago and traveled to Iowa City, Iowa, to the University of Iowa Writers' Workshop, where instructor Paul Engle helped rekindle her love of folk materials. She was already familiar with and impressed by the synthesis of folk culture in Zora Neale Hurston's first novel, *Jonah's Gourd Vine* (1934). She had also read Dunbar's dialect poetry, Sterling A. Brown's folk poetry, and the urban folk material of Langston Hughes's poems, and she had heard her maternal grandmother's stories and folk sayings. Her original idea for an M.A. thesis (conceived while an undergraduate at Northwestern) was a Civil War novel about her great-grandmother. Her final decision was the poetry collection *For My People*, published by Yale University Press in 1942, two years after she received her M.A. from Iowa.

For My People, which won the Yale University Younger Poet's Award, was the first book of poetry published by a black woman since Georgia Douglas Johnson's *The Heart of a Woman and Other Poems* (1918). With this volume Walker became the first American black woman honored in such a prestigious national literary competition. Her identification with the trials of black people and the boldness with which she denounced the evils of racism, particularly in the title poem of *For My People*, parallel the work in the 1940s of poets Brown, Robert Hayden, and Melvin Tolson. Stephen Vincent Benét's foreword recognizes Walker's talent and, indirectly, her indebtedness to folk culture and the cadence of her preacher father's voice. He wrote that the poems are marked by "straightforwardness, directness, [and] reality," and that those qualities are "combined with a controlled intensity of emotion and a language that, at times, even when it [is] most modern, [has] something of the surge of biblical poetry."

The structure of "For My People" is used with minor variations in several other poems in the volume. The ten stanzas are units or strophes of free verse characterized by parallelism, repetition of phrases, and paradox. The first nine stanzas depend upon the completed imperative sentences of the tenth stanza for their full meaning; this tenth stanza demands that a new world be created for black citizens who have been overtly denied by the practices of the present world. The speaker in each stanza functions as a movie camera might, sweeping in randomly organized fashion, focusing on scenes of the black experience. In the third stanza, for example, the speaker frames children "in the clay and dust and sand of Alabama/backyards playing baptizing and preaching and doctor." In the sixth stanza people are thronging streets in Chicago, New York, and New Orleans, "lost disinherited dispossessed, and happy/people filling the cabarets . . . and other people's pockets." The images used are representative of the multitextured collage that is the black experience in America. Implicit in the breathless tumbling effect of the words is the suggestion that, from a historical perspective, efforts at racial development have been futile for the majority of the black population. Failed expectations have resulted in appalling despair and disappointment. Because of Walker's intimate knowledge of the South and of the plight of her people, regardless of geography, she effectively communicates their static condition in a progressive country. The poem urges action, demands sweeping changes, and warns that change eventually may be wrought through violence, a "bloody peace."

The remaining nine poems in the first section of *For My People* are spoken by a narrator in rebellion against provincialism and romanticism, who perceives that the long years of complacency are nearing an end. In "People of Unrest" unrest

is sensed rather than seen. Black people in meta-
phorically languorous positions stare from pil-
lows into the sun, waiting. "Since 1619" consists
of questions designed to spotlight postures that
have inhibited black mobility.

> How many years since 1619 have I been singing
> Spirituals?
> How long have I been praising God and shout-
> ing hallelujahs?
>
> ....
>
> When will I burst from my kennel an angry mon-
> grel,
> Lean and hungry and tired of my dry bones and
> years?

"We Have Been Believers," similar to "For My People" in structure and content, condemns what
black people have believed in–"black gods of an
old land" and "white gods of a new land"–to say
"We have been believers/ . . . too long. Now the
needy no longer weep/and pray; the long-suffering arise, and our fists bleed/against the bars
with a strange insistency."

The last poem in section 1, "Today," is the
only one in the volume in which Walker moves beyond her direct focus on the black experience.
Middle America, "complacently smug in a snug
somnolescence," is oblivious to the warnings of
World War II being sounded from Europe just as
they have proven themselves insensitive to the unrest of black Americans: "I sing of slum scabs on
city faces,/scrawny children scarred by bombs
and dying of hunger,/wretched human scare-
crows strung against lynching stakes. . . . "

Four lyric poems in the first section of *For
My People* express love and longing for the physical beauty of the southern landscape. "My roots
are deep in southern life. . . . I belong with the
smell of fresh pine, with the trail of coon, and
the spring growth of wild onion," the speaker
says in "Sorrow Home." Here, and in "Southern
Song," realism persists, however, and the speaker
knows that black life in the South is marred by racial strife. Two stanzas of lush pastoral imagery
are contrasted with these lines: "I want no mobs
to wrench me from my southern rest; no/forms
to take me in the night and burn my shack and/
make for me a nightmare full of oil and flame."
"Dark Blood" envisions the speaker's origin in nostalgic and romantic images of Africa but concludes with the realistic antithesis of a return to
Mobile, Alabama, to "littered streets and the one-
room shacks." Finally, in "Lineage," a compact
poem praising the strength of grandmothers who

Walker, circa 1970

"followed plows and bent to toil/moved through
fields sowing seed," the speaker ponders a seem-
ing reversal of evolution, since she is weaker than
her foremothers.

The central section of *For My People* is a folk
gallery of ten portraits, among them predictable
black archetypes like "Bad-Man Stagolee" and
"Big John Henry," but also "Poppa Chicken,"
"Mollie Means," and "Kissie Lee." Written in ballad rhythm and style, these narratives feature characters whose deeds have lifted them to heroic
stature in the black community. Some characters,
Bad-Man Stagolee and Kissie Lee, for example,
have flouted the law and escaped punishment.
Others, such as Big John Henry and Gus, the Line-
man, earn their reputations through extraordinary perseverance demonstrated in their jobs.
Poppa Chicken "was a sugah daddy" and Teacher
"a pimp and rake," but their stories contain not
condemnation of their activities but pride because of their toughness. Mollie Means, unlike
the other flesh and blood characters, is cast in
the aura of the supernatural. Walker says Mollie
was a character in the stories her grandmother
told her about a woman or a witch who put a
spell on a young bride. Walker fleshes out the

poem with other details of Mollie's practices, how she "cast her spells and called the dead" and how "farmers feared their crops would blight." The most sustained passage in the poem is the spell put on the bride, and the groom's search to find a conjurer powerful enough to reverse it. Even after she "died at the hands of her evil deed," Mollie's ghost terrorizes the neighborhood.

Some of the remaining six sonnets in the third section of the volume continue the social protest begun in part 1, but in a subjective voice. Unrest, dissatisfaction, and intense anger characterize the mood of the workers. In "Childhood" the speaker observes miners returning from work, "the swing of dinner buckets in their hands/ and grumbling undermining all their words." In "Memory" the speaker sees "shoulders hunched against a sharp concern/And smells a deep and sinister unrest." The volume ends with "the struggle for bread, for pride, for simple dignity."

Walker began teaching in the 1940s. She taught at North Carolina's Livingstone College in 1941 and West Virginia State College in 1942. On 13 June 1943 she married Firnist James Alexander. In that year, too, she began to read her poetry publicly when she was invited by Arthur P. Davis to read "For My People" at Richmond's Virginia Union University, where he was then teaching. After the birth of the first of her four children in 1944 Walker returned to teach at Livingstone for a year. She also resumed the research on her Civil War novel in the 1940s. She began with a trip to the Schomburg Center in 1942. In 1944 she received a Rosenwald Fellowship to further her research. In 1948 Walker was unemployed, living in High Point, North Carolina, and working on the novel. By then she clearly envisioned the development of *Jubilee* as a folk novel and prepared an outline of incidents and chapter headings. (Almost all the chapter headings were supplied by the stories of her grandmother.) In 1949 Walker moved to Jackson, Mississippi, and began her long teaching career at Jackson State College (now Jackson State University).

In the 1950s Walker continued to do research for *Jubilee*. In 1953 she traced her grandmother's family's path from Greenville, Alabama, to Dawson, Georgia. In Greenville she located her grandmother's youngest sister, who had a picture of Walker's great-grandmother, the model for the heroine of *Jubilee*; the family Bible; and the chest that the great-grandmother had carried from the plantation. Walker used the Southern

Historical Collection at the University of North Carolina at Chapel Hill (specifically, the Nelson Tift papers) and the slave narratives in the Martin Collection at North Carolina Central University, Durham. In January 1954 Walker traveled to Yale as a Ford Fellow and revised her story. However, according to her adviser, she retained a major flaw in the fiction: she was telling the story, but her prose was dead. Walker returned to Jackson State and her former teaching job in September 1954. With a fourth baby, she and her husband concentrated on the acquisition of a home for the family. For the next seven years, 1955 to 1962, she and her husband were plagued with medical and financial pressures. During that period, although Walker wrote and published almost nothing, she continued her research by reading until she was saturated in the era covered by the novel.

In 1962 Walker returned to the University of Iowa Writers' Workshop to begin work on a Ph.D. in English. Working with her former adviser, Paul Engle, she planned a program to use the novel as her dissertation. Verlin Cassill showed her how to make the material come alive. Taking courses, teaching freshman English, and doing the other chores doctoral study requires, she found little time for work on *Jubilee*. By fall 1964, however, with major degree requirements behind her, Walker began writing once more. She received a year's salary advance from Jackson State so that she might write without financial hardship. The last sentence was typed on 9 April 1965.

The fictional history of Walker's great-grandmother, here called Vyry, *Jubilee* is divided into three sections: the antebellum years in Georgia on John Dutton's plantation, the Civil War years, and the Reconstruction era. Against a panoramic view of history Walker focuses the plot specifically on Vyry's life as she grows from a little girl to adulthood. In the first section Vyry, the slave, matures, marries and separates from Randall Ware, attempts to escape from slavery with her two children, and is flogged. The second section emphasizes the destruction of war and the upheaval for slaveowner and slaves, while the last section focuses on Vyry as a displaced former slave, searching for a home.

Walker said her research was done "to undergird the oral tradition" and *Jubilee* is primarily known for its realistic depiction of the daily life and folklore of the black slave community. Although there are also quotes from Whittier and

the English romantic poets, she emphasizes the importance of the folk structure of her novel by prefacing each of the fifty-eight chapters with proverbial folk sayings or lines excerpted from spirituals. The narrative is laced with verses of songs sung by Vyry, her guardian, or other slaves. A portion from a sermon is included. The rhymes of slave children are also a part of the narrative. A conjuring episode is told involving the overseer Grimes, suggesting how some folk beliefs were used for protection. Vyry provides a catalogue of herbs and discusses their medicinal and culinary purposes.

Responses to Walker's Civil War story were mixed. Guy Davenport in the *National Review* (4 October 1966) said that "the novel from end to end [is] about a place and a people who never existed." For him Walker had merely recalled all the elements of the southern myth, writing a lot of "tushery that comes out of books, out of Yerby and Margaret Mitchell." He further found "something deeply ironic in a Negro's underwriting the made-up South of the romances, agreeing to every convention of the trade." More justly, Abraham Chapman in the *Saturday Review* (24 September 1966) found "a fidelity to fact and detail" in the depictions of slave life that was better than anything done before. Lester Davis in *Freedomways* (Summer 1967) decided that one could overlook the "sometimes trite and often stilted prose style" because the novel is "a good forthright treatment of a segment of American history about which there has been much hypocrisy and deliberate distortion." He found the "flavor of authenticity . . . convincing and refreshing." Walker's *How I Wrote Jubilee* (1972), a history of the novel's development from her grandmother's oral history, is an indirect response to those critics who compared *Jubilee* with books like Mitchell's *Gone with the Wind* (1936) and who accused Walker of sustaining the southern myth from the black perspective. She answers her detractors by citing the references and historical documents she perused over several years in order to gird her oral story with historical fact.

Walker's second volume of poetry, *Prophets for a New Day*, was published in 1970. She has called *Prophets for a New Day* her civil rights poems, and only two poems in the volume, "Elegy" and "Ballad of the Hoppy Toad," are not about the civil rights movement. Walker begins the volume with two poems in which the speakers are young children; one eight-year-old demonstrator eagerly waits to be arrested with her

group in the fight for equality, and a second one is already jailed and wants no bail. Her point is that these young girls are just as much prophets for a new day as were Nat Turner, Gabriel Prosser, Denmark Vesey, Toussaint L'Ouverture, and John Brown. In "The Ballad of the Free" Walker establishes a biblical allusion and association as an integral part of the fight to end racism: "The serpent is loosed and the hour is come/The last shall be first and the first shall be none/The serpent is loosed and the hour is come."

The title poem, "Prophets for a New Day," and the seven poems which follow it invite obvious comparisons between the biblical prophets and the black leaders who denounced racial injustice and prophesied change during the civil rights struggle of the 1960s. For example, several prophets are linked to specific southern cities marked by racial turmoil: in "Jeremiah," the first poem of the series, Jeremiah "is now a man whose name is Benjamin/Brooding over a city called Atlanta/Preaching the doom of a curse upon the land." Among the poems other prophets mentioned are "Isaiah," "Amos," and "Micah," a poem subtitled "To the memory of Medgar Evers of Mississippi."

In *For My People* Walker urged that activity replace complacency, but in *Prophets for a New Day* she applauds the new day of freedom for black people, focusing on the events, sites, and people of the struggle. Among the poems that recognize southern cities associated with racial turbulence are "Oxford Is A Legend," "Birmingham," "Jackson, Mississippi," and "Sit-Ins." Of these, the latter two are the most accomplished pieces. "Sit-Ins" (Greensboro, North Carolina, in the spring of 1960) is a recognition of "those first bright young to fling [their] . . . names across pages/Of new Southern history/With courage and faith, convictions, and intelligence. . . ." "Jackson, Mississippi" is a lament:

> Here lie three centuries of my eyes and my brains
>   and my hands
> Of my lips and strident demands
> The graves of my dead.
> I give you my heart, Southern City
> For my eyes are full and no tears cry
> And my throat is dusty and dry.

"At the Lincoln Monument in Washington August 28, 1963" draws an analogy between the marchers gathered there and Moses and his people marching out of Egypt. "For Andy Goodman,

Dust jacket for Walker's 1973 volume of poetry (courtesy of Afro-American Collection, Blockson Library, Temple University)

Michael Schwerner and James Chaney," a long lyrical piece, mourns the deaths of the three young civil rights workers murdered in Mississippi on 21 June 1964. "For Malcolm X" recognizes the devastating emptiness left by the death of Malcolm X. In "How Many Silent Centuries Sleep in My Sultry Veins?" the speaker recognizes the varied ancestry that people of color may have.

Three years after *Prophets for a New Day* was published, Broadside Press published *October Journey* (1973), a booklet of only ten poems, of which all but one had been previously published. *October Journey* lacks a thematic arrangement, but all but two of the poems are tributes. "Mary McLeod Bethune," "Paul Laurence Dunbar," "Gwendolyn Brooks," and "Harriet Tubman" are poems that laud the achievements of those admirable persons. "Epitaph for My Father," the longest

poem of the volume, is a commemorative verse to the poet's father. "Ode on the Occasion of the Inauguration of the Sixth President of Jackson State College" pays tribute to those who have administered and taught in historically black colleges throughout the South, often in the face of open hostility. In "Dear Are The Names That Charmed Me In My Youth" the narrator offers personal thanks to unnamed faces who inspired her life to be a "charging promise ringed with rhapsody." The title poem of the volume expresses the beauty of the Southland in the fall, contrasting it with memories of racial oppression:

> I feel the pulse within my throat
> my heart fills up with hungry fear
> while hills and flatlands stark and staring
> before my dark eyes sad and haunting
> appear and disappear.

The last poem of the volume, "A Litany From the Dark People," is a prayer which traces the progress of black people "up from the deepest dungeon and from the darkest night/Into the day of learning and of Education's light."

Editor Paula Giddings conceived the idea for *A Poetic Equation: Conversations Between Nikki Giovanni and Margaret Walker* when she heard Giovanni and Walker on the same program electrify an overflow crowd with readings of their poetry. Walker (clearly the dominant conversationalist) and Giovanni informally discuss a variety of subjects: their personal responses to racism and racial violence; writing, criticism, and film; the future of the black man; Africa; and finally, their children. The most informative and interesting sections are those in which Walker recalls various experiences as a writer and remembers personal anecdotes concerning writers she has known over the years. For example, she discusses her friendship with Richard Wright and analyzes the method he used to write *Native Son*. She remembers her first meeting with Gwendolyn Brooks in the 1930s when both of them lived in Chicago, and her first meetings with Langston Hughes and Ralph Ellison. She speaks minimally of her own published works and of various influences on her development as a poet and novelist.

Retirement from Jackson State University in 1979 has given Walker more time for writing and lecturing. Because of her expertise in black literature and her reputation as a novelist and poet, she is a popular consultant at national conferences and seminars. Recently, Walker was one of three keynote speakers at a conference on the cultural history of black women held in 1984 at Bennett College, Greensboro, North Carolina, and keynote speaker at the international symposium on Wright held at the University of Mississippi in fall 1985.

Among Walker's major projects in retirement has been completion of the book "Richard Wright," whose publication has been delayed by legal entanglements from Wright's widow. Walker is also at work on a collection of her previously published poetry to be titled "This is My Century: The Daemmic Genius." A number of books with Walker as subject are underway by various scholars.

When Benét wrote the introduction to Walker's first book of poetry, he said that he knew she had other books to give. Seven books and nearly forty-five years later, it is expected that Walker has still more books to give, including her autobiography. If she should write no other poems or novels, however, her position as an important chronicler of the black experience and a leading figure in American letters is assured. Walker, however, describes herself in the following terms: "I am a writer, first of all; I hope a poet; certainly an English teacher." And that, undoubtedly, is how generations of readers will also think of her.

References:

Paula Giddings, " 'A Shoulder Hunched Against a Sharp Concern,' " *Black World,* 21 (December 1971): 20-25;

Gloria Hull, "Black Women Poets from Wheatley to Walker," *Negro American Literature Forum,* 9 (Fall 1975): 91-96;

John Griffin Jones, "Margaret Walker Alexander," in his *Mississippi Writers Talking,* 2 volumes (Jackson: University Press of Mississippi, 1982, 1983), II: 120-146;

Charles Rowell, "Poetry, History and Humanism: An Interview with Margaret Walker," *Black World,* 25 (December 1975): 4-17.

Papers:

Galley sheets of *Jubilee* and an uncorrected copy of *A Poetic Equation* are collected at Millsaps-Wilson Library, Millsaps College, Jackson, Mississippi. A Margaret Walker Alexander Room and Collection is housed at Jackson State University, but the bulk of the author's papers are in her personal possession.

Theodore Ward
(15 September 1902-8 May 1983)

Fahamisha Patricia Brown
Boston College

PLAY PRODUCTIONS: *Big White Fog,* Chicago, Great Northern Theatre, April 1938; New York, Lincoln Theatre, 22 October 1940;

Deliver the Goods, New York, Greenwich House, 1942;

Our Lan', New York, Henry Street Playhouse, April 1947; revised, New York, Royale Theatre, September 1947;

John Brown, New York, People's Drama, April 1950;

The Daubers, Chicago, Experimental Black Actors Guild, 1973.

OTHER: Excerpt from *Big White Fog,* in *The Negro Caravan,* edited by Sterling A. Brown, Arthur P. Davis, and Ulysses Lee (New York: Dryden, 1941), pp. 561-571;

"Analysis of a Play: *Our Lan',* by Theodore Ward," in *A Theatre in Your Head,* edited by Kenneth Rowe (New York: Funk & Wagnall, 1960), pp. 256-428;

Excerpt from *The Daubers,* in *Black Scenes,* edited by Alice Childress (Garden City, N. Y.: Doubleday, 1971), pp. 77-89;

Big White Fog, in *Black Theater U.S.A.,* edited by James V. Hatch (New York: Free Press, 1974), pp. 278-319.

PERIODICAL PUBLICATION: Excerpt from *John Brown, Masses and Mainstream,* 2 (October 1949): 36-47.

Theodore Ward (photograph © Camille Billops, courtesy of the Hatch-Billops Collection)

No history of black American theater would be complete without the inclusion of Theodore Ward. One of the first serious black playwrights of the modern period, Ward made play writing and the theater his life's work. Unfortunately, to this day, most of his work has gone unexamined and unproduced. Although his professional reputation was made in a single decade, between 1938 and 1948, Ward's vision of a skillful and historically accurate black theater was to be an animating vision of the New Black Theater Movement of the late 1960s and early 1970s, when he was rediscovered.

Ward was born in Thibodaux, Louisiana, on 15 September 1902, the eighth of eleven children, the son of a schoolteacher mother and an itinerant peddler father. Although Ward managed to acquire only a grade school education, he supplemented it through his extensive reading. (Among the products sold from the back of his father's wagon were books—religious, practical, and classical.) Ward's mother died when he was thirteen, and shortly afterward he ran away from home. He spent his teen years rambling through the United States. Ward earned a living

as a shoe shiner, barbershop porter, bellhop, and busboy. While living outside Salt Lake City he studied the short story and poetry under Louis Zucker in the extension division of the University of Utah, polishing his skills through self-study of an elementary English grammar text. In 1931 Ward won a Zona Gale Scholarship in Creative Writing to the University of Wisconsin at Madison. He remained at Wisconsin for two years, winning a second one-year scholarship on Gale's recommendation. While at Wisconsin Ward wrote at least one play. (His earlier effort at play writing had been thrown into the fire as "the work of the devil" by his highly religious father.)

Ward moved to Chicago in 1935, joining a John Reed Club and working briefly as a recreational director in the Works Progress Administration program at the Abraham Lincoln Centre on Chicago's South Side. In 1937 he wrote "Sick and Tiahd" for a play writing contest sponsored by a labor organization, winning second prize, and in 1940 his *Big White Fog* was selected for production by the Federal Theatre Project.

Big White Fog is a polemical play that explores three philosophies which offer hope to blacks: black nationalism, capitalism, and socialism-communism. The play suggests that socialism-communism is the best choice. Although there had been considerable opposition to the political content of the play, it opened in Chicago in April 1938, having received unqualified support from project director Hallie Flanagan; it ran for ten weeks. The play's exploration of a middle-class black family's encounters with American racism, capitalism, Garveyism, and socialism-communism was attacked by some critics as propaganda. Riot police were put on standby for opening night, but no racial confrontation occurred. Sterling A. Brown has said that *Big White Fog* was the most artistic of the Federal Theatre Project's Negro-unit productions.

When the Federal Theatre Project was being mandated out of existence by the United States Congress, Ward was singing in the chorus of the Chicago unit's production of the Gilbert and Sullivan musical *Swing Mikado*, which was to be sent to New York. Thus, by 1940, Ward had joined the ranks of New York's unemployed theater community. He would remain in New York for almost twenty-five years. In 1940, together with Langston Hughes, Powell Lindsay, George Norford, Theodore Browne, and Owen Dodson as members of the board of directors, Ward founded the Negro Playwrights Company. The purpose of this new company was to "reflect the realities of Negro life and to provide a working theater for Negro artists." In their brochure, "A Professional Theater with an Idea," the founders emphasized their interest in creating a "Negro literature of the drama comparable with reality or truth." For their first production they selected *Big White Fog*, calling it a "representative play by a Negro playwright."

The new production of *Big White Fog* had its New York premiere at the Lincoln Theatre on 22 October 1940 and ran for sixty-four performances. Canada Lee starred as Victor Mason, and Frank Silvera made his acting debut in the production. *Big White Fog* would be the only production of the Negro Playwrights Company because the company was never able to secure sufficient financial backing to mount a second production.

Big White Fog announced the presence of a major writing talent in black theater. The plot revolves around the efforts of the Mason family, headed by Victor Mason, a proud follower of Marcus Garvey, to come to grips with racism in Depression-era America. Although some of the dialogue is pretentious, Ward manages to cram the play with vignettes that transmit the reality of the black American experience. The dreams and ambitions of the family are thwarted by the "big white fog" of racism which prevents Victor's son Lester from achieving his dream of a scholarship to college and his capitalist brother-in-law Dan from making his fortune as an exploitative landlord. Wanda, the daughter, channels her energy into the pursuit of funds to escape but, faced with the needs of her family, finally turns to prostitution. Ward's solution is a multiracial socialist confrontation with the oppressor. In a 1970 letter Ward said, "There was a considerable opposition to the play being produced because it seemed to advocate Communism, when despite my own political outlook at the time, in writing the play I had only sought to present the objective reality as an alternative to the situation and conditions of Victor Mason and his family."

If there are problems in the script they are those of the beginning playwright. Too often Ward's characters pontificate rather than converse. The play's language is occasionally pedantic and inappropriate for its characters and situations. But some of the scenes are vividly accurate in their rendering of family interaction. Although the convergence of so many problems in a single family may seem contrived when merely

Ward in 1976 (photograph © Camille Billops, courtesy of the Hatch-Billops Collection)

listed, somehow the play works. The plight of the Mason family is a recognizable one. Since the competing ideologies of African nationalism, black capitalist assimilation, and Marxist socialism all had their adherents, *Big White Fog* was a play that spoke directly to the community for which it was written.

Critical response to *Big White Fog* was mixed. In general, critics praised the performances in both the Chicago and the New York productions but condemned the play for the nature of its debate and its conclusion. As a whole the New York critics were much more unfavorable in their response to the play. Ward cited a change in the nation's "intellectual climate" as a possible source of the disparity and always believed that neither production had allowed the play to succeed on its own merits. Writing in the *New York Times* (23 October 1940), Brooks Atkinson, while cataloging the play's dramatic flaws, complimented it as "the best serious play of Negro au-

thorship about race problems that this courier has happened to see. . . . Ward writes like a professional in the politically conscious genre."

In 1941 Ward organized a company and attempted to get an early version of *Our Lan'* produced in Chicago, where *Big White Fog* had had a receptive audience. He could not acquire sufficient funds to renovate a theater he had acquired for the performance. Faced with the need to support himself, he took his writing talents to the Writers' War Board. He wanted to produce a play about Frederick Douglass, but the board felt the play's theme was too serious for the Negro troops. From 1942 to 1945 Ward shined shoes, producing only one play, the 1942 *Deliver the Goods*, which showcases the struggle of longshoremen to support the war effort. For a time he also inspected motors in a war plant. A 1945 opportunity to write radio scripts for overseas broadcast by the Office of War Information turned sour when that agency also was abolished by Con-

Amanda Green as Delphine and Moses Gunn as Joshuah in the May 1977 Dartmouth College production of Ward's play Our Lan' *(photograph by Stuart Bratesman, Jr., courtesy of the Hatch-Billops Collection)*

gress. In the mid 1940s he received a Theatre Guild Award on the basis of the draft of *Our Lan'*. The scholarship included membership in a play writing workshop conducted by Kenneth Rowe. By the completion of the workshop Ward had a script that was ready for production. Sponsored by the Theater Guild for a one-week run in April 1947 at the Henry Street Playhouse, *Our Lan'* was enthusiastically received, and the Guild decided to take it to Broadway. A modified version of the play, with a new director, opened on Broadway in September 1947 to considerably less favorable reviews and closed after five weeks. The critics agreed that the play had lost its simplicity.

Our Lan' tells how a small band of freed slaves and their leader, Joshuah Tain, are dispossessed of the land given to them at the close of the Civil War. Ward used the play to explore "how far back in American history there was the clearest expression of the Negro's comprehension of what was necessary for his own salvation." The character of Joshuah Tain is both folkloristically heroic and classically tragic. Moving courageously to his fate, he is a heroic figure doing what must be done against all odds. Reviewing the two New York productions for the *New York Times* (19 April 1947 and 29 September 1947), Brooks Atkinson was moved to call the first production "clearly the best of the plays put on during the season at the Henry Street Playhouse." The multiple scenes of the play are stitched together with traditional slave songs. The love story between Joshuah, a former field hand, and Delphine, a former house slave, parallels the story of the little community's attempts to hold on to the land that has been promised to them and underscores the intersection of the personal with the political.

The play was revived in 1967 and again in 1978. Although written early in his career, *Our Lan'* remains Theodore Ward's greatest achievement.

A National Theater Conference Award in 1947 enabled Ward to complete "Shout Hallelujah!," a slice-of-life drama about black and white construction workers dying of silicosis, which was not produced. In 1948 he received a Guggenheim Fellowship which enabled him to begin research on what he envisioned as his life's achievement, a dramatic rendering of the story of John Brown. Ward completed the bulk of his research at Dartmouth College and in 1950 returned to New York, where the work in progress was produced in a converted garage on the Lower East Side of Manhattan. Although the play apparently never received another public production, Ward continued to polish and refine the script of *John Brown* (alternately titled *Of Human Grandeur*) over the next twenty years. The play was reviewed by Atkinson (*New York Times*, 4 May 1950), who was more impressed by the theater than by the play. He stayed only for one act and panned the play and cast (which included Rod Steiger) thoroughly. Ward himself once acknowledged that his subject might be too large for the stage, but he never gave up on the play.

Ward moved back to Chicago in 1964 and founded the South Side Center for the Performing Arts in 1967. The center's purpose was to "train black youths and adults in theater craftsmanship as well as to provide an outlet for Negro drama which expresses some ritual part of Negro life and spirit." Ward envisioned it as a place that would "reflect and interpret the lives of the people of the surrounding neighborhoods." Serving as the center's general manager and artistic director, he assembled a cast and production staff for a revival of *Our Lan'* in 1967 at the Louis Theater, a converted movie theater. The play ran for ten months in one of Chicago's poorest communities. Productions of two other Ward plays, "Candle in the Wind," the story of a Reconstruction-era Mississippi state senator, and "Whole Hog or Nothing," were scheduled for the 1968-1969 season but never produced, as the center succumbed to lack of funds. A 1978 Rockefeller Foundation grant enabled Ward to take *Our Lan'* to the South in a New Orleans production by the Free Southern Theater. During the play's production period, Ward served as their writer in residence. He died in Chicago on 8 May 1983.

References:

Doris E. Abramson, *Negro Playwrights in the American Theater, 1925-1959* (New York: Columbia University Press, 1969), pp. 109-135, 155-159, 163-164, 269-270;

Sterling A. Brown, "The Federal Theater," in *Anthology of the Afro-American in the Theatre: A Critical Approach*, edited by Lindsay Patterson (Cornwell Heights, Pa.: Publishers Agency, 1968) pp. 101-107;

Sam Greenlee, "Special Report–Black Theater in America: Chicago," *Negro Digest*, 18 (April 1969): 23;

James V. Hatch, Introduction to *Big White Fog*, in his *Black Theater U.S.A.* (New York: Free Press, 1974), pp. 278-280;

Loften Mitchell, *Black Drama: The Story of the American Negro in the Theater* (New York: Hawthorn Books, 1967), pp. 113-114, 133-134;

Eugene Perkins, "Reports on Black Theater USA: Chicago," *Black World*, 22 (April 1973): 31-32.

Papers:

Many of Ward's papers are on file at the Schomburg Center for Research in Black Culture, New York Public Library. The manuscripts of his plays are held in the Hatch-Billops Collection, New York, New York.

Dorothy West

(2 June 1907-   )

SallyAnn H. Ferguson
North Carolina Agricultural and Technical State University

BOOK: *The Living Is Easy* (Boston: Houghton Mifflin, 1948).

OTHER: "The Richer, the Poorer," in *The Best Short Stories by Negro Writers: An Anthology from 1899 to the Present,* edited by Langston Hughes (Boston: Little, Brown, 1967), pp. 130-133;

"Jack in the Pot," in *Harlem: Voices from The Soul of Black America,* edited by John Henrik Clarke (New York: New American Library, 1970).

PERIODICAL PUBLICATIONS: "The Typewriter," *Opportunity,* 4 (July 1926): 220-222, 233-234;

"Hannah Byde," *Messenger,* 8 (July 1926): 197-199;

"An Unimportant Man," *Saturday Evening Quill,* 1 (June 1928): 21-32;

"Prologue to a Life," *Saturday Evening Quill,* 2 (April 1929): 5-10;

"The Black Dress," *Opportunity,* 12 (May 1934): 140, 158;

"Mammy," *Opportunity,* 18 (October 1940): 298-302;

"Elephant's Dance: A Memoir of Wallace Thurman," *Black World,* 20 (November 1970): 77-85.

Dorothy West, 1978 (courtesy of the author)

Although her literary career spans over fifty years, Dorothy West has not received the critical attention her contributions to black American literature merit. Too often critics devote only a few paragraphs to her critically acclaimed novel, *The Living Is Easy* (1948), and largely ignore her some forty published short stories and her editorial achievements. West's writings, however, exemplify the wealth of artistic talent prevalent during and after the Harlem Renaissance and the concern of its participants with the realistic treatment of the black man. She was among the first to explore the ironic possibilities of the black urban life-style, a milieu most short-story writers tended to overlook. In addition, during the 1930s West edited two important magazines, *Challenge* and *New Challenge,* which helped to crystallize the dominant black literary attitudes of the day. Many luminaries of that era were her contributors and friends, including Langston Hughes, Claude McKay, Zora Neale Hurston, Countee Cullen, Arna Bontemps, and Richard Wright. Thus, West was not just a one-novel wonder but a consistent and spirited contributor to the black American literary canon.

West was born 2 June 1907 in Boston, Massachusetts, and grew up at 478 Brookline Avenue, the only child of Rachel Pease Benson and Isaac Christopher West, an ex-slave from Virginia.

After being set free at seven years old, her father, a dark-skinned man with blue eyes, industriously shined shoes and ran errands until, by age ten, he had saved enough money to convince his mother to open a restaurant in Richmond, Virginia. Later he sought better business opportunities in Springfield, Massachusetts, where he owned an ice cream parlor and food store. Isaac West eventually settled in Boston, was listed in Dun & Bradstreet, and ran a wholesale fruit company, becoming known in time as the "Black Banana King" of Boston. Although he incorrectly believed that he would leave his daughter a million dollars, he nevertheless gave her an early life of relative comfort. West's mother, one of twenty-two children, was born in Camden, South Carolina, and brought to Springfield by a teacher who feared her good looks and fair skin would bring her to ruin in the South. As a teenager she often pressed her nose against the window of Isaac West's ice cream parlor, but not until years later did they meet and marry in Boston. Rachel West may have married her husband, a man a generation or more her senior, for his money. His profits provided a living for the extended family—comprised of Rachel West's sisters, brothers, nieces, and nephews—in which West grew up.

At the age of two West began her formal education with private lessons from Bessie Trotter, sister of *Boston Guardian* editor Monroe Trotter, and later from Grace Turner, a proper Bostonian. Young West was so precocious that in 1911 Rachel West told the Boston School Board that her daughter belonged in public school. After tests indicated that the four-year-old could indeed do second-grade work, the board admitted her to the Farragut School. She completed her elementary education at the Martin School in the Boston Mission Hill District. Her early school years were made difficult by poor Irish-American students who called her nigger. Not until West began classes at the Girl's Latin School did the racial taunts stop. There, nonetheless, she experienced the more subtle racism of her middle-class liberal classmates, who seemed friendly enough on campus but who, away from school, preferred looking in shop windows to speaking to her. Undaunted, she graduated in 1923 and then studied journalism and philosophy at Columbia University.

When she was seven West began writing stories. "Promise and Fulfillment," her first short story to be published appeared in the *Boston Post*, which offered a prize for the best story of the

week. Within three years she was winning the prizes regularly. Just before her eighteenth birthday West and her cousin, poet Helene Johnson, entered the *Opportunity* writing contest and received invitations to attend the magazine's awards dinner in New York. West had long viewed New York as "the magic city" that, during numerous summer vacations on Martha's Vineyard, had filled the stories told to her and the other children by composer and family friend Harry T. Burleigh. Therefore, when her mother encouraged her to ignore the invitation because it did not explicitly name her as a prizewinner, she argued that surely the contest sponsors would not send invitations to losers. She and Johnson traveled to New York and settled into the Harlem YWCA room that *Opportunity* provided for them.

When West's submission, "The Typewriter," was published in *Opportunity* in 1926, it launched her as a serious and talented writer (she split the second-place award with Hurston). The biographical sketch that appeared in the 1926 contest-winner issue gives a personal glimpse of West: "I am a rather reticent sort, but I am intensely interested in everything that goes on about me. I love to sit apart and read—as best I can—the souls of my neighbors." She also stated that Fyodor Dostoyevski was her favorite author, and his influence certainly predominates throughout her work. "The Typewriter," for example, deals with a spiritually and economically wasted black father who uses his daughter's typewriting lessons to gain a modicum of personal worth. Each time he pretends to be her boss and dictates a letter, he imagines himself the successful businessman a racist culture prevents him from becoming. For Margaret Perry (1976) "the close identity of father and daughter evokes the Dostoyevskian absorption with childhood and the belief in the incorruptible nature of children." Millie remains oblivious to the rewards her pretense provides for her father and does not perceive that its end causes his death. The depth of West's ironic vision, a salient characteristic of her writing, prompted Edward J. O'Brien to include "The Typewriter" in *The Best Short Stories of 1926*. In the contributors' notes West said her chief interests were plays and people, and her chief abhorrence was most women writers.

"Hannah Byde," which was also published in 1926, shows West's tendency, also from Dostoyevski, to emphasize moral, psychological, and social confinement. It appeared in the *Messenger*, then the official organ of the Brotherhood of

Sleeping Car Porters. "Hannah Byde" illustrates the tragedy suffered by many of West's female characters restricted by both racism and sexism. Often they end up like Hannah, bitterly resigned and "crushed by environment, looking dully down the stretch of drab tomorrows littered with the ruins of shattered dreams." Because she is not white, Hannah's avenues of achievement are greatly narrowed, and her life becomes an empty "uneventual circle" that she, at twenty, tries to enliven by marrying George Byde. In due course he stifles her, but she has no recourse other than passive resignation to her fate and acceptance of an unwanted pregnancy. Throughout this tale West uses verbal irony to underscore the defeat in Hannah's life. For instance, when her husband puts jazz music on the phonograph to "do her good," Hannah, alienated and depressed, hears only "dreadful noises" in this traditional cultural healer.

West remained at the YWCA until anthropologist Franz Boas arranged a fellowship for Hurston, thus enabling West and Johnson—with Isaac West's help—to take over Hurston's apartment in Harlem. Now permanently situated in New York, West associated herself with the numerous artists and intellectuals who flocked to Harlem. At that time influential whites like Carl Van Vechten, H. L. Mencken, and Fannie Hurst were taking black writers seriously, publishing their works, and giving them critical attention. A friend of Rachel West introduced West to Van Vechten, who asked to see samples of her work. Over the years Van Vechten and West corresponded, and she acknowledges that he taught her much about the craft of writing. Hurston, whom Dorothy West had met through the *Opportunity* contest, also took a special liking to the young author and introduced West to her employer, Hurst. Hurst was an eccentric woman whom West alienated by trying to arrange a meeting with her for a friend. After this mistake West never heard from Hurst again. Before the split, however, Hurst furthered West's career by introducing her to Elisabeth Marbury, who later became West's agent. When Marbury died in 1933, George Bye, another well-known agent whom West met through Hurst, took over her career.

In these early days West continued to write short stories, although only a few were published. She began to call herself "the best-known unknown writer of the time," whose "rejections read like acceptances until the end." She often ran into quota systems in white periodicals,

where she was beaten out by the black-story-of-the-issue. With the emergence of the *Saturday Evening Quill,* a magazine of the Boston Quill Club, however, two more of her stories were published. The editor of the *Saturday Evening Quill,* Eugene Gordon, was on the editorial staff of the *Boston Post* and apparently liked their middle-class themes. Like Booker T. Washington, he stressed the Americanism of the Afro-American artist who, he felt, should write of his experiences in this country rather than his African origins. "An Unimportant Man" appeared in the first number of the *Saturday Evening Quill* in 1928. "Prologue to a Life" appeared in the second number of 1929. Both stories show West's continued preoccupation with Dostoyevski and the irony of black urban existence.

The protagonist in "An Unimportant Man" is Zeb, another of West's unaccomplished, frustrated, and childlike black men who have close relationships with their daughters. Through Essie, Zeb expects vicariously to gain self-importance and value. Nearly forty, he knows he is a failure and will not take for a fourth time a bar exam he failed twice before passing on a third try, now nullified by a technicality. He vows to educate his daughter and ensure that she never becomes an "idle dreamer," like himself, who has ended up working as a cook. The irony of the story is found in the fact that Zeb's decision to control Essie's life evidences his willingness to repeat the same mistakes with her that his own mother made with him. She could never accept his mediocrity and thus pushed him into a difficult academic program that he could never master. In contrast, Zeb's successful friend Parker, who had far fewer advantages but an affinity for the law, passed his exams on the first try because "He had known, of course, that he would." The last line of the story—"The room was filled with the echo of sadly mocking laughter"—highlights the irony in Zeb's plans to suppress Essie's natural inclination toward "something that's beautiful" and force her into an academic life. When "An Unimportant Man" reappeared in the 1929 edition of *Copy,* a collection of the published work of Columbia University writing students, West's biographical remarks showed her continuing aspirations for a literary career. She said: "I have no ability nor desire to be other than a writer, though the fact is I whistle beautifully."

During the late 1920s, West began a friendship with editor-novelist Wallace Thurman that lasted until his death in 1934. She saw him as

West at the time of The Living Is Easy, *1948 (courtesy of the author)*

"the most symbolic figure of the Literary Renaissance in Harlem." In a memoir published in the November 1970 issue of *Black World*, she remembered his bad-boy personality, his cynicism, and his memorable, infectious laugh. In 1927 both she and Thurman got bit parts in the original stage production of *Porgy*, directed by Rouben Mamoulian, whom West credits with greatly refining DuBose Heyward's work. Characteristically enough, soon after being hired, Thurman protested the low wages and was fired, even though West and the others received raises as a result of his stand.

West got her role in *Porgy* by writing the Theatre Guild and asking for a position as a writer. She was hired as an extra though she had no experience or interest in acting. West needed this job in order to remain in New York during the Depression year of 1929. Times were difficult, even for her father, so the seventeen-and-a-half dollars she earned every week helped to buy the bologna, hamburger, and crackers for herself and Johnson. When *Porgy* was taken to London dur-

ing the summer of 1929–the first she did not spend on Martha's Vineyard–West went along. The plan was to spend the next year there and then go on to Paris. Unfortunately, this itinerary changed because the London audiences did not understand the actors' speech, and the troupe found itself back in New York after only three months abroad.

In June 1932 West sailed to Russia with a group of twenty-two black Americans, including Langston Hughes, to film *Black and White*, a movie that was supposed to illustrate the mistreatment of blacks in America. The project was never completed, however, because of the controversy it generated, particularly in the media. For example, journalist-novelist George Schuyler claimed, among other things, that the group was the target of a Communist recruitment campaign. His suspicions were aroused when he learned that only two members of the group, Sylvia Garner and Wayland Rudd, had any real acting experience. Seasoned black performers contacted earlier refused to pay their own expenses

West signing copies of her only novel, 1948 (courtesy of Dorothy West Collection, Mugar Memorial Library, Boston University)

to Europe on the promise of contracts after their arrival, thus forcing the organizers of the troupe to recruit black intellectuals as actors. West learned about the trip through the Fellowship of Youth and Peace Reconciliation, an organization for which she had volunteered to address envelopes. Urged by her friend, author Henry Lee Moon, West decided to use the trip to Russia to escape temporarily the many excesses and self-indulgences of the Harlem Renaissance. She had attended too many parties where everybody drank too much, and she had already seen a doctor for a psychosomatic illness which, one morning after such a bash, rendered her unable to move. West decided to travel abroad even though she only had twenty dollars.

Once in Moscow, the group was reimbursed

for their expenses but soon learned that the Russian script did not accurately reflect black American life. Although Langston Hughes tried to rewrite it, he and the others were eventually told by the Russian officials of Meschrabpom Films that the movie was canceled. West always believed that Hugh Cooper, an American then in Russia to build the Dniepostro dam, also influenced the cancellation. According to West, Moon and a friend once overheard him vow to stop the project if the Russians made a film denigrating the American treatment of blacks. In any event, the twenty-two split up, with some returning to America and others like West and Hughes remaining in Russia. In his biography of Hughes (1986), Arnold Rampersad notes that West and Hughes

were involved in some way, though probably not sexually. In an impulsive letter dated 26 May 1933 she proposed marriage to Hughes, saying that she loved him and wanted a child. "Then she would leave Langston to roam the world like the external boy she knew he was meant to be." She eventually got a contract with another filmmaker and stayed in Russia eleven months more until the director singled her out for undeserved praise. Additionally, shortly before leaving, she learned that her father had died after losing his business to large chain stores.

Although she was only twenty-five when she returned from Russia, West felt old and guilty that she had not lived up to earlier literary expectations, for she had published only a few short stories since beginning her career about seven years before. Consequently, on 23 October 1933 she wrote to James Weldon Johnson: "It occurred to me that I could make up for much I have wasted by some way finding space for young dark throats to sing heard songs." Partly to redeem herself, then, she used forty dollars to found and edit *Challenge*. This was the first little magazine of the Depression that sought to bridge the divisions among the older aesthetes like Alain Locke and James Weldon Johnson, her own bohemian Renaissance circle, and the emerging social realists ·like the Chicago group led by Richard Wright. As Walter C. Daniel remarks (*CLA Journal,* June 1976) West intended *Challenge* to "recapture, in the mid-thirties, the literary vitality of the Harlem Renaissance which had not survived the Depression." Johnson, then professor of creative writing at Fisk University, accepted the task, and the result was a sternly instructive lecture. He wrote: "It is a good thing that Dorothy West is doing in instituting a magazine through which the voices of younger Negro writers may be heard. . . . But these younger writers must not be mere dilettantes: they have serious work to do. . . . they need not be propagandists: they need only be sincere artists, disdaining all cheap applause and remaining true to themselves. . . . To those who really desire to become writers let me say: Writing is not only an art, it is also a trade that demands long, arduous and dogged effort for mastery."

For all the talk of "younger Negro writers," the first issue of *Challenge* included surprisingly few. Renaissance stalwarts like Hughes, who led with the story "Little Dog," and Bontemps, who contributed the essay "Saturday Night: Alabama Town" and the story "Barrel Staves," dominated

the issue. Indeed, the first two members relied heavily on works of such well-known authors as Hughes, Bontemps, Cullen, Hurston, Helene Johnson, and McKay. Although originally intended as a monthly, *Challenge* became a quarterly with the appearance of the second number in September 1934, largely because the submissions from the younger writers were, in the editor's view, so incredibly bad as to delay publication. West explained to her readers: "We felt somewhat crazily that the authors must be spoofing and that they didn't really mean us to take their stuff for prose and poetry." By the third issue in May 1935, however, West felt more optimistic about the magazine, since most of the contributors were new and young, if not always black. Seventeen-year-old Frank Yerby contributed two poems, "To a Seagull" and "Draught." White writers such as Myron Mahler and Paul Murray also wrote for the magazine.

The problem of poor writing did not disappear, however, and West addressed this issue directly in the fourth number, which was published in January 1936. She editorialized: "Somebody asked us why *Challenge* was for the most part so pale pink [tame]. We said because the few red articles we did receive were not literature. We care a lot about style. And we think a message is doubly effective when effectively written without bombast or bad spelling." But West was also coming to care about protest. The fourth number together with the fifth, which appeared in June 1936, signaled a shift in West's editorial policy away from the conventional, conservative style and substance of earlier issues to the proletarian stance of the Chicago writers. In the June 1936 number, West made her position explicit: "We would like to print more articles and stories of protest. We have daily contact with the underprivileged. We know their suffering and soul weariness. They have only the meager bread and meat of the dole, and that will not feed their failing spirits."

The sixth and final issue of *Challenge* belatedly appeared in April 1937. West then explained that financial problems and poor submissions caused its nearly yearlong publishing delay. More important, she introduced the Chicago group to her readers and noted that the group held regular meetings to discuss their works and those of others. In response to the "considerable dispraise" directed toward *Challenge* at these gatherings, West offered these critics "a special section in a forthcoming issue that "they may

show us what we have not done by showing us what they can do."

A proposed special section soon evolved into *New Challenge*, an ambitious magazine that listed Dorothy West and Marian Minus as editors and Richard Wright, who actually did much of the work, as associate editor. Although it contained such noteworthy items as Wright's now-famous essay "Blueprint for Negro Writing" and Ralph Ellison's first published piece entitled, "Creative and Cultural Lag," a review of *These Low Grounds* (1937) by Waters Turpin. *New Challenge* soon fell victim to financial problems. Like the earlier Renaissance magazines *Fire!!* and *Harlem*, it could not attract sufficient subscriptions or advertisements and thus went broke after the first issue appeared in the fall of 1937. Additionally, Robert G. O'Meally states in *The Craft of Ralph Ellison* (1980) that the sudden withdrawal of support by the Communist party and troubles between West and Minus caused the Winter 1937 issue of *New Challenge* to go unpublished.

In the year or so after *Challenge* and *New Challenge* folded, Dorothy West worked as a welfare investigator in Harlem. This job probably inspired the story "Mammy," which was published in the October 1940 number of *Opportunity*. The central character is a Depression-era caseworker who both degrades and is degraded by another black for the sake of economic survival. Its thematic structure depends heavily on contrast and parallelism and shows West developing a highly sophisticated ironic style. Early in the story a black elevator operator keeps his job because he insults the black female caseworker who offends a white woman by boldly entering his elevator. He talks rudely to the black woman and "rolls his eyes at his white passenger as if to convey his regret at the discomfort he was causing her." But when the white threat passes, he pleads for understanding from the caseworker. He reasons, "With white folks needin' jobs, us niggers got to eat dirt to hang on." Later in the story the caseworker herself is similarly compromised. She denies the relief request of a deserving old black maid in order not to offend a white woman. Like the elevator operator, she finds herself pleading to a fellow black to "Please, please understand. This is my job." Because the welfare investigator never perceives her kinship to the elevator operator, the dramatic irony of their situation permits the author to illustrate the limitations of racial pride. West elicits the reader's sympathy for these two characters by making it clear that white racism

forces them to take such drastic measures for survival.

After eighteen months as a welfare worker West joined the Works Progress Administration Federal Writers' Project, which provided many literary artists with both a creative outlet and a source of income during the Depression. Given various writing assignments which, unfortunately, were never published, she remained with the project until it ended in the mid 1940s. About the same time, she began writing short stories for the *New York Daily News* and soon became a regular contributor. From 1940 to 1960 she published more than twenty-six stories in this newspaper, the first of which–the often anthologized "Jack in the Pot"–appeared in the "Blue Ribbon Fiction" section. While many of her friends were contemptuous of her association with the lowbrow *New York Daily News*, she argued that it paid the bills. But John Henrik Clarke, who included "Jack in the Pot" in his collection *Harlem: Voices from the Soul of Black America* (1970), acknowledged the artistry and realism of her black American portraits.

Around 1945 West left New York permanently to live on Martha's Vineyard, where she began writing an autobiographical novel, a task to which she brought nearly thirty years of writing experience. *The Living Is Easy* examines the economic and psychological prisons upwardly-mobile blacks create for themselves by pursuing false values. The protagonist and most striking character in the book is light-skinned, predatory Cleo Judson from South Carolina. Throughout life she has a neurotic need to be loved best by her mother who loves her four daughters equally and her husband most of all. For Cleo her share of maternal affection constitutes a rejection of sorts, and throughout her life she compensates for her mistreatment by seeking recognition from and control over others. As a child she pulls outrageous, dangerous, and attention-getting stunts; later, as an adult, she seeks money and prestige among the black elite of Boston. Because he is wealthy enough to provide the social entrée she craves, Cleo marries Bart Judson, the "Black Banana King," a much older man who she does not love. She then brings her three sisters to live in the fine home he gives her, breaking up their marriages in the process. Indeed, winning her sisters away from their husbands even substitutes for Cleo's sexual needs. Discussing Bart with her sister Charity, she confides: "I haven't been near that nigger's room since my sis-

ters walked into this house." But in her attempt to beat Robert, sister Serena's racially oppressed husband, Cleo simultaneously rejects the plight of oppressed southern blacks and consequently triggers the collapse of her own family. The Judson banana business goes bankrupt, and Bart, who measures his worth by his ability to support the family, leaves Boston to find other sources of income. Her three sisters are now forced to work at the menial jobs Cleo despises. The novel ends with Cleo still asking: "Who is there now to love me best? Who?" Significantly, her final question reveals just what makes Cleo Judson and *The Living Is Easy* so memorable and engrossing. It shows a vulnerability to human feeling at odds with her cold, bitchy nature. In other words, the novel portrays a woman who both inflicts and suffers pain.

West further develops the theme of values gone awry through minor characters who, like Cleo, pursue worthless goals. For instance Duchess marries distinguished Bostonian Simeon Binney in order to expiate the sin of her parents' adulterous relationship through his fine family name. But their tragic marriage is never consummated; Duchess becomes mortally ill, and Simeon, who has sold his ideal of black pride for his wife's money, philanders and drinks away his pain. Even Bart Judson, the most admirable character in the book, displays a sometimes questionable value system, especially when he chooses Cleo for his wife on the basis of her good looks and light skin. As a result he finds himself married to a coldhearted woman who berates him as "Mr. Nigger" and rarely lets him into her bed.

The Living Is Easy generally received good notices, and most reviewers found Cleo a distinctive character. To Florence Codman of *Commonweal* (25 June 1948), she was "a woman smitten by the virus of Agrippinas of all races, the predatory female on the loose, a wholly tantalizing creature." Writing in the *New York Herald Tribune* (13 June 1948), Arna Bontemps labeled Cleo a "vixenish heroine" drawn with a "steady hand" and "sardonic wisdom." The unsigned reviewer for *Booklist* (1 June 1948) found the book "not outstanding" but conceded that "the inside view of snobbery among colored people in Boston and the portrayal of an unscrupulous woman hold the interest. . . ." In the *New York Times Book Review* (16 May 1948) Seymour Krim, like Codman, found some of the writing loose but observed that "the important thing about the book is its abundant and special woman's energy and

beat. The beat is a deep one, and it often makes man's seem puny." Writing for *Opportunity* (Summer 1948), Philip Butcher considered Bart Judson the most admirable character in the book but dismissed the others as types rather than people, burdened with the author's tendency toward irony and melodrama. He also claimed that the novel "is disappointingly narrow in scope and shallow in treatment. It lacks the balanced insight Miss West, as a Bostonian, might be expected to bring to it." Nonetheless, he acknowledges that, as a vivid picture of a vicious woman who ruins herself and everyone she loves, "it is no small achievement." In the *Crisis* (October 1948) Moon was far more enthusiastic and wrote: "Miss West has enlarged the canvas of Negro fiction and has treated a phase of Boston life which the popular novels of that city have neglected."

More recent criticism assessments of *The Living Is Easy* have also been largely positive. Although Robert A. Bone (1965) notes narrative weaknesses such as a faltering plot and lack of proportion, he praises the novel for its neatness, economy of style, and occasional brilliance, calling it a "diamond in the rough." He is also impressed with West's capacity for verbal irony, as when her narrator remarks: "Mr. Harnett failed in business and blew his brains out just like a white man. Everybody was a little proud of his suicide." Bone concludes that *The Living Is Easy* is among the top fifteen novels by black Americans. Theodore L. Gross and James A. Emanuel (1968) observe that West did some of the best writing of the 1940s. In their view, *The Living Is Easy* "satirically exposed the shallow wasteful creeds that deteriorate many middle-class Negroes." Noel Schraufnagel (1973) calls West an accommodationist novelist of skill who "reveals the insanity of imitating the false values of white society, while at the same time showing the pervasiveness of this practice."

When in 1982 the Feminist Press reprinted *The Living Is Easy* with an afterword by Adelaide Cromwell Gulliver, Susan McHenry in *Ms.* magazine, like her predecessors, praises West's brisk storytelling and eye for ironic detail. She also stresses the American qualities of the novel and compares West to Theodore Dreiser and Sinclair Lewis. The influence of the Feminist Movement can be seen, however, in the review by Carole Brovoso in the *Village Voice Literary Supplement* (1983). She praises the novel's focus on the special role of the mother in childhood fantasies. "Mysterious talismans given to us at birth, our

mothers are the first symbols we have of what our special magic can create," McHenry writes. Similarly, in "I Sign My Mother's Name," Mary Helen Washington sees a woman discovering her creative voice "through the mediation of a female power–her mother."

Before the 1930s West began writing another novel, "The Wedding," after receiving a grant from the Mary Roberts Rinehart Foundation. The main character is a ninety-year-old near-white woman forced by economics to live with her fair-skinned daughter and hated, dark-skinned son-in-law. When the black power turmoil of the mid 1960s erupted, West stopped work on the book, fearing its middle-class theme would be unfairly criticized. More recently, however, West has resumed writing "The Wedding" with the hope of a fairer evaluation now that tempers have cooled. Now living in semiretirement at Oak Bluffs, Massachusetts, she lectures periodically, gives interviews and continues to write her short stories, which remain uncollected. At this time West contributes a weekly column on such topics as black women and summer residents to the *Martha's Vineyard Gazette*. Entitled "Oak Bluffs," it covers the year-round activities of all Oak Bluffs residents. Even at the age of eighty-one West still demonstrates the energy and creativity that have marked her contributions to black American literature for over a half century.

References:

Robert A. Bone, *The Negro Novel in America*, revised edition (New Haven: Yale University Press, 1965), pp. 116-117, 187-191;

Walter C. Daniel, "*Challenge Magazine:* An Experiment That Failed," *CLA Journal,* 19 (June 1976): 494-503;

Theodore L. Gross and James A. Emanuel, *Dark Symphony: Negro Literature in America* (New York: Free Press, 1968). p. 355;

Genii Guinier, *Black Women Oral History Project Interview with Dorothy West, May 6, 1978* (Cambridge: Schlesinger Library, Radcliffe College, 1981), pp. 1-75;

Abby Johnson and Ronald M. Johnson, *Propaganda and Aesthetics: The Literary Politics of Afro-American Magazines in the Twentieth Century* (Amherst: University of Massachusetts Press, 1979), p. 113;

Robert G. O'Meally, *The Craft of Ralph Ellison* (Cambridge: Harvard University Press, 1980), p. 30;

Margaret Perry, *Silence to the Drums: A Survey of the Literature of the Harlem Renaissance* (Westport, Conn.: Greenwood Press, 1976), p. 132;

Noel Schraufnagel, *From Apology to Protest: The Black American Novel* (De Land, Fla.: Everett-Edwards, 1973), p. 61;

Mary Helen Washington, "I Sign My Mother's Name," in *"Mothering" the Mind: Twelve Studies of Writers and Their Silent Partners,* edited by Ruth Perry and Martine Watson Brownley (New York: Holmes & Meier, 1984), p. 150.

Papers:

West's papers are held in the Mugar Memorial Library, Boston University. Some of her early writings are held in the James Weldon Johnson Collection, Yale University.

Chancellor Williams

(22 December 1905-   )

La Vinia Delois Jennings
University of North Carolina at Chapel Hill

BOOKS: *The Raven* (Philadelphia: Dorrance, 1943);
And If I Were White (Washington, D.C.: Shaw Publications, 1946);
Have You Been to the River? (New York: Exposition Press, 1952);
The Rebirth of African Civilization (Washington, D.C.: Public Affairs Press, 1961);
Problems in African History (Washington, D.C.: Pencraft Books, 1964);
The Destruction of Black Civilization: Great Issues of a Race from 4500 B.C. to 2000 A.D. (Dubuque: Kendall-Hunt, 1971);
The Second Agreement With Hell (New York: Carlton Press, 1979).

OTHER: "Africa," in *Contemporary Sociology,* edited by Joseph Slabey Roucek (New York: Philosophical Library, 1958), pp. 1085-1094;
"Pan-Asiatic and Pan-African Movements," in *Contemporary Political Ideologies,* edited by Roucek (New York: Philosophical Library, 1961), pp. 212-240;
"The Teaching of African History," in *The Teaching of History,* edited by Roucek (New York: Philosophical Library, 1967).

PERIODICAL PUBLICATIONS: "Some Current Problems in African Education," *Journal of Negro Education,* 24 (Winter 1955): 16-25;
"African Democracy and the Leadership Principle," *Journal of Human Relations,* 8 (May 1960): 819-830;
"Educational Obstacles to Africanization in Ghana, Nigeria and Sierra Leone," *Journal of Negro Education,* 30 (Summer 1961): 261-265.

Chancellor Williams (photograph by Sulalman Ellison, courtesy of the Schomburg Center for Research in Black Culture, the New York Public Library, Astor, Lenox and Tilden Foundations)

Although he is primarily known for his contributions to African education and for a controversial history on the destruction of black civilization, historian and sociologist Chancellor Williams began his literary career as a fiction writer. His distinction as an author of fiction lies in his skill at blending fact, interpretation, and conjecture in provocative narratives that explore the psychological motives of his characters.

Chancellor Williams, born in Bennettsville, South Carolina, on 22 December 1905, was the youngest of five children. His father had been a

slave, and his mother was a cook, nurse, and evangelist. In Marlboro Academy, the small, rural elementary school that he attended, he was constantly asking questions about the great disparity between the social positions of blacks and whites; he was told that slavery was the cause of the low socioeconomic conditions of blacks. At the suggestion of his fifth grade teacher, Alice Crosson–whom he credits, along with another teacher, Mami Sawyer, as being the source of his first encouragement and inspiration–Williams solicited subscriptions for the *Crisis*, the magazine of the NAACP, and the *Norfolk Journal and Guide*, the leading southern black newspaper of the day, in order to gain more information relating to black life. The back cover of the *Crisis* provided him with a list of books by Booker T. Washington, W. E. B. Du Bois, George Williams, and other influential black writers. He read extensively in his search for answers to racial questions. Obtaining a more balanced view of America's racial history compelled Williams to reject history as recorded in the southern textbooks which glorified the Confederacy and southern slave masters of the eighteenth and nineteenth centuries. Thus at an early age Williams concluded that hostile or indifferent white historians were incapable of recording fairly and accurately the history of blacks.

As was the case in many southern rural areas, the segregated schools of Marlboro County ended with the eighth grade, so it was necessary for Williams to leave home to further his education. Through the encouragement of L. Melendez King, an attorney who was an 1899 graduate of Howard University's law school, Williams went to Washington, D.C., at the age of fourteen, secured employment, and initially enrolled at Dunbar High School but later switched to Armstrong. In 1925 he entered the school of education at Howard University and graduated in 1930. As a Rosenwald Fellow from 1931 to 1932 Williams studied the cooperative movement in the western United States. In 1934 he returned to Howard University to study for a graduate degree in history and came under the influence of William Leo Hansberry, who founded what may have been the first African studies program, and Charles Wesley. Despite his devotion to courses in his majors Williams resisted overspecialization and took courses, such as science and psychology, that equally interested him. Upon completing his thesis–"The Socio-Economic Status of the Free Negro in the District of Columbia,

1830-1860"–and being awarded the master of arts degree in history in 1935, Williams embarked on his career as an educator, serving as the administrative principal of the Cheltenham School for Boys in Maryland (1935-1937) and teaching in the Washington, D.C., public schools (1939-1941). During this period he also did postgraduate, nonresident study at the Universities of Chicago and Iowa. From 1941 to 1946 he held a series of posts in the federal government, including section chief of the Census Bureau, statistician of the War Relocation Board, and economist in the Office of Price Administration.

During World War II Williams wrote his first book, a historical novel on Edgar Allan Poe entitled *The Raven* (1943). Williams sympathetically recounts Poe's unstable years as a foster son in the wealthy Allan household in Richmond to his arrival in Baltimore just before his early demise under dubious circumstances. A *New York Times* reviewer (9 January 1944) praised the novel as being of "extraordinary quality" despite its "overlong" length and technical clumsiness. The review faults Williams for forever halting his narrative to remind us "how great a man he [Poe] will one day become. . . . The finished portrait as it emerges under Chancellor Williams' pen is extravagant, neurotic and unstable to a degree not easy for any but a psychiatrist to view with uniform sympathy."

Three years after completing *The Raven*, Williams published *And If I Were White* (1946), an extended essay on race relations which was a reply to the "If I Were a Negro" series by prominent white writers. In September of the same year he joined the faculty of Howard University as a teacher in the social sciences program. Upon the completion of his doctoral dissertation in 1949 on the socioeconomic significance of the storefront church movement in the United States since 1920, American University awarded him the Ph.D. in history and sociology.

Williams transformed the empirical research of his doctoral dissertation into a novelized version of the life of black storefront churches, *Have You Been to the River?* (1952), which is told from the viewpoint of Tom Moore, a young professor. It is the story of the rise to power of Charles Amos David–Prophet, founder and leader of the Church of the Apostolic Faith and Saints–and the followers he incites to frenzied obedience. The novel focuses mainly on Liza Jackson–a Mother Leader in the Prophet's organization whose gradual acceptance of the new gos-

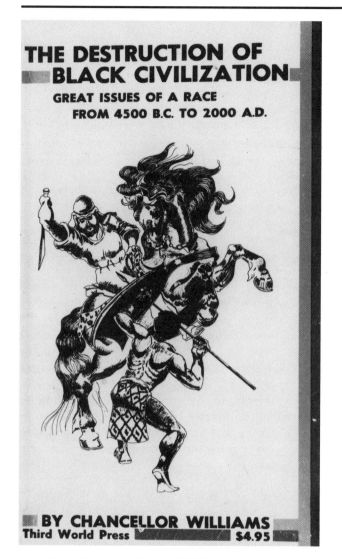

THE DESTRUCTION OF BLACK CIVILIZATION

GREAT ISSUES OF A RACE
FROM 4500 B.C. TO 2000 A.D.

BY CHANCELLOR WILLIAMS
Third World Press $4.95

*Cover for a later edition of Williams's controversial
1971 history*

pel causes her to leave her husband and ruin her children's lives, and so blinds her that only on her deathbed does she realize her folly.

Williams devoted the next two decades to the study of African education and African history. From 1953 to 1954 he researched African education and culture in England as a visiting scholar at Oxford and the University of London. He also worked at the British Museum and Rhodes House and lectured at John Ruskin College. In the late 1950s Williams went to Ghana and began a comprehensive study of African history. The main objective of his field research was to document the independent achievement of the African race and the nature of black civilization prior to Asian or European influences. The result of this field study, during which he con-

ducted, despite British opposition, a massive poll, was *The Rebirth of African Civilization,* published in 1961–the same year he succeeded his mentor Hansberry as professor in Howard University's history department. In 1963 and 1964 another African field study that took him through more than twenty-five countries and allowed him to survey the traditional cultures of 105 language groups culminated in *The Destruction of Black Civilization: Great Issues of a Race from 4500 B.C. to 2000 A.D.* (1971). "Black Odyssey" and "A History of the African People," often mistaken as two additional publications of Williams, are the preliminary titles for works never completed.

In *The Destruction of Black Civilization,* a controversial account of African history that catapulted him to cult-figure status, Williams asks: "If the blacks were among the very first builders of civilization and their land, the birthplace of civilization, what has happened to them since that left them at the bottom of world society?" The answer to this question, Williams asserts, lies in the tendency of Africans to trust outsiders, which led to invasion of African countries and increased penetration into the interiors of the continent; disunity among Africans themselves was also a problem. By the seventeenth century the continent was forced to participate in the slave trade to maintain commerce with the outside world. Concluding with an overview of black history, Williams instructs blacks to learn from their past and present, and he strongly stresses the need for blacks to organize to reclaim their destiny as a great people. A *Black Books Bulletin* review-essay (1973) of *The Destruction of Black Civilization* prophesied that both black and white scholars would attack Williams "for his failure to give more academic weight and scholarship to his book through massive footnoting and lengthy appendices," and indeed critics complained about documentation; they also made accusations that the history was loosely constructed and propagandistic. Conversely, the reviewer for the *Black Scholar* (1973), in a favorable evaluation, stated that "the beauty of the book lies in its ability to give the reader a clear understanding of 6,000 years of African political history without losing sight of specific historical details." Attracting worldwide renown, *The Destruction of Black Civilization* received the Black Academy of Arts and Letters Book Award in 1971, and in 1979, the Twenty-first Century Foundation awarded the first Clarence L. Holte International Biennial Prize to

Chancellor Williams in recognition of his significant and lasting contribution to black heritage.

The Second Agreement with Hell (1979), Williams's third fictional novel, has a nineteenth-century setting mixing real and imagined characters. His protagonist, Steve, a slave who survives the ravages of the Civil War to wrestle with freedom and identity in the South, is the mouthpiece for the ideology of Booker T. Washington. Unlike most slaves who dreamed of escape to the North via Harriet Tubman's Underground Railroad, Steve prefers to carry out his grandfather's vision of true freedom by staying in the South and promoting black self-esteem. To fulfill his objective, Steve has perfected his skills as a woodcraftsman and has secretly learned to read. Incor-

porating factual data and historical personages such as Jefferson Davis and Bennett C. Pickney into his narrative, Williams accurately re-creates the social milieu and political fervor of the period.

References:

Phil W. Petrie, "Dr. Chancellor Williams: Celebrating Our Glorious History," *Essence* (December 1981): 74;

Jacqueline Trescott, "Patriarch of Pride," *Washington Post* (5 March 1980);

Michael R. Winston, *Howard University Department of History 1913-1973* (Washington, D.C.: Howard University, 1973).

Richard Wright

(4 September 1908-28 November 1960)

Edward D. Clark
North Carolina State University

See also the Wright entry in *DLB Documentary Series 2.*

BOOKS: *Uncle Tom's Children: Four Novellas* (New York & London: Harper, 1938; London: Gollancz, 1939); enlarged as *Uncle Tom's Children: Five Long Stories* (New York & London: Harper, 1940);*Native Son* (New York & London: Harper, 1940; London: Gollancz, 1940);

How "Bigger" Was Born (New York: Harper, 1940);

Native Son (The Biography of a Young American): A Play in Ten Scenes, by Wright and Paul Green (New York & London: Harper, 1941; revised by Green, in *Black Drama, An Anthology,* edited by William Brasmer and Dominick Consola, Columbus, Ohio: Merrill, 1970, pp. 70-178);

Twelve Million Black Voices: A Folk History of the Negro in the United States, by Wright, photographs selected by Edwin Rosskam (New York: Viking, 1941; London: Drummond, 1947);

Black Boy: A Record of Childhood and Youth (New York & London: Harper, 1945; London: Gollancz, 1945);

The Outsider (New York: Harper, 1953; London & Sydney: Angus & Robertson, 1953);

Black Power: A Record of Reactions in a Land of Pathos (New York: Harper, 1954; London: Dobson, 1956);

Savage Holiday (New York: Avon, 1954);

Bandoeng 1.500.000.000 d'hommes, translated by Hélène Claireau (Paris: Calmann-Lévy, 1955); republished as *The Color Curtain: A Report on the Bandung Conference* (Cleveland & New York: World, 1956; London: Dobson, 1956);

Pagan Spain: A Report of a Journey into the Past (New York: Harper, 1957; London: Bodley Head, 1960);

White Man, Listen! (Garden City: Doubleday, 1957); enlarged edition, translated by Dominique Guillet as *Ecoute, homme blanc* (Paris: Calmann-Lévy, 1959);

Richard Wright (Special Collections, John Davis Williams Library, University of Mississippi)

The Long Dream (Garden City: Doubleday, 1958; London & Sydney: Angus & Robertson, 1960);

Eight Men (Cleveland & New York: World, 1960);

Lawd Today (New York: Walker, 1963; London: Blond, 1965);

The Man Who Lived Underground: L'homme qui vivait sous terre, by Wright, translated by Claude-Edmonde Magny, edited and with an introduction by Michel Fabre (Paris: Aubier-Flammarion, 1971);

American Hunger (New York: Harper & Row, 1977; London: Gollancz, 1978);

Richard Wright Reader, edited by Ellen Wright and Fabre (New York: Harper & Row, 1978).

PLAY PRODUCTIONS: *Native Son,* by Wright and Paul Green, New York, St. James Theatre, 24 March 1941;

Daddy Goodness, by Wright and Louis Sapin, New York, St. Mark's Playhouse, 4 June 1968.

SCREENPLAY: *Native Son* (Classic Films, 1951), screenplay by Wright.

OTHER: Introduction to J. Saunders Redding's *No Day of Triumph* (New York: Harper, 1942);

Introduction to Nelson Algren's *Never Come Morning* (New York: Harper, 1942);

Introduction to St. Clair Drake and Horace R. Cayton's *Black Metropolis* (New York: Harcourt, Brace, 1945);

Introduction to his *American Hunger,* in *One Hundred Five Greatest Living Authors Present the World's Best,* edited by Whit Burnett (New York: Dial, 1950);

"I Tried to be a Communist," in *The God That Failed,* edited by Richard Crossman (New York: Harper, 1950), pp. 115-163;

Preface to Chester Himes's *Le Croisade de Lee Gordon* (Paris: Correa, 1952);

Introduction to George Padmore's *Pan-Africanism or Communism* (London: Dobson, 1956);

"Five Episodes," in *Soon One Morning,* edited by Herbert Hill (New York: Knopf, 1963), pp. 149-164;

"The American Problem—Its Negro Phase," in *Richard Wright: Impressions and Perspectives,* edited by David Ray and Robert M. Farnsworth (Ann Arbor: University of Michigan Press, 1973), pp. 9-16.

PERIODICAL PUBLICATIONS: "How *Uncle Tom's Children* Grew," *Columbia University Writers' Bulletin,* 2 (May 1938): 15-17;

"What Do I Think of the Theatre?" *New York World-Telegram,* 2 March 1941, p. 20;

"Not My People's War," *New Masses,* 39, no. 13 (17 June 1941): 8-9;

"US Negroes Greet You," *Daily Worker,* 1 September 1941, p. 7;

"Richard Wright Describes the Birth of *Black Boy,*" *New York Post,* 30 November 1944, p. B6;

"Is America Solving Its Race Problem?" *America's Town Meeting of the Air Bulletin,* 11 (24 May 1945): 6-7;

"A Paris les GI Noirs ont appris à connaître et à aimer la liberté," *Samedi-Soir,* 25 May 1946, p. 2;

"Psychiatry Comes to Harlem," *Free World,* 12 (September 1946): 49-51;

"How Jim Crow Feels," *True: The Man's Magazine* (November 1946): 25-27, 154-156;

"Urban Misery in an American City: Juvenile Delinquency in Harlem," *Twice a Year,* no. 14-15 (Fall 1946-Winter 1947): 339-345;

"A World View of the American Negro," *Twice a Year*, no. 14-15 (Fall 1946-Winter 1947): 346-348;

"Introductory Note to *The Respectful Prostitute* by Jean-Paul Sarte," *Art and Action*, no. 10 (1948): 14-16;

"Comrade Strong, Don't You Remember?" *New York Herald Tribune* (European edition), 4 April 1949, p. 3;

"L'homme du Sud," *France Etats-Unis* (December 1950): 2;

"Richard Wright Explains Ideas about Movie Making," *Ebony*, 6 (January 1951): 84-85;

"American Negroes in France," *Crisis*, 58 (June-July 1951): 381-383;

"The Shame of Chicago," *Ebony*, 7 (December 1951): 24-32;

"Le Noir est une creátion du Blanc," *Preuves* (Paris), 8, no. 87 (May 1958): 40-41;

"L'art est mis en question par l'âge atomique," *Arts, Lettres, Spectacles* (Paris), 5 June 1960;

"Harlem," *Les Parisiens*, no. 1 (December 1960): 23.

Any serious discussion of the development of black fiction in modern American literature must include Richard Wright. He was the first black novelist to describe the plight of the urban masses and the first to present this material in the naturalistic tradition. Not only is he the father of the post-World War II black novel, he is also the main precursor of the black arts movement of the 1960s. Ralph Ellison and James Baldwin are but two of many outstanding black writers who profited from his influence. Moreover, he was, as Robert Felgar explains in *Richard Wright* (1980), "perhaps the very first writer to give the white community explanations and themes that cut through its prejudices and forced it to look at the reality of black life in America."

Richard Nathaniel Wright felt victimized by racial discrimination and racial prejudice throughout his life in the United States. He experienced some of the most severe abuses of racial oppression in Mississippi, where he was born on 4 September 1908, on a plantation in Roxie twenty-two miles east of Natchez, to sharecropper Nathan Wright and teacher Ella Wilson Wright. Nathan Wright, like most black sharecroppers, was extremely poor. In 1911 Ella Wright went to Natchez to live with her family while Nathan became an itinerant worker. Later that same year, in an effort to improve their economic status, Nathan Wright loaded his family onto a riverboat at Natchez and migrated to Memphis, Tennessee. Nathan Wright then deserted his family.

Richard Wright lived in Memphis until he was almost eight. As small children he and his younger brother Leon were often hungry and were expected to look out for themselves. The menial jobs that Ella Wright now had to take did not provide adequate income to support the family. Wright's autobiography, *Black Boy* (1945), explains: "I would feel hunger nudging my ribs, twisting my empty guts until they ached. I would grow dizzy and my vision would dim." His mother would send him to beg money from his father, now living with a mistress. In 1914 Ella Wright became ill, and the two brothers were sent to Settlement House, a Methodist orphanage.

Mrs. Wright and her sons moved to Elaine, Arkansas, to live with her sister, Maggie, and Maggie's husband, Silas Hoskins, in the summer of 1916. In late 1916 or early 1917 Silas Hoskins was murdered by whites who coveted his property, and the family fled to West Helena, Arkansas, where they lived in fear in rented rooms for several weeks. Mrs. Wright took the boys to Jackson, Mississippi, for several months in 1917, but they returned to West Helena by the winter of 1918. Further family disintegration occurred after Mrs. Wright suffered a stroke in 1919. Wright reluctantly chose to live with Uncle Clark and Aunt Jody in Greenwood, Mississippi, where he could be near his mother, but restrictions placed on him by his aunt and uncle made him an emotional wreck. On the verge of a nervous breakdown, he was permitted to return to Jackson, where he lived with Grandmother Wilson from early 1920 until late 1925.

Wright's education was greatly disrupted by family disorganization. The frequent moves and Mrs. Wright's illness made regular school attendance impossible. Wright first entered Howe Institute in Memphis, Tennessee, around 1916. In 1920 he enrolled and remained for a year at the Seventh Day Adventist school in Jackson, Mississippi, with his Aunt Addie, a fanatical Seventh Day Adventist, the only teacher. Wright felt stifled by his aunt and his maternal grandmother, who tried to force him to pray that he might find God. He later threatened to leave home because Grandmother Wilson refused to permit him to work on Saturdays, the Adventist Sabbath. Early strife with his aunt and grandmother left him with a permanent, uncompromising hostility toward religious solutions to mundane problems.

Wright in 1933

Traces of this hostility surface in much of his writing.

Wright's first formal education started in September 1921 when he joined a fifth grade class at Jim Hill Public School, Jackson, Mississippi. Within two weeks he was promoted to the sixth grade. In 1923 he enrolled at the Smith-Robinson School, also in Jackson; because of excellent grades he was made part-time supervisor of the class. Wright also showed special interest in and talent for writing, getting his first story, "The Voodoo of Hell's Half Acre," published in 1924 in the *Southern Register,* a black Jackson newspaper. In 1925 Wright was made class valedictorian. Determined not to be called an Uncle Tom, he refused to deliver the assistant principal's carefully prepared valedictory address that would not offend the white school officials and finally convinced the black administrators to let him read essentially what he had written. In September of the same year Wright registered for mathematics, English, and history courses at the new Lanier

High School in Jackson but had to stop attending classes after a few weeks of irregular attendance because he needed to earn money for family expenses.

In November 1925 Wright returned to Memphis with plans to get money to make "the first lap of a journey to a land where [he] could live with a little less fear." The two years he remained in Memphis were especially important, for there he indulged a developing passion for reading. He discovered *Harper's* magazine, the *Atlantic Monthly,* and the *American Mercury.* Through subterfuge he was able to borrow books from the white library. Of special importance to him were H. L. Mencken's *A Book of Prefaces* (1917) and one of his six volumes of *Prejudices* (1919-1927). Wright was particularly impressed with Mencken's vision of the South as hell.

Late in 1927 Wright arrived in Chicago, where he spent a decade that was as important to his development as his nineteen years in the South were. After finally securing employment as a postal clerk, he read other writers and studied their styles during his time off. His job at the post office eliminated by the Great Depression, he went on relief in 1931. In 1932 he began attending meetings of the Chicago John Reed Club, a Communist literary organization whose supposed purpose was to use art for revolutionary ends. Especially interested in the literary contacts made at the meetings, Wright formally joined the Communist party in late 1933 and as a revolutionary poet wrote numerous proletarian poems ("I Have Seen Black Hands," "We of the Streets," "Red Leaves of Red Books," for example) for *New Masses* and other left-wing periodicals.

By 1935 Wright had completed his first novel, "Cesspool," published as *Lawd Today* (1963), and in January 1936 his story "Big Boy Leaves Home" was accepted for publication in *New Caravan.* In February Wright began working with the National Negro Congress, and in April he chaired the South Side Writers' Group, whose membership included Arna Bontemps and Margaret Walker. Wright submitted some of his critical essays and poetry to the group for criticism and read aloud some of his short stories. In 1936 he was also revising "Cesspool."

The year 1937 was a landmark for Wright. After a quarrel with a Communist party leader, he severed ties with the Chicago branch and went to New York in late May to become Harlem editor of the *Daily Worker.* Wright was also upset over repeated rejections of "Cesspool" and other

works. He was happy that during his first year in New York all of his activities involved writing of some kind. In the summer and fall he wrote over two hundred articles for the *Daily Worker*. He helped organize *New Challenge*, a quarterly for works of progressive black authors, and wrote for the first issue "Blueprint for Negro Writing," the most complete and profound statement of his theories on Afro-American writing. Wright also wrote articles for *New Masses*, helped with the New York City Writers' Project, and continued revising the stories that would comprise *Uncle Tom's Children* (1938). The year was also a landmark for Wright because he met and developed a friendship with Ellison that would last for years, and he learned that he would receive the *Story* magazine first prize of five hundred dollars for his short story "Fire and Cloud."

Wright completed his final revision of "Cesspool" in 1937, and he was again disappointed that he could not get a publisher. This heavily-autobiographical first novel, published posthumously, is in some ways more structurally sophisticated than some of Wright's later works. The dreams, fantasies, and conscious behavior of its protagonist are the roots for later Wright themes: black nationalism, problems associated with mid-twentieth-century migration of blacks from the rural South to the industrial urban areas, and the absurdities of the existentialist hero.

Following the general structure of James Joyce's *Ulysses* (1922), Wright restricts the action of *Lawd Today* to one twenty-four-hour period, 12 February 1937, in the life of his protagonist, black postal worker Jake Jackson, who hates his job, his wife, his race, and himself. Since the date is specific, Wright can deal with more than the activities of one ordinary black man. Wright's greatest technical success in the novel is his ironic use of devices to give the novel additional dimension. One device is the newspaper Jake reads at breakfast and in the taxi. Jake's comments on what he reads illustrate his acceptance of some of the worst values of white American society. He sounds like a black George F. Babbitt with his empty clichés of money, worship, and even racism directed against "Jews, Dagoes, Hunkies and Mexicans." The central ironic device is the recurrent use of statements from a radio broadcast celebrating Abraham Lincoln's birthday and the northern victory in the Civil War. The continual stream of phrases contains layers of irony. Not only is the contrast between the importance of the events the broadcast relates and the triviality

of Jake's life, but also the tragic failure of America to fulfill the promise of the idealism of Lincoln and William Lloyd Garrison.

Wright's unsparing naturalistic technique gives a special strength to *Lawd Today*. Jake Jackson's brutal treatment of his wife Lil, the dreary post office building and monotony of the work in it, the elaborate orgies of drinking, feasting, dancing, and sex—all are described in minute detail. These scenes and others successfully evoke the sights, sounds, and smells of Jake Jackson's Chicago. And Wright makes no overt claims for his protagonist as he does in later works: the implications of Jake's blighted and futile existence speak for themselves.

After Wright received the *Story* magazine prize in early 1938, he shelved his manuscript of *Lawd Today* and dismissed his literary agent, John Troustine. He hired Paul Reynolds, the well-known agent of Paul Laurence Dunbar, to represent him. Meanwhile, the Story Press offered Harper all of Wright's prize-entry stories for a book, and Harper published them under Wright's chosen title, *Uncle Tom's Children*, in 1938.

Uncle Tom's Children, Wright's first book to be published, contains four lengthy short stories whose similarities in themes and method give the work unity. Wright's message is that Uncle Tom is dead, and his children will fight for freedom and survival. In "Big Boy Leaves Home," the first and finest story in the collection, Wright skillfully uses natural setting, varied points of view, and thematic richness to make an apparently simple tale about truancy, murder, lynching, and flight one of high artistic merit. Big Boy Morrison, Bobo, and two fellow truant adolescents are enjoying the idyllic countryside, very much in accord with their natural environment, until a white woman discovers them naked, resting after a swim in a creek forbidden to blacks. Black and white fears suddenly translate the Edenic setting into one of violence and murder, terminating with Big Boy killing the white woman's fiancé, after which he hides in a kiln overnight hoping to be ferried away by truck to Chicago the next morning. His hope of safety barely survives the brutal lynching/burning of Bobo by white citizens.

Wright's careful manipulation of viewpoint heightens the intensity of the story. He uses third person viewpoint in the first two sections where the narrative focuses upon the four boys and then upon the boys and the two whites. In the

Dust jacket for Wright's 1940 novel that sold 200,000 copies in less than three weeks

third section Big Boy is the major point of interest. The point of view shifts to first person during Big Boy's reveries in the kiln. The reader sees the lynching of Bobo from Big Boy's peculiar vantage point and, as it were, through his eyes.

"Big Boy Leaves Home" examines many of Wright's major themes: fear, initiation into violence, flight, survival, and freedom. Wright uses a setting and action reminiscent of the story of the Fall in Genesis, but here violent white racism drives Big Boy from the southern garden to uncertain freedom in the North; his initiation into violence and flight add poignancy and depth. There is irony in the title, for Big Boy is not simply leaving home. His survival depends on his flight from home to escape life-threatening racial tensions in his search for justice and freedom. Big Boy Morrison, innocent no longer, and having achieved adulthood through rebellion motivated by fear, is like the protagonists of "Down by the Riverside," "Long Black Song," and "Fire and Cloud," the other stories in the book.

"Down by the Riverside" contains, along with Wright's basic theme of the black man's struggle for survival, the themes of courage and stoic

endurance. Brother Mann confronts natural floods and the floods of racial hatred in his futile efforts to save his pregnant wife and son. When the white Heartfield boy Mann is able to save from the floods identifies him to the authorities as the murderer of his father, Mann rebels by dashing away from his captors, forcing them to shoot him in the back. A serious weakness in "Down by the Riverside" is that it has too many contrived incidents. Mrs. Heartfield does not report the murder of her husband when she seeks help, and the Heartfields turn in Mann as a murderer after his act of saving the boy.

In "Long Black Song," one of Wright's rare works written from the viewpoint of a female protagonist, he successfully integrates plot, character, and imagery. A white traveling salesman seduces a young black mother while her husband, Silas, is away purchasing supplies. When the salesman returns the next day with a friend, Silas, who has gotten the details from Sarah, horsewhips one of the men and kills the other one. The tragic theme is Silas's oppression and his doomed awareness of himself: " 'The White folks ain never gimme a chance. They ain never give no black man a chance. Their ain nothin in yo whole life yuh kin keep from 'em. They take yo lan! They take yo freedom! They take yo women! N Then they take yo life!' " Silas can assert himself only by fighting to the end, thereby becoming master of his own death. Sarah, in contrast to Silas, is a mother earth character who sadly watches a lynch mob burn down their house when Silas refuses to come out but not before he has killed one or two additional men. Hers is an inner rhythm that harmonizes with her memories and wishes. Wright fuses images of the seasons, the days and nights, the lush colors, and the earth rhythms to unfold her character. Sarah has a pastoral vision of the world that brings to mind William Faulkner's Lena Grove or Gertrude Stein's Melanctha. The entire story echoes Wright's experiences in Elaine, Arkansas, where his Uncle Silas was killed by white men.

Whereas the first three stories in *Uncle Tom's Children* describe the efforts of the individual black man against the white mob, "Fire and Cloud" deals with the theme of collective resistance to the white oppressor. The story relates the efforts of a black minister, Rev. Dan Taylor, to get food relief for the near-starving community of a southern town. When Taylor does not agree to stop a protest march, he is kidnapped the night before the march by a group of whites and

brutally beaten; but the whipping inspires him, and an integrated demonstration takes place with the preacher leading it.

Wright forcefully dramatizes the social issues in the dilemma faced by Taylor, emphasizing themes of freedom and the futility of religion. Taylor, in defying the white power structure, moves from religious resignation to social action. He does not reject God, but he does shift his religious emphasis to accomplish recognizable goals. Under his leadership the group acts and is successful. A major weakness in the work is Wright's reliance on stereotypes. The white villains are all hard, cold, and mean; the blacks are simple, unassuming, driven to their desperate actions only by their hunger. Only Taylor seems an authentic human being. The poor whites joining with the protesting blacks at the end make the conclusion more of a Marxist-desired utopia than an event basically related to the story and undercut Taylor's concluding remark, "Freedom belongs to the strong."

Because of the organization and similarity in theme and method the short stories in the 1938 edition of *Uncle Tom's Children* form a unified work of fiction. The 1940 edition is diluted by the addition of the essay, "The Ethics of Living Jim Crow," and the story, "Bright and Morning Star." The essay is out of place and, "Bright and Morning Star" is very different from the four stories in the 1938 version in that it is a polemic. Wright successfully portrays Big Boy Morrison, Brother Mann, and Silas as individuals fighting oppression and Taylor as a group leader. In "Bright and Morning Star," however, he appears too interested in promoting Marxist themes to delineate a strong character.

The publication and favorable reception of *Uncle Tom's Children* improved Wright's status with the Communist party and enabled him to establish a reasonable degree of financial stability. He was appointed to the editorial board of *New Masses,* and Granville Hicks, prominent literary critic and Communist sympathizer, introduced him at leftist teas in Boston. By 6 May 1938 excellent sales had provided him with enough money to move to Harlem, where he began writing *Native Son* (1940).

In 1939 Wright met two white women who, he thought, met his criteria for a wife: Dhimah Rose Meadman and Ellen Poplar. He married Dhimah in August 1939 with Ralph Ellison as best man. The honeymoon was delayed until the spring of 1940. During the honeymoon in Cuerna-

vaca, Mexico, Wright discovered how little he and Dhimah had in common, and they left Mexico separately, never to be reconciled. After his divorce from Dhimah, Wright married Ellen Poplar on 12 March 1941. Their first daughter Julia was born on 15 April 1942.

On the strength of *Uncle Tom's Children* and his completion of a section of *Native Son,* in early 1939 Wright was awarded a Guggenheim Fellowship which made it possible for him to complete *Native Son* for publication by 1 March 1940. The publication of the novel marked the beginning of a black literature that refused to compromise with many white expectations.

Native Son has no chapter divisions but instead consists of three books: "Fear," "Flight," and "Fate," and Wright skillfully uses fear as the controlling motif for the entire work. Three key scenes in book 1 dramatize the theme of fear. The opening, fear-filled scene illustrates the emotional violence manifested by the four members of the Thomas family against one another. All are afraid of a huge rat, and Bigger prolongs the fear (even after he kills it) by swinging the dead rat in front of his sister Vera until she faints. When Bigger joins his street-gang friends until time for a job interview at the residence of the wealthy Daltons, who need a chauffeur, another kind of fear surfaces. The gang plans to rob Blum's Delicatessen, a white man's business, and each gang member becomes afraid. Bigger demonstrates his fear through violence, terrifying Gus with kicks and threats of murder until he thinks the hour set for the robbery has passed. Hired by the Daltons, Bigger's fears mount to hysteria when Mary Dalton's blind mother enters Mary's bedroom, where Bigger has taken her after an evening out drinking with Jan Erlone, her boyfriend, during which she has become drunk. Realizing that he, a black man, is alone in a young white woman's bedroom, in 1940 a crime in most places in America, he places a pillow over Mary's head to prevent her from answering her mother. After his desperate effort results in Mary's accidental death by suffocation, Bigger, still acting out of fear, decapitates her body, stuffs it into the furnace, burns it, and returns home.

In "Flight" Wright emphasizes both Bigger's mental and physical responses to fears initiated in book 1. Bigger begins to rationalize that in killing Mary Dalton he has destroyed symbolically all the oppressive forces that have made his life miserable. He is proud, for "he had murdered and created a new life for himself." Out of fear

Dust jacket for Wright's 1941 Marxist history of black people in America

for his own safety he suggests that Jan Erlone is guilty, a suggestion supported by a ransom note which Bigger sends to the family to lead suspicion from himself. Bigger's fears mount, and he goes to Bessie, his mistress, so that she can comfort him; but she wrings from him a confession of the murder. He instructs her to collect the ransom money. At the Dalton home when the ransom note arrives, and afraid that he might see a vivid image of Mary's face as he had seen it upon the bed, Bigger cannot shake down the furnace ashes. This fear to act leads to the discovery of Mary's charred bones, which makes it necessary for him and Bessie to flee. Deciding that Bessie will become a great liability, Bigger, partially out of fear, brutally murders her. With this premeditated murder Bigger becomes a fearful monster who moves from one tenement to the next, creating fear throughout the black ghetto until the vast police network captures him on a rooftop.

In the first two books point of view is limited to what Bigger sees, feels, and hears. Wright's dramatic dialogue and graphic descriptions of Bigger's actions and surroundings force the reader to take special notice of him. He is not the familiar black victim but the violent at-

tacker and appears to confirm the white man's fantasies of black assault and rape. Bigger is deprived and depraved beyond ordinary humanity.

Book 3, "Fate," mainly an analysis of the action in books 1 and 2, reduces Bigger to a somewhat passive character, thereby eliminating the rapid pacing and extraordinary narrative drive which characterize books 1 and 2. But fear remains the central motif. Wright now focuses not on Bigger's individual fears but on those of other individual blacks and the black and white communities in general. Mrs. Thomas worries over Bigger's fate. She and her minister, the Reverend Hammond, fear for his soul. The prosecution at his trial and the press sensationalize events that arouse public fears, and the Ku Klux Klan burns crosses. Boris A. Max, Bigger's lawyer, explores the causes and effects of fear and racism in his summation, arguing that society is partly to blame for Bigger's crimes. Ironically, what Bigger learns as a result of fear enables him to go to the electric chair declaring in existential terms that what he has done has had value: "It must've been good! When a man kills, it's for something. I didn't know I was really alive in this world until I felt things hard enough to kill for 'em."

Foreshadowing, rich imagery, and symbolism are among the many effective literary devices Wright uses to illuminate his themes. The rat scene is the prime example of foreshadowing. The black rat Bigger fights and kills turns desperately on its enemies when it no longer sees a means of escape. The scene prefigures Bigger's fate. When Bigger leads Bessie to the deserted house to await the ransom money, "something with dry whispering feet flitted across his path, emitting as the rush of its flight died a thin, piping wail of lonely fear." When Bigger is looking for a vacant apartment for a hiding place, he sees a big black rat leap over the snow and looks "wistfully at that gaping black hole through which the rat had darted to safety." Alienated, Bigger himself becomes a trapped rat who futilely fights his pursuers when escape becomes impossible.

Dominant symbols in the novel include the cross, whiteness, and blindness. To emphasize his denial of his mother's Christianity Bigger tears the crucifix from his neck. He later rejects the cross offered him by the Reverend Hammond when the Ku Klux Klan ignites its fiery cross not far from the Dalton residence. The rich religious symbol has been reduced to one level, that of hate and rejection.

Wright consistently uses whiteness to represent Bigger's fear and anxieties. Upon meeting Mrs. Dalton he observes "that her hair and face were completely white; she seemed to him like a ghost." When Bigger returns to the kitchen to get some water, "What he saw made him suck his breath in; Mrs. Dalton in flowing white clothes was standing stone stiff in the middle of the kitchen floor." Later at Mary's bedroom door Mrs. Dalton appears an "awesome blur . . . silent ghost-like." Bigger is never at ease in the presence of Mrs. Dalton and her ubiquitous white cat. Even the weather takes on symbolic overtones. It begins to snow when Bigger flees the Dalton residence. The ice and snowstorms in book 2 are perpetual reminders of the white hostile environment. Bigger, at the end of book 2, is forced on a cross of snow: "Two men stretched his arms out as though about to crucify him; they placed a foot on each of his wrists, making them sink deep down in the snow."

The blindness motif is even more pervasive than that of whiteness. Wright makes all of his characters blind in some way. Mrs. Dalton is physically blind. Racism impairs the moral vision of state prosecutor Buckley. Bigger's limited perception leads him to label all others, especially whites, as blind. Mary Dalton and Jan Erlone believe that the Communist party has all the answers. Mr. Dalton feels that a supply of table tennis tables in the ghetto recreation rooms is an overwhelming humanitarian act. Mrs. Thomas is certain that her religion will provide all solutions.

Native Son sold two hundred thousand copies in under three weeks, breaking a twenty-year record at Harper. Clifton Fadiman in the *New Yorker* compared Wright to Theodore Dreiser and John Steinbeck and praised his "passion and intelligence" that examined "layers of consciousness only Dostoyevski and a few others have penetrated." Henry S. Canby in *Book of the Month Club News* wrote that, "like *Grapes of Wrath* it is a fully realized story . . . uncompromisingly realistic and quite as human as it is Negro." Ralph Ellison in *New Masses* found in it "an artistry, penetration of thought and sheer emotional power that places it in the first rank of American fiction." Jonathan Daniels, Malcolm Cowley, Sterling Brown, and most other eminent black and white critics of the day praised the novel. The few dissenting voices, among them Howard Mumford Jones and David Cohn, had objections that were more personal than literary. While there is yet much critical debate over the place *Native Son* should oc-

cupy in the corpus of great literature, there is a consensus that the novel is one of the classic works of American literature.

The period following publication of *Native Son* was a busy time for Wright. In July 1940 he went to Chicago to do research for the text for a folk history of blacks to accompany photographs selected by Edwin Rosskam. While in Chicago he visited the American Negro Exhibition with Langston Hughes, Bontemps, and Claude McKay. He then went to Chapel Hill, North Carolina, where he and Paul Green collaborated on a dramatic version of *Native Son*. In January 1941 Wright received the prestigious Spingarn Medal for noteworthy achievement by a black. *Native Son* opened on Broadway, with Orson Welles as director, to generally favorable reviews in March 1941. *Twelve Million Black Voices: A Folk History of the Negro in the United States* was published in October 1941 to wide critical acclaim.

Twelve Million Black Voices, the outgrowth of a Works Projects Administration assignment, is a sociological study of American black history and the migration from the rural South to the urban North. The text describes the bondage of blacks from slavery and plantation life to sharecropping and to the factories of the North. Wright emphasizes that in the progression from slavery to the industrialized urban cities blacks have experienced in a few hundred years what whites were exposed to over thousands of years, and blacks should feel proud of their accomplishment. His recurrent themes of freedom, oppression, and survival permeate the work.

Part 1, "Our Strange Birth," traces aspects of black development from 1619 to the Emancipation Proclamation. Wright refers to the slave ships as "floating brothels" and describes the "lecherous crew members as they vented the pent up bestiality of their starved sex lives upon our sisters and wives." He speaks of captivity under Christendom as having "blasted" life, destroying family, traditions, and all the values that had given meaning in Africa before the white man came.

Part 2, "Inheritors of Slavery," covers the period from the Civil War until World War I. Wright discusses the presentness of the racial past, black English, race relations, the importance of books, and the significance of the black church. He explains that the word "Negro," the term by which orally or in print, "we black folk in the United States are usually designated is not really a name at all." It is a white man's word—"a

psychological island whose objectives form the most unanimous fiat in all American history . . . a fiat which artificially and arbitrarily defines, regulates and limits in scope the vital contours of our lives. . . . " Wright's point was made long before the vast majority of Afro-Americans frowned upon "Negro" and "colored."

In part 3, "Death on the City Pavements," Wright discusses the Great Migration, the movement of southern blacks to northern ghettos. He describes the squalid living quarters, most often old houses converted into kitchenettes, which were "seed bed[s] for scarlet fever, dysentery, typhoid . . . pneumonia and malnutrition" and rented "at rates so high they make fabulous fortunes before the houses are too old for habitation."

In "Men in the Making," the concluding section, Wright stresses that black folk are a mirror of all the manifold experiences of America. "What we want, what we represent, what we endure is what America is. If we black folk perish, America will perish." He emphasizes that black and white workers must unite against the classes that exploit them, the Lords of the Land (those who run the plantations) and the Bosses of the Buildings (those who manage the industries). His Marxist explanations are followed by a description of the march toward freedom that could have been written by Carl Sandburg or Walt Whitman. Wright proclaims: "We are with the new tide. We stand at the crossroads. We watch each new procession. . . . Voices are speaking. Men are moving! And we shall be with them."

In *Twelve Million Black Voices* Wright fully identifies with the black experience and convincingly analyzes the roles of blacks in the total American experience. The beautiful lyrical passages that occasionally creep in tend to mitigate temporarily the severity of the naturalistic details, thereby adding a moderating dimension to the work. Wright's extended prose poem, despite its obvious Marxist orientation, is a forceful, saddening, and encouraging black American epic. Uniformly enthusiastic reviewers, Bontemps among them, hailed Wright as a master of poetic prose, belonging to the fine tradition of the Negro spiritual.

While completing *Twelve Million Black Voices* Wright was also writing two novels–"Black Hope" (unpublished) and "The Man Who Lived Underground," which had only its third section published as a short story in 1944. A visit to Fisk University in April 1943 prompted Wright to start a

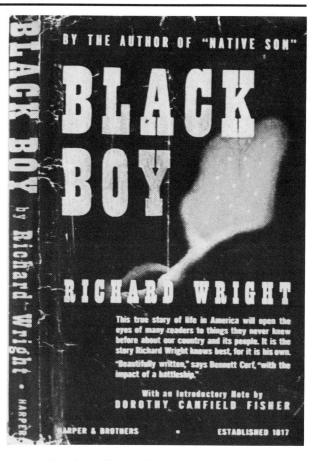

Dust jacket for Wright's 1945 autobiography

still unpublished screenplay, "Melody Unlimited," based on the history of the Fisk Jubilee Singers and highlighting the importance of black colleges as a bridge between black and white. The visit also influenced him to begin his autobiography. On 17 December 1943 he sent Paul Reynolds the manuscript of "American Hunger," which chronicled his life up to his departure from Chicago in 1937. The first section of "American Hunger" was published as *Black Boy: A Record of Childhood and Youth* in 1945; the *Atlantic Monthly* published a part of the second section, which described Wright's membership in and eventual rejection of the Communist party, under the title "I Tried to Be a Communist" in August and September 1944. The second section was not published in its entirety until after Wright's death as *American Hunger* (1977).

In *Black Boy* Wright develops the observations recorded in "The Ethics of Living Jim Crow," the introductory section for the 1940 edition of *Uncle Tom's Children*. The entire autobiography is an espisodically structured yet richly thematic work, similar to a movie documentary, with

Wright as the narrator. It focuses on significant events in his life from the age of four (1912) through nineteen (1927). With some creative license, according to his biographer Michel Fabre, Wright describes and interprets from an adult perspective the economic, familial, educational, and racial handicaps he faced. The first section helps set the tone for the entire autobiography, for throughout *Black Boy* Wright is showing how boredom and different kinds of sickness unite to form unyielding ties of oppression. It describes the house four-year-old Richard set on fire because he was bored and ordered to stay inside and remain quiet. Young Richard temporarily escapes punishment when, terrified, he hides under the house. Fire as a dominant image and symbol and the underground motif permeate many of his works, but they are particularly significant in *Black Boy* because they reinforce its theme, the search for freedom.

Wright relates early familial difficulties. He details how, after a fight with white boys, his mother "lashed so hard and long that I lost consciousness" and " . . . for a long time I was chastened whenever I remembered that my mother had come close to killing me." He remembers hanging a stray kitten to gain triumph over his father: "How could I get back at him? . . . He had said to kill the kitten and I would kill it. I knew that he had not really meant for me to kill the kitten but my deep hate of him urged me toward a literal acceptance of his word."

Wright constantly describes and questions the hunger in his life. He blames his father with a "biological bitterness" for the hunger, "standing at my bedside staring at me." At the foster home, he says, "I was too weak from hunger. . . ." Living with his Uncle Hopkins, at Granny's, nowhere did he feel free from the want of food. One of the more pathetic scenes in the book is near the end of chapter 2 where his only Christmas gift is an orange. He eats it all day long and just before going to bed he tears "the peeling into bits and munched them slowly." Wright laments, "Why did I always have to wait until others were through? I could not understand why some people had enough food and others did not. . . . Hunger was with us always." Midway through *Black Boy* Wright explains, "I vowed that someday I would end this hunger of mine, this apartness, this external difference."

Wright's description of southern whites is totally negative; they are cruel, violent, inhumane persons who will put forth special efforts to de-

base blacks. Such declarations from Wright are not shocking. What does appear rather unusual is Wright's attitude toward blacks. He explains:

> I used to mull over the strange absence of real kindness in Negroes, how unstable was our tenderness, how lacking in genuine passion we were . . . how lacking we were in those intangible sentiments that bind man to man and how shallow was even our despair. . . . I used to brood upon the unconscious irony of those who felt the Negroes led so passional an existence. I saw that what had been taken for our emotional strength was our negative confusions, our flights, our fears, our frenzy under pressure.

This passage and others like it in *Black Boy* suggest to many that Wright lacked racial pride. He did at times have difficulty expressing individual affection for black culture, but he could display admiration for black group achievements as is convincingly shown in *Twelve Million Black Voices*. The fact that Wright is an adult attempting to comprehend almost overwhelming childhood experiences indicates that he is interested in understanding his black culture, not in rejecting it.

Black Boy had phenomenal sales and received tremendous critical praise. By March 1945 it had sold over four hundred thousand copies and was listed at the top of most best-seller lists. Critics from the *New York Times*, the *New York Herald Tribune*, and the *St. Louis Post Dispatch* were among those who wrote glowing reviews. Dorothy Canfield Fisher placed the work on the level with Jean-Jacques Rousseau's *Confessions* and St. Augustine's *Confessions*. Among the thousands of congratulatory letters to Wright was one from William Faulkner, who wrote that "Wright said it well, as well as it could have been in this form." Some blacks expressed mixed acceptance. They felt that Wright spent too much time documenting black despair. A few southern critics made extremely negative remarks concerning the book's account of race relations in the South. Most critics and the general reader concurred that *Black Boy* merits a place on the shelf next to the autobiographies of Benjamin Franklin, Frederick Douglass, and Henry Adams.

The second part of Wright's autobiography, *American Hunger*, like *Black Boy*, explores many of Wright's recurrent themes: manhood, freedom, flight, oppression. Wright focuses on his experiences in Chicago, and he becomes negatively critical of the entire American system, not just the South, as was the case in *Black Boy*, where he at

the end "headed North, full of a hazy notion that life could be lived with dignity."

Perhaps the most significant segments of *American Hunger* deal with Wright's connections with the Communist party and his efforts to retain his integrity despite the party's demands that he sacrifice his artistic aims for the good of the party. After he becomes affiliated with the Chicago John Reed Club, he is upset that he is labeled an intellectual because he reads books other than those endorsed by the party. When he is threatened by the group and scorned even by black Communists, he asks: "Why was it that I was a suspected man because I wanted to reveal the vast physical and spiritual ravages of Negro life. . . . What was the danger in showing the kinship between the sufferings of the Negro and the sufferings of other people?"

Wright explains, "I wanted to be a Communist but my kind of Communist. I wanted to share people's feelings." After much deliberation he asks that his name be removed from the rolls but continues to work for Communist-affiliated organizations. Because of Communist pressure he loses his job at the Federal Negro Theater, and his position with the Federal Writers' Project is jeopardized. The most humiliating experience, however, comes on May Day when a black Communist invites him to join the parade of marchers, and he reluctantly agrees only to be lifted from the sidewalk by party members and "pitched headlong through the air . . . the rows of white and black Communists looking at me with cold eyes of nonrecognition." Wright's spirit is crushed, for he had previously seen communism as a viable alternative to the poverty, hunger, and racism in America. Back at his apartment Wright commences reflecting: "Well, what had I got out of living in the city? What had I got out of living in the South? What had I got out of living in America? I paced the floor, knowing that all I possessed were words and a dim knowledge that my country had shown me no examples of how to live a human life . . . I wanted to build a bridge of words between men and that world outside, that world so distant and elusive that it seemed unreal."

Unlike *Black Boy*, whose ending suggests a success story, *American Hunger* represents the culmination of Wright's disappointment with America. Moral, economic, and racial conditions in Chicago and New York City are but additional proof of the country's failures. Wright insists upon an acute awareness of conditions and radical

Wright and his daughter Julia, 1945 (photograph by Studio Gallery, Stockholm)

changes including a set of values that will respect the rights of everyone. The special importance of *American Hunger* lies in its vivid presentation of Wright's experiences in the North and its explanation of these wider dimensions of his thought.

The remainder of 1945 and the years 1946 and 1947 were extremely busy and highly critical periods for Wright. He traveled abroad, delivered speeches, engaged in debates, reviewed books, and continued to write. In the fall of 1945 he toured the nation delivering lectures about the racial situation. He gave financial aid to black novelist Chester Himes and secured a grant for James Baldwin. He sailed for Paris on 1 May 1946, where he was lionized by the French press and private citizens. In Paris he became friends with Gertrude Stein and many French intellectuals, including Jean-Paul Sartre and Simone de Beauvoir. Wright and Ellen visited Switzerland in November, where he gave interviews and contacted a publisher for the German edition of *Black Boy*. In late 1946 Wright met George Padmore in London. Padmore, the father of African liberation, introduced him to the progressive, militant leaders of the Third World. This meeting had two significant and long-range effects upon Wright. His friendship with Padmore influenced his political thinking and further increased his interest in Africa. Meeting black leaders from all of the English-speaking African countries indi-

cated to Wright that black America's call for freedom was now being echoed throughout the other nonwhite continents of the world, and he concluded that he must visit nonwhite countries.

By January 1947, when the family returned to Manhattan, Wright had become even more dissatisfied with American racial policies. He constantly contrasted the freedom and acceptance he experienced in Paris against the rampant racism he faced in America. Like James Joyce, he felt that he could not expand his artistic and personal freedom unless he exiled himself from the oppressive soil of his native country. Wright and his family returned to Paris in August 1947 and became permanent citizens. Although Wright traveled extensively, France was his home base until his death in 1960. The last fourteen years of his life are especially notable for a shift in ideological emphases: instead of determinism he explored choice; along with racism he emphasized a more metaphysical isolation; in place of colonialism in the Deep South he focused on global oppression. Existentialism and identification with the people of the Third World are outgrowths of his earlier experiences. Though no longer a card-carrying Communist, his writings still reflect Marxist ideals and sympathies.

In 1948 Wright traveled to Milan with Ellen to celebrate Camillo Pellizi's translation of *Native Son* and attended a reception in Turin where *Black Boy* was being translated. He met with principal Italian critics. During a five-day stay in Rome in February 1948 he lectured on Afro-American literature. By this time he had started work again on the manuscript of *The Outsider* (1953) and informed his agent that he wanted to rework it completely.

Upon returning to Paris in May 1948 Wright established himself as a model Parisian intellectual. In interviews he praised the poetry of Gwendolyn Brooks, commented on his favorite novels, *Moby-Dick*, *Ulysses*, and *The Sound and the Fury*, and offered explanations of writers he was currently reading, Franz Kafka, Martin Heidegger, and Soren Kierkegaard among them. Later in the year he stopped working on his new "philosophical" novel, *The Outsider*, and concentrated on acquiring a better understanding of French and German existentialism.

After his second daughter Rachel was born in Paris on 17 January 1949, Wright traveled to Argentina with French director Pierre Cheval to play Bigger Thomas in a film version of *Native Son*. Following his sincere but awkward performance in the 1951 film, an artistic and financial failure, Wright worked with the French American Fellowship, an organization to combat racism in American businesses abroad. The excessive number of hours he spent working with this group further delayed his completing *The Outsider*. Perhaps a greater impediment to its completion was the unfortunate quarrel with James Baldwin over Baldwin's suggestion in "Everybody's Protest Novel" that *Native Son* was merely Harriet Beecher Stowe's *Uncle Tom's Cabin* (1852) in reverse. Wright felt betrayed, and much of his creative energy was involved in his overt hostility toward Baldwin.

Although Wright published no books between 1947 and 1953, he wrote English articles for *Présence Africaine* and French language articles for periodicals such as *France-Observateur* and *Les Temps Modernes*. He also wrote short essays for *Encounter* (England), *Twice a Year*, and *Ebony*. The one work of fiction he published was a short story, "The Man Who Killed a Shadow," later collected in *Eight Men* (1960). During this period he enjoyed rich literary exposure serving on the board of patrons for *Présence Africaine* with Sartre, Albert Camus, and André Gide, all of whom influenced his later works. His purely creative output declined with his move to France, but his political and historical vision certainly deepened.

After almost six years of work Wright finally completed *The Outsider* in London in early 1952. Long and complex, *The Outsider* is perhaps the first consciously existentialist novel written by an American. It is the first Wright novel which does not emphasize racial matters. While the protagonist is black, he is not primarily concerned with his plight as a black; he is a thinking, questioning man in the perplexing twentieth century. Partly autobiographical, *The Outsider* is as much Wright's own spiritual odyssey as it is that of his hero, Cross Damon. Wright's experiences in America, his disaffection with communism, his views on Europe in turmoil based upon his travels during his first year in exile, the long nights spent with Sartre and Beauvoir debating the meaning of freedom, his often deeply felt periods of alienation–all combine to present the picture of a solitary individual intent upon creating the ideal man in the modern world.

Cross Damon feels overwhelmed by tremendous burdens: a wife he no longer loves, a pregnant mistress, and an emotional mother he both loves and hates. When authorities use the overcoat and identification papers he left behind

after climbing from a train crash to identify another victim as him, Damon decides to forget his wife and three sons. After assuming a number of aliases he journeys to New York and becomes involved with the Communist party. Damon moves in with Communists Gil and Eva Blount (because the Blounts wish to desegregate their apartment building managed by the Fascist and racist Langley Herndon) and discovers and reads Eva Blount's diary from which he learns Gil Blount had deceived her by marrying her, not out of love, but because the Communist party had ordered it. Alarmed over this cynical violation of individual rights, Damon vows that the party will not destroy his freedom and humanity. That he has violated Eva's privacy never enters his mind. Later, entering a room ostensibly to stop Blount and Herndon from fighting, Damon kills both men and arranges the clues so that it appears they have killed each other. Damon rationalizes that in destroying the Communist and the Fascist he is killing "gods" who would rob him of his freedom. Only much later does he comprehend that in slaying them—exercising his complete freedom— he has himself assumed the role of a god: "Oh, Christ their disease had reached out and claimed him too. He had been subverted by the contagion of the lawless; he had been defeated by that which he had sought to destroy."

In a desperate attempt to conceal his previous crimes Damon murders a high Communist official who has evidence which will convict him. That Damon has become a demon is further dramatized when district attorney Houston tells him his mother has died, possibly because of his deeds, and then ushers Damon's wife and three sons into the room. Damon (demon) acknowledges no one and nothing. With no positive proof Houston cannot arrest him. Damon, alone, enters the streets of Harlem and hides in theaters until Communist party members track and shoot him down. In a final scene reminiscent of Bigger Thomas's last scenes with his lawyer, Boris A. Max, Damon explains in existentialist terms: "Don't think I'm so odd and strange . . . I'm not. . . . I'm legion . . . I've lived alone, but I'm everywhere." He warns of a new era when men will stop deceiving themselves about their murderous nature and the meaninglessness of life. Dying, Damon is asked by Houston what he found in life. He responds "Nothing. . . . Alone a man is nothing."

In *The Outsider* Wright uses existential tenets to expose the myths by which men often irration-

ally live. Some sections of the novel are little more than existentialist jargon. The novel, however, is an illustration not of Wright's existentialism, but of his rejection of it as an adequate means to cope with the problems of the modern world. Cross Damon equates freedom with power; while exercising his unbridled freedom he murders four human beings and is partially responsible for the deaths of two others. Damon casts aside almost all societal codes of behavior only to realize in the end that human restrictions help humanize man. Neither man nor society can accommodate completely free individuals, for they are threats to human existence.

While thematically rich, *The Outsider* has many obvious flaws. As most contemporary critics noted, there are numerous improbabilities, contrived speeches, and a melodramatic plot. Critics from the *New York Times*, the *New York Herald Tribune*, and *Time Magazine* praised some of the detective story techniques but could not enthusiastically recommend the novel because of its problems. Black writers, the late Lorraine Hansberry among them, called Wright an outsider, outcast from his own people. Only European critics had unqualified praise for the novel, according it a better reception than they did Camus's existential novel *The Stranger* (1942).

The Outsider had scarcely undergone final revision before Wright was back in Paris at work on another book. Wright announced to novelist and fellow expatriate William Gardner Smith that he had completed another novel, one that "like all my future books, I think . . . will take up aspects of the problems broached in *The Outsider*." Wright managed to generate great enthusiasm among his friends for the completed novel, *Savage Holiday* (1954), but had great difficulty getting the work published. Harper, his regular publisher, rejected the book, and his agent Paul Reynolds agreed that it was an inferior work. Avon Books printed a paperback edition of *Savage Holiday* in 1954. The work is especially notable because it is an important black writer's only novel in which all of the major characters are white, and racial concerns are seldom mentioned.

In *The Outsider* Wright emphasizes tenets of existentialism; in *Savage Holiday* he adds Freud. Retired insurance executive Erskine Fowler, an apparently successful man who lives in a fashionable section of New York and is very much respected by his peers, has locked away his feelings and passions because of his inability to accept the fact that he had incestuous desires for his beauti-

Wright, circa 1947, when he moved permanently to France

ful, sexually alluring mother. He also feels guilty about his role in the accidental death of the gorgeous and promiscuous Mrs. Blake's five-year-old son Tony. To assuage his dual grief Fowler hopes to redeem Tony's death by redeeming Mrs. Blake through marriage. Fowler courts and proposes to Mrs. Blake, during which time the long-suppressed Fowler, who wishes to establish a relationship with his mother and possess her sexually, vicariously, through Mrs. Blake, emerges. At the same time he hates Mrs. Blake and vents his sense of outrage against her by killing her: "With machine like motion Erskine lifted the butcher knife and plunged it into her stomach again and again." At this point the novel becomes a Freudian workbook. At the police station where he later reports the murder, Fowler recalls a fantasy he had repressed as a child when his mother scolded him for stabbing a stuffed doll. He decides the stuffed doll represented his mother and concludes that the fantasy arose from an actual occurrence in his childhood when he drew a picture of a dead doll and imagined that he had drawn a picture of his mother. The Freudian

movement has been from mother to doll to Mrs. Blake, and the childhood symbolic act has terminated in an adult symbolic act. Fowler feels that he cannot tell the police why he committed the crime because he cannot explain that his real motives originated from a childhood fantasy.

As Edward Margolies points out in *The Art of Richard Wright* (1969), Wright's ending the book as he does makes one feel that he "has somehow made short shrift of all the problems he had been so laboriously posing throughout the novel." Wright is not able to show that Fowler is in control of his passions because of extreme weaknesses of plot and character; and the too obvious Freudian implications further damage the novel's credibility. Wright reworks some of his favorite themes: freedom, religion as an impotent force, the substitution of violence for love, the presentness of the past; he fails, however, to make them unobtrusive parts of the novel. Since *Savage Holiday* was never published in hardcover, it was not reviewed by the American press. Like *The Outsider*, however, it created excitement in Europe where it was translated into French, Italian, German, and Dutch and received some favorable reviews from the French press.

During 1953, the same year *The Outsider* was published in New York and a few months after completing the first draft of *Savage Holiday*, Wright journeyed through the undeveloped country of the British West African colony of the Gold Coast (later called Ghana) by way of the Canary Islands. *Black Power: A Record of Reactions in a Land of Pathos* (1954), written as a result of that trip, is a very personal book in which Wright draws conclusions about the culture, the people, and the political, social, and economic problems facing the African country. The work has characteristics of a writer's journal of ideas and a travel diary, for Wright includes statistical charts, significant historical data he has gathered from books, dialogue obtained through his questioning of tribal chieftains and British officials, and vivid descriptions of Africans and their country.

In a short introduction, "Apropos Prepossessions," Wright states that the aim of this book is "to pose the problem anew in an area that is proving a decisive example for an entire continent," the problem being whether the West will deal justly with its nonwhite subjects or leave them prey to communism. In doing this Wright reiterates his scorn for religious authority. He reacts to Christian missionary efforts in the same manner that he responded to his Grandmother Wilson's at-

213

tempts to convert him. Just as his grandmother tried to rob him of his individual freedom for her own satisfaction, so were the missionaries attempting to subjugate and exploit for their own purposes. When he and Nigerian Supreme Court Justice Thomas visit a house of prostitution in Las Palmas, Canary Islands, Wright remarks, "It occurred to me that this shabby whorehouse was perhaps the only calm and human spot in this strongly entrenched Catholic city."

In *Black Power* Wright's recommendation for solving the Gold Coast's problems is simplistic. He argues that Kwame Nkrumah has to enlist and rechannel the frustrated religious energies of the detribalized masses into the cause of industrialization and nationhood. The people must be subjected to a form of militarization that will give "form, organization, direction, meaning and a sense of justification to those lives. . . : a temporary discipline that will unite the nations, sweep out the tribal cobwebs, atomize the fetish-ridden past, abolish the mystical and nonsensical family relations." Then Nkrumah and his assistants will be able to use people rather than the dollars of Western capitalists to modernize their industrial economy. History has shown that Wright's do-it-yourself formula could never solve Africa's complex political, economic, and psychological problems.

While Wright does some of his best expository writing in *Black Power,* his tendencies to make hasty generalizations and to assume the superiority of Western traditions at the expense of indigenous African culture mitigate the effectiveness of the book. Wright calls the African "an oblique, a hard to know man who seemed to take a childish pride in trying to create a state of bewilderment in the minds of strangers." He asserts that "the African almost invariably underestimated the person with whom he was dealing; he always placed too much confidence in an evasive reply, thinking that if he denied something, then that something ceased to exist. It was childlike." The postscript to *Black Power* concludes, "I found only one intangible but vitally important element in the heritage of tribal culture that militated against cohesiveness of action: African culture has not developed the personalities of the people to a degree that their egos are stout, hard, sharply defined; there is too much cloudiness that makes for lack of confidence, an absence of focus that renders that mentality incapable of grasping the workaday world." A summer tour through a part of one country on the African con-

tinent hardly qualifies one to make such judgments. In his introduction Wright states that "the West can meanly lose Africa or the West can nobly save Africa." To follow Wright's plan for African independence, Africa must disband her tribes, industrialize, and become technologically competent in order to assume a position of world leadership, or, as Wright really means, it must become like the West. That native Africans might not wish to replace their entire culture with so-called Western advancements does not seem to occur to Wright. A major theme in the work is freedom, but one has to consider what kind of freedom at the expense of which freedom or freedoms.

Neither *Time, Newsweek,* nor the daily *New York Times* reviewed the book, and the *New York Times Book Review* called it a caricature of British colonialism "drawn not from life but from the dreary old arsenal of Marxist slogans." The *New York Herald Tribune Weekly Book Review,* the *Boston Globe,* and the *Chicago Tribune* highly praised the book.

In early 1955, with the help of Gunnar Myrdal, Wright attended the Bandung Conference in Indonesia as a representative for the Congress of Cultural Freedom. He finished his report in June 1955 and in the fall began work on a novel tentatively called "Mississippi," later entitled *The Long Dream* (1958). The report on the conference, first published in France in 1955, was circulated in the United States as *The Color Curtain: A Report on the Bandung Conference* in 1956. In this work Wright expands his thesis from *Black Power* that poor and weak Africans are exploited by oppressive whites to include all nonwhites, particularly Asians. His overriding thesis is that race is the central issue in determining the development of the new nations of Africa and Asia. This book, a much shorter volume than *Black Power,* is comprised of excerpts from official speeches and private interviews and Wright's observations and comments.

Wright focuses on Chou En-lai's major speech before the conference in which Chou concentrated on African-Asian unity rather than East-West political and ideological conflict. As he did in *Black Power,* Wright again offers Western industrialization as the solution to Asia's difficulties: "Is this secular, rational base of thought and feeling in the Western world broad and secure enough to warrant the West's assuming the moral right to interfere sans narrow selfish political motives? My answer is yes."

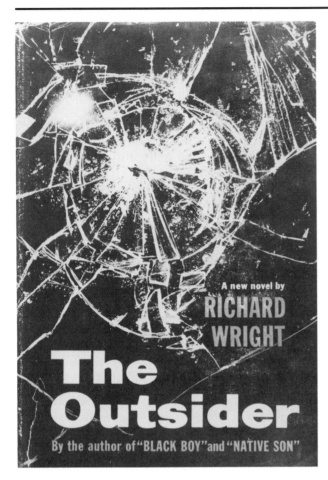

Dust jacket for Wright's 1953 existentialist novel (courtesy of the Afro-American Collection, Blockson Library, Temple University)

Reviews of the book were generally favorable. The *New York Times Book Review* praised everything except Wright's tendency "to exaggerate the racial and religious unity in the Third World and the importance of China." The *Saturday Review* called Wright's analysis an "important contribution" to understanding the conference.

Wright visited Spain from August 1954 until mid December and continued his tour in the spring of 1955. He went to the major cities, Barcelona, Madrid, and Seville among them, and traveled to numerous rural villages. In 1956 he participated in the planning of the First Congress of Negro Artists and Writers held in Paris. He translated Louis Sapin's play *Papa Bon Dieu* (*Daddy Goodness*), which reflects his great interest in black folk cultures, especially the cults of Father Divine and Daddy Grace. On 22 November 1956 Wright began a tour of Scandinavia, and later the same year he completed *White Man, Listen!* (1957).

Pagan Spain: A Report of a Journey into the Past (1957), is the published result of the excursion to Spain. The five-chapter report contains excellent descriptive scenes of Spain's cities and towns and a rich variety of information about Spanish life collected from interviews Wright conducted and public events he attended. An especially effective structural device is his use of a Franco government approved handbook which states the aims and principles of the regime. Wright discusses the Spain he sees and at convenient intervals inserts passages from the handbook, thereby providing an excellent contrast between what he actually observes and the propagandistic explanations in the political guide.

Wright issues some severe condemnations of life in Spain. He is convinced that the methods used to persecute and terrorize Protestants correspond to those used in the American South against blacks and other minorities, and he asserts that the church's views toward sex are the reasons sex is the preoccupation among Spaniards and prostitution is a major industry. Poor wages received by women for honest labor force them to prostitution to satisfy the men who do not receive full gratification from the women they love. Wright concludes that Spain is hopelessly mired in an archaic past, that "the prostitution, the corruption, the economics, the politics had about them a sacred aura. All was religion in Spain."

In *Pagan Spain* Wright adds to his gallery of outsiders people who are not persecuted because of color but because of religion and gender. While the work indicates a broader humane concern, it also shows Wright again making too many hasty generalizations in his evaluation of a country and its ways. He again suggests replacing the indigenous culture of a nation with Western technology and ideals. *Pagan Spain* was a financial failure, but it received critical praise. The *New York Times* discussed Wright's great insight into the rituals of Spain. The *Saturday Review* stressed as a strong point of the book Wright's brilliant analysis of the "unconscious sources of religion."

White Man, Listen!, Richard Wright's last book of nonfiction, consists of a series of lectures delivered between 1950 and 1956 in cities in Italy, Germany, France, and Sweden. The order of essays follows the essential pattern of Wright's fiction: movement from bondage to freedom, and the flight to new or changed circumstances. The four essays warn of the catastrophe that can be-

fall the Western world if it continues to deny full freedom to large segments of the world's population. These lectures recapitulate much of what Wright states in earlier essays and books. In "The Psychological Reactions of Oppressed People," the first and longest of the sections, Wright discusses the missionary zeal which instilled in arrogant Europeans the ideas that they could behave paternalistically toward less developed cultures and that they were perfectly justified in overrunning Asia, Africa, and parts of America. He argues that oppressed people must come from behind their masks and confront the oppressor if they expect to keep "the white shadow of the West" from falling across the rest of the world.

In "Tradition and Industrialization" Wright asserts that Christianity can be viewed favorably only in comparison with the mystical Eastern religious philosophies, which are far worse than the Western ones. He is happy that deluded missionaries brought their Christianity to the Third World because the message they brought was so inappropriate for the Eastern world that in attempting to replace their old beliefs with Western dogma, the Easterners completely lost their religious outlook. Easterners can now say, "Thank you Mr. White Man for freeing me from the rot of my irrational customs and traditions." Wright concludes that this newly purged group must be permitted to act free from Western intervention.

"The Literature of the Negro in the United States" is a historical survey of black American writers. Wright begins by pointing out that Alexandre Dumas and Aleksandr Pushkin are black writers who were fully integrated parts of their respective French and Russian cultures, whereas only one black American writer, Phillis Wheatley, has been able to identify fully with the dominant values of her country. Because black writers in this country have not enjoyed full freedom, freedom is a central theme of Afro-American literature. Black literature as such will disappear when blacks are free, for writing by blacks is a kind of barometer of liberty for Afro-Americans. The more freedom blacks enjoy the more muted the cry for it in their literature. After all "the Negro is America's metaphor," Wright asserts.

The concluding discussion in the book, "The Miracle of Nationalism in the African Gold Coast," is really a condensed version of *Black Power*. Wright tells the Africans to overcome their "ancestor worshipping attitudes" and "mas-

ter the techniques of science." His somewhat paradoxical advice to the continent to throw the West out and then become as Western as possible is another illustration of his failure to see that before man can realize a world larger than race, community, tribe, or state, he must show respectful treatment to all segments of the world's cultures. *White Man, Listen!* is, nevertheless, a very interesting, readable book. It is a provocative exploration of the theme of freedom.

The black press was nearly unanimous in its praise of *White Man, Listen!* J. Saunders Redding wrote in an Associated Press review that Wright "had never written more brilliantly or poignantly." *Time, Newsweek,* and the *Saturday Review* refused to review the work, and the *New York Times* criticized Wright for "treating the white world as a solid block."

By July 1957 Wright had almost finished the second revision of his new novel which he thought of calling "The Double Hearted" or "American Shadow" until his editor at Harper, Edward Aswell, suggested "The Long Dream." By mid February 1958 Wright had made final revisions for "The Long Dream," and he returned to work on "Island of Hallucinations" until *The Long Dream* was published in New York in mid October 1958.

In *The Long Dream,* the first and only published book of a projected trilogy, Wright returns to the southern world of *Black Boy.* The novel focuses on two major concerns: the relationship between Tyree Tucker, a prominent mortician and owner of a house of prostitution, and his son Fishbelly (called Fish), and the complex relationship symbolized by the father as the economic power of the black community and the white police chief as the legal and political power in the city. In each section of a tripartite structure Wright dramatizes events which develop or alter these relationships.

In part 1, "Daydreams and Nightmares," as Fish watches his father examine the corpse of his friend Chris Sims, a young black murdered and castrated by whites for being attracted to a white woman, he expresses his bitter, angry disillusionment with his father and the black community for their passive reactions. In Fish's mind they also underwent castration, and he decides, in a manner which suggests Wright himself in *Black Boy,* that he can accept neither Southern black attitudes nor white ones. The episode that signals Fish's induction into manhood originates at the Clintonville jail, where Fish and a friend have

been arrested for trespassing on a white man's property. When his father comes to get him released, Fish feels humiliated by his subservient behavior before the white officials, but he later realizes that he is released only because of his father's pleas. He then comprehends that Tyree Tucker has been doing all that a black in the South can do and concludes that his secure future is tied in with the acquisition of money and the acceptance of his father's pragmatic philosophy. A central irony is that Fish's maturation is but his accepting his own role as a cheater of other blacks as a way of life, and thus denying them freedom.

The main dramatic event in "Days and Nights," part 2, is the Fourth of July fire at the Grove Dance Hall which takes forty-two lives, including that of Gladys, Fish's mistress. Wright again employs burning, one of his favorite symbols, to bring dramatically to light a corrupt and oppressive business arrangement. The scandal caused by the disaster necessitates a confrontation between Tyree Tucker, who is also the Grove Dance Hall manager, and Gerald Cantley, the white police chief who collects regular payments both to protect prostitution and ignore other violations in the hall. When Tucker attempts to send cancelled checks which show his payments to Chief Cantley to white reformer McWilliams, Tucker is killed in one of Cantley's carefully orchestrated ambushes.

The theme of oppression resurfaces, for Fish now clearly sees that his murdered father followed the same system that the white man uses to oppress and exploit blacks. He retains admiration for his father, however, for he did stand up and strike back at the white oppressor. Ironically enough, Fish will perpetuate his father's oppression and exploitation, for he welcomes the identical corrupt arrangements Tucker had with Cantley and continues to enjoy economic prosperity in Clintonville. Wright creates a mirror effect from one Tucker to the next, symbolizing the continuing fate of the vulnerable southern black.

In "Waking Dream" Fish's long search for his own freedom and dignity evolves into a tragedy. Even though Fish falls on his knees crying that he would not betray a white man, this mirror image of his father's actions does not stop Cantley from having him imprisoned on the false charge of raping a white woman—a terrible irony in that Fish had often imagined raping one. Despite his power in the black community Fish, like his father, cannot defeat the white power struc-

Dust jacket for Wright's posthumously published novel about Jake Jackson, a black postal worker (courtesy of the Afro-American Collection, Blockson Library, Temple University)

ture. Released after serving two and one-half years, Fish, at the first opportunity, leaves for Memphis for a flight to New York and a connecting flight to Paris. An Italian-American on the Paris-bound plane relates to Fish the story of his father's emigration to and successes in America. Fish reflects about himself: "That man's father had come to America and had found a dream; he had been born in America and had found it a nightmare." This last scene clearly shows the particular alienation of the black American and effectively dramatizes Wright's theme of flight from oppression to possible freedom. In "Five Episodes," the only published section of a second part of the planned trilogy, Wright discusses Fish Tucker's life in France.

Two of many noteworthy achievements in *The Long Dream* are Wright's extraordinary portrait of Tyree Tucker and his effective presentation of the black church. Fish Tucker must be labeled the protagonist, but it is Tyree Tucker whom the reader will remember longest. Tyree

Tucker is in turn calculating, cunning, loving, pious, predatory, and saccharine, and at each interval he is convincing. He is a respected leader in the black community, a father who obviously loves his son, a black man who knows when to humble himself before whites, one who dares seduce the mother of a boy recently lynched, and one who prospers off the misery of other blacks. Because he is no one type but a composite of types, he is a fascinating antihero.

Wright never expressed faith in religion, but he was aware of the importance of the black church to the black community. His handling of the funeral services for the forty-two fire victims and Tyree Tucker is extraordinary. At one point in the sermon the Reverend Ragland is explaining to the mourners that their miseries are not caused by whites or corrupt economic and political institutions but by God Himself, and His ways are mysterious. He continues:

> Who dares say how many of us'll be here a year from now? Your future's in the hollow of Gawd's Hands now, there's men in this town who say that they run it. . . . The men who run this town can be white as snow, but we know who's the boss! GAWD'S THE BOSS! And He's more powerful than the president, the governor, the mayor, the chief of police.

Reverend Ragland's sermon fully captures in philosophy and color the spirit of the mid twentieth century rural black church.

The Long Dream received mostly adverse critical reaction. Granville Hicks in the *Saturday Review* referred to the "crude prose style and weak characterization." Redding in the *New York Times* argued that Wright "had been away too long" and that the work "is sensational and fattened by too much iteration." Other critics such as Ted Poston of the *New York Post* and Nick Aaron Ford writing for *Phylon*, agreed that the novel was bad. Roi Ottley in the *Chicago Sunday Tribune* gave the novel one of a few overwhelmingly favorable reviews. He saw *The Long Dream* as a "superb book balanced by Wright's compassion for his people." Though not a great book, *The Long Dream* has many great moments.

Despite overwhelming negative criticism from his agent, Paul Reynolds, of his four-hundred page "Island of Hallucinations" manuscript in February 1959, Wright, in March, outlined this third novel in which Fish was finally to be liberated from his racial conditioning and would become a dominating character. By May

1959 Wright had developed a desire to leave Paris and live in London. He felt French politics had become increasingly submissive to American pressure, and the peaceful Parisian atmosphere he had enjoyed had been shattered by quarrels and attacks instigated by enemies of the expatriate black writers. On 26 June 1959, after a party which marked the French publication of *White Man, Listen!*, Wright became ill, victim of a virulent attack of amoebic dysentery which he had probably contracted during his stay on the Gold Coast. By November 1959 Ellen had found a London apartment, but Wright's illness and "four hassles in twelve days" with British immigration officials made him decide "to abandon any desire to live in England."

On 19 February 1960 Wright learned from Reynolds that the New York premiere of the stage adaptation of *The Long Dream* received such bad reviews that the adapter, Ketti Frings, had decided to cancel other performances. Meanwhile, Wright was running into additional problems trying to get *The Long Dream* published in France. These setbacks prevented his finishing revisions of "Island of Hallucinations," which he needed to get a commitment from Doubleday.

Wright was able to complete two radio scripts and a seventy-page story "Leader Man" for "Ten Men," a title he had proposed to his editor in 1959 for a new collection. The title became *Eight Men* when his editor convinced him that "Leader Man" and "Man and Boy," a new title Wright suggested for the text of *Savage Holiday*, should not be included. Wright aborted his earlier idea to trace the genesis of each story to give the collection a common theme; hence, the works in *Eight Men* display the variety and development in Wright's literary and thematic skills. After dedicating the collection to the friends he had made in Paris, Wright sold the work to World Publishers in March 1960 and eagerly awaited publication, but the collection did not reach the public until two months after his death.

"The Man Who Lived Underground," the most critically acclaimed work in *Eight Men*, brings to mind both Fyodor Dostoyevski's *Letters from the Underworld* (1864) and Victor Hugo's *Les Misérables* (1862). Wright, however, has gone a step beyond them and included all humanity in his underground community. Fred Daniels, a black man escaping from the police, who have wrongly accused him of murder, takes up residence in a sewer. Following a nightmarish experience during which time he sees images of death

and decay around him and views people engaged in deceit and corruption through a crevice, he concludes that the underground where he resides—the sewer—is the actual world of the human heart, and the world above—the metaphysical sewer—is an area where people attempt to conceal the immense darkness of their souls. This emotional experience brings on a sense of guilt, and he rises to the street to announce his guilt to the world. First rejected by a church congregation, he is later mortally wounded by a policeman who exclaims: "You've got to shoot his kind. They'd wreck things."

The work has a black protagonist, but it transcends racial bounds. Its many themes of self-identity, the search for meaning in the world, the need for communication, and alienation are those which concern all mankind. Existentialist tenets—dread, terror, guilt, nausea—are also present, but Wright has successfully made them characteristics of Fred Daniels's personality, not just existentialist clichés as often is the case in *The Outsider*. The excellent paradoxes, light and dark imagery, and other vivid, concrete details combine to make "The Man Who Lived Underground" a superior work of art. Wright's suggestion did not go unnoticed by Ralph Ellison whose subsequent *Invisible Man* (1952) incorporates some of the same structural devices and examines many of the same themes.

The other works in *Eight Men* show great variety. "The Man Who Was Almost a Man" details the struggles of Dave Saunders who purchases a revolver to assure his manhood will be acknowledged. "Big Black Good Man," one of Wright's few humorous stories, develops the theme of black pride through the adventures of a black sailor. "The Man Who Saw the Flood" is an extended vignette which, like "Down by the Riverside," deals with a black tenant family that returns home after a devastating flood. "The Man Who Killed a Shadow" brings to mind *Native Son* in that its central character is a black man who inadvertently kills a white woman, a major difference being the black protagonist in the story is used as a symbol of libidinal abandon. "Man of All Work" is a delightful unproduced radio script about mistaken identity. "Man, Gawd Ain't Like That," a much more ambitious radio script, illustrates much of what Wright says in *Black Power* and *White Man, Listen!* "The Man Who Went to Chicago" is an autobiographical sketch.

The stories in *Eight Men* are also representative of the different stages of Wright's develop-

Dust jacket for the second volume of Wright's autobiography

ment. The ones he wrote in the 1930s ("The Man Who Saw the Flood" and "The Man Who Was Almost a Man") deal with southern workers; the stories of the 1940s ("The Man Who Lived Underground," "The Man Who Went to Chicago," and "The Man Who Killed a Shadow") employ an urban setting to depict blackness, invisibility, outsider or underground status; the stories of the 1950s ("Man of All Work," "Man, Gawd Ain't Like That," and "Big Black Good Man") celebrate a new kind of black nationalism, black virility as opposed to white flabbiness, and a proud awareness of African identity.

During 1959 and 1960, the last two years of his life, Wright was fighting amoebic dysentery, and by February 1960 he was constantly ill. On 19 March 1960, after a roundtable discussion on black theater organized by Claude Planson of the Théatre des Nations, Wright announced to his friend and Dutch translator, Margrit de Sablonière, that he had returned to poetry. He told her, "During my illness I experimented with the Japanese form of poetry called haiku; I wrote some 4,000 of them and am now sifting them out to see if they are any good." Wright had borrowed the four volumes by R. H. Blyth on the art of haiku in order to learn the rules of its composition. He reduced the number of

poems to eight hundred by mid April and sent the eighty-page manuscript to his friend and editor William Targ of World Publishing Company.

Targ's company rejected the poems, but the consolation of writing the haiku enabled Wright to live with illness and to endure the attacks he felt were multiplying against him. In February he had received an unfriendly letter from Sartre. The letter turned out to be a forgery, but it had already greatly hurt Wright. Wright concluded that no reply from either St. Clair Drake or Horace Clayton meant they did not want him to write a new preface for *Black Metropolis*. Wright even came to doubt the friendship of Chester Himes and to question his relationship with Dr. Victor Schwarzmann, his personal physician. His illness and his generally suspicious nature caused him to regard any changes in regular procedures or negative responses to his writing as parts of a general plot against him.

In June 1960 Wright recorded a series of discussions for French radio dealing primarily with his books and literary career but also with the racial situation in the United States and the world, specifically denouncing American policy in Africa. In late September, to cover extra expenses brought on by his daughter Julia's move from London to Paris to attend the Sorbonne, Wright wrote blurbs for record jackets for Nicole Barclay, director of the largest record company in Paris. In spite of his financial straits Wright refused to compromise his principles. He declined participation in a series of programs for Canadian radio because he suspected American control over the programs, and he rejected the proposal of the Congress for Cultural Freedom that he go to India to speak at a conference in memory of Leo Tolstoy for the same reason.

Still interested in literature, Wright offered to help Kyle Onstott get *Mandingo* (1957) published in France. His last display of explosive energy occurred on 8 November 1960 in his polemical lecture, "The Situation of the Black Artist and Intellectual in the United States," delivered to students and members of the American Church in Paris. Wright argued that American society reduced the most militant members of the black community to slaves whenever they wanted to question the racial status quo. He offered as proof the subversive attacks of the Communists against *Native Son* and the quarrels which James Baldwin and other authors sought with him.

On 26 November 1960 Wright talked enthusiastically about *Daddy Goodness* with Langston

Hughes and gave him the manuscript. Two days later, on 28 November 1960, while waiting in the Eugene Gibez Clinic in Paris for extensive medical examinations, Wright died of a heart attack. He is buried in Pere Lachaise, Paris.

Richard Wright is undeniably one of the most important American writers of the twentieth century. His books have been translated into many languages, and millions throughout Asia, Africa, Europe, and the Middle East have read about the experiences of a Mississippi black boy. Through his "travel" books he brought the oppressed peoples of the Third World countries to the attention of the East and the West. Wright more than any other American author illustrates the premise that America's basic ills are those of racism. His significance as an interpreter of the racial problem in imaginative literature led Irving Howe to assert in "Black Boys and Native Sons" (1963) that after *Native Son* appeared, American culture was changed forever. The claim is perhaps excessive, but no black writer between Frederick Douglass and James Baldwin has offered so moving a testimony and delivered so scathing an indictment of America's racial dilemmas to so large an audience as has Richard Wright. Wright elevated the protest novel to a more highly respected art form that numerous other "native sons" have adopted. While some of his work is weak and unsuccessful–especially that completed within the last three years of his life–his best work will continue to attract readers. His three masterpieces–*Uncle Tom's Children, Native Son*, and *Black Boy*–are a crowning achievement for him and for American literature. They are enduring works of art, each of which transcends any one literary classification.

During the 1970s and 1980s scholars and the general public have shown increasing interest in Richard Wright. Critical essays have been written about his writing in prestigious journals. Richard Wright conferences have been held on university campuses from Mississippi to New Jersey. A new film version of *Native Son*, with a screenplay by Richard Wesley, was released in December 1986. Selected Wright novels are required reading in a growing number of American universities and colleges. *The Outsider, American Hunger, The Long Dream*, and other long out-of-print Wright books have been reissued by Harper & Row. Several doctoral dissertations have been accepted, and plans are underway to release more of his unpublished work. Today more and more Americans are reading of Wright's life and prob-

lems as a sensitive, intelligent, black American. The rising interest in Wright suggests, happily, a wider understanding and acceptance of the literary importance of America's native son.

Bibliography:

Charles T. Davis and Michel Fabre, *Richard Wright: A Primary Bibliography* (Boston: G. K. Hall, 1982);

Keneth Kinnamon, et al., *A Richard Wright Bibliography: Fifty Years of Criticism and Commentary: 1933-1982,* (Westport, Conn.: Greenwood Press, 1988).

Biographies:

Constance Webb, *Richard Wright: A Biography* (New York: Putnam's, 1968);

John A. Williams and Dorothy Sterling, *The Most Native of Sons: A Biography of Richard Wright* (Garden City, N.Y.: Doubleday, 1970);

Michel Fabre, *The Unfinished Quest of Richard Wright* (New York: Morrow, 1973).

References:

Richard Abcarian, *Richard Wright's Native Son: A Critical Handbook* (Belmont, Calif.: Wadsworth, 1970);

David Bakish, *Richard Wright* (New York: Ungar, 1973);

James Baldwin, "Everybody's Protest Novel," in his *Notes of a Native Son* (Boston: Beacon, 1955), pp. 85-114;

Baldwin, "Richard Wright," *Encounter,* 16 (April 1961): 58-60;

Robert Bone, *Richard Wright* (Minneapolis: University of Minnesota Press, 1969);

Russell Carl Brignano, *Richard Wright: An Introduction to the Man and His Works* (Pittsburgh: University of Pittsburgh Press, 1970);

Ralph Ellison, "Richard Wright's Blues," in his *Shadow and Act* (New York: Random House, 1964), pp. 77-94;

Michel Fabre, *The World of Richard Wright* (Jackson: University Press of Mississippi, 1985);

Robert Felgar, *Richard Wright* (Boston: Twayne, 1980);

Addison Gayle, Jr., *The Way of the New World: The Black Novel in America* (New York: Anchor/Doubleday, 1975), pp. 165-182;

Gayle, *Richard Wright—Ordeal of a Native Son* (Garden City: Doubleday, 1980);

Yoshinobu Hakutani, ed., *Critical Essays on Richard Wright* (Boston: G. K. Hall, 1982);

Irving Howe, "Black Boys and Native Sons," in his *A World More Attractive* (New York: Horizon, 1963), pp. 98-110;

Joyce A. Joyce, *Richard Wright's Art of Tragedy* (Iowa City: University of Iowa Press, 1986);

Keneth Kinnamon, *The Emergence of Richard Wright* (Urbana: University of Illinois Press, 1972);

Edward Margolies, *The Art of Richard Wright* (Carbondale: Southern Illinois University Press, 1969);

Don McCall, *The Example of Richard Wright* (New York: Harcourt, Brace & World, 1969);

David Ray and Robert M. Farnsworth, eds., *Richard Wright: Impressions and Perspectives* (Ann Arbor: University of Michigan Press, 1973);

John M. Reilly, *Richard Wright: The Critical Reception* (New York: Burt Franklin, 1978);

John A. Williams, *The Most Native of Sons* (Garden City: Doubleday, 1970);

James O. Young, *Black Writers of the Thirties* (Baton Rouge: Louisiana State University Press, 1973), pp. 229-235.

Papers:

The most extensive collection of Wright's papers is in the Richard Wright Archive in the Beinecke Rare Book and Manuscript Library at Yale University. One of the manuscripts of *Black Power* is at Northwestern University. Eighteen letters by Wright are held at Kent State University. Eight of these letters were published (1968) in an unauthorized edition. Rare magazines and newspapers that contain some of Wright's writings are housed in the Schomburg Collection of the New York Public Library, the American Library in Paris, and the Harvard University libraries.

Frank Yerby

(5 September 1916-   )

Jeffrey D. Parker
University of South Carolina

BOOKS: *The Foxes of Harrow* (New York: Dial Press, 1946; London: Heinemann, 1947);
The Vixens (New York: Dial Press, 1947; London: Heinemann, 1948);
The Golden Hawk (New York: Dial Press, 1948; London: Heinemann, 1949);
Pride's Castle (New York: Dial Press, 1949; London: Heinemann, 1950);
Floodtide (New York: Dial Press, 1950; London: Heinemann, 1951);
A Woman Called Fancy (New York: Dial Press, 1951; London: Heinemann, 1952);
The Saracen Blade (New York: Dial Press, 1952; London: Heinemann, 1953);
The Devil's Laughter (New York: Dial Press, 1953; London: Heinemann, 1954);
Benton's Row (New York: Dial Press, 1954; London: Heinemann, 1955);
Bride of Liberty (Garden City, N.Y.: Doubleday, 1954; London: Heinemann, 1955);
The Treasure of Pleasant Valley (New York: Dial Press, 1955; London: Heinemann, 1956);
Captain Rebel (New York: Dial Press, 1956; London: Heinemann, 1957);
Fairoaks (New York: Dial Press, 1957; London: Heinemann, 1958);
The Serpent and the Staff (New York: Dial Press, 1958; London: Heinemann, 1959);
Jarrett's Jade (New York: Dial Press, 1959; London: Heinemann, 1960);
Gillian (New York: Dial Press, 1960; London: Heinemann, 1961);
The Garfield Honor (New York: Dial Press, 1961; London: Heinemann, 1962);
Griffin's Way (New York: Dial Press, 1962; London: Heinemann, 1963);
The Old Gods Laugh: A Modern Romance (New York: Dial Press, 1964; London: Heinemann, 1964);
An Odor of Sanctity (New York: Dial Press, 1965; London: Heinemann, 1966);
Goat Song: A Novel of Ancient Greece (New York: Dial Press, 1967; London: Heinemann, 1968);

Frank Yerby, circa 1950 (courtesy of Dial Press)

Judas, My Brother: The Story of the Thirteenth Disciple (New York: Dial Press, 1969; London: Heinemann, 1969);
Speak Now (New York: Dial Press, 1969; London: Heinemann, 1973);
The Dahomean: An Historical Novel (New York: Dial Press, 1971); republished as *The Man from Dahomey* (London: Heinemann, 1971);
The Girl from Storyville: A Victorian Novel (New York: Dial Press, 1972; London: Heinemann, 1972);
The Voyage Unplanned (New York: Dial Press, 1974; London: Heinemann, 1974);
Tobias and the Angel (New York: Dial Press, 1975; London: Heinemann, 1975);
A Rose for Ana María (New York: Dial Press, 1976; London: Heinemann, 1976);

Dust jacket for Yerby's 1952 novel set during the crusades of the thirteenth century

Dust jacket for Yerby's 1957 novel about Guy Falks, a man who desperately seeks possession of the plantation Fairoaks, which he considers his birthright

Hail the Conquering Hero (New York: Dial Press, 1977; London: Heinemann, 1978);

A Darkness at Ingraham's Crest (New York: Dial Press, 1979; London: Grenada, 1981);

Western: A Saga of the Great Plains (New York: Dial Press, 1982; London: Grenada, 1983);

Devilseed (Garden City, N.Y.: Doubleday, 1984; London: Grenada, 1984);

McKenzie's Hundred (Garden City, N.Y.: Doubleday, 1985; London: Grafton, 1986).

PERIODICAL PUBLICATIONS: "Love Story," *Paineite* (February 1937): 15-16;

"Young Man Afraid," *Fisk Herald*, 31 (October 1937): 15-16;

"A Date With Vera," *Fisk Herald*, 31 (November 1937): 16-17;

"The Thunder of God," *New Anvil* (April-May 1939);

"Health Card," *Harper's*, 188 (May 1944): 448-453;

"White Magnolias," *Phylon*, 5 (Fourth Quarter 1944): 319-326;

"Roads Going Down," *Common Ground*, 5 (Summer 1945): 67-72;

"My Brother Went to College," *Tomorrow*, 5 (January 1946): 9-12;

"The Homecoming," *Common Ground*, 6 (Spring 1946): 41-47;

"How and Why I Write the Costume Novel," *Harper's*, 219 (October 1959): 145-150;

"Frank Back in U.S.," *Jet* (16 June 1960): 4-5.

Frank Yerby is the author of thirty-three novels that have sold over fifty-five million copies in the last forty years. Yerby's first novel, *The Foxes of Harrow* (1946), was filmed by 20th Century-Fox in 1951; *The Golden Hawk* (1948) was filmed by Columbia in 1952; and *The Saracen Blade* (1952) was filmed by Columbia in 1954. *Pride's Castle* (1949) was filmed for television. Although Yerby is an extremely prolific writer, his literary reputation seems to exist only in terms of his popularity. His only work of fiction to achieve serious critical acclaim is the short story "Health Card," for which he received the O. Henry Memorial Award for the best first story in 1944. Since then, Yerby has produced what many critics consider to be only novels of entertainment.

Frank Garvin Yerby was born 5 September 1916 in Augusta, Georgia. His father, Rufus Garvin Yerby, worked as a hotel doorman in Miami and Detroit; because he traveled frequently, the Yerby children were reared for the most part by their mother, Wilhelmina Smythe Yerby. Yerby attended Haines Institute in Augusta, a private black school for elementary and high school grades. He then enrolled at Paine College in Augusta where he majored in English and minored in foreign languages. He received a B.A. degree in English from Paine in 1937 and an M.A. in English from Fisk University in 1938. In 1939 he enrolled at the University of Chicago to begin a Ph.D. program in English. In Chicago Yerby worked with the Federal Writers' Project. It was here that he became acquainted with writers Richard Wright, Margaret Walker, William Attaway, and Arna Bontemps. Yerby continued in this program for nine months, but, because of financial problems, he left and began teaching at Florida A&M University in Tallahassee as an instructor of English. Yerby also taught at Southern University in Baton Rouge, Louisiana, in the same capacity from 1940 to 1941.

Yerby continued writing during this period but was largely unsuccessful at publication except for some short stories in college anthologies and a few poems published in such magazines as *Challenge, Shard,* and *Arts Quarterly*. In 1941 Yerby left the teaching profession and with his wife, Flora Claire Williams (whom he married 2 March 1941), spent 1941 to 1944 working in a defense plant in Dearborn, Michigan. The couple had two sons and two daughters. They were eventually divorced.

During the early 1940s Yerby published six short stories, including "Health Card." This narrative, concerning the injustices done to a black couple by the military, who assume all black women are prostitutes, was submitted to *Harper's* magazine, where it was published in 1944. The publication gave Yerby national attention and resulted in other offers for future publication. Yerby's "My Brother Went To College" was published in *Tomorrow*, January 1946; and "Roads Going Down" and "The Homecoming" were in the Summer 1945 and Spring 1946 issues of *Common Ground* respectively. Of the five stories published during the early 1940s, "White Magnolias," which appeared in *Phylon* in the fourth quarter of 1944, is probably the best. All of Yerby's short stories deal with blacks and their environment, particularly Georgia, but he discovered that most American readers had little or no interest in race problems or in intense discussions of bigotry. As Yerby commented in October of 1959 in an article that appeared in *Harper's* magazine, "The idea dawned on me that to continue to follow the route I had

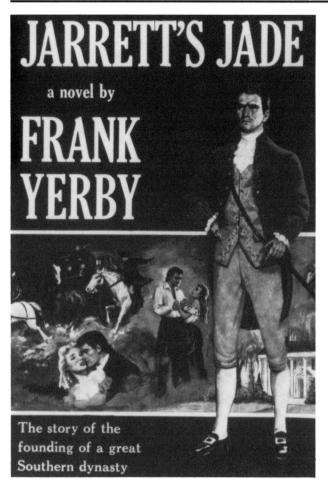

*Dust jacket for Yerby's 1959 novel set in the South just before
the American Revolution*

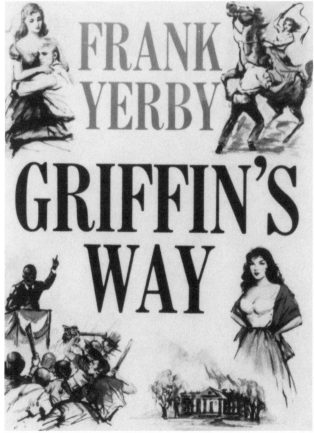

*Dust jacket for Yerby's 1962 novel set in Mississippi during
Reconstruction*

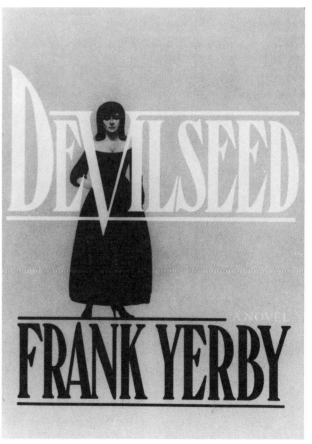

Dust jacket for Yerby's 1964 novel set in a Caribbean country undergoing a revolution

Dust jacket for Yerby's 1984 novel about Mireille Duclos, a San Francisco prostitute in the 1850s who becomes a society matron

mapped out for myself was roughly analogous to shouting one's head off in Mammoth Cave." As a result he decided to write what he came to call a "costume" novel; and while working during the day at the defense plant he wrote at night. In 1946 Dial published *The Foxes of Harrow*.

The Foxes of Harrow contains all the stock ingredients of the southern historical romance: sexual excess, dueling, magnolias, forty-room mansions, financial success, and eventual ruin. Critics found little social significance in Yerby's novel, with the possible exception of Richard Match, who wrote in the *New York Times* that the novel contained "some sympathetic evidences of the Negroes' deep resentment against slavery." Edmund Wilson, commenting in the *New Yorker*, wrote: "Mr. Yerby has packed everything in—passion, politics, Creole society, sex, the clash of races, and war—but he never captures the faintest flutter of the breath of life." The *Christian Science Monitor* reviewer saw "a breathless but lucid rapidity in the action . . . intimate knowledge of the locale and a study of the times . . . imagination, the ability to create clearly defined characters, a lush full-bodied style and, quite naturally, considering [character] Stephen Fox, more than a touch of melodrama." Another critic, Sterling North, who, with a greater degree of foresight than he perhaps realized, wrote that "the author would soon be richer than *The Foxes of Harrow*." By the end of the year over a million copies of the novel had been sold, and reprints appeared in *Negro Digest*, *Omnibook*, and *Liberty*.

In a *New York Times Book Review* interview in June 1982 Yerby noted that he "remembered that nobody ever went broke underestimating the taste of the American public, so I set out to write the worst possible novel it was humanly possible to write and still get published but it sort of got hold of me, and about half way through, I started revising and improving it." Since its publication in 1946 Yerby estimates that *The Foxes of Harrow* has sold between ten and twelve million copies.

Generally speaking, black intellectuals reviewed *The Foxes of Harrow* favorably. Blyden Jackson, writing in the first quarter 1948 issue of *Phylon*, said, "The Negro is coming into his American heritage of assurance." Black and white critics eagerly awaited Yerby's second publication after he had announced that he was writing a novel about the South and Reconstruction, but Yerby continued to follow the costume novel formula. In the Summer 1968 issue of *Massachusetts*

Review Darwin T. Turner wrote, "Yerby did not prove effective as a symbol. He refused to plead for the race; he abandoned America without shrieking that bigotry had exiled him from his home; he earned a fortune writing books and spent his time racing sports cars and lolling on beaches. So corpulent an achiever of the American dream can never personify the Negro intellectual, for the charm of the symbol is its aura of failure."

In the 1959 article in *Harper's* Yerby offered a defense of the novel of entertainment. He said, "The classics of today are very nearly always the best sellers of the past. Thackeray, Dickens, Defoe, Byron, Pope, Fielding . . . the list is endless—enjoyed fabulous popularity in their day . . . having collected a houseful of rejection slips for works about ill-treated factory workers, a people who suffered because of their religion or the color of their skins, I arrived at the awesome conclusion that the reader cares not a snap about such questions, that, moreover, they are none of the novelist's business." He argues that novels written with the express intention to entertain should be considered a legitimate part of literature. Yerby closes this article by noting that "our constitutional right to the pursuit of happiness has not been repealed."

Yerby describes the formulas he uses for writing successful costume novels. The protagonist must be a charming scoundrel, a dominant male, indefatigable. In a physical sense there are three negatives: shortness, baldness, and beardedness. The heroine(s) must have a definable sexuality about her (them) and be tempered to wait out the time it takes to win the affections of the protagonist. The third ingredient of the costume novel is "a strong, exteriorized conflict, personified in a continuing, formidable antagonist or antagonists," within a basic thematic struggle of man against himself, man in relationship with God, and man against death. He argues that "the writer is or should be concerned with individuals. They may be workers, Negroes, Jews, if you will; but they must be living people, with recognizably individual problems, and confronted with individual, personified opposition, not Prejudice, Bigotry, and what-have-you in capital letters. Those problems exist; but they are awfully hard to pin down in an interesting fashion." Yerby mixes his hero, heroine(s), and conflicts with minor characters and a lean plot.

In the article in *Harper's* Yerby addresses what he calls literary sex. He points to the fact

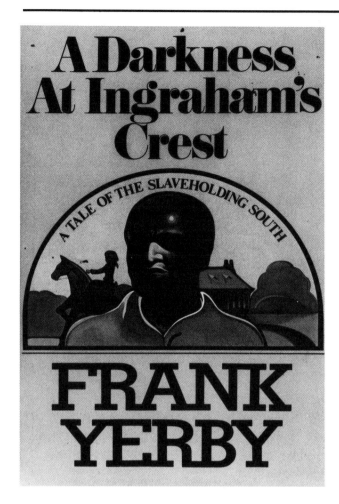

Dust jacket for Yerby's 1979 sequel to The Dahomean
*(1971), about Hwesu, an African ruler who is sold
into slavery*

that the protagonist should be romantic, and his being a romantic means that "in his emotional relationships he should not be too bright. . . ; the action of the costume novel's plot is carried forward by our hero's failure to realize that in any movie of life there are literally dozens, if not hundreds, of women who will do just as well; that if he doesn't win fair Susan's dainty hand; and that very probably he will catch a most interesting variety of hell if he does win it. Which come to think of it, is not unrealistic: emotional maturity is one of the rarest qualities in life."

Stephen Fox, in *The Foxes of Harrow*, is a typical example of the protagonist in Yerby's fiction. For instance, although he is enthusiastically attracted to beautiful women, and they to him, he refuses the free services of a prostitute, Jenny, because she is too young. On the other hand, he robs a drunk named Metoyer and steals his pants. Stephen starts in New Orleans penniless

and ends up a wealthy plantation owner. Hwesu in *A Darkness at Ingraham's Crest* (1979) is a slave who is brought to the South and rechristened Wesley Parks. Incredibly strong, Wes has magic powers from his African ancestors. He continues to strive for freedom, dominating those who would master him, in spite of difficult odds. At one point in the novel, for example, he engineers the rout of a large crowd of vigilantes. All the women, black and white, are attracted to him, and he reciprocates their affection.

Of the heroine Yerby writes that she should be more emotionally immature, or romantic, than the protagonist. She should have an "aura of sex about her." Female characters in Yerby's novels are willing to accept the eccentricities and the infidelities of the male protagonist. The heroine is alternately portrayed as a rather frigid but honorable wife, an unrespectable mistress, a reluctant virgin, or a nymphomaniac.

Yerby's treatment of women in his novels indicates that, in general, women are nothing more than superficial targets for conquest by more "emotionally mature" protagonists. Although Yerby contends that sex in the novel does not necessarily sell books, his work includes a large number of women whose characters reside solely in a sexual context. There exists no female character who is wholly admirable or complete, or any female character who can stand outside of a submissive relationship with a male counterpart. Women are often subjected to sexual and physical abuse. For example, in *An Odor of Sanctity* (1965), Alaric Teudisson, after discovering that his wife, Clothilde, is an adulteress, carves the letters "A" for adulteress, "S" for strumpet, and "W" for whore upon her face.

Fancy Williamson, in his *A Woman Called Fancy* (1951), is somewhat atypical for a Yerby heroine. She flees the Carolina Hills to avoid a marriage to a sixty-five-year-old man arranged by her father to pay his drinking debts. Arriving in Augusta, Georgia, in the spring of 1880, Fancy becomes scandalously linked to one man after another. She plays the role of being a typically submissive woman in order to achieve success.

In an interview for *Ebony* magazine in 1966 Yerby was very defensive. He said he wanted to discuss "the future of the novel as an art form as opposed to using it as a sociological tract to further any cause whatsoever, no matter how worthy, which reduces the thing I love most in life, that is, writing, to mere propaganda." Citing what he feels to be a successful novel that does deal with ra-

BEST SELLERS by FRANK YERBY

THE FOXES OF HARROW. "A flaming story of a charming rogue, and gambler, Stephen Fox, who, starting with nothing more than a $10 gold piece and a pearl stickpin, became an aristocrat in the wickedest city of its time — New Orleans from 1840 to 1865. . . . There are duels, luscious belles, a quadroon mistress, gambling scenes — in short, all the ingredients." —**Los Angeles Times**

THE VIXENS. A story of passion, violence, cruelty, lust and hate in New Orleans after the Civil War when the carpet-baggers and scalawags were ruling Louisiana. "An exciting book . . . a rip-roaring thriller." —**Boston Herald**

FLOODTIDE. "A rich, violent story of Natchez in the heyday of the slave-holding South, of graceful living, of gentlemen planters whose drinking and love-making equalled their violent politics . . . and of lovely ladies."
—**Chicago Tribune**

BENTON'S ROW. The story of four brawling generations of the Bentons of Louisiana from 1842 to the end of the first World War. "This is exciting reading, good Yerby. You'll welcome his latest offering." —**Chicago Tribune**

A WOMAN CALLED FANCY and THE GOLDEN HAWK. (*Double Volume*) A WOMAN CALLED FANCY is the story, set in the deep South of the Eighties, of Fancy, a 19 year-old mountaineer girl with a consuming ambition to be a great lady and of what happened to her and the men around her in her climb to the social heights. "A tension-packed story."—**St. Louis Post-Dispatch.** THE GOLDEN HAWK: "A superb novel of action, love, and revenge in the West Indies of the seventeenth century . . . the story of Kit Gerardo and his attempt to win power, love, and revenge in the New World by the only means open to him, piracy." —**St. Louis Globe Democrat**

CAPTAIN REBEL. "A fast-moving, exciting story of a young Louisianan who becomes the South's outstanding blockade runner during the Civil War. . . . As a rousing adventure story, this is among his best books, perhaps the best." —**Boston Post**

FAIROAKS. The story of Guy Falks, Southern aristocrat who, without knowing it, lived a lie so gloriously that in the end he made it come true. "Yerby's most ambitious novel, his best by far." —**Chicago Tribune**

THE SERPENT AND THE STAFF. A highly entertaining yarn of the turn-of-the-century life and times of Duncan Childers, who claws his way up from a New Orleans gutter to become the most fashionable surgeon in New Orleans. "Yerby possesses the true fictioneer's skill. This is an unrestrained book with violence, hates . . . action and more action." —**St. Louis Post-Dispatch**

JARRETT'S JADE. The story of the founding of a great Southern dynasty by a Scots aristocrat who knew what he wanted and fought for it with a skill and daring and courage that was almost madness. "Another tale which will delight his followers. There's intrigue, romance, action, color and solid drama here." —**Los Angeles Mirror and News**

GILLIAN. "Frank Yerby's event-filled narrative of Geoffry Lynne's quest for the murderer of Gillian, bewitched and bewitching heroine, is highly dramatic and completely engrossing." —**Nashville Banner**

THE GARFIELD HONOR. "Frank Yerby has written a violent stormy novel in *The Garfield Honor*. There are fights, romances, ambition and greed and meanness in this full-flavored tale, and all the usual Yerby verve and color." —**Tulsa World**

Back of dust jacket for Yerby's Griffin's Way *(1962), with blurbs for Yerby's most popular books during the early 1960s*

cial themes, Yerby states that, "*Invisible Man* is not propaganda in any way. It's an artistic job." The tragedy of racism "is a true and important theme, yes, but you've got to find a new way of doing it, as Ellison did. He found a new way of doing it, and he did it wonderfully. It's probably the reason he hasn't written anything else, because he did it so damned well."

In the *Ebony* interview Yerby noted that his most recent novels, *The Old Gods Laugh* (1964) and *An Odor of Sanctity*, were different from his previous works in being historical novels. Discussing the difference between the costume novel and the historical novel Yerby said that "a costume novel may be an historical novel. In fact practically all costume novels are historical novels. But not all historical novels are costume novels. . . . In fact, I think that, in certain ways, it is probably easier to say something in the historical novel than it is in 'serious' novels." It appears then that Yerby is of the opinion that the central focus of the costume novel is to entertain while the historical novel may be used as a vehicle for revealing his particular perception about a particular time and place. No doubt the inclusion of sexual relationships, authentic weapons, financial successes, and the other stock elements of the historical novel have played a large part in Yerby's popularity, but essentially the distinction he makes between his historical and his costume novels is academic.

Although Yerby researches his novels thoroughly, one reviewer felt that in *A Darkness at Ingraham's Crest* Yerby had created "a 350 page novel expanded to include another 350 pages of lecturing" (*Charleston News and Courier*, 11 November 1979). The same article noted, "If in other tales of the antebellum South, a biased picture of the content, ignorant and comical black person was painted, Yerby, through the eyes of the black male protagonist has painted a similar, biased picture of the white man, a sort of racial stereotyping in reverse." Writing for the *Columbia State*, Betty Lynn Compton characterizes the novel as having "the sweep of *Gone With The Wind* and the bitterness of *Roots*, a combination that makes it both entertaining and sickening." From a similar perspective, the *Nashville Tennessean* (18 November 1979) review was titled: "Frank Yerby's Latest Novel Improbable Portrait of the South."

Although Yerby has been accused of abandoning racial themes after the publication of "Health Card," he has continued to write about black characters, but without the rather dogmatic

Yerby, circa 1978 (photograph by Jerry Bauer)

approach required by the novel of social protest. Black characters are of central importance in *Speak Now* (1969), *The Dahomean* (1971), and *A Darkness at Ingraham's Crest*, where they are much like his white protagonists except for conflicts attendant to their race.

Yerby characterizes *Goat Song* (1967) and *Judas, My Brother* (1969) as serious novels. *Goat Song* takes place in ancient Greece, and *Judas, My Brother* contains scenes from Galilee, Jerusalem, and Rome. Of the two novels, *Judas, My Brother* is the most ambitious. The novel is the story of Yeshua (Hebrew for Jesus), the son of a carpenter, and Nathan, who is characterized as a skeptic and a hedonist. Yeshua becomes the leader of a fanatical sect that challenges the Roman Empire and Judaism. Nathan acts as Yeshua's protector until the end and becomes "ironically, his thirteenth disciple." The dust jacket for the novel claims that "thirty years of research have gone into this stunning and admittedly controversial recreation of the beginnings of Christianity."

Judas, My Brother contains "A Word to the Reader" which is extremely significant in questioning the novel's seriousness. "This novel is a demy-

thologized account of the beginnings of Christianity; and therefore, I am sadly aware, sure to be labeled controversial. Actually there is nothing controversial about it.... This novel touches upon only two issues which in a certain sense, might be called controversial: Whether any man truly has the right to impose, by almost imperial fiat, belief in things that simply are not so. To me, irrationality is dangerous; perhaps the most dangerous force stalking through the world today. This novel, then, is one man's plea for an ecumenicism broad enough to include reasonable men; and his effort to defend his modest intellect from intolerable insult.... Beyond this, I hope that you, Reader, will find it also the rattling good tale I intended it to be; for, if you can put it down, whatever the value of its dialectics, I have failed the novelist's primary task."

Yerby's attempt to add another myth, or perhaps a more factual myth, to a body of what he hopes will become a kind of expanded or at least more tolerant theology parallels his defense of the novel of entertainment as having a legitimate place in more serious literature; for all the polemics, *Judas, My Brother* and *Goat Song* are costume novels.

A clear critical assessment of Yerby's accomplishments over the forty some years that he has been writing is a difficult task, in part because of the wide range of topics that he has written about. Yerby's subjects include ancient Greece, the Great Plains, the beginning of Christianity, prostitution, Moorish Spain, and the antebellum South, just to name a few. There seems to be no clear-cut or easily described development of thought in Yerby's fiction. His novels create a mosaic of ideas that appear to be ambitious in terms of subject matter, but they are also written with the purpose of entertainment. He has often expressed resentment over the fact that critics and intellectuals are unable to see the intended seriousness in his novels of entertainment and that the novel of entertainment is a legitimate part of literature, but in fact his research lends a background of authenticity to some rather contrived and formulaic plots. His research rarely provides the reader with insights into making enlightened conclusions, nor does it provide clearer insights into the moral, cultural, and philosophical problems relative to his fiction. Although Yerby has stated that these matters are none of the novelist's business, he must surely be aware that even the novel of entertainment imposes limitations on the

writer. His pattern for success has been the costume novel, and he has written many of these. Although Yerby has written, at least in *A Darkness at Ingraham's Crest,* an indictment against the South and slavery, he has certainly done much to perpetuate the myths surrounding the "Old South." Yerby's reliance on formulas and the fact that at times he has managed to produce a novel a year has also caused many critics to take his content rather lightly, and, as Robert A. Bone put it, "If the Negro novel were really integrated, Frank Yerby would be taken no more seriously than Mickey Spillane."

In 1952 Yerby became an expatriate, and on 27 July 1956 he married Blanca Calle-Perez, a native of Spain, where he now lives. Having published thirty-three novels in thirty-nine years and having had his work translated into fourteen languages, including Japanese and Hebrew, Yerby has stated that he finds the popularity of his novels "both incomprehensible and disquieting." As of 1988, only *The Foxes of Harrow, Western: A Saga of the Great Plains* (1982), *Devilseed* (1984), and *McKenzie's Hundred* (1985) remain in print.

References:

Joseph Benson, "Frank Yerby," in *Southern Writers,* edited by Louis Rubin, Robert Bain, and Joseph M. Flora (Baton Rouge: Louisiana State University Press, 1979), pp. 510-511;

Robert A. Bone, *The Negro Novel in America,* revised edition (New Haven: Yale University Press, 1965), pp. 167-169;

Harvey Breit, *The Writer Observed* (Ohio: World, 1960), pp. 127-129;

H. W. Fuller, "Famous Writer Faces a Challenge," *Ebony,* 21 (June 1966): 188-190;

Hugh M. Gloster, *Negro Voices in American Fiction* (Chapel Hill: University of North Carolina Press, 1948), p. 257;

Russell B. Nye, *The Unembarrassed Muse* (New York: Dial Press, 1970), pp. 47, 51, 54;

Darwin T. Turner, "Frank Yerby as Debunker," *Massachusetts Review,* 20 (Summer 1968): 569-577;

Turner, "Frank Yerby: Golden Debunker," *Black Boots Bulletin,* 1 (1972): 4-9, 30-33;

Turner, "The Negro Novelist at the South," *Southern Humanities Review,* 1 (1967): 21-29.

Papers:
Some of Yerby's manuscripts are held at the Mugar Memorial Library, Boston University.

Appendix I

The Hatch-Billops Collection

The Moorland-Spingarn Research Center

The Schomburg Center For Research In Black Culture

The Hatch-Billops Collection
James Hatch

The Hatch-Billops Collection originated in 1968 when Camille Billops and James Hatch were teaching art and literature respectively at the City College of New York. With the rise of the civil rights movement and a concomitant increase in racial consciousness, a demand arose for courses in black American art, drama, and literature. Finding that very little had been published on the history of the black American cultural arts and that which had been published was often out of print, Hatch and Billops began collecting primary materials.

With a grant from the National Endowment for the Humanities, Hatch and Billops conducted oral histories with black artists in all disciplines—art, cinema, dance, drama, literature, music, and related educational and political topics. Billops began photographing the works of black artists in exhibitions and private collections. To provide background information for her slides a library of books, periodicals, and clippings was assembled. Hatch began to collect black plays and theater programs, and today the black theater collection of published materials is one of the most complete in the world.

As the Hatch-Billops collection grew, word spread to other teachers and institutions, and soon there were requests for copies and for lists of materials and sources in black cultural history. To facilitate sharing the information it soon became apparent that it would be necessary to formalize the collection. Because the books, tapes, and slides had been catalogued, the New York State Board of Regents, after an inspection of the library, granted a charter to Hatch-Billops as a research institution that would serve the public in three ways:

1. to collect and preserve primary and secondary resource materials in the black cultural arts;
2. to provide tools and access to these materials for artists and scholars as well as the general public;
3. to develop and disseminate programs in the arts which would use the resources of the collection.

Housed in a Manhattan loft at 491 Broadway, the collection now contains over one thousand oral history tapes, ten thousand slides of artists and art works, approximately four thousand books, as well as hundreds of theater pro-

James Hatch and Camille Billops (photograph by Adger Cowans, courtesy of the Hatch-Billops Collection)

Billops, Owen Dodson (right), and photographer James Van Der Zee at the time of their collaboration on The Harlem Book of the Dead *(photograph by Jeanie Black, courtesy of the Hatch-Billops Collection)*

grams, art exhibition catalogs, posters, scarce and rare periodicals, and photographs. Among the unpublished plays are the complete dramas of Ted Ward and Owen Dodson, the latter part of a large manuscript collection–the Owen and Edith Dodson Memorial Collection. The materials of the collection do not circulate except in special group shows; however, some of the materials may be duplicated for use in other libraries.

A board of six directors sets policy for the collection and oversees the Friends of Hatch-Billops, a fund-raising group. Other funds come to the library through grants from organizations such as the New York State Council on the Arts, the National Endowment for the Arts, and the National Endowment for the Humanities.

The collection attempts to disseminate some of its history and information through a series of Sunday afternoon salon programs held in the loft. Here individual artists and scholars, such as Dizzy Gillespie, John A. Williams, and Amiri Baraka, have spoken of those who have influenced their lives. These conversations are published annually in the series *Artist and Influence* and are made available to libraries at cost. In this way, the library preserves black histories that might otherwise be lost. The collection has also hosted special seminars on archival preservation of black history, the writing of black biography, contemporary Asian theater, and the images of women in the arts.

The Moorland-Spingarn Research Center

Thomas C. Battle
Howard University

During the latter nineteenth and early twentieth centuries the founding of organizations such as the Bethel Literary and Historical Association (1881), the American Negro Historical Society (1897), the Negro Society for Historical Research (1912), and the Association for the Study of Negro Life and History (1915) stimulated a growing interest in studying black history and culture and collecting sources to document these important aspects of American life. Long the center for black intellectual life, Howard University was a natural seedbed for developing both the discipline of black history and library collections documenting it.

The leading proponent at the university for the development of a research collection on black history separate from the general library collection was Kelly Miller, a professor of mathematics and sociology (1890-1934) and dean of the College of Arts and Sciences (1907-1919). Envisioning a national "Negro-Americana Museum and Library," Dean Miller persuaded his good friend, Rev. Jesse E. Moorland, to donate his exceptional private library on black history to the university for this purpose. Moorland, an alumnus and trustee of Howard, who served as general secretary of the YMCA, announced his gift of some three thousand books, pamphlets, and other historical items in a letter of 18 December 1914 to university president Stephen M. Newman. Moorland noted that his collection was "regarded by many experts as probably the largest and most complete yet gathered by a single individual" and that he was "giving this collection to the University because it is the one place in America where the largest and best library on this subject [of the Negro and slavery] should be constructively established. It is also the place where our young people who have the scholarly instinct should have the privilege of a complete reference library on the subject." In accepting his generous donation, the university's board of trustees created the Moorland Foundation, A Library of Negro Life, and housed it as a special collection in the new library building donated by Andrew Carnegie.

Rev. Jesse E. Moorland (courtesy of the Moorland-Spingarn Research Center, Howard University)

Responses to the establishment of the Moorland Foundation, which represented a conscious decision and effort to pursue and promote the documentation, research, and study of the black experience, were positive and wide-ranging. Librarian of Congress Herbert Putnam noted that the black-related holdings of the Library of Congress would be but a fraction of what Howard University was planning to develop. Although the formative years of the Moorland Foundation were to witness relatively slow development, its establishment provided a solid base for the further

development of a collection documenting black history and culture.

A new era for the Moorland Foundation began in 1930 with the appointment of Dorothy Burnett Porter as director, and its establishment as a research library in 1932. A graduate of Howard University in 1928 and the first black American woman to earn a masters in library science from Columbia University, Porter was to direct the foundation for the next forty-three years. Porter improved the classification scheme, making it more suitable for a special research collection, and developed a wide variety of research tools and authoritative bibliographies based upon her vast knowledge in the field that would become known as black studies. She greatly augmented the collection's holdings. A new library facility in 1939 provided increased research and storage space. During the 1930s the foundation served as a clearinghouse for materials documenting the black experience in a project sponsored and supported by the Works Progress Administration. The result was the compilation of "A Catalogue of Books in the Moorland Foundation" and the preparation of a card file "on all publications by or about the Negro made known to the project workers by cooperating librarians in public, university and private libraries scattered throughout the country."

Since the holdings of the Moorland Foundation were general in nature, the most important landmark in the collection of literary resources was the purchase in 1946 of the private library of Arthur B. Spingarn, a noted bibliophile who served as president of the National Association for the Advancement of Colored People from 1940 to 1965. Spingarn, a widely read scholar of black history and literature who consulted with numerous editors, writers, scholars, diplomats, and booksellers throughout the world during his thirty-five years of collecting, had assembled a collection of works by Negro authors that was unique in its depth, breadth, and quality. In acknowledging the acquisition of Spingarn's library, Howard's president, Mordecai Wyatt Johnson, described it as "the most comprehensive and interesting group of books by Negroes ever collected in the world." Among the Spingarn Collection's treasures are Juan Latino's *Ad Catholicum Pariter et Invictissimum Phillippum dei Gratia Hispaniarum Regum*, published in 1573 at Granada, Spain. The book is a volume of epigrams depicting Phillip V's victory over the Turks, written by a black slave who was one of the outstanding Latin-

ists and humanists of Renaissance Spain and a noted professor at the University of Granada. The collection also includes Armand Lanusse's *Les Cenelles* (1845), the first anthology of Negro poetry in the United States. Perhaps the rarest pieces of early Americana are Phillis Wheatley's broadside, *An Elegiac Poem on the Death of that Celebrated Divine . . . George Whitefield* (1770), and her *Poems* (1773). The collection is particularly important for its works by early black American writers and leaders, including Jupiter Hammon, Benjamin Banneker, Richard Allen, Daniel Coker, Paul Cuffee, David Ruggles, Peter Williams, John Marrant, Absalom Jones, Lemuel Haynes, and David Walker. There are also many works by Afro-Cuban, Afro-Brazilian, and Haitian writers. There is an inscribed volume of Olaudah Equiano (Gustavus Vassa). In the years after the initial purchase of his library Spingarn added hundreds of volumes in an effort to complete it, and the collection grew to contain items in many African languages, such as Swahili, Kikuyu, Zulu, Yoruba, Vai, Ewe, Luganda, Ga, Sotho, Amharic, Hausa, and Xhosa.

Since its acquisition the Spingarn Collection has been maintained separately, and the original Moorland gift has become the general collection to which new additions are made. Although the Spingarn Collection contains the best-known rarities, there is some duplication of holdings, and the Moorland Foundation has the distinction of housing the earliest imprinted title, Nicolas Durand de Villegagnon's *Caroli. V. Imperatioris Expeditio in Africam ad Argieram* (1542).

By 1957 the Moorland Foundation collections had grown to some forty thousand volumes, many of which represent black American contributions to American literature. It had acquired the books and personal papers of Alain Locke, a central figure in the Harlem Renaissance. The Locke Papers are essential to research on this period and include correspondence with most of the major figures, including Langston Hughes, Claude McKay, and Zora Neale Hurston. The Moorland Foundation also acquired the Leigh Whipper Theatre Collection, the Mary O. Williamson Collection on celebrities, the Rose McClendon Memorial Collection of photographs by Carl Van Vechten, and the Mary E. Moore Collection of Negro Authors. In 1958 Moorland acquired Spingarn's collection of Negro music, at the time one of the largest such collections in the world, including works by artists such as Will Marion Cook, Samuel Coleridge-Taylor, Henry T.

Kelly Miller, Howard University professor and dean, who was instrumental in the acquisition of Moorland's Collection (courtesy of the Moorland-Spingarn Research Center, Howard University)

Arthur B. Spingarn, whose library was purchased by Howard University in 1946 (courtesy of the Moorland-Spingarn Research Center, Howard University)

Title page for Juan Latino's book of epigrams, published in 1573. Latino, a black man, was a professor at the University of Granada (courtesy of the Moorland-Spingarn Research Center, Howard University).

Burleigh, Clarence Cameron White, W. C. Handy, William Grant Still, and Howard Swanson. Foreign composers represented are Brazil's Antonio Carlos Gomes; Jose Mauricio Nunes Garcia, regarded as the father of Brazilian music; Justin Elie, Haitian composer of salon music; Amadeo Roldan of Cuba; and world-renowned French violinist Le Chevalier de Saint Georges. It was also about this time that the Moorland Foundation became known as the Moorland-Spingarn Collection, or simply the Negro Collection, to avoid the confusion of those who had mistaken it for a charitable organization. The heightened racial consciousness of the 1960s was important for the collection, which represented the evidence to counter charges that blacks had no meaningful history or literary tradition.

A new phase of development for the Moorland-Spingarn Collection began in 1973. Porter retired in June of that year, although she stayed until September, when Michael R. Winston assumed leadership. Porter in 1933 had described the purposes of the Moorland Foundation:

1. To accumulate, record and preserve material by and about the Negro;
2. To assist interested students of Negro life to pursue the scholarly exploitation of the material in the collection;
3. To instill race pride and race consciousness in Negro youth; and
4. To provide a great reference library on every phase of Negro life.

These basic objectives continued as the foundation of the reorganized Moorland-Spingarn Research Center, and a Manuscript Division was designed to pursue the programmatic, analytical collecting of documentary sources that would enable scholars to probe the deceptively simple surface of black history and culture. The acquisition of personal papers and organizational records not limited to collections of literary significance has resulted in the development of important holdings like the library and personal papers of C. Glenn Carrington, acquired in 1975. A student of Alain Locke at Howard University, where he also studied comparative culture, Carrington sought to develop a collection of books, manu-

Dorothy Burnett Porter, director of the Moorland-Spingarn Research Center from 1930 to 1973 (courtesy of the Moorland-Spingarn Research Center, Howard University)

The Moorland-Spingarn Research Center reading room (courtesy of the Moorland-Spingarn Research Center, Howard University)

scripts, music, and other materials that reflected the ideas of the New Negro Movement. The Carrington Collection, assembled over a period of fifty years, contains more than twenty-two hundred books in fifteen languages, approximately five hundred recordings, and eighteen storage boxes of manuscript materials, photographs, broadsides, prints, periodicals, sheet music, newspapers, and other items. There is an extensive collection of autographed Langston Hughes material in fifteen foreign languages, and there are subject files documenting the lives and careers of blacks in the arts. The works of twentieth-century writers such as James Baldwin, Amiri Baraka, Arna Bontemps, William Stanley Braithwaite, Gwendolyn Brooks, Ed Bullins, Countee Cullen, Owen Dodson, W. E. B. Du Bois, Paul Lau-

rence Dunbar, Nikki Giovanni, Robert Hayden, Zora Neale Hurston, Ted Joans, James Weldon Johnson, John O. Killens, Haki Madhubuti, Claude McKay, Naomi Long Madgett, Paulé Marshall, Gordon Parks, Dudley Randall, Ishmael Reed, Sonia Sanchez, and Richard Wright reflect the diversity of the collection.

The Moorland-Spingarn Research Center is one of America's most valuable cultural warehouses. It not only acquires and preserves an important part of Afro-American heritage but makes these resources available to researchers throughout the world. In its nearly seventy-five years of service to the research community, it has developed an enviable record of success and looks forward to continuing its efforts into the twenty-first century.

The Schomburg Center For Research In Black Culture

Howard Dodson

The flurry of activity by artists and scholars known as the Harlem Renaissance gave impetus to at least two significant cultural events in 1925. The first significant examination of contemporary culture, *The New Negro: An Interpretation*, was published; its editor, Alain Locke, wrote that "Whoever wishes to see the Negro in his essential traits, in the full perspective of his achievement and possibilities, must seek the enlightenment of that self-portraiture which the present developments of Negro culture are offering." The other event was the opening of the Division of Negro Literature, History, and Prints in the 135th Street branch of the New York Public Library. A repository for materials on black life that documented past achievements and served as a foundation for the solicitation of future contributions, this special library was the forerunner of the Schomburg Center for Research in Black Culture, which stands today as one of the world's foremost facilities dedicated to the preservation and interpretation of black cultural artifacts.

From its inception the Schomburg Center has served both as a repository and as a center for black intellectual and artistic activities. Its location in Harlem has given added significance to those roles, for by the early 1920s Harlem had become the "black capital," home to an amalgam of blacks from various parts of the United States, the Caribbean, and Africa. Economic expansion, especially during World War I, increased opportunities for black home ownership; simultaneously, literacy and race consciousness were expanding within the black community. Political consciousness and race pride were heightened by the activities of the National Association for the Advancement of Colored People (NAACP), the National Urban League, and the preachments of Marcus Garvey. More outlets for literature were becoming available through black newspapers and magazines such as the *Crisis*, edited by W. E. B. Du Bois of the NAACP; the Urban League's *Opportunity*, edited by Charles Johnson; and the *Messenger*, edited by A. Philip Randolph of the Brotherhood of Sleeping Car Porters.

*Arthur A. Schomburg (courtesy of the Schomburg Center for
Research in Black Culture, the New York Public Library,
Astor, Lenox and Tilden Foundations)*

Critic Sterling Brown, writing about poets from
1914 to 1936, also captured the concerns of
other black literary figures when he noted their
five major concerns were "(1) a discovery of Africa as a source of race pride, (2) a use of Negro heroes and heroic episodes from American history,
(3) propaganda of protest, (4) a treatment of the
Negro masses with more understanding and less
apology, and (5) franker and deeper self revelation." Black writing during the period sprang
from social concerns as well as literary interests;
and early anthologies of black writings covered a
broad spectrum ranging from poetry to prose to
social and political criticism.

As Harlem became the focal point for black
artistic and intellectual activities, the 135th Street
branch library took on a new dimension. The
New York Public Library had opened the branch
in 1905 in a neighborhood that was predominantly Jewish. Within fifteen years it was half
black. Ernestine Rose, who had developed ser-

vices in other ethnic neighborhoods, was assigned to adapt the library's resources to meet
the needs of the changing community. In 1921
the branch began to sponsor annual art exhibitions which were planned by committees including cultural leaders such as W. E. B. Du Bois,
James Weldon Johnson, and Arthur Schomburg.
It also sponsored lectures and book discussions.
By 1924, however, the library was facing a serious dilemma. The community's heightened interest in materials by and about black people had
begun to strain its limited resources. To meet this
challenge Rose called a community meeting in December 1924, during which a citizen's committee
was created which elected Schomburg, James
Weldon Johnson, Hubert H. Harrison, and John
Nail as officers. The group recommended that
the rarest books be set aside as a Negro reference library. Gifts and loans for the special collection came from the private libraries of noted
black collectors, including John Bruce, Louise Lati-

mer, Harrison, George Young, Charles D. Martin, and Schomburg.

At the formal opening of the Division of Negro Literature, History, and Prints on 8 May 1925, Rose noted the existence of similar collections in the Library of Congress, in the libraries of institutions such as Tuskegee Institute and Howard University, in certain large city reference libraries, and in a few private libraries. She predicted, however, that the collection at the 135th Street library would become one of the largest and most valuable in the world because of its location in Harlem, "the greatest negro city in the world"; and because it would make materials "available equally to scholars, to the man in the street and to school children of all races." As a result of the publicity surrounding the opening of the Negro division and the efforts of Charles S. Johnson, L. Hollingsworth Wood, and Eugene Knickle Jones of the Urban League, the Carnegie Corporation provided a grant of ten thousand dollars for the New York Public Library to purchase Schomburg's personal collection. This acquisition brought the division immediate international stature.

Schomburg continued to augment the collection and also served as an unpaid consultant to the library, addressing staff meetings and assisting young scholars. A second Carnegie grant in 1932 made it possible for him to be hired as curator of the Negro division, a position he held until his death in 1938. In 1940 the library was renamed the Schomburg Collection of Negro Literature, History, and Prints in his honor. Under Schomburg and the collection's first staff member, Catherine Allen Latimer, holdings had been organized and expanded. This work was continued by Lawrence D. Reddick, a noted historian and lecturer, who was appointed to succeed Schomburg in 1939. Reddick initiated lecture series; organized exhibitions and programs to mark special occasions; and began the annual presentation of the Schomburg collection's highly respected Honor Roll in Race Relations Award.

The 1940s were a time of increasing use for the collection. In 1942 the collection moved into the entire top floor of the new 135th Street branch library building. The American Negro Theater staged productions in the basement auditorium, serving as training ground for performers such as Frederick O'Neal, Hilda Simms, Hilda Haynes, Rosetta LeNoire, Earle Hyman, Sidney Poitier, and Harry Belafonte, and for playwrights such as Alice Childress and Abram Hill.

Schomburg and his sister, Dolores, in Puerto Rico, circa 1905 (courtesy of the Schomburg Center for Research in Black Culture, the New York Public Library, Astor, Lenox and Tilden Foundations)

The collection was a primary resource for writers such as Richard Wright and Langston Hughes. Discussions drew the participation of African and Caribbean visitors to the United States who were involved in struggles for self-government, such as Ja Ja Wachuku, former ambassador from Nigeria; George Westermann, former ambassador from Panama; and Kwame Nkrumah, who became the first president of Ghana. The collection was a center for black scholars involved in WPA projects; and later, during the 1950s, provided resources for research done for Kenneth Clark's report on the effect of segregated education on black and white children, which was cited in the U.S. Supreme Court's historic *Brown v. Board of Education* decision in 1954.

From 1948 through the 1970s the collection continued to expand under the guidance of Jean Blackwell Hutson. By 1966, however, it was in serious jeopardy. Materials were deteriorating from overuse by readers, air pollution, and unsatisfactory climatic conditions. Although the collection had been moved back into the entire space in the 135th Street building in 1954, it was overcrowded. Hudson launched a successful campaign to rally support within the New York Public Library and in the black community. In a re-

Inscribed photograph from John Edward Bruce (Bruce Grit) a historian and journalist who was one of the founders of the Negro Society for Historical Research in 1911, to Schomburg (courtesy of the Schomburg Center for Research in Black Culture, the New York Public Library, Astor, Lenox and Tilden Foundations)

Interior of the 135th Street Branch of the New York Public Library, 1928 (photograph by James Van Der Zee, courtesy of the Schomburg Center for Research in Black Culture, the New York Public Library, Astor, Lenox and Tilden Foundations)

organization the Schomburg Collection was designated as part of the research libraries of the New York Public Library in 1972, and its name was changed to the Schomburg Center for Research in Black Culture. Hutson became chief of the center. City and federal grants helped pay for the construction of an expansion which opened in 1980. The efforts of the Schomburg Center were enhanced in the 1970s by the advocacy of the Schomburg Corporation, an umbrella organization formed in 1968 to coordinate the activities of individuals and organizations involved in Schomburg support efforts.

It is hoped that renovation and construction work soon will get under way to convert the old 135th Street building into a facility that will include study and storage space for the Art, Photographs and Prints, and Moving Image and Recorded Sound collections, a 380-seat auditorium, a full exhibition gallery, and a gift shop. Along with the newly renovated Countee Cullen branch library, the expanded Schomburg Center for Research in Black Culture will form a learning and activities complex, completely equipped with contemporary technology and facilities geared to accommodate future growth.

The Resources Of The Schomburg Center

The collection that the New York Public Library acquired from Schomburg in 1926 was unique and well known to artists and scholars dealing with black life. A Puerto Rican of African descent, Schomburg attributed his motivation to collect books to the stinging remark by one of his early teachers in Puerto Rico that the Negro had no history. The collection that he amassed, augmented by searches for rarities in the United States, Europe, and Latin America, established the "three outstanding conclusions" that he said resulted from the systematic and scientific study of the black past:

> First, that the Negro has been throughout the centuries of controversy an active collaborator, and often a pioneer, in the struggle for his own freedom and advancement.
>
> Second, that by virtue of their being regarded as something "exceptional," even by friends and well-wishers, Negroes of attainment and genius have been unfairly disassociated from the group, and group credit lost accordingly.
>
> Third, that the remote racial origins of the Negro, far from being what the race and the world have been given to understand, offer a record of credible group achievement when scientifi-

cally viewed, and more important still, that they are of vital general interest because of their bearing upon the beginnings and early development of culture.

Arthur Schomburg's collection included over five thousand books, three thousand manuscripts, two thousand etchings and portraits, and several thousand pamphlets. Among its treasures was a volume of Latin poetry by Juan Latino published in Spain in 1573. Latino, a full-blooded African, was incumbent of the chair of poetry at the University of Granada during the reign of Philip V. Other rarities included various editions of Gustavus Vassa's autobiography, which provided evidence for Granville Sharpe's attack on slavery in the British colonies in 1796; army orders signed by Toussaint L'Ouverture; certificates of slave sales; and the Spanish manuscript of Soley Balsas (1757), recounting in poetry the life of the African girl who became St. Theresa of Salamanca. There were also the Latin and Dutch treatises of the West African-born Jacobus Eliza Capitein; and *De la litterature des Negres* (1808, French edition) by Abbe Henri Gregoire, the French abolitionist and intellectual. Early black American holdings included Jupiter Hammon's *An Address to the Negroes in the State of New York* (1787); manuscript poems and early editions of works by Phillis Wheatley; sermons by the black pastor Lemuel Haynes to the white congregation that he served in Rutland, Vermont, for thirty years following the Revolutionary War; copies of Benjamin Banneker's almanacs (1792 and 1793); and various editions of William Wells Brown's *Clotel; or, The President's Daughter: A Narrative of Slave Life in the United States* (1853). During Schomburg's tenure as curator the Negro division acquired many valuable items, including the Williamson Collection of Negro Freemasonry.

From its beginning with Schomburg's collection the center's holdings have grown to comprise over five million items, including over one hundred thousand volumes, seventy-five thousand microforms, more than four hundred black newspapers, and over one thousand current periodicals from around the world. Its General Research and Reference collections are used by nearly fifty-five thousand readers annually. Among the special resources available are the vertical file, a reference tool for information contained in flyers, newspaper and magazine clippings, pamphlets, and ephemera, indexed under seven thousand subject headings; the Er-

Exterior of the library, circa 1945 (courtesy of the Schomburg Center for Research in Black Culture, the New York Public Library, Astor, Lenox and Tilden Foundations)

nest D. Kaiser Index to Black Resources, a handwritten card catalog of articles in thousands of issues of magazines and newspapers; the U.S. Federal Population Census (1790 through 1900); the Soundex Index, a name guide to the 1880 and 1900 census records; and a computer terminal which provides access to the Research Libraries Information Network.

The Schomburg Center also maintains several special collections. Developed from Schomburg's original collection, the Rare Books, Manuscript and Archives section allows researchers the opportunity to work directly with original source materials. Its holdings comprise thirty-eight hundred rare books and pamphlets, two hundred forty-five manuscript collections, and over thirteen thousand pieces of sheet music and other rare printed materials. The archives in-

clude the papers of Alexander Crummell, Schomburg, and John Edward Bruce. Other early collections focus on slavery and abolition activities, Haiti, the West Indies, industrial education, and black Freemasonry. The library holds the organizational records of the National Negro Congress, the Civil Rights Congress, the New York Urban League, the Black Academy of Arts and Letters, and the Central Division of Marcus Garvey's Universal Negro Improvement Association. There are also significant collections of personal papers which are especially strong in the areas of history, politics, government, labor, and the arts. The library contains manuscripts of writers Claude McKay, Zora Neale Hurston, Langston Hughes, Richard Wright, Piri Thomas, Larry Neal, Julian Mayfield, and Ben Carruthers; musicians Lawrence Brown, Andy Razaf,

Poet Langston Hughes and Jean Blackwell Hutson, who was later chief of the collection, 1950 (courtesy of the Schomburg Center for the Research in Black Culture, the New York Public Library, Astor, Lenox and Tilden Foundations)

Philippa Schuyler, Clarence Cameron White, and Sammy Heyward; and thespians Eusebia Cosme, John Marriott, and Fredi Washington.

Schomburg was responsible for a number of significant acquisitions for the center's art collection, including bronze busts of an African man and woman by the nineteenth-century French sculptor Charles Cordier; Pietro Calvi's marble and bronze bust of Othello; works from black American artists such as Augusta Savage, William Ernest Braxton, Albert Alexander Smith, and Lois Mailou Jones; and Caribbean artists, including the Cuban-born Pastor Argudin y Pedroso and Teodoro Ramos Blanco. Through the efforts of Alain Locke, Edith Isaacs, publisher of *Theater Arts* magazine, was persuaded to purchase the col-

lection of art developed by Raoul Blondiau, a Belgian diplomat in the Congo (Zaire). A portion of that collection was deposited at the center and designated the Blondiau-Theatre Arts Collection. Other African art holdings include the Eric de Kolb Collection of weaponry from the southern and western areas of Africa; and the Oxmantown Collection of Yoruba art from Nigeria. The art collection also includes important contemporary works by Norman Lewis, Jacob Lawrence, Romare Bearden, Vivian Browne, Ed Clark, Emma Amos, and Herbert Gentry.

The Schomburg Center's photograph collection comprises over two hundred thousand photographs dating from the 1840s to the present, including portraits of black artists of the 1930s

The old 135th Street library and the 1980 addition, circa 1981 (courtesy of the Schomburg Center for Research in Black Culture, the New York Public Library, Astor, Lenox and Tilden Foundations)

Reading room in the Schomburg Center (courtesy of the Schomburg Center for Research in Black Culture, the New York Public Library, Astor, Lenox and Tilden Foundations)

by Marvin and Morgan Smith. There are many photographs of political figures, musicians, actors, athletes, and social activists. Among the documentary photographs are rare images documenting slave and free black life in South America and the Caribbean during the nineteenth and early twentieth centuries; photographs of the Gullah people of South Carolina by Doris Ulmann; Walker Evans's photographs of African art; the work of James Van Der Zee; and the Farm Security Administration photographs of the 1930s and 1940s.

The Moving Image and Recorded Sound collection encompasses musical documentation, oral history recordings, motion pictures, and videotapes. Recordings of early radio broadcasts date from the late 1920s; and there are also early recordings of statements by George Washington Carver, Booker T. Washington, and Marcus Garvey. Recorded music holdings include classics by artists such as Marian Anderson, Roland Hayes, Leontyne Price, Ulysses Kay, William Grant Still, Mamie Smith, Alberta Hunter, and Bessie Smith. Jazz, gospel, reggae, and other contemporary forms are also represented. In addition to American music, materials document the music of Africa, the Caribbean, and other areas of the world where there are people of African descent. Among the film and video holdings are early film classics such as *Scar of Shame* and *The Emperor Jones*, along with documentaries like *The Streets of Greenwood*, which portrays the Student Nonviolent Coordinating Committee in 1962. There is early footage of Noble Sissle, Lena Horne, Kid Ory, Paul Robeson, Count Basie, Ethel Waters, Thelonious Monk, and Billie Holiday. The center has also established an Oral History/Video Documentation Project which videotapes in-house interviews.

Schomburg Center Special Programs

The center has sponsored exhibitions from its inception. Since 1980 the exhibition program has been expanded. An impressive series of exhibitions has been mounted in recent years, with themes such as "Censorship and Black America"; "Art Against Apartheid"; "The Black West"; "Freedom's Journals: A History of the Black Press in New York State"; and "Give Me Your Tired, Your Poor. . . ?: Voluntary Black Migration to the United States," the center's contribution to the Statue of Liberty centennial celebration. Related

forums during some exhibitions have drawn standing-room-only audiences. A traveling exhibition program makes shows available to sister institutions and other interested organizations in the United States, South America, and the Caribbean.

Since 1983 the Schomburg Center has hosted two scholars annually. A grant from the Rockefeller Foundation has made it possible for the center to launch its own Scholars in Residence Program by hosting two scholars for the 1986 and 1987 academic year. Three additional scholars spend short-term residencies ranging from three to six months under other auspices. The scholars work closely with the network of scholars affiliated with the Schomburg Assembly, an interdisciplinary regional association of scholars specializing in African and Afro-American history and culture. Under the auspices of the assembly, they participate in seminars and forums, lecture series, and programs for the general public. As a natural extension of its programs and services, the center, in conjunction with the Phelps-Stokes Fund, administers the Clarence L. Holte Literary Prize, an award presented biennially to a contemporary writer in recognition of a significant contribution to the cultural heritage of Africa and the African diaspora made through published writings in the humanities.

The center's publications include catalogs produced in conjunction with some exhibitions and the *Schomburg Center Journal*, a quarterly publication for donors. A special publication in 1986, *The Schomburg Center for Research in Black Culture: 60th Anniversary Tribute*, included historical data and rare photographs from the center's collection. *The Schomburg Clipping File* has been published on microfiche; primarily a newspaper and periodical clipping file, it also includes typescripts, broadsides, pamphlets, programs, book reviews, menus, and other ephemera. Focused on items from 1925 to 1974 the file is arranged chronologically within each of the 6,950 subject headings.

The Schomburg Center is looking toward the twenty-first century as it expands its services, facilities, and technology to meet the contemporary needs of writers, scholars, artists, and others who are studying and making contributions to black culture. In the tradition established by Schomburg the center continues to be a repository for materials documenting black life and a participant in the evolution of black culture.

My Dear Sir:

Will you, do the kindness to procure for me a copy of the Report of the Committee to investigate the John Brown raid? It was published in 1860. and none but Senators and representatives can now get hold of the Documents. You will do me a great favor if you will procure me one and send it to me at the City Hall.

Respectfully your friend
Fred.k Douglass.

Undated letter in which Frederick Douglass requests a copy of a report on John Brown's Harper's Ferry raid. Douglass had been under suspicion for complicity with Brown (courtesy of the Schomburg Center for Research in Black Culture, the New York Public Library, Astor, Lenox and Tilden Foundations).

1

Negro Literature. The demand for good books by Negro authors is steadily growing, with the awakening of the racial consciousness of the Negro. The time has arrived for the Negro everywhere to read and study the worth-while books of acknowledged Negro scholars and authors who have contributed to the sum of human knowledge by their writings on the achievements, aspiration and aims of the Negro race past and present. The Hunt Publishing Co. is preparing to meet this demand by publishing at an early date. The biography of the learned and erudite scholar linguist diplomat and publicist the late Dr Edward Wilmot Blyden LLD, &c by Fred W Hooke of Sierra Leone WCA to which will be appended a <u>rare</u> contribution from the pen of that eminent Negro scholar entitled The Negro in Sacred History teeming with historical data, and Biblical references to the antiquity, achievements, and greatness of the Negro race, from the time to which the memory of man runneth not. The book will be printed on good paper and will be well bound and will be sold for $125 per copy when printed. As soon as five hundred subscribers have been secured the book will be published and distributed. No progressive Negro can afford to be without a copy of this book. As the publisher has the written authority to reprint

Manuscript for Bruce's editorial soliciting funds to publish Fred W. Hooke's biography of black scholar and diplomat Edward Wilmont Blyden (courtesy of the Schomburg Center for Research in Black Culture, the New York Public Library, Astor, Lenox and Tilden Foundations)

2

the fugitive pamphlets and unpublished mss of this Negro ~~Savant~~ Scholar hitherto
These will from time to time be republished in serial form suitable
for binding at Fifty cents per number we shall endeavor if
~~the~~ our efforts are properly encouraged, thus to reproduce in this way
the book that made Dr Blyden famous, as an author, Christianity Islam and
The Negro Race which is now out of print, and which Negroes of this
generation have only a slight acquaintance with. It is a masterful work
valuable primarily for its rich fund of authentic ~~statement~~ facts touching
the Negro. It is an invaluable book for the student and the scholar
and for all Negroes who owned knew the truth about their race and its
~~than~~ strivings and accomplishments, Those of our readers who
may want these books should send in their orders at once
We anticipate a big sale for them in West Africa the scene of
Dr Blydens early struggles and labors, make money orders payable
to — Hunt & Bruce Publishers
136 St
New York City

Manuscript for a poem published in Alice Moore Dunbar Nelson's 1895 book, Violets and Other Tales *(courtesy of the Schomburg Center for Research in Black Culture, the New York Public Library, Astor, Lenox and Tilden Foundations)*

Song In Spite of Myself.

440

Never love with all your heart,
  It only ends in aching,
And bit by bit to the smallest part,
  That organ will be breaking.

Never love with all your mind,
  It only ends in fretting;
In musing on sweet joys behind,
  Too poignant for forgetting.

Never love with all your soul;
  For such there is no ending,
Though a mind that frets may find control,
  And a shattered heart find mending.

Give but a grain of the heart's rich seed,
  Confine some under cover,
And when Love goes bid him Godspeed,
  And find another lover.

Countee Cullen

Fair copy of a poem by Countee Cullen published in the December 1928 issue of Harper's *(copyright 1929 by Harper & Row Publishers, Inc.; renewed 1957 by Ida M. Cullen; reprinted by permission of Harper & Row Publishers, Inc.; courtesy of the Schomburg Center for Research in Black Culture, the New York Public Library, Astor, Lenox and Tilden Foundations)*

Appendix II

PHYLON (Fourth Quarter, 1950)
The Negro in Literature:
The Current Scene

PHYLON was founded in 1940 by W. E. B. Du Bois as a scholarly journal of comment on world race problems. It was soon recognized as the preeminent journal of black culture in America. Annually in the winter issue, PHYLON published a feature article on the year's literary production by black writers. In issue number 4 for 1950, published in December, the editors commissioned instead an assessment by distinguished critics and scholars of black writing in the first half of the twentieth century. As a gauge of the contemporary attitudes of black intellectuals toward black literature, this issue is unparalleled. In view of their significance, those articles in the December 1950 PHYLON that address the issue's theme–"The Negro in Literature: The Current Scene"–are reprinted here in full.

Preface

One of the major concerns of PHYLON is that of orientation—of "placing" the elements of race and culture. Since those elements are constantly in flux, the task of necessity becomes one of re-examination and revaluation. Perhaps nowhere in the entire complex is the shifting more radical and its analysis more important than in the field of literature. And aside from the significance of the folksay and the more sophisticated imaginative writing as social and cultural barometers, there are the questions of the purpose, vitality, and design inherent in the literature as literature. It was from these tentative formulations then that the editors began moving toward the planning of the present issue.

It was not our aim simply to re-hash the "Negro Renaissance" period—though we felt, as did many of our contributors, that sufficient time had elapsed to allow for a sober appraisal of the forces at work during that period and of the literary end-products. It further seemed to us that, though fifty-year summaries at mid-century are tempting to editors, the establishment of such a frame would almost certainly result in an arid recitation of names and titles which had earned their oblivion, while blurring what appeared to us to be the proper focus. That no single period had been as fruitful as that of the thirties and forties seemed to us beyond argument; and it was this very period which stood in greatest need of examination by a congress of those who had produced its literature, or who were most competent to assess it. We resolved to assemble such a forum in the pages of PHYLON, inviting personalities to address themselves to various aspects of the general subject: "The Negro in Literature: The Current Scene."

Knowing full well that our contributors would formulate and arrive at richer insights and more meaningful questions, the editors began by posing a series of questions which any contributor might use as points of departure—or might ignore altogether. We raised such questions as: What are the promising and unpromising aspects of the Negro's present position in American literature? Are there any aspects of the life of the Negro in America which seem deserving of franker, or deeper, or more objective treatment? Does current literature by and about Negroes seem more or less propagandistic than before? Would you agree with those who feel that the Negro writer, the Negro as subject, and the Negro critic and scholar are moving toward an "unlabeled" future in which they will be measured without regard to racial origin and conditioning?

As we had hoped, the great majority of those whose contributions we invited not only responded enthusiastically, but treated issues of much greater pertinency and complexity than those we had provisionally indicated. The makers of the literature, the scholars, the critics have dealt honestly and, on the whole, effectively, it seems to us, with the achievements, the shortcomings and the discernible future of the Negro in the field of letters.

The contributors arrive at consensus on a surprising number of points in the pages which follow. On other points the groundwork is laid for stimulating controversies which, in our opinion, should be further debated in PHYLON itself, and perhaps in other journals. The editors themselves hope that the statement made by one of the contributors to the effect that this issue of PHYLON "will be a major contribution to critical writing on the Negro" is not too blatantly optimistic. We trust that the issue will in some measure justify so generous a pre-estimate.

—*Mozell C. Hill and M. Carl Holman*

The Negro Writer: Pitfalls and Compensations

William Gardner Smith

This is, as everyone recognizes by now, a world of relativity. We measure the rights of individuals against the rights of the society; the rights of the artist against the rights of his public; the right of free speech against the right of the individual to protection from slander. Degrees of good and evil are measured against other degrees of good and evil.

This apprehension of infinite relativity is, I think, instructive in considering the position of the Negro writer—I speak particularly of the novelist—in American society. For a moment, disregard the mechanical pros and cons, debits and credits—whether it is easier, or more difficult, for a Negro writer to have his work published; consider the purely esthetic question: What handicaps, and what advantages, does the American writer possess by virtue of being a Negro?

Because the handicaps are better known, and perhaps easier to understand, I will consider them first. The Negro writer is, first of all, invariably bitter. There are degrees of this bitterness, ranging from the anger of Richard Wright and the undercurrent of contempt for the white world in Chester Himes to the cruel satire exhibited by George Schuyler in his semi-classic *Black No More*. A writer is a man of sensitivity; otherwise, he would not be a writer. The sensitivities of the Negro writer react, therefore, more strongly against the ignorance, prejudice and discrimination of American society than do those of the average Negro in America.

There are all forms and varieties of this inevitable strain of bitterness in the Negro writer. Sometimes it results in militancy; sometimes in contempt for race and self; sometimes in hatred for the whole of American society, with blindness for the good things contained therein. It is often hard for the Negro writer to resist polemicizing. He is driven often to write a tract, rather than a work of art. So conscious is he of the pervading evil of race prejudice that he feels duty-bound to assault it at every turn, injecting opinion into alleged narration and inserting his philosophy into the mouths of his characters.

Writing of Negroes, the novelist has difficulty with his characterizations. His people usually become walking, talking propaganda, rather than completely rounded individuals. The Negro writer hesitates, perhaps unconsciously, to temper the goodness of his Negro characters with the dialectical "evil." Fearful of re-enforcing stereotypes in the white reader's mind, he often goes to the other extreme, idealizing his characters, making them flat rather than many-sided. Or, conscious of the pitfalls listed above, and anxious to prove that he is not idealizing his Negro characters, the writer goes to the other extreme—in the name of naturalism—and paints the American Negro as an exaggerated Bigger Thomas, with all the stereotyped characteristics emphasized three times over. To strike a compromise—and, incidentally, the truth—is possibly the most difficult feat for a Negro writer. Proof of this is the fact that I have not read one Negro novel which has truthfully represented the many-sided character of the Negro in American society today. Chester Himes, perhaps, has come closer than any other Negro author to such a representation.

It seems that it is difficult for the Negro writer to add to his weighty diatribes the leaven of humor. Writing is an art; the writer works upon the emotions of his reader. Every sentence, every cadence, every description, every scene, produces an emotional response in this reader. Consciously did Shakespeare lead his audiences through one powerful emotion after another to achieve the final, powerful effect of the death of Desdemona at the hands of Othello; consciously did Marlowe lead to the final descent into hell of Faust. In each of these journeys through dramatic experience there were rises and falls; there were moments of stern conflict and moments of relative relaxation; here were moments of tears and moments of relieving laughter.

Too often, however, in Negro novels do we witness the dull procession of crime after crime against the Negro, without relief in humor or otherwise. These monotonous repetitions of offenses against the Negro serve only to bore the reader

260

in time; and in so doing, they defeat the very purpose of the writer, for they become ineffective. One might even say that the chronicles of offenses constitute truth; however, they do not constitute art. And art is the concern of any novelist.

Novels which last through all time are concerned with universal themes. Dostoievski's great Raskolnikov is all of us in the aftermath of great crime; Tolstoi describes the universal ruling class in time of national crisis. The Negro writer is under tremendous pressure to write about the topical and the transient–the plight of the Negro in American society today. It may be that the greatest of such novels will last because of their historical interest It may even be that one or two will last because the writer has managed to infuse into his work some universal elements–as Dickens did, even when writing about the social conditions in the England of his day. But most Negro writers do not inject the universal element. They write only about the here and the now. Thus, their novels come and they go: in ten years, they are forgotten.

At this point, let me emphasize that the drive of the Negro writer to write about purely topical themes is of fantastic strength, and difficult for the non-Negro to appreciate. Starving and land-hungry Chinese want food and land: they are not much concerned about such abstractions as the rights of free speech, habeas corpus, the ballot, etc. When day to day problems press upon the individual, they become, in his mind, paramount. This sense of the immediate problem confronts the Negro writer. But it is significant to note that we do not today consider highly that literature which arose in protest against, say, the system of Feudalism, or even, in the United States, slavery.

*   *   *

But there are compensations for these difficulties confronting the Negro writer. They are great compensations.

Writing is concerned with people, with society and with ethics. Great writing is concerned with the individual in the group or tribe; obedience to or deviation from the laws of that tribe, and the consequences. Usually, by the very process of selection, omission and arrangement of his material, the author implies a judgment– approval or rejection of the laws of the society, be they in legal, ethical or religious form. Basic to such writing, obviously, is some understanding of both the society and the people in it.

To grasp social and individual truth, it is my opinion that the novelist must maintain emotional contact with the basic people of his society. At first glance, this appears a simple thing; but, in reality, it is difficult. Consider the material circumstances of the "successful" writer. He becomes a celebrity. He makes money. Usually, he begins to move in the sphere of people like himself–authors, artists, critics, etc. He purchases a home on Long Island. He no longer uses the subway; for now he has an automobile. He lectures; he speaks at luncheons; he autographs books; he attends cocktail parties; he discusses style, form, and problems of psychology with friends in a rather esoteric circle; and he writes. In a word, he moves, to some degree, into an ivory tower; he becomes, in a fashion, detached from the mainstream of American life.

In times of stability this detachment is often not too harmful: for the moral code remains what it was at the moment of the writer's detachment and, despite its rarification in his new environment, still may serve as the wellspring for vital work. In moments of social crisis, however, the established moral code comes into violent conflict with the desires of the people of society. Thus, immediately prior to the French Revolution, the ethics of Feudalism, though still officially recognized, actually were outdated and in conflict with the democratic tendencies of the people; and thus, today, the individualistic and basically selfish ethic of Capitalism, while still officially proclaimed, is in reality contrary to the socialist tendency which has spread over the world, and even made itself felt in America through Roosevelt's New Deal and Truman's election on a Fair Deal program.

The writer who is detached from society does not perceive this contradiction; and thus is missing from his writing some element of social truth. He is behind the times; he is holding onto a shell. Part of the greatness of Tolstoi is that he perceived the ethical, i.e., social, conflict, and accurately recorded it.

The Negro writer cannot achieve–at least, not as easily as the white American writer–this social detachment, however much he might desire it. The very national prejudice he so despises compels him to remember his social roots, perceive the social reality; in a word, compels him to keep his feet on the ground. He cannot register at the Mayflower Hotel. He cannot loll on the Miami Beach. He cannot ignore disfranchisement, epithets, educational and employment discrimina-

tion, mob violence. He is bound by unbreakable cords to the Negro social group. And so his writing, however poor artistically, must almost invariably contain some elements of social truth.

The Negro writer is endowed by his environment with relative emotional depth. What does a writer write about? We have said: people, and their problems, conflicts, etc. But–what problems, what conflicts? Pick up any popular American magazine or book and you will find out–the problem of whether John D., a thoroughly empty individual, should leave his wife Mary C., a thoroughly empty individual, to marry Jane B., a thoroughly empty individual. To this problem are devoted hundreds of pages; hundreds of thousands of words. And in the end the reader of intelligence must ask the question: So what?

Emotional depth, perception of real problems and real conflicts, is extremely rare in American literature–as it is in American society generally. Instead of issues of significance, our fiction (our serious fiction) is overladen with such trite themes as that of Tennessee Williams' *The Roman Spring of Mrs. Stone*. America's is a superficial civilization: it is soda-pop land, the civilization of television sets and silk stockings and murder mysteries and contempt for art and poetry. It is difficult, out of such environment, to bring forth works with the emotional force of, say, *Crime and Punishment*.

Here again the Negro writer's social experience is, despite its bitterness, also an artistic boon. To live continually with prejudice based on the accident of skin color is no superficial experience; and neither is the reaction produced by such constant exposure superficial. There is a depth and intensity to the emotions of Negroes–as demonstrated in "Negro music"–which is largely lacking in white Americans. How often has the Negro maid or housecleaner come home to laugh at her white mistress' great concern about the color of a hat, the shape of a shoe, keeping up with the next-door Joneses? How often have Negroes, on the job, laughed in amazement at the inane trivialities which occupy the thoughts of their white fellow workers. And this laughter is logical. The Europeans would understand it. For, what man or woman who has seen a lynching, or been close to the furnaces of Dachau, or been rebuffed and rejected because of his skin color, can really seriously concern himself with the insipid and shallow love affair between Susie Bell and Jerry?

Thus, the Negro writer, if he does not make the tragic error of trying to imitate his white counterparts, has in his possession the priceless "gift" of thematic intuition. Provided he permits his writing to swell truthfully from his deepest emotional reaches, he will treat problems of real significance, which can strike a cord in the heart of basic humanity. He will be able to convey suffering without romanticizing; he will be able to describe happiness which is not merely on the surface; he will be able to search out and concretize the hopes and ambitions which are the basic stuff of human existence. And he will, in Hemingway's words, be able to do this "without cheating." For the basic fact about humanity in our age is that it suffers; and only he who suffers with it can truthfully convey its aches and pains, and thwarted desires. And now, speaking only of this period in which now we live, I should like to point out one last advantage which I feel accrues to the writer by virtue of being a Negro. It concerns the international power struggle.

We live, it appears, in an age of struggle between the American brand of Capitalism and the Russian brand of Communism. This is the obvious struggle; and most of the individuals in the world seem to feel that one must choose between one or the other. But is this, really, the root struggle? Or is mankind, the great majority of it, not actually groping for a rational social order, free from the tensions of economic and political crisis, free from war and from dictatorship, in which the individual will be permitted to live according to an ethic all sensible and truly just men can subscribe to?

For a moment, leave the last question. Consider the writer in the American scene, in this day and age. Picture him as being young and filled with ideals; consider him intelligent, sensitive and understanding. Ask the question: Can he approve of American society as it exists today?

I say, on the basis of experience and of individual reaction, no! The young writer will notice many good things, worthy of retention, in the America of today. He will approve of free speech (now being seriously curtailed); he will approve the idea of a free press (even though becoming a monopoly because of the economics involved); he will believe in free artistic expression, realizing that only through freedom can real art survive. But can he approve of the dog-eat-dog existence we glorify by the name of Free Enterprise?–an existence which distorts the personality, turns avarice into virtue and permits the strong to run

roughshod over the weak, profiteering on human misery? Can he approve chronic depressions and endless wars? Can he approve racial and religious prejudice?

The young writer of ideas and ideals, I say, must instantly be repelled by the ugly aspects of American society. The history of our literature will bear this out—at a swift glance, I think of Emily Dickinson, Thoreau, Emerson, Hawthorne, Dos Passos, Faulkner, Henry James, Melville and, recently, Norman Mailer. And, being repelled, the writer seeks a substitute, something which offers hope of cure. Today, at first glance, the only alternative seems to be Russian Communism.

To list the important American writers who have turned from American Capitalism to Communism since the latter part of the nineteenth century would take up more space than this article is permitted. Suffice it to say that nearly every naturalistic writer in America has made this turn. Our young writer of intelligence and ideals, then, makes this turn. He embraces Communism of the Russian brand. And, immediately, he begins to feel uncomfortable.

For he discovers, in the folds of Russian Communism, the evils of dictatorship. He learns about purge trials; and is handed fantastic lies, which insult his intelligence, to justify them. He learns of the stifling of literature, art and music in the Soviet Union. He learns that Hitler is one day evil, the next day (following a pact with the Soviet Union) good, and the next day evil again. He discovers that Roosevelt is today a warmonger, tomorrow a true democrat and peoples' friend, whose "grand design" the Communist Party, U. S. A., seeks only to imitate. He learns that Tito, only yesterday a Communist hero only a little lower than Stalin, has in reality been a spy and a Fascist since 1936. He learns that a book which is "good" today becomes "bad," "bourgeois" and "decadent" tomorrow when the Party Line changes.

In panic does our idealistic and intelligent writer flee from alliance with the Communist Party. And at this point, the advantage of the Negro writer is discovered. For, having become disillusioned with the Soviet dictatorship, where does the white writer turn for political truth? Back to Capitalism, in ninety-nine out of a hundred cases; back to the very decaying system which lately he had left, a system he now calls "Democracy," "Freedom" and "Western Culture." He repeats the performance of John Dos Passos and, more recently and more strikingly (though in another field) Henry Wallace. The things he formerly found unbearable in Capitalism—he now ignores. Prejudice, depressions, imperialism, political chicanery, support of dictators, dog-eat-dog, strong-kill-the-weak philosophy—these things no longer exist. Black becomes white again. And the creative artist is dead! For he is blind.

The Negro writer, too, makes this retreat from Communism—for he, too, is opposed to lies, deceit, dictatorship and the other evils of the Soviet regime. But—and this is the significant point—the Negro writer does not, in most cases, come back to bow at the feet of Capitalism. He cannot, as can the white writer, close his eyes to the evils of the system under which he lives. Seeing the Negro ghetto, feeling the prejudice, his relatives and friends experiencing unemployment, injustice, police brutality, segregation in the South, white supremacy—seeing these things, the Negro writer cannot suddenly kiss the hand which slaps him. Looking at China, at Indo China and at Africa, he cannot avoid the realization that these are people of color, struggling, as he is struggling, for dignity. Again, prejudice has forced him to perceive the real, the ticking world.

Denied many freedoms, robbed of many rights, the Negro—and the Negro writer—rejects those aspects of both American Capitalism and Russian Communism which trample on freedoms and rights. Repelled now by both contending systems, the Negro writer of strength and courage stands firmly as a champion of the basic human issues—dignity, relative security, freedom and the end of savagery between one human being and another. And in this stand he is supported by the mass of human beings the world over.

So add it up. The handicaps are great. Many Negro writers—the majority, I should say, so far—have been unable to overcome them. The work of others is impaired by them. But if the handicaps can be overcome, the advantages remain. And, as I said before, they are great advantages. Because I believe that an increasing number of Negro writers will be able to overcome the disadvantages inherent in their social situation, I predict that a disproportionate percentage of the outstanding writers of the next decade will be Negroes.

Negro Publications and the Writer
Era Bell Thompson

As soon as my berth was made up, I asked the porter for a table. The look of surprise turned into a big proud grin as I opened my typewriter case and went to work. I had noticed how carefully he had handled the machine the night before, how he had said a little louder than necessary, "Do you want your typewriter with you, Miss?"

Busy as I was with my notes, I could not help noticing the interest I was attracting. Hardly a passenger or trainman passed who did not stare at the spectacle of a Negro girl who could not only read reading, but type writing. One or two stopped to satisfy their curiosity, others sent the porter, a more than willing emissary.

"Got everything you need?" he began, solicitously. I had. "Got a lot of work there," he ventured, coming closer. Then, "What kind of work do you do, if I may be so bold?"

"I write for a magazine," I told him.

"Oh! You are that lady who writes! I've heard about you." He reared back, his eyes twinkling. He raised his voice so that the white passengers could hear. "Well, well! What do you know about that! I've already had on my train the beautiful movie star, Lena Horne, the great Negro educator, Mrs. Bethune, the come-upper Mae West, and now I've got you. Yes, sir, I've done carried all the notorious women!"

That was a great day for the Negro in journalism, the day he reached professional status among his own people—with or without notoriety (and I do not know how Mae West got into the act), for on that day a porter gave notice to the world that we, too, have correspondents hopping trains and pounding typewriters; that our magazines and newspapers are now to be reckoned with, no longer ridiculed.

Merchandisers, already vying for the newly discovered Negro buying market, were made even more aware of black dollar potentialities when the colored Associated Publishers, Inc., (seventeen of their twenty-four papers are members of the Audit Bureau of Circulations) acquainted them with the power of the Negro press during last year's American Manufacturer's Association meeting at the Waldorf Astoria. A tape recording told the story of fourteen million Americans with an eleven billion dollar annual income–an untapped market right at their own doorstep which requires no foreign language, no special package labeling, and which annually buys more than the total value of United States domestic exports below the Rio Grande.

Such demonstrations plus intensive campaigns by individual publishers have resulted in increased national advertising which, in turn, has raised our periodicals out of mediocrity and given them a scope and status never before attained. No longer dependent solely upon subscriptions, political handouts and the meager income derived from advertising cheap and questionable products, the Negro press for the first time has the wherewithal to improve itself. National advertising enables it to compete with established newspapers and magazines which have heretofore included Negro readership in with their total circulation count, but made no effort to recognize its vast buying importance.

By the same token the Negro press is also competing with the white press for Negro stories. Seldom does a month go by that some white publication does not carry an article or picture spread extolling the achievements of a darker brother. On the other hand, stories (especially technical and scientific) that appear in Negro publications require the same painstaking preparations given to stories for white publications. So when a white organization, institution or agency tells a Negro editor that his coverage of its activity was better than that of any other publication, that editor knows that although his is a specialized press, aimed at the Negro millions, the quality of his work is no longer measured by a separate rule.

This has resulted in better layout, better printing and greatly improved pictures as well as larger staffs. It spells less sensationalism and race-baiting, more features and fiction. Even humor is finding its rightful place in the pages of the Negro press.

What does all this mean to the Negro writer? It means more markets and also greater competition. It means better training and consequently higher salary. Within the Negro field

alone, there are some two hundred weeklies, a daily, several scholarly and specialized periodicals, three major picture magazines, one digest, a comic, and now a slick confession magazine–all kinds of markets for all kinds of writing.

Both the *Afro-American* and the *Courier* have large magazine sections, and a few of the other weeklies use short stories. The Negro angle is desirable, say most editors of the emancipated Negro press, but they warn against belaboring the subject. Pay among the best of these markets compares favorably with that of white publications. Journalism classes and writers' magazines regularly canvass the Negro field for their literary needs. The Negro press today represents a four million dollar investment, boasts of a two million circulation. But the Negro writer need not stop there.

White journalism has always been open to the Negro, but never to the extent that it is today. Negro and white Abolitionists worked side by side on propaganda journals before the Civil War, and as early as the 1880's Thomas Fortune, founder of the New York *Age,* became assistant editor of the New York *Evening Sun.* During the same period, John S. Durham was a member of the staff of the Philadelphia *Evening Bulletin.* Both Lester A. Walton and Eugene Gordon worked on large Eastern dailies. Charles W. Chesnutt's short stories began to appear in the *Atlantic Monthly* in 1887, but it was a decade and a half later before readers discovered his racial identity. For many years the renowned poet and anthologist William Stanley Braithwaite was a critic for the Boston *Evening Transcript,* interviewing every foremost contemporary British poet who visited America and every foremost American poet.

Today it is quite common in the North for the larger white dailies to employ a Negro reporter and even some of the more liberal Southern papers are following suit. Top white magazines have been more reluctant to accept Ne-

groes on their staffs–or perhaps qualified Negroes have not applied. As far as we know, Earl Brown of *Life* is the only Negro writer on the staff of a leading white magazine. E. Simms Campbell has been one of *Esquire's* most celebrated cartoonists for a good many years, and photographer Gordon Parks is a regular member of the lens crew at *Life.* Walter White broke ground for syndicated columns.

How many other Negroes are similarly employed, or that make their cake and Cadillac money free lancing for the pulps, we do not know. White editors are not as interested, it would seem, in the color of the author as they are in the quality of his work. It is no longer unusual to see the byline of a Negro on a story or article in a white magazine.

Opportunity for Negro writers is here, but far too few are ready. Too few have bothered to prepare themselves for such openings when they do occur. Like the ministry, which is finding less room for the untutored Man of God whose only qualification is his "call" to preach, journalism is also no place for those with only the "urge" to write.

Judging from the unsolicited manuscripts that pass over the desk of the Negro editor, the rate of illiteracy is nearly as high as the number of would-be lions of literature. Second to inability to write correct and effective English is an unwillingness to think in terms other than The Problem. And high on the list are a lack of literary imagination and a sense of humor.

Schools of journalism and special courses in writing are accessible to most potential writers. Certain fellowships and grants are available to those with talent.

Negro journalism has at last come of age. Current opportunities for the Negro writer are more than good and the future holds for those who qualify even greater success–if not downright notoriety.

Some Practical Observations: A Colloquy

Langston Hughes and the Editors

Editors: Mr. Hughes, very few Negro writers in America have chosen, or have felt themselves able to choose, writing as their sole occupation as you have. What has being a Negro meant for you as a writer?

Hughes: Well, for one thing, I think it's pretty obvious that the bulk of my work stems directly from the life of the Negro in America. Since the major aims of my work have been to interpret and comment upon Negro life, and its relations to the problems of Democracy, a major satisfaction for me has been the assurance given me by my readers that I have succeeded in some measure—especially in those areas lightly touched upon, if at all, by the writers who preceded me.

Editors: You certainly must have been asked this next question before: From this vantage point, and as one of the major figures in the "Negro Renaissance," what would you say as to the value of the "Renaissance"? Is there any real truth in the suggestion advanced by some that the "Renaissance" was in certain respects actually a harmful thing for the Negro writer?

Hughes: My feeling would be that the "Renaissance" represented a positive value mainly. It certainly helped a great deal by focusing attention on Negro writers and on literature about Negroes for some six or eight years. It provided a springboard for young Negro writers and for those who wanted to write about Negroes. That impetus in many cases has continued into the present.

Now there may have been certain false values which tended at the time to be over-stressed—perhaps the primitivism and that business of the "color" of Negro life was overdone. But that kind of exaggeration is inevitable, and I doubt that any real harm was done. Those of us who were serious about writing weren't actually affected very much. We knew what we were doing and what we wanted to do. So we went ahead with our work, and whatever false emphasis there was didn't really disturb us.

Editors: You have behind you well over two decades of varied and substantial achievement. How would you say the general situation has

changed for the Negro author in America since you began writing?

Hughes: Oh, in several ways, but the most striking change I would say has occurred in the magazine world. In the past twenty years–and in the case of some publications, in the past five years or so–the field of magazine writing has opened up considerably. For instance, when I first started writing, it was said that the *Saturday Evening Post* would not accept work written by Negroes. Whether or not the *Post* actually followed such a policy, it did seem to be true of certain other magazines. Yet in recent years the *Post* has run pieces by Zora Neale Hurston and Walter White, as well as some of my own work; and in many major magazines articles and stories which take something other than the Octavus Roy Cohen line now appear frequently.

Editors: Would you say that this is one of the gains which may in part be attributed to the "Renaissance"?

Hughes: I think so—though, of course, there are other factors in the picture, including two which I think are often overlooked in accounting for the increased activity among Negro writers and the widening audience to which these writers may address themselves. But it can hardly be disputed that the "Renaissance" did a great deal to make possible a public willing to accept Negro problems and Negro art.

Editors: You spoke just now of two factors which tend to be overlooked. What are they?

Hughes: The first of these is the international fame which Negroes in fields other than literature have won in the last fifteen years or so. The world renown won by such diverse figures as Joe Louis, Marian Anderson, Duke Ellington, and Ralph Bunche has created greater interest abroad in the American Negro. I think this has helped to bring about the present situation in which we find books by Negro writers in this country being translated into other languages and reaching an international audience.

Another factor which will, I believe, become increasingly important is the growth in the number of good Negro bookshops and efficient book-

sellers. Negroes operate at least four first-rate bookstores in New York; there is at least one such bookstore in Atlanta run by Negroes, and this is true of other cities. This, in my opinion, is one of the healthiest developments which could have occurred for the Negro writer and for the Negro reading public.

Editors: We are inclined to agree with you on that–though as difficult to analyze statistically as the influence of the labor and liberal movements in this country–the factors you cite must undoubtedly be recognized as gains for the Negro writer. Granted these and other gains and the access to a wider reading public, in which literary areas would you say Negroes have done the best work in recent years?

Hughes: In the novel and in poetry, I should think. We've had Wright, and Motley, and Ann Petry, and Yerby in the novel. And in addition to the older poets still writing there is a promising group coming along in Bruce McWright, Myron O'Higgins, Margaret Walker, and M. Carl Holman. And, of course, Gwendolyn Brooks, the Pulitzer poet. But here I'm thinking mainly of poets who haven't yet published books. There are three or four good young poets in this category, like Russell Atkins, whose work appeared in *The Poetry of the Negro.*

And in fiction, among those who haven't yet brought out books, there is a really significant talent in Ralph Ellison.

Editors: What about the theatre? You probably have done as much in the theatre as any other contemporary Negro writer. Why haven't there been more plays by Negro authors?

Hughes: We've had some plays, of course. There's Theodore Ward, whom you know of–though he hasn't had any real "success" yet. And George Norford, who had a comedy done by the Group Theatre last year. We haven't made too much progress as writers in the theatre–mainly because it's pretty hard to have professional contacts. Such contacts are indispensable to success in modern playwriting and it's difficult to make headway when the opportunities for achieving the contacts are so limited.

Editors: The lag then, if we may call it that, in playwriting seems due to this difficulty in getting "inside"–a problem which does not seem to be restricted to Negro playwrights alone. The difference may be one of degree.

But are there any other points at which the Negro writer seems not to be making any significant contribution?

Hughes: Well, let me put it this way: it seems to me that there is a crying need for good literary criticism. I can't give the reasons for it, but our great deficiency is this dearth of really good critics. We have almost no books of literary criticism–certainly not recent, competently-done books.

And it's not just literary essays, and books of criticism which are lacking. There is a need for good journalistic articles and for non-fiction works in many fields. In history and in sociology the record is better than elsewhere. Frazier, John Hope Franklin, Cayton, Drake, and others, have done fine work here. I hope to see more good writing in these and other fields.

Editors: The almost inevitable question in any discussion of this kind makes its appearance now: Are there any special problems which face the Negro writer here in America which the white writer is not likely to encounter?

Hughes: I think so. It's pretty clear by now, for example, that the Negro writer has to work especially hard to avoid the appearance of propaganda. Then there is the hypersensitivity arising from the Negro's situation in this country which causes him to take offense at certain realistic portrayals of Negro life.

Editors: There are those problems arising from his materials and his audience, then. But what of marketing problems? It has been suggested, for example, that Negro authors sometimes meet with special difficulties in selling manuscripts. It has even been charged that publishers have insisted on editing of the kind which was, in effect, censorship based on prejudice, or on the willingness to kowtow to the prejudiced reader in the interest of sales.

Hughes: That the Negro writer marketing the fruits of his talent meets with problems which the white writer does not face, I would agree. I would not agree that the field of book publishing is actually involved. Other experienced Negro writers would testify, I believe, that when a writer has done a good book, the publisher usually tends not to alter or limit it in any way–and certainly not with racial considerations in mind.

Editors: If the book publishers deserve a clean bill of health, then where does the Negro writer meet with his "special problems"?

Hughes: The real limitations are in the "tributary" fields where race is definitely a handicapping factor. Hollywood is the Number One example of this, using practically no Negroes as writers. Radio also is a very limited field for the au-

thor who happens to be a Negro. Television, while newer, seems no more likely to be hospitable to Negro writers.

All this means, of course, that unless he is fortunate enough to produce best-sellers the Negro who wishes to write must usually supplement his writing by some occupation which is generally not very closely related to writing. If Negro publications could be, or would be, more generous in the fees paid (or which they should pay) Negro writers, there would be an improvement in the quality of these publications and more Negro writers would be able to earn a living from writing, rather than from teaching and other activities. Failing that, the Negro writer turns in vain to the editorial staffs of other American magazines and of publishing houses. These almost never hire Negroes. Negro book reviewers—even for such publications as the *Times,* the *Herald-Tribune,* and the *Saturday Review of Literature*—are limited by the fact that they are usually given only books about Negroes or by Negroes to review.

Another important source of income for most authors—that of lecturing—is severely limited if the author happens to be a Negro. Only the most liberal women's clubs care to have Negro lecturers—so about seventy-five or eighty percent of this field is closed. And you can count on your hands the white colleges in the southern and border states of this country which will invite Negroes to lecture.

Editors: What you have just said is good strong medicine. And it is certainly not with any desire to palliate it that we pose our final question: As you consider the Negro writer in the field of contemporary letters, what do you find most heartening?

Hughes: There are, as I think I have indicated by some of the things I said earlier, many encouraging aspects which were not present twenty, or ten, or even five years ago. The most heartening thing for me, however, is to see Negroes writing works in the general American field, rather than dwelling on Negro themes solely. Good writing can be done on almost any theme—and I have been pleased to see Motley, Yerby, Petry and Dorothy West presenting in their various ways non-Negro subjects. Dunbar, of course, and others, wrote so-called "white" stories, but until this particular period there have not been so many Negroes writing of characters not drawn from their own race.

Edna Ferber originally wrote stories of Jewish life, but she broadened her perspective and went on to write *So Big, Show Boat* and *Cimarron.* I think we are headed in the direction of similar and perhaps superior achievement.

Poets Who Are Negroes
Gwendolyn Brooks

The Negro poet has impressive advantages. Ready-made subjects—which he may twist as he wills. Great drives. And that inspiriting emotion, like tied hysteria, found only in the general territory of great drives.

Many a Gentile poet, longing for a moving, authoritative and humane subject, longing almost for major indignities because he knows that such make the pen run wild, longing to be "carried away," envies him these.

In the very heart of the superiorities, however, there is a crouching danger. The temptation, sometimes encouraged by ignorance but more often by laziness, to let the mere fact of lofty subject, great drive and high emotion suffice; to present them as such fact as requires no embellishment, no interpretation, no subtlety.

It is like throwing dough to the not-so-hungry mob. The mob will look, may handle, but cannot be expected to eat. Although your product be made of ever so sincere a wheat.

You have got to cook that dough, alter it, until it is unrecognizable. Then the mob will not know it is accepting something that will be good for it. Then it will eat, enjoy, and prosper.

Every Negro poet has "something to say." Simply because he is a Negro; he cannot escape having important things to say. His mere body, for that matter, is an eloquence. His quiet walk down the street is a speech to the people. Is a rebuke, is a plea, is a school.

But no real artist is going to be content with offering raw materials. The Negro poet's most urgent duty, at present, is to polish his technique, his way of presenting his truths and his beauties, that these may be more insinuating, and, therefore, more overwhelming.

Toward Unfettered Creativity: A Note on the Negro Novelist's Coming of Age

Thomas D. Jarrett

In *Annie Allen,* the 1949 Pulitzer prize-winning volume of poetry, Gwendolyn Brooks aptly writes, "People like definite decisions,/Tidy answers, all the little ravelings/Snipped off, the lint removed, they/Hop happily among their roughs. . . ." So it is, I believe, with the recent approach of some Negro critics who, in their attempt to find neat and glowing answers to questions about the present status of Negro fiction, have given considerable notice to the Negro novelist's having come of age. However, if we are to render a fair judgment of the fiction that has been produced by Negroes since 1938, and more especially of that which has been written recently, one candid observation, I believe, should be made at the very outset–too much has been said about the Negro novelist's having come of age rather than about what is still required of him before he can attain maturity in the realm of fiction writing. This point, I believe, demands emphasis, for to date he has not arrived. There are indications that he will arrive in the not too distant future.

Today it is true that the expression "Negro literature" finds less acceptance among intellectual circles than ever before and that the Negro novelist, writing for both whites and Negroes, is realizing more and more that these two audiences are in actuality one. Further, it is true that some Negro writers have concerned themselves with themes that have not required the use of Negro characters in dominant roles and that such themes have attracted the eye of Hollywood. But none of these achievements, noteworthy though they may be, singly and jointly, signal the writer's having come of age. The works of Negro writers, viewed as a whole, are still too narrow in scope; racial hypersensitivity is still too prevalent, as is attested, for example, in Willard Savoy's *Alien Land* (1949), where, because of this, the latter part of the novel becomes an article on "passing;" in J. Saunders Redding's *Stranger and Alone* (1950), about which one critic has recently noted, convincing character portrayal is sacrificed for a "not too

fictional essay on the iniquities and inanities of Negro higher education;" and in Chester Himes' *Lonely Crusade* (1947), an inconsequential account of violence, in which hypersensitivity precludes an artistic presentation of subject matter.

The novels cited above are not unique examples of hypersensitivity and didacticism as practiced by Negro fictionists; others could be cited. Outside the realm of fiction by Negroes, works like Faulkner's *Intruder in the Dust* (1949) (a weakling among his many works that evince artistic strength) and Mrs. Cid Ricketts Sumner's *But the Morning Will Come* (1949) exhibit similar defects and lose much of their effectiveness, well-meaning though they may be, because preachment has subdued artistry. But the point that I especially wish to underscore is this–a deliberate implantation of the didactic element in one's work decreases its effectiveness as a work of art. The fictionist is concerned with truth, as he sees it; but that truth exhibited through the emotions and thoughts of the characters, must be controlled and molded by an artistic process which dismisses, I believe, a computed didacticism. Here, to borrow a phrase from Henry Seidel Canby, many novels by Negroes are still too "fat where they ought to be thin."

From what I have said, I do not mean to imply that the Negro writer should discard his race consciousness; that he cannot easily do. Nor is there the suggestion that he should no longer write about Negroes or about racial problems. As the editors of *Negro Caravan* have put it, "Negro authors, as they mature, must be allowed the privilege and must assume the responsibility of being the ultimate portrayers of their own." One can but note that there is still urgent need for a good "school" novel about Negroes, and that much remains to be written in the area of the historical novel. As far as I know, Redding's *Stranger and Alone* is the only serious attempt at a "school" novel by a Negro writer. Is it too much to expect that in the near future some talented fictionist will give us a more panoramic picture of the

Negro college and college community, its loves, hopes, teacher-student relationship, its fears and frustrations, and an account of the malignant as well as the wholesome forces operating from without and from within? Can this be done without presenting characters that are almost completely negatively equipped? I believe it can. It is true that Worth Tuttle Hedden's *The Other Room* (1947) goes far in this direction; but, looking in from the outside, her view is too limited, and her narrative lacks plausibility. And it is admitted that Bucklin Moon's adeptly woven mosaic in *Without Magnolias* (1949) of all classes of Negroes in a small college town in Florida is a mark not easily surpassed. Yet, one might well ask what a Negro writer, looking from within, might do, if these two writers, who are not Negroes, can go so far.

As regards historical fiction, I believe it is safe to say that the Negro writer's efforts have been feeble. Frank Yerby, undoubtedly a skillful fictionist, made an auspicious entre in *The Foxes of Harrow* (1946), a semi-historical romance; but, exercising his prerogative, he has moved away from the realm of historical fiction and has repeatedly employed a romantic rags-to-riches theme, cemented with triangular romances and bits of historical material. Hollywood has beckoned to him, and he has answered the call. On the other hand, Peter Abrahams (*Wild Conquest,* 1950) and V. S. Reid (*New Day,* 1950) have already demonstrated that they can handle historical material with considerable adeptness; they might well become our first novelists in that area. Given an interest, the writer has at his disposition a wealth of material. The story of the free Negro before and after the Civil War–his relationship with slaves, poor whites, and the planter; his efforts to establish educational institutions for his people–these and other phases of his total story still have not been fully unraveled, although Howard Fast has demonstrated in *Freedom Road* (1944) what can be done with such material. A few free Negroes, fast passing, still remain uninterviewed. The scholarly studies of the free Negro by John Hope Franklin, the late Luther Jackson, and Alrutheus Taylor, for example, are still untapped. And the fictional account of Negro men of stature against the background of their time is still to be written (witness Howard Fast's *Citizen Tom Paine* [1943]). Is it a fancy of the imagination to envision a novel about Frederick Douglass, for example, which would give us the story of the real Douglass, vibrant and colorful, living in a genu-

ine world of his milieu? The material is available. Only the shaper is needed.

More and more, it seems to me, no matter what the subject is, it cannot be gainsaid that before Negro fiction attains full maturity there must be a growing social consciousness and a universality in the treatment of themes; and, concomitantly, there must be a higher regard for literary values if works that are meaningful and vital and of the first order are to be produced.

It may be argued that no writer ever achieves complete objectivity, and that psychological barriers, which need no enumeration here, preclude the Negro writer's attaining an objectivity which other writers might well reach. Certainly this is a limiting factor. However, some Negro writers, still few in number, are breaking down the barrier, and are achieving more and more a catholicity in treatment of themes. In *Native Son* (1940) Richard Wright makes it clear that Bigger Thomas is a Negro, but he makes it equally as clear that he could be "white." His experiences might well have been those of a white youth in the ghettoes of Chicago. The struggle of Lutie Johnson for a better way of life for herself and her son in Ann Petry's *The Street* (1946), despite what would seem to be occasional excessive sermonizing on the plight of Negroes, has undeniable universal appeal. In *Knock on Any Door* (1947), a work in which Willard Motley evinces a superb handling of sustained and meaningful imagery, Nick Romano, a victim of the ulcerous maladies of the city and the slums, might well have been a Negro, although for Motley's purposes he is Italian. William Demby, although lacking maturity in craftsmanship in *Beetlecreek* (1950), is concerned with the "Negro problem" only in a secondary sense; yet one of his main characters is a Negro. He is interested in characters as human beings and, more important, in the barriers that separate human beings. And the struggle between the Boers and the Matabeles in Peter Abrahams's *Wild Conquest* is not conveniently delineated so that the writer might sermonize on race prejudice, et cetera, but rather on the hatred that engulfs the world and the inefficacy of violence in solving problems. Through a balanced portraiture of Boer and Matabele, with their hatreds and friendships, and, above all, through the presentation of positive, believable characters, the author mourns the darkness that covers the earth and records the need of a "one world" outlook. Thus, these novelists, I maintain, writing with craftsmanship and creativity, and employing the

materials that they know best, whether they deal with "white" or "Negro" themes, are tipping the scales away from a kind of "chip-on-the-shoulder" writing, still prevalent, which often offers no answer to anything; but rather, as one Negro critic has well said, in treating the "world I never made" simply concern themselves with the "anatomy of disaster."

It is not enough, then, for the Negro writer to talk barrenly about prejudices and hatred and what is right and wrong in the world. He must, if he chooses to deal with such subjects, evince literary merit. Sounder literary values are needed for full maturity. As he takes his pen in hand, he must not only treat subjects that have universal appeal and relevance, but in doing so, in his delineation of situation, he must not allow the "problem" to prohibit or to becloud his presenting characters who act and react as human beings. Witness, for example, Motley's superb presentation of characters in *Knock on Any Door*. In them the reader finds semblances or recordings of his own observations and experience. True there is social preachment, yet Motley does not step out of the book to present it; but rather by means of analogy and artful pictorialization he sets forth his naturalistic social philosophy and expresses his indictment of society. Through well-chosen symbols, which again and again drive home his ideas with the pierce of an arrow, he makes his main character a tragic exemplum of what can happen to an individual through society's neglect and active participation. Art for Motley is personal, to be sure, but it is not mechanical.

In the foregoing paragraphs, it has not been my intention to set down a hard and fast blueprint for the Negro fictionist of our day, for, in essence, I do not believe that there is one. Rather, I have chosen to mention a few things which I believe he must do if he is to mature. And as I have written, I have not been unmindful of the role that the Negro audience must play in the encouragement of unfettered creativity. This ever-increasing audience must read books rather than merely talk about them and must encourage in every possible way artistry in serious fictional writing rather than suggest through its demands and criticisms that the novelist's major criterion for writing should be the pleading of a "cause" in the guise of fiction. This audience must expect and demand the same of Negro novelists as it does of other novelists. If it does, I believe that it will be pleasantly rewarded in the near future.

Of the novels written by Negroes during 1949 and the first five months of 1950, six, I believe, are worthy of consideration: Savoy's *Alien Land*, Demby's *Beetlecreek*, V. S. Reid's *New Day*, Yerby's *Pride's Castle* (1949), Redding's *Stranger and Alone*, and Abrahams's *Wild Conquest*. Four of these six, *Alien Land, Stranger and Alone, Beetlecreek*, and *New Day* are first novels, and this in itself is significant. Three of these six, *Beetlecreek, New Day*, and *Wild Conquest*, treat themes and employ techniques that are almost wholly new in Negro fiction. William Gardner Smith, after a promising first novel, is now ready with *Anger at Innocence*, a study of tenement life in Philadelphia. These facts in themselves, I believe, reveal that Negro novelists, day by day, are evincing greater potentialities, employing new themes and new techniques, and, above all, as Reid and Abrahams especially show, are giving more attention to literary values. Here then, I believe, is considerable indication that new blood is flowing into the literary hearts of Negro writers. Here is promise; we await fulfillment.

Negro Folk Expression

Sterling A. Brown

For a long time Uncle Remus and his Brer Rabbit tales stood for the Negro folk and their lore. One thing made clear by the resurrection of Uncle Remus in Walt Disney's *Song of the South* is the degree to which he belonged to white people rather than to the Negro folk. A striking contrast to the favored house servant is such a folk character as Huddie Ledbetter, better known as Leadbelly, whose knowingness is stark rather than soft, and whose audience (certainly in his formative years) was his own kind of people, not the white quality. The bitter brew that Leadbelly concocted in the levee camps and jooks and prisons differs from the sugary potions that Remus and the other "uncles" dispensed. Both Uncle Remus and Leadbelly portray sides of the Negro folk, but to round out the portraiture Bessie Smith, Josh White, the Gospel Singing Two Keys, and such big old liars as those heard by E. C. L. Adams in the Congaree swamps and by Zora Neale Hurston in Central Florida are also needed. In any consideration of American Negro folk expression it is important to realize that even before Joel Chandler Harris revealed the antics of Brer Rabbit to America, John Henry was swinging his hammer in the Big Bend Tunnel on the C. & O. Road.

There is rich material on hand for a revaluation of the Negro folk. Out of penitentiaries in the deep South, John and Alan Lomax have brought the musical memories of singers with such names as Iron Head, Clear Rock, and Lightning. From what is more truly folk culture these men and others like John Hammond, Willis James, and John Work have brought hidden singers and songs. The Library of Congress Archives of Folk Music are crammed with solid stuff; the large recording companies are following the lead of small companies like Disc, Folkways and Circle in issuing albums of Negro folk music. Ten years after her tragic death in the Delta, Bessie Smith has been honored in a Town Hall Concert (even now I can hear her surprised cry: "Lord, Lord, Lord!"). And in Carnegie Hall Big Bill has sung blues from the sharecropping country, and Josh White has sung both mellow-blues and sardonic

mockery, and Blind Sonny Terry has blown on his wild harmonica the joys of the fox hunt, of a high-balling train, and the wailing fear of a lost wanderer in a southern swamp. Folk singers of the spirituals, unknown yesterday, have their names placarded now; Harlemites pass around the name of Mahalia Jackson as they used to do that of Mamie Smith; and in the Harlem dancehalls where jazz bands "cut" each other on Saturday nights, spiritual singers battle each other on Sundays to cheering crowds. This commercializing will affect the genuineness of the stuff, but it is getting a hearing for folk material. And an audience for the authentic is growing.

All of this is part of the generally awakened interest in American folk culture, indicated by the diligence and popularity of collectors, anthologists, musicologists, and interpreters. Before its demise the WPA Federal Projects laid in a fine backlog of American folkstuff, and World War II, of course, quickened interest in the American past. Though the furore may have something of the faddish about it, American folklore stands to gain more from enthusiasm and careful study than from the earlier disdain and neglect. The Negro creators of an important segment of American folklore should no longer be subjected to the condescension of the "oh so quaint," "so folksy," school. Looking on Negro lore as exotic *curiosa* becomes almost impossible if the body of available material is thoughtfully considered. Outmoded now are those collectors who could or would find only ingratiating aunties and uncles, most of whose lore consisted in telling how good their white folks were.

With the discarding of the old simplifications, the study of the Negro folk becomes complicated. The field of folklore in general is known to be a battle area, and the Negro front is one of the hottest sectors. One sharply contested point is the problem of definition of the folk; another that of origins. Allies are known to have fallen out and skirmished behind the lines over such minor matters as identifying John Hardy with John Henry. But this is not a battle piece. In general the vexed problems of origin are left for oth-

ers, more competent in that area; strict delimitation of the concepts "folk," "folk literature" and "folk music" are not the purpose here. This essay aims instead to tell what the "folk Negro" (as most students understand the term)* has expressed in story and proverb and song. It is well known that folk culture among Negroes is breaking up. Some of the material (in discussing the blues, for instance) has been transplanted in the cities, but, though inexactly folk, it is used because its roots drew first sustenance from the folk culture.

Collectors, both scholarly and amateur, have long paid tribute to the richness of Negro folk expression. Enthusiasts like Roark Bradford and Zora Hurston overpraise Negro folk speech at the expense of the speech of white Americans. According to Bradford, "The most ignorant Negro can get more said with a half-dozen words than the average United States Senator can say in a two-hour speech." But folk should be compared with folk; and considering the speech of white America to be barren and bleak does injustice to a large part of American folklore, to the gusto of the tall tale, for instance. The folk Negro's imaginativeness and pith can easily be recognized; they stand in no need of dubious comparisons.

In Africa the telling of tales is a time honored custom. The slaves brought the custom with them to the New World. According to the latest scholarship of Melville Herskovits, the body of tales they brought has been retained in relatively undisturbed fashion. These tales were not dangerous; they were a way to ease the time; they could entertain the master class, especially the children. So they were not weeded out as were many of the practices of sorcery, or discouraged as were the tribal languages. In the African cycles the heroes were the jackal or fox, the hare, the tortoise, and the spider. The last, a sort of hairy tarantula, is little used in the lore of the southern Negro, but is hero of the Anansi tales of Jamaica. The African fox, more like our jackal, has become the American fox; the African hare, "Cunnie Rabbit," really a chevrotain, water deerlet, or gazelle, has become the American rabbit with the word cunnie Englished into cunning, and the African tortoise has become the American dry-land turtle or terrapin. In America, Brer Terrapin is a hero second only to Brer Rabbit whom he bests occasionally. Of the hero's victims the African hyena has become the American wolf, and the American fox and bear have joined

the losing side. African animals— lions, leopards, tigers, and monkeys—are still in the cast of characters.

Close parallels to American Negro tales have been found extensively in Africa and the Caribbeans. Nevertheless, folklorists are wary of finding Africa the place of ultimate origin of all of the tales. Many of the basic plots are of great age and spread. Oddly enough, the three stories that Joel Chandler Harris considered unquestionably African, namely: "How the Rabbit Makes a Riding-horse of the Fox," "Why the Alligator's Back Is Rough," and "The Tar Baby Story," have close European counterparts, dating back hundreds of years. "The Tar Baby Story" has been traced to India through a study of nearly three hundred versions. According to Stith Thompson, it reached the Negroes and Indians of America by several paths, the main one being "from India to Africa, where it is a favorite and where it received some characteristic modifications before being taken by slaves to America." In the Congo version a jackal is stuck to a tortoise covered with beeswax; among the Pueblo Indians a coyote catches a rabbit with a gum-covered wooden image.

To indicate the problems facing source-hunters, one of the most popular European stories might be considered here. In the Reynard cycle, and reappearing in Grimm's *Fairy Tales*, is the plot of the fox who played godfather in order to sneak away and eat food that he and the bear have stored in common. Asked the name of his godchildren (for he leaves three times) he answers Well Begun, Half Done and Done. Several collectors found the story in South Carolina, with Brer Rabbit cheating Brer Wolf, and the children variously named: "Fus' Beginnin'," "Half-Way" and "Scrapin' de Bottom," or "Buh Start-um," "Buh Half-um" and "Buh Done-Um." Easy attribution to American slaveowners, however, comes up sharp against the numerous African versions in one of which the rabbit fools his working partner, the antelope, with non-existent children named Uncompleted One, Half-completed One, and Completed One.

All of this illustrates the underlying unity of Old World culture. Africa, then, is not the starting place of all the favorite Negro tales, but was a way-station where they had an extended stop-over. The long association with Asiatic Moslems in East Africa and the penetration of European powers into West Africa beginning with the slave trade affected the native tradition of tale tell-

ing. According to Stith Thompson, "The African finds enjoyment in nearly every kind of European folktale. He may do some queer things with them and change them around so that little more than a skeleton of the original remains and so that it takes the expert eye to discover that they are not actually native. On the other hand he may take the tale over completely with all its foreign trappings." Nevertheless Thompson believes that "the great majority of their [African] tales have certainly had their origin on the soil of central or southern Africa." Regardless of original source, whether in Europe or Africa, American Negro fables have been so modified with new beasts and local color added, different themes, and different experiences, that an almost new, certainly a quite different thing results. Such is the way of written literature where authors took "their own where they found it," and such is even more the way of folktales.

"Den Br' Hoss, an' Br' Jack-ass, an' Br' Cow an' all dem, crowd close roun' Br' Dog, for dem was like yard-chillen, dey is peaceable an' sort o' scary. An' all de creeters what stan' up for Br' Gator scatter out wide away from dere, for dem was woods-chillen, rovin' an' wild." Thus, according to a South Carolina tale, started the big row in the world between the tame and the wild creatures that is never going to stop.

This illustrates the process. The basic incident, the war between domestic and wild animals, is widely used in folktales, from the Orient to the Reynard cycle. But the details, the "entrimmins," according to Uncle Remus, the phrases "yard chillen," and "woods chillen," and the naming of their traits, give the flavor of the low country, where Samuel Stoney and Gertrude Shelby heard the above yarn.

Public recognition of the wealth of American Negro stories came in the late eighties with the appearance of Joel Chandler Harris's Uncle Remus Tales. A few animal tales had seen print earlier, but Harris was the first to give a substantial number. Soon he was besieged with correspondents who told him new tales or variants that they had heard from Negroes. Harris deserves the credit of a pioneer. He insisted that he gave the tales "uncooked," but there is too much evidence of his alterations to accept his word. The tales are not genuine folktales, in the sense of by the folk for the folk, for they are told by an old Uncle to entertain Young Marster. In line with literary trends of the time, Harris made them more sentimental and genteel and less racy than the

folk tell them; he gives much about Negro life and character, valuable for purposes of local color but likely to be taken for granted by the folk; and he uses the devices of a skillful short story writer. Simpler and starker tales, with fewer alterations, have been taken from their native habitat by collectors such as C. C. Jones, Jr. (a contemporary of Harris), Ambrose Gonzales, Elsie Clews Parsons, Guy Johnson, and A. W. Eddins. Negro collectors are few and far between; Charles W. Chesnutt fashioned skillful short stories out of folk beliefs in *The Conjure Woman* (1889); and Thomas Talley, pioneer folk-collector, Arthur Huff Fauset, Zora Neale Hurston and J. Mason Brewer have published collections. Stella Brewer Brooks has written the best study of Joel Chandler Harris as folklorist. But educated Negroes by and large have not been greatly interested. From Harris's day to the present, collectors, being of different race or class or both, have been viewed by the folk with natural distrust.

Nevertheless, a considerable number of tales has been recorded. Many are animal tales; of these all are not strictly fables, which convey an ostensible moral, though some are. Whereas the more efficient Fox, crafty and cruel, hypocritical and scheming, amused the European peasantry, the American Negro slave took Brer Rabbit for hero. The harmless scary creature he invested with a second nature, and made him a practical joker with a streak of cruelty, a daring hunter of devilment, a braggart, a pert wit, a glutton, a lady's man, a wily trickster, knowing most of the answers, and retaining of his true characteristics only his speed on the getaway. Animals noted for greater strength and ferocity are his meat. Brer Fox has degenerated from crafty Reynard into something of a fool, though still a worthy opponent, but Brer Wolf and Brer Bear are numskulls. Commentators have long considered these tales of cunning overcoming strength, of the weakling out-smarting the bully, as a compensatory mechanism, a kind of oblique revenge, the wish fulfillment of an ironic people who could see few ways out of oppression. It might be pointed out that none of the hero-animals in Africa are quite so helpless as the American rabbit. It is unlikely that the slaves did not see pertinence to their own experiences in these tales. Outsmarting was one of the few devices left them. So they made heroes out of the physically powerless who by good sense and quick wit overcame animals of brute strength who were not right bright. "You ain't got no cause to be bigger in de body,

but you sho' is got cause to be bigger in de brain."

With his pardonable fondness for the creature, Joel Chandler Harris placed Brer Rabbit in the limelight. He is less focused on in other collections, though still the star performer. The theme of weakness overcoming strength through cunning remains uppermost. Brer Squirrel escapes from Brer Fox by reminding him to say grace; when the fox closes his eyes, the squirrel is treetop high. Brer Goat foils Brer Wolf, never trusting him from that day to this. Brer Rooster outeats Brer Elephant: "it ain't de man wid de bigges' belly what kin eat de longest." Animals and birds of everyday observation swell the company: the officious yard dog, the fierce bulldog, the hound, another fall-guy for the rabbit; the horse, the mule, the jackass, the bull, the stupid ox; the deer, the raccoon, possum and squirrel; the frog, the crawfish, and many kinds of snakes; the turkey buzzard, the partridge, the blue-jay, the marsh-hen; the mosquito, the hornet, the gnat.

Many tales drive home a point about mankind based on the animals' observed traits. The gnat, riding the bull's horn, says: "I gwine now. Ain't you glad you don't have to tote me puntop yo' horn no more?" The bull answers: "I never know when you come, and I ain't gonna miss you when you gone." The possum tells the raccoon that he can't fight because he is ticklish and has to laugh when in the clutch of his enemy, but the raccoon sees through the rationalization. With his belly full, running in the pasture, Brer Mule dreams that his father was a race-horse, but harnessed to a heavy cart and hungry, he recalls that his father was only a jackass. The ox rebukes the axle wheels for groaning; *he* is the one pulling the load, though he refuses to cry out. "Some men holler if briar scratch his foot, and some men lock their jaws if a knife is sticking in their heart."

Ingenious explanations of animal characteristics and behavior occur in many tales. You never see a blue-jay on Friday because that is the day for his weekly trip to hell; the woodpecker's head is red because Noah caught him pecking holes in the ark and whipped his head with a hammer; the possum's tail is bare because, wanting music on the ark, Ham used the hairs to string a banjo; the alligator's mouth is all out of whack because the dog, God's apprentice helper, was either careless or cruel while wielding the knife in the week of creation, making the alligator and dog eternal

foes; the porpoise's tail is set crossways because with his tail straight up and down the porpoise was too fast, he outsped the sun; Sis Nanny Goat, self sacrificing, allowed all of the other animals to get their tails first, hence, "Kind heart give Sis Nanny Goat a short tail"; the wasp is so shortpatienced because he thinks everybody is laughing at his tiny stomach (he can't laugh himself because he would "bust spang in two").

Though performing other functions in the Old World, animal tales are often considered by American Negroes as "stories for the young uns." Animal stories were by no means the only stock, even in slavery. More realistic tales made direct use of unallegorized human experience. In coastal Georgia the folk still remember the tale of the Eboes who, hating slavery, marched singing into the tidal river and were drowned. The name of Ebo's Landing gives historic color to the tradition. The same folk tell also of the magic hoe that worked itself, and of the flying Africans who changed into birds and soared away to their homeland rather than take the overseer's whipping. Modelled on tales in African folklore, in the New World they take on the quality of dreams of escape.

More widespread in Negro folklore are the tales of the trickster Jack or John. In slavery days he outwits not only the devil but Ole Marster, Ole Miss, and the "patterollers." More recently his competitors have been the grasping landlord, the browbeating tough, and the highhanded sheriff, deputy, and policeman. Sometimes Jack, like Brer Rabbit, comes to grief himself, but oftener he outsmarts the opposition or makes his dare and is long gone. Jack schemes to get out of a whipping or to obtain freedom. Sometimes he is in cahoots with a sharp witted master to take advantage of gullible neighbors. Sometimes the repartee is sharp; a master tells that he dreamt of a heaven set aside for Negroes and found it to be run-down and generally messed-up; Jack retorts with his dream of white folk's heaven, all gleaming and glittering, with streets of gold, but without a solitary person in the place! The tellers aim at comedy, often richly satiric; the hardships of slavery are casually mentioned as if taken for granted by teller and audience; but Ole Marster and Ole Miss and the slaves themselves are ribbed with gusto, with toughminded humor. Pretentiousness and boasting ride for a fall; sentimentality is pricked; all the characters, white and black, master and slave, come "under the same gourd-vine," all are "made out of meat."

A favorite object of lampooning, familiar in general folklore, was the old maid, the master's sister. One of the fanciful plots has her turning into a squinch owl, her long-drawn wails voicing her yearning for a husband, but other tales satirize her bossiness and silliness in down-to-earth situations. The Irish were also satirized. Comparative newcomers with their own brogues and dirty jobs, the Irish were characterized as big dunces. Here, of course, the American Negro shares an Anglo-Saxon tradition. The "po' buckra," the "poor white trash," the "cracker," came in for contempt and hostility in Negro tales, but the stories about them were not often funny.

Exaggeration in the hearty tradition of American tall talk is pervasive. In Zora Hurston's recording, mosquitoes sing like alligators, eat up the cow and then ring the bell for the calf. The plague of the boll-weevil is graphically symbolized: "Old Man Boll Weevil whipped little Willie Boll Weevil 'cause he couldn't carry two rows at a time." Land is so rich that the next morning after a mule is buried, "he had done sprouted li'l jackasses"; it is so poor that "it took nine partridges to holler Bob White" or needed "ten sacks of fertilizer before a church congregation could raise a tune on it." A snail is sent for a doctor. After seven years his sick wife hears a scuffling at the door and cries out her relief. The snail says, "Don't try to rush me–ah' ain't gone yet." He had taken all that time to get to the door. Weather is so hot "till two cakes of ice left the icehouse and went down the street and fainted."

Quite common are the "why" stories; jocular explanation of the creation of the world, the position of woman, the origin of the races. One teller informed Zora Hurston: "And dats why de man makes and de woman takes. You men is still braggin' about yo' strength and de women is sitting on de keys [to kitchen, bedroom, and cradle] and lettin' you blow off 'til she git ready to put de bridle on you." But another informant explains why "de sister in black works harder than anybody else in the world. De white man tells de nigger to work and he takes and tells his wife."

Mythological tales explain the origin of the ocean, where the hurricane comes from, why the wind and waters are at war, why the moon's face is smutty. Others enlarge material from the Bible. Ingenuity is especially exercised on filling in gaps in the creation story. Up in heaven a newcomer tells of the havoc of the Johnstown flood to a bored listener who turns out to be Noah. Peter is humanized more than the other apostles: famished, he brings a huge rock to the Lord to turn into bread and is nonplussed when he hears the pronouncement: "And upon this rock will I found my church." Religion is treated freely, even irreverently, but not to the degree of Roark Bradford's *Ol' Man Adam an' His Chillun*, which is synthetic, not genuine folk-stuff.

Tales about the origin of the races leave little room for chauvinism about a chosen people. The slaves knew at first hand that the black man had a hard road to travel and they tell of the mistakes of creation with sardonic fatalism. Uncle Remus tells how all men were once Negroes, "en 'cordin' ter all de counts w'at I years fokes 'uz gittin' long 'bout ez well in dem days as dey is now." One of Zora Hurston's informants told her that "God made de world and de white folks made work." Another said that the Negro outraced the white man and took the larger of two bundles that God had let down in the road. But the smaller bundle had a writing-pen and ink in it, while the larger bundle had a pick and shovel and hoe and plow and cop-axe in it. "So ever since then de nigger been out in de hot sun, usin' his tools and de white man been sittin' up figgerin', ought's a ought, figger's a figger; all for de white man, none for de nigger."

Irony has been in the stories from the earliest recorded versions, but recent collectors have found it less veiled. Zora Huston retells the yarn of the dogs' convention where a law was passed not to run rabbits any more. But Brer Rabbit stayed cautious: "All de dogs ain't been to no convention and anyhow some of dese fool dogs ain't got no better sense than to run all over dat law and break it up. De rabbit didn't go to school much and he didn't learn but three letters and that trust no mistake. Run every time de bush shake." She tells another of the slaves who saved his master's children from drowning. Old Master sets him free. As he walks off, old master calls to him: "John, de children love yuh." . . . "John, I love yuh." . . . "And Missy *like* yuh!" . . . "But 'member, John, youse a nigger." John kept right on stepping to Canada, answering his master "every time he called 'im, but he consumed on with his bag."

The age-old tale of the deceptive bargain gets added point down in the Brazos Bottom. Brer Rabbit, father of a large, hungry family, is sharecropping for Brer Bear who has him in his power. Brer Rabbit is forced to promise Brer

Bear everything that grows above the ground. But that year he planted potatoes. The second year, Brer Bear settles for root crops, but Brer Rabbit planted oats. The third year, Brer Bear claimed both tops and roots, leaving Brer Rabbit only the middles. As a fine climax, Brer Rabbit planted corn. Another old tale of the goose that the fox threatened to kill for swimming on "his" lake, now ends with Sis Goose taking her just cause to court. "When dey got dere, de sheriff, he was a fox, and de judge, he was a fox, and de attorneys, dey was foxes, and all de jurymen, dey was foxes, too. An' dey tried ole sis goose, and dey convicted her an dey executed her, and dey picked her bones."

There is similar edge in numerous jokes about sharecropping and the law. Landlords who "figure with a crooked pencil" are derided. One sharecropper held back a couple of bales from the reckoning. When told, after elaborate figuring, that he had come out even, he expressed his happiness that he could sell his extra bales. The landlord then cursed him to hell and back, telling him that he had to do all that hard figuring over again. When another sharecropper was told that his return was zero after making a bumper crop, he shut up like a clam. The landlord, distrusting his silence, insisted that he tell him what he was thinking. The sharecropper finally said: "I was just thinking, Mister Charlie, that the next time I say 'Giddap' to a mule again, he's gonna be setting on my lap." Yarnspinners weep in mimicry of the landlord who, in the early days of the New Deal, had to give government checks to his tenants, crying: "After all I've done for you, you so ungrateful that you cashed those checks."

Negroes borrow, of course, from the teeming storehouse of American jokes. Jokes about Negroes are of three types. The first includes those told by whites generally to whites (the kind collected by Irvin Cobb, for instance, and the standbys for after-dinner speakers, with such black face minstrelsy props as watermelon, chicken, razors, excessive fright, murder of the English language, etc.). Some of these may be found among Negroes who will belittle their own for a laugh as quickly as any other people will, but they are not the most popular. The white man's mark on a Negro joke often does not help it. A second type is told by Negroes to whites to gain a point. Sometimes verging on sarcasm, they use the license of the court fool. Then there are jokes strictly for a Negro audience, what John Dollard calls "part of the arsenal of reprisal against white people."

Often too, the joke lays bare what the tellers consider a racial weakness and the outsider must not be let into the family secrets, as it were. Sometimes it pleads the racial cause. Jokes ridicule the myth of "separate but equal"; a Negro gets off free in traffic court by telling the judge that he saw whites drive on the green light so he knew the red light was for him. Hat-in-hand Negroes and workers too zealous on the job are satirized. During the war the jokes, or more truly anecdotes, took on a grimmer tone. One folk hero became the soldier who after being badgered on a bus, faced his tormentors and said, "Well, if I am going to die for democracy, I might as well die for some of it down here in Georgia." One repeated line concerned an epitaph: "Here lies a black man killed by a yellow man while fighting to save democracy for the white man." Many of these anecdotes are bitter; some, dealing with sadistic sheriffs and mobs are gruesome; yet they produce laughter, a sort of laughter out of hell. But they are shared by educated as well as uneducated and though passed along by word of mouth, they take us somewhat afield from the folk.

---

*That is, as a rural people, living in a kind of isolation, without easy contact with the outside world. Sometimes they are cut off from progress geographically (especially the sea-islanders or swamp dwellers or the people on black-county plantations). But even rural Negroes with better communication and transportation facilities are socially isolated by segregation and lack of educational and economic advantages. Unlettered, folk Negroes have a local culture transmitted orally rather than by the printed page.

Criticism at Mid-Century
Ulysses Lee

Despite the scarcity of book-length studies in criticism, there exist well formed ways of looking at the Negro literary artist and at the Negro in American literature. Any current survey of the Negro in America, on whatever level, places considerable emphasis upon literary achievement. Thus, the historian, John Hope Franklin, in *From Slavery to Freedom;* the sociologist, E. Franklin Frazier, in *The Negro in America;* and the journalist, Roi Ottley, in *Black Odyssey* all view his literature as an important part of the Negro's American experience. Though the works may be judged in terms of their historical significance, their contribution to the emergence of a group consciousness, or their adaptability to rather racy reportage, the accounts in these three books are in the direct tradition of literary criticism by Negroes. For criticism has generally been a handmaiden of progress, illuminating not the works themselves but the wonder that they exist, analyzing not the problems and methods of the authors but their effect, actual and probable, upon their audiences, always remembered as comprising both Negro and whites.

The function of literature as a means of interpreting Negro life and attitudes has been central in the developing tradition. It has been generally assumed that the Negro author will use his literary gifts to good ends. If his work does not improve race relations, it is assumed that it should not harm them. Thus, Richard Wright's *Native Son* inspired heated editorial and reader discussion in the columns of the Negro press after its publication in 1940. Such discussions can be healthy signs of growing cultural maturity. But these debates were not concerned with *Native Son*'s virtues or deficiencies as a novel nor with the adequacy of its treatment of its themes. They centered about the moral right of the author to risk a reinforcing of objectionable attitudes about Negroes which might do collective harm; the debaters were disturbed that white readers might see in every Negro another Bigger. Similarly, *Black Boy* was looked at askance in some areas not because it was relatively unbelievable as full and frank autobiography but because it paid no homage to the kinder and gentler aspects which have long been believed to be major characteristics of Negro life.

Its critics have rarely had the opportunity to address themselves to the form and substance of the literature of the Negro. They have usually been too busy as teachers and missionaries to do so. They have had to judge the works with which they are concerned less as literature than as new evidence of advance and achievement, to be shared and gloried in by all members of the race. The Negro artist is viewed as a man knocking at the door of American publishing houses, of American magazines, of American homes and minds. The great hope is that there will be ever widening opportunities for the writer to produce in freedom from racial bonds. Arna Bontemps, commenting on Coutee Cullen, lamented that he "died . . . still clinging to a life-long dream of being an American poet, but still denied part of its fulfillment." But, by the time of Cullen's death, Bontemps continued, "there remained little doubt that some of the poets who followed . . . would be free to write as they were inclined to write or as the spirit moved them, not as representatives of any racial group." The new novelists of the Forties–Willard Motley, Ann Petry, and Frank Yerby–"wrote stories about American people who were not Negroes at all." This, Bontemps concluded, was a "natural thing to do," and few people "knew or cared" that these authors were Negroes.

It is not necessary to discuss either the validity or the accuracy of this point of view to discover within it a major motivation for both the creative artist and the critic who, as in Bontemp's case, are often one and the same person. There is one great difference between minorities in the United States and in most of the rest of the world. In America minorities wish to identify as closely as possible with the goals and concepts of the majority. They wish acceptance and participation in the larger culture on the egalitarian terms underlying the national political and cultural credo. They wish, like Edward Bok, to become "American." They may wish to preserve some part of a minority heritage but they wish this to be looked upon by the rest of the country as a val-

ued contribution to the diversity of American life and not as a mark of shame setting them apart from the mainstream. Elsewhere, and especially in Europe, minorities are separatist. They wish to preserve a national or ethnic culture, with its own language, customs, and, at times, its own political and economic institutions. Negro Americans have been tempted by both types of thinking but, by and large, their aims have been similar to those of other American minorities, except in cases where the apparent hopelessness of achieving the stated goal has forced support for movements for a forty-ninth all-Negro state, for a mass exodus back to Africa, or for an infinite variety of economic, social, or cultural separatist panaceas.

The arts and the artists have been viewed generally as ambassadors of good will. The artist is not only interpreter of one people to another through universal media. He is also a prime exhibit of achievement and of racial potentialities. Twenty-five years ago the terms "New Negro" and "Negro Renaissance" gained wide currency not only because they were conveniently descriptive of the post-World War I ferment with its element of wonder but also because it was important that Americans of the day know that here were Negro artists in larger numbers than before writing plays, novels, and poems, exploiting the materials of their racial heritage just like the white writers of the period. The terms were popularized and given permanence by the critics and by the two great magazines of the day, *Opportunity* and *The Crisis*. How much of the ferment itself was permanent and how much was passing fad was cause for concern by the end of the decade. Sterling Brown, in one of his earlier pieces for *Opportunity* in the series "The Literary Scene: Chronicle and Comment"—a series which was to continue through the Thirties but with lamentably lessening frequency in its later years—predicted from an examination of current publishers' announcements that the many new books promised for 1931 represented a "ballast" preventing the "valuable interest" in Negroes from "flying off on the winds of faddistic caprice." The lists were dominated by sociological and economic titles—Spero and Harris, and Woodson and Greene on Negro labor; T. J. Woofter's and Guy Johnson's studies of St. Helena Island; Charles S. Johnson on the Negro in American civilization; and Louise Kennedy on the migration were all announced for 1931. Two months after Brown's comment, Alain Locke, writing his retrospective

review for the year 1930, attempted to give the "much exploited Negro renaissance," of which he had been a main interpreter, a decent burial along with the "period of inflation and overproduction" of which he then thought the Renaissance a product. "Has the afflatus of Negro self-expression died down?" he asked. "Are we outliving the Negro fad? Has the Negro creative artist wandered into the ambush of the professional exploiters?" These were major questions which were to be asked several times over in the next twenty years.

*   *   *

Through the Thirties and into the Forties there were three critics whose ideas on literature were dominant. These were Benjamin Brawley, Alain Locke, and Sterling Brown. W. E. B. DuBois, as editor of *The Crisis*, had made his critical views known in reviews, in his columns of "Opinion," and in his editorials. In his books and in separate essays he had evaluated literature by and about Negroes. But, like William Stanley Braithwaite, whose twenty-five anthologies of verse and volumes of critical essays had been appearing since 1906, and James Weldon Johnson, whose introduction to the *Book of American Negro Poetry* in 1922 had provided a rationale of the Negro's creative genius leading directly into some of the ideas central to the Renaissance, DuBois after 1931 expressed himself on literary problems only in a manner incidental to his wider interests. Brawley, Locke, and Brown, however, gave the bulk of their attention to literature and to the allied arts.

Benjamin Brawley, in 1910, published in Atlanta a sixty-page booklet with the title *The Negro in Literature and Art*. This booklet, little more than a segregating of biographical and bibliographical material about Negro writers and artists away from the then popular general biographical surveys of Negroes who had "achieved," answered a definite need. The edition was soon exhausted. In 1913, the booklet became, in somewhat altered form, the last chapter in his *A Short History of the American Negro*. In 1918 it became the basis, again altered, of a larger and separate work, *The Negro in Literature and Art in the United States*, in which the author undertook "to treat somewhat more thoroughly than has ever before been attempted the achievement of the Negro in the United States along literary and artistic lines judging by absolute rather than by partial or limited standards." The key word here was "achieve-

ment" and not standards. It was not that Brawley did not have standards. It was rather that his were those of nineteenth century English criticism; too rigid application of these standards would have dulled the "achievement" which he was anxious to demonstrate. His critical standards are more readily apparent in his *New Survey of English Literature,* intended as a classroom text, or in his contributions to *The Home Mission College Review,* which he edited for its full career from 1927 to 1930. There he wrote on English hymns, on Richard Le Gallienne and the "tradition of beauty," on *The Ancient Mariner* as mystical allegory, and on Thomas Noon Talfourd. In his journal he inveighed against the quality of language instruction in high schools while, as editor, he welcomed to his review's pages papers on the value of Greek literature to the ministry and on Carlyle. The Renaissance, in the meantime, was at its height, but Brawley's journal, edited from Raleigh, showed little awareness of it, though it did publish Montgomery Gregory's observations on its course. Gregory pointed out that even in 1928, which Locke was to call the flood-tide year of the Renaissance, "transmutation of our race life into works of artistic beauty" was mainly in the hands of "white alchemists" who, from Harris and his Uncle Remus stories to E. C. L. Adams, Julia Peterkin, DuBose Heyward, and Paul Green had exploited Negro materials while Negroes themselves looked on. "Practically the Negro's only representatives in this forward movement," he wrote, "are a very small group of youthful pioneers centered in the North, in New York City, to be precise. Only a few faint echoes are heard elsewhere in the land. All hail to Countee Cullen and Langston Hughes! But where are their comrades?"

Brawley, while he had no great enthusiasm for what he called the Harlem "obsession" of the writers of the Renaissance, continued to chronicle their works in successive revisions of his books. His two revisions of the Twenties added new bibliographical materials, a new chapter in which James Weldon Johnson was added to his list of "representative writers," and appendices consisting of articles which had appeared in magazines. In the meantime, his conviction, expressed in the 1918 edition, that "every race has its peculiar genius, and that, so far as we can at present judge, the Negro, with all his manual labor, is destined to reach his greatest heights in the field of the artistic" deepened. In his 1929 revision he noted that the main emphasis of his volume had

shifted from "the Art" to "the Literature." In his final revision, published in 1937, he emphasized the notion of a peculiar racial genius, titling the book *The Negro Genius.*

The canvas on which Brawley worked was large. It grew larger through the years as new writers and artists and, finally, architects came to join his procession. As a result, he found little room for the expression of purely critical opinion and that which he expressed seldom changed through the years. Of Chesnutt in the 1918 edition he said, for example, "Mr. Chesnutt writes in simple, clear English, and his methods might well be studied by younger writers who desire to treat, in the guise of fiction, the many searching questions that one meets today in the life of the South." Eleven years and two editions later, he had merely added that Chesnutt, in the meantime, had won a Spingarn award.

Although he remained aloof from the ferment of the Renaissance, it must not be thought that Brawley lacked influence as a critic. His books remained standard. He organized well his information about writers and the opinions that he expressed as critic, while not always representing deep and penetrating analysis, were designed to increase respect for and the audience for the creative work of Negroes. He approached Negro writing as a duty—a duty of the teacher and inspirer of youth. Thus his biography of Dunbar, published in 1936, was more pleasantly sentimental and reminiscent than critical or analytical. In his work he omitted largely the contributions of white authors to the literature of the Negro; while he was not a racial chauvinist, as his companion work in Negro history shows, literature by white authors was outside the scope of his demonstration of Negro achievement. Moreover he may have doubted the ability of white authors to write accurately and justly of the Negro, for he once wrote of the Negro: "The more we think we know him the more unfathomable he is."

The growing New York group of writers of the Twenties had both a critical interpreter in Alain Locke and journals for their earlier productions in *The Crisis,* still edited at the time by W. E. B. DuBois, and *Opportunity,* edited by Charles S. Johnson and, later, by Elmer Carter. Both journals were almost competitively aware of the changes which they were promoting between covers more normally devoted to social chronicle and investigation. *Opportunity* was especially anxious to develop not only creative writers but also a strong critical tradition. In an editor's note to

Eugene Holmes' short study of Jean Toomer in 1932, Elmer Carter declared: "The development of a body of critical opinion within the Negro group must accompany his advance in literature." *Opportunity* has now gone from the scene and *The Crisis* is now but a shadow of her former robust self. But a great many of the writers whom they served to introduce are now, twenty to thirty years later, the major figures of Negro literary expression. Through the Thirties and most of the Forties they were the main vehicles for serious literary criticism as well.

Alain Locke began his continuing career as assessor of the Negro literary and artistic scene with his special issue of the *Survey Graphic* in 1925 and his *The New Negro* which grew out of it. Both of them were central to the recognition that something really was happening in Harlem. Locke had written earlier papers for *Opportunity* and *The Crisis* on the younger literary movement but, after 1925, he became a prolific explorer of the current literature of the Negro and of its potentialities. From 1929 on, until the death of the magazine, he contributed an annual "retrospective review" to *Opportunity,* surveying and attempting to find a unity in the year's literature. He missed but one year; after the passing of *Opportunity* his annual reviews were transferred to PHYLON. The bulk of literature has increased so since he began that his reviews must now be published in two installments.

Through the years Locke's wonder at the acquisition of new themes by Negro writers has not been discarded from his critical credo, though it must be something of a chore to find a slightly new and challenging angle around which to chart a unifying theme in each annual review. Actually the themes have not changed very much. In his 1927 introduction to "Four Negro Poets" in the Simon and Schuster series of "Pamphlet Poets," he declared that "With this generation of Negro poets, a folk temperament flowers and a race experience bears fruit. Race is often a closer spiritual bond than nationality and group experience deeper than an individual's: here we have beauty that is born of long-suffering, truth that is derived from mass emotion and founded in collective vision." The idea of the collective effort, expressing group reactions to stimuli current in the society has continued in the critical work of Alain Locke. He has headed his annual reviews with such suggestive titles as: "We Turn to Prose," "Black Truth and Blacker Beauty," and "The Negro: 'New' or Newer." Through the years he

has dealt with reconciling the problem of a distinctive minority culture co-existing with a larger culture and yet neither obliterated by the larger culture nor completely separate from it. In his 1942 review, under the title "Who and What Is Negro?" he chided the editors of *The Negro Caravan*–Sterling Brown, Arthur Davis, and the present writer–for denying in their critical introduction to their anthology that the term "Negro literature" had validity, since Negro writers as a whole were part of the main stream of American literature. In 1944, in a survey of the American Negro in the nation's culture, he declared that "It is the public and democratic inclusion of the Negro artist in his rightful place in the national culture which must climax this whole historical development." But he added that this would require "full freedom and unrestricted integration of the Negro artist himself, in order that he may be in a position to make his contribution most representative from the point of view of the minority culture and more effectively from the point of view of the national culture itself." The full freedom is apparently personal, so that the artist may live and breathe and absorb as he will; his work will, nevertheless, continue as representative of a specific minority culture within the larger culture, according to this point of view. Writers must therefore continue their awareness of a Negro quality in their heritage and culture, exploiting it fully for a measured contribution to the larger culture.

Sterling Brown, the third and youngest of the formative critics of the Thirties, had barely begun his public career as critic when the Renaissance in its original form died away. Himself a poet, whose *Southern Road* appeared at the beginning of the Great Depression, he shared few of the urban delusions of the central figures of the Renaissance though he followed and understood them fully. Like Brawley, he was physically located away from the great Harlem metropolis during most of the Twenties but, unlike Brawley, he found the time and followed the urge to investigate more fully the Negro folk cultures of semi-rural Virginia, Missouri, and Tennessee while on teaching assignments in those regions. In both his poetry and in his criticism he therefore employed in greater depth a knowledge of the folk sources of literary expression. This knowledge was greater than that of prior and most contemporary interpreters of Negro expression; in addition it was buttressed by what most of his contemporaries also lacked: a thorough grounding in

past and contemporary literatures. The newer traditions of realism and naturalism were not uncongenial to him and his studies in the Irish literary revival had convinced him that major worth for the Negro literary movement lay in the life and expression of the people themselves.

It is not surprising, then, that he saw, in 1930, a sign of hope in the increasing number of serious, scholarly works on the life of the folk and laboring Negro. His series of essays for *Opportunity* covered a wide range of subjects. In them he emphasized the need for an understanding literary audience as well as for knowledge-full authors; he covered the all-important influences of white writers as well as Negro authors. His "The Blues as Folk Poetry," published in the second *Folk-Say;* his pioneering discussions of Negro character, of the perversions of historical fiction; and of the inadequacies of films were all distinguished contributions to the development of a critical credo. This credo is, essentially, that valid literary expression, in whatever form, must be true to its subject matter. The author must therefore forego all literary and social traditions which, either by softening sentimentally or exaggerating for effect, distort the substance for the sake of form, sales, conformity, or anything else which is properly extraneous to the subject matter at hand. He applied this credo in the two booklets, *The Negro in American Fiction* and *Negro Poetry and Drama*, published as Bronze Booklets Numbers Six and Seven in 1937 by the Associates in Negro Folk Education, of which Alain Locke was the moving spirit. These booklets were too restricted in space for the wealth of factual material which Brown literally crammed into them. Poetry and drama together, for example, were treated in one hundred forty-two small pages, including references and discussion questions for each of ten chapters and treating both Negro and white authors. There was little space left for analyses, author by author and work by work. Yet, in penetrating and incisive statements he was able to say a great deal more about the treatment of the Negro in American literature than had been done before. Of E. C. L. Adams, for example: "It is clear that he has overheard, or been allowed to hear, a great deal. And that is why his work is superior to local color." Of the blues: "The genteel turn away from them in distaste, but blues persist with their tense and tonic shrewdness about human nature." And: "Jean Toomer is best as a poet in the beautiful prose of *Cane*."

But there was little room for expatiation in the crowded pages of the Bronze Booklets.

Brown, like most good poets and critics, is an excellent teacher and lecturer. How many times, from New England to the Deep South, he has been called upon to lecture on the Negro in American literature or culture he himself probably does not know. He has responded freely to these requests, thereby fulfilling a major function of the critic in enlarging the audience for the artist and advancing the frontiers of understanding. His classroom lectures are equally filled with critical substance and the platform lectures have served to extend his classroom audiences from his home base at Howard to Atlanta, Minnesota, Vassar, and New York University. But all of this, valuable as it is to those who are fortunate enough to be within earshot, has not served to increase his output of much needed critical writing. With so few volumes of criticism available to the reader it is therefore doubly unfortunate that no enterprising publisher has gathered the best of the *Opportunity* pieces, the blues, historical fiction, and character study essays into a volume where they could be read with profit today.

The Thirties were not devoid of critical volumes treating one or another aspect of Negro writing. In addition to the Brawley and Brown volumes, Nick Aaron Ford published, in 1936, *The Contemporary Negro Novel: A Study in Race Relations*. Essentially a Master's paper with added remarks, this study is barely critical, in a literary sense, for it approaches the novel almost wholly through "Attitudes," "Racial Differences," and "Literary Values." In the concluding pages of his study the author asks: "Since the Negro novelist has not produced even a first rate novel is he not justified in laying aside the pretensions of pure artistry and boldly taking up the cudgel of propaganda?" Since "pure art" is here defined as that which "carries no thesis" and "argues no case," with the alternative faced by the writer being "the task either to elevate the soul or to make glad the heart" (neither of which, the critic says, Negro novels do), it is hardly surprising that the author's answer to his question is yes.

Jay Saunders Redding, two years later, produced *To Make a Poet Black*, a rapid survey beginning with the assertion that the writing of Negroes is a "literature of necessity" in which the writers have had to have "two faces. If they wished to succeed they have been obliged to satisfy two different (and opposed when not opposite) audiences, the black and the white." But,

after so promising a beginning, implying that what follows will deal largely with the sociology of literature, the study quickly lapses into a rapid gloss of literary effort from Hammon to Redding's contemporaries, with scarcely a further bow to the problem so neatly phrased.

Brawley's *Dunbar*, which many found inadequate as a critical biography, found a rival in Victor Lawson's *Dunbar Critically Examined*, published in 1941. Lawson attempted to provide the biocritical analysis which Brawley and other writers had omitted from their studies of the poet. Filled with frequent quotations, comparisons, and presumed sources for Dunbar's work, the study's most useful materials are the biographical notes provided from interviews with Dunbar's contemporaries. Dunbar remains, however, the only Negro writer to have two book-length critical treatments of any sort. Only Douglass rivals him on this point, and none of the Douglass studies attempts a critical evaluation of his writings and speeches as a whole. Fisk University published in 1941 the memorial lectures delivered in his honor by Arthur B. Spingarn, Carl Van Vechten, and Sterling Brown, but these cannot be said to provide a critical estimate of James Weldon Johnson's work.

The most detailed and complete study of a phase of Negro expression in America yet provided is Hugh M. Gloster's *Negro Voices in American Fiction*, published in 1948. Unfortunately this study stops short of the war and post-war periods, thus depriving the author of the advantage of examining the work of the newer novelists of the Forties. Unfortunately as well, since the book, according to the author's statement, "is concerned not so much with literary appraisal as with racial expression, artistic evaluation has been avoided except for the occasional employment of terms indicating the quality of the work." As a result the study is largely of the themes, attitudes, and social and historical background of the works examined. For that reason the book is more valuable as a starting point for future criticism than for its own critical qualities.

*   *   *

No one in the Forties emerged to challenge the critical standing which Brawley, Brown, and Locke had achieved by the mid-Thirties. The War was partly responsible and the disappearance of journals hospitable to critical comment was equally to blame. *Opportunity* and *The Crisis*, having weathered the Great Depression, fell upon evil days in the Forties. Neither, after 1941, continued to play the midwife's role to Negro writing and criticism that had been theirs in the preceding two decades. PHYLON, a product of Du Bois' return to Atlanta, at first concerned itself primarily with the social and economic problems of race and culture at home and abroad, paying an occasional tribute to the arts in the publication of Braithwaite's autobiography, *The House Under Arcturus*, several essays by Hugh M. Gloster later to be used for his book referred to above, and occasional essays on literature or art from a scholarly viewpoint. In the last years of the Forties, however, PHYLON began to take a livelier interest in critical studies. In addition to Alain Locke's annual review of the year's work, this quarterly prints Miles Jefferson's annual appraisal of the year in drama, primarily limited to the Broadway stage. Critical essays by Blyden Jackson, William Couch, William Allen, and Robert A. Smith have been especially valuable. In other journals, John S. Lash, especially on the Negro in films; Philip Butcher on Cable and on contemporary literature; John Lovell on drama; and Ralph Ellison, on Richard Wright and also on films, have been active. But it is too early yet to assess the work of these younger men. Whether they will develop critical credos individually or in concert, whether they will successfully carry out the critical function of receiving and transmitting ideas and standards cannot be told until more of their, and of others', records are in.

This issue of PHYLON itself will be a major contribution to critical writing on the Negro. It has been foolish, perhaps, to undertake this piece without first absorbing the contents of this issue. If this issue deepens and more sharply defines the problems facing the Negro author at mid-century it will have been a worthy addition to the critical writing on the Negro author.

An Essay in Criticism

Blyden Jackson

I think it is a truism that in every regard the Negro writer has been typically American, except, perhaps, in the amount and quality of his work. Whether in absolute or comparative terms, the Negro has not published much in America. Likewise, whether in absolute or comparative terms, his writing has been too often execrable, although throughout the course of Negro literature constant improvement is readily discernible.

Now the problems of both the quantity and the quality of Negro literature are, it seems to me, inextricably intertwined with the problem of the Negro writer's audience. It is nonsense to say that a writer's audience does not influence him, just as nonsensical as it is to hold that writers write—and permit themselves to be published—merely because there is something in them that must come out. And the Negro writer has lacked a helpful audience in two large ways: viz., sympathetically and critically. The lack of a wide sympathetic audience among the only extensive public available to him undoubtedly has inhibited the Negro writer's effective use of symbols; and, of course, creative writing itself is nothing if not symbolic. However, eliminating the iniquities of racial stereotypes, the indispensable propaedeutic for easing the Negro writer's problem in the handling of symbols, must continue to wait upon the combined action of many forces—among them, incidentally, the services of a competent and forthright critical audience. On the other hand the lack of a critical audience is clearly a reflection on Negro literary scholarship more than on anything else.

For Negroes just have not gotten around to real criticism of their own literature. We have done some good things. But all our accomplishments can be quickly demonstrated to be mere prolegomena for the hard, serious, tedious labor of giving our literature the sort of scholarly and critical framework which adds the needed marginal dimensions to the established European literatures. Let us look at the best we have done in criticism. Redding's *To Make a Poet Black* is a rapid summary, mainly historical, moving too hastily to develop adequately his thesis that Negro literature is a literature of necessity, although often enough delighting us with such trenchant *obiter*

dicta as its characterization of Joel Chandler Harris' dialect. Gloster's more recent *Negro Voices in American Fiction* is an excellent reference work, with an especially valuable bibliography, but, again, Gloster is limited by intentions patently as summary as Redding's. Sterling Brown, who has done yeoman work in the area of his choice, has found himself completely occupied with the mere job of getting Negro literature into the field of vision of a wide public. Brawley was always as timid and platitudinous as a Sunday-school pamphlet. James Weldon Johnson was an executive, and his criticism, while often redeemed by his native taste, betrayed that tendency of his disposition as well as his lack of academic scholarship. There is little more to say about Negroes' criticism of their own literature, except that here for Negro students with ability and industry is a veritable green pasture.

Sometimes I have dreamed dreams about what could transpire in the criticism of Negro literature. Dreams can be very magnificent. Dubois, a half century ago at Atlanta, bursting with the enthusiasm of his youth, laid down, it will be remembered, a program for an integrated sociological study of the Negro problem that was to have carried through a hundred years. Incidentally, during the thirteen years that he then stayed at Atlanta, he maintained his program's operation largely according to plan. And I have wished that those of us working with Negro literature might catch some of the magnificence, foolish, arrogant, but, withal, glorious, of young Dubois' Atlanta dreaming. I do not begrudge a single one of the buildings I see going up on Negro campuses. God knows when one wanders around the great university campuses of America and then comes South again he knows all too bitterly how much, in the "segregated but equal" dispensation, we are still on short rations. And if one moves through the parts of Negro ghettoes where most Negroes have to live, perceiving unavoidably the squalor and meanness everywhere, scrofulous hovels jammed together, filthy, unkept streets, bad odors and harsh atmospheres, he will give thanks for every bit of clean turf, every piece of modern plumbing, every gracious con-

tour on the Negro college campus. It is, indeed, always a matter of great wonder to me when I recall where Negroes have been cooped up that we are not all snarling, venomous beasts. After all, how can any man esteem beauty who knows nothing of it? Let us, then, get what we can of beauty on our physical campuses. And yet—I would sometimes that our college budgets did occasionally contemplate a series of studies in our literature. I can at least pretend names for them: The Atlanta University Series of American Negro Writers; the James T. Shephard Editions of Slave Narratives; The Tennessee State College Studies in Negro Literary Acculturation. I can think, too, of individual studies prepared, if not issued also, under the aegis of some Negro school that has somehow or other managed to institute a program of research. This business of dialect—we have now reached a state of cultural assurance sufficient for us to put it in its right perspectives, both linguistically and psychologically. I should like to see it studied. What we know, or ought to know, about the fictional treatment of the Negro middle class, has never been systematically assembled. There are handbooks and anthologies of Negro poetry, but no single intensive studies of separate poems of any Negro poets. And, of course, the possibilities for tracing the relations of Negro literature are, as one would expect, virtually legion. Because Negroes have not written in great volume, or because some people say that Negro art is shallow, a dream like this may seem far-fetched. It is not. One competent and diligent student, Lorenzo Dow Turner, working—one almost wants to say barehanded—in the field of linguistics has shown how rich can be the yield from sources that might easily appear barren to the superficial eye. Moreover, some of the things I suggest have been already attempted. I know, although I have seen neither of them, that within the last several years at least two problems in research have dealt with the all too long neglected slave narratives. Some time ago Brawley did for Chapel Hill a life of Paul Laurence Dunbar, the first of a series, never continued, which Farrison tells me Brawley was to have edited. It is a shockingly inadequate and old-maidish performance, but still it was a start. Certainly the materials to justify a host of enterprises by students of Negro literature do exist. The problem is in getting people who know what to do with these materials, and who, moreover, are prepared to endure the drudgery which sustained scholarship demands.

Indeed our literature is thin, not altogether because of its own inherent limitations, but because we have not enriched it and expanded it with the great accretions of interpretation such as those we are likely to bear in mind every time we engage in the reading of a fairly familiar piece of literature by a white author reputable enough to be in the literary histories. To realize this one need not go to Shakespeare, around whom the critical works are so numerous that they literally do constitute fair-sized libraries. One may select almost at random comparatively minor figures in the kingdom of English letters and still have quite a bit of bibliographical sport with them. But, in terms of the assistance which a good critical audience can provide, Negro literature is starved. Waiving for the moment the possible contributions of diligent research, consider merely the province of aesthetic judgment. There are so many issues to be noted and discussed and argued about in that area alone that we have not set down as fully as we might. There is, for instance, in *One Way to Heaven* the way that Cullen wrote two novels, the really larger one about two "little" people, for all that it simpers occasionally, having much of the charm of a fairy story, but the other—which is not fitted too well into the whole—while worthy of commendation as an attempt healthily to laugh at one's self, too stilted and self-conscious for good satire; or, since we have started with *One Way to Heaven*, there is also the trouble generally that Negro writers have in writing good, convincing conversation, a trouble especially distressing in comedy-of-manners work like the satirical episodes in Cullen's novel where he brings people together for drawing-room talk but gets out of them only a painful burlesque of the brilliant stream of *mots* on which one floats gaily through the ether of Congreve or Wilde or Shaw. And there are countless other items, each of them conceivably a rift to be loaded with ore: like the way in which, for all the nobility of her intentions, because she is herself so naively philistine, so breathless with adoration for good-looking people Nordic style (even when they are tinted with the tar brush), good-looking clothes, good-looking homes and country-club ideas of the *summa bona*, Jessie Fauset's defenses of the Negro middle class backfire into an indictment of her horrid copycatting of the wrong values; or, to speak again of conversation, the verisimilitude as ordinary Negro speech of the talk in Zora Neale Hurston's *Moses, Man of the Mountain,* and the superb rightness of this assimilation of the

Old Testament story to Negro mores when Miss Hurston's retelling of the famous Hebrew legend is diagrammed—as it should be—allegorically, so that other beautiful hits, such as the equation of Moses, from the house of Pharaoh, to our mulatto leadership, or of the grumbling of the Hebrews in the Wilderness to the attitudes the Negro masses take toward Negro leaders, assume their due proportions in this parable about one minority group intimated through the tale of another; or, for perhaps even better art, the life-giving quality of Ann Petry's imagination in *The Street,* an achievement the magnitude of which can be sharply realized by doing such a thing as placing beside Miss Petry's Lutie Johnson—a woman warm and vital whose senses, and will, pulse with a fierce indwelling energy—the still-born and crudely manipulated Mimi Daquin of Walter White's *Flight;* or of the fairly common tendency, exemplified very well in this same *Flight,* for Negro novelists to have conceptions beyond their capacities; or, to make an end of this, of what a gratifying thing can happen when the conception and the capacity go hand-in-glove, as they do in William Gardner Smith's *Last of the Conquerors,* where the particular version of irony conceived by Smith, the irony of a Negro boy finding democratic treatment in an experience of life where he least expected it and which he cannot retrieve, is given just the right pitch by the elegiac tone that Smith gets immediately and sustains admirably in spite of the delicacy of its adjustment.

All around us today the air resounds with calls to integrate the Negro into our national life. Very probably the increasingly favorable reaction to those calls is a sign that both America and its Negroes are reaching a certain maturity. Negro writers are promising to do their bit in keeping pace with the latest trend. Symptomatically, they are losing as never quite before, their exaggerated self-consciousness. Gwendolyn Brooks' *Satin-Legs Smith* represents without apology the South Side of Chicago, but none of his unabashed local color prevents him from representing very well also the diminution of man as a romantic spirit in the machine-made monotony of the modern metropolis. Redding's *Stranger and Alone* is a study of Uncle Tomism, but a study of Uncle Tomism which illuminates *sub specie aeternitatis* the ubiquitous errand-boys for Caesar. The Negro writer, who has always been very American, even in his failings and despite his handicaps, is still responsive to his environment. But there is still too little evidence that Negro criticism developed by literary scholarship is making strenuous efforts to "integrate" itself with any American pattern. For the pattern of American scholarship requires, if nothing else, some activity. We have sent by now a goodly squadron of students to the great graduate schools of America. We are even opening up now graduate schools of our own. Perhaps it may be argued in extenuation of our inertia as productive scholar-critics that our teaching loads are too great and our facilities for research too meager to permit us to do those things which we are really chagrined to leave undone. The argument is objectively sufficient. It faithfully describes current conditions as they statistically are. It is subjectively specious. For it says nothing about our will to change those conditions. It says nothing about our determination to see that integration in American education shall mean not only simply the one-way traffic of Negroes going to white schools, but also the Americanizing in terms of budgets, curricula, physical plants, labor practices, administrative attitudes and scholarly proficiency of Negro schools so that we may reasonably cherish the hope of finding, in some not too far distant day, a fair amount of people who will want a two-way pattern of integration that will let them come to "Negro" schools. And, above all, it says nothing about our resolution to do as much as we can under present conditions to integrate our own literature into the national consciousness.

There really is for us no true absolution. We have shirked overmuch our job. In 1945 PHYLON published a poem by Robert Hayden called "Middle Passage." It was, I thought, a good poem. Its riches are infinite enough to deserve some extended comment. I have never seen a printed reference to it of any consequence. In *The Craft of Fiction* Percy Lubbock notices admiringly Tolstoi's handling of time in *War and Peace.* In that novel, Lubbock points out, we feel the passage of time in two ways. We are aware of its flow from day to day and year to year, bearing away, like a conveyor belt, the span of a person's life. But we are also aware of it as a cycle of generations, a wheel ceaselessly revolving, always taking some generation up, some generation down. Langston Hughes' *Not Without Laughter* is much less bulky than *War and Peace.* Yet in *Not Without Laughter* one finds this same double sense of time, just as one finds, virtually wherever one stops to analyze Hughes' performance here, casements opening out upon the expansive world of universal suggestion created by great art. I have said that Negro literature is often execrable. But

it is far from being so execrable as to deserve the extent of neglect in which we have allowed it to languish. Moreover, I have tried to show that it is frequently critically challenging, and indeed I have hinted that now and then it may reward even the most demanding critic with a moment of rapture. Finally, I have indicated that in my own thinking about the relation of one thing to another in this complex world I can plainly see the development of a criticism around Negro literature as an integrative factor of no little value for the growth of democracy in America. Actually I look forward to the day when a book about Negroes, if someone should chance then to isolate such another incidental group in our social order, will have about the same significance as Marquand's *The Late George Apley* or Guthrie's *The Way West* have now. And I want us, as students and teachers of Negro literature, to have had our share in preparing for that day. I want us to have affected both the quality and the reception of Negro writing in such a way as to hasten that age of felicity. I would have us, indeed, feel toward the development of an energetic scholarly criticism within our own ranks a sense of knightly obligation. And I would add, for all those who see eye to eye with me, "a fair promise of better things"– even to an increase in one's own sense of being personally alive.

New Poets

Margaret Walker

During the past twenty years of literary history in America Negroes have enjoyed unusual prominence as poets. At least ten books of poetry by new poets have received serious critical comment in leading literary magazines and columns. If we can believe the additional comments in anthologies of American poetry and books of literary criticism, Negroes writing poetry have gone a long way toward achieving full literary status as American writers; and they have thus attained a measure of integration into contemporary schools of literary thought.

A backward look into American life during these two decades should provide a reason for this literary development and resurgence. It must also accountably tell the background of such poetry, and at the same time provide a basis for predicting the future of poetry written by Negroes in America. Let us, therefore, consider, first, the socio-economic and political factors which have influenced the poetry of the past twenty years.

During the Twenties we spoke of the New Negro and the Negro Renaissance. At that time such figures as James Weldon Johnson, Langston Hughes, Countee Cullen, Claude McKay, and Jean Toomer emerged as the spokesmen of the New Negro. Rich white patrons or "angels" who could and did underwrite the poetry of Negroes by helping to support Negroes who were interested in writing poetry did so as a fad to amuse themselves and their guests at some of the fabulous parties of the Twenties. They considered the intelligent, sensitive, and creative Negro as the talented tenth, exotic, bizarre, and unusual member of his race; and they indulgently regarded the poetry of the Negro as the prattle of a gifted child. Negro people as a mass showed little appreciation for poetry and offered very little audience for the Negro writing poetry. Whatever Negro people thought about the poetry written about Negro life did not seem to matter. In the final analysis the audience and the significant critics were white. Negroes as a whole knew too little about their own life to analyze correctly and judge astutely their own literary progress as poets. Isolated from the literary life of whites and confused by the segregated pattern of economic and political life, it was only natural that the point of view of these writers was limited. They lacked social perspective and suffered from a kind of literary myopia. They seemed constantly to beg the question of the Negro's humanity, perhaps as an

answer to the white patron's attitude that Negroes are only children anyway. *God's Trombones* by James Weldon Johnson, *The Weary Blues* by Langston Hughes, *Color* and *Copper Sun* by Countee Cullen, and *Harlem Shadows* by Claude McKay were published during the Twenties. Each was received as justification that the Negro race could produce geniuses and that it was nothing short of remarkable that "God should make a poet black and bid him sing." Titles of books as well as eloquent short lyrics such as "0 Black and Unknown Bards," and "I, too, sing America . . . I am the darker brother" all reflected an intense desire to justify the Negro as a human being. These books sold well among whites but none of them ranked in a "best-seller" class. People did not buy poetry, certainly not poetry by Negroes. It was a day of individual literary patronage when a rich "angel" adopted a struggling poor artist and made an exotic plaything out of any "really brilliant Negro."

The halcyon days of individual patronage of the arts were ended with the stockmarket crash at the end of the Twenties. The gay hayride of the flaming and gilded Twenties had come to a jolting stop and the depression of the Thirties began to make its first inroads into American life. Hoover persisted so long in predicting that prosperity was just around the corner that it became a standing joke. Men appeared on street corners selling apples, and there was talk of an American dole such as England had already experienced. Early in 1932 before the repeal of prohibition and the ending of the speakeasies that had been an institution of the Twenties, it was a common sight to see streets of large cities littered with sprawling drunkards. The parks were full of unemployed men, shabby and helpless, wearing beaten and hopeless faces. Grant Park in Chicago was a notable example. Evictions were common and Communism was on the march. What chance did the luxury of art have at such a time?

Roosevelt's New Deal not only averted a bloody social revolution in 1932 and 1933 by bracing the tottering economic structure of the country, but it also ushered into existence the boon to art and letters in the form of the Works Progress Administration. The WPA meant two things of far-reaching significance to Negroes who were writers. It meant, first, (as it meant to whites) money on which to exist and provision for the meager security necessary in order to create art. It meant, second, that Negroes who were creative writers, and poets especially, were no longer entirely isolated from other writers. In cities above the Mason-Dixon line where the Writers Projects drew no color line a new school of black and white writers mushroomed over-night into being.

The cry of these writers was the cry of social protest: protest against the social ills of the day which were unemployment, slums, crime and juvenile delinquency, prejudice, poverty, and disease. The New Deal struggled to alleviate these social ills while the writers led the vanguard of literary protest and agitation for a better world. The decade of the nineteen-thirties therefore became known as the socially-conscious Thirties. Negroes joined the ranks of these socially-conscious writers and Negroes who were writing poetry in particular were poets of social protest. At least three new poets appeared during the Thirties with books of poetry of obvious social significance.

Southern Road by Sterling Brown appeared in 1932. It was chiefly concerned with the plight of Negroes in the South. Ballads in this volume such as the "Slim Greer Series" are some of the finest in the annals of American poetry regardless of the color of the author. One of Mr. Brown's later poems, "Old Lem," which first appeared in magazines and anthologies in the Thirties, is an outstanding example of social protest and clearly reflects the mood of the period.

> I talked to old Lem
> And old Lem said:
>   "They weigh the cotton
>   They store the corn
>   We only good enough
>   To work the rows;
>   They run the commissary
>   They keep the books
>   We gotta be grateful
>   For being cheated;
>   Whippersnapper clerks
>   Call us out of our name
>   We got to say mister
>   To spindling boys
>   They make our figgers
>   Turn somersets
>   We buck in the middle
>   Say, "Thankyuh, sah.'
>   *They don't come by ones*
>   *They don't come by twos*
>   *But they come by tens.*

Black Man's Verse and *I Am the American Negro* by Frank Marshall Davis appeared in 1935 and 1937 respectively. These two volumes of poetry, although technically rough and uneven, were scathing books of social protest. An example of

such social protest may be seen in the following excerpt from one of Mr. Davis' poems, "Portrait of the Cotton South:"

> Well, you remakers of America
> You apostles of Social Change
> Here is pregnant soil
> Here are grass roots of a nation.
> But the crop they grow is Hate and Poverty.
> By themselves they will make no change
> Black men lack the guts
> Po' whites have not the brains
> And the big land owners want Things as They Are.

Black Labor Chant by David Wadsworth Cannon, who died before his volume of verse was published in 1939, celebrated the Negro's joining ranks with the upsurging Labor movement, particularly the CIO, and continued in general in the vein of social protest.

Although the outbreak of the Second World War changed the note of social significance, bringing as it did prosperity at home in the United States, and ushering into the world the Atomic Age, the strong note of anxiety it bred was not felt at first in the literature of the period. For at least a decade longer the poetry of American Negroes continued to reflect the mood of the Thirties. A half dozen books of poetry published during the Forties reflect either a note of social protest or a growing concern with the terrible reality of war.

Heart-Shape in the Dust by Robert Hayden appeared in 1940 followed by *For My People* by Margaret Walker in 1942. *Rendezvous With America* by Melvin Tolson was published in 1944; *A Street in Bronzeville* by Gwendolyn Brooks in 1945; and *Powerful Long Ladder* by Owen Dodson appeared in 1946. The first three poets each reflected in varying degrees the note of social protest in their respective volumes of poetry. The last two poets showed a growing concern with the grim reality of war.

Contrast the tone of the poems of the Twenties with examples of the poetry of the early Forties reflecting as they did the social consciousness of the Thirties. From Robert Hayden's early work, *Heart-Shape in the Dust,* an excerpt from the poem, "Speech," follows:

> Hear me, white brothers,
> Black brothers, hear me:
> I have seen the hand
> Holding the blowtorch
> To the dark, anguish-twisted body;

> I have seen the hand
> Giving the high-sign
> To fire on the white pickets;
> And it was the same hand,
> Brothers, listen to me,
> It was the same hand.

From Margaret Walker's poem, "For My People:"

> For my people standing staring trying to fashion a better way from confusion, from hypocrisy and misunderstanding, trying to fashion a world that will hold all the people, all the faces, all the Adams and Eves and their countless generations;
>
> Let a new earth rise. Let another world be born. Let a bloody peace be written in the sky. Let a second generation full of courage issue forth; let a people loving freedom come to growth. Let a beauty full of healing and a strength of final clenching be the pulsing in our spirits and our blood. Let the martial songs be written, let the dirges disappear. Let a race of men now rise and take control.

From Melvin Tolson's poem, "Dark Symphony:"

> Out of abysses of Illiteracy
> Through labyrinths of Lies,
> Across wastelands of Disease . . .
> We advance!
> Out of dead-ends of Poverty,
> Through wildernesses of Superstition
> Across barricades of Jim Crowism
> We advance!
> With the Peoples of the World . . .
> We advance!

In each of these three illustrations of poetry published during the early Forties may be detected the note of social protest, a growing perspective beyond the point of view of race, and a militant attitude not evidenced in the poets of the Twenties.

Gwendolyn Brooks and Owen Dodson published in 1945 and 1946 and their works show a growing concern with the problem of war. They show more than any of the aforementioned poets a growing global perspective which has become a keynote of current poetry. In her volume, *A Street in Brozeville,* Miss Brooks writes about "Gay Chaps at the Bar:"

> We knew how to order . . .
> But nothing ever taught us to be islands
> . . . . No stout
> Lesson showed how to chat with death. We brought
> No brass fortissimo, among out talents,

To holler down the lions in this air.

In Owen Dodson's poems, "Black Mother Praying," and "Conversation on V," the question of race is presented within the framework of war. The following excerpt is taken from "Conversation on V":

V stands for Victory.
Now what is this here Victory?
It what we get when we fight for it.
Ought to be Freedom, God do know that.

Common Peoples Manifesto by Marcus Christian was published in 1948. It has probably not received as widespread critical notice as it deserves, but in several reviews mention has been made of its "considerable merit." It, too, reflects the social note of protest that was typical of the poetry of the Thirties.

The period of greatest intensification of the social note in poetry written by Negroes extends roughly from 1935 to 1945. Summing up the period, generally speaking, we can see that the New Negro came of age during the Thirties. He grew away from the status of the exotic, the accidentally unusual Negro, the talented tenth of what the white audience chose to consider an otherwise mentally infantile minority group whose masses were illiterate, disfranchised, exploited, and oppressed. Negroes became members of a new school of writers who were no longer isolated because of color, who were integrated around the beliefs that created the New Deal. They were the poets of social protest who began to catch a glimmer of a global perspective, who as spokesmen for their race did not beg the question of their humanity, and who cried out to other peoples over the earth to recognize race prejudice as a weapon that is as dangerous as the atomic bomb in the threat to annihilation of culture and peace in the western world.

Any literary development of the Negro in the Thirties was directly due to his social development. During the Thirties the Negro people made great social strides. The New Deal opened many avenues of opportunity and development to the masses of Negro people. The economic standards of the Negro race rose higher than ever in the history of his life in this country. As a result of free art for all the people a cultural renaissance in all the arts swept the United States. This created a new intelligentsia with a genuine appreciation for the creative arts and a recognition for all cultural values. Labor was stimulated by the

unionization together of black and white labor and this in turn strengthened the political voice of the people. Consequently the literary audience widened and the Negro people themselves grew in intellectual awareness.

Three books published during the Forties, however, show a marked departure from the note of social protest. These books are *From the Shaken Tower* by Bruce McWright, published in Great Britain in 1944; *The Lion and the Archer* by Robert Hayden and Myron O'Higgins, published as a brochure in 1948; and Gwendolyn Brooks' Pulitzer Prize-winning volume, *Annie Allen*, which was published in 1949. Each one of these books is less preoccupied with the theme of race as such. Race is rather used as a point of departure toward a global point of view than as the central theme of one obsessed by race. This global perspective is an important new note in poetry. The tendency is toward internationalism rather than toward nationalism and racism. Because modern inventions have shortened the time involved in transportation and communications to such an amazing degree our world has shrunk to a small community of nations and mankind is forced to recognize the kinship of all peoples. Thus we have a basis for new conceptions that of necessity lead us in new directions.

These new poets of the late Forties also remind us that there are other factors in the writing of poetry that are equally as important as perspective. They focus our attention on craftsmanship with their return to an emphasis on form. The new poetry has universal appeal coupled with another definite mark of neo-classicism, the return to form. They show an emphasis placed on technique rather than subject matter, and a moving toward intellectual themes of psychological and philosophical implications which border on obscurantism. These poems are never primitive, simple, and commonplace.

What technical advances have these poets of our new classical age shown over the poets of the Twenties and the Thirtes?

Looking back to the Twenties one quickly recognizes that the poets of the Negro Renaissance varied technically from the strictly classical and conventional poetry to the utterly unconventional. Countee Cullen was an outstanding example of the true classicist who had been schooled thoroughly in versification and all the types and forms of poetry. His classical education was clearly reflected in his poetry. On the other hand, Langston Hughes introduced the pattern

of the "blues" into poetry. He made no pretense of being the poets' poet, of writing intellectual poetry, or conforming to any particular school of aesthetics. The pattern of the "blues" was, nevertheless, the first new Negro idiom introduced into American poetry since the time of Paul Laurence Dunbar and his Negro dialect that was typical of the ante-bellum plantation life. The poetry of Negroes that was published during the Thirties was primarily free verse. Technically there were no innovations.

Currently, the new poets, however, are so concerned with form that they are often interested in form to the exclusion of everything else and thus are in danger of sacrificing sense for sound, or meaning for music. As a result of this tendency much of recent poetry by white writers in America has been labelled obscurantist. Can this charge be safely levelled at recent poetry by Negroes?

Such a charge has already been levelled at *Annie Allen* when the book was mentioned in a recent issue of PHYLON. It was then stated that the poem, "the birth in a narrow room," has too many elliptical or truncated lines. This seems a minor technical matter of not too great importance since it does not actually destroy the meaning of the poem. The lines under question follow:

> Weeps out of western country something new.
> Blurred and stupendous. Wanted and unplanned.
> Winks. Twines, and weakly winks
> Upon the milk-glass fruit bowl, iron pot,
> The bashful china child tipping forever
> Yellow apron and spilling pretty cherries.

Does this make sense? Obviously when one reads the entire poem in terms of the title, the poem does make sense, and that should be all that really matters.

The fact that Miss Brooks dispays an excellent knowledge of form, whether in the versatile handling of types of forms of poetry included in *Annie Allen* or in the metrical variations in the volume, can be readily seen as proof of this new emphasis upon conventional form. She skillfully handles a number of stanzaic forms including couplets, quatrains, the Italian Terza Rima, and even in "The Anniad," the difficult rime-royal or the seven line stanza named for Chaucer. Here is a perfect example:

> Think of thaumaturgic lass
> Looking in her looking-glass

> At the unembroidered brown;
> Printing bastard roses there;
> Then emotionally aware
> Of the black and boisterous hair
> Tamimg all that anger down.

In addition to these conventional forms she includes several poems written in free verse as well as occasional lines of blank verse. In regard to types she includes short lyrics, ballads, and sonnets written with veteran aplomb. As a whole, *Annie Allen* is a fine delineation of the character of a young Negro woman from childhood through adolescence to complete maturity, but with slight racial exceptions it could apply to any female of a certain class and society. The entire volume is tinged with an highly sophisticated humor and is not only technically sure but also vindicates the promise of *A Street in Bronzeville*. Coming after the long hue and cry of white writers that Negroes as poets lack form and intellectual acumen, Miss Brooks' careful craftsmanship and sensitive understanding reflected in *Annie Allen* are not only personal triumphs but a racial vindication.

There may be more reason to level the charge of obscurantism at the poetry of Myron O'Higgins in *The Lion and the Archer*, written in collaboration with Robert Hayden. Although the vocabulary is no more intellectual than that of Miss Brooks, and there are several magnificent poems in this brochure–new in note, and vital–there seems more obscurity and ambiguity in the use of poetic symbols and imagery, as for example:

> But that day in between
> comes back with two lean cats
> who run in checkered terror
> through a poolroom door
> and bolting from a scream
> a keen knife marks with sudden red
> the gaming green
> . . . a purple billiard ball
> explodes the color scheme.

Robert Hayden shows a decided growth and advance in this volume over his first, *Heart-Shape in the Dust*, which was uneven and lacked the grasp of a true Negro idiom which he seemed to be seeking at that time. His sense of choric movement and his understanding and perspective of peoples have increased to a telling degree and he writes now with due maturity and power:

Now as skin-and-bones Europe hurts all over from
    the swastika's
hexentanz: oh think of Anton, Anton brittle, Anton
    crystalline;
think what the winter moon, the leper beauty of a
    Gothic tale, must see:
the ice-azure likeness of a young man reading,
    carved most craftily.

In Bruce McWright there is authentic reporting of World War II but even the title of his book, *From the Shaken Tower*, reflects the questions of our present-day age. War has further denounced the ivory towers because war is the grim reality that ends the romantic dreams and airy castle building. The poets of the Thirties said that ivory towers were not fit habitations for poets anyway; they should be social prophets, preachers, teachers, and leaders. Now, with the threat of annihilation hanging over the civilized world of western culture, whether by atomic or hydrogen bomb, with the tremendous wave of social revolution sweeping through the world, men have felt themselves spiritually bankrupt. There is therefore a wave of religious revival, especially in America, whether through fear and hysteria, or from a genuine desire for inner self analysis, reflection and introspective knowledge that may lead, thereby, to a spiritual panacea which we seek for the ills of the world. Whether to Catholicism, Existentialism, or Communism, modern man is turning to some definite belief around which to integrate his life and give it true wholeness and meaning. Consequently there has already been noted among white writers a decided religious revival. Whereas Marxism was the intellectual fad of the Thirties, religion has become the intellectual fad at present in America where the political and economic structures have definitely reverted to an extremely conservative position. The religious pathway of T. S. Eliot, prophet of the spiritual wasteland, technical pioneer, and most influential name among poets during the Thirties, has been followed by W. H. Auden. Robert Lowell, a Pulitzer Prize poet of a few years ago, is a Catholic convert. Thus far no Negro recently writing poetry has reflected this religious revival, but we may well expect this tendency.

Negroes not only have grown up as poets technically with volumes of poetry showing a growing concern with craftsmanship, social perspective, and intellectual maturity, but they have also begun to reap the rewards in the form of laurels due them for their labors. They have received a greater measure of consideration from literary critics and judges of literary competitions than ever before in the history of writing by Negroes in America. Not only have Negroes succeeded in winning many philanthropic grants such as Rosenwalds and Guggenheims which have provided the wherewithal to pursue creative projects and develop burgeoning talents, but also many other honors and awards have been granted to poets of the Negro race. These have included grants from the Academy of Arts and Letters and the Yale Award for a promising younger poet. Now in 1950 has come the signal achievement with the awarding of the Pulitzer Prize for Poetry to Gwendolyn Brooks for her volume, *Annie Allen*. This is the first time in the history of this Prize that a Negro has won this national honor. With this announcement comes not only the recognition of the fact that poetry by Negroes has come of age but also that the Negro has finally achieved full status in the literary world as an American poet.

What, then, is the future of the Negro writing poetry in America? It would seem from these remarks that the outlook is bright and hopeful. It is a fact that some of the most significant poetry written in America during the past two decades has been written by Negroes. Now, what is the promise? Is there hope that it will be fulfilled? Is the Negro as a poet doomed to annihilation because he is part of a doomed Western world, or is that Western culture really doomed? Is our society already a fascist society? If it is, what hope has our literature? If these are only bogey-men, then whither are we turning? Is our path toward religious revival, neo-classicism, internationalism as a result of global perspectives and world government, or what?

From such young poets as M. Carl Holman must come the answer. Deeply concerned with the psychological, yet aware of our physical world, he shares a growing understanding of our spiritual problems with some of the most mature craftsmen practicing the art of poetry. He bears watching as a poet who is technically aware and intellectually worthy of his salt.

If we are truly in a transitional stage of social evolution, a state of flux, of cataclysmic socioeconomic and political upheaval that will ultimately and inevitably shape our literary life, this will soon be clear. Now, the shape of our emerging society is dimly shadowed by many imponderables. The future of the Negro writing poetry in America is bright only if the future of the world is bright, and if he with the rest of his world can

survive the deadly conflicts that threaten him and his total freedom, the awful anticipation of which now hangs over his head like the sword of Damocles.

Negro Poets, Then and Now

Arna Bontemps

The poetry of the Negro is hard to pin down. Like his music, from spirituals and gospel songs to blues, jazz and be-bop, it is likely to be marked by a certain special riff, an extra glide, a kick where none is expected and a beat for which there is no notation. It follows the literary traditions of the language it uses, but it does not hold them sacred. As a result, there has been a tendency for critics to put it in a category by itself, outside the main body of American poetry.

But Negroes take to poetry as they do to music. In the Harlem Renaissance poetry led the way for the other arts. It touched off the awakening that brought novelists, painters, sculptors, dancers, dramatists and scholars of many kinds to the notice of a nation that had nearly forgotten about the gifts of its Negro people. And almost the first utterance of the revival struck a note that disturbed poetic traditions:

> I've known rivers ancient as the world and older than the
> flow of human blood in human veins.

Soon thereafter the same generation responded to a poem that had been written even earlier and which Claude McKay included in his *Harlem Shadows* under the title of "Flame-Heart" in 1922. "So much have I forgotten in ten years," the first stanza began. It closed with

> I have forgotten much, but still remember
> The poinsettia's red, blood-red in warm December.

And before these notes subsided, Countee Cullen raised his voice:

> O lovers never barter love
> For gold or fertile lands,

> For love is meat and love is drink,
> And love heeds love's commands.
> And love is shelter from the rain,
> And scowling stormy skies;
> Who casts off love must break his heart,
> And rue it till he dies.

The Renaissance was on, and it was richly quotable, with Helene Johnson saying:

> Ah little road, brown as my race is brown,
> Dust of the dust, they must not bruise you down.

And Jean Toomer:

> Pour O pour that parting soul in song,
> O pour it in the sawdust glow of night. . . .
> And let the valley carry it along.

And Frank Horne:

> I buried you deeper last night
> You with your tears and your tangled hair.

And Georgia Douglas Johnson:

> I'm folding up my little dreams
> Within my heart tonight.

And Donald Jeffrey Hayes:

> No rock along the road but knows
> The inquisition of his toes;
> No journey's end but what can say:
> He paused and rested here a day!

And Waring Cuney:

> She does not know
> Her beauty,

She thinks her brown body
Has no glory.

But in those days a good many of the group went to The Dark Tower to weep because they felt an injustice in the critics' insistence upon calling them Negro poets instead of just poets. That attitude was particularly displeasing to Countee Cullen. But some who are writing today are not so sure. Considering the general state of poetry, the isolation of so many major poets from the everyday problems of mankind, their private language, their rarified metaphysical subject matter, one or two Negroes have even dared to suggest that being a Negro poet may not be so bad after all. Certainly there is nothing noticeably tragic about the lusty singers who carry the tunes today.

Gwendolyn Brooks, twice a Guggenheim fellow, once recipient of a grant from the American Academy of Arts and Letters, and more recently a Pulitzer Prize winner, has gathered a basket of laurels while keeping house for her husband and her young son in Chicago. Of all the post-Renaissance group of Negro poets in the U. S. she has received the most substantial critical approval. Her early poems won prizes in the Midwestern Writers' Conference and at Northwestern University, and after the publication of her collection *A Street in Bronzeville* in 1945 she was selected by *Mademoiselle* as one of the ten American women of the year. *Annie Allen,* her second book of poems, became the first by a Negro American poet to win the Pulitzer honor.

Comparable distinctions are probably in store for several of Miss Brooks' contemporaries. Robert E. Hayden, a member of the English faculty at Fisk University, received the Hopwood Award at the University of Michigan in 1938 and again in 1942. The Special Services Committee of Ann Arbor gave him a fellowship in 1946 and the Julius Rosenwald Fund selected him for one in 1947. His poems have appeared in *The Atlantic Monthly, Poetry, Cross Section* and other periodicals and anthologies. A first collection of them was called *Heart-Shape in the Dust* and was published in 1940 in Detroit. Seriously dedicated to his work, Hayden is a conscious artist rather than a spontaneous one, a deliberate worker, a careful polisher. While he does not scorn Negro themes and has used them in his most successful poems to date, he woud like his work to stand or fall by objective poetic standards. As was the case with Countee Cullen, one gets the impression that

Hayden is bothered by this Negro thing. He would like to be considered simply as a poet.

The opposite is true of Frank Marshall Davis and Melvin Beaunearus Tolson. The very titles of Davis' books tell his story: *Black Man's Verse, I Am the American Negro* and *47th Street.* The poetry is about as the titles would indicate. Its main quality is ruggedness. Perhaps this is not surprising in a poet who worked with street construction gangs in his youth and who has since lived the rough-and-tumble life of a newspaper man. He helped to start the Atlanta *Daily World* before beginning a long connection with the *Associated Negro Press* in 1935. Jazz music and the Negro's struggle for civil rights are his great concerns aside from journalism and poetry.

Tolson too is on the rugged side, and racial awareness emerges from nearly every line he has written. He never worked with street gangs, but during his twenty-two years on the faculty of Wiley College he barnstormed with many a winning debating team as its coach. He tried to promote little theatre groups among the sharecroppers in the surrounding country. And he is now doing some of the same things at Langston University. As a poet he first attracted attention when his "Dark Symphony" won a prize at the Negro American Exposition in Chicago and later appeared in the *Atlantic Monthly.* A volume of his poems followed, under the title *Rendezvous With America,* and it is so clearly and unmistakably Negro in every way that the government of Liberia recently reached across the sea to place a laurel wreath on the poet's brow. It has named Tolson its poet laureate.

Somewhere between Hayden and Tolson, in subject matter as in prosody, are Margaret Walker and Owen Dodson, both awkward fits for any rigid category. Margaret Walker is the vivacious daughter of a southern minister and attended Gilbert Academy in New Orleans before going to Northwestern University. The State University of Iowa gave her a Master's degree in creative writing, accepting a collection of her poems in place of a thesis. This same sheaf of poems, when entered in the Yale University Younger Poets competition, won the prize in 1942 and was published as *For My People.* A Rosenwald Fellowship, a lecture tour, and other exciting honors and adventures followed. Miss Walker is now teaching at Jackson College in Mississippi.

Dodson's father was a Brooklyn minister. Educated there, at Bates College and at Yale University, where he earned a Master of Fine Arts de-

gree, Dodson saw two of his plays produced at Yale before he went out to teach and direct drama at various Negro colleges, including Howard University, where he is now located. *Powerful Long Ladder*, his first book, was a collection of poems. His poems have appeared in a number of magazines, and he too has benefited by a Rosenwald Fellowship.

A still younger group is already taking shape. To it belong such writers as Moses Carl Holman and Bruce McWright. Of these Myron O'Higgins seems nearest to recognition at this date, and Bette Latimer is the youngest. Both of these have had magazine and anthology publication, and O'Higgins is co-author with Robert Hayden of the attractive brochure *The Lion and the Archer*. He has been a Rosenwald Fellow. Bette Latimer graduated from Fisk in 1948, the year of her twenty-first birthday. Another newcomer is Mason Jordan Mason whose work is not widely known but whose admirers are most outspoken. Of none of the new group have more exciting things been predicted. A book of his poems is promised by the Twayne Publishers, Inc., whose poetry editor is John Ciardi.

As a whole, however, neither members of the post-Renaissance group nor the youngest group were as precocious as Langston Hughes and Countee Cullen, Claude McKay and Paul Laurence Dunbar. Hughes wrote "The Negro Speaks of Rivers" the summer after his graduation from Central High School in Cleveland. It has been translated into a dozen or two languages. Countee Cullen wrote "I Have a Rendezvous with Life" as a high school student at De Witt Clinton in New York, the poems of his first book while an undergraduate at New York University. The *Songs of Jamaica* by Claude McKay were written by the time he was nineteen, and all the poems in Dunbar's first book were apparently written before he reached twenty-one. Cullen and Hughes achieved important books at twenty-two and twenty-four respectively, books which received serious attention and widespread approval among top critics everywhere.

By far the most productive of the survivors of the Harlem Renaissance poets is Langston Hughes, of course. But Sterling Brown, who belongs to the same age group, though his poetry came to notice a little later, is still active, a distinguished teacher at Howard University as well as a respected critic and a poet with a deep feeling for folk materials. He is unsurpassed as a teller of tales and a reader of his own narrative verse

and character pieces, and the University of Minnesota and Vassar College have both borrowed him for semesters on their campuses. Donald Jeffrey Hayes, the quality of whose lyrics remains dulcet, lives quietly in Atlantic City, but continues to contribute short lyrics to magazines like *Harper's Bazaar*, *Good Housekeeping* and *This Week*. Neither racial nor highbrow, Hayes' position among Negro poets is in some respects like that of Frank Yerby among fiction writers. His hobby is setting his own lyrics to music. Helene Johnson, youngest of the Harlem group, stopped publishing poetry long ago, despite the promise of her early verse. She lives in Brooklyn with her husband and children. Clarissa Scott Delany, beautiful daughter of Emmett Scott and first wife of Hubert Delany, died young. And Frank Horne still turns a few poignant phrases in verse between his duties as a housing expert in the government at Washington.

There is also among us a sedate and unobtrusive company of mature singers whose careers go back, in at least one case, to the turn of this century and whose quiet achievements have encouraged other subsequent groups of Negro American poets. William Stanley Braithwaite stands out among these. A selected edition of Braithwaite's poems has just been published by Coward-McCann, calling to mind again such early collections as his *Lyrics of Life and Love* (1904) and *The House of Falling Leaves* (1908) as well as his famous series of annual *Anthologies of Magazine Verse*, 1913 to 1929, in which the works of American poets like Edgar Lee Masters, Vachel Lindsay, Carl Sandburg and many others were introduced to book readers. During all those years Braithwaite's service to poetry in the United States was of the greatest importance. He was seldom thought of as a Negro, but eventually recognition came from this direction as well. Now in his aerie at 409 Edgecomb Avenue in Harlem this veteran singer devotes his time to biographical and critical studies.

Angelina W. Grimké, Anne Spencer, Georgia Douglas Johnson and Jessie Redmond Fauset, all younger than Braithwaite, also belong to a span of singing years that began before the Renaissance in Harlem and reaches to the present. All are women of unusual charm—and reticence. Since her retirement as teacher of English in the Dunbar High School in Washington, D. C., Miss Grimké has lived in New York City. Anne Spencer, a librarian in Lynchburg, Virginia, was once described by another poet as "a lady in her gar-

den." She has more than justified this by recently announcing a crowning achievement: a pink candy-striped Chinese peony, eight years from seed. Georgia Douglas Johnson worked with an organization of women in behalf of the Republican candidates in the last elections. Many other poets, past and present, have found politics quite compatible with creative composition. One gathers that Georgia Douglas Johnson's has not flagged as a result. Jessie Redmond Fauset, an influence in the Harlem Renaissance by reason of her literary editorship of the *Crisis* as well as her four well-known novels, now appears to have returned to poetry, an even earlier love.

In the nation as a whole the suffering poet is still a prevailing type. There is no premium on sensitiveness. And the lot of the Negro poet has much in common with the plight of the whole species. This explains, no doubt, the tendency of some writers of poetry to apologize for the habit, others to keep it a secret. All have to face the hard problem of making a living. Since the income from poetry is extremely small, one may wonder how poets manage to keep body and soul together.

Well, Pauli Murray, one member of the young group, is a distinguished lawyer. Frank Horne, as has been indicated, continues in government service. Some, like Moses Carl Holman, Robert Hayden, Melvin B. Tolson and Sterling Brown, are college professors. Others, Helene Johnson and Gwendolyn Brooks, are housewives. Richard Wright, a sometime poet, is an important American novelist and probably the most distinguished American now living on the Left Bank in Paris. Myron O'Higgins and Bette Darcie Latimer are at the age of youthful pilgrimages and journeys.

Langston Hughes is the only Negro poet since Dunbar who has succeeded in making a living from poetry. But a poem must be used many ways to yield enough sustenance to keep a hearty individual like Mr. Hughes in the kind of food he likes. Therefore it is not surprising to find his poems being danced by Pearl Primus on the stage while they are sung by Juanita Hall in night clubs and on radio and television and by Murial Rahn in Town Hall concerts and while Paul Robeson is reciting "Freedom Train" in the United States, the West Indies and Central America. But it is a living, and as a result Mr. Hughes has had only one job—one semester as guest professor at Atlanta University—since the publication of *The Weary Blues*, his first book, in 1926. Poetry has turned a pretty penny for the Negro who spoke of rivers the summer after graduating from high school in 1920. And there is an eager and talented band of newer singers who hope that it will do as much for them.

Phylon Profile, XXII: Carl Van Vechten

George S. Schuyler

A great revolution has taken place in American race relations in the past quarter century, and while this phenomenon is ascribed to many causes by various authorities on the subject, perhaps the most prepotent has been the individual effort of Carl Van Vechten.

Changes may be brought about by social forces and mass action, but all changes begin in somebody's mind and move outward like ripples in a millpond to the farthest shores, once the revolutionary idea has been accepted. Tall, white-maned Carl Van Vechten, still suave and benign at seventy, has done more than any single person in this country to create the atmosphere of acceptance of the Negro.

Styles in thinking, like styles in clothing, shoes, and house furnishings, are the creation of a few individuals. More importantly, a new style in thinking requires disciples and the speed of their own conversion depends upon the personality and reputation of the father of the idea.

Many inspired white people before Van Vechten had devoted their lives to fighting color prejudice and bettering race relations, and without them and their influence the Negro here would have been well nigh eliminated by the white Neanderthal element. They were the quintessence of the American conscience.

Unlike them, however, the Sage of Central Park West did not approach the darker brethren as a problem over which to moan and sob but as more exotic and colorful Anglo-Saxons, considerably closer to the stirring drumbeats out of the green jungles of Africa and possessed of hitherto shackeled genius, so far unhonored and unsung but eminently worthy of investigation, appreciation and acceptance.

His attitude was not that of indignant belligerence toward the Negro-phobists among the civilized minority that shapes opinion the world over, but rather an attitude of pitying condescension toward those who were unaware, through ignorance or negligence, of the artistic, spiritual and cultural gifts of colored Americans.

It was one thing to utter anguished roars against the evils of peonage, discrimination, segregation and lynching but quite another to contend that these blacks were richly endowed Americans who had so much to offer spiritually and culturally to our civilization if permitted to do so.

His attack was not directed against the masses but against the upper classes who influence and direct the masses. As he said, "Break the taboo on the highest levels and finally that progress will seep down to the masses."

His attack was explosively effective because of his unprecedented technique which has been widely adopted and promoted by his disciples. As one picture is worth ten thousand words, so one association with an exceptional Negro has the impact greater than a ton of pro-Negro propaganda. Carl Van Vechten devoted himself to bringing together, physically and intellectually, the writers, actors, dancers, musicians, singers and composers of both "races" on a plane of equality.

"The more the two races get together," he held, "the better it is for race relations. Getting together should be on all levels and in all institutions." He was able to do this more effectively than others because he was already world famous as a successful critic of the ballet, of music and of the theater, and the best-selling author of a half dozen books on music and such works as *The Tattooed Countess, The Blind Bow Boy, Sacred and Profane Memories, Peter Whiffle, Spider Boy, The Tiger in the House, Lords of the Housetops* and numerous light and learned essays.

The literary lights, the stars of the ballet, the kings and queens of the theater, the painters, sculptors and editors who had attained envious preeminence frequented his salons on West 55th Street and later on Central Park West; and to this company Van Vechten introduced their darker opposite numbers. Here they rubbed shoulders, sipped cocktails, nibbled hors d'oeuvres, conversed, sang and danced without self-consciousness. What was at first an innovation and a novelty soon became commonplace, an institution.

Such salons in the early twenties were rare to the point of being revolutionary. At the time it was most difficult for Negroes to purchase a ticket for an orchestra seat in a theater, even in

298

Harlem, and it was with the greatest difficulty that a colored American in New York could get service in a downtown restaurant. Except at Coney Island, beaches were closed to Negroes and few were the other places that would tolerate their patronage. The freedom of the North was pretty much of a mockery, and this was particularly true of employment. This was the time when the production of O'Neill's *All God's Children Got Wings* was being denounced editorially in leading "liberal" newspapers, and the current Mayor of New York was refusing permission for colored and white children to appear in the first scene.

Most of the white people of Van Vechten's circle knew Negroes only as domestics and had never had them as associates. It was extremely daring for a white person to dine publicly with a Negro, and certainly to dance with one; but if those of the upper crust could be weaned over to such social acceptance, it was likely that a trend would be started which would eventually embrace the majority of those whites who shaped public opinion and set the social pace.

To this laudable endeavor Carl Van Vechten and his famous actress wife, Fania Marinoff, devoted themselves as assiduously as any sincere revolutionists could. With Machiavellian design the doyen of the dilettanti made it smart to be interracial. Once the idea took hold it spread in geometrical progression. Racial bias was eliminated on the higher levels and the Van Vechten philosophy spread like a forest fire, consuming great stands of racial snobbery along the way. Where there had been doubt and skepticism, there grew tolerance, curiosity, understanding and appreciation among both racial groups. Those who came as mere faddists left as fellow travelers of interracialism.

Indeed, it is interesting to compare the revolutionary methods of Carl Van Vechten in America with those of Willi Muenzenberg in Germany. For ten years after the Communist overthrow of the Kerensky government in Russia, the Red policy abroad was "No collaboration with the bourgeoisie," and everybody who bathed regularly, wore a white collar and did not have the palms of his hands covered with callouses was anathema to the Communists worshipping the Proletarian God. Willi Muenzenberg was the first Communist to discern that the Comrades were thus failing to utilize what could become a tremendous asset.

So Muenzenberg invented the fellow traveler. He cultivated the artistic and cultured circles, saw that they got recognition and publicity through his immense publishing facilities and influences, made it fashionable to become proletarian utopians and fight for "democracy": that is to say, totalitarianism. He believed that ten times more influential people could be made propagandists for Communism than there were card-carrying Communists, and time has confirmed him to the hilt.

With far different objectives but similar techniques, Van Vechten won over the same class in this country to acceptance of the Negro and appreciation of his potentialities and contributions. His disciples were the minority that tell the majority what to think, wear, see and hear, and they have multiplied tremendously in the past quarter century. It has now become smart to be tolerant, understanding and appreciative interracially, and if any one person can be credited with bringing about this revolution it is Carl Van Vechten. You cannot have equality unless it is desired, and it will not be desired unless the idea is first accepted, which will not happen at the bottom until it first happens at the top.

Of course, it took more than salons to do the job. After all, there is a limit to the number of people who can be invited even to Madison Square Garden. Fortunately, Carl Van Vechten had a powerful and potent pen. He had been influential in the world of opinion since he lost his first job with the Chicago *American* in 1906 for "lowering the tone of the Hearst papers." Coming from Cedar Rapids, Iowa, where his father had helped found a school for Negroes and where he had first become acquainted with Negroes through a Mr. Oliphant, he met more colored people, including a singer, Carita Day (Carrie Washington) whose talent impressed him.

When he moved to New York and became assistant music critic of the New York *Times*, he met the incomparable Bert Williams and other talented Negro artists in the course of his work. At the same time as H. L. Mencken and George Jean Nathan were first attracting widespread attention as literary and dramatic critics, Van Vechten was winning laurels for his urbane and penetrating criticism of contemporary music. He not only knew this music (he played the piano even as a boy) but was friendly with those who were composing, singing and playing it.

It was then that he inevitably became introduced to jazz, the greatest native American

music, and those who sang and played it. Indeed, he was one of the pioneers in discovering the worth of this music and was certainly the first to write understandingly and enthusiastically about it in the media read by those who set the style in everything. In such de luxe publications as *Vanity Fair*, a swank, slick paper periodical avidly read by the cognoscenti of the day, he introduced Ethel Waters and the three Smith girls, Mamie, Clara and Bessie, who were packing Negro theaters to the rafters but were yet undiscovered by the "superior" race. No evidence of Negro talent in arts and letters escaped his eagle eye or his interested attention. Always a man of great enthusiasms, he plunged into this new field with a zealot's obsession. Then when he met Walter White after the publication of the latter's *Fire in the Flint*, and through him the monumental James Weldon Johnson, his enthusiastic interest became incandescent.

He attended a dance given by the National Association for the Advancement of Colored People and met the fledgling poets, Countee Cullen and Langston Hughes, and writers like Zora Neale Hurston, Eric Walrond and Rudolph Fisher who were just breaking their shells, and Jessie Fauset, whose novel *There Is Confusion* was to become a landmark of the Negro Renaissance.

Within a month Van Vechten had become a regular visitor to Harlem, knew every important Negro and a whole lot who were not. This was his first time to meet the Negro intelligentsia, the colored folk who were like the whites with whom he was wont to associate. He was fascinated by the almost Parisian sophistication of the educated Negroes, by their keen minds, by the smartness and taste of their dress and furnishings. Here were Negroes who had high standards, who were abreast of the best in literature, who were a credit to American culture, and yet who were held apart from the mainstream of national life.

How could he make the rest of America understand this sophisticated, exotic, striving microcosm of American society? How could he capture the attention of the civilized minority everywhere and make them see what he had seen and heard and felt? It was with this in mind that he went to work on a novel of Harlem life–not the Harlem of fetid slums which later writers have dwelt upon *ad nauseum*, but a civilization as unknown to white folks as some Himalayan kingdom.

The novel was published in 1926 as *Nigger Heaven* and attained immediate preeminence on the best-selling lists. The reaction to the book gave eloquent testimony to the contemporary status of interracialism. The whites were astonished, delighted, incredulous; some Negro critics gagged at the sardonic title while others rejoiced that at last the reading public was getting a fairly accurate portrait of Negro urban life, its polish as well as its pitfalls, its joy as well as its grief. The gulf that existed between colored and white society was revealed by the amazement of whites that such a society existed without their knowledge, and by the naive delight of Negroes in a realistic portrayal of their lives.

There is a story that one wealthy white matron in Oklahoma City asked her Negro maid: "Is it true that there are Negroes in New York who live like those described in this book?"

"Why, Madam," the maid replied, "there are Negroes in Oklahoma City who live like that!"

The Negroes who objected to *Nigger Heaven* were mostly those who had not read it but disliked the title. James Weldon Johnson, Alice Dunbar Nelson and the writer were the only Negro reviewers who approved it without reservation, but the novel was nevertheless widely read by colored people. James Weldon Johnson held that no other title would have been so appropriate because of its tragic irony. One of the most violent critics was Dr. W. E. B. DuBois.

The novel succeeded in getting Van Vechten a much wider audience for his viewpoint than he could ever have obtained by personal contact in his apartment between white and colored people. With the ice thus broken, many road blocks to Negro acceptance were destroyed. It is noteworthy that today there is scarcely a prominent white person in the country who does not say that he or she personally has no prejudice against Negroes.

Because he felt that a critic could not be truly objective after forty, Van Vechten stopped his musical criticism at that age after writing numerous books of penetrating observations on music and music makers. At the age of fifty he abandoned the writing of novels because he felt that he had nothing more of importance to say. But being an active person and still tremendously interested in the Negro and his acceptance by the white society, he turned to photography. After all, while most white people had heard and read about outstanding Negroes, few had seen how they looked. At that time the picture of a Negro, no matter how prominent,

rarely appeared in the columns of a newspaper or magazine of general circulation.

With his usual enthusiastic concentration, Van Vechten devoted himself to photographing the outstanding Negroes of the day. He had been interested in photography since the end of the nineteenth century and by this time he was an expert. Throughout the Franklin Roosevelt and Harry Truman eras, he has given most of his attention to this task.

The result has been a tremendous volume of fine photographs of the most outstanding colored and white artists of the day in the theater, painting, sculpture, belles lettres, journalism, music and the theater. To be sure that these photographs receive wide circulation, Van Vechten has had them printed on postcards. It is not unusual to open one's mail box some morning and find a brief note from Van Vechten on the back of one of those postcards. In this way the eminent critic has reached thousands of people with wonderful photographs of Ethel Waters, Philippa Schuyler, Walter White, Marian Anderson, Avon Long and scores of others too numerous to mention.

Indeed, these photographs became so numerous that it led Van Vechten inevitably into the exhibiting of them. They have been shown almost everywhere and undoubtedly they have contributed much to breaking down barriers between the races. In these pictures of artistic and cultured Negroes he carries a message almost as effective as the essays and books he has written and the soirees he has held in his artistic, colorful and book-lined apartment on Central Park West.

Over one hundred of these photographs of outstanding Negroes were placed on exhibition at Wadleigh High School in New York City in 1949, as the Jerome Peterson Memorial Collection. He wanted to show the young people of all races how many distinguished Negroes there are in the world. He succeeded beyond all expectations.

In 1947 he presented to Howard University the Rose McClendon Memorial Collection of Photographs of Celebrated Negroes, some one hundred and seventy in all.

In 1941 he began the James Weldon Johnson Collection of Negro Arts and Letters to Yale University. It consisted of manuscripts, letters, photographs, songs and other material, and contains the major portion of James Weldon Johnson's memorabilia. Included are also many rare phonograph records.

In 1949 Fisk University was the grateful recipient of the Carl Van Vechten Gallery of Fine Arts which contained numerous books and manuscripts, the finest collection of its kind in the South. This was supplemented by the George Gershwin Collection of Music and Musical Literature to the same institution of learning. Along with this was the Florine Stettsheimer Memorial Collection of books about the fine arts. To Yale University went the Anna Marble Pollock Memorial Library on books about cats. To make sure that those who did not frequent libraries and museums would be sure to see his huge collection of photographs of notable Negroes, Mr. Van Vechten arranged an exhibition of intimate photographic studies in the windows of the Roger Kent stores in Rockefeller Plaza, in New York. Here could be seen the pictures of Marian Anderson, Leo Coleman, Joe Louis, Edward Matthews, Willard Motley, Paul Robeson, Bessie Smith, Josh White and Walter White, along with photographs of the leading white artists of stage, screen, the ballet and literature.

Many honors and testimonials have been given to the racial revolutionist of Central Park West by Negroes and whites who understand and appreciate his quiet and effective work for interracial amity. They range all the way from scrolls by Yale University to a testimonial dinner by the James Weldon Johnson Literary Guild at the Port Arthur Restaurant in Chinatown, New York City. They are just a small token of the gratitude of those who appreciate what his efforts have meant in breaking down the inhibitions, prejudices and snobbery that hampered the development of a healthy understanding and acknowledgment of the contribution of the Depressed Tenth to American culture and civilization.

Today, rich in years and knowledge, he holds open house for his friends and disciples in the vast drawing room of his colorful apartment on Central Park West, with the oil portrait of himself as a much younger man looking down benignly upon the scene. Easily he moves among his guests, replenishing glasses, conversing with this one and that, dropping a *bon mot* or a mordant observation here and there among his friends and worshippers, with an occasional aside to his petite spouse, Fania Marinoff, the perfect hostess, who has retired from the theater but will always be of it.

His great legacy to future generations is the honor of having boldly entered where lesser men feared to tread; and despite the carping criticism

and sneering of the bigoted, having wrought a real revolution in white men's thinking about the Negro. His has been a labor of love and admiration, unlike the hateful efforts of more sinister propagandists proclaiming more ambitious and far-reaching goals in which they really did not believe.

His efforts have been and still are the triumph of sincerity and appreciation over bigotry and snobbery. No one today can meet and talk with him and his wonderful wife without being spiritually and intellectually enriched. No one can know of what he has accomplished in healing America's greatest wound without a feeling of deepest appreciation. For here was and is a man who, without hope or desire of mundane reward, labored in the vineyard and brought forth such bounty as men have rarely seen.

Lounging lazily on the broad settee facing his fireplace, he remarks as if to himself, that he would like to see all separation, all barriers, all handicaps removed, and all Americans regardless of color or creed, united as brothers in mutual understanding and cooperation.

"I'd like it to be," he murmurs, "–well, like my house. Colored people come in and out, play an important role in my life–but there is no problem. Just people."

Race and the Negro Writer

Hugh M. Gloster

From the beginnings of his active authorship in this country the Negro writer has been preoccupied with racial issues and materials. This obsession with race is not hard to explain, because the tragic plight of the colored population of the United States has forced the Negro writer to stand with his people and to voice their sufferings, reverses, triumphs, and aspirations. The inhumanities of slavery, the restrictions of segregation, the frustrations of prejudice and injustice, the debasements of concubinage and bastardy, the ravages of persecution and lynching– these have constituted the bitter experience of American black folk; and it is only natural that the Negro writer has focused upon the themes of racial defense, protest, and glorification.

While propaganda from inside sources has frequently assisted colored people in their struggle toward equality and freedom, the preponderating use of racial subject matter has handicapped the Negro writer in at least four important ways. In the first place, it has retarded his attainment of a cosmic grasp of the varied experiences, humorous as well as tragic, through which individuals pass in this life. Second, it has diminished his philosophical perspective to the extent that he has made only meager contributions to national and world ideologies. Third, it has usually limited his literary range to the moods and substance of race in the United States. Fourth and finally, it has helped certain critics and publishers to lure him into the deadly trap of cultural segregation by advising him that the black ghetto is his proper milieu and that he will write best when he is most Negroid. Incidentally, this insidious counsel, repeated many times in an attempt to stabilize cultural separation, has been propagated so effectively that the abandonment of black stereotypes by the Negro writer is traditionally viewed by many Americans as an artistic desertion of the race.

In spite of the limiting and crippling effects of racial hypersensitivity and Jim-Crow esthetics, the Negro writer has gradually loosened the shackles that have held him in mental bondage for the past two centuries. In recent years the emancipatory process has been accelerated through the efforts of such authors as Richard Wright, Ann Petry, Gwendolyn Brooks, Willard Motley, Frank Yerby, and Zora Neale Hurston. In *Native Son* (1940) Wright treats the old subject of Negro degradation and persecution but transcends the color line by identifying his downtrodden protagonist with underprivileged youth of other lands and races:

More than anything else, as a writer, I was fascinated by the similarity of the emotional tensions of Bigger in America and Bigger in Nazi Germany and Bigger in old Russia. All Bigger Thomases, white and black, felt tense, afraid, nervous, hysterical, and restless.

This successful blending of class and race experience suggests that Wright's sympathies are comprehensive enough to include all exploited people; and *Native Son* illustrates, perhaps more effectively than any other novel by an American Negro, that it is possible to attack racial oppression and at the same time provide truthful implications for all mankind. In *The Street* (1946), a stirring record of delinquency in Harlem, and in *Annie Allen* (1949), a Pulitzer Prize-winning account of human fortunes in South Chicago, Ann Petry and Gwendolyn Brooks, respectively, disclose the common human denominators of passion, marriage, motherhood, and disillusionment in the lives of contemporary Negro women. Also lifting his work to the universal plane by representing humanity through an individual, Willard Motley reports the downfall and death of Nick Romano in *Knock on Any Door* (1947). In this important contribution to world literature the symbolic victim of organized society is an Italian boy who rapidly degenerates after his impoverished family moves to the slums of Chicago's West Side. With his motto of "Live fast, die young, and have a good-looking corpse," Nick could be any dissolute youth in any corrupt metropolis. Writing entertaining romances for big money profits, Frank Yerby has produced in rapid succession five novels that are ideologically and esthetically unimportant but nevertheless noteworthy as the first series of best-seller triumphs by an American Negro writer in the field of general fiction. Following Yerby into the mainstream but not approaching his financial success have come Ann Petry with *Country Place* (1947), an account of clandestine love in a small New England town, and Zora Neale Hurston with *Seraph on the Suwanee* (1946), a local-color title of romance and marriage among Florida Crackers. Wright, Mrs. Petry, Miss Brooks, Motley, Yerby, and Miss Hurston are tillers of broader fields than the circumscribed areas of racial life.

The gradual emancipation of the Negro writer from the fetters of racial chauvinism and cultural isolation has recently been facilitated by the rapid extension of democratic ideas and attitudes in this country and abroad. Despite the persistence of the plantation tradition with its apotheosis of slavery as a felicitous existence for the irresponsible "darky," the publishing and writing professions have exhibited an increasingly liberal attitude toward the Negro as author and as subject. During the past five years, for example, such firms as D. Appleton-Century Company, the Dial Press, Houghton Mifflin Company, and Charles Scribner's Sons have published Negro-authored books in the field of general fiction; and in advertisements of these works the practice has been to make no mention of the racial identity of the writers. Throughout the country, moreover, white authors are manifesting a growing disposition to describe frankly and understandingly the social and intellectual dilemmas of colored people. Even Southerners are treating Negro life with increasing honesty and objectivity, and Georgia-born Lillian Smith's *Killers of the Dream* (1949) may be regarded as a harbinger of an unbiased approach to racial subject matter by writers living below the Mason-Dixon Line. That the social conscience is disturbed not only in the United States but in other countries as well is convincingly demonstrated in Alan Paton's *Cry, the Beloved Country* (1946), an epochal novel which records the interactions of South African natives and whites with the insight and courage that characterize the universal approach.

The main point of this essay is not that the Negro writer should suppress his ethnic individuality or relinquish racial subject matter. The chief emphasis is that he should consider all life as his proper milieu, treat race from the universal point of view, and shun the cultural insularity that results from racial preoccupation and Jim-Crow esthetics. If a liberal English clergyman can deal realistically and understandingly with the experience of South Africans in *Cry, the Beloved Country*, the broad-minded Negro artist can similarly handle the comedy and tragedy of his own racial group and of other folk as well. The Negro writer is also an American writer, a man of letters as free as any of his national confreres to tap the rich literary resources of our land and its people. To accept the principle that racial experience is the only natural province of the Negro writer is to approve an artistic double standard that is just as confining and demoralizing in American literature as is segregation in American life.

The Negro Writer–Shadow and Substance

J. Saunders Redding

Season it as you will, the thought that the Negro American is different from other people, and especially from other Americans, is still unpalatable to most Negroes. But a rather inexorable logic both explains the aversion (for of course Negro "differentness" was and is largely responsible for the social ills that beset him) and supports the notion. The Negro is different. An iron ring of historical circumstances has made him so. Slavery, organized terrorism, discrimination, prejudice–the point need not be labored.

But the differentness has little depth. It goes only so far as the superficies, as lineament rather than character. It does not reach down into the biology. It does not thrust deep into the idioplasm, into the matrix of emotion. It transforms nothing fundamental. It does not make the Negro a monster. That he has long borne a monstrous reputation (and that individuals in the race have lived up to it) would be entirely beside the point were it not for the patent fact that this imputation set artificial bounds to the Negro's thinking about himself and to the thinking of whites about him. And this itself would be of no consequence except that it led the Negro, as creator, into the *cul de sac* of insincerity and dishonesty and, as audience, into the aversion mentioned above.

It has been until very recently a vicious circle. The aversion has had the result of leaving the Negro writer with an audience only disingenuously his: an audience which he has had to trick, to bait, to lure. I take it that these terms carry the very strongest connotations of improbity and hypocrisy. In the very earliest and in some later days it was the lure of imitativeness. Take Wheatley and Watkins and Whitfield and Braithwaite, and James Weldon Johnson when he wrote for the *Century*. In Dunbar's day it was the lure of dialect and the contrived comic, and Dunbar is a self-confessed dissembler. In the Twenties and Thirties it was the lure of the naughty peep-show, the sensational and gross, and the most financially successful and the most often commented-upon Negro writers, Claude McKay and Wallace Thurman, were hucksters of

filth. Only now and then did Negro writers working in Negro material deal sincerely and/or profoundly with Negro life. When they did, or tried to, they were rejected. Sutton Griggs and Charles Chestnutt. The first novel that James Weldon Johnson wrote and could never find a publisher for. The novel, *The Autobiography of An Ex-Coloured Man*, which he wrote and published first at his own expense in 1912.

But I think that the day of all this is past or fast passing. The social and intellectual and spiritual climate of Roosevelt's New Deal and of the world's second war was exactly tempered to produce a change in the outlook of the American Negro. This change is reflected in his writing over the last fifteen years. (It is also reflected, but less importantly, in writing by whites about Negroes.) And I think that the ethnocentric compulsions to racial chauvinism and racial escape and cultural and empirical denial are weakened and that the American Negro writer's progress is toward realistic idealism and a sort of scientific humanism, and these, I think, are the highest goals of most of the world's creative effort.

But let me not simply bandy these terms about. By progress toward realistic idealism and scientific humanism, I mean the engagement of the imagination, the intellect, the passions and the will in transforming the real–say, a people or a social philosophy–into something no less real but more rewarding and fulfilling. Out of the obscure and sometimes not fully realized potentials, which the creative mind recognizes intuitively and which are based in realities, spiritual and emotional as well as physical, the realistic idealist seeks to establish desired actualities. Realistic idealism is Dewey's pragmatism, Gilson's Catholicism, and Finkelstein and Koestler's Judaism translated in terms of art rather than of social philosophy.

There is inevitably some relation between a people's daily exertion to live and what they hope to make of life; some relation between effort and ideal. There is proof of this in every great social or moral movement, and sometimes in economic movements, like the late lamented technocracy–all of which owe their origins to a

congruity between what is—the real, and what could be—the ideal.

It is true that this congruity is sometimes destroyed by fanaticism, or cynicism, or the use of the wrong means to attain the desired end, and then the real and the ideal become separated and grow into conflict. Because of the resurgence of the Klan spirit, because of the political cynicism, of period 1900 through Hoover, because of the corruption of justice, because of a thousand daily sneers at a despised people's dream of equality, the separation and conflict between the real and the ideal was happening to the Negro. Then the New Deal and World War Two put a stop to it.

Do not question how. It was because of the very nature of the principles of Roosevelt's revolution, and it was because of the creed for the establishment of which the whole English-speaking world declared itself to be fighting. And so the Negro, but more especially the Negro writer, found himself being slowly liberated from racial chains by the very impulses which he had been re-viled for feeling. With his liberation he could begin to see himself as in no fundamental way different and particular. He could begin to explain himself and his motives and his character in terms of conditioning forces common to all humanity. Virtue, let us say, he could begin to see now was not ludicrous because a Negro possessed it. Treason was no more monstrous—and no less so—because it was committed by a Negro; adultery no more sinful; lying no more reprehensible; cowardice no more shameful. He began to see that the values were human, not racial. And he began to prove this by testing them in creatures of his own imagination who were not Negro.

But at the same time he began to see this, he saw also, I think and hope, that within his special observation and within his special category of race-experience there is still a mine of creative material, and that this material, no longer artificially bounded by fear and shame, is full of lessons and of truth for the world.

A Blueprint for Negro Authors

Nick Aaron Ford

If the Negro author's past achievements have not been great, at least they have been motivated by great intentions. He has created the kind of literature that Walt Whitman had in mind when he said, "Literature is big only in one way–when used as an aid in the growth of the humanities–a furthering of the cause of the masses–a means whereby men may be revealed to each other as brothers."

But as we face the second half of the twentieth century, there is a babel of voices seeking to direct the harassed author. There is widespread dissatisfaction not only with the failure of these authors to achieve a maturity in artistic technique, but also with the limited goals some of them seemingly have set for themselves. In this welter of confusion I dare suggest a blueprint for writers who wish to accept the glorious opportunities and grave responsibilities of the next half century.

The first of my requirements is a mastery of craftsmanship. The past record in this respect is dismal. Despite one hundred and ninety years of effort, no American Negro poet has achieved a status comparable to such first-rate white poets as Robert Frost or Edwin Arlington Robinson. In the field of drama the record is almost nil. Only in fiction, and that within the last decade, has the Negro author achieved first-rate distinction.

The chief weakness of these writers has been in the area of craftsmanship and design rather than theme. No Negro author before the advent of Richard Wright's *Native Son* (1940) had deserved a listing among first-rate American novelists. Only Frank Yerby and Willard Motley have earned such a place since. Other authors have treated equally potent themes, but mastery of the art of fiction has been lacking. For the most part, the style is heavy and laborious, more suitable to a sociological treatise than to a novel. They fail in the three major essentials of good craftsmanship–namely, the ability to invent interesting and natural conversation, the ability to create memorable characters, and the ability to construct unforgettable scenes through the creation of pity and terror.

In addition to Wright, Yerby, and Motley, there are five other novelists who possess one or more of these qualities to a considerable degree, and who, if they continue to improve, will achieve first rank in the near future: they are William Attaway, Ann Petry, Arna Bontemps, William Gardner Smith, and J. Saunders Redding.

My second requirement for the Negro author is the continued use of racial themes. In certain quarters a great clamor has arisen for Negro authors to abandon racial material and launch out in the "universal depths." It is the belief of this school of thought that a writer's preoccupation with materials dealing with his own race is an admission that he is incapable of dealing with any other. It further maintains that such a writer is adding fuel to the fires of race consciousness, segregation, and racial proscription. To counteract these sinister forces, the writer must treat universal themes, and leave to white authors the exploitation of subject matter dealing with Negro life.

In my opinion such perverted reasoning is pure sophistry. In all ages and climates of man's civilization, one of the major purposes of literature has been to represent the thought and actions of men with as much truth to life as is possible. Naturally a writer can portray life that he feels deeply and understands minutely with a greater degree of genuineness and truth than he can life which is more foreign to his experience. I cannot believe that a Negro, sensitive, as all artists must be, can feel and understand anything in America as minutely and as truthfully as he can the effects of race. Then, why should he not write about that which he knows best? No white man or woman can understand the tragedy, the pathos, and the humor of being a Negro in America as well as a talented Negro. Sir Philip Sidney's advice to the young poet, "Look in thy heart, and write," has not yet been proved either invalid or unwise.

Furthermore, the record shows that up to this point, at least, the most powerful and most significant poetry, drama, and fiction by Negro authors have been based on racial themes. Ann

306

Petry's second novel, which logically should have been better than the first, is greatly inferior to *The Street* both in design and execution. She had to be so concerned with conjuring up vicarious experiences of a white society with which she was not minutely familiar that she lost the naturalness of expression necessary to good art. Zora Neale Hurston's *Seraph on the Suwanne,* which portrays life among white Floridians, is almost unbelievably inferior to her two novels of Negro life. Even Frank Yerby achieved greater artistic perfection in *The Foxes of Harrow* and *The Vixens,* both of which have a background of Negro life and action, than he did in *The Golden Hawk* and *Pride's Castle,* which completely ignore the racial angle.

Professor Harry A. Overstreet of New York City College was right when he said, "The whites need to know the Negro and like him. A special obligation, therefore, is upon the Negro writer to turn to the story as a means whereby he may make his people known."

My third requirement for the Negro author is the use of social propaganda subordinated so skillfully to the purposes of art that it will not insult the average intelligent reader. I do not think it is sufficient for the Negro author to treat racial themes with no regard to their deeper social implications as was done by Countee Cullen in *One Way to Heaven* and Zora Neale Hurston in *Jonah's Gourd Vine* and *Their Eyes Were Watching God.*

Is propaganda a legitimate ingredient of literature? Albert Guerard, in *Art for Art's Sake,* says, "An artist does not suffer from being identified with a cause; if the cause is himself, a vital part of himself, it is also a fit element of his art. He suffers most from not being identified with his cause, from adopting and serving a purpose which remains alien to his personality."

In *The Great Tradition* Granville Hicks maintains, "In the whole history of American literature one can scarcely think of a writer, commonly recognized as great, who did not immerse himself in the life of the times, who did not concern himself with the problems of his age."

Tolstoi, in *What Is Art?,* declares, "We know that the well being of man lies in union with his fellowmen.... Art should transform this perception into feeling."

If one accepts the conclusions of the three critics quoted above, as I certainly do, he must also accept propaganda as a legitimate ingredient of serious literature. But I do not advocate art for the sake of propaganda. I demand a proper subordination and the observance of good taste.

An example of the violation of the limitations I place upon this requirement may be seen in the poetry of Frank Marshall Davis. His propaganda, though based on sound critical analysis, is so blunt and militant that it has little chance of winning sympathetic consideration. In addition, much of it offends good taste. Such bitter iconoclasm as the following quotation from "Christ Is a Dixie Nigger" goes beyond the bounds which I have prescribed:

> Your pink priests who whine about Pilate and
>   Judas and Gethsemane I'd like to hog-tie and
>   dump into the stinking cells to write a New Tes-
>   tament around the Scottsboro Boys.
> Subdivide your million dollar temples into liquor
>   taverns and high class whore-houses.... My
>   nigger Christ can't get past the door anyway.
> Remember this, you wise guys.
> Your tales about Jesus of Nazareth are no go
>   with me.... I've got a dozen Christs in Dixie
>   all bloody and black.

With his extraordinary imagination and his marvelous skill in the use of words, Davis could make a favorable impression in the world of poetry, provided he curb his bitterness and temper his cynicism with reasonable restraint.

My fourth requirement grows out of the third. One of the best methods of subordinating propaganda to art is the skillful use of symbolism. By this means the Negro author can fight the battles of his race with subtlety and popularity. Willard Motley, in presenting the story of an Italian minority in *Knock on Any Door,* has symbolized the problems of all minorities, including his own race.

But the chief symbolist among Negro authors is Frank Yerby. Starting his literary career in 1944 with "Health Card," a bitter story of America's rejection of the Negro as a dignified human being, which won for him an O Henry Memorial Prize, he has steadily progressed from complete absorption in a racial theme to complete abandonment of racial material. But in all of his nonracial writings he has substituted a racial symbol, the symbol of rejection.

He finds in the social rebels of the white race, in men and women who because of birth, or manner of livelihood, or disregard of social and moral proprieties have become pariahs among their own people, an archetype of racial rejection. But these white rejectees fight back. They build industrial empires, or pile up huge mountains of illicit wealth, or become swashbuck-

ling pirates who defy the laws of the smug and the respectable. Thus, symbolically the white rejectees get their revenge on a proud and haughty society, and through them the rejected Negro can feel a sense of vicarious triumph.

I conclude with the challenging words of J. Donald Adams: "Sometimes I think the wheel has turned full circle, and that writers must be the fighters now. They really stand at Armageddon, and must battle for the Lord. They, more than anyone else perhaps, can be effective in preserving the values that are threatened."

The Forties: A Decade of Growth

Charles H. Nichols, Jr.

The decade just past began auspiciously with the publication of Richard Wright's *Native Son* and closed, no less auspiciously, with the Pulitzer-Prize-winning book of poems, *Annie Allen*, by Gwendolyn Brooks. The Negro writer in America has featured as prominently in the literature of the Forties as has the Negro subject. And it is my impression that the work of these Negro writers has a number of positive values.

Essentially, I should like to defend two main contentions: first, that in the Forties the Negro author has, by and large, increased his knowledge of his craft–in the novel and in poetry especially; second, that the literature produced by Negroes in recent years has achieved a variety of subject matter almost unknown in the past. This is not to say that the writings under consideration represent in any definite sense a great and permanent literature. These tendencies indicate only that in his literary efforts the Negro is surely coming of age–though, happily, not as a Negro (whatever the racial tag implies). For there can be no doubt that the work of the group will be increasingly "assessed without too much regard to racial origin and conditioning."

That the novelists of our time–Richard Wright, Saunders Redding, Willard Motley, Ann Petry, and Chester Himes–are superior to their predecessors in their capacity to write seems to me patent. The novels they have produced have smoothness of style as well as conviction, subtlety as well as strength, depth of meaning as well as rare insight into character. For these authors are beyond the special pleading, the sentimentality, the white hot protest of the "New Negro Renais-sance," and that feverish search for the exotic which Hugh Gloster has so aptly called "the Van Vechten vogue." They have revealed their meanings in sharply drawn dramatic situations which, while often based on their racial experiences, have universal significance. All this is high praise, but I wish only to indicate how far we have come from *Plum Bun* and *The Autobiography of an Ex-Coloured Man*. *Native Son* has achieved a permanent place in American literature not only because its theme is universal, but because its prose is instinct with life, shorn of pretense and flabbiness, with all the freshness and tang of people talking. *The Street, If He Hollers Let Him Go, Knock on Any Door*, and *Stranger and Alone* have, in varying degrees, the same sensitive portrayal of character, the same immediacy and economy in technique. Chester Himes is, perhaps, given to somewhat melodramatic situations (particularly in *Lonely Crusade* where the structure and purpose of the novel are not clearly realized). Saunders Redding, after the splendid promise of *No Day of Triumph*, has presented in Shelton Howden a character not quite clothed in flesh and blood, but has created memorable characters, vivid scenes from Negro college life–all described with such competence and sure artistry that his first novel is a notable achievement.

In poetry this mastery of craftsmanship is extraordinary. The best work of Gwendolyn Brooks, Margaret Walker, Owen Dodson and M. Carl Holman places them in the front rank of our contemporary poets. The magnificent cadences of Margaret Walker's "Delta," "For My People," "Today" and "Our Need" with their pow-

erful imagery give clear promise of permanent value. It is a pity that Miss Walker has produced so little since 1942. *A Street in Bronzeville* and *Annie Allen* are strikingly original, for, as J. Saunders Redding has written, this is "a poetic talent that expresses itself with intensity, with a richness and aptness of imagery and with glowing warmth." M. Carl Holman often achieves a compactness of expression and an originality of diction which are unusual. But for an occasionally obscure piece, his work is remarkable. The latest poems of Countee Cullen and Langston Hughes are disappointing, at times even banal and trite, and unfortunately we have heard nothing from Sterling Brown for some time. It is regrettable that the total amount of significant poetry by Negroes is so small.

In the drama the paucity of material is even more disturbing. Apart from the stage version of *Native Son*, Langston Hughes' adaptation of *Mulatto* (*The Barrier*) and a play or two by Owen Dodson (*Divine Comedy* and *Bayou Legend*), there has been no play worthy of the name written by a Negro and performed during the last decade. The work of Randolph Edmonds is turgid and loose, too much given to hackneyed situations and bombastic, set speeches. This dearth of plays is especially unfortunate in view of the continued interest in works by and about Negroes on Broadway. *Deep Are the Roots, Anna Lucasta, St. Louis Woman, The Respectful Prostitute* and *Lost in the Stars*—to say nothing of a number of motion pictures—have indicated how eagerly the American public will listen to the playwright who is able to capitalize on the racial theme.

But the Negro writer is turning more and more to broader themes. Dorothy Canfield Fisher wrote of Richard Wright, "The author of this book, as has no other American writer, wrestles with utter sincerity with the Dostoievski subject—a human soul in hell because it is sick with a deadly spiritual sickness." This is a universal theme of the greatest possible significance for our time. It is, in a sense, the theme of Willard Motley's *Knock on Any Door* and of Saunders

Redding's *Stranger and Alone*. It is to be found in Camus and John Hersey and other authors all over the modern world, plagued as we all are by fear, hate, insecurity and the threat of war. Thus the novelists and poets of the Negro group, employing a variety of subjects, are seeing the age-old struggle of their people in its proper perspective: within the broad human struggle for a decent and meaningful life. Not only are these writers exploring many more aspects of Negro experience, but in such works as *The Foxes of Harrow, Pride's Castle, Knock on Any Door,* and *Country Place* they are not even primarily concerned with Negro life. Merely to mention such works is to point out the breadth of view that has characterized the Forties. Only Yerby's themes seem backward-looking. For though Frank Yerby has achieved considerable popularity and, in his novels, recaptures the historical milieu well, his work is in the tradition of nineteenth century romantic fiction, overwritten, turgid, and, in its total effect, tends to reinforce aristocratic biases which should have died a century ago.

In biography, autobiography and the serious essay there have been many important things produced which there is no space to mention. One can only deplore the sensation-mongering, the lack of integrity and accuracy, the yellow journalism of which the Negro press is still all too guilty. It is a very real question whether the Negro newspaper has not already outlived its usefulness.

It would appear, then, that, in the main, a heartening maturity has come to Negro letters in the last decade. The racial pride, the Quixotic radicalisms, the propaganda, the adolescent sense of emancipation and defiance, the bizarre aspects of the "New Negro Renaissance" have given way to a deeper, subtler tone, a more universal quality, and a more impressive technique in the literature written by the group. But the total production of the group is small. We need to improve the quality of our contribution to American letters; we need, too, to provide new outlets for the promising young writers whose aspirations, insights and ideas have too seldom found a voice.

No Kafka in the South
L. D. Reddick

A few seasons ago, Franz Kafka was all the rage in New York—and, no doubt, in other places, too. In those days almost everywhere one went—especially in the houses off Park Avenue, in "the Village," or in and about the universities—little groups could be seen clustered, discussing what Kafka really meant.

The scene is familiar: a varied-looking, rather oddly dressed group, half-sitting, half-lounging on sofas, chairs, hassocks, or the floor; smoking cigarettes or strangely-shaped pipes; sipping liquor lightly; but most of all, uttering an unbroken flow of words.

These "bull sessions," at times, were flights from the interminable political pros and cons; and then, again, they were sometimes continuations of politics in literary terms. The Jewish Question or the Negro Question was bound to come up before the evening was over.

Along with the rest, I read *The Trial, The Castle,* and "The Metamorphosis" and crowded in to hear what my colleague, Erich Fromm, had to say about the symbolism of these works.

In this sense, I was filled with Kafka when I left New York. And I was provincial enough to assume that there were such Kafka groups everywhere else. Actually, out of the "Big Town," I was to go six months before I encountered another Kafka "fan."

Perhaps, it is not possible to move from Manhattan down to Atlanta without undergoing some sort of psychological circumcision. The ritual is performed daily on those "natives" whose wild will to live must be reduced to the laws and customs of the local "culture." It is painful enough for those who realize what goes on, what happens to themselves and to others; but it is horrifying (for me, at least) to see so many who, apparently, are not at all aware that they are, in fact, being castrated. Acquiescence for these lost ones has come so quietly, so well-cushioned, so well-cloaked that memory surrendered its hold on that day of submission long, long ago.

There were always a few, though, who knew that it was not necessary for them to live the kind of lives that they saw almost everybody living.

Under these circumstances, Kafka began to take on new meaning. I re-read him. I could see in Atlanta, Georgia, much that he described as of Prague. This was particularly true when the Negro intellectual and the black bourgeoise were looked at through a Kafka lens. There were, for example, the same exclusion and rejection—more devastating in its less obvious forms. Negroes in Atlanta, like Jews—surely German Jews—in Czechoslovakia, never feel that they are a part of their whole city or town or village; they are always "native-foreigners," so to speak. They are seldom allowed (or allow themselves) to think even about the whole community and its people. Often when a local calamity occurs—a fire, a "cave in" or a collision—Negroes will ask each other, "were any Colored people hurt?" The answer will give them their cue to be sad or indifferent, if not inwardly happy.

More than enough is apparent and crude but the plague of intangible, partly-imaginary persecutions is worse. It is not so much the fact of what actually happens as it is the apprehension of what may happen. The gestures and the shadows are in effect more disturbing than the substance.

Little children notice the humiliating poses that their parents and their teachers (have to) take, from time to time. Black kids fight each other yet step back when some white imp taunts them. Young and pretty brown-skin girls fear to act up and put on as other young and pretty girls do; that is, they dare not take for granted the prerogative of the American woman: that the world was made for her! Even the gay, young Colored men of Georgia do not joke about blondes, as do all men elsewhere in America. I heard one college professor say that his best days are those during which he does not see a white face. That may well be.

Many a sensitive Negro in the South—and without doubt in other places, too—must have felt or dreamed that he was a cockroach (as in "The Metamorphosis") or that he is daily called upon to face trial on charges that are never stated, by an accuser he can never confront (*The Trial*) or that as he pursues some ever-receding hilltop, a

vast invisible leprosy eats away life, his life (*The Castle*).

The parallels to Kafka seem to be limitless; however, there are sufficient reversals to make the theme fresh. For instance, the Negro communities of the South are relatively poor and culturally retarded while the Prague Jew was economically and culturally ahead of his fellow citizens. Again, the double rejection in Atlanta (or Nashville, Tennessee) of the Negro intellectual is as Negro (by the white majority) and as intellectual (by the masses) whereas the German Jews in Kafka's Prague were rejected as Jews (by the Czechs) and then as Germans (also by the Czechs).

In the South there is a special paradox in that the lower-class Negro protects the middle-class Negro while the latter "leads" and "restrains" the former. There is a fierce affection and ambivalence about it all.

All this is to ask: why has no Negro writer turned these dramatic situations into literature? No picture exists in our novels of the Negro intellectual and there are only fragments of the materially successful Negro business man or professional.

It would be wrong to say that no one in this whole domain has been adequately perceptive. A great many have known "the anguish of the marrow, the ague of the skeleton." John Hope, the educational pioneer of Atlanta University, must have felt deeply about his life and life about him. "You've got to leave Georgia (from time to time) in order to stay here," he used to say.

W. E. B. Du Bois lived in Atlanta, Georgia, at least at the University there, for a decade; then fled; after two more decades returned, then fled again. He walled himself inside a stern discipline and an outer chill and formality that included goatee and cane. He poured himself into his work, producing pioneer and "objective" sociologies. His spirit came forth somewhat in that beautiful book, *Souls of Blackfolk*, and broke loose completely in "A Litany of Atlanta":

> Whither? North is greed and South is blood; within, the coward, and without, the liar. Whither? To death?
> Whither? To life? But not this life, dear God, not this.

Poet William Stanley Braithwaite, Boston-born and Boston-bred, was also there for a decade. And yet, somehow, he never wrote a line (that I have seen) that revealed or betrayed his inner feelings.

The failure of Kafka conditions to produce a Kafka may be inexplicable. Nevertheless, there are several leads that may give us a possible clue to the mystery–if such it is.

First, there is the literary tradition of the Negro community. All over America and in the South particularly–it is an oral tradition, not written. Negroes told the Bre'r Rabbit stories; a white newspaper man wrote them down. The conversation of Negroes is often naturally brilliant. Dick Wright was talking about this when he said that the figures of speech of the teen-agers in a Chicago Southside boys club were "as forceful and colorful as any ever used by English-speaking people."

This is also true of some of the students and teachers in the colleges. They may read their lessons and speak their lectures but when they communicate for fun, they talk very well. Even Negro intellectuals tend to read and talk, rather than read and write.

This disinclination to write on the part of literate persons of color leads to a second consideration. It is, maybe, a bit more direct than the first. There seems not to be, by such individuals, the slightest realization that their subjective experiences–the spiritual loneliness and suffocation–are anything that anybody anywhere would care to read about. Many would be ashamed to admit that they feel the way they do about their world. They will talk, though, to their friends and without striving to do so, reveal the beauty and pity of it all. This, too, this literary bashfulness, is of one piece with the not-belongingness of the marginal outsider.

Finally, everyone knows that writing in America, more than anywhere else on earth, is a commodity. What do readers expect of "Negro literature?" Or better, what do publishers expect readers to expect? Something wild, sensational, filled out with muscle and bone action, loud or tearful music. Look at the novels of Negro life that have sold. From *Uncle Tom's Cabin* to *Nigger Heaven* to *Strange Fruit*–has there been a subtle one in the lot? Even *Native Son* was read by many as a murder-mystery.

Negro authors who have done best-sellers have deserted the Negro theme (vide: Frank Yerby and Willard Motley). The tangential Negro novels are even more external and lurid (from the standpoint of Negro characterization). *Gone with the Wind*–a more modern re-statement of *The*

Leopard's Spots text—still remains the champion world-wide seller. Like its predecessors, contemporaries and successors, it is based, quite obviously, on the prevailing stereotypes. It is difficult to persuade a publisher with his head filled with the commercial success of such works to read a manuscript that runs counter to these fashions or to consider what to him is "making Negroes act like brooding white men."

Perhaps our Southern Kafka does exist. It may be that he is merely unpublished.

A Major Problem of Negro Authors in Their March Toward Belles-Lettres

G. Lewis Chandler

United States, your banner wears
   Two emblems—one of fame;
Alas, the other that it bears
   Reminds us of your shame.
Your standard's constellation types
   White freedom by its stars;
But what's the meaning of the stripes?
   They mean your Negroes' scars.
      —THOMAS CAMPBELL (1777-1844)

"Why haven't they produced a Robinson, a Frost, a Howells, a Melville, a Lewis—even a Longfellow?" "They can dance and they can sing; but they can't write." "If they are judged by their literature alone, they might as well be written off as having no mind at all." "It's time they produce belles-lettres in sufficient quantity and high quality; they write nothing but propaganda."

Such expressions are not uncommon whenever the literary accomplishments of the American Negro are discussed.

To struggle for about one hundred and eighty-five years for recognition and acceptance seems a long time. Perhaps it is. But not for literacy and for creative, imaginative literature. One does not have to be a literary scholar to know that the establishment of belles-lettres evolves slowly, that the emergence of a truly great literary artist or the flourishing of a school of such artists invariably comes to light only after the passing of many centuries of a people's existence—only after that people achieves or seriously approaches unity and integration. As old as is the civilization of France—"the schoolmaster of Western Europe in the matter of conscientious de-

votion to linguistic and literary form and style"—the first truly great names in French poetry—Arnaut Daniel, Bertram de Born, Piere Vidal, Jaupe Rudel—did not appear until the twelfth and thirteenth centuries. It is true that excellent folk material (the splendid "Song of Roland," the best of the celebrated *chansons de gestes* group, for example) had been produced long before the thirteenth century; but outstanding, individual authorship was late in arriving. This is also true of Russian literature. Old as Russia is, she had to wait for the late eighteenth century, when Alexander Pushkin (her first poet of international stature) was born. And it was not until the nineteenth century that a Russian literary galaxy, consisting of Gogol, Turgenev, Goncharov, Dostoievski, and Tolstoi, was developed. Germany, too, after centuries of popular oral literature and national separateness, was long in producing first-rate writers. It is true that Germany's Walther Von der Vogelweide, a twelfth century poet, should be considered great by any high literary measure. But it was in the last part of the eighteenth- and early nineteenth-centuries that Germany, impelled by the need for national unity and integration, came into literary hegemony with Klopstock, Wieland, Lessing, Herder, Schiller, Kant, and Goethe. Again, over nine hundred years in the civilized part of her history passed before England contributed a Chaucer and a Gower to the Literary Hall of Fame. And her first great literary outburst, coincidental with her massive surge for national unity under Elizabeth, came some eight hundred years after the death

of the Venerable Bede–a very long time, but seemingly a necessary long time in the realm of belles-lettres.

What about America? Nearly three hundred years after Jamestown, America defensively pinned her hopes for world recognition in creative literature on that small group which included Hawthorne, Poe, Melville, Twain, Lowell, and Thoreau.

With reference to Negro literature, the foregoing may prove at least one thing: that it is unfair to brand the Negro (out of abject slavery less than ninety years and in known authorship for about one hundred and eight years) as a failure in the field of belles-lettres. To the contrary, the facts, indeed, seem to indicate an indigenous talent of the Negro for creative writing. About thirteen years after Jupiter Hammon, the first known American Negro poet, published "An Evening Thought" in 1760, the precocious Phillis Wheatley produced *Poems on Various Subjects*, gaining for herself a surprised but appreciative audience in both America and England–an audience that ranked her at least with Anne Bradstreet, the outstanding American poet before Freneau. Only eighty-eight years after the death of Wheatley, Paul Laurence Dunbar, one of America's leading interpreters of lowly life, was born to win not only the attention and praise of America's greatest critic of the day, William Dean Howells, but to achieve worldwide recognition as an artist. Something of the same thing can be said of Dunbar's contemporaries: William Stanley Braithwaite and Charles W. Chesnutt, both of whom witnessed in the 1920's the rise and acclaim of a large group of young Negro Renaissance writers, such as Hughes, McKay, Cullen, Toomer, Fisher, Brown, Fauset. The 1930's yielded Margaret Walker, Zora N. Hurston, and Richard Wright. The 1940's saw the emergence of not only the popular Frank Yerby and the much discussed Willard Motley and J. Saunders Redding but also Gwendolyn Brooks, the first Negro poet to win the Pulitzer Prize. All this in about one hundred and eighty years of authorship! From Jupiter Hammon and Phillis Wheatley to Gwendolyn Brooks in poetry; from William Wells Brown, the generally-acknowledged first Negro fictionist, to Yerby and Redding; from the crude prose of Briton Hammon to the refined style of Du Bois and Alain Locke–this indicates definite growth and progress toward belles-lettres. It seems, therefore, unfair and untrue to say the Negro has

done little or nothing in belles-lettres or to lament that he has not produced writers of the stature of classic Americans: Moody, Holmes, Hawthorne, James, Robinson, Frost, Twain, Lowell, Lewis, Whitman, O'Neill. Prejudiced English reviewers and critics of the nineteenth century made the same mistake about American writers. Modern American reviewers and critics in appraising the literary contributions of the Negro must not repeat this glaring error in critical, objective judgment and historical perspective.

But irresponsible criticism is not the major problem facing the Negro literary artist. Nor is it primarily lack of training and experience, or a predilection for propaganda, or for racial themes, or for sociological, not artistic, treatment, of material. Admittedly, these are some of his handicaps–mere concomitants, however, of a basic problem and shame in American democracy–segregation.

Segregation creates inequalities, dependence, subservience, vicious colonialism, and racism. Among writers, it tends to encourage the production of only utilitarian, promotional literature. When the American colonies were subservient to and segregated by England, they produced, with few exceptions, no eminent samples of belles-lettres. The Roger Williamses, the Cotton Mathers, the John Dickinsons, the Michael Wigglesworths, the Benjamin Franklins, the Crèvecoeurs, even the Philip Freneaus, wrote much that was promotional, little that was divorced from the practical, from the need to protest and vindicate. Similarly, Negro authors from George Moses Horton to Frances E. W. Harper, to Frederick Douglass, to Carter Woodson, to Walter White, to Richard Wright have often been diverted from imaginative writing by the enveloping demands of a segregative, enslaving pattern amid which they have lived. The creative vigor of American literature could not develop in an atmosphere of separateness and subservience. It grew luxuriantly, however, after Emerson, Bryant, Noah Webster, and others destroyed literary colonialism in demanding artistic and linguistic independence as well as national integration for America. Likewise the annihilation of segregation in American society and culture will accelerate the advance of American authors (Negro and white) toward creative achievement. This is no idle prophecy, no wishful thinking. We see concrete evidences of its validity. It is indeed no accident that since 1920 Negro authorship has made significant progress. World War I gave the Negro

his first big chance to strike at segregation. The literary result was the remarkable promise and outburst of the Negro Renaissance. Then came the Depression Decade, when white and black discovered no color barriers in starvation. The positive literary by-product of this period was the appearance of writers like Richard Wright, Zora Neale Hurston, and Margaret Walker. World War II, offering America unprecedented world leadership, provided the Negro with a third opportunity as he took his cause to the Supreme Court and, as he won integration in the armed forces and in some phases of public education. Gwendolyn

Brooks and Frank Yerby may be regarded as the literary symbols of these triumphs. Who, therefore, can deny that, as a result of other successful assaults on segregation, Negro authorship will attain full stature–and in record time! And then America can honestly reply to Thomas Campbell:

> Those stripes in my banner do not mean Negro scars;
> They mean justice, freedom, integration without bars.

The Threshold of Maturity

N. P. Tillman

Has the Negro writer come of age? Here is a question that will produce a wide range of answers, first, because of disagreement on definitions and, second, because of differences of opinions within each camp. Such a query, however, has practical value, for it causes us not only to look at the Negro writer and his medium, but also to evaluate his work in terms of broad literary standards.

Anyone who is familiar with the writings of Negroes from the colonial period to the present would have to admit that it is a long artistic journey from Phillis Wheatley to Richard Wright, and that several positive gains have been registered on the way. Two or three of these advance steps come readily to mind.

For instance, the American reading public accepts a book by a Negro now on much the same basis as it receives a book by a white author. Consequently, the Negro writer has a more direct line to the publisher than ever before, for the primary aim of the publisher is to feed the demands of the book buyers.

The second gain is somewhat related to the first. The American market no longer demands a specific type of story from a Negro author, so that he has a wide choice of material and approach both within and outside the Negro group. This freeing of the writer from narrow lim-

itations is resulting in a broadening of his point of view and, indeed, in his seeing the Negro in a better pespective; and it will surely result in his writing better fiction about Negroes when he chooses them as his subjects.

There is no intention here to hold that Negroes should not write about Negroes. It is simply wrong to insist that an artist must limit his art to his own group if he is to get a hearing. Especially has this attitude been stifling to the Negro author in America, because it has made him so thoroughly a part of his subject that he has been usually unable to view it objectively. Hence, most of the fiction written by Negroes reads like a direct personal protest against discrimination rather than an artistic presentation of a segment of life that reveals to us how discrimination warps the individual and affects society in the large.

Only in a measure has the Negro writer been responsible for the advances discussed. They have come about largely as a result of the social growth of America itself; and this move toward national maturity can be attributed to a number of causes. It is evident that they will figure greatly in accelerating the development of the Negro writer, if he can seize the advantage.

Some thirty years ago, Mencken charged that one could practically omit the Southern part

of the United States without affecting the position of American letters. Perhaps the southerner had been so engrossed in advancing a theory that he lost sight of his task as a creative artist. Today in an honest anthology of the best in American fiction, drama and poetry, there might be no Negro entry. But this does not mean that the Negro writer in some instances is far behind his white contemporary in talent. It does mean that it takes time and hard work as well as talent to reach the top in any of the arts. And there are some good examples of living Negro authors who hold out a high promise.

Has the Negro writer of fiction come of age? I would rather say that, on the whole, he is on the threshold of maturity. He has yet to master the technique of his art. But with a ready market and freedom of choice of material, he has now, as never before in America, a happy combination of circumstances conducive to his growth. He can now, if he chooses, center his efforts on writing like an artist.

The Literature of the Negro:
A Social Scientist's Appraisal

Ira De A. Reid

Since I am neither a creative writer nor a literary critic, I must slip into my professional toga as a sociologist in this evaluation of the propaganda theme in the literature of Negro life. Because I find it singularly difficult to build and wrap my opinions in the neat idea-packages provided by the Editors, I fear that in discussing propaganda I am also peering into the packages of "values" and "labels" and "objective treatment." Knowing this and risking the editorial blue pencil, I shall attempt to cast my discussion within the limits of what social scientists now label the *natural history* of a situation.

If we were to examine the development of the literature of Negro life, the perspectives of time, place and measurable social change, I think we might assay it in terms of the specific as well as the general interests it seems to reveal. Assuming that this literature was at once purposeful and marketable, it seems possible to delineate the changes in the intellectual mood and temper of its producer as well as its market within a framework of four major socio-literary-type structures.

First of all, there is the ATTENTION-GETTING LITERATURE. This, I suppose, is the major propaganda effort in the works on Negro life. It seeks to invite attention to the problems of enslavement, caste-like segregation, discrimination and other typical adjustment-forms in a race-centered society. This literature is geared to a "Lo! the poor Negro" type of symbol. Its typical gesture is one of breast-beating, or a head bowed down in misery. Once the hallmark of all literature in this field, it is now a less conspicuous general literary form, and is one of the chief weapons of this age's "cause-and-purpose" writing, the literature of the pamphleteers, the human relations agencies, the racial pressure groups.

The literature of new peoples in a new land is also a LITERATURE OF ANCHORAGE. Efforts on the parts of scholars, dreamers, rebels and "race-happy" persons to relate their present to an historically accepted past, are indeed typical of propagandistic literature. It may be that the works identify the currently poorly-accepted Negro with the ancient and glorious histories of the kingdoms of the Nile River or the Guinea Coast or with the Bantu people. It may be a biographical or an autobiographical datum that portrays the subject as a descendant of an African prince (never identifying the subject with any one of his several wives), or as a descendant of a mixed biological union (seldom a white mother, usually a wealthy or politically important white father), or, as is the current fashion, as the descendant of a slave. This literature is not to be regarded as mere banality. It provided anchorage

for a people that needed such security in a culture that was so ancestry-first boat-and-homeland minded.

The PROOF-PROVIDING LITERATURE, ranging in forms from that of esoteric history to validated scientific theories, tends to support the thesis that persons of color have been and now are human, possessed of intellects and skills, emotions and achievements since the early days of what we now call civilization. This literature of pride and group-ego-inflation is a very important part of American literature in general, and is not peculiar to that under specific consideration. It does seem significant, however, that so much of the literature of the past thirty years has been given to providing evidence that despite (or because of) their visible or invisible genotypical differences, the colored peoples are predestined to be the accursed among men.

These aforementioned forms seem to provide an adequate framework within which to interpret most of the past literature on Negro life. They have been written by folk with both labels—white and non-white. It seems, however, that the present literary productions might be classified as the LITERATURE OF ART AND SCIENCE. Of course it is not an entirely new phase of literary production. It is, however, a more abundant one. Again, the writers have borne the racial labels, but the labels have been less meaningful. Here are to be found the creative literature, the belles-lettres, the scientific writings, the literature that provides clues to social experience and social action. Within this structure are to be found the work of the scholar as well as that of the "pot-boiler" writer, of the scientist as well as of the "huckster," of the creative artist and of the purveyor of traits from a folk culture. Their wares are in plentiful supply and are in inter- and intra-racial competition with wider producer and consumer markets than any other type of Negro life literature.

The possibilities of a literature dealing with the life and ways of Negro peoples in the Western world seem beyond comprehension. Certainly the potentials of that life have not been fully explored either in the literary or the scientific writings of our time. We seem to have reached the end of a period when most of the fiction dealt with the theme that the Negro is "tricked by life and made a fool of." Much of the literature whether written by Negroes or whites continues to portray an image of the Negro Image (to paraphrase Harry Overstreet), that is of a group "confused and disconcerted by the facts of life." Moods of pessimism, racial breast-beating, portrayal of the ugliness of life as if it were the reality of Negro group existence, all have been over-used as vehicles of the racial theme.

A literature of the future is going to demand a more fulsome appraisal of life as it is lived, in a style and with a meaning that requires imagination, skill and social understanding. And, to shed my prophetic caul, I expect that literature to require above all, a more discerning social intelligence than much of our literature now portrays. I expect it to deal with such items as the transitoriness of the racial experience; the great emphasis placed upon leisure; the semantic mumbo-jumbo of group adjustment; the dual morality that has attended the perpetuation of racial separatism; self-hate within the sub-group; the voids that attend our present programs of tolerance; how we have created what Erich Fromm calls "marketplace personalities;" how it happens that despite all the pessimism, the ugliness, the dream-shattering, and the breast-beating—the group survives as a dynamic social unity. Or, I see that literature seeking an answer to the thesis advanced by Allen Tate—"The Negro arrived too late with too little to expect too much from the American harvest."

Well, as I rethink the above words, my dream grows dim. There is reason to conclude that the dynamics of race-group adjustment in the Western world provide such a wealth of material, of so great significance for human understanding and survival that he who plumbs it, and who can portray any of its value-implications in essay, drama, poetry, novel, biography, or scientific writing may be "labeled" white, colored, European, or Fijian, but the label will have a new socially approved meaning. That too, it seems, is of essence.

Self-Criticism: The Third Dimension in Culture

Alain Locke

The symposium section in this issue of PHY-LON, which I have had the opportunity of reading in manuscript, seems to signal the emergence of a long-awaited stage in Negro cultural development. For these eight essays analyzing our literary output and its implications mark a considerable step forward toward objective self-criticism. This is a necessary and welcome sign of cultural maturity. It was predicated twenty-five years ago as one of the objectives of the so-called Negro Renaissance, along with the companion aim of objective self-expression, but unfortunately such criticism was not forthcoming in any large volume. Its lack was unquestionably indicative of a certain lingering immaturity, the reasons for which it will be interesting to assess a little later on. For the moment it may be noted that the conditions which delayed it may also have been considerably responsible for the admitted shortcomings of our literary and artistic output in the Nineteen-twenties, thirties, and forties. Indeed this seems to be the present consensus of the new criticism which is so significantly emerging.

It is now obvious in retrospect, as many of these articles point out, that for many generations Negro creative expression was inevitably imitative and marked with a double provincialism of cultural immaturity and a racial sense of subordination. It ran a one-dimensional gamut from self-pity through sentimental appeal to hortatory moralizing and rhetorical threat—a child's gamut of tears, sobs, sulks and passionate protest. All of us probably expected too much of the Negro Renaissance, but its new vitality of independence, pride and self-respect, its scoff and defiance of prejudice and limitations were so welcome and heartening.

Like the adolescence it was, the New Negro era was gawky and pimply, indiscreet and over-confident, vainglorious and irresponsible; but its testy dynamic gave the Negro new spiritual stature and an added dimension of self-reliance. As several of the critics point out, adolescence was mistaken for manhood, so there was in the creative expression of the Twenties and Thirties pride without poise, vision without true perspective, self-esteem without the necessary tempering of full self-understanding.

Beginning with the broader social identifications of *Native Son,* and the social discoveries of common-denominator human universals between Negro situations and others, these critics rightly claim, artistic expression with Negroes has become increasingly sounder, more objective and less racialistic—in the limiting sense of chauvinism—but withal even more racial in the better sense of being more deeply felt and projected. This third dimension of objective universality, they feel, is the ultimate desideratum for a literature that seeks universal appeal and acceptance. I agree. In fact, have always agreed, though this is neither the time nor place for self-justifying quotations.

Suffice it to say that even in 1925, some original proponents of the "Negro Renaissance" forecast the position which seems to be the new consensus of the "new criticism." That is, that when the racial themes are imposed upon the Negro author either from within or without, they become an intolerable and limiting artistic ghetto, but that accepted by choice, either on the ground of best known material or preferred opportunity, they stake off a cultural bonanza. Mr. Gloster, for example, does well to inveigh against the triple snares of "race defense, protest and glorification," but it still remains that Negro life and experience contain one of the unworked mines of American dramatic and fictional material, overworked and shabby as their superficial exploitation has been. For both the white and the Negro author in this area, the era of pan-mining is about over or should be; the promising techniques are now deep-mining and better artistic smelting of the crude ore. In provincial and chauvinistic rendering, of which we have been offered far too much, especially from Negro authors, as Messrs. Redding and Reddick bravely point out,

Negro materials pan out shallow, brittle and unrefined. But in objective, thoroughly humanized treatment they still promise artistic gold fit for universal currency. The necessary alchemy is, of course, universalized rendering, for in universalized particularity there has always resided the world's greatest and most enduring art.

Though rare, this quality has appeared sporadically in Negro writing. Mr. Chandler is right in giving us the proper historical perspective, however, by reminding us how long it took American literature itself to achieve this dimension of universalized power and insight. Perhaps it would be invidious to be too specific for the current generation, though I think all would agree that the first two chapters of *Native Son* had such quality, not to mention how and why the book as a whole lost these virtues as it became more and more involved in propagandist formulae. I am personally surprised that no one referred to the phenomenal early appearance of such "universal particularity" in Jean Toomer's *Cane* in 1923. Here was something admirably removed from what Mr. Chandler calls very aptly "promotional literature," but it is Negro through and through as well as deeply and movingly human. It was also exempt from any limitation of provincialism although it gave local color convincingly. To wish for more of this is to ask for the transmuting quality of expert craftsmanship combined with broad perspective or intuitive insight, one or the other. For we must remember the two ways in which Russian literature achieved its great era; through the cosmopolitan way of Turgenev, Tolstoi and Chekov and the nativist way of Dostoievski, Gogol and Gorgki, each of which produced great writing and universal understanding for Russian experience.

Our problem now seems to be how to translate this new insight into creative action. So far as a body of sound criticism can point the way, we have in this group of critical essays the beginnings of a new objective criticism, and henceforth can have little excuse if a considerable part of our creative expression does not follow its lead and guidance. At least we have within our artistic grasp the final resolution of the old dilemma of the proper attitude of the Negro writer toward race materials. Agreeing that this should be, to quote Mr. Gloster, "to consider all life as his proper milieu, yet treat race (when he chooses) from the universal point of view, shunning the cultural isolation that results from racial preoccupation and Jim-Crow esthetics," we have as a net re-

sult, however, the mandate: Give us Negro life and experience in all the arts but with a third dimension of universalized common-denominator humanity.

A final word or so of constructive criticism may be in order. Let us start with the shameful fact that out of the whole range of Negro experience, the very areas on which the Negro author has almost monopolistic control, there has been little else than strange silence. On this matter, Mr. Reddick hints provocatively. I will venture to speak even more plainly on my own responsibility. Three tabus that seal doors that must be broken through to release greatly original and moving revelations about Negro life and experience remain unbroken, partly through convention-ridden cowardice, partly through misconceived protective strategy. If William March and Erskine Caldwell, Lillian Smith and William Faulkner can boldly break with the tribal tabus of the White South to release the full potentials of Southern drama and fiction, so in turn must the Negro author boldly break the seals of analogous Negro conventionality. Of course, easier said than done! The Negro intellectual is still largely in psychological bondage not only, as Reddick puts it, "to the laws and customs of the local (Southern) culture," but to the fear of breaking the tabus of Puritanism, Philistinism and falsely conceived conventions of "race respectability." Consciously and subconsciously, these repressions work great artistic harm, especially the fear of being accused of group disloyalty and "misrepresentation" in portraying the full gamut of Negro type, character and thinking. We are still in the throes of counter-stereotypes.

The releasing formula is to realize that in all human things we are basically and inevitably human, and that even the special racial complexities and overtones are only interesting variants. Why, then, this protective silence about the ambivalences of the Negro upper classes, about the dilemmas of intra-group prejudice and rivalry, about the dramatic inner paradoxes of mixed heritage, both biological and cultural, or the tragic breach between the Negro elite and the Negro masses, or the conflict between integration and vested-interest separatism in the present-day life of the Negro? These, among others, are the great themes, but they moulder in closed closets like family skeletons rather than shine brightly as the Aladdin's lamps that they really are.

To break such tabus is the crucial artistic question of the moment, the wrath of the Negro

Rotarians, preachers, college presidents and journalists notwithstanding. It is this inner tyranny that must next be conquered, now that the outer tyrannies of prejudice and intellectual ostracism are being so suddenly relaxed. I am far from suggesting that even a considerable part of this revelation will be morally risqué or socially explosive; some of it will be, of course. But I do sense a strange and widely diffused feeling that many of these situations are Masonic secrets–things to be talked about, but not written or officially disclosed. Maybe, now that a few Negro authors have demonstrated the possibility of financial independence and success as writers, some of our younger talents can shake free of the white-collar servitudes of job dependency on the one hand and conventional "race loyalty" on the other. If so, we may confidently anticipate an era of fuller and more objective presentation by Negro authors of their versions of contemporary living in general and Negro life and experience in particular.

Books for Further Reading

Abramson, Doris E. *Negro Playwrights in the American Theatre: 1925-1959.* New York and London: Columbia University Press, 1969.

Baker, Houston A., Jr. *Blues, Ideology, and Afro-American Literature.* Chicago and London: University of Chicago Press, 1984.

Baker. *The Journey Back: Issues in Black Literature and Criticism.* Chicago: University of Chicago Press, 1980.

Baker. *Singers of Daybreak: Studies in Black American Literature.* Washington, D.C.: Howard University Press, 1974.

Bell, Bernard. *The Afro-American Novel and Its Tradition.* Amherst: University of Massachusetts Press, 1987.

Bigsby, C. W. E. *The Second Black Renaissance: Essays in Black Literature.* Westport, Conn.: Greenwood, 1980.

Bone, Robert A. *The Negro Novel in America,* revised edition. New Haven and London: Yale University Press, 1965.

Byerman, Keith. *Fingering the Jagged Grain: Tradition and Form in Recent Black Fiction.* Athens: University of Georgia Press, 1985.

Callahan, John F. *In the African-American Grain: The Pursuit of Voice in Twentieth-Century Black Fiction.* Urbana and Chicago: University of Illinois Press, 1988.

Campbell, Jane. *Mythic Black Fiction: The Transformation of History.* Knoxville: University of Tennessee Press, 1986.

Christian, Barbara. *Black Feminist Criticism: Perspectives on Black Women Writers.* New York: Pergamon Press, 1985.

Cooke, Michael G. *Afro-American Literature in the Twentieth Century: The Achievement of Intimacy.* New Haven: Yale University Press, 1984.

Cruse, Harold. *The Crisis of the Negro Intellectual.* New York: Morrow, 1967.

Dixon, Melvin. *Ride Out the Wilderness: Geography and Identity in Afro-American Literature.* Urbana and Chicago: University of Illinois Press, 1987.

Evans, James H., Jr. *Spiritual Empowerment in Afro-American Literature: Frederick Douglass, Rebecca Jackson, Booker T. Washington, Richard Wright and Toni Morrison.* Lewiston, N.Y.: Mellen Press, 1987.

Evans, Mari, ed. *Black Women Writers (1950-1980): A Critical Evaluation.* Garden City, N.Y.: Anchor Press, Doubleday, 1984.

321

Gates, Henry Louis, Jr., ed. *Black Literature and Literary Theory*. New York: Methuen, 1984.

Gayle, Addison, Jr. *The Way of the New World: The Black Novel in America*. Garden City, N.Y.: Anchor Press, Doubleday, 1975.

Gibson, Donald. *The Politics of Literary Expression: A Study of Major Black Writers*. Westport, Conn.: Greenwood, 1981.

Gibson, ed. *Five Black Writers: Essays on Wright, Ellison, Baldwin, Hughes, and LeRoi Jones*. New York: New York University Press, 1970.

Gysin, Fritz. *The Grotesque in American Negro Fiction: Jean Toomer, Richard Wright, and Ralph Ellison*. Bern: Francke, 1975.

Harper, Michael S., and Robert B. Stepto. *Chant of Saints: A Gathering of Afro-American Literature, Art, and Scholarship*. Urbana: University of Illinois Press, 1979.

Harris, Trudier. *Exorcising Blackness: Historical and Literary Lynching and Burning Rituals*. Bloomington: Indiana University Press, 1984.

Hemenway, Robert, ed. *The Black Novelist*. Columbus, Ohio: Charles Merrill, 1970.

Henderson, Stephen. *Understanding the New Black Poetry: Black Speech and Black Music as Poetic References*. New York: William Morrow, 1973.

Hughes, Carl Milton. *The Negro Novelist: A Discussion of the Writings of American Negro Novelists, 1940-1950*. New York: Citadel Press, 1953.

Jackson, Blyden. *The Waiting Years: Essays on American Negro Literature*. Baton Rouge: Louisiana State University Press, 1976.

Jackson, and Louis D. Rubin, Jr. *Black Poetry in America: Two Essays in Historical Interpretation*. Baton Rouge: Louisiana State University Press, 1974.

Kinnamon, Keneth. *The Emergence of Richard Wright: A Study in Literature and Society*. Chicago: University of Illinois Press, 1972.

Klotman, Phyllis Rauch. *Another Man Gone: The Black Runner in Contemporary Afro-American Literature*. Port Washington, N.Y.: Kennikat Press, 1977.

Lee, Robert A., ed. *Black Fiction: New Studies in the Afro-American Novel Since 1945*. New York: Barnes & Noble, 1980.

Major, Clarence. *The Dark and Feeling: Black American Writers and Their Work*. New York: Third Press, 1974.

Margolies, Edward. *Native Sons: A Critical Study of Twentieth-Century Negro American Authors*. Philadelphia and New York: J. B. Lippincott, 1968.

McCall, Dan. *The Example of Richard Wright*. New York: Harcourt, Brace & World, 1969.

Miller, R. Baxter, ed. *Black American Literature and Humanism*. Lexington: University Press of Kentucky, 1981.

Miller, ed. *Black American Poets Between Worlds, 1940-1960.* Knoxville: University of Tennessee Press, 1986.

Mitchell, Loften. *Black Drama: The Story of the American Negro in the Theatre.* New York: Hawthorne, 1967.

O'Brien, John, ed. *Interviews with Black Writers.* New York: Liveright, 1973.

Payne, Ladell. *Black Novelists and the Southern Literary Tradition.* Athens: University of Georgia Press, 1981.

Pryse, Marjorie, and Hortense J. Spillers, eds. *Conjuring: Black Women, Fiction, and Literary Tradition.* Bloomington: Indiana University Press, 1985.

Schraufnagel, Noel. *From Apology to Protest: The Black American Novel.* De Land, Fla.: Everett-Edwards, 1973.

Smith, Valerie. *Self-Discovery and Authority in Afro-American Narrative.* Cambridge, Mass.: Harvard University Press, 1987.

Sollors, Werner. *Beyond Ethnicity: Consent and Descent in American Culture.* New York: Oxford University Press, 1986.

Stepto, Robert B. *From Behind the Veil: A Study of Afro-American Narrative.* Urbana: University of Illinois Press, 1979.

Tate, Claudia, ed. *Black Women Writers at Work.* New York: Continuum, 1983.

Wade-Gayles, Gloria. *No Crystal Stair: Visions of Race and Sex in Black Women's Fiction.* New York: Pilgrim Press, 1984.

Contributors

Katherine H. Adams ....*Loyola University in New Orleans*
Sandra Carlton Alexander ....*North Carolina Agricultural and Technical*
                                                                            State University
Thomas C. Battle ....*Howard University*
Fahamisha Patricia Brown ....*Boston College*
Steven R. Carter ....*University of Puerto Rico*
Edward D. Clark ....*North Carolina State University*
Leonard J. Deutsch ....*Marshall University*
Howard Dodson ....*Schomburg Center for Research in Black Culture*
Robert M. Farnsworth ....*University of Missouri at Kansas City*
SallyAnn H. Ferguson ....*North Carolina Agricultural and Technical*
                                                                            State University
Robert E. Fleming ....*University of New Mexico*
Samuel B. Garren ....*North Carolina Agricultural and Technical*
                                                                            State University
James V. Hatch ....*City College of New York*
Kathleen A. Hauke ....*University of Nairobi*
Jacquelyn Jackson ....*Middle Tennessee State University*
La Vinia Delois Jennings ....*University of North Carolina at Chapel Hill*
Norma R. Jones ....*Alcorn State University*
George E. Kent ....*University of Chicago*
Jeffrey D. Parker ....*University of South Carolina*
Kathy A. Perkins ....*University of California, Los Angeles*
Joyce Pettis ....*North Carolina State University*
Ralph Reckley ....*Morgan State University*
Robert P. Sedlack ....*DePauw University*
Thelma Barnaby Thompson ....*University of the District of Columbia*
Clara Robie Williams ....*Atlanta, Georgia*
Ora Williams ....*California State University, Long Beach*
Mary B. Zeigler ....*Kennesaw College*

Cumulative Index

Dictionary of Literary Biography, Volumes 1-76
Dictionary of Literary Biography Yearbook, 1980-1987
Dictionary of Literary Biography Documentary Series, Volumes 1-4

Cumulative Index

DLB before number: *Dictionary of Literary Biography*, Volumes 1-76
Y before number: *Dictionary of Literary Biography Yearbook*, 1980-1987
DS before number: *Dictionary of Literary Biography Documentary Series*, Volumes 1-4

A

Abbey Press DLB-49

The Abbey Theatre and Irish
    Drama, 1900-1945 .... DLB-10

Abbot, Willis J. 1863-1934.................. DLB-29

Abbott, Jacob 1803-1879 ....DLB-1

Abbott, Robert S. 1868-1940 .... DLB-29

Abelard-Schuman DLB-46

Abell, Arunah S. 1806-1888 .... DLB-43

Abercrombie, Lascelles 1881-1938............. DLB-19

Abrams, M. H. 1912- DLB-67

Abse, Dannie 1923- DLB-27

Academy Chicago Publishers DLB-46

Ace Books................................... DLB-46

Acorn, Milton 1923-1986.................... DLB-53

Actors Theatre of Louisville....................DLB-7

Adair, James 1709?-1783? DLB-30

Adamic, Louis 1898-1951.......................DLB-9

Adams, Alice 1926- Y-86

Adams, Brooks 1848-1927.................... DLB-47

Adams, Charles Francis, Jr. 1835-1915 .... DLB-47

Adams, Douglas 1952- Y-83

Adams, Franklin P. 1881-1960 .... DLB-29

Adams, Henry 1838-1918 ....DLB-12, 47

Adams, Herbert Baxter 1850-1901 .... DLB-47

Adams, J. S. and C. [publishing house]........ DLB-49

Adams, James Truslow 1878-1949............. DLB-17

Adams, John 1735-1826 .... DLB-31

Adams, John Quincy 1767-1848............... DLB-37

Adams, Léonie 1899- DLB-48

Adams, Samuel 1722-1803 ....DLB-31, 43

Adams, William Taylor 1822-1897 .... DLB-42

Adcock, Fleur 1934- DLB-40

Ade, George 1866-1944 ....DLB-11, 25

Adeler, Max (see Clark, Charles Heber)

Advance Publishing Company................. DLB-49

AE 1867-1935 .... DLB-19

Aesthetic Poetry (1873), by Walter Pater DLB-35

Afro-American Literary Critics:
    An Introduction DLB-33

Agassiz, Jean Louis Rodolphe 1807-1873........DLB-1

Agee, James 1909-1955.....................DLB-2, 26

Aiken, Conrad 1889-1973 ....DLB-9, 45

Ainsworth, William Harrison 1805-1882....... DLB-21

Aitken, Robert [publishing house]............. DLB-49

Akins, Zoë 1886-1958 .... DLB-26

Alain-Fournier 1886-1914 .... DLB-65

Alba, Nanina 1915-1968...................... DLB-41

Albee, Edward 1928- DLB-7

Alcott, Amos Bronson 1799-1888...............DLB-1

Alcott, Louisa May 1832-1888 ....DLB-1, 42

Alcott, William Andrus 1798-1859...............DLB-1

Alden, Isabella 1841-1930 .... DLB-42

Alden, John B. [publishing house]............. DLB-49

Alden, Beardsley and Company DLB-49

Aldington, Richard 1892-1962..............DLB-20, 36

Aldis, Dorothy 1896-1966 .... DLB-22

Aldiss, Brian W. 1925- DLB-14

Aldrich, Thomas Bailey 1836-1907.........DLB-42, 71

Alexander, Charles Wesley
    [publishing house] DLB-49

Alexander, James 1691-1756 .... DLB-24

Alexander, Lloyd 1924- DLB-52

Alger, Horatio, Jr. 1832-1899 .... DLB-42

Algonquin Books of Chapel Hill.............. DLB-46

B

D

H

I

J

K

Cumulative Index

N

S

Cumulative Index

T

Cumulative Index

U

V

Y